For Us, but Not to Us

For Us, but Not to Us

Essays on Creation, Covenant, and Context
in Honor of John H. Walton

Edited by
Adam E. Miglio, Caryn A. Reeder,
Joshua T. Walton, & Kenneth C. Way

PICKWICK *Publications* · Eugene, Oregon

FOR US, BUT NOT TO US
Essays on Creation, Covenant, and Context in Honor of John H. Walton

Copyright © 2020 Wipf and Stock Publishers. All rights reserved. Except for brief quotations in critical publications or reviews, no part of this book may be reproduced in any manner without prior written permission from the publisher. Write: Permissions, Wipf and Stock Publishers, 199 W. 8th Ave., Suite 3, Eugene, OR 97401.

Pickwick Publications
An Imprint of Wipf and Stock Publishers
199 W. 8th Ave., Suite 3
Eugene, OR 97401

www.wipfandstock.com

PAPERBACK ISBN: 978-1-5326-9371-7
HARDCOVER ISBN: 978-1-5326-9372-4
EBOOK ISBN: 978-1-5326-9373-1

Cataloguing-in-Publication data:

Names: Miglio, Adam E., editor. | Reeder, Caryn A., editor. | Walton, Joshua T., editor. | Way, Kenneth C., editor.

Title: For us but not to us : essays on creation, covenant, and context in honor of John H. Walton / edited by Adam E. Miglio, Caryn A. Reeder, Joshua T. Walton, and Kenneth C. Way.

Description: Eugene, OR: Pickwick Publications, 2020. | Includes bibliographical references and index.

Identifiers: ISBN 978-1-5326-9371-7 (paperback). | ISBN 978-1-5326-9372-4 (hardcover). | ISBN 978-1-5326-9373-1 (ebook).

Subjects: LCSH: Walton, John H. | Bible—Old Testament—Criticism, interpretation, etc. | Creation—Biblical teaching. | Covenant theology—Biblical teaching.

Classification: BS1188 F55 2020 (print). | BS1188 (ebook).

Manufactured in the U.S.A.　09/25/20

Artwork: "Israelite Cosmology," courtesy of J. Harvey Walton. Originally published in John H. Walton and Andrew E. Hill, *Old Testament Today: A Journey from Ancient Context to Contemporary Relevance*. 2nd ed. (Grand Rapids: Zondervan, 2013) 62.

Scripture quotations marked (ASV) are from the American Standard Version Bible, which is in the public domain.

Scripture quotations marked (ESV) are from the ESV® Bible (The Holy Bible, English Standard Version®), copyright © 2001 by Crossway, a publishing ministry of Good News Publishers. Used by permission. All rights reserved.

Scripture quotations marked (LEB) are from the *Lexham English Bible*. Copyright 2012 Logos Bible Software. Lexham is a registered trademark of Logos Bible Software.

Scripture quotations marked (NIV) are taken from the Holy Bible, NEW INTERNATIONAL VERSION®, NIV® Copyright © 1973, 1978, 1984, 2011 by Biblica, Inc.® Used by permission. All rights reserved worldwide.

Scripture quotations marked (NJPS) are reprinted from *Tanakh: The New JPS Translation According to the Traditional Hebrew Text*. Copyright © 1985, 1999 by The Jewish Publication Society with the permission of the publisher

Scripture quotations marked (NRSV) are from the New Revised Standard Version Bible, copyright © 1989 National Council of the Churches of Christ in the United States of America. Used by permission. All rights reserved worldwide.

Scripture quotations marked (RSV) are from the Revised Standard Version of the Bible, copyright © 1946, 1952, and 1971 National Council of the Churches of Christ in the United States of America. Used by permission. All rights reserved worldwide.

Scripture quotations not from any of the preceding versions are translated by the authors of the individual essays.

Contents

List of Figures | vii

List of Tables | viii

Acknowledgments | ix

Abbreviations | x

Contributors | xv

A Tribute to John H. Walton | xvii
  Adam E. Miglio, Caryn A. Reeder, Joshua T. Walton, and Kenneth C. Way

The Publications of John H. Walton (1978–2019) | xxi
  Shawn Virgil Goodwin

PART 1: CREATION | 1

1. **Sense of a Beginning: The Role of Beginnings in the Israelite Historical Résumés** | 3
   Aubrey Buster

2. **Back to the Beginning: Verbal Syntax and Semantics in Genesis 1:1–3** | 22
   John A. Cook

3. **Stretching Out the Heavens: The Background and Use of a Creational Metaphor** | 37
   Brittany Kim

4. **The Image of God in the Shalom of God** | 57
   Alexander N. Kirk

5. **Mr. Darwin's Bible** | 73
   David N. Lincicum

6. **The Image of God: Human Identity in the Cosmic Temple** | 87
   Ryan S. Peterson

7. **Praise the LORD, the (un)Creator of Heaven and Earth: Psalm 105's Depiction of YHWH's Sovereignty in the Egyptian Plagues** | 99
   Michelle A. Stinson

PART 2: COVENANT | 111

   8. The Difference God Makes for Considering
      Scripture, Creation, and Covenant | 113
      Christopher R. J. Holmes

   9. The Lost World of the Exodus: Functional Ontology
      and the Creation of a Nation | 126
      Carmen Joy Imes

  10. An Enduring House (Terms and Conditions Apply):
      Potential Northern Extensions of the Davidic Covenant | 142
      R. Jesse Pruett

  11. Israel's Relationship with Nature and with YHWH
      in the Book of Hosea | 158
      Eric J. Tully

  12. The Theological Implications of Covenant as Vassal Treaty in Israel | 174
      J. Harvey Walton

PART 3: CONTEXT | 197

  13. Taking Care of Dead Kings: Isaiah 26 and the King of Life | 199
      Hannah Clardy

  14. Jesus and Ritual Impurity in Mark's Gospel | 217
      Seth M. Ehorn

  15. On Identifying the "Dragon's Spring" in Jerusalem (Neh 2:13) | 234
      Kyle H. Keimer

  16. Metaphor and Meaning in Psalm 23:
      Provisions for "a Table in the Presence of My Enemies" | 245
      Adam E. Miglio

  17. The Patriarchs' Altar-Building as Anticipation
      of the Israelite Conquest | 254
      Benjamin J. Noonan

  18. Jesus the Slave: The Gender of a Christological Metaphor
      in Luke and Paul | 276
      Caryn A. Reeder

  19. The Sword of YHWH: The Human Use of Divine Weapons
      in the Ancient Near East and the Hebrew Bible | 293
      Charlie Trimm

  20. David's Census and the Fate of the Canaanites | 305
      Joshua T. Walton

  21. The Lost World of Lexical Semantics:
      Samson's Spectacle in Judges 16:25 | 321
      Kenneth C. Way

  22. The Victory of YHWH in the Temple of Dagon (1 Samuel 5:1-5) | 335
      Jonathon Wylie

Figures

Figure 19.1: Amun holding divine weapon before Ramses III | 295
Figure 19.2: Horus holding divine weapon before Ramses II | 295

Tables

Table 1.1: Starting Points for Historical Résumés | 13
Table 7.1: Comparison of Egyptian Plague Orders | 102
Table 7.2: Comparison of Ordering of Events in Genesis 1 and Psalm 105 | 105
Table 11.1: The Three-Phase Structure in Hosea | 160
Table 11.2: Hosea's Accusation against Israel in 2:2–8 [4–10] | 161
Table 11.3: Two Connected Relationships | 165
Table 11.4: Eschatological Restoration in Hosea 2:14–23 [16–25] | 168
Table 17.1: Synopsis of the Patriarchal Altar-Building Accounts | 266
Table 21.1: Lexical Base | 323
Table 21.2: Synchronic Nuances | 328

Acknowledgments

CREATING A *FESTSCHRIFT* IS a collaborative endeavor, and a number of people devoted their time, expertise, and resources to the project. The Alumni Association at Wheaton College provided a generous grant to assist with the costs of editing and publication. Emily Varner and James Cuénod gave expert editorial assistance. Jonathan (J. Harvey) Walton contributed original art depicting Israelite cosmology. The editors are grateful for all of these essential tributes toward *For Us, but Not to Us*.

Abbreviations

General

AD	*Anno Domini*, "in the year of the Lord" = CE
ANE	Ancient Near East
BC	Before Christ = BCE
BCE	Before Common Era
BM	British Museum
ca.	*circa*, "approximately"
CE	Common Era
CSB	Holman Christian Standard Bible, 2nd ed.
ESV	English Standard Version
LBH	Late Biblical Hebrew
LEB	Lexham English Bible
LXX	Septuagint
MT	Masoretic Text
NASB	New American Standard Bible
NET	New English Translation/The NET Bible
NIV	New International Version
NJPS	TANAKH: The Holy Scriptures: The New Jewish Publication Society Translation
NKJV	New King James Version
NLT	New Living Translation
NRSV	New Revised Standard Version
NT	New Testament
OT	Old Testament

Abbreviations

RS	Ras Shamra (= Ugarit)
RSV	Revised Standard Version
SBL	Society of Biblical Literature

Journals and Reference Works

ABD	*The Anchor Bible Dictionary*. Edited by David Noel Freedman. 6 vols. New York: Doubleday, 1992
AEL	*Ancient Egyptian Literature*. Miriam Lichtheim. 3 vols. Berkeley: University of California Press, 1973, 1976, 1980
ANET	*Ancient Near Eastern Texts Relating to the Old Testament*. Edited by James B. Pritchard. 3rd ed. Princeton: Princeton University Press, 1969
AOAT	Alter Orient und Altes Testament
ARAB	*Ancient Records of Assyria and Babylonia*. Daniel David Luckenbill. 2 vols. Chicago: University of Chicago Press, 1926–27
ARM	Archives Royales de Mari
BA	*Biblical Archaeologist*
BAR	*Biblical Archaeology Review*
BASOR	*Bulletin of the American Schools of Oriental Research*
BBR	*Bulletin for Biblical Research*
BDAG	*A Greek–English Lexicon of the New Testament and Other Early Christian Literature*. Frederick William Danker et al. 3rd ed. Chicago: University of Chicago Press, 2000
BDB	*Hebrew and English Lexicon of the Old Testament*. Francis Brown, S. R. Driver, and Charles A. Briggs. Oxford: Clarendon, 1907
Bib	*Biblica*
BRev	*Bible Review*
BSac	*Bibliotheca Sacra*
BT	*The Bible Translator*
BZ	*Biblische Zeitschrift*
BZAW	*Beihefte zur Zeitschrift für die alttestamentliche Wissenschaft*
CAD	*The Assyrian Dictionary of the Oriental Institute of the University of Chicago*. 21 vols. Chicago: Oriental Institute, 1956–2010
CBQ	*Catholic Biblical Quarterly*
CHANE	*Culture and History of the Ancient Near East*

Abbreviations

COS	*The Context of Scripture.* Edited by William W. Hallo and K. Lawson Younger Jr. 4 vols. Leiden: Brill, 1997–2016
CTH	*Catalogue des textes hittites*
CTJ	*Calvin Theological Journal*
DCH	*The Dictionary of Classical Hebrew.* Edited by David J. A. Clines. 9 vols. Sheffield: Sheffield Phoenix, 1993–2016
DDD	*Dictionary of Deities and Demons in the Bible.* Edited by Karel van der Toorn et al. Grand Rapids: Eerdmans, 1999
DUL	*A Dictionary of the Ugaritic Language in the Alphabetic Tradition.* Gregorio del Olmo Lete and Joaquín Sanmartín et al. 3rd rev. ed. Leiden: Brill, 2015
EI	*Eretz-Israel*
FAT	Forschungen zur Alten Testament
GKC	*Gesenius' Hebrew Grammar.* Wilhelm Gesenius. Edited by E. Kautzsch. Edited and translated by A. E. Cowley. Oxford: Clarendon, 1910
GTJ	*Grace Theological Journal*
HALOT	*The Hebrew and Aramaic Lexicon of the Old Testament.* Ludwig Koehler and Walter Baumgartner. 5 vols. Leiden: Brill, 1994–2000
HBT	*Horizons in Biblical Theology*
HeBAI	*Hebrew Bible and Ancient Israel*
HSM	Harvard Semitic Monographs
HTR	*Harvard Theological Review*
HUCA	*Hebrew Union College Annual*
IBHS	*An Introduction to Biblical Hebrew Syntax.* Bruce K. Waltke and Michael Patrick O'Connor. Winona Lake, IN: Eisenbrauns, 1990
ICC	International Critical Commentary
IEJ	*Israel Exploration Journal*
IJST	*International Journal of Systematic Theology*
IJT	*Indian Journal of Theology*
Int	*Interpretation: A Journal of Bible and Theology*
IVPBBCOT	*The IVP Bible Background Commentary: Old Testament.* John H. Walton et al. Downers Grove, IL: InterVarsity, 2000
JANEBL	*Journal for Ancient Near Eastern and Biblical Law*
JANER	*Journal of Ancient Near Eastern Religions*
JAOS	*Journal of the American Oriental Society*
JBL	*Journal of Biblical Literature*

Abbreviations

JBQ	*Jewish Bible Quarterly*
JCS	*Journal of Cuneiform Studies*
JESOT	*Journal for the Evangelical Study of the Old Testament*
JETS	*Journal of the Evangelical Theological Society*
JHB	*Journal of the History of Biology*
JHS	*Journal of Hebrew Scriptures*
JNES	*Journal of Near Eastern Studies*
JNSL	*Journal of Northwest Semitic Languages*
JPOS	*Journal of the Palestine Oriental Society*
JSNT	*Journal for the Study of the New Testament*
JSOT	*Journal for the Study of the Old Testament*
JSOTSup	Journal for the Study of the Old Testament Supplement Series
JSS	*Journal of Semitic Studies*
JTI	*Journal of Theological Interpretation*
JTS	*Journal of Theological Studies*
KAI	*Kanaanäische und aramäische Inschriften*
KTU	Die keilalphabetischen Texte aus Ugarit
KUB	Keilschrifturkunden aus Boghazköi
LCL	Loeb Classical Library
LHBOTS	Library of Hebrew Bible / Old Testament Studies
MARG	Mitteilungen für Anthropologie und Religionsgeschichte
NEAEHL	*The New Encyclopedia of Archaeological Excavations in the Holy Land.* Edited by Ephraim Stern et al. 5 vols. Jerusalem: Israel Exploration Society, 1993–2008
NICNT	New International Commentary on the New Testament
NICOT	New International Commentary on the Old Testament
NIDOTTE	*The New International Dictionary of Old Testament Theology and Exegesis.* Edited by Willem A. VanGemeren. 5 vols. Grand Rapids: Zondervan, 1990
NovT	*Novum Testamentum*
NTS	*New Testament Studies*
OBO	Orbis Biblicus et Orientalis
OEANE	*The Oxford Encyclopedia of Archaeology in the Near East.* Edited by Eric M. Meyers. 5 vols. Oxford: Oxford University Press, 1997

Abbreviations

OrAnt	*Oriens Antiquus*
OTE	*Old Testament Essays*
OTL	Old Testament Library
RIMA	Royal Inscriptions of Mesopotamia: Assyrian Periods
RIME	Royal Inscriptions of Mesopotamia: Early Periods
RINAP	Royal Inscriptions of the Neo-Assyrian Period
SAA	State Archives of Assyria
SAAB	*State Archives of Assyria Bulletin*
SBJT	*Southern Baptist Journal of Theology*
SBLWAW	SBL Writings from the Ancient World
SHBC	Smyth & Helwys Bible Commentary
TDOT	*Theological Dictionary of the Old Testament.* Edited by G. Johannes Botterweck et al. 16 vols. Grand Rapids: Eerdmans, 1974–2018
TLOT	*Theological Lexicon of the Old Testament.* Edited by Ernst Jenni and Claus Westermann. 3 vols. Translated by Mark E. Biddle. Peabody, MA: Hendrickson, 1997
TynBul	*Tyndale Bulletin*
UF	*Ugarit-Forschungen*
UT	*Ugaritic Textbook.* Cyrus H. Gordon. Analecta Orientalia 38. Rome: Pontifical Biblical Institute, 1965
VT	*Vetus Testamentum*
VTSup	Vetus Testamentum Supplements
WBC	Word Biblical Commentary
WTJ	*Westminster Theological Journal*
ZABR	*Zeitschrift für altorientalische und biblische Rechtsgeschichte*
ZAW	*Zeitschrift für die alttestamentliche Wissenschaft*
ZIBBCOT	*Zondervan Illustrated Bible Backgrounds Commentary: Old Testament.* Edited by John H. Walton. 5 vols. Grand Rapids: Zondervan, 2009
ZTK	*Zeitschrift für Theologie und Kirche*

Contributors

Aubrey Buster, Assistant Professor of Old Testament, Wheaton College, Wheaton, Illinois

Hannah Clardy, Junior Research Associate in Old Testament, Tyndale House, Cambridge, United Kingdom

John A. Cook, Professor of Old Testament and Director of Hebrew Language Instruction, Asbury Theological Seminary, Wilmore, Kentucky; Research Fellow, University of the Free State, Bloemfontein, South Africa

Seth M. Ehorn, Visiting Assistant Professor of Greek Language and New Testament at Wheaton College, Wheaton, Illinois

Shawn Virgil Goodwin, Metadata Analyst at ATLA

Christopher R. J. Holmes, Associate Professor of Systematic Theology at University of Otago, Dunedin, New Zealand

Carmen Joy Imes, Associate Professor of Old Testament at Prairie College, Three Hills, Alberta, Canada

Kyle H. Keimer, Senior Lecturer in the Archaeology, History, and Language of Ancient Israel at Macquarie University, Sydney, Australia

Brittany Kim, Adjunct Professor at North Park Theological Seminary, Chicago, Illinois

Alexander N. Kirk, Professor of New Testament at Sekolah Tinggi Teologi Injili Indonesia, Yogyakarta, Indonesia

David N. Lincicum, The Rev. John A. O'Brien Associate Professor of Theology at University of Notre Dame, Notre Dame, Indiana

Adam E. Miglio, Associate Professor of Archaeology at Wheaton College, Wheaton, Illinois

Benjamin J. Noonan, Associate Professor of Old Testament and Hebrew at Columbia Biblical Seminary, Columbia International University, Columbia, South Carolina

Contributors

Ryan S. Peterson, Associate Professor of Theology at Talbot School of Theology, Biola University, La Mirada, California

R. Jesse Pruett, PhD Candidate at University of Wisconsin-Madison, Madison, Wisconsin

Caryn A. Reeder, Professor of New Testament at Westmont College, Santa Barbara, California

Michelle A. Stinson, Associate Professor of Old Testament at Simpson University, Redding, California

Charlie Trimm, Associate Professor of Old Testament at Talbot School of Theology, Biola University, La Mirada, California

Eric J. Tully, Associate Professor of Old Testament and Semitic Languages at Trinity Evangelical Divinity School, Trinity International University, Deerfield, Illinois

J. Harvey Walton, PhD Candidate at University of St. Andrews, School of Divinity, Scotland, United Kingdom

Joshua T. Walton, Adjunct Faculty at Capital University, Columbus, Ohio

Kenneth C. Way, Professor of Old Testament and Semitics at Talbot School of Theology, Biola University, La Mirada, California

Jonathon Wylie, Upper School Faculty, Covenant School, Huntington, West Virginia

A Tribute to John H. Walton

Adam E. Miglio, Caryn A. Reeder,
Joshua T. Walton, and Kenneth C. Way

"For us, but not to us" succinctly captures John H. Walton's approach to Scripture. The phrase places value on both contemporary and ancient contexts of the biblical text, and it also reminds contemporary readers that they are not the implied audience of the human authors or editors. Walton's vocational calling centers on training biblical interpreters to put aside their own cultural presuppositions in order to comprehend the ancient world of the text to the best of their ability by using all of the resources at their disposal—whether historical, archaeological, cultural, literary, or linguistic.

This hermeneutic, recently termed "cognitive environment criticism,"[1] is implicit in Walton's earlier publications, such as *Ancient Israelite Literature in its Cultural Context* (1989) and *The IVP Bible Background Commentary: Old Testament* (2000). However, the phrase "*for* us, but not *to* us" does not appear in print, as far as we can tell, until 2008 when it is found in the final sentence of his article, fittingly titled, "Interpreting the Bible as an Ancient Near Eastern Document" (based on a paper presented in January 2004).[2] The phrase (and several variations) subsequently appears throughout Walton's *Lost World* volumes and in his *Old Testament Theology for Christians: From Ancient Context to Enduring Belief* (2017).[3]

---

1. See Walton, *Ancient Near Eastern Thought and the Old Testament* (2nd ed., 2018), 11, 18; Walton, *Old Testament Theology for Christians*, 16.

2. In Block, ed., *Israel: Ancient Kingdom or Late Invention?*, 327. The full quote: "Comparative study does not impose something foreign upon the text; rather it seeks to rediscover that which is intrinsic to the text. This dimension may not be taken for granted, because in many ways we are foreign to the text, for the Bible was written *for* us but not *to* us" (Walton's italics).

3. For Walton's *Old Testament Theology*, see p. 5. For references in the *Lost World* series, see Longman and Walton, *Lost World of the Flood*, vii, 9; Walton, *Lost World of Adam and Eve*, 19; Walton, *Lost World of Genesis One*, 9, 21; Walton and Sandy, *Lost World of Scripture*, 52; Walton and Walton, *Lost World of the Israelite Conquest*, 7, 9; Walton and Walton, *Lost World of the Torah*, 13, 103. The phrase also appears in Keener and Walton, *NIV Cultural Backgrounds Study Bible*, iii; Walton and Walton, *Demons and Spirits*, 15. Another volume that captures the essence of the phrase in its subtitle is Walton and Hill, *Old Testament Today: A Journey from Ancient Context to Contemporary Relevance* (2nd ed., 2013).

The phrase "for us" echoes the Apostle Paul's frequent reminder that the Hebrew Scriptures are "for us," that is, "for our sake" or "for our instruction" (see Rom 4:24; 1 Cor 9:10; cf. Rom 15:4; 1 Cor 10:6, 11). The "us/our" in these texts refers to the church, to whom Walton's publications are primarily directed. While he engages with the wider academy, he usually writes *for Christians*, particularly evangelical Christians, so that they can effectively interpret progressive revelation by employing a "christotelic" approach to the Old Testament.[4]

Yet while Scripture is "for us," it is "not to us"; it is ancient people's mail, so to speak. Christians must stay cognizant of the fact that God's self-revelation is culturally embedded.[5] For this reason, it is essential to develop the skills of a "cultural broker"[6] when engaging Scripture. As Walton explains,

> [I]f we are to interpret Scripture so as to receive the full impact of God's authoritative message, *we have to set our cultural river aside and try to understand the cultural river of the ancient people* to whom the text was addressed. The Bible was written to the people of ancient Israel in the language of ancient Israel; therefore, its message operates according to the logic of ancient Israel.[7]

In other words, "we cannot seek to construe *their* world in *our* terms."[8]

Our subtitle for this honorary volume, *Essays on Creation, Covenant, and Context*, is designed to capture Walton's primary research trajectories and to serve as rallying topics for our various contributors. Although "charts" might be added to this series of c-words, in light of Walton's now famous *Chronological and Background Charts of the Old Testament* (1978, 1994), we have contented ourselves with offering only occasional supplementary tables in some of our peer-reviewed essays. Walton is probably best known for his fresh perspectives on "creation" and cosmology (see *NIV Application Commentary: Genesis*; *Lost World of Genesis One*; *Genesis 1 as Ancient Cosmology*), but "covenant" is an equally important theme in Walton's groundbreaking work (see *Covenant: God's Purpose, God's Plan*; *Lost World of the Israelite Conquest*; *Old Testament Theology for Christians*; *Lost World of the Torah*). We are using "context" intentionally as a broad term in order to accommodate various essays that employ aspects of Walton's interpretive methods (described above), especially those

---

4. See Walton, *Old Testament Theology for Christians*, 5–6, 22. For an example of christotelic interpretation, see Walton's discussion of the first four commandments in "Interpreting the Bible as an Ancient Near Eastern Document," in Block, ed., *Israel: Ancient Kingdom or Late Invention?*, 324–25.

5. See Walton and Walton, *Lost World of the Torah*, 11; cf. Longman and Walton, *Lost World of the Flood*, 3, 6–7.

6. Walton and Walton, *Lost World of the Torah*, 12.

7. Walton and Walton, *Lost World of the Torah*, 14 (italics added). For the metaphor of a "cultural river," see also Longman and Walton, *Lost World of the Flood*, 6–7, 179; Walton and Walton, *Lost World of the Israelite Conquest*, 8–10, 254.

8. Walton, *Genesis 1 as Ancient Cosmology*, 6 (Walton's italics).

engaging additional c-words like culture, cultural river, comparative studies, cognitive environment, or even children's curricula.

Our richly diverse group of contributors reflect Walton's influence on theologians, archaeologists, historians, and New Testament scholars in addition to scholars of Hebrew Bible and the ancient Near East (with its many sub-disciplines). During his two decades of teaching at Moody Bible Institute (1981–2001) and another two decades of teaching at Wheaton College (2001–present), Walton has inspired many undergraduate and graduate women and men to pursue careers in biblical and related studies. Walton significantly influenced all of the contributors to this volume, whether they studied in his classroom, worked as his research assistants, explored the Holy Land with him, or even grew up in his home. Over the last twenty years, these contributors have also come to know one another through the annual SBL breakfasts that Walton has hosted for his ever-growing number of students and students-now-colleagues from across the world. May Walton's tribe continue to increase!

We are all deeply grateful to John H. Walton for his generous investments in our lives. None of us would be who we are or where we are today without his gifts of time, encouragement, inspiring teaching, and mentorship. Many of us are also beneficiaries of John's and Kim's nurturing hospitality and supportive presence at various milestones of our lives. Somewhat like the Bible, the Waltons have been there "for us," but this collection of academic essays is "not to us." It is a *Festschrift* ("commemorative publication"), and we offer it as a מנחה ("tribute") to John H. Walton, to honor him in recognition of forty years of loyal service to God and the church.

Bibliography

Block, Daniel I., ed. *Israel: Ancient Kingdom or Late Invention?* Nashville: Broadman & Holman, 2008.

Keener, Craig S., and John H. Walton. *NIV Cultural Backgrounds Study Bible.* Grand Rapids: Zondervan, 2016.

Longman, Tremper, III, and John H. Walton. *The Lost World of the Flood: Mythology, Theology, and the Deluge Debate.* Downers Grove, IL: InterVarsity, 2018.

Walton, John H. *Ancient Near Eastern Thought and the Old Testament: Introducing the Conceptual World of the Hebrew Bible.* 2nd ed. Grand Rapids: Baker, 2018.

———. *Genesis 1 as Ancient Cosmology.* Winona Lake, IN: Eisenbrauns, 2011.

———. *The Lost World of Adam and Eve: Genesis 2–3 and the Human Origins Debate.* Downers Grove, IL: InterVarsity, 2015.

———. *The Lost World of Genesis One: Ancient Cosmology and the Origins Debate.* Downers Grove, IL: InterVarsity, 2009.

———. *Old Testament Theology for Christians: From Ancient Context to Enduring Belief.* Downers Grove, IL: InterVarsity, 2017.

Walton, John H., and Andrew E. Hill. *Old Testament Today: A Journey from Ancient Context to Contemporary Relevance.* 2nd ed. Grand Rapids: Zondervan, 2013.

Walton, John H., and D. Brent Sandy. *The Lost World of Scripture: Ancient Literary Culture and Biblical Authority*. Downers Grove, IL: InterVarsity, 2013.

Walton, John H., and J. Harvey Walton. *Demons and Spirits in Biblical Theology: Reading the Biblical Text in Its Cultural and Literary Context*. Eugene, OR: Cascade Books, 2019.

———. *The Lost World of the Israelite Conquest: Covenant, Retribution, and the Fate of the Canaanites*. Downers Grove, IL: InterVarsity, 2017.

———. *The Lost World of the Torah: Law as Covenant and Wisdom in Ancient Context*. Downers Grove, IL: InterVarsity, 2019.

The Publications of John H. Walton (1978–2019)

Shawn Virgil Goodwin

Books

1978. *Chronological and Background Charts of the Old Testament*. Grand Rapids: Zondervan. (Rev. and exp. ed., 1994).

1982. *Jonah*. Grand Rapids: Lamplighter.

1988. *Obadiah, Jonah*. Grand Rapids: Zondervan. (With Bryan Beyer).

1989. *Ancient Israelite Literature in Its Cultural Context: A Survey of Parallels between Biblical and Ancient Near Eastern Texts*. Grand Rapids: Zondervan.

1991. *A Survey of the Old Testament*. Grand Rapids: Zondervan. (With Andrew Hill. 2nd ed., 2000; 3rd ed., 2009).

1994. *Covenant: God's Purpose, God's Plan*. Grand Rapids: Zondervan.

1997. *IVP Bible Background Commentary: Genesis—Deuteronomy*. Downers Grove, IL: InterVarsity. (With Victor H. Matthews).

2000. *IVP Bible Background Commentary: Old Testament*. Downers Grove, IL: InterVarsity. (With Victor H. Matthews and Mark W. Chavalas).

2001. *Genesis: From Biblical Text . . . to Contemporary Life*. NIV Application Commentary. Grand Rapids: Zondervan.

2004. *Old Testament Today: A Journey from Original Meaning to Contemporary Significance*. Grand Rapids: Zondervan. (With Andrew E. Hill. 2nd ed., 2014).

2006a. *Ancient Near Eastern Thought and the Old Testament: Introducing the Conceptual World of the Hebrew Bible*. Grand Rapids: Baker Academic. (2nd ed., 2018).

2006b. *The Essential Bible Companion Key Insights for Reading God's Word*. Grand Rapids: Zondervan. (With Mark L. Strauss and Ted Cooper, Jr).

2008. *Jonah*. Edited by Tremper III Longman and David E. Garland. The Expositor's Bible Commentary. Rev. ed. 8. Grand Rapids: Zondervan.

2009a. *Genesis: The Covenant Comes to Life*. Grand Rapids: Zondervan. (With Janet Nygren).

2009b. *The Lost World of Genesis One: Ancient Cosmology and the Origins Debate*. Downers Grove, IL: InterVarsity.

2010. *The Bible Story Handbook: A Resource for Teaching 175 Stories from the Bible*. Wheaton, IL: Crossway. (With Kim Walton).

2011. *Genesis 1 as Ancient Cosmology*. Winona Lake, IN: Eisenbrauns.

2012. *Job: From Biblical Text ... to Contemporary Life*. NIV Application Commentary. Grand Rapids: Zondervan.

2013a. *Four Views on the Historical Adam*. Grand Rapids: Zondervan. (With Denis O. Lamoureux, C. John Collins, William D. Barrick, Gregory A. Boyd, Philip Graham Ryken, Matthew Barrett, and Ardel B. Caneday).

2013b. *The Lost World of Scripture: Ancient Literary Culture and Biblical Authority*. Downers Grove, IL: InterVarsity. (With Brent Sandy).

2015a. *A Brief Survey of the Bible: Discovering the Big Picture of God's Story from Genesis to Revelation*. Grand Rapids: Zondervan. (With Mark L. Strauss).

2015b. *How to Read Job*. Downers Grove, IL: InterVarsity. (With Tremper Longman III).

2015c. *The Lost World of Adam and Eve: Genesis 2–3 and the Human Origins Debate*. Downers Grove, IL: IVP Academic. (With N. T. Wright).

2016. *NIV Cultural Backgrounds Study Bible*. Grand Rapids: Zondervan. (With Craig S. Keener).

2017. *The Lost World of the Israelite Conquest: Covenant, Retribution, and the Fate of the Canaanites*. Downers Grove, IL: InterVarsity. (With J. Harvey Walton).

2018. *The Lost World of the Flood: Mythology, Theology, and the Deluge Debate*. Downers Grove, IL: InterVarsity. (With Tremper Longman III and Stephen O. Moshier).

2019a. *Demons and Spirits in Biblical Theology: Reading the Biblical Text in Its Cultural and Literary Context*. Eugene, OR: Cascade Books. (With J. Harvey Walton).

2019b. *The Lost World of the Torah: Law as Covenant and Wisdom in Ancient Context*. Downers Grove, IL: InterVarsity. (With J. Harvey Walton).

Books Edited

2009. *Zondervan Illustrated Bible Backgrounds Commentary: Old Testament*. 5 vols. Grand Rapids: Zondervan.

2013. *Teach the Text Commentary Series*. 21 vols. Grand Rapids: Baker. (With Mark L. Strauss and Rosalie de Rosset).

2014. *Windows to the Ancient World of the Hebrew Bible: Essays in Honor of Samuel Greengus*. Winona Lake, IN: Eisenbrauns. (With Bill T. Arnold and Nancy L. Erickson).

2018. *Behind the Scenes of the Old Testament: Cultural, Social, and Historical Contexts*. Grand Rapids: Baker. (With Jonathan S. Greer and John W. Hilber).

Articles

1981. "The Antediluvian Section of the Sumerian King List and Genesis 5." *BA* 44:207–8.

1985. "New Observations on the Date of Isaiah." *JETS* 28:129–32.

1986. "The Four Kingdoms of Daniel." *JETS* 29:25–36.

1987a. "Deuteronomy: An Exposition of the Spirit of the Law." *Grace Theological Journal* 8:213–25.

1987b. "Isa 7:14: What's in a Name?" *JETS* 30:289–306.

1988. "The Decree of Darius the Mede in Daniel 6." *JETS* 31:279–86.

1989. "Vision Narrative Wordplay and Jeremiah 24." *VT* 39:508–9.

1991a. "Eighth Century Chronology Revisited." Evangelical Theological Society Papers (Theological Research Exchange Network no. ETS-4312).

1991b. "The Place of the *Hutqaṭṭēl* within the D-Stem Group and Its Implications in Deuteronomy 24:4." *Hebrew Studies* 32:7–17.

1991c. "Psalms: A Cantata about the Davidic Covenant." *JETS* 34:21–31.

1992b. "The Object Lesson of Jonah 4:5–7 and the Purpose of the Book of Jonah." *BBR* 2:47–57.

1993. "Bible-Based Curricula and the Crisis of Scriptural Authority." *Christian Education Journal* 13:83–94. (with Laurie D. Bailey, and Craig Williford).

1996. "The Mesopotamian Background of the Tower of Babel Account and Its Implications." *BBR* 5:155–75.

2001. "Equilibrium and the Sacred Compass: The Structure of Leviticus." *BBR* 11:293–304.

2002. "Inspired Subjectivity and Hermeneutical Objectivity." *The Master's Seminary Journal* 13:65–77.

2003. "The Imagery of the Substitute King Ritual in Isaiah's Fourth Servant Song." *JBL* 122:734–43.

2005a. "Common Sense Lexicography and 1 Timothy 2:12–15." Evangelical Theological Society Papers (Theological Research Exchange Network no. ETS-0234).

2005b. "Perspectives on the Nature of Prophetic Literature." Evangelical Theological Society Papers (Theological Research Exchange Network no. ETS-3915).

2007. "Theories of Origins: A Multi- and Interdisciplinary Course for Undergraduates at Wheaton College." *Perspectives on Science and Christian Faith* 59:289–96. (With Stephen O. Moshier, Dean Arnold, Larry L. Funck, Raymond J. Lewis, Albert J. Smith, and William R. Wharton).

2008. "Creation in Genesis 1:1—2:3 and the Ancient Near East: Order out of Disorder after Chaoskampf." *CTJ* 43:48–63.

2012. "Human Origins and the Bible." *Zygon* 47:875–89.

2015a. "An Expanded View of Biblical Authority: A Response to Van Kuiken." *JETS* 58:693–95. (with D. Brent Sandy).

2015b. "Response to Richard Averbeck." *Themelios* 40:240–42.

2016a. "Response to Provan." *Ex Auditu* 32:22–25.

2016b. "The Role of the Ancient Near East and Modern Science in Interpretation." *The City*, December. https://hbu.edu/news-and-events/2016/12/02/the-role-of-the-ancient-near-east-and-modern-science-in-interpretation.

2017a. "Abraham's Troubling Test." *Bible Study Magazine*, July/August:12–13.

2017b. "Hermeneutical Humility and Origins in Genesis." *Cultural Encounters* 12:34–43.

2018. "Current Hot Topics in Old Testament: Joshua's Conquest." *Didaktikos* 2:41–42.

2019. "Understanding Torah: Ancient Legal Text, Covenant Stipulation, and Christian Scripture." *BBR* 29:1–18.

Book Chapters

1990. "The Sons of God in Genesis 6:1–4." In *The Genesis Debate: Persistent Questions about Creation and the Flood*, edited by Ronald F. Youngblood, 184–209. Grand Rapids: Baker.

1994a. "Cultural Background of the Old Testament." In *Foundations for Biblical Interpretation: A Complete Library of Tools and Resources*, edited by David S. Dockery, K. A. Mathews, and Robert Bryan Sloan, 255–73. Nashville: Broadman & Holman.

1994b. "Joshua 10:12–15 and Mesopotamian Celestial Omen Texts." In *Faith, Tradition, and History: Old Testament Historiography in Its Near Eastern Context*, edited by Alan R. Millard, James Karl Hoffmeier, and David W. Baker, 181–90. Winona Lake, IN: Eisenbrauns.

1997. "Principles for Productive Word Study." In *New International Dictionary of Old Testament Theology and Exegesis*, edited by Willem A. VanGemeren, 1:161–71. Grand Rapids: Zondervan.

2001. "The Anzu Myth as Relevant Background for Daniel 7?" In *The Book of Daniel: Composition and Reception*, edited by John J. Collins and Peter W. Flint, 69–89. Supplements to Vetus Testamentum 83/1. Leiden: Brill.

2008. "Interpreting the Bible as an Ancient Near Eastern Document." In *Israel: Ancient Kingdom or Late Invention?*, edited by Daniel Isaac Block, 298–327. Nashville: Broadman & Holman.

2011. "The Ancient Near Eastern Background of the Spirit of the Lord in the Old Testament." In *Presence, Power, and Promise: The Role of the Spirit of God in the Old Testament*, edited by David G. Firth and Paul D. Wegner, 38–67. Downers Grove, IL: InterVarsity.

2012. "The Decalogue Structure of Deuteronomic Law." In *Interpreting Deuteronomy: Issues and Approaches*, edited by David G. Firth and Philip Johnston, 93–117. Nottingham, UK: Inter-Varsity.

2013a. "A Historical Adam: Archetypal Creation View." In *Four Views on the Historical Adam*, edited by Matthew Barrett and Ardel B. Caneday, 89–118. Grand Rapids: Zondervan.

2013b. "Reading Genesis 1 as Ancient Cosmology." In *Reading Genesis 1–2: An Evangelical Conversation*, edited by J. Daryl Charles, 141–69. Peabody, MA: Hendrickson.

2014. "Demons in Mesopotamia and Israel: Exploring the Category of Non-Divine but Supernatural Entities." In *Windows to the Ancient World of the Hebrew Bible Essays in Honor of Samuel Greengus*, edited by Bill T. Arnold, Nancy Erickson, and John H. Walton, 229–46. Winona Lake, IN: Eisenbrauns.

2017a. "Biblical Interpretation: What Is the Nature of Biblical Authority?" In *Old-Earth or Evolutionary Creation?: Discussing Origins with Reasons to Believe and BioLogos*, edited by Kenneth Keathley, 27–48. Downers Grove, IL: InterVarsity.

2017b. "The Tower of Babel and the Covenant: Rhetorical Strategy in Genesis Based on Theological and Comparative Analysis." In *Evangelical Scholarship, Retrospects and Prospects: Essays in Honor of Stanley N. Gundry*, edited by Dirk R. Buursma, Katya Covrett, and Verlyn D. Verbrugge, 109–18. Grand Rapids: Zondervan.

2018a. "Cosmic Origins: Genesis 1:1—2:4." In *Understanding Scientific Theories of Origins: Cosmology, Geology, and Biology in Christian Perspective*, edited by Robert C. Bishop, 99–116. Downers Grove, IL: InterVarsity.

2018b. "Creation. New Creation, and the So-Called Mission of God." In *Creation and Doxology: The Beginning and End of God's Good World*. Edited by Gerald L. Hiestand and Todd A. Wilson, 133–44. Downers Grove, IL: InterVarsity.

2018c. "The Genesis Flood." In *Understanding Scientific Theories of Origins: Cosmology, Geology, and Biology in Christian Perspective*, edited by Robert C. Bishop, 237–44. Downers Grove, IL: InterVarsity.

2018d. "Human Origins: Genesis 2–3." In *Understanding Scientific Theories of Origins: Cosmology, Geology, and Biology in Christian Perspective*, edited by Robert C. Bishop, 547–57. Downers Grove, IL: InterVarsity.

2018e. "Interactions in the Ancient Cognitive Environment." In *Behind the Scenes of the Old Testament: Cultural, Social, and Historical Contexts*, edited by Jonathan S. Greer, John W. Hilber, and John H. Walton, 333–39. Grand Rapids: Baker Academic.

2018f. "Origins in Genesis: Claims of an Ancient Text in a Modern Scientific World." In *Knowing Creation: Perspectives from Theology, Philosophy and Science*, edited Andrew B. Torrance and Thomas H. McCall, 107–22. Grand Rapids: Zondervan.

2018g. "Principles and Methods of Biblical Interpretation." In *Understanding Scientific Theories of Origins: Cosmology, Geology, and Biology in Christian Perspective*, edited by Robert C. Bishop, 9–13. Downers Grove, IL: InterVarsity.

2018h. "The Temple in Context." In *Behind the Scenes of the Old Testament: Cultural, Social, and Historical Contexts*, edited by Jonathan S. Greer, John W. Hilber, and John H. Walton, 349–55. Grand Rapids: Baker Academic.

The Publications of John H. Walton (1978–2019)

Reference Work Contributions

1979. *The International Standard Bible Encyclopedia*, edited by Geoffrey W. Bromiley. Fully revised. Grand Rapids: Eerdmans. (Select articles).

1988. *Baker Encyclopedia of the Bible*, edited by Walter A. Elwell and Barry J. Beitzel. Grand Rapids: Baker. (Select articles).

1991. *The Complete Bible Study Tool Kit*, edited by John F. Balchin, David Field, and Tremper Longman. Downers Grove, IL: InterVarsity. ("Unpacking the Old Testament," 19–38).

1997. *New International Dictionary of Old Testament Theology & Exegesis*, edited by Willem A. VanGemeren. 5 vols. Grand Rapids: Zondervan. (Select articles).

2003. *Dictionary of the Old Testament: Pentateuch*, edited by T. Desmond Alexander and David W. Baker. Downers Grove, IL: InterVarsity. ("Creation," 155–68; "Eden, Garden of," 202–7; "Exodus, Date of," 258–72; "Flood," 315–26; "Serpent," 736–39; "Sons of God, Daughters of Man," 793–98).

2005a. *Dictionary of the Old Testament: Historical Books*, edited by Bill T. Arnold and H. G. M Williamson. Downers Grove, IL: InterVarsity. ("Genealogies," 309–16).

2005b. *Dictionary for Theological Interpretation of the Bible*, edited by Kevin J. Vanhoozer, Craig G. Bartholomew, Daniel J. Treier, and N. T. Wright. Grand Rapids: Baker Academic. ("Ancient Near Eastern Background Studies," 40–45; "Etymology," 200–202; "Jonah, Book of," 401–4).

2008. *Dictionary of the Old Testament: Wisdom, Poetry & Writings*, edited by Tremper Longman and Peter Enns. Downers Grove, IL: Nottingham, UK: Inter-Varsity. ("Job 1: Book of," 333–46; "Retribution," 647–55; "Satan," 714–17).

2009. *Zondervan Illustrated Bible Backgrounds Commentary: Old Testament*, edited by John H. Walton. Grand Rapids: Zondervan. ("Methodology: An Introductory Essay," 1:viii–xv; "Genesis," 1:2–159; "Jonah," 5:100–119; "Zechariah," 5:202–31 [with Kenneth G. Hoglund]).

2011a. *The Eerdmans Companion to the Bible*, edited by Gordon D. Fee and Robert L. Hubbard. Grand Rapids: Eerdmans. ("Flood Stories in the Bible and the Ancient Near East," 86–87).

2011b. *The Baker Illustrated Bible Handbook*, edited by J. Daniel Hays and J. Scott Duvall. Grand Rapids: Baker. ("Other Flood Accounts in the Ancient Near East," 47).

2016. *Encyclopedia of the Bible and Its Reception*, edited by Dale C. Allison Jr. et al. Berlin: de Gruyter. ("Immortality: 1. Ancient Near East and Hebrew Bible/Old Testament," 12:1008–11).

2017. *Dictionary of Christianity and Science: The Definitive Reference for the Intersection of Christian Faith and Contemporary Science*, edited by Paul Copan, Tremper Longman, Christopher L. Reese, and Michael G. Strauss. Grand Rapids: Zondervan. ("Cosmology, Ancient," 116–20).

Reviews

1986. Review of *The History of Israel and Judah in Old Testament Times* by François Castel. *JETS* 29:505–7.

1990. Review of *A New Chronology for the Kings of Israel and Judah and Its Implications for Biblical History and Literature* by John H. Hayes, Paul K. Hooker. *JAOS* 110:767–70.

1992a. Review of *Character and Ideology in the Book of Esther* by Michael V. Fox, *Ashland Theological Journal* 24:111–13.

1992b. Review of *The Bible in the Light of Cuneiform Literature: Scripture in Context III* by William W. Hallo. *Hebrew Studies* 33:130–32.

1996. Review of *Deuteronomy* by Eugene Merrill. *JETS* 39:469–71.

1999. Review of *The Torah: Theology and Social History of Old Testament Law* by Frank Crüsemann. *JETS* 42:714–16.

2000. Review of *Gods, Goddesses, and Images of God in Ancient Israel* by Othmar Keel and Christoph Uehlinger. *JETS* 43:535–37.

2011. Review of *The Seven Pillars of Creation: The Bible, Science, and the Ecology of Wonder* by William P. Brown. *Perspectives on Science and Christian Faith* 63:138–39.

2013. Review of *The Book of Genesis: Composition, Reception, and Interpretation* by Craig A. Evans. *BBR* 23:580–84.

2014. "Can the Bible Survive Science?" Review of *The Nature of Creation: Examining the Bible and Science* by Mark Harris. *Marginalia: Los Angeles Review of Books*. June 24, 2014. http://marginalia.lareviewofbooks.org/can-bible-survive-science-john-walton/.

2015. Review of *What Really Happened in the Garden of Eden?* by Ziony Zevit. *Review of Biblical Literature* [http://www.bookreviews.org].

Children's Books

1986a. *Abraham and His Big Family*. Elgin, IL: Chariot. (With Kim Walton, illustrated by Alice Craig).

1986b. *Jonah and the Big Fish*. Elgin, IL: Chariot. (With Kim Walton, illustrated by Alice Craig).

1986c. *Moses and the Mighty Plagues*. Elgin, IL: Chariot. (With Kim Walton, illustrated by Alice Craig).

1987a. *Adam & Eve in the Garden*. Elgin, IL: Chariot. (With Kim Walton, illustrated by Alice Craig).

1987b. *Daniel and the Lions*. Elgin, IL: Chariot. (With Kim Walton, illustrated by Alice Craig).

1987c. *David Fights Goliath*. Elgin, IL: Chariot. (With Kim Walton, illustrated by Alice Craig).

1987d. *Elijah and the Contest.* Elgin, IL: Chariot. (With Kim Walton, illustrated by Alice Craig).

1987e. *Jeroboam and the Golden Calves.* Elgin, IL: Chariot. (With Kim Walton, illustrated by Alice Craig).

1987f. *Jesus, God's Son, Is Born.* Elgin, IL: Chariot. (With Kim Walton, illustrated by Alice Craig).

1987g. *Paul and the Bright Light.* Elgin, IL: Chariot. (With Kim Walton, illustrated by Alice Craig).

1987h. *Samuel and the Voice in the Night.* Elgin, IL: Chariot. (With Kim Walton, illustrated by Alice Craig).

1993. *The Tiny Tots Bible Story Book.* Elgin, IL: Chariot. (With Kim Walton, illustrated by Alice Craig; collection of all of the individual Bible stories).

1995a. *God and the World He Made.* Elgin, IL: Chariot. (With Kim Walton, illustrated by Alice Craig).

1995b. *Noah and the Flood.* Elgin, IL: Chariot. (With Kim Walton, illustrated by Alice Craig).

Part 1

Creation

1

Sense of a Beginning
The Role of Beginnings in the Israelite Historical Résumés

AUBREY BUSTER

Men can do nothing without the make-believe of a beginning.
—GEORGE ELIOT, *DANIEL DERONDA*

IT IS WITH GREAT pleasure that I dedicate this essay to John Walton, who has spent much of his career helping us think better about *beginnings,* the beginning of the Bible, and its relationship to the beginning of the cosmos. For this, the guild owes him a great debt of gratitude. As for me personally, however, I would like to thank him primarily for his role as a teacher. It was in John's classes that I learned the thrill of discovery that came with a carefully and consistently applied method, and it was his class on Genesis that led to my first serious interest in pursuing a career in biblical studies.

Introduction

One of the primary difficulties of teaching introductory courses in Hebrew Bible is deciding how to cover an immense amount of material in the course of a single semester. Usually, this results in a "book-a-day" approach, with some minor prophets grouped together. A frequent exception to this general rule, however, is the book of Genesis, to which I have discovered I need to give two or even three days, double or triple the time given to even biblical books of a similar length, such as Jeremiah or Isaiah. This is not because the book of Genesis is inherently more complex or more theologically important than any other book in the canon. It is simply because my students have significantly more pre-conceptions about what is contained in this book, its opening eleven chapters in particular. If they have come from a faith tradition that emphasizes the regular reading of scripture, many of them have started (and re-started) their "Bible in a Year" reading plans at this point. Sunday school classes begin here. Debates concerning the relationship between the beginning of a sacred book and the beginning of "everything" begin here.

My students are not alone in this. Beginnings in general play an outsized role in remembering. It is easier for most students from the United States to remember the first president than to list those who follow. Figures who are attached to the "beginnings" of things tend to attract cultural mythologies that are often difficult to debunk. It is common knowledge at this point in our history that Christopher Columbus did not *discover* America. Yet as a figure associated with the "beginning" of a colonized North America, Columbus has come to stand for more than simply a man who did or did not undertake a series of actions that we are free to celebrate or condemn.[1] Moving beyond history, this quirk of human memory extends to the opening lines of literary works outside of the Bible. As literary scholar Peter Rabinowitz quips, "if you ask someone familiar with *Pride and Prejudice* to quote a line from the novel, the odds are that you will get the opening sentence."[2]

Beginnings also play an important role in biblical studies. Much of scholarship on the Hebrew Bible focuses, not on the narrative beginnings of biblical books, but on constructing proposals for their *origins,* defined in terms of authorship or in terms of the most original component pieces of each respective biblical text. Simply put, beginnings matter. Because of their importance, they are also usually culturally established. If you ask a Jew or a Christian to name the "beginning" of the Bible, they would likely respond with Gen 1:1. But if you asked an ancient Israelite to tell the beginning of *their* story, what image or event would come to mind? This is, of course, an impossible question to answer. We cannot conduct a Pew survey of ancient Israelites in this regard. What we do have is a remarkable array of texts in the Hebrew Bible that preserve performances of schematic versions of Israel's history. We cannot be entirely sure whether the performances preserved in our Bible represent "common knowledge" among Israelites at any particular point in their history. But we do have evidence for the regular communal recitation of history as a cultural practice, both in the Hebrew Bible and in Second Temple Judaism. In each case, the historical reviews rehearse a cultural *master narrative,* the "authoritative account of some extended segment of history," an account that is assumed to be accepted by the community who hears it.[3] These abbreviated rehearsals of Israel's master narrative, however, begin at several different places. The brevity and variety of these "historical résumés" offer the

---

1. See, for example, Schuman et al., "Elite Revisionists," 2–29.
2. Rabinowitz, "Reading Beginnings and Endings," 300.
3. Newsom, "Rhyme and Reason," 217.

opportunity to observe how the selection of a particular starting point influences the content and arrangement of the rest of the story.

In the following essay, I will pose two questions: the first question is, how do different beginnings shape the way that the story is told? In this section of the essay, I will present a selection of theoretical insights focused on the questions of beginning and the way in which a narrative's beginning both sets up and determines the content of the story that is to follow. This overview is necessarily selective, but it will at least suggest some of the various roles that beginnings play in the configuration and interpretation of stories. Secondly, I will turn to the historical résumés in the Hebrew Bible to interrogate the roles of beginnings in the stories that Israel told about herself. While each of these recitals plays an important rhetorical role in its respective individual narrative or anthological context, by surveying them as a series we can also see the most common ways in which Israel referred to the beginnings of her own life with God.

Functions of Beginnings

Beginnings as National Origins

Beginnings are often understood as *origins,* that is as "an external event that originally constituted an object, situation, or being."[4] This understanding of beginning as origin profoundly influences the readings of the beginning of the Hebrew Bible, which opens with the origin story *par excellence,* the creation of the heavens and the earth. The identification of beginnings with an origin goes far beyond disputes concerning the age of the earth, however, or the relationship of faith with science. It is, instead, a *perspective* on beginnings that is native to human thought. As Niels Buch Leander observes, "Understood as origin, a beginning is intended to provide explanation."[5]

Even in traditions that do not claim to articulate the absolute origin of everything ("In the beginning, God created the heavens and the earth"), origin stories play a powerful explanatory role. The story of "where we came from" is often assumed to offer some significant insight into "who we are." As Anthony Smith observes, myths of common origin answer questions of similarity and belonging. The questions "why are we alike? Why are we one community?" are answered with a response that has to do with *origin*: "because we came from the same place, at a definite period of time and are descended from the self-same ancestor."[6] The memory of a community's origin, however that origin is imagined, constitutes the "event that marks the group's emergence as an independent social entity."[7] Whether the relationship to the ancestor is real or

---

4. Leander, "To Begin with the Beginning," 16.
5. Leander, "To Begin with the Beginning," 16.
6. Smith, *Ethnic Origins,* 24.
7. Zerubavel, *Recovered Roots,* 7.

imagined is ultimately inconsequential to the rhetoric of cultural texts: their recollection of a common ancestor or a common constitutive event, a common *beginning point,* can be powerful enough to transcend present social differences.

The weight of the understanding that that which comes *first* in a story carries extraordinary explanatory weight can be seen in the tradition of biblical interpretation. The presentation of the world and humans as they were first created plays an outsized role in interpreting what follows. To Jews and Christians, the narratives in the primeval history function as foundational statements about who *we* are and how we have arrived to where we are today. The understanding of beginnings as origins, particularly the national origins of Israel and Judah, is also native to biblical studies. For example, Thomas Römer and Konrad Schmid understand the various beginning points of Israel's story in the historical résumés, to be reviewed below, as concomitant with Israel's varied self-understanding of her own national and political origins.[8] They use the multiple beginning points referred to in the résumés, and alluded to in other modes of discourse, to argue for competing social groups in Israel who claim for themselves allegiance to a certain ancestor, Abraham, Jacob, or Joseph, or epoch-making event, such as the exodus. For both groups, beginnings understood as origins function to explain central aspects of group identity.

Beginnings as Discontinuities or Temporal Thresholds

Such an approach to beginnings, that is, the assumption that the beginning points of stories outline alternative claims to origin that in turn unify and define social groups, is not, however, the only way to understand beginnings. In fact, the controversy about the relationship of "beginnings" to "origins," which has sometimes existed as an unchallenged assumption in biblical studies, was one of the central schisms in 20th-century philosophy and literature.[9] It stands at the very heart of the post-structuralist critique of a metaphysical perspective. Instead of a singular origin, to which, in theory, all could be traced, figures such as Jacques Derrida and Michel Foucault distinguished between "origins" as ultimate externally imposed beginnings and other internal "beginnings," the various inaugurations of internal shifts and change.[10]

In his influential essay on "Nietzsche, Genealogy, and History," Foucault articulates this central distinction between an "origin," defined as the ultimate beginning, and what he dubs "genealogy." The concept of an "origin" emphasizes continuity: to

---

8. Römer, "Résumer l'histoire," 21–39; Schmid, *Genesis and the Moses Story.*

9. Leander, *Sense of a Beginning,* 31.

10. Foucault, "Nietzsche, Genealogy, History," 76–100; Foucault, *The Order of Things,* 328–35; Derrida, "Structure, Sign, and Play," 278–93. I am grateful to Adam Miglio for pointing out the way that Gilles Deleuze and Felix Guatarri also radicalize an approach to origins through their construction of a distinction between *arborescent* and *rhizomatic* knowledge in *A Thousand Plateaus.* Furthermore, Marc Van der Meiroop relates their *rhizomatic* construction of knowledge to Mesopotamian epistemology in *Philosophy Before the Greeks,* 222–23.

search for an *origin* often assumes that if one finds what came first, one has discovered a fundamental principle that remains consistent in all that follows.[11] Genealogy, on the other hand, a concept that Foucault develops from Nietzsche, is a method designed to trace the many connecting and intersecting *shifts* that lead to where one finds oneself in the present: to "identify the accidents, the minute deviations—or conversely, the complete reversals—the errors, the false appraisals, and the faulty calculations that gave birth to those things that ... have value for us."[12] Instead of "origins," Foucault identifies a series of *termini a quo* (temporal thresholds), points of the inauguration of a change. In each case, these changes might be considered the "beginning" of something new, but it is a beginning that cannot be disconnected from what came before. There is no imagining of an origin *ex nihilo*.

The result of this theoretical shift is an emphasis on *many* beginnings. It is the task of the critic or of the historian to trace these temporal thresholds astutely. This central idea that one should not search for an explanatory origin but for *many* beginnings has recently found a thought-provoking analogy in a study by Sara Milstein on the archaeology of textual openings in texts from the ancient Near East, including the Hebrew Bible.[13] Milstein examines the common practice of "revision by introduction" in the ancient Near East, whereby a scribe would transform the meaning of a work by the addition of a new beginning. This editorial act is clear in texts that are preserved in extant manuscript copies both *with* and *without* particular beginnings, such as the Sumerian King List, the Epic of Etana, the Community Rule, and the Gilgamesh Epic.[14] But for many of her examples, particularly those from the Hebrew Bible, she engages in a project of textual archaeology, whereby she discovers the textual fissures, the "minute deviations ... or conversely, the complete reversals," that mark the addition of a new beginning.[15]

Beginnings as Rhetoric

The viewpoints above attempt to define beginnings according to what they *are*. But perhaps a better question is what do beginnings *do?* Instead of a concern for beginnings as first principles, rhetorical analyses of beginning have focused on the way in which beginnings and origins play a powerful formative function for communities. Attending to beginnings as rhetorical strategies introduces a shift in emphasis, if not in kind. I noted above that a claim to common origins functions as a powerful act of establishing communal unity. But descriptions of origins are not self-apparent. As Kenneth Burke expresses, the selection of "any given terminology is a *reflection* of

---

11. Foucault, "Nietzsche, Genealogy, History," 77; cf. Foucault, *The Order of Things*, 329.
12. Foucault, "Nietzsche, Genealogy, History," 81.
13. Milstein, *Tracking the Master Scribe*.
14. Milstein, *Tracking the Master Scribe*, 43–146.
15. Milstein, *Tracking the Master Scribe*, 147–206.

reality" but it is also a "*selection* of reality; and to this extent it must function as a *deflection* of reality."[16] A rhetorical approach to beginnings recognizes that the information that the author or orator presents at the beginning is always an act of emphasis that foregrounds certain aspects of reality but simultaneously downplays or erases others. The choice of a beginning point is an influential decision. In the following, I would like to divide the primary rhetorical forces of beginning into three categories: familial definition, logical/temporal priority, and constitutional principles. These should not be understood as an *exhaustive* list, but rather a selection of three representative "types" of rhetoric associated with beginnings.

Familial definition is the act of articulating the "definition of a substance in terms of ancestral cause."[17] What things *are* is determined by what they *were*.[18] The relationship of this definition to that of understanding beginnings as a common origin, described above, is clear. The attention to the description of origins as a *rhetorical* move, however, highlights the ways in which particular *aspects* of these sources of origin can be foregrounded or hidden in an attempt to accentuate a particular aspect of the present characterization. It is not just who your ancestors *are*, but how they are *described* that determines the influence on the present characterization of an individual or group. Furthermore the concept of "family," a concept which is, strictly speaking, grounded in both genetic links and the social structure of kinship relationships, does not need to have a biological basis. That is, claims to a common origin are not only constructed by strictly genetically defined groups. They are also constructed by social groups who might share a nationality or a belief.[19]

Family definition is only one potential rhetorical force of a given beginning point. Beginnings can also be significant for their claim to *temporal* and *logical* priority. Burke describes a fundamental confusion between temporal and logical firsts, whereby that which comes *before*, in chronological terms, often becomes associated with coming *before*, as a predictable cause. In this way, the "*logical* idea of a thing's essence can be translated into a temporal or narrative equivalent by statement in terms of the thing's source or beginnings."[20] The confusion of logical and temporal priority is also a feature of habits of historical explanation: that which came before can easily be re-interpreted as a cause. This statement does not necessarily need to be made explicit: sometimes, to order things one *before* another is to suggest a causal relationship between them.

Finally, beginnings can function as *constitutional principles*, a concept most influentially developed by James Boyd White in his theory of "constitutive rhetoric." This role played by beginnings is worth reflecting on a little bit more extensively as it will

16. Burke, "Terministic Screens," 45.
17. Burke, *A Grammar of Motives*, 26.
18. Burke, *Attitudes Toward History*, 66.
19. See Anderson, *Imagined Communities*, 1–7.
20. Burke, *A Rhetoric of Motives*, 13.

function as a key component of describing the role of the exodus as a "constitutional principle" of Israel's self-understanding. Constitutional principles differ from claims to origin or familial definition, in that, rather than strictly outlining *identity*, they outline a fundamental *motivation*. That is, such principles outline certain "desires, commands, or wishes"[21] that might be embodied in a particular community. White uses the example of the opening of the *Iliad*: the epic begins with an opposition between two men over a woman. This opening scene is not only the starting point of the story, but it is also the very grounds for the action that will comprise the entirety of the *Iliad*. It introduces the significance of the conflict, "what it means for Agamemnon . . . or for Achilles."[22] It is a *ground* for further action. Burke similarly defines "constitutional principles" as "an act or body of acts, done by agents, and designed to serve as motivational ground of subsequent actions, it being thus an instrument for the shaping of human relations."[23] To begin a story, or to describe the beginning of a community by delineating such constitutional principles, places the emphasis not primarily on the character's or community's origins, that is, how they *came to* exist, but on the purpose for *which* they exist in the story or in the community.

Beginnings as an Act of Literary Configuration

If a rhetorical analysis of beginnings describes the way that beginning points *persuade* and *identify*, literary analysis will focus on the ways that beginnings *introduce* and *cohere* with what follows. Beginnings serve as the first introduction to the story, the starting point of a literary whole that will also have an artificially imposed end. Analyses of beginning from a literary perspective have therefore focused on the *formal* and the *hermeneutic* role of beginnings as the first act of narrative configuration.

Paul Ricoeur, in his landmark study on time and narrative, observes that the beginnings, middles, and ends of stories are achieved only by virtue of "poetic composition," that is, through intentional acts of narrative selection and configuration.[24] The storyteller selects from what was a mere series of events, one occurring after the other, and arranges these events into a temporally defined whole with an artificially imposed beginning and end. It is an act of meaning-making, the first "act of judgment which manages to hold [events] together rather than reviewing them *seriatim*."[25] This "act of judgment" makes a claim that the events that make up the beginning, middle, and end, *do*, in fact, *go together*. Based on this, Ricoeur identifies two formal criteria for beginnings, each of which relates them to the subsequent flow and closure of the

---

21. Burke, *A Grammar of Motives*, 360.
22. White, *Heracles' Bow*, 38.
23. Burke, *A Grammar of Motives*, 341.
24. Ricoeur, *Time and Narrative*, 38.
25. Mink, "The Autonomy of Historical Understanding," 37.

plot: he argues that stories, to comprise a meaningful whole, must demonstrate *followability* and *concordance*.

Followability implies that the middle and the end satisfactorily flow from the beginning and that the sequence is intelligible and meaningful.[26] Concordance describes the internal coherence of each of the elements of the story that move us from the beginning to the end.[27] It is the concordance of the elements within the story that grants to it a meaning. The significance of beginnings then, in light of an emphasis on narrative configuration of time, is their relationship to the rest of the story. Beginnings and endings cannot be understood apart from one another.

This formal role, however, cannot be considered apart from the *hermeneutic* role that beginnings play. It is perhaps more accurate to say that beginnings, rather than possessing formal coherence with the end, craft the *expectation* of this coherence. As Said expresses, there is a "necessary certainty, a genetic optimism, that continuity is possible *as intended* by the act of beginning."[28] The first lines inform the reader concerning what kind of story this is going to be. This expectation of coherence also works retrospectively; as we read, we attempt to make sense of the story in light of the beginning and in anticipation of the end. This expectation and ability to craft coherence out of beginnings and endings is a feature of meaning making, as Kermode calls it, a result of our "considerable imaginative investments in coherent patterns."[29] Peter Rabinowitz therefore accurately highlights the interpretive role of beginnings: they occupy "privileged positions," places of special emphasis for both authors and readers.[30] The opening sets up the "narrative parameters of fiction," the perspective from which the story will be told, its tone, and indicators of where the reader should focus. Following the principle of concordance, these initial parameters also often "determine . . . the conditions for closure."[31] The opening serves as the most memorable signal, along with paratextual clues such as the title, of where the story will lead us. The beginning is the only part of the story that we have in our minds the entire time that we are reading it, and in so doing frames our encounter with the entire story.

The hermeneutic power of beginnings is demonstrated in a particularly notable way in the phenomenon of "revision through introduction" in ancient Near Eastern texts. Here I will return to Sara Milstein's work that was already introduced above. In *Tracking the Master Scribe* she analyzes several cases in which beginnings were *added* to works in order to re-frame previously existing texts. She identifies this strategy of revision as one of the most important techniques of the transformation of texts available to scribes. The reason for this is that the beginning is a site of extraordinary

---

26. Ricoeur, *Time and Narrative*, 66.
27. Ricoeur, *Time and Narrative*, 38–45.
28. Said, "Beginnings," 264; cf. Perry, "Literary Dynamics," 50–58.
29. Kermode, *Sense of an Ending*, 17.
30. Rabinowitz, "Reading Beginnings and Endings," 300.
31. Leander, *Sense of a Beginning*, 46.

interpretive influence: "the front of the text was not simply a convenient place for supplementation," she observes, "it was a crucial site for reshaping the work and the audience's reception of that work."[32] If the beginning indicates how the rest of the work is read, then adding a new beginning can shape the interpretation of the entire work, even if the remainder of the text remains unchanged.

So too, in highly schematized works like the Israelite historical résumés, the concept of narrative concordance becomes a primary principle of story-telling. The beginning and the ending do not only "go together well"; the first episode described functions as a template for the rest of the episodes in the résumé. One gets the sense in some of the résumés that history hardly moves *beyond* its starting point at all. Eric Voegelin identifies this type of narrative construction in biblical stories as "paradigmatic," that is, when "single events become paradigms of God's ways with man [sic] in the world."[33] In this case, the explanatory and formal functions of the "beginning" reach a point of rhetorical perfection: the pattern discerned in the first episode becomes the pattern through which the rest of the story is told.

Beginnings as an Act of Commemoration

Finally, before I turn to the beginnings of the historical résumés themselves, I will consider the significance of beginnings in public acts of commemoration. This category possesses a special pride of place within this essay, as my texts of choice are explicitly commemorative in nature. That is, the Israelite historical résumés claim to recall, often in ritual contexts, a presumably well-known tale for a people group for whom it has great importance. The beginning point(s) of the historical résumés marks the place where, in some cases, the people reciting the résumé situate their *own* beginning. Here we return full circle to the category that opened this essay, beginnings understood as origins. It is common for public commemorative activity to coalesce around points of origin. Analyzing beginnings from the perspective of memory studies draws attention to the way that beginning points are socially constructed, often through these repeated acts of commemoration. Furthermore, commemorated beginnings tend to obscure that which came before; any event that preceded the remembered "starting point" is consigned to the status of *pre-history* and is often therefore forgotten.

The forgetfulness constructed by commemorative acts has recently become a subject of great interest. In the United States, for example, the holiday known as Columbus Day traditionally marked what was understood an important historic event: Christopher Columbus's "discovery" of America. "Beginning" American history here, however, has often obscured the immense history of the people who were already living on the North American continent. A revolution in revisionist history has recently called into question the popular hegemony of identifying the moment of Columbus'

---

32. Milstein, *Tracking the Master Scribe*, 40.
33. Hogan, "Editor's Introduction," 5.

purported discovery in 1492 as "America's Founding Event."[34] Part of this revolution is the commitment by some to alter the commemorative holiday, by *remembering a different starting point*. Several cities have now replaced "Columbus Day" with "Indigenous People's Day."[35] In this way, they are using national rituals of commemoration to encourage national awareness of an often-forgotten aspect of American history, and to figuratively move the beginning point *backwards*.[36]

What the slow transformation of Columbus Day illustrates is that constructing "beginnings" is a "highly ambitious sociomnemonic act."[37] The assignment of a beginning also assigns the limits of remembering. When a group decides where to begin a story, they also decide to not tell or retell that which preceded. For novels, this is a decision with potentially very little social impact. For the commemoration of events important for or constitutive of the cultural group, it is very significant indeed.

Where Do the Historical Résumés Begin?

With this theoretical background in place, I turn to my second question to ask where the Israelite historical résumés begin and what effect the beginning point has on the configuration of the following narrative. Why are the historical résumés a good test case for this question of beginnings? In part it is because the résumés claim to retell the central events of Israel's history, what Carol Newsom calls Israel's "master narrative," the "authoritative account of some extended segment of history."[38] So too, as Zerubavel observes, commemorative activity tends to be concentrated around points of origin.[39] It is therefore informative for the question of Israel's own historical self-understanding to ask where she locates her beginning in these commemorative ceremonies, which are often portrayed in the text as orally performed public events. While these performances re-describe traditional material (there is no radically revisionist

---

34. Fulford, *The Triumph of Narrative*, 36.

35. The difficulty of adjusting public opinion after decades of commemorative activity, however, is documented by Schuman, "Elite Revisionists," 2–29. Other significant attempts to establish a "new beginning" can be seen in the attempts by France in the 1790s to replace the Christian designations of era (BC/AD) with a French Republic era, beginning in 1792, or the establishment by some Germans of "Zero hour" (*Stunde Null*) in 1945 as an attempt to craft a new political identity as they emerged from the shadow of their recent Nazi past. See Zerubavel, *Time Maps*, 91; cf. Koonz, "Between Memory and Oblivion, 262; Andrews, "Making the Revolutionary Calendar," 517–23; Zerubavel, *Hidden Rhythms*, 86–87.

36. The origins of Columbus Day *itself* reveals the power of origin stories: the holiday was established in light of racially-motivated violence against Italian-Americans in the South. Commemorating the Italian Christopher Columbus as the first "American" granted Italian-Americans a "formative role in the nation-building narrative." Staples, "How Italians Became 'White.'" I am grateful to Adam Miglio for bringing this article to my attention.

37. Zerubavel, *Time Maps*, 89.

38. Newsom, "Rhyme and Reason," 217.

39. Zerubavel, *Time Maps*, 89–110.

history among them),[40] they also begin their recollections at different points in Israel's history. The beginning points of the résumé fall into roughly three categories: those that begin with events surrounding the exodus, those that begin with the patriarchs, and those that begin with creation. This divergence in beginning point has intrigued many scholars, most of whom use this as a data point to speculate concerning the origins of the longer narrative sources that comprise the Pentateuch/Hexateuch.[41] It is precisely due to their *limited variety*, however, that they present such an intriguing case study for analyzing the role that beginnings play in configuring the following story.[42] As I stated above, my goal is not to discover the "beginnings" of the Hebrew Bible, but to ask how different beginnings shape the way the story is told in each respective retelling.

As with my overview of theories related to beginnings, so too my discussion of the résumés will be selective. I present a table below that lists the starting points for each of the historical résumés.

Deuteronomy 6:20–25	Exodus
Deuteronomy 26:5b–9	Patriarchal Ancestors ("a wandering Aramean")
Joshua 24:2–15	Patriarchal Ancestors (Abraham and Terah)
1 Samuel 12:6–17	Exodus
Psalm 78	Exodus
Psalm 105	Patriarchal Ancestors (Abraham and Jacob)
Psalm 106	Exodus
Psalm 135:8–11	Exodus
Psalm 136	Creation
Ezekiel 20:3–32	Exodus
Neh 9:6–37	Creation

Table 1.1: Starting Points for Historical Résumés

40. Ezekiel 20 has sometimes been called a revisionist history, but even its narrative structure still relies on the same events as many other historical résumés, the exodus from Egypt and the wilderness wanderings.

41. Kreuzer, *Die Frühgeschichte Israels;* cf. Lauha, *Die Geschichtsmotive,* 34–35; Kühlewein, *Geschichte in den Psalmen,* 158; Schmid, *Genesis and the Moses Story,* 70–73.

42. For an analysis of how the résumé demonstrates narrative and historical configuration more generally, see Newsom, "Rhyme and Reason," 215–33.

Part 1: Creation

As can be seen from the selection of texts above, the exodus is the most frequent starting point for the historical résumé (6), closely followed by those that begin with one of Israel's patriarchal ancestors (3), and finally two (2) that begin with God's creation of the world. In the following analysis, my primary focus will be on the way in which the beginning point determines the direction and content of what follows, as well as to ask if there are any patterns determined *by* the selection of the beginning point itself. I will set aside for now questions that have to do with the relationship of these events to the development of the Pentateuch.

Exodus

The exodus is the most common starting point for Israel's commemorations of their history. The role of the exodus as the *first* event in a series provides an instructive example of how the beginning plays a formal role as the first act of configuration. While scholars who study narrative often note the way that the beginning outlines the *possibilities* of narrative direction in the story, the exodus event commonly provides a determinative narrative template for the historical episodes that follow. That is, when it stands as the first event, it serves as the first in a series of repeating paradigms of human and divine action.

The paradigmatic role of the exodus event is clearly illustrated in 1 Sam 12. As Newsom observes, 1 Sam 12 presents a "rhyming history" that organizes "the relevant history according to three cycles of similarly structured events."[43] The exodus is the first cycle of this rhyming history, and it sets the pattern for what is to follow. This pattern is *Israelite action → foreign oppression → cry of the Israelites → divine salvation*. In order to establish this pattern, the description of the exodus begins, not with divine activity, but with Jacob's descent into Egypt. In each iteration of the pattern, it is Israel's actions that lead to their foreign oppression. Jacob's descent is the first Israelite action that leads to their foreign oppression, and it stands in parallel to their action in v. 9, in which they forget God and are sold into the hands of foreign kings. The paradigm established by Samuel's description of these two events frames his assessment of the Israelites' present request for a king. By identifying a historical *pattern* beginning with the exodus, Samuel suggests a "cause and effect relationship" the force of which will determine the outcome of their present act of denying Yahweh's kingship through their request for a human king.[44]

It is notable that the exodus, which stands as Yahweh's act of divine redemption *par excellence* in the narrative contained in the book of Exodus, is used in several cases in the historical résumés as a paradigm that foregrounds *human* action. In both Pss 78 and 106, the description of the exodus is quite literally *preceded* by a statement concerning the Israelite's incorrect response to it. Before the exodus is even described

---

43. Newsom, "Rhyme and Reason," 220.
44. Newsom, "Rhyme and Reason," 220.

in Ps 78, it is described as the object of Israel's forgetfulness: v. 11, the verse that introduces the first of two historical summaries in the psalm reads "they forgot his works, and the wonders that he had shown them." A similar rhetorical technique is used in Ps 106: the theme of the résumé is presented summarily in v. 6 "Both we and our ancestors have sinned; we have committed iniquity, and have acted wickedly." This summary statement then leads into their first act of "sin": they did not remember the wonders of God in Egypt (Ps 106:7). That the focus of Ps 106 is on a paradigm of *human* action is clear even in terms of a grammatical analysis. The Israelites are the subject of the verb in vv. 7, 12–14, 16, 19–21, 24–25, 28–30, and 32–39, and in every case, the action that they enact is one of sin against Yahweh. In both Pss 78 and 106, it is the Israelite response to the exodus event that forms the first instance of a paradigm that will repeat throughout the psalm. In these cases, then, the beginning plays the introductory role *par excellence*. A single event has not only become, in Voegelin's terms, "paradigms of God's ways with man [sic] in the world,"[45] but also and primarily "paradigms of humanity's ways with God." It is as if the beginning reveals all that one needs to know about the characters involved.

Ezekiel 20 also begins with the exodus and uses the exodus as the basis for a repeating historical pattern. As Daniel Block demonstrates, Ezekiel frames his review of Israel's history in a repeating triptych, describing three historical events: Israel's sojourn in Egypt, the first desert generation, and the second desert generation. In each "panel" of the triptych, Yahweh *acts*, the people *revolt* against Yahweh's commands, Yahweh resolves to punish, but then relents for the "honor of my name."[46] Yet Ezekiel's idiosyncratic presentation and adjudication of events has earned this résumé the title of a "revisionist history," and it remains one of the most infamous interpretive cruxes in the entire book. In Ezekiel's recital of history, even typical "high points" in Israel's tradition are framed negatively, and events that are not referenced elsewhere contribute to its unrelentingly dismal view of Israel's actions: for example, Ezekiel reports idol worship in Egypt before the exodus, idol worship that is not recorded elsewhere, and he describes the giving of the law itself as an event that was "not good." He presents both significant historical and theological anomalies in his narrative. Newsom has identified this as an imaginative attempt to invent "the only past that can account for this present," that is the less than ideal present experienced by the author of Ezekiel.[47] Block labels the historical résumé a *parody*: that is a "deliberate skewing and distorting of the sacred traditions," a distortion that presumably would have been understood by the audience.[48] One might frame these anomalies, additionally, as an alternative understanding of *beginnings* as *cause*. If the exodus, as we have seen, is frequently considered a prototype of action in the historical résumés, that is, a prototype whose

---

45. Hogan, "Editor's Introduction," 5.
46. Block, *The Book of Ezekiel*, 620–24.
47. Newsom, "Rhyme and Reason," 225.
48. Block, *The Book of Ezekiel*, 613.

pattern is *projected* onto later history, Ezekiel *retrojects* later history onto the prototypical event itself. That is, Ezekiel 20 "discovers" the roots of Israel's evil already in Egypt.[49] The characterization that is going to be revealed in history, Israel's idolatrous tendencies, and that which is going to be the result, the law as an instrument that will measure Israel's shortcomings, are transformed into prior causes. The fact that something has *resulted* from an event, in terms of temporal ordering, causes the first event to be interpreted as a *cause*. As Burke observes, in narrative "mode[s] of expression, things deemed to be most basic" can be described as "*first in time.*"[50]

In the examples above, the exodus as beginning functions as a paradigm for divine and human action. In Deut 6:20, the exodus instead presents the "constitutional principles" for Israel's polity. The exodus is the first event in an abbreviated narrative that answers the question: "What is the meaning of the decrees and the statutes and the ordinances that the Lord our God has commanded you?" (Deut 6:20).[51] The exodus is therefore presented as the event that undergirds adherence to the laws and statutes. In this sense it provides the basis for Israel's *motivation*. To attend to motivation shifts emphasis from *identity*, that is, who we are, to agency, *what then should we do?* The exodus event is not construed as an origin story *per se* in these résumés. It is used, strictly speaking, as a constitutional act, not the *birth* of Israel, but the event that crafts Israel's common, collective motivations as the people of God. This is, in part, why the exodus is repeatedly appealed to in public commemorative ceremonies. These ceremonies served not only as *knowledge-providing* and *confirming* ceremonies, but also as *hortatory* and *persuasive* ceremonies designed to motivate action in the present.

Patriarchal Ancestors: Statement of Origin

If the exodus functions as either a paradigmatic event or a constitutional principle when it begins a résumé, references to the patriarchal ancestors function primarily as statements of origin, conveying upon the listening audience a particular *status*. This function is clearest in Ps 105. In Ps 105, the résumé begins with the covenant given to Abraham, Isaac, and Jacob, along with the grant of the land (Ps 105:8–11; cf. v. 6). The psalm links the listening audience to their primordial ancestors through several acts of explicit identification: the audience is described by the psalm as the "offspring of Abraham" and the "sons of Jacob" (v.6). The significance of this claim to familial origin and its continuity in the present is confirmed by the reference to an "everlasting covenant" (בְּרִית עוֹלָם), one that endures "for a thousand generations" (לְאֶלֶף דּוֹר). In the case of Ps 105, Foucault's *critique* of claims to origin, that they emphasize a radical continuity

---

49. Eric Jarrard observes that this act of retrojection also serves to establish a "long-standing, habitual inclination towards Israelite rebellion and idolatry," one that counters more idyllic presentations of Israel's life with God in Jeremiah and Hosea. See Jarrard, "Beyond Use and Abuse of History," 9.

50. Burke, *Language as Symbolic Action*, 206.

51. All Scripture quotations are my own translations.

in which "beings followed one another in so tightly knit an order, upon so continuous a fabric, that in going from one point of this succession to another one would have moved within a quasi-identity,"[52] appears to correspond to the psalm's claim exactly. It is Israel's relationship to an originary patriarch and the everlasting nature of the covenant that inaugurated the relationship between God and Israel that determines the end result of all of the historical events described in the psalm. The beginning directly foreshadows the ending: the land promise to the patriarchs described in Ps 105:11 is then restated in the fulfillment formula in v. 42. To borrow Leander's formulation, it is clear that the beginning of this story, understood as Israel's origin, is intended to provide the explanation for all events that follow and that lead to Israel's present.[53]

Notably, while the events retold in Deut 26:5–9 overlap significantly with those narrated in a portion of Ps 105, by including a reference to the patriarchs, the exodus, and the entry into the land, the resulting tenor of the story told is very different. Rather than emphasizing continuity with previous generations, the story in Deut 26:5–9 hinges on an utter transformation from "father" to "sons." In contrast to Ps 105, the first "father" in this brief historical creed is *unnamed*. There is no reference to the covenant made between God and the patriarchs, nor to the related promise of the land. This "father" is further described with the Gentilic designation אֲרַמִּי, which, however historically accurate it might be, is a rare and rarely adopted ethnic term for Israel.[54] In this case, the beginning serves not primarily to identify an unchanging characterization or to provide familial definition but as what Burke calls a *terministic screen*, a strategic choice of terms through which the remainder of the story will be read. As noted in the first half of this paper, this selection of terms is both a selection and a deflection of reality.[55] The recollection of Israel's first ancestor serves to set up a narrative of dramatic transformation, from a few to a great nation, and from weakness to strength. If a more recent proposal by Janzen is correct, that the debated term אֹבֵד, which is translated in most English translations as "wandering" should instead be translated as "starving," then the transformation in Israel's status from the beginning to the end of the review becomes even more clearly delineated.[56] The characterization of the father as *lacking food* (v. 5) leads into a celebration of *great abundance* (vv. 9–11). The choice of terms is very likely determined by the ritual setting in which this review is recited, the offering of the first fruits. In comparing Ps 105 to Deut 26, both traditional statements of Israel's history that connect her to her ancestry in order to make a claim about the present, one can see that the way *in which* it describes the

---

52. Foucault, *The Order of Things*, 329.
53. Leander, "To Begin with the Beginning," 16.
54. Kitchen, "Aram, Arameans," 55–59; Gibson, "Light from Mari," 44–62; Gibson, "Observations," 217–38; Craigie, *The Book of Deuteronomy*, 321–22.
55. Burke, "Terministic Screens," 45.
56. Janzen, "The Wandering Aramean," 359–75.

beginning, even as it describes the same event as the beginning point, determines the remainder of the story.

Not all links to an ancestor are used to characterize the present generation positively. If Ps 105 emphasizes the *positive* role of identification with an ancestor, Josh 24 identifies the *threat* that an ancestry can pose. It highlights the way in which claims to origin function as rhetorical moves: particular aspects of a genealogy or figures within a genealogy can be foregrounded or hidden in an attempt to accentuate a particular aspect of characterization for the present generation. In Ps 105, connection with Abraham implies a connection to covenant promises. In Josh 24, *Abraham's* father is remembered, and with him, an anxiety around Abraham's Mesopotamian origin and original allegiance to Mesopotamian gods. The challenge posed in Josh 24 is one of a question of *allegiances.* Israel is portrayed at the beginning of the recital as potential members of *two* identities: one identity, traced to Abraham's father Terah, is characterized by allegiance to a foreign deity (v. 2). The other, traced to Yahweh's "taking" of Abraham *away* from his land of origin and granting to him a family, is characterized by the opportunity to ally oneself to Yahweh (v. 3). The historical recital therefore concludes with a declaration of allegiance: the ambiguity of allegiance engendered by their origin will be ended only by an act of explicit identification (v. 15).

Creation: Divine Singularity

In light of the considerable role that the creation narratives have played in traditional interpretations of the Hebrew Bible as a whole, it is noteworthy that creation is the least frequent starting point among the historical résumés. Furthermore, neither of the historical résumés that begin with creation, Ps 136 and Neh 9, refer to any of the narratives involving humans in Gen 2–3 or to the other narratives in the primeval history, the "fall," the flood, or the construction of the Tower of Babel. The profound literary role that Gen 1–11 plays in the canonical form of the Hebrew Bible is therefore almost completely lacking in these regularly recited forms of Israel's history.[57] In each case, when the historical résumés begin with creation, the reference to creation characterizes not *humans* and their role in the created order, but *Yahweh* and Yahweh's utterly unique role in the cosmos. References to Yahweh's creative activity in both cases correspond closely to statements about Yahweh's singularity using the term לְבַד "alone" (Neh 9:6a; Ps 136:4). In both Neh 9 and Ps 136, this statement of Yahweh's uniqueness is immediately followed by a description of Yahweh's creating the heavens and their hosts, the earth, and the waters (Neh 9:6b; Ps 136:4–9). In the historical

---

57. This has been observed by several scholars. For example, Kreuzer, in his critique of von Rad's theory of the "little historical credo" finds it surprising that Von Rad emphasized the absence of the Sinai pericope in the "creeds," while ignoring entirely the absence of the creation story. See Kreuzer, *Die Frühgeschichte Israels*, 24–25.

résumés then, creation functions primarily to support claims to Yahweh's singularity. It is not used as a paradigm for human activity.

A later exception to this rule demonstrates the distinction and marks a potential development in the use of the primeval history in Second Temple literature. While creation remains a paradigm of divine character in the canonical résumés, the third-second-century BCE recital, Words of the Luminaries (4Q504–506), features Adam, described as "our father" and the first of the Israelite ancestors, as the first recipient of a divine commandment and the first transgressor of that commandment (4Q504 I, 4–9). The actions of Adam provide the template for later Israelite actions, culminating in the exile, which is described in language reminiscent of that first sin (4Q504 XV, 15). The prominent role of Adam in this recital calls into question his absence in the canonical résumés, and the marked preference that they demonstrate for *Abraham* and *Jacob* as "our father," and for the exodus as the event that functions as the most common paradigm for later interactions between God and Israel.

Conclusion

When in *Alice and Wonderland*, the white rabbit asks the King of Hearts where he should begin his account, the King answers seriously to "begin at the beginning ... and then go on till you come to the end: then stop."[58] We very easily pick up on Lewis Carroll's intended humor at this point in the story. Beginnings are by no means self-evident. That being said, beginning points do matter. They affect the way that we interpret stories, the way that we remember periods of time, and the way that we think of ourselves and the groups of which we are a part. So too, Israel repeatedly reflected on her own beginnings, her beginnings as a people, and the beginnings of her relationship with God. There is no single interpretive key to understanding the influence of beginning points on a story. But the historical résumés offer a fruitful perspective on the ways in which beginnings shape stories and the way in which they shape national and religious identities. As I have attempted to demonstrate, an awareness of the varied perspectives that interpreters can have on beginning points might help us to critically examine our own assumptions regarding beginning points in the Hebrew Bible. And for those religious communities who identify the stories in the Hebrew Bible as their own, it might also illumine some of our assumptions about the way we narrate *our own* beginnings.

---

58. Carroll, *Alice in Wonderland*, 94.

Part 1: Creation

Bibliography

Anderson, Benedict. *Imagined Communities: Reflections on the Origin and Spread of Nationalism*. New York: Verso, 1991.

Andrews, George G. "Making the Revolutionary Calendar." *American Historical Review* 36 (1931) 517–23.

Block, Daniel. *The Book of Ezekiel: Chapters 1–24*. NICOT. Grand Rapids: Eerdmans, 1997.

Burke, Kenneth. *Attitudes toward History*. Los Altos, CA: Hermes, 1959.

———. *A Grammar of Motives*. Berkeley: University of California Press, 1945.

———. *Language as Symbolic Action: Essays on Life, Literature, and Method*. Berkeley: University of California Press, 1966.

———. "Terministic Screens." In *Language as Symbolic Action*, 44–62. Berkeley: University of California Press, 1966.

Carroll, Lewis. *Alice in Wonderland*. New York: Norton, 1992.

Craigie, Peter C. *The Book of Deuteronomy*. NICOT. Grand Rapids: Eerdmans, 1976.

Deleuze, Gilles, and Félix Guattari. *A Thousand Plateaus: Capitalism and Schizophrenia*. Minneapolis: University of Minnesota Press, 1987.

Derrida, Jacques. "Structure, Sign, and Play in the Human Sciences." In *Writing and Difference*, translated by Alan Bass, 278–93. Chicago: University of Chicago Press, 1978.

Foucault, Michel. "Nietzsche, Genealogy, History." In *The Foucault Reader*, edited by Paul Rabinow, 76–100. New York: Pantheon, 1984.

———. *The Order of Things: An Archeology of the Human Sciences*. New York: Random House, 1973.

Fulford, Robert. *The Triumph of Narrative: Storytelling in the Age of Mass Culture*. New York: Broadway, 1999.

Gibson, John C.L. "Observations on Some Important Ethnic Terms in the Pentateuch." *JNES* 20 (1961) 217–38.

———. "Light from Mari on the Patriarchs." *JSS* 7 (1962) 44–62.

Hogan, Maurice P. "Editor's Introduction." In *Order and History; Volume 1: Israel and Revelation*, edited by Maurice P. Hogan, 1–14. The Collected Works of Eric Voegelin 14. Columbia: University of Missouri Press, 2001.

Janzen, J. Gerald. "The Wandering Aramean Reconsidered." *VT* 44 (1994) 359–75.

Jarrard, Eric. "Beyond Use and Abuse of History: Constructed Memory in Ezekiel 20." Paper presented at the Annual Meeting of the SBL, Denver, CO, 17 Nov 2018.

Kermode, Frank. *Sense of an Ending*. Oxford: Oxford University Press, 1967.

Kitchen, Kenneth A. "Aram, Arameans." In *New Bible Dictionary*, edited by J. D. Douglas, 55–59. Grand Rapids: Eerdmans, 1962.

Koonz, Claudia. "Between Memory and Oblivion: Concentration Camps in German Memory." In *Commemorations: The Politics of National Identity*, edited by John R. Gillis, 258–80. Princeton: Princeton University Press, 1994.

Kreuzer, Siegfried. *Die Frühgeschichte Israels in Bekenntnis und Verkündigung des Alten Testaments*. BZAW 178. Berlin: de Gruyter, 1989.

Kühlewein, Johannes. *Geschichte in den Psalmen*. Stuttgart: Calwer, 1973.

Lauha, Aarre. *Die Geschichtsmotive in den alttestamentlichen Psalmen*. Annales Academiae Scientiarum Fennicae, B56, 1. Helsinki: 1945.

Leander, Niels Buch. *The Sense of a Beginning: Theory of the Literary Opening*. Copenhagen: Museum Tusculanum Press, 2018.

———. "To Begin with the Beginning: Birth, Origin, and Narrative Inception." In *Narrative Beginnings: Theories and Practices*, edited by Brian Richardson, 15–28. Lincoln: University of Nebraska Press, 2008.

Milstein, Sara. *Tracking the Master Scribe: Revision through Introduction in Biblical and Mesopotamian Literature*. Oxford: Oxford University Press, 2016.

Mink, Louis O. "The Autonomy of Historical Understanding." *History and Theory* 5 (1966) 24–47.

Newsom, Carol A. "Rhyme and Reason: The Historical Résumé in Israelite and Early Jewish Thought." In *Israel's Prophets and Israel's Past: Essays on the Relationship of Prophetic Texts and Israelite History in Honor of John H. Hayes*, edited by Brad E. Kelle and Megan B. Moore, 215–33. LHBOTS 446. London: T. & T. Clark, 2006.

Perry, Menakhem. "Literary Dynamics: How the Order of a Text Creates Its Meaning [With an Analysis of Faulkner's 'A Rose for Emily']." *Poetics Today* 1.1–2 (1979) 35–64.

Rabinowitz, Peter. "Reading Beginnings and Endings." In *Narrative Dynamics: Essays on Time, Plot, Closure, and Frames*, edited by Brian Richardson, 300–313. Columbus: Ohio State University Press, 2002.

Ricoeur, Paul. *Time and Narrative*. Translated by Kathleen McLaughlin and David Pellauer. Vol. 1. 3 vols. Chicago: University of Chicago Press, 1984.

Römer, Thomas. "Résumer l'histoire en l'inventant: Formes et fonctions des 'sommaires historiques' de l'Ancien Testament." *Revue de Théologie et de Philosophie* 43 (1993) 21–39.

Said, Edward. "Beginnings." In *Narrative Dynamics: Essays on Time, Plot, Closure, and Frames*, edited by Brian Richardson, 256–66. Columbus: Ohio State University Press, 2002.

Schmid, Konrad. *Genesis and the Moses Story: Israel's Dual Origins in the Hebrew Bible*. Winona Lake, IN: Eisenbrauns, 2010.

Schuman, Howard, et al. "Elite Revisionists and Popular Beliefs: Christopher Columbus, Hero or Villain?" *Public Opinion Quarterly* 69 (2005) 2–29.

Smith, Anthony D. *The Ethnic Origins of Nations*. Oxford: Blackwell, 1986.

Staples, Brent. "How Italians Became 'White.'" *New York Times* (October 12, 2019). https://www.nytimes.com/interactive/2019/10/12/opinion/columbus-day-italian-american-racism.html

Van der Meiroop, Marc. *Philosophy before the Greeks: The Pursuit of Truth in Ancient Babylonia*. Princeton: Princeton University Press, 2017.

White, James Boyd. *Heracles' Bow: Essays on the Rhetoric and Poetics of the Law*. Madison: University of Wisconsin Press, 1985.

Zerubavel, Eviatar. *Hidden Rhythms: Schedules and Calendars in Social Life*. Chicago: University of Chicago Press, 1981.

———. *Time Maps*. Chicago: University of Chicago Press, 2003.

Zerubavel, Yael. *Recovered Roots: Collective Memory and the Making of Israeli National Tradition*. Chicago: University of Chicago Press, 1995.

2

Back to the Beginning

Verbal Syntax and Semantics in Genesis 1:1–3

JOHN A. COOK

SEVERAL DECADES AND MORE ago I was a student in John Walton's Genesis class—a student with no intention to pursue Old Testament or Hebrew studies. I recall my amazement as John opened his Hebrew Bible and began to translate on the fly from Genesis 1 as he explained the creation account. For Bible college students, most of whom aspired to master biblical languages, it was a feat that left most of us in awe. For myself, it was a critical juncture that relit my love of ancient languages from the glowing ember that remained from high school Latin. After embarking on a new quest to master Biblical Hebrew, I experienced the additional joy of having John as a Hebrew teacher for a semester. I recall his enthusiasm over receiving the newly published Waltke and O'Connor syntax volume that same year,[1] which I promptly purchased, following his lead. Given John's instrumental role in guiding my professional trajectory, first in Genesis class and then in Hebrew grammar, it seems a fitting tribute to address here the grammar of Genesis 1:1–3.

Genesis 1:1–3

The interpretive issues in these verses are manifold, and the commentary on them immense. In this paper, my focus is specifically on elucidating the semantics and discourse-pragmatics of the four historical interpretive options, each of which differs

---

1. Waltke and O'Connor, *Biblical Hebrew Syntax*.

in how they conceive of the temporal relationships among the lead predicates in each verse. I list these options below with representative translations.[2]

1. Three successive events: *God created . . . The earth was . . . God said . . .*

    "In the beginning God created the heavens and the earth. 2 The earth was without form and void, and darkness was upon the face of the deep; and the Spirit of God was moving over the face of the waters. 3 And God said, 'Let there be light'; and there was light." (RSV)

2. First event is a title for the chapter, and the second event sets the scene for the third: *God created: The earth was . . . God said . . .*

    "In the beginning, God created the heavens and the earth—2 Now the earth was formless and empty, and darkness was over the face of the deep. And the Spirit of God was hovering over the surface of the waters. 3 And God said, 'Let there be light!' And there was light." (LEB)[3]

3. First event is subordinate to the second, followed by the third: *When God created . . . , the earth was . . . Then God said . . .*

    "In the beginning when God created the heavens and the earth, 2 the earth was a formless void and darkness covered the face of the deep, while a wind from God swept over the face of the waters. 3 Then God said, 'Let there be light'; and there was light." (NRSV)

4. First event is subordinate to the third, and the second is parenthetical: *When God created . . .*

    (the earth was . . .), then God said.

    "When God began to create heaven and earth—2 the earth being unformed and void, with darkness over the surface of the deep and a wind from God sweeping over the water—3 God said, 'Let there be light'; and there was light." (NJPS)

The clauses in these verses, given in Hebrew in (5) below, differ from each other significantly.

5. Gen 1:1–3

1 בְּרֵאשִׁית בָּרָא אֱלֹהִים אֵת הַשָּׁמַיִם וְאֵת הָאָרֶץ
2 וְהָאָרֶץ הָיְתָה תֹהוּ וָבֹהוּ וְחֹשֶׁךְ עַל־פְּנֵי תְהוֹם וְרוּחַ אֱלֹהִים מְרַחֶפֶת עַל־פְּנֵי הַמָּיִם
3 וַיֹּאמֶר אֱלֹהִים יְהִי אוֹר וַיְהִי־אוֹר

---

2. For discussions of these four options and their history, see Westermann, *Genesis 1–11*, 93–98; Wenham, *Genesis 1–15*, 11, 13; Hamilton, *Genesis 1–17*, 103-8. I am not claiming that the translation committees necessarily associated their translations with these linguistic analyses, only that the translations are suitably compatible with these analyses respectively.

3. I am assuming that the m-dash after verse 1 in the Lexham English Bible (LEB) is meant to set it off from the following as a title sentence. Otherwise, the RSV and similar translations may be construed either according to (1) or (2).

Part 1: Creation

Verse 1 consists of a verb-subject ordered clause with a perfect (or *qatal*) verb that is preceded by the temporal prepositional phrase בראשית. By contrast, the second verse begins with a *waw*-prefixed subject-verb ordered clause with the perfect conjugation of the stative copular verb. The two subsequent clauses in verse 2 belong with first clause in ways that will be discussed further below: they consist of a subject-predicate null copula (or verbless) locative clause (i.e., the copular complement is a locative prepositional phrase), and a subject-predicate participle clause, which I analyze as featuring a null copula supporting the participle.[4] Finally, verse 3 features a verb-subject ordered clause with past narrative (*wayyiqtol*) predication.

Hebrew grammars have a long tradition of addressing the interpretation of sequences of verbal forms. The notion that verbal sequences are significant originates in large part with theories regarding the *waw*-prefixed forms.[5] Labels for the *waw*-prefixed forms such as conversive, relative, inductive, consecutive, and sequential all signal the idea that these verbal conjugations are in some way dependent on the preceding verb form for the determination of the temporal contours of the discourse and even the event semantics of the *waw*-prefixed clause itself. For example, the variety of consecutive or sequential theories all posit a semantic "advancement" of the discourse time by the *waw*-prefixed verb forms, often rendered as 'and then'. The nineteenth-century relative and inductive theories posited that the semantics (tense-aspect-mood) of the *waw*-prefixed forms were based on or conveyed from the preceding verb. Thus, the order or sequence of verbal forms was taken to be significant not just for interpreting the discourse but the individual clause and predication. Even the medieval conversive theory depended on observing the sequence of verbs in order to distinguish between the conversive *waw* and the conjunctive *waw*.[6]

Attention to the interpretation of *waw*-prefixed forms based on their sequential context, has led to an understanding that the sequence of the other verbal forms is likewise significant for grasping the temporal flow and pragmatics of the discourse. Thus, grammars feature categories like the "disjunctive" perfect verb, which breaks up a sequence of past narrative verbs and "indirect volitives" to describe the sequencing of various volitive forms.[7] These traditional explanations almost universally suffer from oversimplification and overgeneralization at the same time.[8]

Nevertheless, these approaches correctly highlight the importance of analyzing interclausal relationships in discourse. Many forays have been made by linguists into the analysis of the semantics and pragmatics of successive clauses in discourse, which

---

4. See Cook, "Participle and Stative."

5. Many labels are employed for these forms, including the *waw*-consecutive imperfect and perfect, and *wayyiqtol* and *weqatal*. For an explanation of my terms for these forms—*past narrative* for the former and *irreal perfect* for the latter—see Cook, *Time and the Biblical Hebrew Verb*, chap. 3.

6. For a brief survey of these theories, see Cook, *Time and the Biblical Hebrew Verb*, 83–93.

7. On the perfect in disjunctive clauses, see Matlock, "The Perfect," 132; on the indirect volitive patterns, see Joüon, *Grammar of Biblical Hebrew*, §116.

8. For a critique, see Cook, "Semantics of Verbal Pragmatics."

represents a departure from the sentence-based analysis typical especially of early semantic studies. Semantic theories, such as discourse representation theory, have emerged directly in response to the failure of earlier theories to account for inter-clausal relationships such as antecedent reference and the temporal relationships among events.[9] It is on this last issue and the related one of discourse foreground and background that the interpretive differences outlined above with respect to Gen 1:1–3 revolve.

Event Relationships in Discourse

To appreciate the semantic and discourse-pragmatic differences among the four interpretive options, it is necessary to examine the temporal relationships among successively reported clauses in narrative discourse, as well as the related distinction of foreground-background.

Event Ordering in Time

As a starting point, successively reported events may temporally relate to each other in three basic ways, as given in (6).

6. Given events A and B reported in that order, they may relate in terms of:

   a. **Succession:** event A occurs (or begins) prior to event B occurring (or beginning).
      Ex., *Jared left and (then) Colin left. Jared fell asleep and (then) Colin arrived.*

   b. **Reversal:** event B occurs (or begins) prior to event A occurring (or beginning).
      Ex., *Jared arrived, but Colin had left (already). Jared arrived, but Colin had become ill.*

   c. **Overlap:** event A or B occurs within the timeframe of the other.
      Ex., *Jared visited Colin, and he was sick. Colin was sick, and Jared visited him.*

Discourse, especially narrative types, seem to universally default to an iconically successive ordering of events, as in (6a).[10] That is, the speaker or narrator relates events in the order in which they occurred. Temporally successive expressions such as this are defined by the irreversibility property, which means that the reverse reporting of the events in (6a) yield a different interpretation of the flow of events. Because of this default reading of reported events, events reported out of order require special marking, such as

---

9. See Kamp, "Discourse Representation Theory."

10. Brown and Yule (*Discourse Analysis*, 125) call iconic ordering the *ordo naturalis* of narrative discourse. This default seems related to the conversational manner principle "be orderly" noted by Grice, *Way of Words*, 27.

the past perfect construction in (6b). By contrast, in (6c) both events are reported with the simple past, as are the events in (6a), but they are interpreted as overlapping.

Over the past half-century or so, studies have slowly refined our understanding of how temporal succession and temporal overlap are linguistically signaled. While earlier studies focused on single contributing factors, such as situation aspect (e.g., achievement and accomplishment events effect temporal succession, whereas activities and states do not) or viewpoint aspect (e.g., perfective viewpoint effects temporal succession, whereas imperfective and progressive do not),[11] eventually the notion of (un)boundedness was identified as the fundamental feature accounting for the temporal ordering of events. Boundedness refers to the event property of having reached a temporal boundary, and linguists have concluded that only bounded events can effect temporal succession; by contrast, unbounded events are interpreted as overlapping with juxtaposed events.[12] Utilizing this concept of boundedness avoids any simplistic linking of temporal succession to a particular verb type (situation aspect) or conjugation.[13] Instead, boundedness can be linguistically signaled by various and combined factors, including situation aspect, viewpoint aspect, temporal adverbs, and pragmatic context.

The basic principles of boundedness are summarized in (7), with accompanying examples.

7. Principles of (un)boundedness

   a. Imperfective/progressive aspect + any situation type = *unbounded*.
      Ex., *Colin was sick/working/building a house/winning, and Jared arrived.* Jared's arrival is interpreted as occurring within the timeframe of Colin's situation, whether a state *(sick)*, activity *(working)*, accomplishment *(building a house)*, or achievement *(winning)*.[14]

   b. Perfective aspect + achievements/accomplishments/activities[15] = *bounded*.
      Ex., *Colin won/built a building/worked, and Jared arrived.*

---

11. The traditional situation aspects referred to in the literature are state, activity, accomplishment, and achievement. Viewpoint aspects include the perfective-imperfective distinction as well as the progressive (treated here as semantically equivalent to the imperfective) and varieties of the perfect or anterior. For a detailed discussion, see Cook, *Time and the Biblical Hebrew Verb*, chap. 1.

12. See especially Depraetere, "(Un)boundedness and (A)telicity."

13. In particular, (un)boundedness is crucially distinct on the one hand from (a)telicity, which is a property used to distinguish situation types, and on the other hand from (im)perfectivity, which are viewpoint aspects.

14. For the purposes of illustration, I am employing English Simple Past as expressing perfective aspect and the Progressive gram as expressing imperfective. While these are not perfective and imperfective grams, they are semantically similar enough to be used to illustrate the contrasts discussed here.

15. Smith, "Activities," nuances the case of perfective aspect with activities by calling them "implicitly" bounded. She notes that in contrast to perfective aspect with accomplishments and achievements, activities with perfective aspect are more sensitive to (non-linguistic) contextual factors with respect to whether they are interpreted as bounded or unbounded.

    c. Perfective aspect + states = *unbounded*.
       Ex., *Colin was sick, and Jared arrived.*

Each of these cases represents the default interpretation of these events, which means that any of them can be altered by adverbial modification overtly expressing temporal boundedness, overlay, or reversal. For example, adding a durative phrase like *for two days* to an imperfective/progressive expression like *Colin was sick* overtly expresses a temporal boundary, so that the following event is now temporally successive with it: *Colin was sick for two days, and (then) Jared arrived.*[16] Expressions with a default bounded interpretation are most frequently changed to overlapping or reversed events by employing subordinate temporal expressions that expressly coordinate or reverse the time of the two events, as in *While Colin worked, Jared arrived* and *Before Colin won, Jared arrived.*

Real world knowledge and the content of clauses may also play a part in how the clauses are temporally related to each other. One such relationship that is relevant to this discussion but lies outside the basic taxonomy given in (6) is when an event encompasses one or more subevents, such as in (8a). Note that switching the initial clause to the end of the discourse, as in (8b), has no effect on the interpretation, even though we would expect it would based on the principles in (7), suggesting that the real world knowledge of what "work" entails for Amantha plays a role in the interpretation of the temporal relationship among these events.[17]

8. Events with subevents

    a. *Amantha worked hard all day: she answered e-mails, organized the office, and shipped the day's orders.*

    b. *She answered e-mails, organized the office, and shipped the day's orders; Amantha worked hard all day.*

Foreground and Background

The foreground-background distinction is a very different sort of concept than boundedness. It is not semantic but psycholinguistic, pertaining to the way in which we perceive, organize, and relate events: we classify related clusters of events as more or less salient to the development of the episode. Terms like the "main line" of the narrative get at the same idea, and hint at the notion that foregrounded events relate

---

16. Note that Colin may have still been sick when Jared arrived (in the narrative world), but the clause itself only presents a bounded event comprising the first two days of his illness.

17. The subevents may be interpreted as temporally successive or overlaid depending on real-world knowledge. Thus, in (8a), the subevents appear to be unordered and could be reported in a different order without a difference in meaning. By contrast, if the events included *she packaged the day's orders and shipped them*, knowledge of the logical order of packaging and shipping demands a successive interpretation or at least those two events.

directly to one another, whereas background events lie, well, in the background. How precisely foreground events relate to each other is linked to boundedness and temporal succession: such events are better candidates for the foreground of a narrative insofar as they "move" the sequence of events forward, often with logical relationships such as cause-effect. By contrast, background events provide "supporting" material by way of providing contexts and motivations for foregrounded events. The example in (9) illustrates well the foreground-background distinction.

9. Gen 31:31–33[18]

וַיַּ֤עַן יַעֲקֹב֙ וַיֹּ֣אמֶר לְלָבָ֔ן כִּ֣י יָרֵ֔אתִי כִּ֣י אָמַ֔רְתִּי פֶּן־תִּגְזֹ֥ל אֶת־בְּנוֹתֶ֖יךָ מֵעִמִּֽי: עִם֩ אֲשֶׁ֨ר תִּמְצָ֜א אֶת־אֱלֹהֶ֗יךָ לֹ֣א יִֽחְיֶה֒ נֶ֣גֶד אַחֵ֧ינוּ הַכֶּר־לְךָ֛ מָ֥ה עִמָּדִ֖י וְקַֽח־לָ֑ךְ וְלֹֽא־יָדַ֣ע יַעֲקֹ֔ב כִּ֥י רָחֵ֖ל גְּנָבָֽתַם: וַיָּבֹ֨א לָבָ֜ן בְּאֹ֥הֶל יַעֲקֹ֣ב ׀ וּבְאֹ֣הֶל לֵאָ֗ה וּבְאֹ֛הֶל שְׁתֵּ֥י הָאֲמָהֹ֖ת וְלֹ֣א מָצָ֑א וַיֵּצֵא֙ מֵאֹ֣הֶל לֵאָ֔ה וַיָּבֹ֖א בְּאֹ֥הֶל רָחֵֽל:

Jacob answered and said to Laban, "I was afraid, because I thought, lest you take your daughters away from me. The one with whom you find your deities will not live! Before our kinsmen, identify for yourself what is with me and take it for yourself." *Now Jacob did not know that Rachel had stolen them.* So Laban entered into the tent of Jacob and into the tent of Leah and into the tent of the two handmaids. But he did not find them. And he exited the tent of Leah and entered the tent of Rachel.

When Laban overtakes Jacob fleeing with his family, he asks why he left secretly and accuses him of stealing his household idols. The foreground continues with the past narrative double speech introduction וַיַּ֤עַן יַעֲקֹב֙ וַיֹּ֣אמֶר in verse 31, in which Jacob explains his fear of losing his family and challenges Laban to find his household idols among his family's possessions. Between the embedded speech and the continuation of the foreground narrative with וַיָּבֹ֨א לָבָ֜ן in verse 33, the narrator injects the following as background that explains Jacob's rash vow to kill whoever of his family has the idols: לֹֽא־יָדַ֣ע יַעֲקֹ֔ב כִּ֥י רָחֵ֖ל גְּנָבָֽתַם. While the interruption of the string of past narrative foreground verbs signals this background material, it is not as simple as that contrast, particularly because that contrast is motivated by the negative, with which the past narrative is incompatible.[19] Rather, the background information is mainly signaled by the departure from the default temporal successive ordering of the foreground: the stative clause לֹֽא־יָדַ֣ע יַעֲקֹ֔ב overlaps both the time of Jacob and Laban's exchange and Laban's subsequent search, and the perfect verb in the complement clause כִּ֥י רָחֵ֖ל גְּנָבָֽתַם contextually must refer to Rachel's action prior to fleeing, so it is in reverse order with the surrounding events.

---

18. Translations are those of the author, unless otherwise noted.

19. At the same time, negated clauses are ranked as relatively less salient irrealis expressions that typically belong to the background (see discourse salience rankings in Cook, *Time and the Biblical Hebrew Verb*, 151, 154).

While there is a strong correlation between temporal succession and foreground, it is not exclusive. For example, consider the passage in (10).

10. Gen 29:15–18

וַיֹּ֤אמֶר לָבָן֙ לְיַעֲקֹ֔ב הֲכִי־אָחִ֣י אַ֔תָּה וַעֲבַדְתַּ֖נִי חִנָּ֑ם הַגִּ֣ידָה לִּ֔י מַה־מַּשְׂכֻּרְתֶּֽךָ: וּלְלָבָ֖ן שְׁתֵּ֣י בָנ֑וֹת שֵׁ֤ם הַגְּדֹלָה֙ לֵאָ֔ה וְשֵׁ֥ם הַקְּטַנָּ֖ה רָחֵֽל: וְעֵינֵ֥י לֵאָ֖ה רַכּ֑וֹת וְרָחֵל֙ הָֽיְתָ֔ה יְפַת־תֹּ֖אַר וִיפַ֥ת מַרְאֶֽה: וַיֶּאֱהַ֥ב יַעֲקֹ֖ב אֶת־רָחֵ֑ל וַיֹּ֗אמֶר אֶֽעֱבָדְךָ֙ שֶׁ֣בַע שָׁנִ֔ים בְּרָחֵ֥ל בִּתְּךָ֖ הַקְּטַנָּֽה:

Laban said to Jacob, "Is it because you are my kin that you should serve me for nothing? Tell me what your wage is?" Now Laban had two daughters. The name of the elder was Leah and the name of the younger was Rachel. The eyes of Leah were weak; Rachel was beautiful of form and beautiful of sight. *Jacob loved Rachel* and said, "I will serve you seven years in exchange for Rachel, your younger daughter."

Laban's speech is introduced by the foregrounding past narrative וַיֹּ֤אמֶר in verse 15. Verses 16–17 then provide background context to the offer Laban extends, consisting of stative null copula clauses recalling the character of Rachel and introducing her older sister Leah. Verse 18 resumes the foreground with וַיֶּאֱהַב, clearly marked as such by the use of the past narrative conjugation.[20] If the narrator wanted this to be background, continuing with a perfect verb אָהַב would have served well with a past stative or past inchoative sense: 'now Jacob loved Rachel' or 'Jacob had fallen in love with Rachel'. Instead, the event must be taken as a past stative thrust atypically into the foreground by the past narrative conjugation, signaling that this is crucial information in the temporally and causally linked foreground of the narrative that continues with Jacob's asking for Rachel as a wife.[21]

Interpretive Options and Genesis 1:1–3

With the above linguistic framework about the semantics of event relationships in narrative time and the discourse distinction between foreground and background, we are in a better position to explicate the nuanced differences between the four grammatical options for understanding Gen 1:1–3. My focus here is on the semantic and pragmatic nuances of the interclausal relationships, and not primarily on syntax, nor on lexical semantics or extra-linguistic factors such as theological motivations. There

---

20. For my argument that the past narrative (*wayyiqtol*) conjugation always expresses foregrounded events, see Cook, *Time and the Biblical Hebrew Verb*, 289–98 and Cook, "Semantics of Verbal Pragmatics."

21. The past narrative with a stative can express an inchoative sense as well as the perfect ('Jacob fell in love with Rachel'), but the default ordering of the narrative foreground with an inchoative rendering suggests that Jacob fell in love with Rachel right there and then. Rather, the stative forces temporal overlay with the surrounding discourse while the past narrative forces the high-salience foregrounding of the event, despite its departure from the *ordo naturalis* of the narrative.

is one central syntactic issue that divides the options into two: the question of whether verse 1 is taken as a subordinate clause or not. On this matter, commentators have long recognized both options are grammatical,[22] and Holmstedt has ably analyzed the syntax of these verses in this regard and come to a similar conclusion, which I endorse.[23] Therefore, I will not dwell on this matter further.

The semantic-pragmatic issues center on verse 2 and the relationship its clauses have with the verses on either side. Is verse 2 foreground, temporally successive with verse 1, which reports the first act of creation (interpretation 1)? Or does verse 2 set the scene for the initial foregrounded event of verse 3, and verse 1 lies outside of the narrative proper as a title (interpretation 2)? Is verse 2 part of the foreground as the independent clause upon which the scene-setting background clause of verse 1 depends (interpretation 3)? Or does verse 2 serve as background parenthetical material, interrupting the subordinate verse 1 and its main clause of verse 3?

Despite the central issue resting on verse 2, comparatively viewed, it is helpful to examine these four interpretations in two pairs that eliminate the differences of syntax: those that take verse 1 as an independent clause and those that take it as a subordinate clause. For each pair, we want to explicate the temporal relationship among the clauses, determine their foreground/background status, and investigate whether each is grammatical or not and whether there are any parallel structures in the Hebrew Bible that might be used to validate their grammaticality.

Gen 1:1 as an Independent Clause

The traditional interpretation in 1 treats the events in these verses as temporally successive foregrounded events, or as Wenham states it, "synchronically, i.e., v 1: first creative act; v 2: consequence of v 1; v 3: first creative word."[24] The central striking feature of this construal is that it excludes temporal overlay between the stative expressions in verse 2 and the bounded event of verse 1. That is, it is read as *God created . . . (then) the earth was . . .* This is particularly striking because at the same time, the events of verse 2 are interpreted as overlapping with each other and overlapping the succeeding event in verse 3. Of course, it stands to reason that the stative copula, null copula, and progressive participle clauses in verse 2 would overlap each other and the surrounding bounded events, as they are all unbounded. Hence, at the moment that *God said* (verse 3), *the earth was . . . darkness (was) . . . and the spirit of God (was) hovering . . .* (verse 2). The situation of course immediately alters with God's speaking, but arguably these unbounded events overlay with at least some of the intervals of time of God's speech.[25]

---

22. For example, Westermann, *Genesis 1–11*, 95.
23. Holmstedt, "Syntax of Gen 1.1–3."
24. Wenham, *Genesis 1–15*, 13.
25. On the analysis of events in terms of moments and intervals, see Cook, *Time and the Biblical Hebrew Verb*, chap. 1.

In turn then, it is semantically unexpected that the unbounded situations of verse 2 do not also overlap the event of verse 1. Stative predicates in the perfect conjugation admit a successive understanding through an inchoative rendering (e.g., *the earth became*), just as they also allow an out-of-order reading as a past perfect (e.g., *the earth had been*), but an inchoative (not to mention past perfect) reading is not what the traditional view adopts. Rather, it is the rendering advocated by the largely defunct "gap theory" view, which envisions an undetermined amount of time between God's creative act in verse 1 and the earth falling into the state of affairs in verse 2.

On closer examination, it is the traditional view's extra-linguistic understanding of the event in verse 1 that motivates the unexpected successive reading with verse 2: the situation in verse 2 cannot overlap with verse 1, because the materials required do not exist until they are "created" in verse 1. For an analogy, compare the two statements in (11).

11.

    a. *Evan painted a house; the house was big.*

    b. *Evan built a house; the house was big.*

Although the second clause in each is identical, they are not interpreted in the same way: in (11a) the state of the house being big overlaps with Evan's painting the house; by contrast, because Evan is bringing the house into material existence by building it in (11b), the statement that the house was big cannot apply to it until the first event is completed (bounded). Similarly, until the earth (or the heavens and the earth) are completed, the state of affairs of verse 2 cannot properly apply. Of course, it is possible to understand the predicate of verse 1 differently: if ברא does not refer to bringing into material existence, analogous with (11b), but refers to something else, analogous with (11a), such as *God organized the heavens and the earth*, then the situations of verse 2 will be understood to overlap with the events on either side of it. Thus, the matter of the traditional interpretation really turns on the lexical-semantic understanding of ברא. Traditionally ברא has been understood to refer to material creation, a view defended especially by those desiring to preserve an idea of *creatio ex nihilo* in this verse. Walton has cogently argued that the term does not refer to material creation, but refers, instead, to bringing something into functional existence.[26]

The motivating force for interpretation 2 likewise lies in how the predicate in verse 1 is extralinguistically understood. In this case, it is taken to apply to all the following events in the chapter, bookending the account with the statements in 2:1–3. Construed in this way, the predicate in the first verse stands outside the foreground-background distinction altogether, on a different discourse level as it were. In this interpretation, verse 2 functions as the initial scene-setting background clause to the first foregrounded clause of the account, the past narrative in verse 3. The unbounded

---

26. Walton, *Genesis One*, proposition 3; *Genesis 1*, 127–33.

situations in verse 2 are understood to overlay the past narrative event of verse 3 in precisely the same way as in interpretation 1. Meanwhile, these unbounded events cannot overlay with any preceding ones, simply because there are none.

The oddity of the construal of the events of verse 1 and 2 as temporally successive (interpretation 1) is reinforced by a dearth of evidence of any parallels to this interpretation.[27] I have been unable to find any clear cases in which a subject-perfect non-bounded clause is successive to a preceding one. Not only is it typical that subject-perfect verb clauses function in ways contrastive with past narrative in narrative discourse (i.e., background and non-temporally successive events), but the stativity of היה makes it an unlikely candidate for appearing in a string of successive clauses unless it is interpreted as inchoative. Even in episode-initial thetic expressions, such as in Gen 3:1, given in (12), arguably the situation overlaps to some extent with the necessary backdrop of Genesis 2.[28]

12. Gen 3:1

וְהַנָּחָשׁ הָיָה עָרוּם מִכֹּל חַיַּת הַשָּׂדֶה אֲשֶׁר עָשָׂה יְהוָה אֱלֹהִים

Now the snake was craftier than all the beasts of the field that Yhwh God had made.

Even in the rare instance that subject-perfect היה serves as foreground, more typical than thetic statements like the one in (12), are cases where it follows a past narrative, to express two closely related or even contrastive events. This applies not only to היה but to other subject-perfect clauses, as illustrated in (13).[29]

13. Gen 4:2b–5a

וַיְהִי־הֶבֶל רֹעֵה צֹאן וְקַיִן הָיָה עֹבֵד אֲדָמָה: וַיְהִי מִקֵּץ יָמִים וַיָּבֵא קַיִן מִפְּרִי הָאֲדָמָה מִנְחָה לַיהוָה: וְהֶבֶל הֵבִיא גַם־הוּא מִבְּכֹרוֹת צֹאנוֹ וּמֵחֶלְבֵהֶן וַיִּשַׁע יְהוָה אֶל־הֶבֶל וְאֶל־מִנְחָתוֹ: וְאֶל־קַיִן וְאֶל־מִנְחָתוֹ לֹא שָׁעָה

Abel was a herder of sheep, and Cain was a tiller of the soil. After a while, Cain brought a gift to Yhwh from the produce of the ground, and Abel brought, he also, some of the firstborn of his flock and from their fat. Yhwh regarded Abel and his gift, but Cain and his gift he did not regard.

---

27. There are few cases of immediately successive independent perfect clauses outside of genealogical contexts (e.g., Genesis 10), and in the cases I was able to find, the events are not temporally successive and usually one or both clauses are background material (e.g., Gen 13:12; 14:2–3; 15:17; 24:1; 31:25; 34:5; 44:3–4).

28. For other episodes in Genesis beginning with a subject-perfect verb, see 4:1; 15:1; 21:1; 24:1; 39:1; 43:1.

29. See also Gen 11:3; 31:47. On occasion two perfect verbs are used to express correlative or contrastive events: e.g., Gen 13:12; 31:25. In both patterns, the events temporally overlap with each other.

By contrast, episodes sometimes begin with summary statements, as illustrated by the example in (14).

14. Gen 22:1

וַיְהִי אַחַר הַדְּבָרִים הָאֵלֶּה וְהָאֱלֹהִים נִסָּה אֶת־אַבְרָהָם

After these things, God tested Abraham.

The Akedah story crucially begins with a statement by the narrator that what follows was only a test; God was not actually intending Abraham to kill Isaac. It serves as a title, similar to the way that interpretation 2 argues Gen 1:1 functions.

Gen 1:1 as a Subordinate Clause

Interpretations 3 and 4 both treat verse 1 as a subordinate, background clause. They differ in whether they take it as subordinate to the initial clause in verse 2 or in verse 3. In both cases, the predicate of the subordinate clause overlays that of the main clause by virtue of its subordinate temporal syntax and semantics. As discussed above, certain situation types and viewpoint aspects have default bounded readings. Temporal subordination is a common strategy used to override the default successive readings of bounded events, as illustrated by the examples in (15).

15.

    a. *Evan painted the house, and he said, "It's big."*

    b. *Evan said, "It's big," and he painted the house.*

    c. *While Evan painted the house, he said, "It's big."*

    d. *Evan said "It's big," while he painted the house.*

In (15a) the events are bounded and temporally successive. If we reverse them, as in (15b), the sense is altered. By contrast, constructed with a temporal subordinate clause, the order of the subordinate and main clauses can be reversed without any change in meaning, as shown in (15c–d).

This subordinate strategy is unnecessary to effect temporal overlay if one of the predicates is unbounded, as illustrated by the example in (11a) above. A subordinate strategy is thus unnecessary to create temporal overlay between the event of verse 1 and the stative and progressive predicates in verse 2. By contrast, this is the only way to effect temporal overlay between *created* in verse 1 and *said* in verse 3. In both cases, however, the subordinating strategy clearly denotes verse 1 as background to its foregrounded main clause, whether in verse 2 or in verse 3. Although the event in verse 3 is already clearly marked as foregrounded by the past narrative conjugation, the stative and progressive situations of verse 2 lend themselves to a background reading insofar as boundedness and temporal succession are closely correlated with narrative foreground. Nevertheless, it is possible to find a rationale for subordinating verse 1 to verse 2 on the assumption that verse 2 is foregrounded, despite the stative/progressive semantics of the predicates, to highlight the state of the earth at the beginning of God's creative activity.[30]

In contrast to this foregrounded status given to verse 2 by interpretation 3, 4 relegates it to the backgrounded parenthetical material. As Holmstedt notes, parenthesis consists of "non-at-issue" or background material and it interrupts the syntax—here, interrupting the sequence of subordinate (verse 1) and its main clause (verse 3).[31]

As in the case of the above comparison between the first two interpretive options, there is a stark contrast between the second two options in terms of comparable constructions in the Hebrew Bible. On the one hand, examples of episodes beginning with a temporal clause subordinate to a following subject-verb perfect clause are not forthcoming. On the other hand, temporal clauses subordinate to past narrative verbs, as illustrated in (16), are ubiquitous.[32]

16. Gen 24:52

וַיְהִי כַּאֲשֶׁר שָׁמַע עֶבֶד אַבְרָהָם אֶת־דִּבְרֵיהֶם וַיִּשְׁתַּחוּ אַרְצָה לַיהוָה:

When the servant of Abraham heard their words, he bowed to the ground to Yhwh.

More importantly, an example paralleling Gen 1:1–3 even more closely can be found in Josh 23:1, given in (17).

17. Josh 23:1–2

וַיְהִי מִיָּמִים רַבִּים אַחֲרֵי אֲשֶׁר־הֵנִיחַ יְהוָה לְיִשְׂרָאֵל מִכָּל־אֹיְבֵיהֶם מִסָּבִיב וִיהוֹשֻׁעַ זָקֵן בָּא בַּיָּמִים: וַיִּקְרָא יְהוֹשֻׁעַ לְכָל־יִשְׂרָאֵל

After many days, after Yhwh gave rest to Israel from all their enemies all around, (Joshua was/had become old; he [had] advanced in years) Joshua summoned all Israel . . .

As in Gen 1:1–3, in the example from Joshua in (17), it must be decided whether the initial subordinate expression is subordinate to the subject-verb perfect clause or the following past narrative clause.[33] The stative expression וִיהוֹשֻׁעַ זָקֵן, just as וְהָאָרֶץ הָיְתָה,

---

30. The case would be similarly atypical as the one in (10); however, in contrast to that case, here there is no clear foreground indicator apart from the assumption that the backgrounded verse 1 is subordinate to a foregrounded independent clause.

31. Holmstedt, "Syntax of Gen 1.1–3." Holmstedt, "Parenthesis."

32. See also Gen 6:1; 20:13; 27:1; 30:25; etc. The initial ויהי is immaterial to the case, as evident from examples like Gen 22:4 that lack it, indicating that the prepositional phrase is subordinate to the following past narrative verb.

33. The initial ויהי is immaterial to the case, as evident from examples like Gen 15:1 that lack it. As in Gen 15:1, so here, the prepositional phrase is syntactically subordinate to the following verb, not the initial ויהי, which serves as a discourse-pragmatic marker (see Cook, *Time and the Biblical Hebrew*

can be interpreted in a number of ways that are contextually determined. In both cases, an inchoative sense that effects temporal succession seems an odd fit: Joshua did not become old only after Yhwh gave rest to Israel. A past-perfect rendering, as the perfect verb in (9) receives, is possible here in Josh 23:1, indicating that by the time Yhwh had given rest to Israel, Joshua had already become old. A similar sense is possible for Gen 1:2, suggesting that when God began to create, the earth was already, and had been for some undetermined time prior, in the state of affairs expressed by verse 2.[34]

Regardless of the contextual options, neither of these stative expressions is a likely candidate for a foregrounded independent clause to which the initial clause is subordinate. In both cases, the narrative proper begins with a dynamic event—*God said*; *Joshua summoned*—and the subordination of the initial clause to this past narrative foreground event follows the typical pattern. The intervening stative expression, as expected, overlaps both of the other events (whether rendered as simple past or past-perfect), which are coordinated by the temporal subordinate structure: at the time that God created the heavens and the earth, which is coterminous with his speaking, the earth was/had been . . . ; at the time after which Yhwh gave rest to Israel, which is coordinate with the time Joshua summoned Israel, Joshua was/had become old. Given its background, temporal overlay status, combined with its interruptive placement between a subordinate and main clause, it stands to reason that in both cases, the intervening stative expression is parenthetical.[35]

Summary and Conclusions

Four interpretive options for Gen 1:1–3 have long been entertained among biblical scholars and theologians. Comparative literary motives, theological motives, as well as syntactic and lexical semantic factors have motivated these different readings. In this brief study, I have turned to the semantics and pragmatics of the interrelationship of the events in these verses to explicate the nuanced differences among them, and

---

Verb, 309–12). Instances of prepositional phrases without an initial ויהי proceeding past narrative verbs (e.g., Gen 22:4) confirm this analysis insofar as they demonstrate that the past narrative is not exclusively clause initial, but may be preceded by adjunct modifiers.

34. It is also possible for the perfect verbs in each case to express a combined inchoative past-perfect meaning of *had become*. In contrast to the simple past-perfect or simple past renderings, this would put the pragmatic focus on the earlier dynamic event of *becoming* rather than on the static state of affairs of *being*. This strikes me as unsuitable to the context, where the pragmatic function of the parenthetical material is more salient to the following foreground event than the preceding subordinate clause. This distinction appears to stem from past-perfect dynamic (inchoative) events as indicating a reversal of temporal order *with a previously reported event*. Since the previously reported event is subordinate and therefore coordinate with the following foregrounded event, heading a temporally successive narrative, it gives an odd sense.

35. The accompanying בָּא בַּיָּמִים clause in Josh 23:1 is part of the parenthesis, as it accompanies this stative expression elsewhere (Gen 24:1; Josh 13:1; 1 Kgs 1:1).

pinpoint the factors motivating one interpretation over another. Both the semantic/pragmatic analysis and an examination of parallel structures in the Hebrew Bible suggest that one choice in each pair of syntactic construals is preferable or more natural to the grammar of Biblical Hebrew: reading verse 1 as an independent clause is only plausible if read as a title event that encompasses the entirety of the creation narrative that follows; similarly, treating verse 1 as a subordinate clause is most plausible if read with verse 3 as its governing clause, in contrast to verse 2. The latter is then understood reasonably as a parenthetical expression.

Bibliography

Brown, Gillian, and George Yule. *Discourse Analysis*. Cambridge: Cambridge University Press, 1983.

Cook, John A. "The Semantics of Verbal Pragmatics: Clarifying the Roles of *Wayyiqtol* and *Weqatal* in Biblical Hebrew Prose." *JSS* 49 (2004) 247–73.

———. "The Participle and Stative in Typological Perspective." *JNSL* 34 (2008) 1–19.

———. *Time and the Biblical Hebrew Verb: The Expression of Tense, Aspect, and Modality in Biblical Hebrew*. Winona Lake, IN: Eisenbrauns, 2012.

Depraetere, Ilse. "On the Necessity of Distinguishing between (Un)boundedness and (a)telicity." *Linguistics and Philosophy* 18 (1995) 1–19.

Grice, H. P. *Studies in the Way of Words*. Cambridge: Harvard University Press, 1975.

Hamilton, Victor P. *The Book of Genesis: Chapters 1–17*. NICOT. Grand Rapids: Eerdmans, 1990.

Holmstedt, Robert D., "Parenthesis in Biblical Hebrew as noncoordinative nonsubordination." *Brill's Journal of Afroasiatic Languages and Linguistics* 12 (2020): 99–118.

———. "The Syntax of Gen 1.1–3." To appear in Festschrift for Mats Eskhults. Studia Semitica Upsaliensia in Acta Universitatis Upsaliensis.

Joüon, Paul. *A Grammar of Biblical Hebrew*. 2nd ed. Translated by T. Muraoka. Rome: Pontifical Biblical Institute, 2006.

Kamp, Hans, Josef van Genabith, and Uwe Reyle. "Discourse Representation Theory." In *Handbook of Philosophical Logic*, edited by Dov M. Gabby and Franz Guenthner, 125–394. Dordrecht: Springer, 2011.

Matlock, Michael D. "The Perfect (*Qatal*)." In *"Where Shall Wisdom be Found?" a Grammatical Tribute to Professor Stephen a. Kaufman*, edited by Hélène Dallaire, Benjamin J. Noonan, and Jennifer E. Noonan, 127–37. Winona Lake, IN: Eisenbrauns, 2017.

Smith, Carlota S. "Activities: States or Events?" *Linguistics and Philosophy* 22 (1999) 479–508.

Waltke, Bruce K., and M. O'Connor. *An Introduction to Biblical Hebrew Syntax*. Winona Lake, IN: Eisenbrauns, 1990.

Walton, John H. *The Lost World of Genesis One: Ancient Cosmology and the Origins Debate*. Downers Grove, IL: IVP Academic, 2009.

———. *Genesis 1 as Ancient Cosmology*. Winona Lake, IN: Eisenbrauns, 2011.

Wenham, Gordon J. *Genesis 1–15*. WBC 1. Waco, TX: Word, 1987.

Westermann, Claus. *Genesis 1–11: A Commentary*. Translated by John J. Scullion. Continental Commentaries. Minneapolis: Augsburg, 1984.

3

Stretching Out the Heavens
The Background and Use of a Creational Metaphor

BRITTANY KIM

As I sat in John Walton's Old Testament backgrounds class in the first year of my Master's program at Wheaton College, a new world stretched out before me—the world of the ancient Near East. John masterfully spoke and various realms emerged: a three-tiered cosmos, temple, and state. Again he spoke, and the realms were populated with gods and goddesses of the sky, earth, and netherworld; priests, divine images, and rituals; divinely ordained kings, legal lists, and omens. He explained strange and puzzling features of the Old Testament by showing how they fit together with aspects of the ancient Near Eastern world, each according to its kind, but he also revealed how the Old Testament was set apart as unique, a reflection of its divine Creator. And it was very good.

I have had the opportunity to learn from John not only in class and in his published works but also in many lively and stimulating discussions over meals. I am so thankful for all the insights I have gained from him about creation and the ancient Near East, exegesis and theology, scholarship and life, as well as for his unceasing encouragement and support. I dedicate this essay to John, a wise mentor and faithful friend, as he approaches his years of retirement rest.

The OT metaphor of YHWH stretching out the heavens (נטה שמים and related phrases)[1] has been examined most extensively in a 1972 essay by Norman Habel, which

---

1. Isa 40:22; 42:5; 44:24; 45:12; 48:13; 51:13; Jer 10:12 // 51:15; Zech 12:1; Ps 18:10 [9] // 2 Sam 22:10; Ps 104:2; 144:5; Job 9:8; 26:7. Some scholars also emend the unusual phrase נטע שמים ("planting the heavens") in Isa 51:16 to נטה שמים (e.g., Blenkinsopp, *Isaiah 40–55*, 330), but there is little evidence for the emendation (see further Koole, *Isaiah 49–55*, 191).

focuses on its association with Israel's tabernacle traditions.² This essay builds on Habel's work with an exploration of the paired phrase רקע הארץ, typically translated "spreads out the earth" (Isa 42:5; 44:24; cf. Ps 136:6), proposing a different understanding that offers further connections with the tabernacle or temple. I also evaluate ANE parallels that have been suggested as a possible background for the metaphor, and finally, I examine how the metaphor functions in its literary contexts within the OT.

The Background of the Metaphor of YHWH Stretching Out the Heavens

Israel's Tabernacle Traditions à la Habel

The metaphor of YHWH stretching out the heavens appears more frequently in Isaiah 40–55 than in any other corpus. Its first occurrence in 40:22 is the most expansive and forms the lens through which we should read later references to the metaphor in this section of Isaiah.³ The verse describes YHWH as:⁴

> The one who sits above the circle of the earth,
> And its inhabitants are like grasshoppers,
> The one who stretched out the heavens like a curtain (הנוטה כדק שמים)
> And who spread them out like a tent to dwell in (וימתחם כאהל לשבת).

Both דק and מתח are *hapax legomena*, but they seem to function as poetic complements to אהל ("tent") and נטה ("stretch out"), respectively.⁵ Elsewhere, אהל appears as the object of נטה to describe someone "stretching out a tent" to set it up, or in other words "pitching a tent." Typically, these tents are human dwellings (e.g., Gen 12:8; 35:21; Judg 4:11), but as Habel observes, a few passages use נטה to describe people pitching sacred tents (Exod 33:7; 2 Sam 6:17; 1 Chr 15:1; 16:1; also 2 Chr 1:4).⁶ Moreover, אהל is frequently used in conjunction with the tabernacle in other contexts (e.g., Exod 26:7, 12–13; 40:19, 22; Num 3:7–8; 2 Sam 7:6). These lexical associations with the tabernacle suggest that Isa 40:22 presents the image of YHWH stretching out the heavens in order to erect a heavenly tabernacle.⁷ There he "sits" (ישב) enthroned "above the circle of the earth" to exercise his rule over the whole cosmos.⁸ This parallels

---

2. Habel, "He Who Stretches," 417–30; see also Hartenstein, "JHWH, Erschaffer des Himmels," 383–409, though his aim is broader.

3. See also Hartenstein, "JHWH, Erschaffer des Himmels," 402.

4. All translations of the biblical text are mine unless otherwise noted.

5. Modern commentators interpret דק as something made of fabric: "net" in Goldingay and Payne, *Isaiah 40–55*, 1:120; "gauze" in Paul, *Isaiah 40–66*, 149; "thin cloth" or "veil" in Koole, *Isaiah 40–48*, 108–9; and "curtain" in *DCH* ("דק," *DCH* 2:460).

6. Habel, "He Who Stretches," 426.

7. See Habel, "He Who Stretches," 430.

8. See Habel, "He Who Stretches," 420.

the tabernacle and temple traditions, which depict YHWH as sitting (ישב) enthroned upon the cherubim in the Most Holy Place to exercise his rule over Israel (e.g., Ps 99:1; 1 Sam 4:4; 2 Kgs 19:15 // Isa 37:16).[9]

Similarly, Psalm 104:2b–3a describes YHWH as the one:

> Who stretches out the heavens like a curtain (נוטה שמים כיריעה),
> Who lays the beams of his upper chambers on the waters.

According to Goldingay, v. 3a indicates that "Yhwh's dwelling lay *above* the dome of the heavens" and was "firmly fixed." Therefore, the curtain in v. 2b is not related to his abode.[10] However, I am not convinced that these must refer to two separate structures. As Habel suggests, they may offer parallel depictions of YHWH's dwelling place, the former evoking the image of the tabernacle and the latter suggesting a structure of greater permanence like the temple.[11] After all, the word used for "curtain" in v. 2b (יריעה) also appears frequently in connection with the earthly tabernacle (e.g., Exod 26:1–10; Num 4:25; cf. 2 Sam 7:2).[12] The imagery of Psalm 104 reflects the same connection between YHWH stretching out the heavens and the creation of his divine abode as found in Isaiah, suggesting that this imagery may be constitutive of how the metaphor was more generally conceptualized in Israelite thought.

Habel sees further tabernacle/temple associations with נטה שמים in Ps 18, where the phrase appears along with the image of YHWH riding on a cherub (v. 11 [10]), recalling the cherubim carved into the cover on the ark of the covenant upon which YHWH sits enthroned (Exod 37:7–9; 2 Sam 6:2).[13] Psalm 18:7 [6] speaks of YHWH hearing the psalmist's plea for help "from his temple" (היכל). Since YHWH responds by coming down from the heavens in v. 10 [9], the "temple" where he is located when he hears the psalmist's plea is likely his heavenly dwelling, not the temple in Jerusalem.[14]

The Paired Phrase רקע הארץ and Further Tabernacle/Temple Associations

The metaphor of YHWH stretching out the heavens often appears in conjunction with the declaration that YHWH "made (עשׂה) the earth" (Isa 45:12; Jer 10:12; 51:15) or

---

9. See also Goldingay, *Message of Isaiah 40–55*, 56.

10. Goldingay, *Psalms*, 3:184, italics mine. He argues further that "if anything, this is the tent where the world's inhabitants will live." See also Koole, *Isaiah 40–48*, 110.

11. Habel, "He Who Stretches," 423.

12. See also Barker, "Waters of the Earth," 69–70; Berlin, "Wisdom of Creation," 77.

13. Habel, "He Who Stretches," 425–26, though he suggests that Exod 37 and 2 Sam 6 reflect different traditions.

14. Habel, "He Who Stretches," 425; see also Wilson, *Psalms*, 1:41 n. 15; Craigie, *Psalms 1–50*, 174; Goldingay, *Psalms*, 1:259. Longman, by contrast, views it as the earthly temple, citing Solomon's temple dedication prayer, which speaks of the people praying in distress toward the "house that [Solomon] built" and of YHWH "hear[ing]" from heaven" (1 Kgs 8:44–45; *Psalms*, 113). But even if that is the case, the verse assumes a strong connection between the earthly temple and YHWH's heavenly dwelling place.

"laid [its] foundations" (יסד, Isa 51:13; Zech 12:1; Ps 104:5; cf. Isa 48:13). Two texts, however, pair נטה שמים with the rare phrase רקע הארץ (Isa 42:5; 44:24; cf. Ps 136:5–6). Translators typically render רקע הארץ as "spread out the earth," relying on the parallel with נטה to determine the meaning of רקע.[15] However, in the three other places where רקע appears in the *qal*, it clearly means "to stamp down" or "trample" (2 Sam 22:43; Ezek 6:11; 25:6). In the *piel*, the verb means "to hammer out" or "overlay with" metal, as in the creation of cultic objects (Exod 39:3; Num 16:39 [17:4]; Isa 40:19).[16] The *hiphil* is found only in Job 37:18a, which English versions typically translate as "*spread out* the skies" like the *qal* form in רקע הארץ.[17] The description of the skies as "hard as a cast [metal] mirror" in v. 18b, however, suggests that the *hiphil* of רקע functions in a similar way as the *piel* to portray the image of "hammering out the skies."[18] The noun רקיע ("firmament") in Gen 1:6 is probably also derived from this meaning of the verb, on the understanding that the רקיע is a hard (perhaps metal) surface. This coheres with the common assumption in the ancient world that there was a solid vault in the sky.[19]

None of these occurrences of רקע support the meaning "to spread out," indicating a need to reexamine רקע הארץ. Commenting on Ps 136:6, Hans-Joachim Kraus translates the phrase as "who founded the earth," contending that "the verb denotes solidification and hardening of an element." However, he does not explain or justify his understanding.[20] By contrast, a few commentaries on Isaiah interpret the phrase as "the one who beats out the earth," following the verb's use to designate "hammering out metal."[21] However, that use of the verb appears elsewhere only in the *piel* and *hiphil*.

15. Aside from the English versions, see, e.g., "רקע," *DCH* 7:555; Hess, "רקע," *NIDOTTE* 3:1200; Blenkinsopp, *Isaiah 40–55*, 208; Allen, *Psalms 101–50*, 293; Habel, "He Who Stretches," 418; Janzen, "On the Moral Nature," 474 n. 32.

16. See also the sole occurrence of the passive *pual* to describe "hammered" silver (Jer 10:9).

17. See the NRSV, ESV, NASB, and NIV; also "רקע," *DCH* 7:555.

18. See Longman, *Job*, 407–8; Greenstein, *Job*, 159; Hartley, *Job*, 482. Although Walton seems to understand the verb as meaning "spread out" here, he may be right that the use of the *hiphil*, which often has a causative meaning, "puts Job in the position of control and cause with God as his instrument" (*Job*, 370).

19. See further Seely, "Firmament and the Water Above," 227–40. By contrast, Walton argues on the basis of Job 37:18 that "*šeḥaqim* ['skies'] pertains to the solid sky" and that "*raqiaʿ* refers to the space created when the *šeḥaqim* were put in place" (*Job*, 371).

20. Kraus, *Psalms 60–150*, 495, 498; see also Hossfeld and Zenger, *Psalms 3*, 502. There is some support for this translation in the LXX, which renders רקע הארץ as στερεόω ("to make strong"); the Vg., with *firmāre* ("to make firm") in Isa 42:5 and Ps 135:6 [136:6] and *stabilīr* ("to make firm, establish") in Isa 44:24; and the Tg., with שכלל ("founded") in Isa 42:5 and 44:24.

21. Goldingay and Payne, *Isaiah 40–55*, 1:223–25; see also Goldingay, *Psalms*, 3:591; Oswalt, *Isaiah 40–66*, 115–17; Watts, *Isaiah 34–66*, 646; Westermann, *Isaiah 40–66*, 99; Whybray, *Isaiah 40–66*, 74. Smith connects the ideas of spreading and hammering, saying that the verb "was also used in 40:19 to refer to the action of a craftsman who 'beats out, spreads out' gold into a thin layer to cover the wood of an idol" (*Isaiah 40–66*, 166 n. 281; cf. Paul, *Isaiah 40–66*, 246; Ludwig, "Establishing of the Earth," 347–48). But "spread out" does not adequately capture the sense of the verb when it is applied to hammering out metal.

Therefore, I contend that the verb should be translated in the same way as its other occurrences in the *qal* stem, leading to the portrait of YHWH as the one "who stamped down the earth." Jan Koole, citing Franciscus Zorell's Hebrew lexicon, mentions this meaning of the verb with reference to the phrase רקע הארץ.[22] Yet Koole retains the conventional translation "who spread out the earth" with no further comment.

The translation I propose evokes the image of YHWH creating the various topographical features of the earth by stamping down its surface with his feet.[23] If YHWH stretches out the heavens to erect a heavenly tabernacle where he sits enthroned (as in Isa 40:22), then correspondingly he stamps down the earth to fashion not only a dwelling place for humanity (see 42:5b) but also as a place for his feet to rest. The portrait coheres with the description of heaven as YHWH's throne and earth as his footstool in Isa 66:1. Elsewhere in Isaiah, YHWH's feet rest in the earthly temple. That image is most explicit in 60:13 (cf. Ezek 43:7). But it may also be implied in 6:1, where the prophet narrates a vision of YHWH "seated on a throne, high and lifted up, and the hem [of his robe] filled the temple." If the temple contains the bottom hem of his robe, then surely his feet are there too. Similarly, in 1 Chr 28:2, the ark of the covenant is described as YHWH's "footstool," and in a few poetic passages his "footstool" may refer either to the ark or to the temple sanctuary more broadly (Ps 99:5; 132:7; Lam 2:1).[24]

Habel connects the statement that David "established (כון) a place for the ark of God and stretched out (נטה) a tent for it" in 1 Chr 15:1 with the affirmation that YHWH "established (כון) the world" and "stretched out (נטה) the heavens" in Jer 10:12. While Habel's identification of a symbolic ritual in 1 Chr 15:1 is debatable,[25] the OT draws a clear correspondence between the ark and the earth, where YHWH's feet rest, and between the earthly tabernacle/temple and YHWH's heavenly sanctuary, where he dwells. After all, as John Walton notes, throughout the ANE, "the temple on earth was considered only a type of the larger, archetypal cosmic temple, [so] many images and symbols evoke the relationship between temple and cosmos."[26]

Proposed Ancient Near Eastern Parallels

Other scholars seek a background for the metaphor of YHWH stretching out the heavens in ANE parallels. However, since they offer little-to-no discussion of the proposed parallels, further attention is needed to determine whether the ANE texts

---

22. Koole, *Isaiah 40–48*, 226. Zorell offers the definition "quasi calcando pedibus rem *extendit simul et firmavit*" ("רָקַע," *Lexicon Hebraicum Veteris Testamenti*, 789).

23. Psalm 136:6 specifies that YHWH "stamped down the earth upon the waters," reflecting the ancient view that there were waters under the earth.

24. See further Goldingay, *Psalms*, 3:550.

25. Habel, "He Who Stretches," 426–27.

26. Walton, *Ancient Near Eastern Thought*, 85; see also Habel, "He Who Stretches," 427, as well as the association between the sanctuary and the heavens and earth in Ps 78:69 (on which, see Ludwig, "Establishing of the Earth," 354; Goldingay, *Psalms*, 2:513).

Part 1: Creation

provide a helpful background for understanding the biblical use of the metaphor. First, Shalom Paul suggests a parallel in the second-millennium Babylonian lament concerning innocent suffering, *Ludlul Bēl Nēmeqi*, which describes the dwelling place of humanity as:[27]

> Wherever the earth is laid, and the heavens are stretched out (*rit-pa-šu*)

This text uses the adjective *ritpāšu*, meaning "extended, vast," to describe the heavens,[28] which does not demonstrate close lexical correspondence with נטה. However, it forms a stronger parallel with the declaration that YHWH "extended (טפח) the heavens" in Isa 48:13,[29] particularly in light of the paired claim that YHWH "laid the foundations of the earth." The context of this line in *Ludlul Bēl Nēmeqi* extols Marduk (along with his wife *Ṣarpānītum*) as having the unmatched power to bring the dead to life, paralleling YHWH's claims to sovereignty in Isa 40–55. However, *Ludlul Bēl Nēmeqi* does not identify the creator of the cosmos; instead the reference to the heavens and earth merely indicates the realm within which people offer praise to Marduk. The difference is even more striking in light of the emphasis Isa 48:13 places on YHWH's creative action by making his "hand"/"right hand" the subject of its verbs of creation. Therefore, the usefulness of this text as a parallel is quite limited.

David Baker suggests a second parallel in Amherst Papyrus 63.[30] This document contains around thirty-five Babylonian, Syrian, and Jewish texts, one of which appears to be a much-altered version of the biblical Ps 20.[31] The texts are written in Aramaic but transcribed in a demotic script, which has made them difficult to translate. Although the papyrus itself dates to the fourth century BCE, the compositions it contains may date to the seventh century.[32]

The proposed parallel comes in a prayer whose translation and meaning are debated. Richard Steiner and Charles F. Nims understand it as "a farmer's prayer for the rising of the Nile," translating the first two lines as:[33]

> 1 Be go[od], our father, Mar of [Arash], to your [e]x[il]ed tenant farmer.
> 2 You stretched out the heavens, Mar, [you] s[et] the stars in place,

---

27. Paul, *Isaiah 40–66*, 150; translation taken from Lambert, *Babylonian Wisdom Literature*, 58–59 (IV.37).

28. *CAD* R 382.

29. The Hebrew verb טפח is a *hapax legomenon*; on this meaning, see "טפח," *DCH* 3:373.

30. Baker, "Isaiah," 4:136.

31. See Amherst Papyrus 63 XII.11–19.

32. Van der Toorn, "Egyptian Papyrus," 32–39, 66, 68.

33. Steiner and Nims, "Aramaic Text," 36–37 (Col. X); see also the older translation by Steiner in *COS* 1.99:316.

By contrast, Karel van der Toorn views the poem as a hymn depicting the Aramean god Bethel as a storm god reminiscent of Baal.³⁴ He renders these lines as:³⁵

> 1 From the Lebanon, Lord, from Rash, You strike the entire earth.
> 2 You lift up the skies, O Lord. You attack the stars and make (them) dark.

Both readings identify the initial verb in line 2 as the Aramaic *mtḥ*. Van der Toorn acknowledges that this verb could be a cognate of the Hebrew מתח, which is used as a parallel to נטה in Isa 40:22, and that is clearly how Steiner and Nims understand it. However, van der Toorn prefers to interpret the verb in light of the Akkadian *matāḫu* ("to pick up, to lift") because "'stretching out the heavens,' reads like an act of creation, but the entire context suggests divine warfare."³⁶ Even if van der Toorn is right about the meaning of the prayer, however, that would not rule out interpreting the verb in light of the Hebrew cognate. After all, נטה שמים is connected with divine warrior imagery in Ps 18:10 [9] (// 2 Sam 22:10; cf. Ps 144:5).

In fact, there are significant similarities between Ps 18 and this prayer in Amherst Papyrus 63, as van der Toorn understands it. Both portray their respective G/god as a storm deity, who responds to the plight of the petitioner by employing meteorological weapons to rout his or her enemies.³⁷ They also both describe the petitioner as being brought into "a broad place" and ask questions to highlight the G/god's incomparability.³⁸ Perhaps then *mtḥ* is used in this poem in a way similar to נטה in Ps 18. However, given the familiarity with Ps 20 reflected in Amherst Papyrus 63, the poem may derive this idiom from biblical usage and so would not provide any background for understanding the biblical metaphor. In any case, the difficulties surrounding the text urge caution about drawing any firm conclusions.

Finally, Joseph Riordan and Friedhelm Hartenstein find a parallel to YHWH stretching out the heavens in *Enuma Elish*.³⁹ After Marduk slays the goddess Tiamat, it says in IV.137–40:⁴⁰

> 137 He split her into two like a dried fish:
> 138 One half of her he set up and stretched out (*uṣ-ṣal-lil*) as the heavens.
> 139 He stretched (*iš-du-ud*) the skin and appointed a watch.
> 140 With the instruction not to let her waters escape.

---

34. Van der Toorn, *Papyrus Amherst 63*, 153 (identifying it as Col. XI).
35. Van der Toorn, *Papyrus Amherst 63*, 152.
36. Van der Toorn, *Papyrus Amherst 63*, 152.
37. See Ps 18:8–16 [7–15]; Amherst Papyrus 63 XI.1–6.
38. See Ps 18:20, 32 [19, 31]; Amherst Papyrus 63 XI.13, 17.
39. Riordan, "Of Gods and Men," 63 n. 10; Hartenstein, "JHWH, Erschaffer des Himmels," 402.
40. Lambert, *Babylonian Creation Myths*, 94–95.

Part 1: Creation

The phrase translated as "stretched out as the heavens" in line 138 uses the Akkadian verb *ṣullulu*, which means "to roof (a building), to put on top."[41] Therefore, it does not closely parallel the Hebrew נטה. However, the verb *šadādu*, which is used to describe how Marduk "stretched the skin" in line 139, corresponds more closely to נטה with the meaning "to pull taut, stretch."[42] Since Tiamat's body is composed of water, Lambert contends that her skin functions like the רקיע ("firmament") in Gen 1:6–8. Marduk stretches it out to hold back the celestial waters above, separating them from the waters below as he creates the earth from the other half of her body.[43]

Intriguingly, LXX Ps 103:2b [MT 104:2b] describes YHWH as "stretching out heaven like a skin (δέρρις)," with "skin" replacing the MT's "curtain" (יריעה). In the MT יריעה frequently denotes the curtains of the tabernacle. The LXX often translates יריעה with αὐλαία ("curtain," e.g., Exod 26:1–6), but it uses δέρρις ("skin") instead when the text specifies that the curtain is to be made out of the hides of animals (see Exod 26:7–13). So while LXX Ps 103:2b [MT 104:2b] may seem to form a closer parallel with *Enuma Elish*, its aim is probably to evoke the image of tabernacle curtains like the MT.

In *Enuma Elish* Marduk's defeat of Tiamat and subsequent creation of the heavens and earth demonstrate his greatness among the gods, a theme that is prominent in biblical references to YHWH stretching out the heavens. However, while Marduk creates the heavens out of Tiamat's body, stretching out the skin as a barrier to keep her waters back, the OT does not identify any material used by YHWH. Instead Isa 40:22 employs a simile to portray the heavens as the curtains of a celestial tent.[44] Moreover, in *Enuma Elish* the creation of the heavens and the earth emerges out of divine conflict and as somewhat of an afterthought.[45] By contrast, YHWH stretches out the heavens with clear intentionality and almost always without struggle.[46] Finally, immediately after creating the heavens, Marduk sets Anu, Enlil, and Ea in their shrines (IV.141–46) and places the constellations in the sky, but nowhere does the text suggest that he created the heavens as his own dwelling place as in Isa 40:22.[47] In fact, Marduk later announces his intention to build himself an abode in the city of Babylon (V.117–30), but ultimately the lower gods (the Anunnaki) build both the city and dwelling for him as a grateful response for his creation of humanity to relieve the burden of their toil (VI.1–10, 47–73).

---

41. *CAD* Ṣ 239. Dalley, *Myths from Mesopotamia*, 255, therefore renders the line as "Half of her he put up to roof the sky."

42. *CAD* Š/1 22. Like נטה, it can be used for stretching out curtains.

43. Lambert, *Babylonian Creation Myths*, 171.

44. Even LXX Ps 103:2b speaks of YHWH "stretching out the heavens *like* a skin [curtain]," not *from* a skin.

45. See Blenkinsopp, "Protological Language," 508.

46. See further below.

47. While Anu clearly resides in the heaven and Ea is connected with the primordial waters of the Apsû, the location where Enlil is situated (Ešarra) is less clear. Lambert connects the abodes of the three gods with a three-tiered heaven known from other Babylonian texts ("Mesopotamian Creation Stories," 22–23).

Of the suggested parallels, *Enuma Elish* offers the most fruitful comparison with the biblical text. Riordan argues that Isa 40–55 "mimics and subverts the rhetoric and ideology of creation" in *Enuma Elish* by presenting YHWH "as a 'mirror-image' of Marduk, thus countering his claims to supremacy," and he cites the image of stretching out the heavens as one example of the link between them.[48] Although I do not think the parallels with *Enuma Elish* are strong enough to demonstrate literary dependence, it seems likely that Isa 40–55 is polemically engaging with Babylonian religious ideology. Therefore, it is instructive to compare the biblical metaphor of YHWH stretching out the heavens with Marduk's actions in *Enuma Elish* since they reflect the significant differences between Israelite and Babylonian views of creation.

The Use of the Metaphor in the OT

Isaiah 40–55

In the monotheistic context of Isa 40–55, the metaphor of YHWH stretching out the heavens is connected not to his elevation above other gods, as with Marduk in *Enuma Elish*, but to the argument that no other gods exist. Isaiah 40 asks, "To whom will you liken God, or what likeness will you compare with him?" (v. 18) and then launches into a critique of idols (vv. 19–20). Whereas the idols *are created* by craftsmen (vv. 19–20), YHWH is the *creator* of the universe (vv. 22, 26, 28). The image of YHWH stretching out the heavens also highlights his sovereignty over the human rulers who have sent his people into exile. From YHWH's vantage point seated in his heavenly tent, even the mighty kings of the earth appear only as "grasshoppers" (v. 22), so he "makes rulers as nothing" (v. 23). Among these images, the metaphor of YHWH stretching out the heavens provides grounds for trusting that he has the power to bring his people back from exile (vv. 9–11).

The metaphor appears next in 42:1–9. After describing servant Israel's responsibility to "establish justice (משפט) on earth" (v. 4),[49] v. 5 declares:

> Thus says the God, YHWH,
> Who created the heavens and stretched them out (נטה שמים),
> Who stamped down (רקע) the earth and its produce,[50]
> Who gives breath to the people upon it
> And spirit to those who walk on it.

---

48. Riordan, "Of Gods and Men," 60–61; similarly, Blenkinsopp, "Protological Language," 507; Lessing, "Yahweh Versus Marduk," 240; Hartenstein, "JHWH, Erschaffer des Himmels," 400–402; Janzen, "On the Moral Nature," 473.

49. For the identity of the servant here as Israel, see 41:8–9; also Kim, *Lengthen Your Tent-Cords*, 138–39.

50. On any translation of רקע, the verb does not fit naturally with the second object, "its produce" (צאצאיה), which probably refers to the plants that spring up from the earth. Thus the line involves a zeugma (see further Paul, *Isaiah 40–66*, 188; also Koole, *Isaiah 40–48*, 227, who suggests that צאצאיה may include the earth's animal life).

Part 1: Creation

YHWH will enable servant Israel to accomplish their mission (vv. 6-9). Since YHWH created his heavenly tabernacle and stamped down the earth, he now sits enthroned in the heavens to rule the cosmos. Therefore, the whole earth and the people of all nations are within his jurisdiction, and he has both the right and the ability to bring about worldwide justice through his servant. While the theme of other gods is less prominent in this passage, v. 8 declares that YHWH does not share his glory with "idols." When he accomplishes his plan, he alone will get the praise.

The metaphor recurs in the context of a taunt against the idols and their makers in 43:22—45:8. This passage presents a contest with the gods of the nations, in which both sides are to bring out their witnesses in order to determine who has the power to declare what will happen and then bring it about (see 43:8-13; 44:6-11; cf. 41:21-29). Whereas the other gods have no witnesses who can vindicate them, YHWH calls his own people to witness to his proclamation that Cyrus will restore Jerusalem (44:24—45:8). When YHWH fulfills his promise, they will have ample proof of his sovereignty.

Against this background, 44:24 says:

> Thus says YHWH, your Redeemer,
> And the one who formed you from the womb,
> "I am YHWH, who made everything,
> Who stretched out the heavens alone (נטה שמים לבדי),
> Who stamped down (רקע) the earth by myself."

Here the additions to the creation formula are instructive. YHWH created the cosmos "alone" (// "by myself"), evidencing his claim to be the only true God who can act in history. And surely, the God who "stretched out the heavens" is able to coopt a foreign ruler to accomplish his plan of redemption for his people. Moreover, if he "stamped down the earth," then he must also have the ability to manipulate its features by drying up the waters of chaos to free his people from Babylonian exile. After all, he once parted the waters of the Re(e)d Sea to free them from Egypt (v. 27).[51] The passage indicates that YHWH will support and elevate "his anointed" Cyrus not only for *his* people's sake, but also so that *all* people will recognize his uncontested claims to deity (45:1-7). And through Cyrus, the creator God will bring about a new creation for Zion.[52]

It seems, however, that YHWH's people were not keen on the idea of a foreign messiah because in 45:9-10, YHWH declares "woe" against a pot who questions its maker and against children who question their parents about their (pro)creation. Identifying himself as "the Holy One of Israel and the One who forms him," YHWH sarcastically goads his people to "ask me of things to come concerning my children,

---

51. Blenkinsopp also sees a reference here to "the primordial chaos overcome by the god at the beginning of time" (*Isaiah 40-55*, 248). While there may be an allusion to creation here, it carries no hint of struggle. YHWH simply speaks to the deep, and presumably it obeys his command.

52. See Ludwig, "Establishing of the Earth," 355.

and command me concerning the work of my hands (ידי)!" (v. 11).[53] Then in v. 12 he reminds them of his résumé:

> I made the earth,
> And people upon it I created.
> I, by my hands, stretched out the heavens (אני ידי נטו שמים),
> And all their host I commanded.

The implication is that Israel has no right to challenge the plans of the sovereign creator God. The same "hands" (ידי) that stretched out the heavens are now at work at the potter's kiln, shaping Israel into a pot of the artist's own design. Observing the majestic heavens should give Israel reason to trust in the creative abilities of the potter to fashion a beautiful work of art. Furthermore, if God commands the host of heaven, then it is nothing for him to command human kings to do his bidding (v. 13).[54]

The theme of YHWH's contest with the nations is picked up again in Isa 48, where YHWH expresses frustration with his people for their persistent obstinacy and rebellion. They are more prone to attribute acts of deliverance to their idols (v. 5) than to bear witness to YHWH's power (vv. 6–8). Therefore, he pleads with them to listen as he asserts his sole claim to sovereignty, "I am he; I am the first, and I am the last" (v. 12). Then he supports that claim by pointing to his creation of the cosmos in v. 13:

> And my hand laid the foundation of the earth,
> And my right hand extended the heavens (וימיני טפחה שמים).
> When I call to them,
> They all stand together.

This passage uses the *hapax legomenon* טפח rather than נטה, though it seems to be a synonym, meaning "extend" or "spread out."[55] As in 45:12, YHWH emphasizes that he spread out the heavens with his own hand, though here he specifies his right hand as a symbol of power. The third line seems to refer to YHWH calling the heavens, now signifying the heavenly hosts, who stand to attention at his command.[56] So YHWH's act of spreading out the heavens is linked to the creation of a heavenly army. If the heavenly hosts listen to his call and await his instructions, then certainly Israel, whom YHWH "called" (v. 12), should "gather" and "listen" to him (v. 14a).[57] Once again YHWH demonstrates his sovereignty by reiterating his plan to use Cyrus to

---

53. On this translation, see further Kim, *Lengthen Your Tent-Cords*, 28.

54. See also Wardlaw, "Significance of Creation," 461.

55. See "טפח," *DCH* 3:373; Hamilton, "טפח," *NIDOTTE* 2:382; Koole, *Isaiah 40–48*, 580; Blenkinsopp, *Isaiah 40–55*, 293.

56. Note the reference to the heavenly "host" (צבא) in the context of "stretch[ing] out the earth" in 40:26 (Goldingay, *Message of Isaiah 40–55*, 352; cf. Oswalt, *Isaiah 40–46*, 275–76).

57. On Israel as the audience here, see Goldingay, *Message of Isaiah 40–55*, 352; Blenkinsopp, *Isaiah 40–55*, 293.

Part 1: Creation

defeat the Babylonians. The fact that he is the God who created all things provides a ground for the striking claim that he "loves" Cyrus (v. 14).[58]

The metaphor is found one final time in 51:9—52:12, which begins with a plea for YHWH's arm to "awake" and "put on strength" as he when he "cut Rahab to pieces" and "pierced the dragon" (v. 9). The references to YHWH defeating a chaos monster have led some interpreters to connect the text with Marduk's defeat of Tiamat in *Enuma Elish*.[59] However, vv. 9–10 focus not on creation but on YHWH redeeming his people at the exodus by drying up the waters of the Re(e)d Sea.[60] YHWH responds to his people's entreaty by assuring them of his comfort but then rebukes them in v. 13a:

> But you forget YHWH your Maker,
> Who stretched out the heavens (נוטה שמים)
> And laid the foundations of the earth.

As in 40:22, here the image of YHWH stretching out the heavens is used in connection with his sovereignty over earthly rulers. Israel's constant "dread" at the "wrath of the oppressor" (v. 13b) demonstrates that they are not taking into account the fact that YHWH created not only them, but also the whole cosmos. Their oppressor is nothing compared to YHWH (v. 13c),[61] so they should trust in YHWH's ability to deliver them (v. 14). The creator God has the power to "stir up" the waters of chaos (v. 15), presumably to use them as an instrument of warfare against Israel's enemy. So throughout Isa 40–55, the metaphor of YHWH stretching out the heavens is employed to highlight YHWH's sovereignty over the other (so-called) gods and human rulers and to emphasize his ability to deliver his people by defeating their enemies.

Other Prophetic Texts

Outside of Isaiah, the metaphor is found in the prophetic corpus only in Jer 10:12 // 51:15 and Zech 12:1. Intriguingly, while Jer 10 speaks of the coming destruction of Jerusalem by the Babylonians, the metaphor of YHWH stretching out the heavens appears in a section of five verses (10:12–16) that have also been inserted into the oracle against Babylon in chs. 50–51 (51:15–19). As in Isa 40–55, in Jer 10 the metaphor occurs in the context of asserting YHWH's sovereignty over the so-called gods of the nations. In v. 11 YHWH instructs the prophet to tell the people, "The gods who did not make the heavens and the earth, these will perish from the earth and from under

---

58. See Ludwig, "Establishing of the Earth," 355. Here, however, Isaiah does not mention Cyrus by name as in 44:28; 45:1.
59. See, e.g., Westermann, *Isaiah 40–66*, 241–42.
60. See further Smith, *Isaiah 40–66*, 404; Lessing, "Yahweh Versus Marduk," 239.
61. Cf. the image of people as grasshoppers from YHWH's perspective in 40:22.

the heavens."[62] Then v. 12 speaks of the true creator of the cosmos, who though unnamed, is clearly to be identified as YHWH:

> The one who made the earth by his strength,
> Who established the world by his wisdom,
> And by his understanding stretched out the heavens (ובתבונתו נטה שמים).

In contrast to the impotent idols (vv. 3–5), who are a "work (מעשׂה) of mockery" (v. 15), YHWH "made (עשׂה) the earth by his strength" (v. 12). And whereas the idols cannot offer any true instruction (v. 8),[63] YHWH created the heavens with "understanding" (v. 12). Unlike Isa 40–55, however, here YHWH's sovereignty over creation does not provide a reason for Judah to trust in his coming deliverance. Instead, it is connected to his proclamation of judgment leading to exile (vv. 17–18), which prompts personified Jerusalem to lament in v. 20:[64]

> My tent (אהלי) is destroyed and all my tent-cords (מיתרי) are broken;
> My children (בני) are gone from me and are no more.
> There is no one to stretch out my tent again (אין־נטה עוד אהלי)
> Or set up my curtains (יריעותי).

The tent could symbolize the temple (here portrayed as the tabernacle),[65] but it probably refers to the habitation of Jerusalem more broadly.[66] Either way, although Jerusalem insists that there is "no one to stretch out [her] tent" since her "children" (i.e., inhabitants) have gone away into exile, the repetition of נטה from v. 12 may suggest an unvoiced hope. Perhaps YHWH, the God who "stretched out the heavens" may one day "stretch out" Jerusalem's tent again.[67]

In the context of Jer 51, the declaration that YHWH "made the earth (ארץ)" (v. 15) forms a striking contrast with the description of Babylon as a "destroying mountain ... who destroys the whole earth" (ארץ, v. 25). Therefore, YHWH, who once "stretched (נטה) out the heavens" (v. 15), now declares to Babylon, "I will stretch out (נטה) my hand against you" (v. 25). Here the portrait of YHWH as creator of the

---

62. On this translation with its understanding of the difficult syntactical placement of אלה at the end of the verse as a resumptive pronoun referring to the "gods," see Lundbom, *Jeremiah 1–20*, 594. This verse is one of the few Aramaic passages in the OT, on which see further Holladay, *Jeremiah 1*, 324–25.

63. See further Holladay, *Jeremiah 1*, 332.

64. Alternatively, the speaker could be Judah (see further, Lundbom, *Jeremiah 1–20*, 603).

65. Holladay, *Jeremiah 1*, 342.

66. Lundbom, *Jeremiah 1–20*, 605. Note that in 4:20 Jerusalem (or Judah) laments the destruction of her "tents" in the plural.

67. Within the larger canon, the response to this hope comes in Isa 54:2, where YHWH invites Jerusalem to take part in her own restoration by making preparations for an influx of new "children" (בני, v. 1): "Enlarge the place of your tent (אהלך), and let the curtains (יריעות) of your dwellings stretch out (יטו). Do not hold back; lengthen your tent-cords (מיתריך) and strengthen your tent-pegs."

Part 1: Creation

cosmos suggests first that he has the right to judge all nations,[68] particularly when they threaten his created order, and second that Babylon will be no match for the powerful divine hand capable of forming the heavens.

Finally, in Zechariah 12 the metaphor occurs in an oracle promising YHWH's deliverance of Jerusalem when "all the nations of the earth gather against her" (v. 3). His promise is grounded in his identity in v. 1b:

> Thus says YHWH,
> Who stretched out the heavens (נטה שמים)
> And who laid the foundations (יסד) of the earth
> And who formed the spirit (רוח) of man within him:

As in other prophetic passages, here YHWH's creation of both the cosmos and humankind demonstrates his lordship over all nations and also highlights his sovereign ability to accomplish Jerusalem's deliverance.[69]

Intriguingly, this passage shares some intertextual connections with Isa 51. Both Isa 51:13 and Zech 12:1 describe YHWH as stretching out the heavens and laying the foundations of the earth, and only in these two verses in the OT do the verbs נטה and יסד appear together.[70] Also, in Zech 12:2 YHWH declares that he will "make Jerusalem a goblet of staggering (סף־רעל) for all peoples." In Isa 51:17 YHWH calls Jerusalem, who has drunk from "the cup of staggering (כוס התרעלה)," to awake. Then in vv. 22–23 he says that he has "taken the cup of staggering (כוס התרעלה) out of her hand" and promises to give it to her enemies. It seems likely that Zech 12 is intentionally recalling Isa 51, which was fulfilled in Babylon's defeat by Persia and the return of the exiles, in order to buttress the people's trust that YHWH will deliver them from the nations who threaten them at the time of Zechariah.[71] The combination of נטה שמים with YHWH putting "spirit" (רוח) in people also parallels Isa 42:5,[72] and it may recall his aim to bring about worldwide justice—in this case by vindicating Jerusalem in the face of threats from enemy nations.[73]

Psalms and Job

In the Psalms and Job, נטה שמים and related phrases are used in two distinct but related ways. First, two passages portray YHWH stretching out the heavens at creation, as in the prophetic texts already examined. Psalm 104 describes YHWH as "clothed

---

68. See Fretheim, *Jeremiah*, 638.
69. See Meyers and Meyers, *Zechariah 9–14*, 311; Klein, *Zechariah*, 350–51.
70. See Boda, *Zechariah*, 693.
71. Boda, *Zechariah*, 693.
72. See Boda, *Zechariah*, 694; Mitchell, "Note on the Creation Formula," 307.
73. Like servant Israel in Isa 42:1–4, here "the clans of Judah" play a role in bringing about God's justice. However, they do so by "devour[ing] . . . all the surrounding peoples" (Zech 12:6), in contrast to the non-violent context of the Isaianic passage.

with splendor and majesty" (v. 1), suggesting the image of a king.[74] The divine king "stretched out the heavens" to create his heavenly abode (v. 2) and "set the earth on its foundations" (v. 5) to produce a fully ordered cosmos.[75] By making the earth stable and fixing limits for the waters (vv. 6–9), he provides a secure and fit place for his creatures to dwell. From his heavenly palace, he providentially cares for all of his subjects, including the non-human creatures who inhabit sky, earth, and sea (vv. 10–30).

The second reference comes in Job 26:7, in a text with a significantly different tone than the passages examined thus far. In Job 26–28, Job offers an ironic response to Bildad's brief final speech, declaring, "how you have helped one who has no strength!" (God?; 26:2). He then proceeds to accentuate God's sovereign creative power, though without ever naming him, referring in v. 7 to:

> The one who stretched out Zaphon over chaos (נטה צפון על־תהו),
> Who hung the earth over nothing (בלי־מה).

Although צפון can mean "north," here it is more likely a reference to the sacred mountain Zaphon, where the Canaanite god Baal dwelt (see also Ps 48:3 [2]). In the ANE the cosmic mountain, which stretched up to the heavens, was seen as the place where heaven and earth met. And given that elsewhere in the OT it is the "heavens" that are stretched out, it seems likely that Zaphon is used to stand for the heavens, or more particularly for God's sacred dwelling in the heavens.[76] This understanding is further supported by the parallel description of the earth's creation. The unusual references to "chaos" (תהו) and "nothing" (בלי־מה) in this context may suggest the primordial waters (see the use of תהו in Gen 1:2).[77]

Unlike the prophetic references to YHWH stretching out the heavens, here the image is combined with a creational image of cosmic battle as v. 12 declares, "by his strength he stilled the sea, and by his understanding he crushed Rahab." However, Ayali-Darshan observes that these two elements appear in an inverted order. Rather than God's defeat of the chaos monster Rahab leading to his creation of the heavens and earth, which would parallel *Enuma Elish* (see also Ps 74:13–17; 89:10–13 [9–12]), here creation precedes the cosmic conflict.[78] While the reason for this structure is unclear, it effectively downplays any connection between God's defeat of Rahab and his act of stretching out Zaphon. In the context of the Joban dialogues, this portrait of God as creator serves to highlight his transcendence and inaccessibility. He is a God who cannot be grasped by the "wisdom" of Job's friends, nor can he be called to account, even though he has "denied justice" to Job (27:2). Ultimately, however, the

---

74. See Goldingay, *Psalms*, 3:183; Estes, *Psalms 73–150*, 272.

75. On the text of Ps 104:2, see p. 39.

76. For the former, see Walton, *Job*, 251; Balentine, *Job*, 389. For the latter, see Hartley, *Job*, 365–66; Clines, *Job 21–37*, 636.

77. Ayali-Darshan, "Question of the Order," 410; similarly, Walton, *Job*, 252–53.

78. Ayali-Darshan, "Question of the Order," 403–9.

transcendent God will prove not to be completely inaccessible when he speaks to Job from the whirlwind (chs. 38–41).

A few passages use the metaphor in a second way to describe YHWH as stretching out the heavens in order to leave his heavenly abode and step down to earth so that he can execute judgment on human adversaries (Ps 18:10 [9] // 2 Sam 22:10; Ps 144:5; Job 9:8). In these texts, "parted the heavens" is an appropriate translation. First, Ps 18:10 [9] declares:

> And he parted the heavens and came down (ויט שמים וירד),
> And thick darkness was under his feet.

Given the description of YHWH's heavenly dwelling as a "temple" in v. 7 [6],[79] this verse may offer a parallel image of YHWH's heavenly abode as a tabernacle, whose entrance curtains YHWH pulls apart so that he can exit.[80] His emergence from the heavens results in a storm theophany that combines darkness with fiery brightness (vv. 10b–13 [9b–12]). As he rides down on a cherub-steed, he employs the lightning and wind as weapons against the psalmist's enemies, thereby bringing deliverance.

Psalm 144, which is dependent on Ps 18,[81] presents an entreaty that YHWH would intervene in a current situation of distress as in that earlier psalm. In v. 5, the psalmist pleads:

> YHWH, part[82] your heavens (יהוה הט־שמיך ותרד) and come down;
> Touch the mountains so that they smoke.

The psalmist calls on YHWH to descend from his heavenly dwelling and scatter the psalmist's enemies, using lightning as a weapon (v. 6).[83] This image forms a contrast to the more desperate cries of the lamenter in Isa 63:19b [64:1b], who calls for YHWH to "rend (קרע) the heavens and come down." The latter verse evokes the image of YHWH tearing the curtains of his heavenly tabernacle in his haste to come rescue his people.

The final use of the metaphor is found in Job's first response to Bildad in Job 9–10. Although 9:8 is typically understood as describing God's creation of the heavens,[84]

---

79. See further on p. 39.

80. Habel tries to connect these two psalms to the use of נטה שמים as a creational metaphor elsewhere, saying with regard to Ps 144 that "when YHWH comes he first 'prepares' his celestial abode by 'stretching out' the heavens where he displays his glorious presence" ("He Who Stretches," 424). However, whereas elsewhere the phrase is typically paralleled by a reference to YHWH creating the earth, here it is paired with ירד ("came down"). This suggests that the "stretching" of the heavens has a different purpose here (see further Goldingay, *Psalms*, 3:686 n. 16; Cross and Freedman, "Royal Song of Thanksgiving," 24 n. 23).

81. See further Goldingay, *Psalms*, 3:683.

82. This is the only occurrence of the phrase נטה שמים where נטה appears in the *hiphil* stem, but there does not seem to be any difference in meaning between its use here and in Ps 18:10 [9].

83. Allen, *Psalms 101–50*, 364.

84. The NRSV is representative when it translates v. 8a as "who alone stretched out the heavens";

Walton argues convincingly that the context of divine judgment necessitates reading the verse along the lines of Ps 18:10 [9] and 144:5.[85] Therefore, the verse describes God as:

> The one who parts the heavens by himself,
> And tramples the waves of the sea[86]

Indeed, like Ps 18:8–12 [7–11], Job 9:6–7 portrays an earthquake and depicts God coming under cover of darkness, though it goes a bit further in using imagery that suggests the undoing of creation. Rather than God simply using darkness to conceal himself (Ps 18:12 [11]), here he "speaks to the sun, and it does not shine; and he seals off the stars" (Job 9:7).[87] In Balentine's view, Job "can see that God is empowered to turn creation upside down and to replace order with chaos."[88]

The more ominous tone may be due to the fact that unlike the psalmist, Job does not envision God coming down from the heavens to rescue him but instead sees himself as the object of divine judgment. He despairs that despite his innocence, he cannot vindicate himself before such a terrifyingly powerful God (vv. 15, 20), who "destroys the blameless and the wicked" (v. 22). Readers of the book are aware of what Job is not—God does not part the heavens to come down and attack Job. His suffering comes from the hand of the *satan* (1:6–12; 2:1–6). Nevertheless, it also describes God as allowing his suffering and preserves God's sovereign transcendent freedom to govern the cosmos as he sees fit.

Conclusion

Habel rightly draws our attention to how the metaphor of YHWH stretching out the heavens connects with Israel's tabernacle traditions. Understanding the paired phrase רקע הארץ as an image of YHWH stamping down the earth to prepare a place for his feet to rest evokes the image of a cosmic temple portrayed in passages like Isa 66:1, further contributing to Habel's argument. While some scholars have suggested ANE parallels for the metaphor, only *Enuma Elish* provides a helpful comparison. In *Enuma*

---

see also Balentine, *Job*, 167; Clines, *Job 1–20*, 230; Seow, *Job 1–21*, 557–58.

85. Walton, *Job*, 168–70.

86. Many commentators see here a mythological portrayal of YHWH's defeat of a sea monster or watery chaos (cf. the reference to Rahab in v. 13; e.g., Clines, *Job 1–20*, 230–31; Balentine, *Job*, 167). Even if that is the case, the focus here is on his defeat over historical (rather than primordial) forces of chaos. Walton observes that a Baal stele depicts "the storm god walking on the waves of the sea as he strides forth with his lightning bolts in hand" (*Job*, 169); see also Hab 3:15. Other passages describe YHWH "tread[ing] on the heights of the earth" when he comes in judgment (Mic 1:3; Amos 4:13).

87. Job 9:5–6 may also indicate that God "moves mountains . . . and overturns them" and "makes the earth shake *from* its place"; however, Walton reads these verses as saying that God "traverses the mountains . . . and overthrows [his enemies]. He causes the earth to tremble *in* its place" (*Job*, 170, italics mine).

88. Balentine, *Job*, 167; see also Tönsing, "Creation Language," 441.

Elish the metaphor is connected to the supremacy of Marduk over the other gods, but the OT uses the metaphor to emphasize YHWH's status as the only true God. In Jer 10:12 the sovereign might YHWH demonstrated in stretching out the heavens is directed against his own people, and Job also views God's creative power as threatening (26:7; cf. 9:8). However, elsewhere YHWH's creation of a heavenly tabernacle where he sits enthroned is connected to his providential care for creation (Ps 104:2) and provides a foundation for trusting that he has the ability to redeem his people (Isa 40–55; Zech 12:1; cf. Jer 51:15). Indeed, the Psalms offer hope that God will hear his people when they call to him in his heavenly dwelling and that he will "part" the curtains to come down and deliver them in their distress (Ps 18:10 [9] // 2 Sam 22:10; Ps 144:5).

Bibliography

Allen, Leslie C. *Psalms 101–50*. Rev. ed. WBC 21. Nashville: Nelson, 2018.

Ayali-Darshan, Noga. "The Question of the Order of Job 26,7–13 and the Cosmogonic Tradition of Zaphon," *ZAW* 126 (2014) 402–17.

Baker, David W. "Isaiah." In *ZIBBCOT*, edited by John H. Walton, 4:2–227. Grand Rapids: Zondervan, 2009.

Balentine, Samuel E. *Job*. SHBC. Macon, GA: Smyth & Helwys, 2006.

Barker, David G. "The Waters of the Earth: An Exegetical Study of Psalm 104:1–9." *GTJ* 7 (1986) 57–80.

Berlin, Adele. "The Wisdom of Creation in Psalm 104." In *Seeking Out the Wisdom of the Ancients*, edited by Ronald L. Troxel et al., 71–83. Winona Lake, IN: Eisenbrauns, 2005.

Blenkinsopp, Joseph. "The Cosmological and Protological Language of Deutero-Isaiah." *CBQ* 73 (2011) 493–510.

———. *Isaiah 40–55: A New Translation with Introduction and Commentary*. Anchor Bible 19a. New York: Doubleday, 2002.

Boda, Mark J. *The Book of Zechariah*. NICOT. Grand Rapids: Eerdmans, 2016.

Clines, David J. A. *Job 1–20*. WBC 17. Dallas: Word, 1989.

———. *Job 21–37*. WBC 18A. Grand Rapids: Zondervan, 2006.

Clines, David J. A., ed. *DCH*. 8 vols. Sheffield: Sheffield Phoenix, 1993–2014.

Craigie, Peter C. *Psalms 1–50*. 2nd ed. WBC 19. Grand Rapids: Zondervan, 2004.

Cross, Frank Moore Jr., and David Noel Freedman. "A Royal Song of Thanksgiving: II Samuel 22 = Psalm 18a." *JBL* 72 (1953) 15–34.

Dalley, Stephanie. *Myths from Mesopotamia: Creation, the Flood, Gilgamesh, and Others*. Rev. ed. Oxford: Oxford University Press, 2000.

Estes, Daniel J. *Psalms 73–150*. NAC 13. Nashville: Broadman & Holman, 2019.

Fretheim, Terence E. *Jeremiah*. SHBC. Macon, GA: Smyth & Helwys, 2002.

Gelb, Ignace J., et al., eds. *The Assyrian Dictionary of the Oriental Institute of the University of Chicago*. 21 vols. Chicago: Oriental Institute, 1956–2011.

Goldingay, John. *The Message of Isaiah 40–55: A Literary-Theological Commentary*. New York: T. & T. Clark, 2005.

———. *Psalms*. 3 vols. Baker Commentary on the Old Testament. Grand Rapids: Baker Academic, 2006–2008.

Goldingay, John, and David Payne. *Isaiah 40–55: A Critical and Exegetical Commentary*. 2 vols. ICC. London: T. & T. Clark, 2006.

Greenstein, Edward L. *Job: A New Translation*. New Haven: Yale University Press, 2019.

Habel, Norman C. "'He Who Stretches Out the Heavens.'" *CBQ* 34 (1972) 417–30.

Hallo, William W., ed. *Canonical Compositions from the Biblical World*. Vol. 1 of *COS*. Leiden: Brill, 1997.

Hartenstein, Friedhelm. "JHWH, Erschaffer des Himmels: Zu Herkunft und Bedeutung eines monotheistischen Kernarguments." *ZTK* 110 (2013) 383–409.

Hartley, John E. *The Book of Job*. NICOT. Grand Rapids: Eerdmans, 1988.

Holladay, William L. *Jeremiah 1: A Commentary on the Book of the Prophet Jeremiah Chapters 1–25*. Hermeneia. Philadelphia: Fortress, 1986.

Hossfeld, Frank-Lothar, and Erich Zenger. *Psalms 3: A Commentary on Psalms 101–150*. Translated by Linda M. Maloney. Hermeneia. Minneapolis: Fortress, 2011.

Hutton, Jeremy M. "Isaiah 51:9–11 and the Rhetorical Appropriation and Subversion of Hostile Theologies." *JBL* 126 (2007) 271–303.

Janzen, J. Gerald. "On the Moral Nature of God's Power: Yahweh and the Sea in Job and Deutero-Isaiah." *CBQ* 56 (1994) 458–78.

Kim, Brittany. *"Lengthen Your Tent-Cords": The Metaphorical World of Israel's Household in the Book of Isaiah*. Siphrut 23. University Park, PA: Eisenbrauns, 2018.

Klein, George L. *Zechariah*. NAC 21B. Nashville: B&H, 2008.

Koole, Jan L. *Isaiah III*. Translated by Anthony P. Runia. 3 vols. Historical Commentary on the Old Testament. Kampen: Kok Pharos, 1997.

Kraus, Hans-Joachim. *Psalms 60–150*. Translated by Hilton C. Oswald. Continental Commentaries. Minneapolis: Fortress, 1993.

Lambert, W. G. *Babylonian Creation Myths*. Winona Lake, IN: Eisenbrauns, 2013.

———. *Babylonian Wisdom Literature*. Oxford: Oxford University Press, 1960. Repr. Winona Lake, IN: Eisenbrauns, 1996.

———. "Mesopotamian Creation Stories." In *Imagining Creation*, edited by Markham J. Geller and Mineke Schipper, 15–59. Leiden: Brill, 2008.

Lessing, R. Reed. "Yahweh Versus Marduk: Creation Theology in Isaiah 40–55." *Concordia Journal* (2010) 234–44.

Longman, Tremper, III. *Job*. Baker Commentary on the Old Testament. Grand Rapids: Baker Academic, 2012.

———. *Psalms*. Tyndale Old Testament Commentaries. Downers Grove, IL: InterVarsity, 2014.

Ludwig, Theodore M. "The Traditions of the Establishing of the Earth in Deutero-Isaiah." *JBL* 92 (1973) 345–57.

Lundbom, Jack R. *Jeremiah 1–20: A New Translation with Introduction and Commentary*. Anchor Bible 21A. New York: Doubleday, 1999.

Meyers, Carol L., and Eric M. Meyers, *Zechariah 9–14*. Anchor Bible 25C. New York: Doubleday, 1993.

Mitchell, Christine. "A Note on the Creation Formula in Zechariah 12:1–8; Isaiah 42:5–6; and Old Persian Inscriptions." *JBL* 133 (2014) 305–8.

Oswalt, John N. *The Book of Isaiah: Chapters 40–66*. NICOT. Grand Rapids: Eerdmans, 1998.

Paul, Shalom M. *Isaiah 40–66: Translation and Commentary*. Eerdmans Critical Commentary. Grand Rapids: Eerdmans, 2012.

Part 1: Creation

Riordan, Joseph. "Of Gods and Men: Creation and Divinity in Deutero-Isaiah and *Enūma Eliš*." *Conversations with the Biblical World* 36 (2016) 137–53.

Seely, Paul H. "The Firmament and the Water Above, Part I: The Meaning of *raqiaʿ* in Gen 1:6–8." *WTJ* 53 (1991) 227–40.

Seow, C. L. *Job 1–21: Interpretation and Commentary*. Illuminations. Grand Rapids: Eerdmans, 2013.

Smith, Gary V. *Isaiah 40–66*. NAC 15B. Nashville: B&H, 2009.

Steiner, Richard C., and Charles F. Nims. "The Aramaic Text in Demotic Script: Text, Translation, and Notes." 2017. Pages 1–92. http://repository.yu.edu/handle/20.500.12202/51.

Tönsing, D. L. "The Use of Creation Language in Job 3, 9 and 38 and the Meaning of Suffering." *Scriptura* 59 (1996) 435–49.

Van der Toorn, Karel. "Egyptian Papyrus Sheds New Light on Jewish History." *BAR* 44.4 (2018) 32–39 66, 68. https://www.baslibrary.org/biblical-archaeology-review/44/4/3.

———. *Papyrus Amherst 63*. AOAT 448. Münster: Ugarit-Verlag, 2018.

VanGemeren, Willem A., ed. *NIDOTTE*. 5 vols. Grand Rapids: Zondervan, 1997.

Walton, John. *Ancient Near Eastern Thought and the Old Testament: Introducing the Conceptual World of the Hebrew Bible*. 2nd ed. Grand Rapids: Baker Academic, 2018.

———. *Job*. NIV Application Commentary. Grand Rapids: Zondervan, 2012.

Wardlaw, Terrance R. Jr. "The Significance of Creation in the Book of Isaiah." *JETS* 59 (2016) 449–71.

Watts, John D. W. *Isaiah 34–66*. WBC 25. Rev. ed. Waco, TX: Word, 2005.

Westermann, Claus. *Isaiah 40–66*. Translated by David M. G. Stalker. Old Testament Library. Philadelphia: Westminster, 1969.

Whybray, R. N. *Isaiah 40–66*. New Century Bible. Grand Rapids: Eerdmans, 1975.

Wilson, Gerald H. *Psalms*. 2 vols. NIV Application Commentary. Grand Rapids: Zondervan, 2002.

Zorell, Franciscus. *Lexicon Hebraicum Veteris Testamenti*. Rome: Editrice Pontificio Istituto Biblico, 1989.

4

The Image of God in the Shalom of God

Alexander N. Kirk

THE LAST SEVERAL DECADES have brought about a sea change in the way that the "image of God" (Gen 1:26–27; 9:6) is understood, with the majority of Old Testament scholars now agreeing that the concept refers to a functional role or status rather than inherent human capacities.[1] Nevertheless, the tide of scholarly consensus has not yet turned from an individualistic conception of the image to a more corporate one. This essay will contend that *humankind* is created as the (singular) image of God; individual human beings are not created as distinct images (plural) of God per se. As John Walton has stressed, "We are not individually his images; we are corporately his image."[2] In addition, it will be proposed that the functioning of human society that is envisioned by this concept is best understood within the biblical-theological framework of "shalom" (שָׁלוֹם).[3]

---

1. This is not to deny that certain human capacities—such as reason, morality, conscience, relationality, freedom, etc.—are presupposed in the concept of being created as God's image. Yet these capacities are not the direct referent of the term. For histories of interpretation, see Grenz, *Social God*, 142–82; Middleton, *Liberating Image*, 18–29; and Herring, *Divine Substitution*, 87–95, among others. Peterson has recently suggested that the image of God refers to human "identity"—a term that encompasses both functional and ontological aspects of being human (*Human Identity*, 65–66). Compare Lints, *Identity and Idolatry*, 34–42.

2. *Old Testament Theology*, 86. This essay is dedicated to John Walton with gratitude for provoking my curiosity and shaping my theology. In courses he taught, the Old Testament came alive.

3. By "shalom" I mean "the webbing together of God, humans, and all creation in justice, fulfillment, and delight" (Plantinga, *Not the Way*, 10) or "the functioning and flourishing of the entire created order according to God's revealed purposes for it" (DeVine, *Shalom*, 1). For basic introductions to the Hebrew word, see Yoder, *Shalom*, 10–19 and Leiter, *Neglected Voices*, 22–30. Like DeVine, I am employing the concept of shalom to comprehend a larger reality than is denoted by any one instance of the Hebrew word (*Shalom*, 1).

Part 1: Creation

In what follows, three key texts in Genesis 1–11 will be revisited in light of the entire Old Testament to demonstrate that God created humankind to reflect his glory throughout the earth in a peaceful and flourishing civilization.[4] The essay will conclude with a very brief discussion of the New Testament's development of the image of God and an exhortation to readers.

Genesis 1:26–29

The most foundational text for understanding the "image of God" is Gen 1:26–29. Almost every Hebrew word in this passage has given rise to a mountain of secondary literature. A thorough exposition of these verses cannot be attempted here, but a few comments on specific words and ideas that are germane to my argument will be offered.

Verse 26 begins, "Then God said, 'Let us make humankind as our image, according to our likeness, so that it might rule'" (וַיֹּאמֶר אֱלֹהִים נַעֲשֶׂה אָדָם בְּצַלְמֵנוּ כִּדְמוּתֵנוּ וְיִרְדּוּ).[5] In announcing that humankind will be made "as our image" (בְּצַלְמֵנוּ), the biblical author employs a term, צֶלֶם, that most commonly refers to a cultic statue. However, scholars are quick to point out that the related Akkadian term *ṣalmu* can also refer to a king as the image of a god.[6] What commonality between cult images and kings allows the term *ṣalmu* to refer to either? Both cult image and king may visually represent a god, but perhaps more importantly, both occupy a position between heavenly and earthly realms, mediating between the two. Cult images and kings may be considered linchpins for the operation of the two realms in tandem.[7] With regard to the king in particular, Walton claims that his major responsibility in the ancient world was "to maintain order in the part of the cosmos that he could affect: his kingdom."[8]

Therefore, in assigning this royal (and priestly) status or position to humankind, God is commissioning them to fulfill a similar role to the ancient Near Eastern king

---

4. Compare Wolters, *Creation Regained*, 41–42. Likewise, Middleton asserts: "the human calling as *imago Dei* is itself developmental and transformative and may be helpfully understood as equivalent to the labor or work of forming culture or developing civilization . . . The human task thus reflects in significant ways the divine artisan portrayed in Genesis 1 as artfully constructing a world" (*Liberating Image*, 89).

5. All translations of Scripture are my own and are based on the Hebrew text of the Leningrad Codex and the NA28 Greek text. To make clear certain exegetical points, my translations are intentionally literal, sometimes even woodenly so. The translation of Gen 1:26a above reads the preposition בּ as a *beth essentiae* and the second ו as marking purpose.

6. For a thorough discussion, see Herring, *Divine Substitution*, 38–43.

7. For a good summary of the critical role of cult images in the regions and religions of the ancient Near East, see Hundley, *Gods in Dwellings*, 363–72. At least one ancient text refers to a priest as the very image of Marduk (see Herring, *Divine Substitution*, 44–47). Priests likewise played a key role in negotiating the relationship between heavenly and earthly realms. Genesis 1–2 seems to assign humanity a priestly role in sacred space—for which, see Walton, *Adam and Eve*, 104–15.

8. *Ancient Near Eastern Thought*, 265.

and even, in some ways, a similar role to the cult image: humankind was charged with the responsibility of creating and maintaining order in the earthly realm by virtue of its relationship to the heavenly realm. Why would God create such an agent? God's intention in establishing order on earth through humankind is for the worldwide manifestation and praise of his own glory—God intends his image to "fill the earth" (Gen 1:28).

The second word to consider is אָדָם, which in verses 26 and 27 is a collective singular, referring to all of humankind and not to "Adam," the first created human being. This notion is explicitly and repeatedly confirmed by the plural suffixes in Gen 5:2: "male and female he created *them*, and he blessed *them* and gave *them* the name אָדָם in the day *they* were created." Nevertheless, this observation has not been given the interpretive weight it warrants. Commentators and theologians still frequently declare that Adam and Eve were individually created in the image of God.[9] The terms "image" (צֶלֶם) and "likeness" (דְּמוּת) do not occur in Genesis 2 at all, however, so this interpretive move may represent an illegitimate conflation of the two chapters or perhaps unintentional slippage, as the second creation account unduly influences the interpretation of the first.[10]

In Gen 1:26 and 28 we read that humankind receives dominion over fish, birds, livestock, and wild game.[11] The verb that is used, "to rule" (רדה), often has harsh connotations elsewhere in the Torah, describing dominion over slaves or enemies.[12] In the present context, the verb probably stresses the unrivaled authority and power that humankind is to exercise on earth; in all created realms, there are none to challenge humanity's primacy. Although domestication of certain animals could be in view in the injunction to rule, the broader idea is that all creatures are submitted to humankind for humanity's benefit and welfare or, at least, that no creatures vie against them.[13]

---

9. For example, see Gladd, *From Adam to the Church*, which was published in December 2019: "In the first creation account, Adam is created in the image and likeness of God, whereas in the second account Adam receives the 'breath of life'" (13).

10. While McDowell helpfully highlights thematic similarities between Gen 1 and 2, and certain similarities between Gen 2 and Mesopotamian *mīs pî pīt pî* and Egyptian *wpt-r* rituals, I do not find her thesis convincing that "the first man was, on some level, *an* 'image of God'" (*Image of God*, 2; italics added).

11. For this understanding of רֶמֶשׂ as "wild game," see Walton, *Genesis*, 341–42. This category would include animals such as "wild cattle, antelope, fallow deer, gazelle, and ibex" and possibly rabbits (342).

12. Compare Lev 25:43, 46, 53; 26:17; and Num 24:19. The verb כבש ("subdue") in Gen 1:28 is even more forceful.

13. While the "sea monsters" (תַּנִּין; Gen 1:21) and "(predatory) beasts" (חַיָּה; Gen 1:24–25) are not listed among the classes of animals over which humankind is to rule (Gen 1:26, 28), it is declared that humankind shall rule over all the earth, so, at the least, these creatures were not created to antagonize humankind or reduce their number. These creatures may have been omitted from the list because they serve no useful function for humankind, either before or after the sin of Adam and Eve. In Ps 8:7–9 MT it is declared that Yahweh has "put all things under humankind's feet . . . whatever moves through the paths of the seas."

Part 1: Creation

After humanity's sin, the situation changes. Genesis 1:26 and 28 may be helpfully contrasted with Gen 9:2 and 5, the latter indicating that the animal kingdom is now in rebellion against humankind's rightful rule and poses a threat to human life.[14] Wild animals, especially those inhabiting desolate places, often represent forces of chaos in the Old Testament. They occupy ruins and invade lands ravaged by war.[15] Thus, their presence indicates a lack of shalom.[16] Therefore, humankind's total subjugation of all animals in Gen 1:26 and 28 has less to do with ecological stewardship than with a secure and unchallenged dominion over the natural realm—a dominion that is conducive to human flourishing.

Conspicuous by its absence in Gen 1:26–28 is any notion that one human or group of humans—such as a king or nation—is to rule over others. Rather, it is implied that all humankind rule together. This is often referred to as the "democratization" of the image of God in the Old Testament.[17] Whereas in the ancient Near East kings were typically considered to function as the images of the gods, in Genesis this privileged role is given to all. Later in Israel's history, in warning Israel against the consequences of accepting a human king like the other nations, the prophet Samuel foretells how the king will exploit the nation and make the people his slaves (1 Sam 8:10–18). The vision of human society in Gen 1:26–29, though in seed form, is diametrically opposed to this common ancient practice. Yet God will eventually fulfill his original vision for human society through an idealized king, who will bring about shalom by ruling justly and on behalf of the oppressed.[18]

A corporate conception of the image of God may also be seen in the phrase "let *us* make humankind as *our* image" (נַעֲשֶׂה אָדָם בְּצַלְמֵנוּ; Gen 1:26), the plural forms of which have occasioned much debate among interpreters. I agree with those who discern a reference here to the heavenly court or "divine council."[19] The primary ob-

---

14. Compare Gen 37:20, 33; Exod 23:29; Lev 26:22; Deut 7:22; and especially Lev 26:6, "I will grant shalom in the land . . . and I will remove harmful beasts from the land." Notice also Ezek 34:25, 28: "I will make with them a covenant of shalom and remove harmful beasts from the land so that they might dwell in the wilderness securely and sleep in the forests . . . And they will no longer be plunder for the nations and the beasts of the land will not devour them. They will dwell securely and none will cause them to fear." See also Walton, *Genesis*, 127n14.

15. Compare Pss 44:20; 63:11; Isa 13:21–22; 14:23; 23:13; 34:11–15; Jer 9:10; 10:22; 49:33; 50:39; 51:37; Lam 5:18; Ezek 13:4; Zeph 2:14–15; and Mal 1:3.

16. See the texts in the previous footnote as well as verses such as Job 30:29; Song 2:15; and Isa 35:7.

17. See Levenson, *Creation*, 114–16 for a defense of this notion. Furthermore, as Mathews observes, "Human life, unlike the lower orders, is not instructed specifically to reproduce 'after its kind.' . . . The text's silence also infers that mankind is only of one kind. Since humanity is of one sort, the unity of the human race is prominently noted and, concomitantly, dismisses any notion that certain peoples are inherently superior or inferior" (*Genesis*, 174). Unlike McDowell, I do not think that the lack of the phrase "according to its kind" in Gen 1:26–28 indicates that "humanity was made according to *God's kind*" ("In the Image," 38; italics original).

18. See, for example, Ps 72:1–19; Isa 11:1–9; and Ezek 34:1–31. Compare Rev 3:21; 5:10; 20:6; 22:5.

19. See, for example, Wenham, *Genesis*, 28; Middleton, *Liberating Image*, 55–60; Heiser, *Unseen*

jection to this view is that it seems to imply that humankind was made by and in the image of the entire divine council, including Yahweh *and* all his attendant heavenly beings.[20] The Old Testament consistently portrays Yahweh alone as the creator of the heavens and earth, although heavenly beings are said to be present at the creation of the earth (see Job 38:7). So the phrase "let us make" probably is nothing more than Yahweh's public pronouncement of his intention to create, made in the presence of the divine council.[21]

Yet it must be asked, why would the divine council be alluded to in this verse at all? This question is especially pointed since the next verse, Gen 1:27, reverts to the singular suffix: "So God created humankind as *his own* image (בְּצַלְמוֹ)." The implicit assertion of the word "as *our* image" (בְּצַלְמֵנוּ; Gen 1:26) may be that humanity is created to reflect the well-ordered and harmonious "society" of the heavens, in which relationships are not broken or even strained by a jealous competitiveness. Genesis's vision of tranquility in the divine realm strongly contrasts with other ancient Near Eastern worldviews.[22] Understood in this way, the declaration "Let us make humankind as our image" (Gen 1:26) finds a striking parallel in Jesus' prayer, "let your kingdom come, let your will be done, as in heaven, so also upon the earth" (Matt 6:10). The lack of war and division in the divine council is to be reflected in a shalom on earth among humankind.

The passage continues with the assertion "male and female he created them" (Gen 1:27), which has also engendered much discussion and debate. In my view, not only does this phrase strike the note of democratization mentioned earlier—men and women alike are dignified with the status of being God's image—but also, this binary points toward the most basic building blocks of human society. Sexual differentiation is essential for the covenant of marriage, procreation, and the constitution of families. As Stanley Grenz contends, human sexuality "spurs individuals to seek community through relationships. The drive toward bonding that is characteristic of human life constitutes the foundation for various expressions of human community ... The ultimate goal of sexuality, and hence of the impulse toward bonding, is participation in the fullness of community."[23] Therefore, the image of God does not directly denote a human's capacity for relationships, but it does presuppose the relational bonds that are

---

Realm, 38–40; and Walton, *Old Testament Theology*, 35–43.

20. For this objection, see Clines, "Image of God," 66–67, who is followed by many commentators. It is noteworthy that a long tradition of ancient Jewish commentary was not dissuaded by this objection.

21. Compare references to the divine council in Gen 3:22 and 11:7. Psalm 8:6 MT is also very instructive: "You have made [humankind] a little lower than the gods (אלהים)."

22. See Walton's discussion of "theomachy" in *Ancient Cosmology*, 68–74. Compare Middleton, *Liberating Image*, 270: "But Genesis 1 does not just relativize the creation-by-combat motif. Rather, by its alternative depiction of God's nonviolent creative power at the start of the biblical canon, the text signals the creator's original intent for shalom and blessing at the outset of human history, prior to the rise of human (or divine) violence."

23. *The Social God*, 280.

necessary for any human society or civilization. The glory of God is thus displayed not only in individual words and deeds, but more importantly in a web of relationships, at the communal level. No single human being can reflect the likeness of God by himself or herself.[24]

A corporate conception of the image of God, read within a biblical theology of shalom, also prompts us to reconsider the command/blessing "bear fruit and become numerous" (Gen 1:28). This phrase, typically translated "be fruitful and multiply," is often interpreted as a reference to rapid biological reproduction and thus simply as a *means* to filling the earth and subduing it. It is reasoned that humankind could neither fill the earth nor subdue it without a sufficient human population. This is undoubtedly true; however, the hendiadys connotes more than biological fertility. The verbs "bearing fruit" (פרה) and "becoming numerous" (רבה), together and apart, also refer to the "swarming" activity of civilization (Gen 9:7; Exod 1:7), nation-building (Gen 17:6, 20; 28:3; 35:11; 48:4), agricultural abundance (Gen 26:22; 49:22–26; Lev 26:4–10; Deut 6:3; 7:3; 30:16), material wealth (Gen 47:27; Deut 30:5), military strength (Exod 1:10, 12, 20), security, and political peace (Lev 26:5–9).[25] These societal characteristics correspond to the biblical vision of shalom, which Mark DeVine describes as "settled community life."[26]

Most importantly, "bearing fruit" assumes a right relationship to God and may be contrasted with a root producing poisonous and bitter fruit—that is, covenant unfaithfulness (Deut 29:18–19)—that God will judge with burning, sickness, brimstone, and salt, so that the land becomes a desolate waste where nothing is sown and nothing can sprout (Deut 29:23).[27] When viewed in this way, the phrase "bear fruit and become numerous" describes the role of being the image of God as much as "ruling" or "subduing" does. Bearing fruit and becoming numerous is not just the biological *means* to manifesting God's presence on earth; the verbs themselves evoke civilizational expanse and development—concepts that are inherent to the functioning of God's image on earth.

---

24. Compare Baker, *Covenant*, 76. Contra Mathews, *Genesis*, 173 and Levering, who insists that "*each* individual human is in the image of God" and that "the image of God is in the soul's powers of knowing and loving" (*Doctrine of Creation*, 155; italics original).

25. Likewise, "subduing" the earth may refer to concrete human activities such as mining and irrigation (Walton, *Genesis*, 132), which are the purview of civilized societies.

26. *Shalom*, 3.

27. Compare Deut 28:16. Arnold suggests that the command "be fruitful and multiply" (פְּרוּ וּרְבוּ) is "a verbal play, which may be intended to bring to mind the nominal hendiadys 'formless void' (תֹהוּ וָבֹהוּ)" (*Genesis*, 43). If so, the shalom of civilizational flourishing may be contrasted with *nonorder* and even the *disorder* of the devastation and desolation following war (compare Walton, *Old Testament Theology*, 184–86). For the latter idea, see especially Jer 4:19–31, which also employs the Hebrew pair, תֹהוּ וָבֹהוּ. "The sound of the trumpet you have heard, O my soul, the alarm of war. Collapse upon collapse is proclaimed because the whole land is devastated . . . I looked on the earth and behold, formlessness and void . . . I looked and behold, there was no human . . . I looked and behold, the orchard was a wilderness and all the cities were laid waste before Yahweh" (4:19–20, 23, 25, 26).

Finally, God's gracious provision of seed-bearing plants and fruit trees (Gen 1:29) ensures that humankind will have a sustainable and abundant source of food. Once again, the ancient Near Eastern "Great Symbiosis" is turned on its head by the biblical text, as God provides for the material needs of humankind rather than vice versa.[28] The implication of Gen 1:29 is that humanity's rule over the earth is a "dominion of dependence" upon God.[29]

This cursory explication of various aspects of Gen 1:26–29 has illuminated three levels of relationship that are integral to the image of God: humankind was created to be properly reverent toward God and in dependence upon him, properly related to one another in a just and righteous society, and properly installed over the earth, including all of its animal populations.[30] One might capture this vision of harmonious vertical and horizontal relationships with the term "order," as Walton does, but the preferred term of the Old Testament seems to be "shalom"—the state of the world when everything is as it should be, when relationships between all three levels are functioning as intended.[31] Even though no single occurrence of שָׁלוֹם in the Old Testament may capture "the full scope of these three relational dimensions,"[32] the Hebrew term commends itself for use in this way because of its broad semantic range. In different contexts the term could be variously translated as "peace," "prosperity," "welfare," "safety," "harmony," "health," or "wholeness."[33] Therefore, it appears as if humankind functioning as the image of God cannot be fully comprehended apart from a "constellative anthropology"[34] and the holistic framework of shalom. In other words, what is needed is a wider frame of reference.

If humankind created as the image of God is such a foundational theological concept, then why does the terminology of צֶלֶם אֱלֹהִים disappear in the remainder of the Old Testament? Richard Lints argues that "the emphasis upon the divine presence

---

28. See Walton, *Ancient Near Eastern Thought*, 99 and *Ancient Cosmology*, 78, 196–97. Compare Middleton, *Liberating Image*, 210.

29. This phrase is taken from Hafemann, *God of Promise*, 29.

30. These three levels are also noted by Jančovič, "Imago Dei," 201 and especially McConville: "The idea of humanity as being in the 'image of God' has its context in a depiction of the interrelationships of God and all created things" (*Being Human*, 14–15; compare also page 25).

31. Walton contends that "order" is *the* "pivotal concept" in Genesis's creation account (*Old Testament Theology*, 77). Walton's *Old Testament Theology*, according to a digital search, has 329 occurrences of the word "order," but only 9 occurrences of "peace" and zero occurrences of the word "shalom." Ollenberger, "Creation and Peace," also connects the concepts of order and peace in Gen 1–11, though not exactly as I do. The biblical concept of "rest" is also closely related to order and shalom.

32. DeVine, *Shalom*, 1.

33. For the complexity and expansiveness of the term שָׁלוֹם, see especially Talmon, "Signification," 75–115.

34. This term was coined by Jan Assmann. "A constellative anthropology stresses the ties, roles, and functions that bind the constituent parts together. It abhors the ideas of isolation, solitude, self-sufficiency, and independence, and considers them symptoms of death, dissolution, and destruction. Life is interdependence, interconnection, and communication within those webs of interaction and interlocution that constitute reality" ("A Dialogue," 386, as quoted by Walton, *Ancient Near Eastern Thought*, 111).

replaced an earlier emphasis upon the divine image."[35] While this seems partly correct, and without becoming entangled in questions of source criticism, I would suggest that the concept of humanity created as the image of God can most clearly be seen in those biblical passages that describe humankind in an idealized harmony with God and the natural realm—that is, those passages especially in the book of Psalms and in Isaiah that picture shalom. In this sense, the image of God is an eschatological concept, casting a vision for what God intended for humankind at creation and what he will one day bring to pass.[36]

The corporate nature of the image of God, as confirmed thus far from various angles, may be further illustrated with a metaphor. Commentators on the book of Genesis and theologians are quick to employ the metaphor of "mirrors" when describing the design of human beings.[37] The metaphor is a useful one: it communicates the idea that humans reflect a glory from above; this glory is not self-generated. Yet this metaphor may be improved by conceiving of humankind as forming a single, massive *parabolic* mirror, constructed from a multitude of tiny panels. While each segment of the larger mirror does reflect light, the overall structure is designed and fitted together so that the sum is greater than the parts.[38] As human beings, we are created to be properly oriented toward the sun, but also correctly aligned with one another in a human society and suitably constructed on top of the earth. Only when the entire mirror is arranged and angled properly can it reflect with maximal brightness, as it was designed to do. This metaphor reveals the deficiency in individualistic conceptions of the image of God. Such conceptions fail to encompass the broader purpose and inherently communal design of God in creation.

Genesis 5:1–5

While the term "image" (צֶלֶם) is foregrounded in Gen 1:26–29, occurring three times, the term "likeness" (דְּמוּת) becomes more prominent in Gen 5:1–3. Why? Commentators who posit that these nouns and the prepositions ב and כ are interchangeable and

---

35. *Identity and Idolatry*, 74.

36. Therefore, I agree with Briggs that "Genesis uses the phrase 'image of God' to set us reading the canonical narrative with certain questions in mind" ("Image," 123), though I believe that much more can be understood from Gen 1–11 concerning the meaning of the phrase than Briggs allows. With regard to shalom, Talmon writes, "The envisaged restoration of the *pax salomonica* in 'the days to come' is probably the most important aspect of the conception of 'peace' in biblical literature" ("Signification," 106–7).

37. This metaphor was alluded to by Augustine but significantly expanded and emphasized by John Calvin (Grenz, *Social God*, 166).

38. Compare Brown, *Creation*, 65: "One should not even identify the *imago* as an individual matter at all. Human beings were created, according to Genesis 1, as a plurality, and out of this plurality arose culture . . . However it is to be defined, culture is something more complex than the simple sum of human individuals."

essentially synonymous in these two passages need not wrestle with this question.[39] However, although these nouns and prepositions are undoubtedly semantically similar, there are good reasons to think that distinctions remain.[40] Ultimately, the matter will be decided by which interpretation of the texts is most insightful and compelling.

A new section is started in Gen 5:1 with the words, "This is the book of the generations of humankind. In the day when God created humankind, in the likeness (בִּדְמוּת) of God he made it."[41] This is followed in verse 3 with the statement, "When Adam had lived 130 years, he fathered a son in his own likeness (בִּדְמוּתוֹ)." Three recent articles have demonstrated how these verses conceive of the likeness of humankind to God in the manner of a son's likeness to his father.[42] In other words, Gen 5:1 makes a claim about the divine "parentage" of God and the term דְּמוּת, in this instance, taps into the pervasive biblical concept of kinship.

Yet in what respect in these verses is the proverb true, "like father, like son"? Obviously, a biological son almost always has some physical resemblance to his father, though this fact is not emphasized in the Old Testament. What is far more important is the concern that a son resemble his father morally or ethically—what we might refer to as the "spiritual formation" of a child by its parent. This formation will occur when father and son are in a proper relationship in which a father authoritatively but lovingly commands his son and the son gives honor to his father by obeying him. When this dynamic is broken, it is lamentable: "A wise son makes a father glad, but a foolish son grieves his mother" (Prov 10:1).[43]

It must be remembered that God creating humankind in his likeness is just as much of an *expectation* as God creating humankind in his image is. Whether or not humankind actually brings order to the earth as his image has no bearing on the fact that this is the status and commission that has been conferred upon them. Likewise, whether or not humankind actually resembles God morally in learning his ways has no bearing on the fact that this ethical obligation has been created. When read in this way, God's creation of humankind in his likeness is parallel to the expectation that Abraham is "known" (ידע) in order that "he may command his children and his household after him to guard the way of Yahweh by doing righteousness and justice" (Gen 18:19). Abraham, God's "son" by covenant, is expected to practice justice just as the Judge of all the earth is (Gen 18:25), and just as Abraham's children after him are.

---

39. This is the majority position, represented by scholars such as Wenham, *Genesis*, 28–29; Mathews, *Genesis*, 167; and Kilner, *Dignity and Destiny*, 89–91.

40. See Herring, *Divine Substitution*, 108–18, which is largely dependent on Garr, *Image and Likeness*, 95–178.

41. Reading both occurrences of אָדָם in this verse as generic references to all humankind is also considered and favored by McDowell, "In the Image," 35n21.

42. See Crouch "Divine Parentage," Ortlund, "Image of Adam," and McDowell "In the Image."

43. The close ethical link between father and son is indirectly evidenced in Ezek 18:1–20. Compare also the proverbial statement, "a son honors his father" (Mal 1:6), by which it is meant, a son *ought* to honor his father.

Part 1: Creation

The lines of parental authority and moral instruction may be hinted at in Gen 4:26, the verse immediately preceding Gen 5:1. After Cain's descendants plunge into violence and chaos (4:23–24), Gen 4:26 offers a ray of hope: "To Seth, to him also, a son was born and he called his name Enosh. At that time, humankind began (הוּחַל) to call on the name of Yahweh" (4:26).[44] I do not view it as a coincidence that humankind's first recorded act of devotion to Yahweh after the murder of Abel follows hard on the heels of Seth naming his son. From Gen 4:26—5:3 we learn that God names humankind, Adam names Seth, and Seth names Enosh—all acts of parental authority. Likewise, we are to infer that Enosh was created in Seth's likeness, as Seth was created in Adam's likeness, and humankind was created in God's likeness. Hope for the world is preserved through this righteous line as humankind begins to call on the name of Yahweh.

If this analysis is on target, it may explain why דְּמוּת is used only once in Gen 1:26–29 and with the preposition כ, and why צֶלֶם is used only once in Gen 5:1–3 with the same preposition. According to Randall Garr, the preposition כ "expresses a similarity or approximation between otherwise *dis*similar and *non*identical entities."[45] In Gen 1:26 humankind is similar in a way to God amongst his divine council, although the plural suffix of כִּדְמוּתֵנוּ strains the moral resemblance and thus the preposition כ is employed.[46] Since the divine council is not mentioned in the construction "in the likeness of God" (בִּדְמוּת אֱלֹהִים; Gen 5:1), the resemblance can be stated more directly with the preposition ב. Likewise, the direct and repeated affirmation of humankind "as God's image" (בְּצֶלֶם אֱלֹהִים) in Gen 1:27 becomes more oblique in Gen 5:3 when it is stated that Adam fathered a son "according to his image" (כְּצַלְמוֹ). Seth may indeed "represent" Adam in carrying on his name and legacy—compare Gen 48:16, for example—but Seth does not function as the "image of Adam" in the way that humankind functions as the image of God. Rather than using the typical language of Adam "transmitting," "passing down," or "transferring" the image of God to Seth by fathering him, it may be more accurate to say that Adam "incorporates" Seth into humankind, which is the image of God on earth. After all, that which is born of humankind is humankind (compare John 3:6).

The notion of humankind created as the image of God is not entirely absent from Gen 5, as a comparison of this chapter with the *Sumerian King List* and even the observation that kings are nowhere mentioned in Gen 1–11 indicates that all of humankind has taken the place of kings in the development of civilization.[47] Never-

---

44. The verb הוּחַל is third person singular in form and its subject is not stated. The LXX identifies the subject as Enosh. I have taken the subject to be "humankind" as the name "Enosh" (אֱנוֹשׁ), like "Adam," can also be used to refer generically to humankind. Compare Ps 8:5 MT and Mathews, *Genesis*, 291–92.

45. *Image and Likeness*, 98; italics original.

46. Certainly angels do God's bidding (see, for example, Ps 103:20), which means that a moral comparison between humankind and the divine council is not inappropriate.

47. See Middleton, *Liberating Image*, 213–14, and Walton, *Genesis*, 278, respectively.

theless, the focus of Gen 5:1–3 is more on the concept of "likeness," while Gen 1:26–29 focuses on the "image." As Stephen Herring has posited, the syntactical differences between these two passages "likely highlight the functional component of Gen 1:26–27 and the genealogical emphasis of Gen 5."[48] A close comparison of these passages has sharpened our understanding of both terms, "image" and "likeness."

Genesis 9:1–7

In Gen 9:1–7 there is further evidence for the view that the image of God should be construed corporately and within a broader theology of shalom. First, we may simply note that this entire section is addressed to Noah and his sons, who together represent all of humankind after the flood. Noah does not receive these instructions by himself, even though God has been speaking to Noah individually up until this point (compare Gen 6:13; 7:1; 8:15). This confirms that God's command/blessing of "bear fruit and become numerous" (9:1) is addressed to humankind, not to individuals per se. While humankind will now rule over the animal kingdom through "fear and terror" (9:2) due to the fracture between humankind and the natural realm introduced through sin, the goal is still that humankind would not experience any threat to their security and well-being from animals, as before. This rift will not be fully healed until the eschatological reign and shalom of the Messiah (see especially Isa 11:6–9).

Verses 5 and 6 are of particular interest: "Indeed, for your blood—that is, your life—I will require an account; from the hand of every animal I will require an account and from the hand of a person—that is, from the hand of a man, his brother—I will require an account for the life of a person. For the one shedding the blood of humankind, by humankind will his blood be shed, for as the image of God (בְּצֶלֶם אֱלֹהִים) he made humankind." Although the Hebrew grammar in these verses is unwieldy, the meaning is relatively straightforward: if beast or man kills a human being, God authorizes meting out the punishment of death to the offender. This authorization is based upon the fact of humankind being created as the image of God.

Typically, these verses are interpreted individualistically. Commentators stress that a human being is given the right to kill a murderer based on the sanctity of each individual's human life. An individual person has dignity and worth because he or she is created *in* the image of God. While the dignity and worth of every single human being is clearly taught in the Old Testament, Gen 9:5–6 should be interpreted corporately. The

---

48. *Divine Substitution*, 122n198. Likewise, Gentry provocatively suggests that "the relationship between humans and God is best captured by the term sonship. The relationship between humans and the creation may be expressed by the terms kingship and servanthood" ("Kingdom through Covenant," 32).

power of capital punishment is given to society, not individuals per se.[49] For example, the nation as a whole, not just an offended individual, was expected to stone rebels.[50]

Furthermore, the appeal to the image of God is not primarily an appeal to the sanctity of an individual human being, as if a sin has been committed primarily against a person's inherent worth before God. Rather, murder is more a violation of the communal trust, the shalom that God intends for human society. This can be seen in the clarifying phrase "from the hand of a man, his brother" (מִיַּד אִישׁ אָחִיו; Gen 9:5)—that is, the victim is the "brother" of the killer. The phrase evokes Yahweh's interaction with Cain, in which he asks, "Where is Abel, *your brother*?" and Cain ironically replies, "I do not know; am I the guardian of my brother?!" (Gen 4:9). The fact that Abel is Cain's brother is emphasized six times in Gen 4:8–12. Cain was wrong to kill Abel because they are bonded by blood; this is a violation of relationship, not of Abel's "right to life" per se. Likewise, in Gen 9:5–6 murder is a punishable offense because of the relational obligations that bind humankind and are created by God.[51] A society characterized by murder cannot properly reflect the glory of God.

In this vein, it must also be significant that as humankind begins to become numerous on the face of the ground (Gen 6:1), it is the evil of humankind that becomes great (6:5), not the name of Yahweh. More specifically, it is stated that "the earth was ruined in the sight of God and the earth was filled with *violence* (חָמָס)" (6:11; cf. Gen 4:23–24). The passage continues, "So God said to Noah, 'The end of all flesh has come in front of me, for the earth is filled with violence (חָמָס) in front of them; behold, I will ruin them along with the earth'" (6:13).

The evil and violence of humankind is the polar opposite of the peace or shalom that God intends when he creates humankind as the image of God; it is a stain upon the earth, it defiles God's good creation. In prophetic perspective, however, God will one day cleanse the earth so that "violence will no longer be heard in your land, nor oppression or destruction within your borders" (Isa 60:18), the day when he restores humankind to perfect shalom (Isa 60:1–22). In other words, the prohibition of manslaying based on the creation of humankind as the image of God points toward God's desire for shalom and the ultimate triumph of God over human violence. Genesis 9:5–6 focus on the intended sanctity of human *society*, not the sanctity of individual human life, though one may reasonably infer the latter from the former.

49. Compare Mathews, *Genesis*, 405: "Exacting retribution is not a personal matter but a societal obligation." Mathews then poses a well-known conundrum: "After establishing the inviolability of human life, how can the divine directive at the same time exact killing the criminal who also is the divine 'image'?" (406). This tension may be at least partially relieved by interpreting the image of God corporately. Restoring shalom by purging a murderer from society does not violate the image of God but rather upholds it.

50. See Lev 20:2; 24:14–16, 23; Num 15:35–36; and Deut 21:21.

51. Baker, *Covenant*, 125–28 offers a similar interpretation of Gen 9:5–6. "To murder is to make permanent a rejection of the covenant that binds murderer and victim. We who seek to remain within the covenant are bound to apply justice to the one who has offended against the unity of the covenant" (128).

Development in the New Testament

The concept of the image of God is developed in the New Testament, especially with regard to Jesus, the Son of God. Nevertheless, the text that most directly pertains to the creation of humankind as the image of God, Jas 3:8–9, may attest to a corporate conception of that image, even though it is actually the term "likeness" (ὁμοίωσις) that is used: "but as for the tongue, no one among people is able to tame it—it is restless evil, full of deadly poison. With it we bless our Lord and Father and with it we curse people who are made according to the likeness of God." The use of ὁμοίωσις in Jas 3:9—a *hapax legomenon* in the NT—is a clear allusion to Gen 1:26. It should therefore be noted that "people" (ἀνθρώπους) is plural, even though James uses this term in the singular in his letter when referring to people generically.[52] James could easily have written, "we curse *a person* who is made according to the likeness of God."

Furthermore, in describing the tongue as "full of deadly poison" (3:8) and in equating verbal altercations with murder (4:2), James argues against misuse of the tongue as a threat to the solidarity, justice, and peace of the community. Therefore, it is possible that cursing people is judged to be incompatible with God's design in creation not primarily because individuals are created with God-given likeness and therefore possess inherent worth, but rather because humankind has been created to reflect God's moral likeness in their communal dimension.[53]

The fact that Jesus himself is called "the image of God" (εἰκὼν τοῦ θεοῦ; 2 Cor 4:4; Col 1:15), may seem to unravel my entire thesis—at least from the perspective of the New Testament—that humankind is created corporately as the image of God. However, it is critical to bear in mind the difference between the Son of God who is an "imprint-image" and the children of God who are a "likeness-image."[54] Even in his singularity, the Son may be said to be the image of the invisible God precisely because he is the firstborn of all creation (Col 1:15). Just as Jesus cannot be the "head" without a body, so too perhaps he cannot fully be the image of God without being preeminent among a people reconciled by his blood (Col 1:18–20).[55] To change the

---

52. See Jas 1:7, 19; 2:20, 24. Likewise, despite all the interpretive knots in 1 Cor 11:7 ("A man ought not to cover his head since he is the image and glory of God (εἰκὼν καὶ δόξα θεοῦ ὑπάρχων)," it is at least clear that the term ἀνήρ is being used archetypally with implications for all men. The term does not imply that an individual male person is the image of God in himself.

53. According to Kilner, "Genesis 9:6 and James 3:9, more directly suggest that particular people have 'image' status, with the protections that affords, in that people are often killed or cursed one at a time" (*Dignity and Destiny*, 86–87). This is a *non sequitur*. Even though individuals are killed or cursed, the protection they are afforded in these verses seems to be on the basis of their solidarity with humankind.

54. This terminology is taken from Kilner, *Dignity and Destiny*, 59. Unlike humankind, Jesus is "Lord" (κύριος; 2 Cor 4:5), the firstborn of all creation (Col 1:15), by whom all things were created (Col 1:16), in whom all the fullness of deity dwells bodily (Col 2:9), and who is the exact imprint of God's nature (Heb 1:3), etc. In other words, there is a categorical difference between how Jesus is the image of God and how humankind is, and we ought not make hasty deductions about the latter from the former.

55. Walton rightly sees an analogy between the image of God and the body of Christ: "It is

metaphor, though Jesus is certainly the focal point of the parabolic mirror, with the rest of the mirror transformed into *his* image (2 Cor 3:18), the Messiah can only shine with the glory that God intends for him when he is surrounded by a people who are concentrated on him and are aligned with God's purposes.[56] The cross elevates Jesus to the center of the parabolic mirror, but it also connects him to it.

A biblical theology of the image of God must be carried to the end, to the glorious vision of shalom in Rev 21–22. The description of the new heaven and new earth is one of a purified *civilization*, a perfected and praise-filled human society happily settled, where heavenly and earthly realms are finally and fully merged. It is only in this *communal* fulfillment of our hope that the image of God finds its ultimate expression.

Conclusion

John Walton persuasively articulates the need to be immersed in a different cultural river than our own when interpreting the Old Testament.[57] Hopefully this essay has confirmed that the cultural river in which the book of Genesis flows has a much stronger communal current than contemporary American society.[58] In interpreting Gen 1:26–29, we must realize that "the *imago dei* is not merely relational; it is not simply the I-Thou relationship of two persons standing face-to-face. Instead, it is ultimately communal."[59]

Therefore, in interpreting concepts such as the "image of God," we must deliberately place ourselves in a foreign frame of mind. We must swim upstream against our own culture and hundreds of years of the Western interpretive tradition, which have conditioned us to think in individualistic terms.[60] Thus, in understanding that the Bible was written "for *us*, but not to *us*," we must not neglect the import of those plural pronouns.

---

humanity as a whole that functions to bring order, that represents the presence of God on earth, and that has the God-given status. In this way, the image of God can be compared to the New Testament concept of the body of Christ. None of us individually is the body of Christ, but we are all part of the body of Christ" (*Old Testament Theology*, 87–88).

56. For similar commentary on Rom 8:29, see Grenz, *Social God*, 231–32. As he says, "Rom. 8:29 delineates the final exegesis of Gen. 1:26–27" (231). For an entire monograph supporting and expounding upon this claim, see now Jacob, *Conformed to the Image*.

57. See especially his *Ancient Near Eastern Thought*, 6–7.

58. According to Walton, in the ancient cultural river we would find the current of "identity within community" (*Old Testament Theology*, 75). I write this essay from Indonesia, which also displays a strong collectivist culture. Living here has shaped the way I read the Bible.

59. Grenz, *The Social God*, 303.

60. For a theological history of this "turn inward," see Grenz, *Social God*, 60–97. Compare also the word of caution in Lints, *Identity and Idolatry*, 127n68.

Bibliography

Arnold, Bill T. *Genesis*. New Cambridge Bible Commentary. Cambridge: Cambridge University Press, 2009.

Assmann, Jan. "A Dialogue between Self and Soul: Papyrus Berlin 3024." In *Self, Soul, and Body in Religious Experience*, edited by Albert I. Baumgartner et al., 384–403. Studies in the History of Religions 78. Leiden: Brill, 1998.

Baker, Doug P. *Covenant and Community: Our Role as the Image of God*. Eugene, OR: Wipf & Stock, 2008.

Briggs, Richard S. "Humans in the Image of God and Other Things Genesis Does not Make Clear." *JTI* 4 (2010) 111–26.

Brown, William P. *The Seven Pillars of Creation: The Bible, Science, and the Ecology of Wonder*. Oxford: Oxford University Press, 2010.

Clines, D. J. A. "The Image of God in Man." *TynBul* 19 (1968) 53–103.

Crouch, C. L. "Genesis 1:26–27 as a Statement of Humanity's Divine Parentage." *JTS* 61 (2010) 1–15.

DeVine, Mark. *Shalom Yesterday, Today, and Forever: Embracing All Three Dimensions of Creation and Redemption*. Eugene, OR: Wipf & Stock, 2019.

Garr, W. Randall. *In His Own Image and Likeness: Humanity, Divinity, and Monotheism*. CHANE 1. Leiden: Brill, 2003.

Gentry, Peter J. "Kingdom through Covenant: Humanity as the Divine Image." *SBJT* 12 (2008) 16–42.

Gladd, Benjamin L. *From Adam and Israel to the Church: A Biblical Theology of the People of God*. Essential Studies in Biblical Theology. Downers Grove, IL: InterVarsity, 2019.

Grenz, Stanley J. *The Social God and the Relational Self: A Trinitarian Theology of the Imago Dei*. Louisville: Westminster John Knox, 2001.

Hafemann, Scott J. *The God of Promise and the Life of Faith: Understanding the Heart of the Bible*. Wheaton, IL: Crossway, 2001.

Heiser, Michael S. *The Unseen Realm: Recovering the Supernatural Worldview of the Bible*. Bellingham, WA: Lexham, 2015.

Herring, Stephen L. *Divine Substitution: Humanity as the Manifestation of Deity in the Hebrew Bible and the Ancient Near East*. FRLANT 247. Göttingen: Vandenhoeck & Ruprecht, 2013.

Hundley, Michael B. *Gods in Dwellings: Temples and Divine Presence in the Ancient Near East*. Writings of the Ancient World Supplements 3. Atlanta: Society of Bible Literature, 2013.

Jacob, Haley Goranson. *Conformed to the Image of His Son: Reconsidering Paul's Theology of Glory in Romans*. Downers Grove, IL: InterVarsity, 2018.

Jančovič, Jozef. "Imago Dei: An Exegetical and Theological Reappraisal." *ET-Studies* 10 (2019) 183–206.

Kilner, John F. *Dignity and Destiny: Humanity in the Image of God*. Grand Rapids: Eerdmans, 2015.

Leiter, David A. *Neglected Voices: Peace in the Old Testament*. Scottdale, PA: Herald, 2007.

Levenson, Jon D. *Creation and the Persistence of Evil: The Jewish Drama of Divine Omnipotence*. Princeton: Princeton University Press, 1988.

Levering, Matthew. *Engaging the Doctrine of Creation: Cosmos, Creatures, and the Wise and Good Creator*. Grand Rapids: Baker Academic, 2017.

Lints, Richard. *Identity and Idolatry: The Image of God and Its Inversion*. New Studies in Biblical Theology 36. Downers Grove, IL: InterVarsity, 2015.

Part 1: Creation

Mathews, Kenneth A. *Genesis 1–11:26*. NAC 1A. Nashville: Broadman & Holman, 1996.

McConville, J. Gordon. *Being Human in God's World: An Old Testament Theology of Humanity*. Grand Rapids: Baker Academic, 2016.

McDowell, Catherine L. *The Image of God in the Garden of Eden: The Creation of Humankind in Genesis 2:5—3:24 in Light of the* mīs pî pīt pî *and* wpt-r *Rituals of Mesopotamia and Ancient Egypt*. Siphrut 15. Winona Lake, IN: Eisenbrauns, 2015.

———. "In the Image of God He Created Them." In *The Image of God in an Image Driven Age: Explorations in Theological Anthropology*, edited by Beth Felker Jones et al., 29–46. Downers Grove, IL: InterVarsity, 2016.

Middleton, J. Richard. *The Liberating Image: The* Imago Dei *in Genesis 1*. Grand Rapids: Brazos, 2005.

Ollenberger, Ben C. "Creation and Peace: Creator and Creature in Genesis 1–11." In *The Old Testament in the Life of God's People: Essays in Honor of Elmer A. Martens*, edited by Jon Isaak, 143–58. Winona Lake, IN: Eisenbrauns, 2009.

Ortlund, Gavin. "Image of Adam, Son of God: Genesis 5:3 and Luke 3:38 in Intercanonical Dialogue." *JETS* 57 (2014) 673–88.

Peterson, Ryan S. *The* Imago Dei *as Human Identity: A Theological Interpretation*. JTISup 14. Winona Lake, IN: Eisenbrauns, 2016.

Plantinga, Cornelius, Jr. *Not the Way It's Supposed to Be: A Breviary of Sin*. Grand Rapids, Eerdmans, 1995.

Talmon, Shemaryahu. "The Signification of שלום and Its Semantic Field in the Hebrew Bible." In *The Quest for Context and Meaning: Studies in Biblical Intertextuality in Honor of James A. Sanders*, edited by Craig A. Evans and Shemaryahu Talmon, 75–115. Biblical Interpretation Series 28. Leiden: Brill, 1997.

Yoder, Perry B. *Shalom: The Bible's Word for Salvation, Justice, and Peace*. Eugene, OR: Wipf & Stock, 2017.

Walton, John H. *Ancient Near Eastern Thought and the Old Testament: Introducing the Conceptual World of the Hebrew Bible*. 2nd ed. Grand Rapids: Baker Academic, 2018.

———. *Genesis*. NIV Application Commentary. Grand Rapids: Zondervan, 2001.

———. *Genesis 1 as Ancient Cosmology*. Winona Lake, IN: Eisenbrauns, 2011.

———. *Old Testament Theology for Christians: From Ancient Context to Enduring Belief*. Downers Grove, IL: InterVarsity, 2017.

———. *The Lost World of Adam and Eve: Genesis 2–3 and the Human Origins Debate*. Downers Grove, IL: InterVarsity, 2015.

Wenham, Gordon J. *Genesis 1–15*. WBC 1. Waco, TX: Word, 1987.

Wolters, Albert M. *Creation Regained: Biblical Basics for a Reformational Worldview*. 2nd ed. Grand Rapids: Eerdmans, 2005.

5

Mr. Darwin's Bible

DAVID N. LINCICUM

CHARLES DARWIN (12 FEBRUARY 1809—19 April 1882) was an astute observer of geological and biological change in a period of widespread Christian devotion in Victorian England. He is most well-known for his influential proposal that natural selection is the mechanism that drives the evolutionary process, but interest in Darwin has not been reserved for his scientific accomplishments; rather, numerous readers have nurtured profoundly biographical curiosity, beginning within his own lifetime. Given the conflicts between his evolutionary views and certain traditions of reading the Bible in general, and the book of Genesis in particular, an interested public has wanted to know just what Darwin himself believed. The evolution of Darwin's personal religious views has been well studied,[1] but in this essay I take up one particular angle of approach to the general question of Darwin's religious belief: his views on and use of the Bible, which shift demonstrably over time. As Timothy Larsen has programmatically demonstrated, the Bible was ubiquitous in Victorian public discourse, read intensively by atheist and pious alike, from low-church evangelicals to Anglo-Catholics to Unitarians and anti-Christian apologists.[2] In this sea of biblical literacy, what did Darwin himself make of the good book?[3]

---

1. For example, see Phipps, "Darwin and Cambridge Natural Theology"; Brooke, "The Relations between Darwin's Science and his Religion"; Brown, "The Evolution of Darwin's Theism"; Moore, "Of Love and Death: Why Darwin 'gave up Christianity'"; Thomson, *Private Doubt, Public Dilemma*, 65–94.

2. Larsen, *A People of One Book*; Larsen, "The Bible and Belief in Victorian Britain."

3. It is a pleasure to dedicate this essay to a scholar and teacher who has done so much to help his students and the reading public understand the claims of Genesis in their own right.

Part 1: Creation

'Quite Orthodox': Darwin's Early Encounters with the Bible

Our earliest evidence for Darwin's encounter with the Bible can be found in a correspondence with his elder sister, Caroline Darwin. Influenced more by their mother's warm-hearted Unitarianism than by their father's unbelief, Caroline wrote to her brother: "dear Charles I hope you read the bible [sic] & not only because you think it wrong not to read it, but with the wish of learning there what is necessary to feel & do to go to heaven after you die. I am sure I gain more by praying over a few verses than by reading simply—many chapters—I suppose you do not feel prepared yet to take the sacrament."[4] In a letter a couple weeks later, seventeen-year-old Charles replied, "I have tried to follow your advice about the Bible, what part of the Bible do you like best? I like the Gospels. Do you know which of them is generally reckoned the best?"[5] She advises in reply, "I must say dear Charles how glad I am you have been studying the bible—I agree in liking St Johns the best of the Gospels I am very fond of that short Epistle of St. James, as well as St. Johns—I often regret myself that when I was younger & fuller of pursuits & high spirits I was not more religious—but it is very difficult to be so habitually."[6] In this brief and pleasant exchange, we observe a Charles Darwin who appears pious in his intentions, if not particularly well versed in biblical literature.

In a retrospective autobiographical account written at the end of his life, between the years 1876 and 1881,[7] Darwin looked back to his years in Cambridge (1828–1831), shortly after this, when he was, like so many Victorian undergraduates of the monied classes, ostensibly preparing for Anglican ministry: "I read with care Pearson on the Creeds & a few other books on divinity; & as I did not then in the least doubt the strict & literal truth of every word in the Bible, I soon persuaded myself that our Creed must be fully accepted. It never struck me how illogical it was to say that I believed in what I could not understand & what is in fact unintelligible ... Considering how fiercely I have been attacked by the orthodox, it seems ludicrous that I once intended to be a clergyman."[8] Although his incredulity in retrospect colors

---

4. Caroline Darwin to Charles Darwin, 22 March 1826. This and all subsequent references to Darwin's correspondence are drawn from the remarkable "Darwin Correspondence Project" (www.darwinproject.ac.uk), hosted at the Cambridge University Library. My thanks are also due to Rosemary Clarkson, associated with the project, for her help in fielding queries related to this essay.

5. Charles Darwin to Caroline Darwin, 8 April 1826.

6. Caroline Darwin to Charles Darwin, 11 April 1826.

7. A censored version of this autobiography, suppressing some of Darwin's forthright sentiments about religion, was first published in Francis Darwin, ed., *The Life and Letters of Charles Darwin* 1:307–13. An unexpurgated edition of the autobiographical remarks was first published by Darwin's granddaughter in the mid-twentieth century: Barlow, *The Autobiography of Charles Darwin*, which itself is now superseded by the edition in Secord, ed., *Evolutionary Writings*, 349–425. References to this piece will follow Secord's edition. On the family controversy surrounding his autobiographical passages on religion, see Moore, "Of Love and Death," 199–201. See also Colp Jr., "Notes on Charles Darwin's 'Autobiography.'"

8. *Evolutionary Writings*, 375–76. On this period in Darwin's life, see Thomson, *The Young Charles*

his account, through contemporary correspondence it is possible to confirm Darwin's erstwhile belief. After the death of his second cousin Mary Ann Bristowe, he wrote to her brother and his friend, William Darwin Fox: "as far as anyone can, by his own good principles & religion be supported under such a misfortune, you, I am assured, well know where to look for such support. And after so pure & holy a comfort as the Bible affords, I am equally assured how useless the sympathy of all friends must appear, although it be as heartfelt & sincere, as I hope you believe me capable of feeling."[9] The pure and untroubled trust in the Bible is unmistakable in this early correspondence. He had also studied Greek, enough to "translate Homer & the Greek Testament with moderate facility," even if he found greater pleasure in studying the works of the natural theologian William Paley.[10]

By the time he graduated from Cambridge, Darwin was quite sure that he would prefer the life of a scientist to that of a parson (even if he had several teachers who were ordained Anglicans and scientists at the same time). Once his father consented to offer his permission, he joined the fateful expedition of the H.M.S. Beagle (1831–1836) as the ship's naturalist. He confesses that "[w]hile on board the Beagle I was quite orthodox, & I remember being heartily laughed at by several of the officers (though themselves orthodox) for quoting the Bible as an unanswerable authority on some point of morality."[11] On the voyage, Darwin brought along *Das neue Testament* in order to learn German, and also used his reading of the Bible to keep up his Greek: "French & Spanish, Mathematics, & a little Classics, perhaps not more than Greek Testament on Sundays."[12]

Losing His Religion

In his autobiography, Darwin locates the period of his crisis of faith in the Bible to the time after his journey on the Beagle and before his marriage (2 Oct 1836—29 Jan 1839), when, he says, "I was led to think much about religion."[13] The most substantial passage about the Bible in all of Darwin's writings follows; we must consider this in pieces. First Darwin expresses criticism of the Old Testament in a twofold manner:

> But I had gradually come by this time (i.e. 1836 to 1839) to see that the Old Testament, from its manifestly false history of the world, with the Tower of Babel, the rain-bow as a sign &c &c, & from its attributing to God the feelings

---

Darwin, 84-97.

9. Charles Darwin to William Darwin Fox, 23 April 1829.

10. *Evolutionary Writings*, 376.

11. *Evolutionary Writings*, 391.

12. Keynes, ed., *Charles Darwin's Beagle Diary*, 13 (entry from 13 December 1831).

13. *Evolutionary Writings*, 391. Cf. Darwin's journal of 1838: "*All September* read a good deal on many subject [*sic*]; thought much upon religion" (Burkhardt and Smith, et al., eds., *The Correspondence of Charles Darwin, Volume 2: 1837–1843*, 432).

of a revengeful tyrant, was no more to be trusted than the sacred books of the Hindoos or the beliefs of any barbarian.

The critique here is both historical and moral. Historically, Darwin expresses his disbelief in the account of Genesis 1–11 in particular, deeming it "manifestly false," presumably a judgment rendered with respect to historicity. He also expresses a sense of moral misfit between what should be attributed to a god, and what the Old Testament depicts God as doing—acting, in Darwin's phrase, as a "revengeful tyrant." Both of these critiques are commonplace positions that found widespread repetitions both within and beyond the established church, even if they were also the subject of ongoing theological debate.[14] Darwin goes on to lodge a series of further objections:

> The question then continually rose before my mind & would not be banished,—is it credible that if God were now to make a revelation to the Hindoos, would he permit it to be connected with the belief in Vishnu, Siva &c, as Christianity is connected with the Old Testament. This appeared to me utterly incredible. By further reflecting that the clearest evidence would be requisite to make any sane man believe in the miracles by which Christianity is supported,—that the more we know of the fixed laws of nature the more incredible do miracles become,—that the men at that time were ignorant & credulous to a degree almost incomprehensible by us—that the Gospels can not be proved to have been written simultaneously with the events,—that they differ in many important details, far too important as it seemed to me to be admitted as the usual inaccuracies of eye-witnesses—by such reflections as these which I give not as having the least novelty or value, but as they influenced me, I gradually came to disbelieve in Christianity as a divine revelation.[15]

The staccato enumeration of objections to Christian faith threatens to obscure their individuality. We see here, first, an objection to the connection and continuity between the Old and New Testaments, followed by two objections against miracles: a lack of evidence for them, and a conviction that understanding the fixed laws of the natural world precludes or diminishes the possibility of belief in miracles. In these objections, Darwin seems to recall the famous objections of David Hume: "A miracle is a violation of the laws of nature; and as a firm and unalterable experience has established these laws, the proof against a miracle, from the very nature of the fact, is as entire as any argument from experience can possibly be imagined . . . no testimony is sufficient to establish a miracle, unless the testimony be of such a kind, that its falsehood would be more miraculous, than the fact, which it endeavours to establish."[16] Darwin next points to the ignorance and credulity of observers in antiquity, the

---

14. For the former, one might note, influentially, Goodwin, "On the Mosaic Cosmogony"; Colenso, *The Pentateuch and Book of Joshua Critically Examined*; cf. Rogerson, "What Difference Did Darwin Make?". For the latter, Althoz, "The Warfare of Conscience with Theology."

15. *Evolutionary Writings*, 391–92.

16. Hume, *An Enquiry Concerning Human Understanding*, X.90–91.

removal in time of the composition of the Gospels from the events they relate, and the differences between them. Some of these objections may well have been in Darwin's mind already by the late 1830s, but it seems likely that he is telescoping in retrospection a series of objections that accumulated over the course of his life. For example, when Samuel Butler in 1865, some thirty years later, sent to Darwin his pamphlet, *The Evidence for the Resurrection of Jesus Christ*,[17] in which he critiqued the evangelists for the differences among them, Darwin replied, "I am much obliged to you for so kindly sending me your 'Evidence &c–' We have read it with much interest. It seems to me written with much force, vigour & clearness; & the main argument is to me quite new. I particularly agree with all you say in your preface."[18]

Darwin goes on to say, "I was very unwilling to give up my belief.—I feel sure of this for I can well remember often & often inventing day-dreams of old letters between distinguished Romans & manuscripts being discovered at Pompeii or elsewhere which confirmed in the most striking manner all that was written in the Gospels. But I found it more & more difficult, with free scope given to my imagination to invent evidence which would suffice to convince me."[19] This reluctance to give up his belief may be in part due to the effects a loss of Christian faith might have had on his burgeoning romance with Emma Wedgewood, who retained her Unitarian Christian commitment throughout her lifelong marriage to Darwin. In an important correspondence about religious matters that Darwin retained and treasured throughout his life, Emma weighs the toll that religious differences might take on them, while expressing gratitude for Charles's frank admission of his doubts to her. In the end, she concludes "It is perhaps foolish of me to say this much but my own dear Charley we now do belong to each other & I cannot help being open with you." She then goes on to ask him, "Will you do me a favour? yes I am sure you will, it is to read our Saviours farewell discourse to his disciples which begins at the end of the 13th Chap of John. It is so full of love to them & devotion & every beautiful feeling. It is the part of the New Testament I love best. This is a whim of mine it would give me great pleasure, though I can hardly tell why I don't wish you to give me your opinion about it."[20] We do not have Charles Darwin's reaction to reading the farewell discourse, but Emma and Charles were married in January 1839, and lived happily together in spite of their religious differences.

The final objection Darwin enumerates in his autobiographical reflections seems to have been the most weighty. He writes:

> Thus disbelief crept over me at a very slow rate, but was at last complete. The rate was so slow that I felt no distress, & have never since doubted even for a single second that my conclusion was correct. I can hardly see how anyone

17. Butler, *Evidence for the Resurrection of Jesus Christ*.
18. Charles Darwin to Samuel Butler, 30 September 1865.
19. Charles Darwin to Samuel Butler, 30 September 1865.
20. Emma Wedgwood to Charles Darwin, 21–22 November 1838; cf. also Emma Darwin to Charles Darwin, ca. February 1839.

ought to wish Christianity to be true; for if so, the plain language of the text seems to show that the men who do not believe, & this would include my Father, Brother & almost all my best friends, will be everlastingly punished. And this is a damnable doctrine.[21]

As James Moore has argued, particularly after losing his father, who did not believe in Christianity, and daughter[22] in close succession, the moral objections dealt the final blow to Darwin's faith.[23] Whatever the precise reasons for his ultimate break, the objection to hell as conscious everlasting punishment was widespread in Unitarian circles, and made inroads into more mainstream forms of Christian belief in the course of the nineteenth century as well, particularly after F. D. Maurice lodged his famous reservations in his *Theological Essays*.[24]

In sum, the autobiographical reflections on the loss of his Christian faith seem, as Darwin himself says, not to "hav[e] the least novelty," in the landscape of the nineteenth century, but appear as a coalescence of objections that circulated freely within Victorian culture more broadly.

The Persistence of the Biblical

It might be possible to read Darwin's retrospective account of the loss of his Christian faith and think that after the late 1830s (or a decade later if one follows Moore's redating), he simply discarded all vestiges of biblical idiom. But Darwin remained a theist for most of his life, though late in his life he confesses to alternating between thinking of himself as a theist or an agnostic.[25]

Throughout the latter half of the 1830s and 1840s, Darwin's notebooks, unpublished in his lifetime, offer evidence of him working toward his theory of natural selection and the determination of the origin of species. In particular, we find a persistent critique of the view that species arise by 'simple creation.'[26] He also takes aim against the miraculous creation of humanity.[27] While these positions are clearly developed in contradistinction to a certain reading of Genesis that Darwin wishes to contest, he persists in speaking of the 'Creator' throughout his notebooks, in draft essays, and in the *Origin of Species* itself. In the conclusion to the 1844 'Essay' that preceded the *Origin*, Darwin writes:

21. *Evolutionary Writings*, 392.
22. Note Darwin's moving memorial to his daughter (CUL DAR 210.13 = *Life and Letters* 1:132–34).
23. Moore, "Of Love and Death."
24. Maurice, *Theological Essays*, 377–407; cf. Rowell, *Hell and the Victorians*.
25. *Evolutionary Writings*, 396.
26. Barrett, et al., eds., *Charles Darwin's Notebooks*, e.g., B84 (p. 192), B115 (p. 198), B243 (p. 231), D25 (p. 338); D115 (p. 370), etc.
27. C55 (pp. 256–57).

It accords with what we know of the laws impressed by the Creator on matter that the production and extinction of forms should, like the birth and death of individuals, be the result of secondary means. It is derogatory that the Creator of countless Universes should have made by individual acts of His will the myriads of creeping parasites and worms, which since the earliest dawn of life have swarmed over the land and in the depths of the ocean ... From death, famine, and the struggle for existence, we see that the most exalted end which we are capable of conceiving, namely, the creation of the higher animals, has directly proceeded. Doubtless, our first impression is to disbelieve that any secondary law could produce infinitely numerous organic beings, each characterized by the most exquisite workmanship and widely extended adaptations: it at first accords better with our faculties to suppose that each required the fiat of a Creator. There is a grandeur in this view of life with its several powers of growth, reproduction and of sensation, having been originally breathed into matter under a few forms, perhaps into only one and that whilst this planet has gone cycling onwards according to the fixed laws of gravity and whilst land and water have gone on replacing each other—that from so simple an origin, through the selection of infinitesimal varieties, endless forms most beautiful and most wonderful have been evolved.[28]

If this vision of creation contests the picture of Genesis 1 (where precisely a divine fiat accomplishes creation in stages), it still ascribes 'grandeur' to a creator who works through secondary causes. While the 1859 *Origin of Species* does not retain the entire conclusion of the 1844 essay, key parts of it are retained.[29] The *Origin* also persists in polemicizing against the view that species were created individually, or by miracle,[30] but at the same time does so subtly, without directly calling attention to the conflict between traditional understanding of Genesis and the view that Darwin is proposing. And in the end, Darwin frames his results as a contribution to understanding the creator: "To my mind it accords better with what we know of the laws impressed on matter by the Creator, that the production and extinction of the past and present inhabitants of the world should have been due to secondary causes, like those determining the birth and death of the individual."[31] All this suggests that John

---

28. In Francis Darwin, ed., *The Foundations of* The Origin of Species, 254–55.

29. Esp. the final sentence of the book, and its echo of Gen 2:7: "There is grandeur in this view of life, with its several powers, having been originally breathed into a few forms or into one; and that, whilst this planet has gone cycling on according to the fixed law of gravity, from so simple a beginning endless forms most beautiful and most wonderful have been, and are being, evolved." See Darwin, *On the Origin of Species*, 490; cf. 484.

30. See *On the Origin of Species*, 129, 133, 167, 185, 203, 244, 315, 372, 437, 471, 478, 483, 487–88 etc. He also refers to the "Creator" (188–89, 413). Note the reference to miraculous acts of creation: "species are produced and exterminated by slowly acting and still existing causes, and not by miraculous acts of creation and by catastrophes" (487).

31. *On the Origin of Species*, 488. Cf. also his statement that, "The whole history of the world, as at present known, although of a length quite incomprehensible by us, will hereafter be recognized

Durant is not wrong to suggest that, "The *Origin of Species* is the last great work of Victorian natural theology."[32]

Why does Darwin allow the conflict between his model of the origination of species and that presupposed in the dominant interpretation of Genesis to remain unexpressed? It is certainly not because Darwin was unaware of the conflict, nor, as the reception of the book demonstrates, were his readers unaware of the potential conflict.[33] As he prepared *Origin* for publication, he wrote to his friend and senior colleague, the eminent geologist Charles Lyell, and sought advice about his dealings with his publisher, John Murray, who was himself a devout Christian: "Would you advise me to tell Murray that my Book is not more *un*-orthodox, than the subject makes inevitable. That I do not discuss origin of man.—That I do not bring in any discussions about Genesis &c, & only give facts, & such conclusions from them, as seem to me fair.—Or had I better say *nothing* to Murray, & assume that he cannot object to this much unorthodoxy, which in fact is not more than any Geological Treatise, which runs slap counter to Genesis."[34] Darwin in the end apparently did not offer Murray any particular warning,[35] and the instinct not to bring conflict into focus seems characteristic of Darwin's approach, at least in his public writings. Darwin later wrote, "Many years ago, I was strongly advised by a friend never to introduce anything about religion in my works, if I wished to advance science in England; and this led me not to consider the mutual bearings of the two subjects."[36] In an interesting letter to his son George, who had apparently written an essay on religion and moral sense and sought his father's advice on publication, Darwin urged him not to publish it. He cites the example of John Stuart Mill, who by "never expressing his religious convictions" was enabled to influence "the present age in the manner in which he has done." He also mentions Lyell who "is most firmly convinced that he has shaken the faith in the Deluge &c far more efficiently by never having said a word against the Bible, than if he had acted otherwise." He finally cites the example of Voltaire whom Darwin thinks, following John Morley, might have achieved more success in his attacks on Christianity if they had been less direct and rather "slow & silent side attacks."[37]

---

as a mere fragment of time, compared with the ages which have elapsed since the first creature, the progenitor of innumerable extinct and living descendants, was created" (488).

32. Durant, "Darwinism and Divinity," 16.

33. For the reception of Darwin's ideas, see, inter alia, Ellegård, *Darwin and the General Reader*, esp. 155–73; Moore, *The Post-Darwinian Controversies*; Durant, "Darwinism and Divinity"; Ryan, ed., *Darwinism and Theology in America*; Bezanson, *How Free Can Religion Be?*, 80–102; Robbins and Cohen, eds., *Darwin and the Bible*; Turner and Lofthouse, *European Intellectual History*, 102–20. For the broader climate of change in the nineteenth century, see Schaefer, "The Science of Life."

34. Darwin to Charles Lyell, 28 March 1859; cf. also Nickerson, "Darwin's Publisher."

35. Lyell's reply is lost but Darwin's letter of 30 March 1859 thanks him for advice about Murray, and it seems that he sent along his work without any warning of its heterodoxy.

36. *Life and Letters*, 1: 306; cf. Brooke, "The Relations between Darwin's Science and his Religion," 41.

37. Charles Darwin to George Darwin, 21 October 1873.

Nevertheless, despite Darwin's unbelief, we can see from reading notebooks Darwin kept from 1838 to 1860 that he sometimes read or re-read works of theological scholarship.[38] His notebooks have entries for Milman's *History of Christianity* (marked as 'read') in 1840; Paley's *Evidences of Christianity* and his *Natural Theology* (both revisited from Darwin's earlier years, now in 1841 and 1843 respectively). In 1848 he found Neander's life of St. Bernard "interesting," and in 1851 he read and found "excellent" the book by Francis William Newman (the brother of the more famous John Henry Newman), *Phases of Faith*, which was a record of his loss of traditional Christian faith—a narrative that no doubt resonated with Darwin.

Moreover, the Old Testament remained a source of ethnographic detail or anecdotes, which occasionally featured in his writing. Darwin makes notes to this effect in his notebooks,[39] and in *On the Origin of Species*, adduces Genesis as proof for human selection in breeding: "From passages in Genesis, it is clear that the colour of domestic animals was at that early period attended to," alongside evidence from "an ancient Chinese encyclopaedia," "some of the Roman writers," and "savages in South Africa."[40] In an 1872 work, *The Expression of the Emotions in Man and Animals*, Darwin quoted the Bible as evidence of blushing, citing Jeremiah 6:15 and Ezra 9:6.[41] His German translator, Julius Victor Carus, wrote to Darwin to urge him not to employ these passages as evidence for blushing, i.e., reddening of the face, on the basis of the Hebrew terms used (בוש), and the second edition was clarified with an alternative reference to Psalm 34:5 (i.e., 34:6, נהר).[42]

If Darwin was markedly guarded in his public writings with respect to religion, among friends and in personal correspondence he was more candid. Already in 1857, Darwin wrote privately to a friend disparagingly of James Dwight Dana that "I believe, poor fellow, he believes in 1st Chr. of Genesis, so great allowances must be made for him."[43] But at roughly the same time, he writes to his son, William Erasmus Darwin, while the latter was in school: "Mamma desires that you will read the Chapters *very well*; & the dear old Mammy must be obeyed," with reference to the daily biblical reading assignments for sixth form pupils.[44]

Darwin enjoyed a large correspondence with numerous interlocutors after the publication of *Origin* and his other works in evolutionary theory. One prominent

---

38. Vorzimmer, "The Darwin Reading Notebooks (1838–1860)," superseded in the edition of Darwin's reading notebooks at the Darwin Correspondence Project (https://www.darwinproject.ac.uk/people/about-darwin/what-darwin-read/darwin-s-reading-notebooks, accessed 30 January 2020); cf. Stevens, "Darwin's Humane Reading."

39. Notebook C219 (p. 308); see also the invocation of the Genesis story about breeding in D104e (p. 364).

40. *On the Origin of Species*, 34.

41. Darwin, *The Expression of the Emotions in Man and Animals*, 316 and 322 respectively.

42. Julius Victor Carus to Charles Darwin, 24 October 1872; cf. p. 335 of the second edition.

43. Darwin to J. D. Hooker, 25 December 1857.

44. Charles Darwin to William Erasmus Darwin, 17 February 1857.

reaction among some religious scientists was to protest that it was possible to square Christian belief with the results of scientific endeavor, as is evident from the thousands of signatories of *The Declaration of Students of the Natural and Physical Sciences*.[45] But Darwin himself did not warm to such attempts to accommodate natural selection to the biblical record. He refused attempts to co-opt his theories into defenses of Genesis, and wrote to one correspondent who had sent to him such an attempt, "Almost any statement & fact can be reconciled by stretching the statements & facts; & this seemed to me the case throughout the article.—But I am weary of all these various attempts to reconcile, what I believe to be irreconcileable."[46] Another time he flatly declared, "I do not believe in metempsychosis nor in Genesis."[47] In later years he became more frank still in his correspondence. When asked by Nicolai Mengden whether he believed in Christ and the supernatural, Darwin replied, "Science has nothing to do with Christ, except in so far as the habit of scientific research makes a man cautious in admitting evidence. For myself, I do not believe that there ever has been any Revelation. As for a future life every man must judge for himself between conflicting vague probabilities."[48] Similarly he replies to another inquirer, Frederick McDermott, "I am sorry to have to inform you that I do not believe in the Bible as a divine revelation, & therefore not in Jesus Christ as the son of God."[49]

Darwin only rarely refers to works of biblical criticism, and the dominant impression is simply that he is a man of science who no longer gives much consideration to biblical or theological questions.[50] At one point, he wrote to Leonard Horner, who had offered a presidential address to the Geological Society of London, and Darwin expressed his surprise that the printing of the date 4004 BC in standard editions of the English Bible was in fact due to Archbishop James Ussher, rather than, as Darwin had assumed, ingredient to the biblical text itself.[51] This is not to say that Darwin thought that science and theology should keep to their distinct spheres. Rather, in a letter to John Brodie Innes, who had sent him a sermon by E. B. Pusey that disputed evolution, Darwin replied "I hardly see how religion & science can be kept as distinct as he

---

45. *The Declaration of Students of the Natural and Physical Sciences*.
46. Darwin to Bartholomew James Sulivan, 24 May 1861.
47. Darwin to John Crawfurd, 7 April 1861.
48. Darwin to Mengden, 5 June 1879.
49. Darwin to McDermott, 24 November 1880.
50. Nearly the only examples I have been able to find: on 11 May 1855 to J. D. Hooker, Darwin points his correspondent to an article on Job published in the *Westminster Review* (written by James Anthony Froud but published anonymously), which expressed praise for German biblical criticism, in contradistinction to English conservatism. In a letter to J. D. Hooker, 26 July 1863, Darwin writes, "I never thought of Jesus & absence of family affection:—I hear Rénan has discussed this," presumably a reference to Ernst Rénan's recently published *Vie de Jésus*.
51. Darwin to Horner, 20 March 1861. Cf. Horner, "Anniversary Address of the President." Although Ussher has been much maligned for the suggestion, there was a widespread Renaissance attempt to fix the date of creation; see the classic article by Patrides, "Renaissance Estimates of the Year of Creation."

desires, as geology has to treat of the history of the Earth & Biology that of Man.—But I most wholly agree with you that there is no reason why the disciples of either school should attack each other with bitterness, though each upholding strictly their beliefs."[52]

Darwin, like many Victorians who otherwise lost their Christian faith, continued to admire the ethical vision of the Sermon on the Mount, even if he suggests that it is a natural rather than a revealed morality, as in a passage from *The Descent of Man*:

> The ennobling belief in God is not universal with man; and the belief in active spiritual agencies naturally follows from his other mental powers. The moral sense perhaps affords the best and highest distinction between man and the lower animals; but I need not say anything on this head, as I have so lately endeavoured to shew that the social instincts,—the prime principle of man's moral constitution—with the aid of active intellectual powers and the effects of habit, naturally lead to the golden rule, 'As ye would that men should do to you, do ye to them likewise;' and this lies at the foundation of morality.[53]

In his autobiographical reflections, likewise, he confessed that he found the morality of the New Testament "beautiful," but also alleged that, "it can hardly be denied that its perfection depends in part on the interpretation which we now put on metaphors & allegories."[54]

Finally, it seems as though Darwin retained a certain fondness for the occasional biblical idiom. In a notebook entry speaking of biological inheritance, Darwin echoes Num 14:18 in writing, "Verily the faults of the fathers, corporeal & bodily are visited upon the children."[55] When describing the origin of life, he echoes Gen 2:7 in referring to "some one primordial form, into which life was first breathed."[56] Darwin was delighted when Rabbi Naphtali Levy, a Polish emigré to London, sent him a midrashic account of Genesis which attempted to demonstrate that Darwin's ideas were latent in Genesis itself.[57] As he remarked in his autobiography, referring to the reception of the *Origin*, "Even an essay in Hebrew has appeared on it, showing that the theory is contained in the Old Testament!"[58] According to a later recollection by his friend Louisa Nash, Darwin referred to this as "the best bit of praise I ever received."[59] And as he aged, he joked to his friend and second cousin W. D. Fox, "I feel as old as Methusalem [sic],"[60] and echoed the canticle of the aged Simeon (Luke 2:29–32) in describing the

---

52. Darwin to Innes, 27 November 1878.
53. *Evolutionary Writings*, 255.
54. *Evolutionary Writings*, 392.
55. Notebook M73 (p. 536).
56. *On the Origin of Species*, 484.
57. On this exchange, see Dodson, "*Toldot Adam*"; Colp Jr. and Kohn, "'A Real Curiosity.'"
58. *Evolutionary Writings*, 412.
59. Quoted in Colp Jr. and Kohn, "A Real Curiosity," 1719.
60. Letter to W. D. Fox, 11 May 1874.

few publication prospects he had remaining in his old age: "My strength will then probably be exhausted, & I shall be ready to exclaim '*nunc dimittis*.'"[61]

Conclusion

In the end, Darwin contributed decisively to our understanding of the history of the natural world, and so exercised a fateful impact on the hermeneutical attempt to grasp the meaning of Genesis in the contemporary world.[62] But unlike many figures in Victorian culture, Darwin did not leave behind a voluminous oeuvre detailing his attempts to come to terms with that hermeneutical situation. He was, above all, a naturalist and left with some relief the negotiation of theological and biblical claims to others. Nonetheless, his own autobiographical reflections thematize what he takes to be problems with the biblical record, and a portion of Darwin's readers were quick to exacerbate the tensions between Darwin and the Bible. Of course, Darwin did not benefit as he might have from the discoveries in the ancient Near East that by his day were already starting to call into question some interpretative assumptions about the genre and purpose of the creation accounts. Darwin died an agnostic,[63] and one can only guess at what a more sophisticated understanding of Genesis might have enabled the great scientist to conceive. Nevertheless, the Bible haunted Darwin even in his unbelief.

Bibliography

Althoz, Josef L. "The Warfare of Conscience with Theology." In *The Mind and Art of Victorian England*, 58–76. Minneapolis: University of Minnesota Press, 1976.

Anonymous. *The Declaration of Students of the Natural and Physical Sciences*. London: Simpkin, Marshall, 1865.

Barlow, Nora. *The Autobiography of Charles Darwin, 1809–1882*. New York: Harcourt, Brace & World, 1958.

Barrett, Paul H. et al., eds. *Charles Darwin's Notebooks, 1836–1844: Geology, Transmutation of Species, Metaphysical Enquiries*. Ithaca, NY: Cornell University Press, 1987.

Bezanson, Randall P. "Darwin versus Genesis." In *How Free Can Religion Be?*, 80–102. Champaign, IL: University of Illinois Press, 2006.

Briggs, Richard S. "The Hermeneutics of Reading Genesis after Darwin." In *Reading Genesis after Darwin*, edited by Stephen C. Barton and David Wilkinson, 57–72. Oxford: Oxford University Press, 2009.

Brooke, John Hedley. "The Relations between Darwin's Science and His Religion." In *Darwinism and Divinity: Essays on Evolution and Religious Belief*, edited by John Durant, 40–75. Oxford: Blackwell, 1985.

Brown, Frank Burch. "The Evolution of Darwin's Theism." *JHB* 19 (1986) 1–45.

---

61. *Evolutionary Writings*, 419.

62. Cf. Briggs, "The Hermeneutics of Reading Genesis After Darwin."

63. For the legendary (false) story that Darwin (re-)converted to Christianity on his deathbed, see Moore, *The Darwin Legend*.

Burkhardt, F. and Sydney Smith et al., eds. *The Correspondence of Charles Darwin, Volume 2: 1837–1843.* Cambridge: Cambridge University Press, 1986.

Butler, Samuel. *The Evidence for the Resurrection of Jesus Christ.* London: The Author, 1865.

Colenso, John William. *The Pentateuch and Book of Joshua Critically Examined.* London: Longman, Green, Longman, Roberts, & Green, 1862.

Colp, Ralph, Jr., and David Kohn. "'A Real Curiosity': Charles Darwin Reflects on a Communication from Rabbi Naphtali Levy." *The European Legacy* 1 (1996) 1716–27.

Colp Jr., Ralph. "Notes on Charles Darwin's 'Autobiography.'" *JHB* 18 (1985) 357–401.

Darwin, Charles. *On the Origin of Species: A Facsimile of the First Edition.* Edited by Ernst Mayr. Cambridge: Harvard University Press, 1964 [orig. 1859].

Darwin, Charles. *The Expression of the Emotions in Man and Animals.* London: Murray, 1872.

Darwin, Francis, ed. *The Life and Letters of Charles Darwin, Including an Autobiographical Chapter.* 3 vols. London: Murray, 1887.

Darwin, Francis, ed. *The Foundations of* The Origin of Species: *Two Essays Written in 1842 and 1844.* Cambridge: Cambridge University Press, 1909.

Dodson, Edward O. "*Toldot Adam:* A Little-Known Chapter in the History of Darwinism." *Perspectives on Science and Christian Faith* 52 (2000) 47–54.

Durant, John. "Darwinism and Divinity: A Century of Debate." In *Darwinism and Divinity: Essays on Evolution and Religious Belief,* edited by John Durant, 9–39. Oxford: Blackwell, 1985.

Ellegård, Alvar. *Darwin and the General Reader: The Reception of Darwin's Theory of Evolution in the British Periodical Press, 1859–1872.* Gothenburg Studies in English 8. Göteborg: Almqvist & Wiksell, 1958.

Froud, James Anthony. "The Book of Job." *Westminster Review* n.s. 4 (October 1853) 417–50.

Goodwin, C. W. "On the Mosaic Cosmogony." In *Essays and Reviews,* 207–53. London: Parker, 1860.

Horner, Leonard. "Anniversary Address of the President." *Quarterly Journal of the Geological Society of London* 17 (1861) xxxi–lxxii.

Hume, David. *An Enquiry Concerning Human Understanding.* Edited by L. A. Selby-Bigge. 2nd ed. Oxford: Clarendon, 1902.

Keynes, Richard Darwin, ed. *Charles Darwin's Beagle Diary.* Cambridge: Cambridge University Press, 1988.

Larsen, Timothy. "The Bible and Belief in Victorian Britain." *Cahiers victoriens et édouardiens* 76 Automne (2012) 11–25.

Larsen, Timothy. *A People of One Book: The Bible and the Victorians.* Oxford: Oxford University Press, 2011.

Maurice, F. D. *Theological Essays.* 4th ed. London: MacMillan, 1881 [orig. 1853].

Moore, James R. "Of Love and Death: Why Darwin 'gave up Christianity.'" In *History, Humanity and Evolution: Essays for John C. Greene,* edited by James R. Moore, 195–229. Cambridge: Cambridge University Press, 1989.

Moore, James R. *The Post-Darwinian Controversies: A Study of the Protestant Struggle to Come to Terms with Darwin in Great Britain and America, 1870–1900.* Cambridge: Cambridge University Press, 1979.

Moore, James R. *The Darwin Legend.* Grand Rapids: Baker, 1994.

Nickerson, Sylvia. "Darwin's Publisher: John Murray III at the Intersection of Science and Religion." In *Rethinking History, Science, and Religion: An Exploration of Conflict and the Complexity Principle*, edited by Bernard Lightman, 110–28. Pittsburgh: University of Pittsburgh Press, 2019.

Patrides, C. A. "Renaissance Estimates of the Year of Creation." *Huntington Library Quarterly* 26 (1963) 315–22.

Phipps, William E. "Darwin and Cambridge Natural Theology." *Bios* 54.4 (1983) 218–27.

Robbins, Richard H., and Mark Nathan Cohen, eds. *Darwin and the Bible: The Cultural Confrontation*. Boston: Pearson, 2009.

Rogerson, John. "What Difference Did Darwin Make? The Interpretation of Genesis in the Nineteenth Century." In *Reading Genesis after Darwin*, edited by Stephen C. Barton and David Wilkinson, 75–92. Oxford: Oxford University Press, 2009.

Rowell, Geoffrey. *Hell and the Victorians: A Study of the Nineteenth-Century Theological Controversies Concerning Eternal Punishment and the Future Life*. Oxford: Oxford University Press, 1974.

Ryan, Frank X., ed. *Darwinism and Theology in America: 1850–1930*. Vol. 3, *Science and Religion*. Bristol: Thoemmes, 2002.

Schaefer, Donovan O. "The Science of Life." In *The Oxford Handbook of Nineteenth-Century Christian Thought*, edited by Joel D. S. Rasmussen, Judith Wolfe, and Johannes Zachhuber, 89–107. Oxford: Oxford University Press, 2017.

Secord, James A., ed. *Charles Darwin: Evolutionary Writings*. Oxford: Oxford University Press, 2008.

Stevens, L. Robert. "Darwin's Humane Reading: The Anaesthetic Man Reconsidered." *Victorian Studies* 26 (1982) 51–63.

Thomson, Keith. *Private Doubt, Public Dilemma: Religion and Science since Jefferson and Darwin*. New Haven: Yale University Press, 2015.

Thomson, Keith. *The Young Charles Darwin*. New Haven: Yale University Press, 2009.

Turner, Frank M., and Richard A. Lofthouse. *European Intellectual History from Rousseau to Nietzsche*. New Haven: Yale University Press, 2014.

Vorzimmer, Peter J. "The Darwin Reading Notebooks (1838–1860)." *JHB* 10 (1977) 107–53.

6

The Image of God

Human Identity in the Cosmic Temple

Ryan S. Peterson

In a range of books, John Walton has illuminated the landscape of Gen 1 by attending carefully to the conceptual backgrounds of the text as well as its theological foreground. In this essay, I focus specifically on the meaning of the image of God in Gen 1–2. I describe the development that has been evident in Walton's scholarship on the topic. Then, I engage constructively Walton's most recent interpretive proposal. I am very much indebted to Walton in my formation as a theologian. Throughout my undergraduate education, Walton demonstrated that the purpose of the biblical texts is theological—they are meant to teach us about God and God's relation to God's people. Scripture is a living word about God, and this word is received well when the biblical texts are interpreted rightly. These are convictions that I continue to hold and to teach to my students. Walton's perspectives have shaped my own understanding for over 20 years now. I was fortunate enough to have taken Walton's course on the Psalms as a first semester freshman. I was warned that doing so would require real discipline, and it did. After that, I enrolled in as many of Walton's courses as I could. One of those courses was on Genesis as Walton was developing the material that would appear first in his NIV Application Commentary. I have been studying the book of Genesis ever since, and my own understanding has taken shape in dialogue with Walton's. Even when I disagree with Walton, I find the dialogue fruitful.

Part 1: Creation

Hermeneutics

One of the central tenets of Walton's work has been his insistence that "our doctrinal affirmations about Scripture (authority, inerrancy, infallibility, etc.) attach to the intended message of the human communicators (as it was given by the divine communicator)."[1] This is a common affirmation among evangelicals who believe that God inspired human authors to communicate God's abiding message using their own languages and their own contexts. Perhaps what sets Walton apart in his commitment to this affirmation is the distinction he makes between the "framework" of the communication and its "content."[2] That is, the message of the author should not be confused with the culturally-conditioned structure of the message. So, for example, Walton argues that "it is no surprise that Israel believed in a solid sky and that God accommodated to that model in his communication to Israel. But since the text's message is not an assertion of the true shape of cosmic geography, we can safely reject those details without jeopardizing authority or inerrancy."[3] A successful interpreter will differentiate between the structure of the communication and its theological content.

There is a profound advantage in this approach. This approach invites the interpreter to do the hard work needed to read ancient texts in their own literary contexts and idioms. The biblical texts require, and reward, readings that attend to the various ways these texts interface with their historical, cultural, and literary contexts. The meaning of the texts is opened up when these contextual factors are taken into consideration.

Of course, the meaning of the biblical texts is not given *by* these contexts themselves. Rather, the meaning is given *in* these contexts. Therefore, while the contextual factors are significant, the meaning does not exist on the level of context. The meaning of the texts is ultimately theological. The authors communicate truths about God and God's relation to God's people and the world. Like all authors, biblical authors use the conventions of their own language and literature. But the message of the biblical authors is unique. They are inspired by God to speak faithfully about God.

Walton's construal of inspiration and biblical hermeneutics motivates careful scholarly interaction with the biblical texts. However, there is also a danger in this approach in that it takes biblical interpretation out of the hands of those without the expertise to investigate its historical, cultural, and literary contexts. While the meaning of the text is theological, getting at the meaning of the text requires analysis of the text's contextual framework. And most Bible readers do not have sufficient knowledge to analyze the text's contextual framework so that they can differentiate the structure of communication from its content.

---

1. Walton, *Adam and Eve*, 19. This point is made throughout Walton's works. I am using *The Lost World of Adam and Eve* here because it offers a concise summary of his hermeneutical approach.
2. Walton, *Adam and Eve*, 20.
3. Walton, *Adam and Eve*, 20.

To take steps toward overcoming this problem, Walton suggests that the differences between structure and content are material differences. The structure of the message is not theological. At the level of structure, the authors share metaphysical assumptions with others in their cultural contexts. However, even while they use these assumptions to teach theological truths, the authors do not affirm these assumptions as theological truths. The content of the message is the theological truths themselves. These theological truths transcend historical, cultural, and literary contexts. They are as true for us today as they were for the original authors and audiences. They are truths about God and God's relation to God's people. On Walton's account, even given the inerrancy of Scripture, we are free to think differently from the authors about those things that they adopt from their own contexts for strictly communicative purposes.

Walton offers an interpretive strategy for teasing apart the structural framework from the theological truths. This strategy is to differentiate between those things the authors explicitly affirm and those things the authors simply adopt from their contexts.[4] Such differentiation allows the reader to identify the truths the authors intended to communicate. For example, God's acts, when affirmed, must be understood as real divine events. The Bible is not often interested in explaining how God did these acts.[5] Nevertheless, to be faithful to Scripture we must affirm that God did what is affirmed even if we are not sure by what means God did what is affirmed.

Therefore, three distinctions are important here. First, there is a material distinction between the theological interests of the texts and their contextual framework. Second, there is an interpretive distinction between the affirmations of the text and those aspects of the communication that are merely adopted from the authors' contexts. Third, there is a distinction between the events affirmed and the means of accomplishing those events. Scripture is interested in affirming transcendent and particular theological realities, and it does so through several literary media that are variously influenced by their historical, cultural, and literary contexts.

Regarding these contexts, Walton is interested in the shared "cognitive environment" that shapes the literature of the ancient Near East.[6] Familiarity with this cognitive environment helps the interpreter notice when something out of the ordinary is being affirmed. The theological teaching of the biblical texts can be discerned most easily in the cases where Israel's conception of God and God's relation to humanity is unique. For example, "In Genesis, God is outside the cosmos, not inside or a part of it, and he has no origin."[7] This is unique in ancient Near Eastern literature. Reflecting on this uniqueness, Walton observes that:

---

4. Walton, *Adam and Eve*, 21.
5. Walton, *Adam and Eve*, 21.
6. Walton, *Ancient Cosmology*.
7. Walton, *Ancient Cosmology*, 177.

Though the shape of the cosmos is seen in terms quite similar to the literature of the ancient Near East, the elements of the cosmos have no corresponding deities, and the structure of the cosmos is radically different. By the way in which Genesis 1 uses the shared ancient Near Eastern cognitive environment, it asks the same questions that lie behind all of the other ancient cosmologies and operates from the same metaphysical platform but gives quite different answers that reflect the uniqueness of the Israelite world view and theology.[8]

Interpreting the Image of God

Applying his methodology, Walton discerns that Gen 1–3 is a temple text. Indeed, in comparison to other ancient Near Eastern literature, Gen 1–3 is unique in what it is saying about the temple and the image of God. But in order to understand these unique affirmations, one first needs to recognize the temple themes that would have been apparent to those in the cognitive environment of the ancient Near East. In *Genesis*, Walton had already developed several aspects of the view that is more strongly affirmed in *Genesis 1 as Ancient Cosmology* and *The Lost World* books.[9] He notes the way Isaiah 66 portrays the cosmos as a temple, drawing upon the works of Jon Levenson, Michael Fishbane, and Moshe Weinfeld. This section of the commentary focuses on God's rest upon completion of creation, and the parallel rest that God takes up in the temple.

In his discussion of the image of God in *Genesis*, Walton makes a number of key observations. First, an image is "a representative in physical form."[10] Second, drawing on Gen 5:1–3, an image of God has the capacity "not only to serve as God's vice-regents (his representatives containing his essence), but also the capacity to be and act like him;" humans are "created with the potential to mirror divine attributes."[11] Third, "We might deduce that reason, conscience, self-awareness, and spiritual discernment are the tools he has provided so that we may accomplish that goal rather than actually defining the image."[12] Walton deftly notes the importance of humanity's physicality, humanity's aptitude for mimesis, and several human intellectual and spiritual capacities that support growth in reflection of God's character.

I have argued elsewhere that logical order is important when interpreting humanity's creation in the image of God.[13] God does not *discover* the image of God in humanity, as though humanity existed before God made the assessment that humanity should be made in God's image. Rather, God's intention to create humanity in

8. Walton, *Ancient Cosmology*, 178.
9. Walton, *Genesis*, esp. 147–52.
10. Walton, *Genesis*, 130.
11. Walton, *Genesis*, 131.
12. Walton, *Genesis*, 131.
13. Peterson, *The* Imago Dei *as Human Identity*.

God's image is logically prior to humanity's special manner of existence. That is, the very reason humanity exists is that God wanted to place an image of God in the cosmic temple. Humanity's existence takes the form that it does because this form enables humanity to be a living image of God.

That humanity is a living image of God is significant throughout the Old Testament. For example, in Isaiah 44 the prophet declares that there is only one God, one Rock. God's people are living witnesses to this truth, and they are pleased to acknowledge that they belong to the Lord. The living images of God know and love the living God. Those who make idols, on the other hand, take metal or wood, form it, and then throw themselves down before it. They become like the idols, witnesses who are without knowledge or sight. Idolaters become blind as they worship the creature rather than the creator.[14] The second commandment in Exod 20 can be interpreted along these lines as well. God has already made a living image of himself in the cosmic temple. Therefore, it is wrong to make a carved image, or a likeness of anything in heaven, on earth, or under the earth for worship. God has made his own image, and God wants this living image to bear witness to God's life and character.

Walton's reflections on the image of God fit very nicely within the logical order of the text. God's desire (so to speak) was to create a responsive creature who would reflect his character and represent his interests in the world. God gave that creature the physical and spiritual existence necessary for this responsive and representative action.

This logical order is illuminated by interpreting the image of God as human identity. The image of God does not refer primarily to human ontology, be that spiritual or physical, or human dominion, or the roles of priest and ambassador. Rather, human ontology and human function follow from humanity's identity in creation. In Gen 1–2, the meaning of the image of God is underdetermined. Much more knowledge of God and humanity is needed in order to understand the reality toward which the text is pointing. The basic structure of human existence is described in the text. In Gen 1, we are directed to consider the well-known phenomena of human existence: humans are male and female, called to reproduce and exercise dominion over other creatures. What Genesis 1 adds to the phenomena themselves is their *raison d'etre*. Human phenomena take the form that they do because God has made humans in God's image. Again, logical order is important. The phenomena follow from humanity's identity within creation. One would not be able to infer from the phenomena the fact that humans are made in God's image. This is a theological affirmation by the author that explains the unity and purpose of human phenomena.

Over the past 5 years, the term "identity" has gained traction in interpretations of the image of God.[15] The virtue of the term "identity" is that it indicates that the mean-

---

14. See Beale, *We Become What We Worship*.

15. For examples, see Lints, *Identity and Idolatry*; McDowell, "In the Image of God He Created Them" in *The Image of God in an Image Driven Age*, eds. Jones and Barbeau, pp. 29–46; Treier, *Introducing Evangelical Theology*; Farris, *An Introduction to Theological Anthropology*.

ing of the image of God is something central to a person's existence. It has to do with who they are, and not merely what they do. The difficulty with the term "identity" is that the term is used diversely. It is even used equivocally. This diversity of usage creates ambiguity around the term. There is a kind of fuzziness around the claim that human identity has to do with being made in God's image. Are we talking about personal identity, social identity, corporate identity? Moreover, are identities stable and unchanging? Are they fluid and always changing? The term "identity" can be used to say both things.

It is instructive to engage Walton's recent inclusion of identity-language in his interpretation of the image of God. In his earlier work, Walton argued that the various creational scenes in Gen 1 are primarily about function (based on a functional ontology common in the ancient Near East rather than a Western conception of ontology or teleology). His emphasis on function was illuminating. Several scholars have pushed back, suggesting that function is intertwined with ontology and teleology in Gen 1. In other words, Gen 1 is interested in existence, ends, and function. Nevertheless, to one degree or another most evangelical scholars have accommodated Walton's thesis that function is a key component of the interests of Gen 1.

Likewise, Walton has accommodated at least some of the pushback to his view. In his *Old Testament Theology for Christians*, he uses a range of terms in his discussion of the image of God. Helpfully, Walton notes three ways that images were used in ancient Near Eastern cultures that illuminate the significance of the image of God in Scripture. First, with respect to "the image of God that was manufactured to manifest his presence—the cult image." Second, "the image of God that is found in people (usually the king)." Third, "the image of the king that is represented in reliefs and statues and used in a variety of ways."[16] This categorization is helpful because the three different uses have not always been distinguished clearly. These uses of images help to clarify the meaning of imaging in the ancient Near East. After discussing the textual uses of each category, Walton concludes: "From these briefly summarized examples, we can observe that the concept of image in the ancient world expressed ideas of function, substitution, representation, mediation, status, and identity."[17]

Walton argues that in Scripture the image of God is a status conferred on humanity. He defines status as "something that is conferred on someone and about which they have no choice."[18] This is distinguished from identity, which he suggests "reflects how they choose to see themselves and what they want others to see in them."[19] Here is the payoff of this distinction: "The image of God in the Old Testament is therefore seen as a status given by God. So, in conferring the status, God identifies people with him. In doing so, he is revealing the identity that humans should adopt if they want to

16. Walton, *Theology*, 84.
17. Walton, *Theology*, 85.
18. Walton, *Theology*, 86.
19. Walton, *Theology*, 86.

conceive of themselves in a way that will allow them to properly understand how they should live in order to serve the purpose for which God has created them."[20] Further, "Whether someone is spiritually unregenerate, physically limited, mentally incapacitated, old or young, high functioning or low functioning, all who are human have the status 'image of God.' The image is not genetic or biological. We cannot lose it or fail to achieve it. As long as we are human we are part of the corporate image of God."[21]

Walton provides terminology to describe the two sides of identity-language as it is used currently in academic and popular discourse. "Status" refers to that which is fixed by God, and "identity" to one's self-identification with a status. Moreover, the term "status" allows Walton to conclude that every person is made in God's image without limiting God's image to any specific part or aspect of the person. This serves his interest in offering a reading that can be integrated with contemporary science— for Walton, humans could be materially continuous with other earthly creatures when analyzed through scientific measures without compromising humanity's status as God's image, since that status is conferred by God. The status of humanity, since it is granted externally, need not interrupt the natural condition of the creature.

There is a potential disadvantage to Walton's terminology, however; "status" may convey something a bit too alien to Genesis 1. Genesis 1 moves us to see that everything in creation, including humanity, is designed to serve God's purposes. Humanity is made to be God's representative image in the world. The image of God is not an extrinsic status here, but a real condition of relation and existence. Humanity's manner of existence is designed by God to facilitate humanity's creaturely identity.

Like "identity," the meaning of the term "status" is difficult to pin down. It can indicate something earned or unearned. For example, the Fifa Ballon d'Or is given to the best player in world football (soccer). The winner of the award receives a certain status. However, the status is not merely given; it is earned. On the other hand, my children have the status of being in my family. There is nothing they can do to change that fact. But being in my family is not a status given to them apart from the natural condition of their existence. Rather, it is the natural condition of their existence. It is part of their identity. They are my children, and therefore they have the status that comes with being my children, for good or ill. A third example complicates things further. Perhaps the most common way we use the term "status" is with respect to social media and its demand for status updates. In this case, statuses are always changing based on human experiences. As these examples show, the term "status" does not clarify whether one's station is earned, natural, fixed, or fluid. Walton is clear about his use of the term. However, I am not sure a wide use of the term "status" to describe the image of God would be useful doctrinally.

Nevertheless, Walton's dual emphasis is important. God determines the nature of humanity's existence and humanity's relation to him. Also, we are expected to learn

---

20. Walton, *Theology*, 86.
21. Walton, *Theology*, 86.

and embrace the reality of our existence. Humans are knowing and acknowledging creatures. To be whole, we need to understand ourselves. Our anthropology must include the opportunity for humans to come to know—to know ourselves personally, our kind corporately, and our relation to God theologically. The term "identity" is often used to refer to self-understanding, as Walton uses it. However, one's self-understanding can be wrong. We would not want to say that one's faulty self-understanding is the person's true identity, but rather that the person with a faulty self-understanding misunderstands her identity. This situation suggests that we should differentiate between a person's self-understanding and her identity. In our self-understandings we often suppose a certain identity. This is part of the process of self-interpretation or self-discovery. Gen 1's teaching that humans are made in God's image indicates that God has determined a common identity for humanity, and humans are invited to embrace this reality as part of their self-understanding and their understanding of others. Every person is asked to discover her identity in relation to God.

In my work to date, I have chosen to use the term "identity" to refer primarily to God's determination of human existence and secondarily to a human person's self-understanding as a creature of God. One's creaturely identity is given by God. One comes to understand and embrace that identity, so that it becomes the person's self-understanding. Academic literature has used the term "identity" in both ways, and I have found it useful to do the same. What God has determined to be true of humanity really is the case. Fundamentally, we are creatures made in God's image. However, our knowledge of this reality is often inadequate. It must be learned and embraced through attention to God and God's word. The inadequacy of our self-understanding implies that there is a distance between the reality of our identity and our understanding of it. This distance helps us make sense of a number of contemporary pastoral issues.

We are created in the image of God. This is humanity's fundamental identity as a creature in the cosmic temple. This identity cannot be lost or diminished, though one can rebel against it or embrace it. It is not identified with just one part of human existence. Rather, each aspect of human existence makes sense in light of this identity.

I have suggested that humanity's creation in the image of God is a corporate identity revealed through the biblical narratives. The very concept of a corporate narrative identity has been questioned, however, since each individual human has a different personal narrative identity. But in Scripture, our different stories are subsumed into a larger theological narrative. All humans share the same creaturely identity. This creaturely identity is established at humanity's special creation and it persists into the eschaton. Successful fulfillment of human identity is compromised by sin and death. Christ fulfills humanity's identity since he is the very image of God, and his redemption of humanity establishes the conditions for others to live in the fullness of this identity. Union with Christ is necessary for the image of God to be fulfilled in others.

Richard Bauckham clarifies Scripture's portrayal of Jesus's identity.[22]

---

22. Bauckham, *God Crucified: Monotheism and Christology in the New Testament*.

> The dominance of the distinction between 'functional' and 'ontic' Christology has made it seem unproblematic to say that for early Christology Jesus exercises the 'functions' of divine lordship without being regarded as 'ontically' divine. In fact, such a distinction is highly problematic from the point of view of early Jewish monotheism, for in this understanding of the unique divine identity, the unique sovereignty of God was not a mere 'function' which God could delegate to someone else. It was one of the key identifying characteristics of the unique divine identity, which distinguished the one God from all other reality. The unique divine sovereignty is a matter of *who God is*. Jesus' participation in the unique divine sovereignty is therefore also not just a matter of what Jesus does, but of *who Jesus is* in relation to God.[23]

This rich description of Jesus's identity parallels my claim about humanity's identity in God's image. First, Scripture's interest is "who Jesus is in relation to God." In the same way, the interest of Gen 1:26–30 is humanity in relation to God. Second, Jesus's identity implies an ontology and various functions, but this identity is communicated prior to ontology and function. In the same way, humanity's identity implies an ontology and various functions, but human identity is logically prior to ontology and function. Third, the identifying characteristics of God's identity distinguish God from all other reality. Humanity's identifying characteristics distinguish it from other earthly creatures.

The reality of humanity's identity as a created image of God in the cosmic temple is determined by God's creative act. God uses Scripture to shape human understanding of this identity.

Extending the Interpretation of the Image of God

In concert with many Old Testament scholars, I recognize that the image of God is tied very closely to human function in Genesis 1. In fact, one could argue that humans need to reproduce and fill the earth in order to fulfill their function throughout the world. Humans need to be everywhere to represent God everywhere. The text affirms human dominion to be a good thing because human dominion should reflect God's dominion, which is a good thing. God's dominion leads to the flourishing of his creatures. Likewise, human dominion should lead to the flourishing of earthly creatures. However, the rest of the Hebrew Bible describes a state of affairs in which human dominion does not reflect God's dominion. Humans abuse power, exercising control in destructive and oppressive ways. This is a departure from humanity's first calling—the calling to represent God, the true king. Humanity's station as representative of God remains after humanity's fall into sin, but life-giving dominion is rarely evidenced.

Further, the call to imitate God's dominion is a paradigmatic calling. It is not meant to exhaust the meaning of the image of God. Instead, it establishes one aspect

---

23. Bauckham, *God Crucified*, 41.

of humanity's calling, and it exemplifies the pattern for further reflection on the reality that humans are made in God's image. Genesis 1 is a text about God's dominion. God speaks, and creatures exist. God commands, and creation is brought into order God blesses, and the world flourishes. Humans are meant to reflect God's life-giving dominion in our own action. Our dominion is tiny in comparison to God's creation-establishing dominion. Yet, it is a creaturely picture of something true of God.

This initial pattern of analysis should shape further reflection. Gen 1 anticipates fuller revelation of God, and the fullness of divine revelation has implications for fulfillment of human identity. Humans are meant to image God, and therefore knowledge of God is meant to be pictured through faithful human existence in the world.

Such extension of the image of God is found as early as Gen 2–3. As Catherine McDowell has shown in *The Image of God in the Garden of Eden*, the Eden narrative includes an account of God forming and breathing life into an image.[24] She demonstrates this by comparing the biblical account to accounts in the Mesopotamian and Egyptian literature, and she finds that humanity is clearly portrayed as an image of God in Gen 2 even though neither צלם nor דמות is used in the narrative. Humans are intended to take up the role of representing God in the world as living images of the living God.

In both the Old and New Testaments, this is especially striking in the case of holiness because God's holiness is *sui generis*. Nevertheless, God calls humans to reflect God's holiness since humans are images of God in the cosmic temple. Therefore, we are intended to represent God's character in creaturely ways. That God's holiness is *sui generis* implies that human imitation of God's holiness is analogical rather than univocal. Because God is holy in God's own life and toward God's people, then God's people should participate in God's holiness. This divinely granted holiness through participation shines forth in active imitation of God's character. Humans cannot participate in the attributes of God by possessing them the way God possesses them. But humans can participate in a creaturely way in those attributes that God shares with us. Consider McDowell's comments on Lev 19:

> the first two verses and the repetition of 'I am the LORD' and 'I am the LORD your God' (fifteen times in thirty-seven verses!) make it clear what binds these laws together: each of them highlights a particular manifestation of God's holiness that Israel was to imitate. In doing so, they were to be a living manifestation of God's original intention for humanity . . . God's people were intended to live out their identity . . . by the way they lived their lives, including how they dealt with money, how they treated their employees, how they conducted business and how they used their wealth to care for the poor.[25]

---

24. McDowell, *The Image of God in the Garden of Eden*.
25. McDowell, "In the Image of God He Created Them," 43.

The examples in Leviticus illustrate the reality that humans are intended to imitate God's character because we are made in God's image. Genesis 1 and its anthropological descriptions set the stage so that we can interpret the rest of the Scriptures accordingly. Humans are made in God's image. This reality should drive us to want to know, love, and participate in fellowship with God.

The New Testament texts that refer to the image of God are in continuity with Gen 1. Humans are representatives of God in the cosmic temple, and therefore we are meant to know God and reflect God's character in our lives. First John 3:2 has perhaps been the most prominent New Testament passage referred to in discussions of the image of God: "we are God's children now, and what we will be has not yet appeared; but we know that when he appears we shall be like him, because we shall see him as he is." This passage provides an eschatological context for the sanctification described in other texts, such as Eph 4:23–24 and Col 3:10, and it emphasizes the revelatory means of transformation. Genesis 1 shows a pattern of knowledge and imitation. First John 3:2 describes the fulfillment through knowledge and conformation.

Conclusion and Appreciation

Walton's identification of the temple context and the theological content needed for interpreting humanity's creation in the image of God in Gen 1 has been fruitful for exegetical and theological developments related to interpreting Gen 2–3, Lev 19, and related New Testament texts. The lines of continuity between the Old and New Testaments are illuminated by Walton's theological concentration and careful exegesis. Genesis 1 reveals the reality of human existence and calls for humans to embrace this reality, living in accordance with it. This is true for all people, even though it is not known by all people.

Insofar as there is a common word in Scripture spoken to all people about God and about our relation to God, perhaps we should say that Scripture is written to all of humanity. What we share in common as humans is greater than what separates us. This reality may encourage everyone, whether trained academically or not, to read the Bible theologically. As John Webster says, a reader's "hermeneutical situation"[26] conditions appropriate readings of Scripture. Insofar as all humans share the same hermeneutical situation—being creatures of God, made in God's image, living in this particular cosmic temple in relation to the same God—then it will be appropriate for all humans at all times to make certain interpretive moves. These fundamental samenesses need to govern our understandings of historical, linguistic, and cultural differences. Because of the samenesses in our human hermeneutical situation, I think there is great promise for resonance between the best theological interpretations of

---

26. Webster, "Hermeneutics in Modern Theology: Some Doctrinal Reflections," *Word and Church*, 58–65. For commentary, see Sarisky, "The Ontology of Scripture and the Ethics of Interpretation in the Theology of John Webster," 62.

Scripture across time and place. Indeed, Christian readers should benefit from careful contemporary exegesis and from retrieval of classical theological readings of Scripture.

In this essay, I have endeavored to show the fruit of constructive engagement with Walton's interpretation of the image of God. But I also want to say something about the whole. Walton's work has been a work of love—teaching and scholarship given to his students and to all who wish to read Scripture well. Chief among these gifts is Walton's energetic insistence that the purpose of Scripture is theological. The Bible reveals God and God's purposes for God's people. This conviction regarding the reality and availability of divine revelation gives vitality to Walton's work.[27]

Bibliography

Bauckham, Richard. *God Crucified: Monotheism and Christology in the New Testament*. Grand Rapids: Eerdmans, 1998.

Beale, G. K. *We Become What We Worship: A Biblical Theology of Idolatry*. Downers Grove, IL: IVP Academic, 2008.

Farris, Joshua. *An Introduction to Theological Anthropology: Humans, Both Creaturely and Divine*. Grand Rapids: Baker Academic, 2020.

Lints, Richard. *Identity and Idolatry: The Image of God and Its Inversion*. New Studies in Biblical Theology. Downers Grove, IL: IVP Academic, 2015.

McDowell, Catherine. "In the Image of God He Created Them: How Genesis 1:26–27 Defines the Divine–Human Relationship and Why It Matters." In *The Image of God in an Image Driven Age: Explorations in Theological Anthropology*, edited by Beth Felker Jones and Jeffrey W. Barbeau, 29–46. Downers Grove, IL: IVP Academic, 2016.

McDowell, Catherine L. *The Image of God in the Garden of Eden: The Creation of Humankind in Genesis 2:5—3:24 in Light of the* mīs pî pīt pî *and* wpt-r *Rituals of Mesopotamia and Ancient Egypt*. Winona Lake, IN: Eisenbrauns, 2015.

Peterson, Ryan S. *The Imago Dei as Human Identity: A Theological Interpretation*. Journal of Theological Interpretation Supplements 14. Winona Lake, IN: Eisenbrauns, 2016.

Sarisky, Darren. "The Ontology of Scripture and the Ethics of Interpretation in the Theology of John Webster." *IJST* 21 (2019) 59–77.

Treier, Daniel J. *Introducing Evangelical Theology*. Grand Rapids: Baker, 2019.

Walton, John. *Genesis*. NIV Application Commentary Series. Grand Rapids: Zondervan, 2001.

———. *Genesis 1 as Ancient Cosmology*. Winona Lake, IN: Eisenbrauns, 2011.

———. *The Lost World of Adam and Eve*. Downers Grove, IL: IVP Academic, 2015.

———. *Old Testament Theology for Christians: From Ancient Context to Enduring Belief*. Downers Grove, IL: IVP Academic, 2017.

Webster, John. *Word and Church: Essays in Christian Dogmatics*. London: T. & T. Clark, 2006.

---

27. I am grateful for the comments I received after a presentation of some of this material at the Copenhagen Lutheran School of Theology. Input from Johannes Heule was especially helpful. I am also grateful for Caryn Reeder's insightful comments on an earlier draft of this chapter.

7

Praise the LORD, the (un)Creator of Heaven and Earth

Psalm 105's Depiction of YHWH's Sovereignty in the Egyptian Plagues[1]

Michelle A. Stinson

Introduction

Bookended with calls to praise (vv. 1–6, 45b), Psalm 105 invites its audience to reconsider the works of YHWH through an extended historical recital spanning from God's covenant promise of land to Abraham to Israel's arrival at the land of Canaan (vv. 7–45a).[2] Berlin contends that the main focus of Psalm 105 is "the promise of the land to the forebears of Israel, a promise that is eternal and unconditional and that therefore is still in force, undiminished, in the time of the exiles to whom the psalm is directed."[3] References to land occur with noted frequency across Psalm 105. The

---

1. This essay is dedicated to Dr. John Walton to thank him for many years of generous hospitality at his annual SBL breakfasts.

2. The text offers no description of Israel actually possessing the land; instead, the psalm celebrates its impending accomplishment (v. 44). Considering the psalmist's choice of other events in this recital, Clifford observes: "It retells those traditions which underscore the fidelity of God to the people at times when they did not in fact possess the land" (Clifford, "Style and Purpose in Psalm 105," 427).

3. Berlin, "Interpreting Torah Traditions in Psalm 105," 25. She adds: "I use the term 'exiles' to refer to the exile and/or postexilic audience, living either in Babylonia or in the Land of Israel under Persian rule—all these people considered themselves to be in exile in some sense, regardless of their geographic location" (p. 25). There is a growing consensus of assigning an exilic or postexilic date to Psalm 105. As Brettler notes: "Though a wide variety of dates have been offered for the psalm, a consensus began to develop in the late 1970s and early 1980s that it is exilic" (Brettler, "The Poet as Historian: The Plague Tradition in Psalm 105," 20).

word ארץ appears ten times spread across the composition (vv. 7, 11, 16, 23, 27, 30, 32, 35, 36, 44; v. 12 pronoun referent).[4] Explicit statements of YHWH's covenant promise of land occur at the beginning and end of the historical recital (vv. 8–11, 42–45a) with the theme of land as an undercurrent of the psalm as a whole.

Often overlooked by scholars is the fact that the very first occurrence of the term "land" (ארץ) in Psalm 105 is not a reference to the covenantal promise, but instead a statement of YHWH's sovereign reign: "He is the LORD our God; his judgments are in all the earth" (v. 7).[5] Ceresko observes that for the psalmist, it is YHWH's sovereign rule over all the earth (בכל־הארץ, v. 7) that establishes the basis for YHWH's gift of a particular land to a particular people (v. 11).[6] In this chapter, I will demonstrate how the psalmist's depiction of the Egyptian plague account (vv. 26–36) provides additional evidence for this argument for YHWH's sovereignty.[7] Unique to the psalmist's recounting of the plagues (cf. Exodus 7–11 and Psalm 78:44–51), darkness appears first with the remaining plagues unfolding in an order that moves from heaven to the waters to the land, a progression that mirrors the Genesis account of creation. Here in Psalm 105's plague account, the creation order is being systematically dismantled as a sign of divine judgment on Israel's enemies.[8] This chapter will argue that the psalmist's depiction of the plagues as an undoing of creation functions rhetorically to provide a creational foundation to the psalmist's larger argument for YHWH's ability to keep his enduring covenant promise of land.

Psalm 105: Issues of Form and Structure

Many scholars consider Psalm 105 as some type of hymn, be this an "imperative" hymn,[9] or a "hymn of praise."[10] Drawing from its content, others view it as a historical

---

4. In addition to the word "land" (ארץ), the psalmist uses the terms "territory/borders" (גבול) in vv. 31 and 33 and "ground" (אדמה) in v. 35.

5. Tucker, for example, limits the psalmist's concern to territorial issues of land. He largely ignores the reference to ארץ in verse 7 and limits his discussion of the plagues to issues of land possession: "the psalm appears rooted in the land, and the peoples who inhabit it." (Tucker, "Revisiting the Plagues in Psalm CV," 404).

6. Ceresko observes: "Because Yahweh rules over *all* the earth . . . he can make an eternal pledge . . . to give a part of that earth . . . to Abraham's descendants" (Ceresko, "A Poetic Analysis of Ps 105," 31, emphasis in original. This point is restated again on pp. 44–45).

7. Ceresko restricts his discussion of the plague account to its role in the strophic structure of the psalm (Ceresko, "A Poetic Analysis of Ps 105," 36–37, 42–43).

8. The dismantling of the creation order also occurs in Jeremiah 4:23–26, but here in an oracle of judgement on the land of Israel. See van Ruiten, "Back to Chaos: The Relationship Between Jeremiah 4:23–26 and Genesis 1," 21–30.

9. Allen notes: "In form Ps 105 is an expanded hymn of the imperatival style" (Allen, *Psalms 101–150*, 53). He follows Crüsemann, *Studien zur Formgeschichte von Hymnus und Danklied in Israel*, 76 and Westermann, *Praise and Lament in the Psalms*, 122–24, 140.

10. Mays observes: "In form and function, Psalm 105 is a hymn of praise . . . Verses 1–6 are the extended summons to praise, and verses 12–45 compose the content of praise" (Mays, *Psalms*, 338).

psalm,[11] or according to Gunkel, a "legend."[12] Kraus, offering a moderating position, sees it as a fusion of both hymn and history.[13]

Scholars tend to view this psalm as a unified whole, displaying little or no redactional activity.[14] The psalm has three main sections—an Introduction (vv. 1–11) and two geographically informed "movements" (Israel's move from Canaan to Egypt, vv. 12–22, followed by the move from Egypt back to Canaan, vv. 24–45).[15] Within this larger framework, proposals offered for the psalm's divisions exhibit strong continuity, mostly consisting of 7–8 strophes.[16] After the introduction (vv. 1–11), the psalm follows a "generally chronological development."[17]

Psalm 105's Plague Account

The main concern of this chapter is Psalm 105's depiction of the Egyptian "plagues" (vv. 26–36).[18] It is striking that there are only three passages in the Hebrew Bible that

---

11. Fensham observes that Psalm 105 fits the category of psalms that "give a fairly extensive description of history and which present the history as a unity. It is a presentation of history in a fixed chronological order or scheme. Only when this is a characteristic, can we talk of Psalms of history" (Fensham, "Neh. 9 and Pss. 105, 106, 135 and 136: Post-exilic Historical Traditions in Poetic Form," 36).

12. Gunkel groups Psalm 78, 105, and 106 together as "legends," assuming that these are late constructions utilizing the Pentateuchal narratives often with inclusion of deeds of a miraculous nature (Gunkel and Begrich, *An Introduction to the Psalms*, 247–49).

13. Kraus designates the psalm as belonging to "the category of history psalms presented in hymnic style (cf. Psalms 78 and 105)" (Kraus, *Psalms 60–150*, 308).

14. After critiquing Martin Leuenberger's proposal for a literary redaction of the psalm (i.e., vv. 1, 2–5, 45 assigned to a later redaction), Hossfeld concludes: "Thus, we remain convinced of the unity of Psalm 105" (Hossfeld and Zenger, *Psalms 3*, 66).

15. Ceresko, "A Poetic Analysis of Ps 105," 22–23, 26. Verse 23—with its ambiguous reference to Israel/Jacob being in Egypt—functions as a "hinge" for the two sections. Hossfeld offers a helpful discussion of the issue embedded in v. 23: "There are some uncertainties at the end of the Joseph story and the beginning of the story of the nation, depending on how one interprets 'Israel/Jacob' in v. 23: either as a designation for the patriarch Jacob, in which case the verse is still part of the story of Joseph, or as a designation for the people (at least in v 23b); in that case v. 23 opens the history of the nation. Because v. 24 alludes to Exod. 1:7, it is popular to follow the pentateuchal book division and begin the history of the people in v. 24" (Hossfeld and Zenger, *Psalm 3*, 67).

16. Hossfeld divides the psalm into the following sections (1–3//4–7//8–11//12–15//16–23//24–38//39–41//42–45); see Hossfeld and Zenger, *Psalm 3*, 66–67. Clifford prefers to join 1–6//7–11//12–15//16–22//23–38//39–45; see Clifford, *Psalms 73–150*, 153–55. The main two points where disagreement over divisions occurs are the position of v. 23 (see discussion above) and v. 7. The positioning of verse 7 has much to do with how one sees the significance of "land" (ארץ) in the psalm's argument. Clifford, followed by Ceresko, sees the concept of land as key to the argument of the psalm as a whole and places v. 7 as the opening verse of the psalm's actual recital.

17. Ceresco, "A Poetic Analysis of Ps 105," 24.

18. Choosing a designation for these events that precede Israel's departure from Egypt can be a linguistic conundrum. The collective phrase "signs and wonders" (used in Psalm 105:27) proves cumbersome. I have chosen to employ the common term "plague" (נגע) for ease of designation, although this term does not appear in Psalm 105. Interestingly, the term "plague" (נגע) occurs in Exodus only as a designation for the death of the first-born (Exod 11:1).

provide a listing of the Egyptian "plagues": Exodus 7–11, Psalm 78:44–51, and Psalm 105:26–36.[19] Although there is substantial overlap in the accounts, the descriptions of the plagues in these three texts vary in sequence, number, and content. Table 1 offers a visual aid for comparing the three accounts.

Exodus	Psalm 105	Psalm 78
	Darkness (9)	
1. Water to Blood	Water to Blood (1)	Water to Blood (1)
		Swarms of flies (4)
2. Frogs	Frogs (2)	Frogs (2)
3. Gnats	Swarms of flies, Gnats (4, 3)?	–
4. Swarms of flies	cf. above	cf. above
5. Animal Pestilence	–	?
6. Boils	–	–
		Locusts (8)
7. Hail	Hail (7)	Hail (7)
8. Locusts	Locusts (8)	cf. above
9. Darkness	cf. above	–
10. Death of First Born	Death of First Born (10)	Death of First Born (10)

Table 7.1: Comparison of Egyptian Plague Orders[20]

19. Psalm 135:8–9 and 136:10 make mention of the plagues, but only to an individual plague—the slaying of the first-born. Lemmelijn also includes the plague account featured in the Wisdom of Solomon in his discussion (cf. Wis 11:5–15; 16–19). See Lemmelijn, "Genesis' Creation Narrative: The Literary Model for the So-Called Plague Tradition?," 407–19.

20. Note that the numbers in parentheses refer back to the ordering in Exodus. Many scholars work with the assumption that the Pentateuch was in existence at the time, available to the psalmist, and utilized in the construction of this text. Margulis contends that Psalm 105 "presupposes the Pentateuchal narrative as presently constituted" (Margulis, "The Plagues Tradition in Psalm 105," 496); see also Berlin, "Interpreting Torah Traditions in Psalm 105," 22. In addition, Psalm 105 reflects elements of both P and J/non-P material lending support to the possibility that the psalmist knew the entire Torah narrative. Brettler, however, argues against this position based on the selection and arrangement of the plagues. He queries: "It is unclear, however, why a plague narrative based on Exodus would look like Ps 105—specifically, why would darkness be the first plague, why would the order of swarms

Since a discussion of all three accounts would prove impossible given space considerations,[21] I will simply consider Psalm 105's distinctives. Psalm 105's depiction of the plagues departs from the Exodus account in two distinct ways—the order and the number of plagues. The most notable feature of Psalm 105's ordering of the plagues is the relocation of the Plague of Darkness from position nine in Exodus to the initial position in this account. The only other change in the order of the plagues in Ps 105 is a minor one—the swarms of flies (P4) appear before the plague of gnats (P3) and these are paired in a single line (v. 31).

Determining the exact number of plagues in Psalm 105 presents some difficulty. Like Psalm 78, Psalm 105 omits the plague of boils (P6). In addition, the plague of animal pestilence (P5) is absent.[22] The final number of plagues rests primarily on whether or not one divides the swarms of flies and gnats into two plagues or just one. If these are seen as two separate plagues, the total becomes eight.[23] If they are combined, the plagues total seven—a number with symbolic significance for completeness.[24]

A Proposal to Explain the Psalmist's Depiction of the Plagues

Proposals for explaining the inclusion and ordering of the plagues in Psalm 105 vary greatly. Some scholars explain the ordering based on the psalmist's use of an independent source,[25] while others suggest that random human error may be at play.[26] Specifically regarding the repositioning of the plague of darkness, Briggs and others propose a case for the arbitrary reinsertion of an omitted plague by the glossator at

---

(ערב) and lice (כנים) be reversed (v. 31) and why would pestilence (דבר) be omitted?" (Brettler, "The Poet as Historian: The Plague Tradition in Psalm 105," 21). These concerns will be addressed in the remainder of this chapter.

21. For an extended examination of these three plague accounts, see Stinson, "'A Table in the Wilderness?': The Rhetorical Function of Food Language in Psalm 78," 159–96.

22. The presence of the plague of animal pestilence in Psalm 78 is contested by many. For a proposal for its inclusion in Ps 78, see Stinson, "'A Table in the Wilderness?': The Rhetorical Function of Food Language in Psalm 78," 179–83.

23. See Hossfeld and Zenger, *Psalm 3*, 67. This is the position I also hold.

24. Loewenstamm critiques an over-reliance on the Pentateuchal ordering of the plagues over against the psalm's own structure. He argues: "The verse 'He spoke and there came swarms; lice [gnats] throughout their country' (v. 31) does not . . . indicate two plagues but only one, as can be seen clearly from the obvious similarity between this verse and one closely following: 'He spoke, and there came locusts; grasshoppers without number' (v. 34). Psalm 105, it is now apparent, also enumerates seven plagues: darkness, blood, frogs, swarms (including lice [gnats]), hail, locusts and the slaying of the firstborn" (Loewenstamm, *The Evolution of the Exodus Tradition*, 82).

25. Loewenstamm holds that the psalmist relied on a tradition other than the Pentateuch: "We cannot be sure whether Ps 105 is later than the Pentateuch or not; but in either case, it reflects a poetic tradition which precedes the Pentateuch" (Loewenstamm, "The Number of Plagues in Psalm 105," 38).

26. Fensham gives voice to the simplest of these explanations: "It is possible that the poet of Ps. 105 has written from memory with the result that certain plagues changed places and certain were omitted" (Fensham, "Neh. 9 and Pss. 105, 106, 135 and 136: Post-exilic Historical Traditions in Poetic Form," 41).

the beginning of the account.²⁷ Kirkpatrick contends that the plague of darkness was moved to a place of primacy because it was as a result of this plague that the Egyptians were convinced of YHWH's power (see Exodus 11:3).²⁸ Others look within the text of Psalm 105 itself for a possible explanation for the placement of the plague of darkness. Based on the psalm's literary structure, Clifford posits: "Presumably, it was done to contrast the land of Egypt with the desert: God's first act for Israel in the wilderness is to light their darkness with fire (v. 39), whereas God's first act against Egypt is to turn their light to darkness."²⁹ Of these options, no proposal offers a sufficient explanation for the psalmist's refashioning of the plague account and its purpose within the psalm as a whole.³⁰ Berlin contends that scholars must "take seriously the work of the ancient interpreter, both as an exegete and as a creative literary artist—to understand what he did with his traditional material and what he accomplished by doing it."³¹ It is in considering the rhetorical motivations of the psalmist, then, that one may find a way forward.

The remainder of this chapter considers an alternative explanation for Psalm 105's reordering and depiction of the plagues—namely, that it is rhetorically motivated.³² As in Genesis 1 where YHWH's sovereign power is displayed as he systematically *assembles* a good world through his spoken word, so here in Psalm 105, YHWH's sovereignty is shown in creation's intentional *dismantling*. On a rhetorical level, the psalmist's account of the plagues emphasizes YHWH's sovereign rule in the following ways. (1) Here, the One who created the heavens and the earth can—as an expression

---

27. Briggs suggests: "The glossator inserts one which has been omitted in the original, here at the beginning, out of its proper order in the narrative" (Briggs, *A Critical and Exegetical Commentary on the Book of Psalms, Volume 2*, 346). Hossfeld critiques the logic of this view: "The whole series of plagues is introduced in v. 28 by the ninth plague, which prompted J. Wellhausen to look upon the verse as a later addition to the text. In this he is followed by H. Gunkel. However, this belongs to the sort of text improvements which collapses for the sole reason that it is just as inexplicable that a later glossator should have inserted it in the wrong place" (Hossfeld and Zenger, *Psalms 3*, 29, n. 15).

28. Kirkpatrick has suggested that the purpose of this calamity was to "inspire the worshipers of the sun-god with the sense of Jehovah's power" (Kirkpatrick, *The Book of Psalms, Book 4 and 5*, 621). In an attempt to explain the phrase "they did not rebel against his word" (ולא־מרו את־דברוו) in verse 28b immediately following the plague of darkness (v. 28a), Kirkpatrick speculates that the subject of this phrase is the Egyptians.

29. Clifford, *Psalms 73–150*, 155. While this offers an interesting literary connection, Clifford fails to explain any of the other ordering features in the two passages he considers.

30. As will be seen below, Lee offers a compelling explanation for the psalmist's reordering of the plagues. However, he fails to address the purpose of this reordering within the larger argument of Psalm 105. Lee concludes his essay by noting that his study can shed light "on the proper conception of both faith in a God of creation and faith in a God in history" (Lee, "Genesis I and the Plagues Tradition in Psalm CV," 263). However, Lee fails to draw out these connections.

31. Berlin, "Interpreting Torah Traditions in Psalm 105," 22.

32. In this study, I use the term "rhetorical" to refer to a text's suasive force versus its purely poetic or aesthetic features. While literary features contribute to a text's rhetorical force, I use the term "rhetorical" to refer to the persuasive power of texts to influence an audience's attitudes, actions, or behaviors. See Fox, "The Rhetoric of Ezekiel's Vision of the Valley of the Bones," 1–4.

of divine judgment—also dismantle the heavens and the earth. (2) Unlike in Exodus 7–11, YHWH here in Psalm 105 is directly engaged in the unfolding of the plagues. (3) This dismantling of the created order in Egypt (vv. 26–36) is followed by YHWH's act of re-creation (vv. 39–41) through the provision for Israel's physical needs in the wilderness. In these three ways, the psalmist draws the audience's attention to YHWH's sovereign power in and over creation as additional evidence for his ability to keep his covenant promise of land.

YHWH's Sovereignty Shown in the Dis-Ordering of Creation

By moving the plague of darkness to the beginning of the account (v. 28), the psalmist is able to show a gradual unraveling of the events of creation depicted in Genesis 1. By presenting YHWH's judgment on Egypt as a systematic dismantling of creation, the psalmist shows YHWH's abiding sovereignty in and over his creation.[33] Table 2 offers a helpful summary of the events as seen in Genesis 1 and Psalm 105.

Day	Genesis 1	Psalm 105
1 + 4 Heaven	Light + Luminaries (Sun, Moon, Stars)	Darkness (v. 28a) + It became dark (v. 28b)
2 + 5 Waters	Water separated + Life populates water	Waters turned to blood (v. 29a) + Fish in water died (v. 29b)
3 + 6 Earth	(a) Dry land made + Living creatures according to their kinds	(a) Land swarmed with frogs, flies and gnats (vv. 30–31)
	(b) Vegetation multiplies + Man was created	(b) Vegetation destroyed (vv. 32–35) + Egyptian first-born died (v. 36)

Table 7.2: Comparison of Ordering of Events in Genesis 1 and Psalm 105[34]

33. Ziony Zevit argues a similar point in regards to Gen 1 and the account of the plagues in Exodus, namely, "what Yahweh demonstrated through the plagues was that he was lord of creation" (Zevit, "The Priestly Redaction and Interpretation of the Plague Narrative in Exodus," 198). Zevit's argument is based on the cumulative effect of the plagues, not by their specific ordering. He also acknowledges the deficiencies of his argument: "The hypothesis that Pr interpreted the plague traditions in the light of the creation narratives of the primeval history does not clarify the significance or the position of boils in the plague sequence; nor does it explain the position of darkness in the sequence" (p. 211). As will be seen in what follows, Psalm 105's selection and ordering of the plagues coheres much closer to Gen 1.

34. I am indebted to Archie Lee for this visual presentation of the relevant material (Lee, "Genesis I and the Plagues Tradition in Psalm CV," 259). This table reflects Lee's modification of the material appearing in Anderson, "A Stylistic Study of the Priestly Creation Story," 157. My own study expands on Lee's observations to explain the rhetorical function of the re-casted plague account within the broader argument of the psalm as a whole.

Part 1: Creation

Similar to Genesis 1, Psalm 105 exhibits a movement from the heavens, to the waters, to the earth. But also within the psalmist's ordering, one finds correspondences within the days of creation described in Genesis 1. Just as God brought forth light on Day One and on Day Four set the sun and the moon and the stars to give light upon the earth, so he shows his power in sending forth darkness (v. 28a) and restricting the luminaries in their appointed tasks in the heavens (v. 28b).[35] The fresh waters established on Day Two are now polluted (v. 29a) and the fish that live in them die (v. 29b), a direct reversal of the command to the fish on Day Five: "Be fruitful and multiply and fill the waters in the seas" (Gen 1:22a). The separation of Land and Sea that occurs on Day Three are instead brought together as frogs, flies, and gnats (all creatures whose lives are dependent on water) now swarm upon the earth (v. 30–31).[36] In addition, instead of the multiplication of vegetation on the land as seen on Day Three, Psalm 105:35 presents a picture of the total consumption of all the plants of the land and the fruit of the ground by locusts and grasshoppers.[37] And lastly, just as the final divine act on Day Six is the creation of the first man and woman, so here in Psalm 105, it is the death of the first-born that stands as the climax and conclusion to the plagues against Egypt. By recasting the plague account in the guise of Genesis 1, the psalmist is able to present the plagues on the land of Egypt as an "undoing of the heavens and the earth." In this judgment, YHWH displays his enduring sovereignty over creation itself.

YHWH's Sovereignty Shown through Direct Involvement in the Plagues

The psalmist's rendering of the plagues is also intentionally crafted to emphasize YHWH's direct involvement in this undoing of creation. In the Exodus account of the plagues, Moses and Aaron serve as the human agents for enacting YHWH's commands.[38] Within Psalm 105's depiction of the plagues, Moses and Aaron are mentioned briefly at the start of the account (v. 26); however, as the account continues, their presence is ignored. For here in Psalm 105, YHWH directly conducts the plagues, needing no human agent acting on his behalf. It is YHWH who *sent* darkness (v. 28), *turned* waters to blood (v. 29a), *caused the fish to die* (v. 29b).[39] He *spoke* and

---

35. While this is not the only solution offered for this reference "they did not rebel against his words" (ולא־מרו את־דבריו) in 28b, I would argue that seeing the luminaries as the subject makes good sense when seen within the structure of Gen 1. This proposal helps to explain the plural verbal form (i.e. the *kethiv*) used in the psalm.

36. Hossfeld and Zenger, *Psalms 3*, 72–73.

37. Berlin observes that the psalmist's use of the terms עשׂב ("grass") and פרי ("fruit") in verse 35 provides both a parallel to the destruction of the locust plague in the Exodus account (Exod 10:15), as well as a reference back to the creation account where these are "the two species of vegetation that represent the totality of the plant world (Gn 1.12)" (Berlin, "Interpreting Torah Traditions in Psalm 105," 23). This combination of terms occurs only in Gen 1:11, 12, 29; Exod 10:15; Ps 72:16; 105:35.

38. Throughout the narrative, Moses and Aaron are commanded to perform an action (e.g., raise their staff, strike the water/dust, etc.) that would result in the designated plague.

39. Goldingay comments on the psalmist's use of the *hiphil* in verse 29b. He observes that by

there were swarms of flies and gnats (v. 31). He *gave* hail for rain (v. 32), *struck* vines/fig trees, *shattered* their trees (v. 33). He *spoke* again and locusts came (v. 34); he *struck down* the first born of land (v. 36).⁴⁰ The psalmist recounts the events with a succession of 3ms verbs with the result that, as Kraus observes, "the sovereign rule of Yahweh [is] emphasized by the verbal beginnings of sentences."⁴¹ In addition, YHWH's sovereignty is shown through a direct correlation between divine word and resulting action. Genesis 1 establishes a pattern of spoken word ("and God said," ויאמר אלהים) and resulting fulfillment ("and it was so," ויהי כן).⁴² In Psalm 105, the direct link of divine word and result ("he spoke and there came," אמר ויבא) occurs in the descriptions of the swarms of flies and gnats (v. 31) and with the locusts (v. 34).⁴³ The psalmist's depiction of YHWH as the active agent in the plague account offers additional support for his sovereign power over the created world.

YHWH's Sovereignty Shown through Acts of Re-creation

Psalm 105's short depiction of Israel's journey through the wilderness (vv. 39–41) is also crafted to depict YHWH's sovereign control of creation. After dismantling the created order in Egypt, YHWH provides for Israel's needs in the wilderness as an act of re-creation.⁴⁴ YHWH who brought darkness in v. 28, now brings fire "to light" (להאיר) the night (v. 39b). After decimating the agricultural lands of Egypt (vv. 32–35), YHWH now provides unexpected food from above—quail and bread from heaven (לחם שמים) in v. 40. In addition, with the same ease of turning the waters of Egypt to

---

changing the Exodus' *qal* to a *hiphil* form (cf. Exod 7:18, 21 "the fish die") the psalmist places the "explicit emphasis on Yhwh's sovereign action" (Goldingay, *Psalms 90–150*, 214).

40. As Hossfeld observes: "Dominant throughout is the subject who causes the plagues, YHWH—absent only in the case of the plague of frogs (v. 30) and the description of the effects of the plague of locusts (v. 35)" (Hossfeld and Zenger, *Psalms 3*, 67).

41. Kraus, *Psalms 60–150*, 311.

42. We find this linguistic pattern associated with the acts of creating the expanse (Gen 1:6/7; Day 2), waters (Gen 1:9; Day 3), vegetation (Gen 1:11; Day 3), lights in sky (Gen 1:14/15; Day 4), living creatures (Gen 1:24; Day 6), and in the provision of food for humanity and the animals (Gen 1:29/30; Day 6).

43. It is worthy of note that this convention of spoken word and the surety of its accomplishment appeared first in the opening movement of Psalm 105's recital, here as a statement of YHWH's trustworthiness to keep his promise of land by recalling his word of promise: "He is mindful of his covenant forever, of the word that he commanded, for a thousand generations, the covenant that he made with Abraham, his sworn promise to Isaac, which he confirmed to Jacob as a statute, to Israel as an everlasting covenant, saying, 'To you I will give the land of Canaan as your portion for an inheritance'" (vv. 8–11, NRSV).

44. One finds a similar re-creation following the de-creation brought about by the flood (Genesis 6–8). Regarding the divine promises found in Gen 8:22, Walton observes God's reaffirmation of the functional order established in the opening days of creation: time, weather, and food (Walton, *Genesis 1 as Ancient Cosmology*, 165). It is interesting to note that here in Psalm 105 two of these arenas are addressed—time (light) and food (manna/quail)—although these divine gifts are pictured as contrary to their excepted spheres—light (at night) and food (from the heavens).

blood (v. 29), YHWH turns to a desert rock to provide waters that flow like "a river" (נהר, v. 41) to satisfy Israel's thirst. On the heels of the plagues, this account of divine provision for Israel offers an ironic reversal of the judgment experienced by Egypt in the plagues (vv. 26–36). Here YHWH proclaims his sovereignty over creation as he draws upon the resources of the heavens—quail and heavenly bread—and the earth—water from a rock—to meet the needs of his people.

Conclusion

In this chapter, I have proposed that the psalmist's depiction of the plagues as an "undoing" of the creation order serves to emphasize YHWH's enduring sovereignty over creation itself. This proclamation of divine sovereignty, rooted in a creational foundation, provides additional evidence in support of YHWH's trustworthiness to keep his covenant promise of land—the key argument of the psalm as a whole (vv. 8–11).[45] To a people in exile, YHWH's promise of land must have felt like an elusive hope. In order to bolster this argument, the psalmist reminds the audience that it is the "Creator of the heavens and the earth" who stands behind this promise.

Bibliography

Allen, Leslie C. *Psalms 101–150*. WBC 21. Nashville: Nelson, 2002.

Anderson, Bernhard. "A Stylistic Study of the Priestly Creation Story." In *Canon and Authority: Essays in Old Testament Religion and Theology*, edited by George W. Coats and Burke O. Long, 148–62. Philadelphia: Fortress, 1977.

Berlin, Adele. "Interpreting Torah Traditions in Psalm 105." In *Jewish Biblical Interpretation and Cultural Exchange: Comparative Exegesis in Context*, edited by Natalie B. Dohrmann and David Stern, 20–36. Philadelphia: University of Pennsylvania Press, 2008.

Brettler, Marc Z. "The Poet as Historian: The Plague Tradition in Psalm 105." In *Bringing the Hidden to Light: The Process of Interpretation, Studies in Honor of Stephen A. Geller*, edited by Kathryn F. Kravitz and Diane M. Sharon, 19–28. Winona Lake, IN: Eisenbrauns, 2007.

Briggs, Charles A. *A Critical and Exegetical Commentary on the Book of Psalms*. Vol. 2. ICC. New York: Scribner, 1907.

Ceresco, A. R. "A Poetic Analysis of Ps 105, with Attention to Its Use of Irony." *Bib* 64 (1983) 20–46.

Clifford, Richard J. *Psalms 73–150*, AOTC. Nashville: Abingdon, 2003.

———. "Style and Purpose in Psalm 105." *Bib* 60 (1979) 420–27.

Crüsemann, F. *Studien zur Formgeschichte von Hymnus und Danklied in Israel*. WMANT 32. Neukirchen-Vluyn: Neukirchener, 1969.

---

45. Longman and Walton find a similar rhetorical connection between creation, re-creation, and covenant in Genesis 1–11. Regarding the inclusion of the flood narrative, they note that the narrator "is showing how God had worked to bring about order in the past (creation and flood). This serves as an introduction to Yahweh's strategy to advance order yet again through the covenant" (Longman and Walton, *The Lost World of the Flood*, 120).

Fensham, Frank Charles. "Neh. 9 and Pss. 105, 106, 135 and 136: Post-exilic Historical Traditions in Poetic Form." *JNSL* 9 (1981) 35–51.

Fox, Michael V. "The Rhetoric of Ezekiel's Vision of the Valley of the Bones." *HUCA* 51 (1980) 1–15.

Goldingay, John. *Psalms 90–150*, BCOTWP. Grand Rapids: Baker Academic, 2008.

Gunkel, Hermann, and Joachim Begrich. *An Introduction to Psalms: The Genres of the Religious Lyric of Israel*. Translated by James D. Nogalski. Mercer Library of Biblical Studies. Macon, GA: Mercer University Press, 1998.

Hossfeld, Frank-Lothar, and Erich Zenger. *Psalms 3: A Commentary on Psalm 101–150*. trans. Linda M. Maloney. Hermeneia. Minneapolis: Fortress, 2011.

Kirkpatrick, A. F. *The Book of Psalms, Book 4 and 5, Psalms 90–150*. Cambridge: Cambridge University Press, 1912.

Kraus, Hans-Joachim. *Psalms 60–150: A Commentary*. Translated by Hilton C. Oswald. Continental Commentaries Minneapolis: Augsburg, 1989.

Lee, Archie. C. C. "Genesis I and the Plagues Tradition in Psalm CV." *VT* 40 (1990) 257–63.

Lemmelijn, Bénédicte. "Genesis' Creation Narrative: The Literary Model for the So-Called Plague Tradition?" In *Studies in the Book of Genesis: Literature, Redaction and History*, BETL 155, edited by André Wénin, 407–19. Leuven: Leuven University Press, 2001.

Loewenstamm, Samuel E. *The Evolution of the Exodus Tradition*, trans. Baruch J. Schwartz. Jerusalem: Magnus, 1992.

———. "The Number of Plagues in Psalm 105." *Bib* 52 (1971) 34–38.

Longman, Tremper, III, and John H. Walton. *The Lost World of the Flood: Mythology, Theology, and the Deluge Debate*. Downers Grove, IL: InterVarsity, 2018.

Margulis, B. B. "The Plagues Tradition in Psalm 105." *Bib* 50 (1969) 491–96.

Mays, James Luther. *Psalms*. Interpretation. Louisville: John Knox, 1994.

Ruiten, Jacques T. A. G. M. van. "Back to Chaos: The Relationship between Jeremiah 4:23–26 and Genesis 1." In *The Creation of Heaven and Earth: Re-interpretations of Genesis 1 in the Context of Judaism, Ancient Philosophy, Christianity, and Modern Physics*, edited by George H. van Kooten, 21–30. Themes in Biblical Narrative 8. Leiden: Brill, 2005.

Stinson, Michelle A., "'A Table in the Wilderness?': The Rhetorical Function of Food Language in Psalm 78." PhD diss., University of Bristol, 2017.

Tucker, W. Dennis, Jr. "Revisiting the Plagues in Psalm CV." *VT* 55 (2005) 401–11.

Walton, John H. *Genesis 1 as Ancient Cosmology*. University Park: Pennsylvania State University Press, 2010.

Westermann, Claus. *Praise and Lament in the Psalms*. Translated by Keith R. Crim and Richard N. Soulen. Atlanta: John Knox, 1981.

Zevit, Ziony. "The Priestly Redaction and Interpretation of the Plague Narrative in Exodus." *JQR* 67 (1976) 193–211.

Part 2

Covenant

8

The Difference God Makes for Considering Scripture, Creation, and Covenant

CHRISTOPHER R. J. HOLMES

Introduction

I AM GRATEFUL TO Professor John Walton. He introduced me, as an undergraduate in the mid 1990s, to the riches of Old Testament Scripture. His love for Scripture, and the care with which he handles it, are contagious. In this chapter, I show my appreciation for Walton by critically engaging his summative work, *Old Testament Theology for Christians: From Ancient Context to Enduring Belief*. I do so in dialogue with the late and well-known British theologian, John Webster. I use Webster's work so as to test some of Walton's basic assumptions about Scripture, creation, and covenant as well as the way that these theological themes relate to one another. Moving with and beyond Webster, I argue that Walton's groundwork could be enriched by applying a more sustained theocentricity from the perspective of systematic theology. My interaction with Walton's work is undertaken with the notion that the best complement one can pay a former teacher is that of taking their work seriously, that is on its own terms, but not, in so doing, remaining bound by necessity to it. In his approach to Old Testament Theology, Walton acknowledges that the type of biblical theology he explores is more descriptive than synthetic, and pertains more to the past and historical developments than the present.[1] In this chapter I examine the implications of Walton's work in light of a more synthetic perspective for modern Christian thought and practice, showing that the decisive matter in thinking through the nature of Scripture, creation, and covenant is God. God matters most. By reflecting upon the way in which God is the

---

1. Walton, *Old Testament Theology*, 13.

Part 2: Covenant

key to understanding Scripture's nature as well as the relation between creation and covenant, our thinking is sanctified and enriched. It is also rendered more transparent to the biblical testimony.

A Communicative God

Regarding the central message of scripture, Walton affirms that "the most important message of the Old Testament is found in what it teaches about God."[2] I think that this claim can be productively clarified and expanded within the framework of the theological doctrine of God. The Old Testament, as with the New, is Holy Scripture, God's written Word. This is a theological claim, best made in relation to the doctrine of God. Let me explain. God employs textual emissaries and ambassadors because God is a communicative God. God is love, and because God is love he freely gives life to and addresses creatures. The ultimate author of the text of Holy Scripture is God. God speaks as God, as the very plenitude of being itself, through Scripture and thus through the writings of these human agents. God is not in need of creatures but creates them, speaks to them through Scripture, and upholds them in being through the preaching and sacraments of the church because God is life, love, beauty, goodness, and truth *in se*. God is not a contingent being but rather creates contingent beings in order that they may share in his nature and love him as the beings they are.

Why is this important to think about, especially in relation to bibliology? As John Webster has argued in his now classic discussion of Scripture's character in *Holy Scripture: A Dogmatic Sketch*, "the proper location for a Christian theological account of the nature of Holy Scripture is the Christian doctrine of God."[3] The God we encounter in Scripture is profoundly loquacious. His desire to communicate with us who are not God is reflective of what and who he is, the supremely good Trinity, Father, Son, and Spirit. Accordingly, Scripture's contingent character is not to be worried about. What Walton calls "historical inquiry" is important insofar as it helps us appreciate that the characters, events, and indeed narrative of Scripture are located in a particular time and place.[4] And yet, unless "historical inquiry" is subservient to matters metaphysical, indeed the metaphysics of the divine life, then assertions about Scripture as Scripture—God's written Word—remain less than robust. Without considering God, it is, in other words, impossible to answer the question of why there is something and not nothing, and why the something includes Scripture? The doctrine of Scripture assumes an ultimate horizon and that is God. Scripture has a basic principle of intelligibility, and that is God. Scripture is the living voice of God.

When "issues of interpretation are subservient to issues of the matter of the text," then, following Webster, the actual "matter of the text," which is God and his

2. Walton, *Old Testament Theology*, 29.
3. Webster, *Holy Scripture*, 39.
4. Walton, *Old Testament Theology*, 25.

self-communication, is transcendent of the voice of the human author(s)/redactors.[5] In Joseph Cardinal Ratzinger's words, "a text can say more than its author himself was capable of conceiving at the moment of writing it."[6] The Old Testament authors, as with the New Testament authors, are the means by which God speaks. They speak as they do because of God. Their voice is the voice of the living God, which is not to suggest for a moment that their voice competes with his voice. God addresses us through their voices. If such is the case, then, what unlocks, ultimately, "the theology revealed in the Old Testament for Christians," is God.[7] That these texts speak to Jews (and Gentiles) as they do is because of God. As Ratzinger notes, "faith [in God] is truly the spirit out of which Scripture was born and is therefore the only door that leads into its inner heart."[8]

If God is the ultimate author of Scripture, then we must strive to be intimate to God if we are to hear God's voice, scripturally speaking, and respond in faith.[9] A given human author's intention matters, to be sure, but the author's intention is radically subservient to God's, though God's voice and that of the human authors do not contend with one another. There is, without doubt, a kind of non-competitive asymmetry that exists between the two. We see this dynamic at work, for example, in the Servant Songs in second Isaiah, specifically Isa 53:2–3. An approach that ignores this dynamic, privileging the human voice in accordance with the canons of modern historical criticism, is embodied in the commentary of the late Roman Catholic biblical scholar Joseph Blenkinsopp. He writes of these verses: we see "a co-religionist who had come to believe in the Servant's mission and message, one who in all probability was a disciple, speaks about the origin and appearance of the Servant, the sufferings he endured, and his heroic and silent submission to death."[10] Blenkinsopp's sole concern is the author's context; the author's message is purely historical in nature. The text's significance and horizon are indeed exhausted by its context.

A quite different approach, one that recognizes God speaking in and through the human voice, is embodied by the twentieth century Swiss Reformed theologian Karl Barth. Of this passage he writes, "Jesus Christ does present this aspect of Himself, and He always presents this aspect first." Barth continues, asking, "Who sees and believes that the One who has been abased is the One who is exalted, that this very man is very God?"[11] The Servant is Jesus Christ; the horizon of significance is ultimately him. It

---

5. Webster, *Holy Scripture*, 81. Webster understands the "matter" in more Christological terms than do I. Nonetheless, the point stands because interpretation stands downstream of God, in particular God's will to communicate with creatures.

6. Ratzinger, "Biblical Interpretation," 26.

7. Walton, *Old Testament Theology*, 26.

8. See Ratzinger, "Biblical Interpretation," 29.

9. Walton, *Old Testament Theology*, 5.

10. Blenkinsopp, *Isaiah 40–55*, 349.

11. Barth, *CD* II/1, 665–66.

is Jesus who is "the suffering God and triumphant man, the beauty of God which is the beauty of Jesus Christ." In this, Barth very much follows the lead of Calvin. Calvin comments though in a way that highlights the importance of faith, "Hence we see that we must not judge the glory of Christ by human view but must discern by faith what the Holy Scriptures teach about him."[12] Calvin, like Barth, assumes that the Servant is Jesus Christ, that the prophet's voice is God's, and that the passage crystallizes the importance of Christ's passion and death. They both affirm that the prophet is speaking of Jesus Christ, full stop. In so doing, they are not imposing upon the text but rather receiving the Servant's message in all of its christological fullness. As the evangelical biblical scholar of Isaiah, J. Alec Motyer notes, "Nothing but divine revelation can make the Servant known and draw us to him." And Motyer, like Calvin, appreciates the urgency of faith: "it was not easy to believe that he [the Servant] could be the Lord come to save."[13]

We have human authors and texts because we have God. The prophets and apostles have the authority that they do and speak as they do because of God. As Augustine notes, "'O man, what my scripture says, I say.'"[14] God appoints them and elects to speak through them. For bibliology, there is nothing more important than God, which is true of all Christian teachings. Accordingly, when we read, we do not so much think in terms of a lens—an "Israelite" as opposed to a "Christian" lens, to use Walton's language—but rather in terms of mortification and vivification.[15] Are we the kind of people who, by the regenerative work of the Spirit, are able to hear? Do we even want to hear the words of the prophets and apostles as the Word of the Lord? The answers to these questions are as much spiritual as intellectual.

To be sure, Walton is right to draw attention to the likelihood of our misunderstanding "some of what is going on as we navigate ancient language and culture." We do (and will) miss out on some things. This is because "the Old Testament *is* an ancient text written to another culture."[16] But again, there are also other reasons why we will miss out on things, one of which is our hard heartedness. I would like to supplement Walton's identification of historical and cultural barriers by focusing also on spiritual barriers. Receiving the Old Testament Word of the Lord is as much an endeavor in cultural and historical understanding as one of spiritual discernment. The Old Testament's purpose is to equip us to love God and to love our neighbor in relation to God. Its reason for being is that we might live before God in the fear and holiness of God to the glory of God.

With respect to Scripture, the intention that is the most important is God's. Indeed, why does God employ authors in the first place? God employs them because it

12. Calvin, *Isaiah*, 322.
13. Motyer, *Isaiah*, 429, 427.
14. Augustine, *Confessions*, 300.
15. Walton, *Old Testament Theology*, 25, 26.
16. Walton, *Old Testament Theology*, 269.

is his will to do so. The text's authority has to do with God, not with the merits or lack thereof of the human authors and redactors. "Historical inquiry" is important insofar as it helps us appreciate the contingencies employed by God to speak his Word, but historical inquiry yields little theological fruit unless undergirded by a robust sense of God's grandeur. Why is there something (a creation) and not nothing? The answer is God. Why is there a history of God with creatures (the covenant)? The answer is God. Why are the great acts of creation, sustenance, redemption, and perfection recorded, scripturally speaking? The answer is God.

The God who spoke to "our ancestors," to use the language of Hebrews, speaks today (Heb 1:1). The Old Testament authors are the means by which God speaks. The same of course is true of the New Testament. Their voice is annexed to his voice, which is not to suggest that his voice strives with their voice. When a Christian community sings the Psalms, for example, they sing the Psalms of Israel, the same Psalms that are sung by the synagogue. The same God is being worshipped by both Christians and Jews through the Psalms of Israel. And yet, the Christian community understands in faith that the Psalms, following Dietrich Bonhoeffer's lead, "have [first] to do with Jesus Christ."[17] All of Scripture has to do with Christ, and Christ, of course, has to do with God the Father: "God from God, Light from Light," to use the Creedal language. When considering Scripture and how to receive it as such, the matter of whose texts these are is decisive.

Put differently, the audience for the Old Testament as well as the New is the people of God. Of course, the church and synagogue differ profoundly over the identity of Jesus Christ, and yet they are one—one hopes—in listening to the Hebrew scriptures as the Word of God. There is, accordingly, a kind of universality to the Old Testament. The God who addresses his people through these texts has an "audience" in mind, and that audience is, ultimately, all people, Jews and Gentiles. His scriptural Word creates a people, and these texts before us are *of* his covenant people but *from* him. Where is the Old Testament (as with the New Testament) from? They are from God.

Regenerated Hearing

Reading Scripture is a spiritual undertaking. It involves the mortification and vivification in Word and Spirit of our intellect, mind, and will. There is no getting around this. To receive Scripture as the living voice of God means, as Ratzinger argues, "the demand for readiness to open oneself to the dynamism of the Word."[18] Or, to use Webster's perceptive language, "the textual word which is the concern of exegesis . . . announces itself in its own proper communicative vigour."[19] The reason many Christians are impatient with or indifferent to the Old Testament reflects a spiritual

---

17. Ratzinger, "Biblical Interpretation," 29; Bonhoeffer, *Prayerbook*, 157.
18. Ratzinger, "Biblical Interpretation," 21.
19. Webster, *Holy Scripture*, 82.

pathology. Greater than the hermeneutical problem is the spiritual problem. We (the Christian community) assume that there is not a Word to hear in the Old Testament Scriptures. We lack humility. We forget "that the deeds that occurred in the Old Testament have their basis in a future deed in light of which it first becomes possible to understand them correctly."[20] That future deed is of course Jesus Christ, "through" whom and "for" whom are "all things," the "through" including Scripture (Col 1:16).

Furthermore, Jesus is from God; the Son is eternally generated by the Father. The question of Jesus' origin is the question that animates the Fourth Gospel—"Where are you from?"[21] Are you from above, that is from the Father, or from below, from the prince of demons? The same question may be posed of Scripture. Where is it from? From above, that is from God? Or, from below, that is from us? Scripture is from God, as is the case with creation and covenant. And yet, this Word from God takes textual form; it is, in a secondary sense, from us. But how do we receive the words of men as the Word of God? How do we receive these textual words as from above? The key is open hands and ears as supplied by the Spirit. Such transparency encourages what Webster calls "a relinquishment of willed mastery of the text."[22] The reader(s), in other words, needs to be reborn if she is to receive this text as from above. What is true in matters of Christology is true in matters of bibliology.

To say this in another way, when a Christian community prays, sings, and chants the Psalms, they engage with that which bears Christ. The audience for the Psalms is the people of God, both Christians and Jews. Jews and Christians are one in singing the Psalms as God's gift. The Psalms in all of their particularity have a wide horizon, and that is because of God, their ultimate source and condition for reception. The God who blesses his people Israel and in turn the church with the Psalter blesses them with human words—mostly David's words—that are nonetheless words from God. To be sure, the contextual "home" of these texts is the Temple. However, these texts, as with all of Scripture, transcend their original *sitz im leben* because of God. What is definitive for them, which is also true of creation and covenant, as we will consider in a moment, is God, for God is a loquacious God, a communicative God. The decisive principle for receiving Scripture as Scripture is God. Metaphysical inquiry is the context for all other forms of inquiry, whether they be hermeneutical, historical, philological, etc.

Moving forward, let us consider why there is something and not nothing, and why God's covenantal determination to restore this something from the ravages of nothingness demands the same kind of unrelenting theocentrism as does our consideration of bibliology. As we will see, the relationship between creation and covenant is best elucidated in relation to God. The Scriptures tell us about the heart of why there

---

20. Ratzinger, "Biblical Interpretation," 24.

21. See, e.g., John 9:29; 19:9. The latter runs, "He [Pilate] entered his headquarters again and asked Jesus, 'Where are you from?' But Jesus gave him no answer."

22. Webster, *Holy Scripture*, 88.

is something. There is something because of God, for God creates this something in order to share his life with it. Relationship is not only "the goal," as Walton notes, but the beginning of creation and covenant as well, for God creates what exists in such a way that it is a participated reality.[23] What exists *is* in relationship to God, though the reverse is not true. God does not exist in relationship to what he has made; creation is not necessary to God. And so, let us turn to creation, in order to explore how it, like Scripture, has its intelligibility, first and foremost, in relation to God.

The Triune Creator and Covenant-maker

The first truth to affirm is that the created order is caused by God. The heart of a doctrine of creation is God. We have Scripture because God is communicative, and we have a created order (something) because of what Webster calls the "infinite uncreated and wholly realized movement of God's life in himself."[24] Accordingly, God does not create something because God is in need of completion, just as God does not speak to us in Scripture because God is lonely and therefore requires a covenant partner. God's aseity and impassibility is "an affirmation that the world has value in itself."[25] As Walton helpfully notes, the Old Testament firmly rejects what he terms "the Great Symbiosis" wherein it is "the responsibility of the humans . . . to meet the needs of the gods."[26] God does not speak a world into being in order to assuage some compulsion, which is good news! Creation is not "intrinsic to God's fullness."[27] Rather, God creates not only because of who he is—Trinity—but what he is—love. Creation makes sense with respect to the who and what of God.

In terms of the what of God, why does God create? Because he is good, goodness itself. Goodness is what God is. God creates a heaven and earth that are very good because God is exceedingly good. It is in the very nature of divine goodness to give of itself. Moreover, the supremely good God who creates is Trinity, Father, Son, and Spirit. This is who God is. Articulation of the identity of the Creator is important, of course, but so too is the being of the God who creates. Yes, it is appropriate to describe God in agential terms, but equally important is description of God in being terms. It is fitting to speak of God as being in act "but by 'act' here we do not restrict ourselves to those acts whereby God establishes, preserves, redeems and perfects creatures, for we also—primarily—refer to the infinite underivative movement of God in himself."[28]

In greater detail, the created order is from the Father, the first person of the holy and blessed Trinity. He of course creates through the Son, the agent of creation, and in

23. Walton, *Old Testament Theology*, 68.
24. Webster, "Trinity and Creation," 4.
25. Webster, "Trinity and Creation," 13.
26. Walton, *Old Testament Theology*, 102.
27. Webster, "Trinity and Creation," 12.
28. Webster, "Trinity and Creation," 7.

the Spirit, the perfecter of creation, the Lord and giver of life. The Scriptures, in telling us who creates the something, also tell us why there is something and not nothing. There is something because of God, God's will to have a covenant partner who loves and praises him. God creates a world that is important in and of itself. God's relation "to created being is gratuitous."[29]

What might this imply for understanding the relationship between creation and covenant? First and foremost, it infers that God creates with a view to covenant; God desires to be in covenant relationship with us, though not of course because God is needy. God does not speak into being a world in order to address a lack.[30] Rather, God the Father creates us through Christ and in the Spirit with a view to our being his friends. As Webster notes, "the founding condition of creation and its history is the Son or Word who as very God shares in the undivided divine essence."[31] The creation of the world thus makes sense, first and foremost, in relation to the Father as the fount of deity in the divine life and thus "the originating cause of creatures."[32] Second, creation also makes sense with respect to the Word as "the exemplary and efficient" cause and, third, the Spirit as the "perfecting" cause.[33] Covenant is "the most distinguishing feature of Old Testament theology," to be sure, but the covenant assumes a context which is the created order whose basic presupposition is the triune God.[34] This motif, as readers will know, is frequently found in the Old Testament, for example Ezek 37:27: "I will be their God, and they shall be my people."

The covenant, as Walton helpfully notes, is the means by which we "participate in God's plans and purposes."[35] This is a prevalent theme in Walton's account. The covenant is a participatory reality, standing at the center of God's designs. Yahweh, by way of the covenant, "*enlists Israel*" in the service of his will, which is that he might indwell them. Indeed, he created the world for a people who would know and adore him.[36] Men, women, and children, created in his image and restored to his likeness, are the crowning glory of his work. God's work in relation to the world is not static. Creation and covenant have their reason for being in God. God is and remains their principle. The creator is always at work maintaining order, upholding what he has made in order that it might fulfill his purposes by sharing in the history of the covenant.

---

29. This is not to say that what exists, in terms of human persons, necessarily exists in a saving relationship to God.

30. The Old Testament firmly rejects what Walton calls "the Great Symbiosis" wherein it is "the responsibility of the humans . . . to meet the needs of the gods." See Walton, *Old Testament Theology*, 102.

31. Webster, "Trinity and Creation," 18.

32. Webster, "Trinity and Creation," 17.

33. Webster, "Trinity and Creation," 18.

34. Walton, *Old Testament Theology*, 65.

35. Walton, *Old Testament Theology*, 45.

36. Walton, *Old Testament Theology*, 58.

Just so, the covenant is not the end game. It is as Walton notes "a mechanism" by which God reveals himself and prepares us for his indwelling.[37] As with the tabernacle and the temple, the covenant serves God's overarching purpose, that is, the creation of a people whom he inhabits in all his sublime glory. Accordingly, the covenant assumes God; God is its principle of intelligibility, as is the case with creation. Yes, the covenant confers a status, but as Walton reminds us, the law of the covenant—Torah—exhorts us to be covenant partners. The covenant contains an imperative, a do this—for example, "be holy" (Lev 11:44). Herein we see a key link between the doctrine of creation and the covenant. Both contain a call. To live as one created is to live as *God's* covenant partner. This is the summons that Israel's election bestows upon it, and the summons that the church receives in Christ.

Our awareness of the graciousness of this covenantal call is heightened by attention to the ancient Near Eastern context. God does not call Israel into existence because he is destitute. Herein lies the chief difference between Israel and Israel's neighbors. The gods of Israel's neighbors needed worshippers to make them whole: "the relationship in the ancient Near East was a utilitarian codependence."[38] Israel's God, thankfully, does not need Israel. Instead, he graciously gives Israel "a role in his plan and purposes."[39] God elects Abraham and his descendants simply because he is good, not because he has issues to be worked out. By living in covenant partnership with God, the people "preserve his presence among them."[40] Walton, in a helpful move, notes that "sacred space implies divine presence, and divine presence establishes sacred space."[41] God's establishment of such a space among his people finds its fulfillment in what Paul calls the "all in all" of God in 1 Cor 15:28.

Not surprisingly, the law—the Torah as encapsulated in the Decalogue—is the means by which a holy people are formed, a people among whom God dwells. This is not to suggest that the law has an agency of its own. Rather, God's gives Israel the law so that it might "know how to live in the presence of a holy God and as his covenant people."[42] On the one hand, Israel's holiness denotes a status, an indicative; after all, it is God who sets them apart from the nations. On the other hand, that status includes an imperative, "You shall have no other gods before me" (Exod 20:3). "God's people," Walton avers, "are supposed to reflect his identity."[43] As God's people strive to align themselves with who he reveals himself to be, God presents himself to them. The covenant, and the law as the means by which we are formed into God's covenant partners, restores order. The result, as Walton argues, is the "reestablishment" of the presence

---

37. Walton, *Old Testament Theology*, 105.
38. Walton, *Old Testament Theology*, 151.
39. Walton, *Old Testament Theology*, 112.
40. Walton, *Old Testament Theology*, 148.
41. Walton, *Old Testament Theology*, 149.
42. Walton, *Old Testament Theology*, 164.
43. Walton, *Old Testament Theology*, 175.

lost at Eden.[44] Even so, the great distance between the creator and creature remains intact. Creation is a free act, as is God's rehabilitation of lost creatures through the covenant. The covenant does not erase the distinction between creator and creatures but rather restores it to its proper shape. Sinners that we are, we collapse the distinction. The gift of covenant is a restoration of the distinction intrinsic to creation, what Webster calls "an ever greater disproportion" that is intrinsic to our being as creatures before God.[45]

Concluding Remarks

Part of what is a bit odd, at least to me as a theologian, is Walton's notion of theology. Of theologians, he writes that they "are often, in the end, more interested in defining true beliefs for today than in exegetical determinations of an author's intention in context."[46] I demur. Theology is not so much in the business of defining true belief but rather of seeking faithful understanding of the truth that Holy Scripture presents. This involves to some degree a defining, but to think of theology's tasks in those terms is somewhat reductive. Theology reflects the quest for and is a fruit of "a regenerate intelligence," an intelligence that presents in a praise filled way the great truths of God and how all things relate to God in the light of the fulfillment of God's covenantal purposes in Jesus Christ.[47] Theology involves unfolding, prayerfully, the logic, content, and borders of Christian belief in faithful submission to Scripture. The great teachers of the church catholic are preachers (and quite often teachers of preachers) and as such exegetes, Augustine, Thomas Aquinas, and Calvin being exemplary in this regard. As a theologian, my vocation is to encourage students and parishioners to enter into Holy Scripture, receiving its witness to God with a sanctified heart and mind. The end of study of the sacred page is God and the gaining of spiritual sight by which we might see God and present the fruits of what we see to others.

From this perspective, at the end of the day I am not so much concerned with determining the "author's intention in context" but rather of hearing that author as a witness to God's life-giving Word, Jesus Christ.[48] That being so, the author's words witness in the Spirit to the Word. This is what allows Jesus to say, as he does in Luke 24:44, that "the law of Moses, the prophets, and the psalms" wrote things about him that must be fulfilled. Put differently, the author's intentions are subservient to the

---

44. Walton, *Old Testament Theology*, 218.

45. Webster, "Trinity and Creation," 14. This has resonances with Erich Przywara's magisterial work *Analogia Entis: Metaphysics: Original Structure and Universal Rhythm*. He argues therein in part that God is so set apart from creatures that he is in them, without belonging to them, without entering into their essence "such that created being is genuinely 'set-apart' by its own inner 'essentiality.'" See *Analogia Entis*, 292.

46. Walton, *Old Testament Theology*, 276.

47. Webster, "OMNIA," 3.

48. Walton, *Old Testament Theology*, 276.

Word's intention. The Word, the Lord Jesus Christ, elects their words to bear witness to him, in and by the purifying power of the Spirit. An exegete cannot, as Walton notes, be indifferent to analysis of "the contextual intentions" of the authors. However, that is only one dimension of what I think exegesis is. To exegete a passage is also to take seriously whose words these ultimately are—the Lord's—and why they exist—to bear witness to him in order that we be drawn to a life of loving covenant fellowship with him.

I am, as a theologian, deeply invested in what Walton rightly describes as "theological truth."[49] That said, I do not have the grammatical, linguistic, philological, and historical knowledge that he has. That is not only true of myself but of nearly every other theologian I know. We theologians are not preoccupied with an understanding of the context—small "c." That said, we are interested in the ultimate Context—capital "C"—the Word made flesh, consubstantial with the Father, "the reason for and pattern of the production of creatures."[50] It is this Context that elucidates the context.

The Word speaks to us, together with his Father in their Spirit, through these textual witnesses. The witness of Moses, the prophets, and the psalms takes place in a context. But that context is only intelligible in light of the Context of contexts—God's desire to reveal and to communicate to us something of what and who he is—triune love itself. God matters most, whether it be in terms of a doctrine of Scripture, or an account of creation and the covenant and their interrelation.

The covenant is theocentric and as such a participatory reality. The same is true of the created order: God does not create us as spectators but rather as covenantal partners. God establishes reality, which is himself, and the means—the covenant—by which to enter into his reality and share in his life. And that covenant is not isolated from Christ. The new covenant as fulfilled in him denotes the radicalization and *telos* of God's old covenant intentions to indwell us. The New Covenant is not a "plan b" but a further instantiation of the only plan that God has had all along, namely, for God to be ours and we to be his.[51] The covenant in the dimensions of both Old and New is radically theocentric. The transcendent God—maker of heaven and earth, of all things visible and invisible, wills to indwell us, to be "all in all" (1 Cor 15:28). This of course beggar's belief but part of the gift of Walton's distinguished career is his encouragement of many, many students to taste and to see that the Lord of the covenant—who beggars belief—is good, really very good. Walton's writing and teaching ministry has taken up texts that many of us find difficult and obscure so as to show us how they reflect God's intentions and God's faithfulness to indwell us. That said, the emphasis upon historical inquiry and authorial intentionality would only be enhanced by a greater focus on whose texts these are, namely God's, and why it is that we have scriptural texts in the first place.

49. Walton, *Old Testament Theology*, 281.
50. Webster, "Trinity and Creation," 18.
51. Webster, "Trinity and Creation," 294.

Part 2: Covenant

There is (again) much good news in all of this. Resting upon a strong commitment to divine aseity, the God we encounter in the Old Testament is in no need of us. He is good in and of himself. He communicates goodness to us as the love he is by causing the created order as a theatre of his glory, and as the place where he wills to dwell among us. This is not at all like the other gods encountered in the ancient Near East. Walton's extraordinary knowledge of that lost world helps us to see in no uncertain terms how unique and unusual Israel's God is, calling a people into being not because he needs them but because he is love and loves them accordingly. The Old Testament is not obsolete but revelatory of God and God's purposes, functioning as God's Word then and now.[52] The Old Testament is theological through and through, for it has to do with God, and using historical inquiry to uncover that is important and useful, so long as such inquiry is governed by a strong commitment to what Scripture is and how Scripture's ontology defines its reception.

It would indeed be altogether easy, at first glance, to gravitate toward the New Testament simply because what is New seems better, to many of us anyhow. Walton's many writings are devoted toward reminding us that the New is not better but different. The Old provides a "formal articulation" of the covenantal framework of God with respect to his people, and the New, the fulfillment of the promise upon which the Old rests.[53] The God we encounter therein wills to be intimate with and to us as he is. Without the Old Testament, we would be unaware of the depths of God's majestic kindness and patience, his freedom in creating a world and people for himself. We would also be oblivious to the irrevocability of his purposes, and indifferent toward his will as embodied in the promise: "I will be their God, and they will be my people" (Ezek 37:27). That said, a more sustained theocentricity, along the lines suggested by Webster, takes us to a deeper place whereby we see what kind of people we must become if we are to receive the Lord's scriptural testimony to himself as our maker, upholder, and perfecter in all the blessings of life in covenant fellowship.

Bibliography

Augustine. *Confessions*. Translated by Henry Chadwick. Oxford: Oxford University Press, 1992.
Barth, Karl. *Church Dogmatics*. Edited by G. W. Bromiley and T. F. Torrance. Vol. II.1, *The Doctrine of God*. Edinburgh: T. & T. Clark, 1957.
Blenkinsopp, Joseph. *Isaiah 40–55*. AB 19A; New York: Doubleday, 2002.
Bonhoeffer, Dietrich. *Life Together and Prayerbook of the Bible*. Edited by Geffrey B. Kelly. Translated by James H. Burtness. Dietrich Bonhoeffer Works 5. Minneapolis: Fortress, 1996.
Calvin, John. *Isaiah*. Crossway Classic Commentary Series. Wheaton, IL: Crossway, 2000.

---

52. Webster, "Trinity and Creation," 25.
53. Walton, *Old Testament Theology*, 26.

Motyer, J. Alec. *The Prophecy of Isaiah: An Introduction & Commentary*. Downers Grove, IL: InterVarsity, 1993.

Ratzinger, Joseph Cardinal. "Biblical Interpretation in Conflict: On the Foundations and the Itinerary of Exegesis Today." In *Biblical Interpretation in Crisis: The Ratzinger Conference on Bible and Church*, edited by Richard John Neuhaus, 1–23. Grand Rapids: Eerdmans, 1989.

Walton, John H. *Old Testament Theology for Christians: From Ancient Context to Enduring Belief*. Downers Grove, IL: InterVarsity, 2017.

Webster, John. *Holy Scripture: A Dogmatic Sketch*. Cambridge: Cambridge University Press, 2003.

———. "Omnia . . . Pertractantur in Sacra Doctrina Sub Ratione Dei. On the Matter of Christian Theology." In *God without Measure: Working Papers in Christian Theology*. London: T. & T. Clark, 2016.

———. "Trinity and Creation." *IJST* 12 (2010) 4–19.

9

The Lost World of the Exodus
Functional Ontology and the Creation of a Nation

Carmen Joy Imes

John Walton has almost single-handedly changed the face of Evangelical Old Testament studies in two significant ways: (1) by bringing the ancient Near Eastern cognitive environment to bear on the biblical text, and (2) by making scholarship on Bible backgrounds accessible to students and laypeople. Three especially helpful resources are his *Zondervan Illustrated Bible Backgrounds Commentary: Old Testament*, *The IVP Bible Background Commentary: Old Testament*, and the *Cultural Backgrounds Study Bible*, which I use in all my classes. However, I suspect Walton will be remembered most for his *Lost World* series, where he has pioneered a genre all his own, beginning with *The Lost World of Genesis One*. Although Walton and I do not always agree, I owe him a great debt of gratitude for his illuminating work on Old Testament backgrounds. It was my privilege to study under him at Wheaton College in 2011, and I have continued to learn from his writings in the years since. I can scarcely imagine where I would be without his influence.

My essay borrows the structure of Walton's *Lost World* books by heading each section with a proposition. My aim is to consider his insights regarding the functional ontology of creation in Genesis in relation to the Exodus narratives. My claims are not ground-breaking—others have noted the features of Exodus that mimic the Genesis creation stories—but this may be the first attempt to explore more fully the notion of functional ontology in the context of Israel's birth as a nation.

What is meant by functional ontology? H. H. Schmid claimed decades ago already that "In the ancient Near East creation faith did not deal only, indeed not even primarily, with the origin of the world. Rather, it was concerned above all with the present world and the natural environment of humanity now."[1] Schmid recognized that material origins were not primarily in view, but rather humanity's function and purpose. It is this claim which Walton has most fully developed in his *Genesis 1 as Ancient Cosmology* and *The Lost World of Genesis One*. As Walton explains, "In the ancient Near East, creation involves bringing order and organization to the cosmos."[2] The issue is not so much that something *exists* (that's ontology proper), but rather the question of what it exists *for*—what is its *telos* or *raison d'être*.

Proposition 1: Exodus is a Creation Story

Creation is far more central to biblical theology than many assume. Schmid calls it the "fundamental theme" of biblical theology.[3] Redemption and creation are deeply intertwined. While Genesis recounts the creation of the cosmos, Exodus recounts the creation of the nation of Israel. Intertextual links bring this out. In the opening chapter of Exodus, we observe that the creation mandate from Gen 1:28 to "be *fruitful* [פרה] and *multiply* [רבה], *fill* [מלא] the *earth* [ארץ] and subdue it" is in the beginning stages of fulfillment.[4] In addition to these four key terms from Gen 1:28, the narrator of Exodus includes several more key words from Genesis 1. In Egypt "the children of Israel were *fruitful* [פרה] and they *teemed* [שרץ; cf. Gen 1:20–21] and they *increased* [רבה] and became *very*, *very* [מאד; Gen 1:31] numerous, and the *land* [ארץ] was *filled* [מלא] with them" (Exod 1:7, author's translation). By echoing key words from Genesis 1, the narrator ensures we hear this new narrative against the backdrop of creation.

As they were leaving Egypt, YHWH commanded them to celebrate a sacred annual festival in which they rested on the first and the *seventh* day, ensuring that their commemoration of redemption re-enacted creation (Exod 12:16). The pattern of seventh-day rest continued as they began their new life as a nation with YHWH's instruction to *consecrate* every *seventh* day (Exod 16:23). At Sinai, God issued the covenant stipulations as ten words (Exod 34:28), corresponding to the ten times God spoke in Genesis 1 and thereby implying that Sinai is the setting for a new creative act.[5] In addition, Moses spent six days on the mountain, and God spoke to him on the seventh to give him the tabernacle instructions (Exod 24:16), reflecting the seven-day structure of Genesis 1.[6]

Aside from these lexical links, we can observe the transformation that happens in Exodus. At the beginning of the book, although the Hebrews were numerous, they

---

1. Schmid, "Creation, Righteousness, and Salvation," 103.
2. Walton, *Genesis 1 as Ancient Cosmology*, 27.
3. Schmid, "Creation, Righteousness, and Salvation," 111.
4. All Scripture quotations are from the NIV unless otherwise noted.
5. On the ten speech-acts of creation, see Blocher, *In the Beginning*, 33.
6. For a thorough discussion, see Boorer, *Vision of the Priestly Narrative*, 138. Also see Proposition 8 below.

lacked agency and a place of their own. After Sinai, they still lacked a permanent home, but they were a nation, complete with a god, a portable temple at which to worship, cultic functionaries, civic leadership, and a constitution outlining their responsibilities as YHWH's covenant people. YHWH had brought into being a new nation. This view from 30,000 feet may be traced out in the particulars of the Exodus story.

Proposition 2: The Beginning State in Exodus 1 is Nonfunctional

In Exodus 1, the narrator paints an inverted picture for us of God's creation design. As mentioned above, it first appears that the Israelites are fulfilling the creation mandate of Genesis 1:28: "Be fruitful and increase in number; fill the earth . . ." The proliferation of words for the numerical growth of the Israelites in Egypt in Exod 1:7 is striking. However, God had not told humans only to multiply. They were also to "subdue" the earth by governing other living creatures, namely animals (Gen 1:28; cf. Exod 1:14). The fulfillment of this creation mandate faltered in Egypt, as those in power subdued and oppressed their fellow humans, the Hebrews. Following human rebellion in the garden, God had declared that interpersonal enmity and oppression would result (Gen 3:15–16). In Exodus, those curses became national in scope, resulting in painful toil and sweat rather than satisfying labor (Exod 1:12–14; cf. Gen 3:17–19, 23). The dark side of human rebellion was on full display. God designed humans to labor freely and creatively and to benefit from their own work (Gen 2:15–16, 19–20), but in Egypt the labor of the Israelites was harsh. Ruthless taskmasters oppressed them. Pharaoh ordered his taskmasters explicitly to deal "wisely" with the Hebrews (Exod 1:10), exhibiting the twisted logic resulting from the archetypal rebellion in Genesis, a desire to define good and evil apart from God. In short, humanity could neither flourish nor fulfill their creation mandate. Terence Fretheim calls Pharaoh's efforts to control the Israelites "fundamentally anti-life and anticreation."[7] The upshot is that "God's very purposes in creation are being subverted and God's mission is threatened."[8] Against this demoralizing backdrop God acted to redeem God's own people.

Proposition 3: Like Cosmology, Nationhood is Function Oriented

One of Walton's most profound and paradigm-shifting contributions to scholarship is his contention that the Genesis creation account concerns functional, rather than material, origins.[9] While he affirms his belief that God made the material cosmos, Walton claims that ancient Near Eastern people were not wondering about the origin of matter, but rather about their place, or function, in the cosmos. That is, their concern was not with *material* ontology, but with *functional* ontology. By investigating other

---

7. Fretheim, *What Kind of God?*, 225.
8. Fretheim, 231.
9. Walton, *The Lost World of Genesis One*.

creation accounts from the ancient Near East, Walton concludes, "cosmic creation in the ancient world was not viewed primarily as a process by which matter was brought into being but as a process by which functions, roles, order, jurisdiction, organization, and stability were established."[10] Accordingly, "the principal acts of creation are naming, separating, and temple building."[11]

This functional paradigm is illuminating for our reading of Exodus. In Exodus, YHWH revealed his name, separated the Hebrews from the Egyptians, gave them a function or role in relation to the nations, put them under new jurisdiction, and instructed them to build a portable temple so God could live among them. Exodus fits Walton's criteria for an ANE creation story. It is not a matter of their material origin. Did the Hebrews already exist before the book of Exodus? Of course. By the time we reach Exodus 1 we have already followed Abraham's family line for several generations. God had promised to bless them with many descendants, land, and a position of influence over other nations (Gen 12:1–3), a promise that God reiterated with each subsequent generation (Gen 26:3–4, 23; 28:13–15). However, by the end of Genesis, the descendants of Jacob were no more than an extended family (note the mention of Joseph's "father's family" in Gen 50:22). And though Joseph addressed "the Israelites" (Gen 50:25), they consisted of only "his brothers" (Gen 50:24). As the book of Exodus begins, the term "Israelites" designates the family descended from Jacob, renamed Israel. They did not even merit the distinction of being an "enemy" of Egypt as a people (see Exod 1:10). Though numerous, they were small potatoes. Their family history was not a matter of state importance (Exod 1:8).

The Egyptians had imposed a modicum of order by appointing some of the Israelites as "overseers" of forced labor (Exod 5:14). However, we have little indication of the Israelites' internal social organization aside from the mention of "Hebrew midwives" in 1:15, "elders" in Exod 4:29, which could refer to aged people rather than official leaders, and "heads of their families" in 6:14. However, YHWH brought them out of Egypt organized by military units ("all YHWH's divisions" [כל־צבאות יהוה]; see 12:41; and "their divisions" in 6:26; cf. 7:4). In the act of leaving Egypt, under the direction of YHWH's servant, Moses, the Israelites exerted opposition to Pharaoh by means of a defiant social structure, a functional step toward nationhood. The narrator provides little information about that structure, but the sense is that they are God's army.

As a corollary to the proposition that nationhood is function oriented, it is helpful to consider the concept of *ḥerem*, which involves the dissolving or dismantling of social structures that ensure the survival of national identity. If nationhood is function oriented, then loss of national function implies loss of nationhood. In their *The Lost World of the Israelite Conquest*, John and J. Harvey Walton contend just this—that the point of *ḥerem* is not the elimination of people, but rather the erasure of national identity via the dismantling of society. This is why the Israelites drive out the inhabitants of

---

10. Walton, *Genesis 1 as Ancient Cosmology*, 34.
11. Walton, 34.

a city but do not pursue those who flee.[12] The Sinai instructions enjoin the Israelites to destroy pagan *implements of worship*—their idols and sacred stones—and "drive out" the inhabitants of the land, not to kill them (Exod 23:23–33). They are not to make covenants with them or share the land with them "because the worship of their gods will certainly be a snare" (v. 33). If the dissolution of a nation does not necessarily involve slaughter of individuals but rather the destruction of cultic implements and the displacement of people, then the creation of a nation would conversely involve the establishment of a place and means of worship and the opportunity to occupy land of their own. This is the heart of the Exodus story.

Proposition 4: Moses' Origin Story Anticipates Israel's Origin Story

The symmetry between Moses' personal origin story and Israel's is illuminating. Moses escaped from Pharaoh twice—once as an infant through dangerous waters due to the subversive ingenuity of the women in his life, and again as an adult when he began to identify with the Hebrews and to take up their cause. His first crime was being a Hebrew baby boy (Exod 1:16). His second crime was righteous anger against injustice that resulted in the death of an Egyptian (Exod 2:11–12). He fled from Pharaoh by leaving Egypt and traveling through the desert. Then he encountered the visible manifestation of the presence of YHWH at Mt. Sinai (Exod 3:2). During this encounter, YHWH identified himself and commissioned Moses for a divinely-appointed task: return to Egypt to confront Pharaoh and rescue the Israelites (Exod 3:10).

His return to Egypt set the second origin story in motion. The Israelites escaped from Pharaoh—first with his permission and then as he chased them through dangerous waters (Exod 12:31–32; 14:5–23). Like Moses, they left Egypt and traveled through the desert. Then they encountered the visible manifestation of the presence of YHWH at Mt. Sinai (Exod 19:16–19). During this encounter, YHWH identified himself and commissioned the Israelites for a divinely-appointed task: serving as YHWH's *segullah* (סגלה), or special ambassador, among the nations (Exod 19:3–6; 20:2, 7).

At its core, Moses' story is one in which he grew into the role God had set out for him to do, from near death in his infancy to national leadership as YHWH's representative. Israel's story recapitulated Moses' story. They transitioned from near death by Pharaoh's hand to international leadership as YHWH's representative. More on this below.

Proposition 5: The Ten Plagues were an Act of Uncreation

All ten of the "plagues," or signs, in Egypt disrupted creation order. The first plague affects "every gathering of their waters" (כל־מקוה מימיהם; Exod 7:19; cf. Gen 1:10),

---

12. Walton and Walton, *Lost World of the Israelite Conquest*, 176–77.

using the jussive form of the verb "let them be blood" (ויהיו־דם; Exod 7:19; cf. Gen 1:3, 6, 14) to echo the creation story while undoing it.[13] Life-giving water became undrinkable for seven days, signaling that each of the plagues that followed would be acts of un-creation (7:25 [8:3]). Frogs, normally water-dwelling, swarmed on land, moving beyond the boundaries of the water in which they were created to swarm (שרץ; Exod 7:28 [8:3]; cf. Gen 1:20). Flies crowded the air.[14] Livestock died. Dust penetrated human and animal skin, causing boils, as if the very material from which they were made attacked them. Hail obliterated growing plants. Locusts infested everything, destroying vegetation. Light became darkness, erasing the rhythmic alternation between day and night. And finally, firstborn children died. Each strike enacted step-by-step a reversion to a disordered world.

Terence Fretheim highlights the connections between the plagues and creation, noting that the plagues were "ecological signs" that pointed beyond themselves to impending disaster.[15] The passage through the sea was the climax of Israel's deliverance from Egypt. Here the contrast between divided waters for Israel's safe passage on "dry land" and chaotic sea waters that swallowed the Egyptians is striking. Although the narrator did not choose the same word for division of sea waters as the separation of water from land in Genesis 1, the connection to Gen 1:9–10 is strengthened by the use of the same relatively rare term for "dry land" (יבשה) paired with "seas" (ים; see Exod 14:16, 21, 27).[16] At the conclusion of the plagues and the sea crossing, Israel found themselves in the wilderness, a place of non-order or non-existence, where "essential institutions do not yet exist."[17] Fretheim points out that Israel's crossing of the Reed Sea was later construed as a creation event (see Ps 74:12–14 and Isa 51:9–10) in which the sea monster was cut to pieces, echoing ANE creation myths as a divine/cosmic battle.[18] The tradition inextricably linked liberation from Egypt with God as Creator, since redemption was accomplished by means of the created world—water, creatures, weather, and darkness/light.[19] The day the Hebrews left Egypt initiated a new calendar year, signaling their fresh start as a new nation (Exod 12:1–2).[20] The same is true of the

13. Zevit, "The Priestly Redaction," 199–201.

14. Zevit, 201–2.

15. Fretheim, *What Kind of God?*, 227.

16. יבשה ("dry land") occurs 14x in the HB, and nearly always refers to either creation or the sea crossing, with the possible exception of Isa 44:3 and Jonah 1:9, 13; 2:11. It could be argued that Jonah is resisting creational order when he flees by ship.

17. See Walton, *Genesis 1 as Ancient Cosmology*, 25, 27. Quoting Clifford, *Creation Accounts in the ANE and the Bible*, 64.

18. Fretheim, *What Kind of God?*, 239. He lists other texts where the chaos monster is equated with Egypt or Pharaoh: Ezek 29:3–5; 32:2–8; Ps 87:4; Isa 30:7; Jer 46:7–8.

19. See Landes, "Creation and Liberation," 137.

20. Noted by LeFebvre, *Liturgy of Creation*, 62. LeFebvre also notes that the dimensions of the ark make it a "floating 'temple'" so that "both of these stories feature the construction of a mobile sanctuary that carries God's people through a barren wilderness to a new land of bounty, where a mountaintop altar is (to be) constructed for worship" (*Liturgy of Creation*, 76).

flood, which ended on "the first day of the first month" (Gen 8:13–14). In both cases, humans emerged from chaos through watery destruction into new creation. The institution of the Passover ritual as liturgy in the midst of the account of the exodus rendered this event timeless, ensuring that subsequent generations would regularly recover and re-enact the creation of the nation.[21]

Proposition 6: Torah was the Divine Word that Brought Order to Chaos

John Walton and I take somewhat different approaches to Old Testament law. I envision a more robust role for the law in moral formation and demonstrating the character of God to a watching world.[22] However, we agree on two major premises. First, the laws given at Sinai did not function legislatively, but were meant to generate wise deliberation on situations as they arose. Second, and most pertinent to this study, biblical law was intended to bring order to chaos. H. H. Schmid claims that "legal order belongs to the order of creation," and obedience results in the blessing of "the harmonious . . . world order given in creation."[23]

I have already noted the disorder in Egypt. When YHWH delivered Israel, a void resulted that was reminiscent of the opening of Genesis 1—"formless and void" (תהו ובהו, Gen 1:2). The problem after Egypt was no longer oppression, but rather emptiness. Redemption restored Israel to a pre-created state, ready for a new work of God. *What is expected of the people now that their Egyptian taskmasters have been left behind? Who is in charge now? How will this new society be structured?* The disequilibration resulting from their deliverance opened a new opportunity. YHWH created something new by restoring order.

As noted above, in Genesis 1 the word of God brought order to the cosmos. God spoke ten times, and the result was "very good." In the wilderness of Sinai, God spoke ten more "words" to bring about social order to the fledgling nation (Exodus 20; cf. 34:28).[24] God set boundaries around proper worship, proper representation, Sabbath rest, family honor, marriage, as well as the life, property, and reputation of the neighbor. These words functioned as covenant stipulations that formalized expectations for the people who now belonged to YHWH. Sexual intimacy was not a free-for-all; each marriage bed was protected. Worship was not a choose-your-own-adventure; exclusive loyalty to YHWH was required, and worship was to be expressed in carefully

---

21. For a full development of the paradigmatic "hermeneutics of time" evoked by ritual, see Boorer, *Vision of the Priestly Narrative*, 217–453. See also Fretheim, *Exodus*, 133–36.

22. Walton and Walton, *The Lost World of the Torah*. Cf. Imes, *Bearing God's Name*, 40–69, 180–83.

23. Schmid, "Creation, Righteousness, and Salvation," 104, 110.

24. The Hebrew Bible never refers to these as the "Ten Commandments" but only as the "Ten Words," resulting in the English word "Decalogue." Of course the Hebrew דבר (or "word") can be more than just a single logism, but can refer to a "matter" or "thing."

prescribed forms. The ten words curbed greed so that no member of the covenant community overreached or stepped out of bounds. Like the רקיע that separated sky from water, and the dry land that emerged when the chaotic waters gathered in obedience to God's command (Gen 1:9), so YHWH's commands at Sinai established the proper domains of each member of the community, ensuring that those with power did not exploit those without.[25]

Even the calendar rhythms of this new nation echoed the order of creation. Their memorial festival took place on the seventh day after a week of eating unleavened bread to commemorate the Passover/exodus event (12:15; 34:18). During Israel's travels through the wilderness YHWH provided food for six days, followed by a seventh day rest, training them to honor the cessation of labor on the seventh day and trust in God's provision (16:26–30). Resting on the seventh day was not arbitrary or coincidental; it intentionally echoed God's own creative work (20:10) and became a mark of national identity that set Israel apart (31:15; 35:2). Sabbath observance was so central to their national identity that they were to maintain it even during the harvest (34:21). Anticipating their possession of the land, the Sinai instructions also dictated a Sabbath-shaped pattern on a larger scale: in the seventh year servants were to be set free (21:2) and land was to lie fallow (23:11–12).

Proposition 7: Sinai Established Identity and Function for Israel as a New Nation

Sinai did more than establish boundaries to bring order to chaos. At Sinai, YHWH established Israel's identity and function as a nation. The key indication of this new role was YHWH's announcement in Exod 19:4–6:

> You yourselves have seen what I did to Egypt, and how I carried you on eagles' wings and brought you to myself. Now if you obey me fully and keep my covenant, then out of all nations you will be my treasured possession [סגלה]. Although the whole earth is mine, you will be for me a kingdom of priests and a holy nation.

The covenantal context was explicit: "if you . . . keep my covenant" (ברית, 19:5). The means of conveying covenant stipulations was standard: "[YHWH] gave [Moses] the two tablets of the covenant law" (עדות, 31:18).[26] Given this context, YHWH's choice of the Israelites as a *segullah* was significant, considering the use of this term and its cognates in treaties in the wider region. Like *segullah*, both the Ugaritic *sgl*

---

25. Block, "You Shall Not Covet."

26. The Hebrew is often translated as "testimony," but it is not an aural testimony that is implied. In the ancient Near East, the tablets on which a treaty was written were known as '*adê* tablets,' and were deposited in the temple where the gods could be reminded of their duty to enforce them. See Kalluveettil, *Declaration and Covenant*, 31; Lauinger, "Esarhaddon's Succession Treaty at Tayinat: A Biographical Sketch," 87. For more bibliography, see Imes, *Bearing YHWH's Name at Sinai*, 122.

and the Akkadian *sikiltu* could refer to an accumulated treasure, but could also apply metaphorically to a vassal, indicating their special status as the sovereign's representative who carries out his or her will.[27] At Sinai, Israel's national identity was clarified in a way that highlighted their *raison d'être*.

As Fretheim rightly insists, "The Sinai covenant is a matter, not of the people's status, but of their vocation."[28] This, too, echoes creation. For Fretheim, both redemption and law are a matter of conformity to creation order. Redemption from Egypt liberates people by restoring their creation identity.[29] Obedience to the law restores creation order. Fretheim rightly insists that, "The object of Israel's ethic is not asceticism or removal from the sphere of creation but immersion within the very sphere that has been reclaimed by God's redemptive work. Israel now joins God in seeking to keep right what God has put right, and to extend that rightness into every sphere of daily life."[30]

Indeed, the laws at Sinai have implications for every conceivable aspect of life for the Israelites, a virtual catalogue of scenarios in which they were to live as YHWH's *segullah*. Each sphere was properly ordered by the law so that the nations could discover what YHWH was like.

Proposition 8: The Construction of the Tabernacle Echoed the Creation Event

While at Sinai, YHWH not only announced divine expectations for the people's behavior, bringing order to their society, but he also instructed them to build a tabernacle so that he may dwell in their midst. As noted earlier, temple building was thought to be one of the "principal acts of creation."[31] The tabernacle brought physical order to community space and facilitated proper worship. Garden imagery and other creation-related language abounded in the tabernacle, so that the connections with creation are unmistakable.[32] Note the following examples:[33]

---

27. Weinfeld, *Deuteronomy and the Deuteronomic School*, 69 n1, 226 n2; Propp, *Exodus 19–40*, 157; Greenberg, "Hebrew S^{e}gullā : Akkadian *Sikiltu*," 172–74; Wiseman, "Abban and Alalaḫ"; Wildberger, *Jahwes Eigentumsvolk*, 99–100.

28. Fretheim, *What Kind of God?*, 243.

29. Fretheim, 240.

30. Fretheim, 244.

31. Walton, *Genesis 1 as Ancient Cosmology*, 34.

32. Whether the echoes go the other direction, too, is a matter of debate. For the argument that Genesis 1 establishes a cosmic temple, see Walton, *Genesis 1 as Ancient Cosmology*. For the argument that Genesis 1 is not a temple-creation text, see Block, "Eden: A Temple?"

33. For a list of potential connections between creation and temple that includes passages outside of Exodus, see Block, "Eden: A Temple?," 6–7. Note that Block does not see the garden as anticipating the temple, but rather that the temple echoes the garden. He calls the echoes "nonreciprocating" (ibid., 21).

- Just as YHWH *consecrated* the seventh day of creation (Gen 2:13), so he *consecrated* the tabernacle (Exod 40:9–13).

- Just as *cherubim* guarded the way to the tree of life after Adam and Eve's rebellion (Gen 3:24), so three-dimensional *cherubim* guarded the most sacred ark of the covenant (Exod 25:18), while woven *cherubim* adorned the curtains of the inner sanctuary, guarding access to the most holy place (Exod 26:1).[34]

- Just as the *tree* of life was a central feature of the garden (Gen 2:9), so a lampstand styled as a *tree* with buds and blossoms illuminated the sanctuary. The lampstand contained *seven* lamps to *light* the holy place (Exod 25:31–37).[35]

- Just as *gold* and *onyx* abounded in the garden (Gen 2:12), so *gold* and other precious metals covered the furniture and frame of the tent (Exod 26:37) and decorated the high priest's uniform (Exod 28:5–6). The high priest also wore *onyx* and other precious stones (Exod 28:9, 17–19).

- Just as the creation days proceeded from *evening* to *morning* (Gen 3:5), so the priests were to keep the lamps lit "from *evening* till *morning*" (Exod 27:21).[36]

- The priestly garments bestowed "dignity and honor" on those who wore them (Exod 28:40), reversing the shameful nakedness resulting from the archetypal humans' disobedience (Gen 3:7–8).

- Just as God granted permission for the archetypal humans in the garden to eat some fruit but prohibited other fruit (Gen 2:16–17), so the priestly ordination ceremony included food items that were to be eaten and other food that must not be eaten (Exod 29:31–34).

- The emphatic infinitive absolute construction ("dying you will die") appears in God's prohibition of eating from the tree in Gen 2:17 as well as at Sinai, where YHWH warned the people not approach the divine presence. Echoing Eve, he told them not even to *touch* the mountain of God's presence, or they would *surely die* (Exod 19:12–13; cf. Gen 3:3). Somewhat less emphatically, YHWH later warned the priests to follow protocol to keep from dying (e.g., Exod 28:35, 43; 30:20–21).

---

34. The deep *blues and purples* of the fabrics woven with *gold* threads inside the holy place may also be intended to mimic the sky with its sparkling stars (26:1).

35. Less certain are the allusions to fruit and fragrance: While specific types of fruit are not mentioned in the garden (Gen 1:29; 2:9), the *pomegranates* that adorned the hem of the high-priestly robe echo the fruitfulness of creation (Exod 28:33). The fragrant recipe for incense to be used in the tabernacle (30:34–38) may also be intended as an echo of Eden, given that the garden contained "bdellium," which is thought to be a fragrant resin (Gen 2:12). Another possibility is that bdellium is a word for bronze, in which case it would connect to the bronze of the tabernacle. For bibliography, see Block, "Eden: A Temple?," 13, n.51. Solomon's temple amplified the garden imagery by including palm trees, flowers, carved pomegranates and lilies, gourds, and other plants (1 Kings 6–7). Noted by Beale, *Temple and Church's Mission*, 71–72.

36. The priestly role of the archetypal human "to serve and to keep" (Gen 2:15) is often noted, but since the key lexemes do not appear in Exodus with reference to the priests, I have not included them in this list.

Part 2: Covenant

Notably, YHWH chose Bezalel to craft the implements of the tabernacle. He was a man filled with God's "spirit" (רוח [Exod 31:3]; cf. Gen 1:2 and 2:7) and with "knowledge" (דעת [Exod 31:3], a word which previously only appears in Gen 2:17) and "skill" that mimics God's own creative work (מלאכה; Exod 31:3, cf. Gen 2:2–3). Genesis reverberates in this description. YHWH filled Bezalel with God's own spirit and imbued him with divine wisdom, knowledge, and creative skill.[37]

YHWH issued all these tabernacle instructions as commands to be obeyed, reminding us of the divine command in Eden (e.g. Exod 31:6; cf. Gen 2:16).[38] The book of Exodus includes not only instructions for crafting the tabernacle, but also a detailed account of their fulfillment. Unlike the humans in the garden of Eden, Moses, Bezalel, and Oholiab carefully obeyed these commands. The tabernacle instructions further evoke creation because both are deliberately structured around the number seven:

- YHWH issued the tabernacle instructions on Moses' *seventh* day on the mountain, after six days of waiting (24:16).

- The priests' ordination ceremony spanned *seven* days, during which they were clothed with new garments, echoing God's compassionate act of clothing Adam and Eve in the garden (Exod 29:30, 35; Lev 8:33; cf. Gen 3:21).

- The ordination ceremony also involved *seven* days of atonement on the altar, making possible the presence of God in the midst of the people (29:37). And the *seven*-day ceremony was to be repeated for Aaron's successors (29:30).

- At the conclusion of the tabernacle instructions YHWH issued a reminder of the importance of *Sabbath* observance. The Israelites were not to do the prescribed building on the day God prescribed for rest. Their rest was to be an enduring sign of the covenant. The explicit motivation was creation: "in six days the LORD made the heavens and the earth, and on the seventh day he rested and was refreshed" (Exod 31:18). Other than the Sabbath, no other laws were combined with these building instructions, dramatically underscoring the intentional link between the building of the tabernacle and God's own creative work.

- Even more remarkably, the reminder of *Sabbath* observance is the *seventh* of YHWH's recorded speeches that make up the tabernacle instructions. The first six instruct them to work and the *seventh* instructs them to rest.[39]

Block also notes that YHWH *finished* creating (כלה; Gen 2:1) and *finished* the tabernacle instructions (כלה; Exod 31:18) and that the inauguration of the tabernacle occurred on the first day of the first month, which aligns the inauguration with the exit from Egypt and "signals a new creation and the beginning of a new era in cosmic

---

37. He even gave Bezalel a co-worker, as in the garden (Exod 31:6; cf. Gen 2:18), though the same lexemes do not appear.

38. God issued very few commands in the intervening chapters (e.g., Gen 9:4–6; 17:1, 9–14).

39. See Exod 25:1; 30:11, 17, 22, 34; 31:1, 12. As listed in Block, "Eden: A Temple?," 18.

history."[40] Given these abundant connections, it is no stretch to see the tabernacle construction as a creation account. The new thing YHWH is creating is the nation of Israel, complete with a proper temple.

Proposition 9: Like Creation, the Tabernacle Established the Proximity of Divine Presence

Suzanne Boorer rightly claims that "the purpose of the exodus, the freeing of Israel from Egypt, is so that YHWH can be present among them."[41] The restoration of divine presence was the resolution to the oldest human problem. The life-giving presence of God with the man and woman in the garden of Eden was rather understated until the humans alienated themselves from God in Genesis 3. But by watching the negative consequences of their rebellion, we discover the magnitude of what they lost. God had walked among them without causing them fear or danger (Gen 3:8–10). They had been naked and unashamed. However, their disobedience forfeited this peaceful presence. Now they hid from God and tried to avoid responsibility by shifting blame. Their sin resulted in the curse of separation from God's presence, the forfeiture of blessing, the loss of fruitfulness of the ground, and antagonism toward each other. They were exiled from the garden.

The Hebrews' sojourn in Egypt was also an exile of sorts. They were separated from the promised land as well as from the physical places where YHWH had appeared to their ancestors. By deliberately echoing the creation story, the tabernacle instructions ignite hope for the restoration of God's presence in Israel's midst. YHWH explicitly stated that purpose: "Then have them make a sanctuary for me, and I will dwell among them" (Exod 25:8).

The result of the tabernacle construction and priestly ordination was this: "There I will meet you and speak to you; there also I will meet with the Israelites, and the place will be consecrated by my glory" (29:43). The restoration was at hand when YHWH dwelt among them again (29:45–46).

Proposition 10: Israel's National Creation Anticipated Their "Rest" in the Land

David Clines was correct when he said that the theme of the Pentateuch is "the *partial* fulfillment . . . of the promise to or blessing of the patriarchs."[42] The act of creation resulting in a new nation was not entirely complete until they found "rest" in the land in Joshua's day (Exod 33:14; Deut 25:19). Just as the culmination of God's six days of creative work was *rest* on the seventh day, so the culmination of Israel's creation as a

40. Block, 18.
41. Boorer, *Vision of the Priestly Narrative*, 156.
42. Clines, *The Theme of the Pentateuch*, 29, emphasis added.

nation was *rest*. Rest was achieved when the battles were finished and the land was in their possession (Josh 11:23). An intriguing confirmation of this occurred on the way to Sinai, when they fought against the Amalekites. As long as Moses' arms were in the air, the Israelites prevailed. When he "rested" (נוח) his hands, the Amalekites prevailed (Exod 17:11; cf. Sabbath "rest" in 20:11). Rest must wait until the battle is won.

The practice of Sabbath observance offered a taste of the rest that was to come. In this regard, the differences between the Exodus Decalogue and the Deuteronomy Decalogue are instructive. In Exodus, the motivation for keeping the Sabbath was the pattern of creation, in which YHWH "rested" on the seventh day (Exod 20:11–12). In Deuteronomy, the motivation was the fact that YHWH delivered them from slavery in Egypt (Deut 5:12–14). That is, they were not to continue living as slaves. This motivational shift could have meant the elimination of "rest" language, since in the Exodus Decalogue the "rest" is confined to the description of YHWH's "rest" as Creator, but Moses inserted a new purpose clause between the command and the motivation: "so that your male and female servants may *rest*, as you do" (v. 14). This addition maintained the link between Sabbath and rest. However, while the Sabbath provided a glimpse of rest, the ultimate rest awaited entrance into the promised land.

Exodus 33:14 announced that "rest" was still to come. In Moses' farewell sermon, he repeatedly linked "rest" with possession of the land and safety from enemy threat (Deut 3:20; 12:10; 25:19). This theme reappears in Joshua 1:13, 15 as they prepared to enter the land. By the end of Joshua, "rest" had been achieved (Josh 21:44; 22:4). The repeated emphasis on "rest" as a fulfillment of God's promise of land possession strengthens the link between the creation account in Genesis, and the creation of the nation of Israel in Exodus, which anticipates the day they will have land of their own. To put it another way, in Exodus they are residents without a domain to fill, or inhabitants without a habitation.

Conclusion

In what sense might we claim that this world of the Exodus has been "lost"? And what is at stake in our losing it? Two implications are worth considering. First, the Exodus has largely been seen as the "redemption" of the people of God, and by placing the emphasis on redemption, we have lost sight of how the story is infused with creation language. Those searching for a "center" for Old Testament theology have often struggled to coordinate creation and redemption, or wisdom and covenant. This brief foray into Exodus as a creation story suggests that the two themes are interdependent. The Genesis account anticipates and shows the need for redemption, while redemption is unveiled in creation-shaped ways. Of course, my proposal is not new. What may be new is my suggestion that both Genesis and Exodus should be read as advocating functional, rather than material, creation—an ontology of proper and purposeful order.

The second implication worth considering is the vocational clarity that results from reading Exodus as a creation story. If Genesis highlights the functional ontology of all humans as God's image, appointed to govern creation, Exodus highlights the functional ontology of God's covenant people, appointed to represent YHWH to the nations. This vocational focus casts Israel's election in its proper light—not as a claim of superior or inviolable status, but as a solemn responsibility. The giving of the law at Sinai brought order to chaos. The degree to which Israel lived faithfully to the covenant is the degree to which they fulfilled their vocation as YHWH's treasured possession.

The differences between the motivations for the Sabbath command in Exodus and Deuteronomy are one way to illustrate both of these implications while reinforcing my larger claim about the functional ontology of the creation story in Exodus. At Sinai, YHWH pointed back to the first creation account as motivation to rest (Exod 20:11). On the plains of Moab, Moses reiterated the Sabbath command by pointing back to the *second* creation account—to the story of Israel's rescue from slavery in Egypt (Deut 5:15). Both concern creation. Israel's redemption is the reason they must live by a creation-shaped Sabbath rhythm. The fact that Moses delivered this second Sabbath command to the subsequent generation has profound implications for national identity. The exodus is *their* story—"*you* were slaves in Egypt"—even if they were not physically present. They are part of this nation, so the national history is theirs.

The motivational shift between these two versions of the Sabbath command is less jarring when we recognize the link between creation and redemption. YHWH's redeeming act was the beginning of a new chapter in the larger story, one that began "on the first day of the first month." Deliverance redefined Israel as a nation, and it profoundly shaped their way of life—that is, it had *functional* implications. Their task was no longer to work ceaselessly for someone else's profit, nor were they to adopt the persona of an Egyptian taskmaster for their life in freedom, doing to others what had been done to them. Their freedom was the beginning of a new way of life marked by the character and action-in-history of the deity who harnessed creation to rescue them and create something new. Each Sabbath reminded them of their vocation as a free people because the heads of every household were responsible to ensure that all the members of their household could rest: "On [the Sabbath] you shall not do any work, neither you, nor your son or daughter, nor your male or female servant, nor your ox, your donkey or any of your animals, nor any foreigner residing in your towns, *so that your male and female servants may rest, as you do*" (Deut 5:14b, emphasis added). In the exodus, God demonstrated the interconnectedness of creation and redemption while articulating in practical ways how this new nation was to fulfill their *raison d'être* in the world.

Part 2: Covenant

Bibliography

Beale, G. K. *The Temple and the Church's Mission: A Biblical Theology of the Dwelling Place of God*. New Studies in Biblical Theology. Downers Grove, IL: IVP, 2004.

Blocher, Henri. *In the Beginning: The Opening Chapters of Genesis*. Downers Grove, IL: IVP, 1984.

Block, Daniel I. "Eden: A Temple? A Reassessment of the Biblical Evidence." In *From Creation to New Creation: Biblical Theology and Exegesis*, edited by Daniel M. Gurtner and Benjamin L. Gladd, 3–29. Peabody, MA: Hendrickson, 2013.

———. "'You Shall not Covet Your Neighbor's Wife': A Study in Deuteronomic Domestic Ideology." In *The Gospel according to Moses: Theological and Ethical Reflections on the Book of Deuteronomy*, 137–68. Eugene, OR: Cascade Books, 2012.

Boorer, Suzanne. *The Vision of the Priestly Narrative: Its Genre and Hermeneutics of Time*. Ancient Israel and Its Literature 21. Atlanta: SBL, 2016.

Clifford, Richard J. *Creation Accounts in the Ancient Near East and the Bible*. CBQMS 26. Washington, DC: Catholic Biblical Association, 1994.

Clines, David J. A. *The Theme of the Pentateuch*. 2nd ed. JSOTSup 10. Sheffield: JSOT, 1978.

Fretheim, Terence E. *Exodus*. Interpretation. Louisville: Westminster John Knox, 2010.

———. *What Kind of God?: Collected Essays of Terence E. Fretheim*. Edited by Michael J. Chan and Brent A. Strawn. Siphrut 14. Winona Lake, IN: Eisenbrauns, 2015.

Greenberg, Moshe. "Hebrew *Segullā*: Akkadian *Sikiltu*." *JAOS* 71 (1951) 172–74.

Imes, Carmen Joy. *Bearing God's Name: Why Sinai Still Matters*. Downers Grove, IL: IVP, 2019.

———. *Bearing YHWH's Name at Sinai: A Reexamination of the Name Command of the Decalogue*. BBRSup 19. University Park, PA: Eisenbrauns, 2018.

Kalluveettil, Paul. *Declaration and Covenant: A Comprehensive Review of Covenant Formulae from the Old Testament and the Ancient Near East*. AnBib 88. Rome: Biblical Institute, 1982.

Landes, George M. "Creation and Liberation." In *Creation in the Old Testament*, edited by Bernhard W. Anderson, 6:135–51. Issues in Religion and Theology. Philadelphia: Fortress, 1984.

Lauinger, Jacob. "Esarhaddon's Succession Treaty at Tayinat: A Biographical Sketch." Paper presented at the annual meeting of the SBL in Chicago, 2012.

LeFebvre, Michael. *The Liturgy of Creation: Understanding Calendars in Old Testament Context*. Downers Grove, IL: IVP, 2019.

Propp, William H. C. *Exodus 19–40*. AB 2A. New York: Doubleday, 2006.

Schmid, H. H. "Creation, Righteousness, and Salvation: 'Creation Theology' as the Broad Horizon of Biblical Theology." In *Creation in the Old Testament*, edited by Bernhard W. Anderson. Issues in Religion and Theology 6. Philadelphia: Fortress, 1984.

Walton, John H. *Genesis 1 as Ancient Cosmology*. Winona Lake, IN: Eisenbrauns, 2011.

———. *The Lost World of Genesis One: Ancient Cosmology and the Origins Debate*. Downers Grove, IL: IVP Academic, 2009.

Walton, John H., and J. Harvey Walton. *The Lost World of the Israelite Conquest: Covenant, Retribution, and the Fate of the Canaanites*. Downers Grove, IL: IVP, 2017.

———. *The Lost World of the Torah: Law as Covenant and Wisdom in Ancient Context*. Downers Grove, IL: InterVarsity, 2019.

Weinfeld, Moshe. *Deuteronomy and the Deuteronomic School*. Oxford: Oxford University Press, 1972.

Wildberger, Hans. *Jahwes Eigentumsvolk: Eine Studie zur Traditionsgeschichte und Theologie des Erwählungsgedankens*. ATANT 37. Zurich: Zwingli, 1960.

Wiseman, Donald J. "Abban and Alalaḫ." *JCS* 12.4 (1958) 124–29.

Zevit, Ziony. "The Priestly Redaction and Interpretation of the Plague Narrative in Exodus." *JQR* 67 (1976): 193–211.

10

An Enduring House (Terms and Conditions Apply)

Potential Northern Extensions of the Davidic Covenant

R. Jesse Pruett

THE INAUGURATION OF THE Davidic covenant (2 Sam 7) undoubtedly stands as one of the most significant narratives in the Hebrew Bible. Occurring at the apex of David's reign, the event solidifies his divinely sanctioned rule and establishes the succession of his descendants to the throne after his death. In his study of the biblical covenants, John Walton concludes that the election of David and his descendants as divinely sanctioned kings identifies them as the "human vice-regent[s] and representative[s]" of Yahweh's kingship over Israel.[1] He further argues that, in this role, they serve as "covenant administrators" charged with maintaining an appropriate representation of Yahweh by ensuring the covenant obedience of the people of Israel.[2] In return for their fidelity to this commission, the Davidic kings are promised divine support for their rule as well as political and military success. For the next several centuries, this covenant remained the political foundation for rule in Jerusalem until the dissolution of the monarchy in the Babylonian Exile.[3] However, while dominant in the narrative

---

1. Walton, *Covenant*, 66. I am greatly indebted to Professor Walton for his mentorship during my time at Wheaton College. His passion for his students, his devotion to his scholarship, and his service of the Church are all qualities that I hope to emulate in my own career. I am blessed to have been and to continue to be one of his students and am honored to participate in this volume.

2. Walton, *Covenant*, 68–72.

3. The Hebrew Bible does contain hints of the continuation of the Davidic line beyond the formal dissolution of the monarchy through the survival of Jehoiachin in the court of Babylon (2 Kgs 25:27–30) and the role of Davidic descendants in the Persian administration of post-exilic Jerusalem (e.g. Shealtiel and Zerubbabel).

of the Deuteronomistic History, the covenant between Yahweh and the Davidic line is not the only royal covenant described in the biblical text. Following the division of the United Monarchy, there are at least two attempts to establish a royal covenant between Yahweh and a monarch from the Northern Kingdom: once with Jeroboam and once with Jehu. Much like David, these two figures are divinely selected and commissioned to their respective kingships and receive significant dynastic promises during their lifetimes. While not replacing the covenant with David,[4] these attempts represent extensions of the benefits and responsibilities of divinely sanctioned kingship to two individuals outside of the Davidic line. However, neither figure is ultimately able to attain the status and stability of David and his descendants. The following study will analyze the accounts of these two kings and the presentation of their respective covenants, giving special attention (1) to their similarities with David in their elections to kingship and the dynastic promises they receive and (2) to the nature of their inability to fulfill their covenantal obligations and the consequences that result from this failure.[5] Following this survey, the study will conclude with a discussion of the implications that these two extensions have for an understanding of the larger biblical concept of covenant.

Jeroboam: A Failed Extension

The first attempted covenant with a northern king occurs in the context of the division of the United Monarchy. In response to apostasy on the part of David's son Solomon, Yahweh removes a portion of the Israelite kingdom from Davidic control and designates Jeroboam as the ruler of this newly separated territory. As part of his royal election, Jeroboam also receives a conditional dynastic promise that is intended to serve as the foundation for his own rule and that of his descendants. Unfortunately for the new king, he quickly violates his covenant obligations, and his kingdom suffers greatly as a result.

---

4. Despite the drastic reduction of David's kingdom due to the division of the United Monarchy, his dynasty continues and even outlasts the independent existence of the Northern Kingdom and its many dynasties.

5. Due to the focus of this study on the narrative characterization of both kings and the implications of their dynastic promises for the overall notion of biblical covenant, this survey will reflect a synchronic reading of the text. While a diachronic study would help identify the rhetorical purpose of each text or level of the text in its respective historical setting, these considerations are outside the scope of this limited study. For studies that analyze the historical development of either or both of the Jeroboam and Jehu accounts, see Beal, *The Deuteronomist's Prophet*; Campbell, *Of Prophets and Kings*; Finkelstein, "A Corpus of North Israelite Texts"; Hutton, *Transjordanian Palimpsest*; Kasari, *Nathan's Promise in 2 Samuel 7*; Knauf, "Jeroboam ben Nimshi"; Knoppers, *Two Nations Under God*; Lamb, *Righteous Jehu*; McKenzie, *The Trouble with Kings*; Mettinger, *King and Messiah*; Robker, *The Jehu Revolution*; Römer, "How Jeroboam II became Jeroboam I"; Rükl, *A Sure House*; and Schniedewind, *Society and the Promise to David*.

Part 2: Covenant

Election and Promise: A Prophetic Encounter and a Torn Garment

When Jeroboam first appears in the narrative, he is introduced as an Ephratite[6] and a member of Solomon's administration (1 Kgs 11:26). Due to his industrious qualities, he is promoted by the king to a position over a *corvée* labor force in the North (11:27b–28). During his departure from Jerusalem, he encounters Ahijah, a Shilonite prophet, at a solitary location in the open country. Approaching Jeroboam, the prophet takes a new garment,[7] tears it into twelve pieces, and instructs Jeroboam to take ten of the pieces (11:29–31a). The prophet then delivers an oracle that interprets the tearing of the garment as a prophetic sign act indicative of Yahweh's plan to tear a portion of the kingdom away from Solomon and give it to Jeroboam as punishment for the former's cultic infidelity (11:31b, 33).[8] As part of his oracle, Ahijah also extends a conditional promise of an enduring dynasty to the newly designated king that is contingent upon his own obedience to Yahweh (11:38).

This prophetic encounter is significant for the present study due to its establishment of several connections between Jeroboam and the figure of David within the scene. First, both individuals are designated for kingship by prophetic figures acting on behalf of Yahweh (cf. 1 Sam 16:1–13). Second, the sign act of the torn garment recalls Samuel's prophetic rejection of Saul in 1 Sam 15. In this context, the accidental tearing of the prophet's garment is also interpreted as an illustration of Yahweh's intent to remove the kingdom from one individual and transfer it to another, in this case Saul to David (15:27–28).[9] Finally, the dynastic promise to Jeroboam references Yahweh's

---

6. The reference to Jeroboam as an אֶפְרָתִי has typically been interpreted as an Ephraimite tribal designation placing the figure among the Northern tribes (*BDB*, 68; Cogan, *1 Kings*, 337; DeVries, *1 Kings*, 150). However, noting the use of the term to designate the origin of David (1 Sam 17:12) and the association of the parallel geographic term אֶפְרָתָה with Bethlehem (Gen 35:19; Mic 5:1), Mark Leuchter suggests that Jeroboam was actually from the same region as David (Leuchter, "Jeroboam the Ephratite," 60–62). This intriguing suggestion would further augment the comparisons between David and Jeroboam found in the surrounding text (see below).

7. Though ambiguous in the Hebrew text, the garment is typically interpreted as belonging to the prophet, thereby indicating likely foreknowledge of the event (Campbell, *Of Prophets and Kings*, 88 n. 54). This fact is made explicit in the LXX translation of the episode. However, some scholars suggest that the garment actually belonged to Jeroboam, though this remains a minority opinion (Cogan, *1 Kings*, 339).

8. Ahijah's oracle also features a qualification of the promise to Jeroboam that delays its fulfillment until the reign of Solomon's son and reserves one tribe for David's descendants (11:32–36, 39). The tribal limitation reflects Yahweh's promise to David that, although he would punish iniquity on the part of his descendants, he would never completely remove the kingdom from David's line as he had previously done with the dynasty of Saul (2 Sam 7:14–16). However, the reservation of one tribe for David does also introduce a numerical inconsistency into the present text since Jeroboam is only instructed to take ten of the garment's twelve pieces. Various solutions to this issue have been suggested, ranging from historical explanations (often involving the exclusion of Benjamin, Simeon, or Levi) to redactional hypotheses. For a survey of these options, see Nelson, *Double Redaction*, 109–16.

9. This parallel is substantiated by the use of the verb קרע to refer to the actual tearing of the garment and the metaphorical tearing of the kingdom in both contexts (1 Sam 15:27–28; 1 Kgs 11:11–13, 30–31). However, it should be noted that some variance does exist to distinguish the two episodes.

previous promise to David. As narrated by Ahijah, if Jeroboam will remain faithful to Yahweh like David (כַּאֲשֶׁר עָשָׂה דָוִד עַבְדִּי; "just as David, my servant did"; 1 Kgs 11:38), God will give him a dynasty like David's (וּבָנִיתִי לְךָ בַיִת־נֶאֱמָן כַּאֲשֶׁר בָּנִיתִי לְדָוִד; "I will build an enduring house for you just as I built for David"; 11:38). In this context, the collocation of the noun בַּיִת with a *niphal* form of the verb אמן is significant since it provides a lexical link to the contents of the Davidic covenant (2 Sam 7:16).¹⁰ Additionally, this collocation also appears in Abigail's speech to David in which she affirms the intent of the deity to establish his eventual rule over Israel (1 Sam 25:28).¹¹ By casting Jeroboam's dynastic promise in the mold of the covenant with David, the narrative presents the hope that Jeroboam's kingdom will experience the same stability as its southern counterpart.¹²

The connections between Jeroboam and David are not just limited to this prophetic scene but also dominate the surrounding narrative. First, the initial characterization of Jeroboam as an industrious member of Solomon's regime who catches the eye of his sovereign (1 Kgs 11:28) parallels David's own ascent in the court of Saul due to his military successes (1 Sam 16–18).¹³ Additionally, neither figure actively pursues kingship. Instead, both are passively designated by prophetic figures and ascend to the throne as a result of divine orchestration.¹⁴ Finally, both figures are forced to flee

---

Whereas Samuel's garment is torn accidentally, Ahijah purposefully rends his. Further, Samuel's sign act is directed to the individual from whom the kingdom is torn while Ahijah's is stated to the individual who will receive the kingship (Leuchter, "Jeroboam the Ephratite," 53 n.11). Finally, the terminology for the garment is distinct in each narrative: Saul tears Samuel's מְעִיל while Ahijah tears his שַׂלְמָה. However, these distinctions do not challenge the significance of the parallel as they stem from the narrative concerns in each context. Most notably, the use of שַׂלְמָה in the second act is likely intended as a pun on Solomon's name (Leuchter, "Jeroboam the Ephratite," 53).

10. It should be noted that the collocation in 1 Kgs 11 is not an exact parallel to the one preserved in 2 Sam 7. In Abijah's oracle, the verb is as an attributive participle that modifies the preceding noun for house. However, in 2 Sam 7, the verb is a *weqatal* with the noun, modified by a second person singular masculine suffix, as its subject (וְנֶאֱמַן בֵּיתְךָ). This is however a minor distinction and does not damage the strength of the parallel. The form of the collocation in 1 Sam 25, however, is an exact parallel to the form in 1 Kgs 11.

11. The collocation also occurs in the prophetic condemnation of Elide priesthood (1 Sam 2:35). In this context, the deity promises to build a בַּיִת נֶאֱמָן for a future כֹּהֵן נֶאֱמָן ("faithful priest") who will be raised up as a cultic replacement for Eli and his house.

12. One issue with the comparison between the two dynastic promises is the conditionality of Ahijah's oracle and the apparent unconditional nature of Yahweh's promise to David. In the larger narrative, this distinction can be attributed to their respective locations in the careers of each king. In Jeroboam's case, the promise at the beginning of his career serves as a hypothetical that is dependent on his subsequent actions. In this location, it parallels similar promises made to Solomon at various stages of his career (1 Kgs 2:1–4; 9:4–5). For David, the promise occurs at the apex of his rule. At this point, the promise is presented as already confirmed because of David's prior fidelity to the deity (cf. 1 Kgs 3:6; 15:4–5; see Walton, *Covenant*, 115 for this conclusion).

13. Ash, "Ideology of the Founder," 18; Leuchter, "Jeroboam the Ephratite, 52.

14. Perhaps the only significant distinction between the two figures in their prophetic designations is the absence of anointing in the Jeroboam narrative. It is possible that an original account of Jeroboam's anointing has been omitted at some point in the redactional history of the text due to the

the service of their overlords due to homicidal intent on the part of their masters (1 Kgs 11:40; 1 Sam 18–26).[15] By means of this comparison, Jeroboam is thus portrayed as a second David who will soon establish a new Israelite dynasty under the aegis of divine election. In the subsequent chapter, Ahijah's oracle is fulfilled, and Jeroboam is inaugurated as king during a pan-Israelite rebellion against Solomon's son, Rehoboam (1 Kgs 12:1–24).[16] Given the Davidic characterization of Jeroboam, the narrative now presents a question as to whether the new king will follow the example of his predecessor, remain faithful to his covenant obligations, and thus receive the benefits of divinely sanctioned kingship or not.

Failure: Two Prophetic Encounters and an Oracle of Doom

The narrative immediately answers this question with an extended depiction of the failure of Jeroboam's dynasty. This depiction features a direct narrative condemnation of the Israelite king and two prophetic encounters that predict his downfall. The downward spiral begins in the immediate context of Jeroboam's royal inauguration. After the successful division of the United Monarchy, the text continues with the king's consolidation of his rule through the construction of a royal city at Shechem and the establishment of a cult specific to his new kingdom. Given the importance of the latter act, the narrative focuses on the king's cultic reforms. Noting the possibility that continued pilgrimage to the Jerusalem Temple might motivate his subjects to return to Rehoboam, Jeroboam constructs two golden calves, which he subsequently proclaims as images of Yahweh, and erects shrines for these images in Dan and Bethel at the borders of his kingdom (12:28–30). He further ordains non-Levitical priests for the shrines and inaugurates a new festival, effectively abolishing the Jerusalem cultic calendar for his subjects (12:31–33).[17] With this reform of image, shrine, and festival,

---

potential embarrassment of the association of the rite with the ultimate villain of Israelite kingship. However, the fact that the text preserves the anointing of Jehu, also a Northern king, mitigates somewhat against this conclusion. It is also likely that Jeroboam was never anointed by the prophet in the original story (Mettinger, *King and Messiah*, 193). In any case, the absence of this rite does not infringe significantly on the efficacy of the comparison.

15. Ash, "Ideology of the Founder," 18–19; Frisch, "Comparison with David," 17–18.

16. Jeroboam's association with the rebellion is ambiguous in the current text of MT. According to 12:20, he had recently returned from Egypt (see also 12:2) and had to be summoned to the pan-Israelite assembly at which the rebellion occurs in order for the people to make him king. However, 12:3 and 12:20 place him at the assembly among the congregation. Similar tension is present in various Greek versions of the account as well (see Knoppers, *Two Nations Under One God*, 206–23). While there is potential evidence for two different accounts of the event in the original text (Campbell, *Of Prophets and Kings*, 89 n. 55; Cogan, *1 Kings*, 347), the inclusion of Jeroboam at the convocation in 12:2–3 and 12:20 could alternatively reflect the corruption of MT to assimilate the text to one of the divergent Greek witnesses (Knoppers, *Two Nations Under One God*, 216–17). If the latter explanation is correct, the absence of Jeroboam from the convocation would highlight his passive role in his ascension to kingship and thereby further substantiate his comparison to David.

17. The dating of Jeroboam's new festival to the fifteenth day of the eighth month indicates its

Jeroboam effectively divorces his new kingdom from any religious connection to its southern counterpart. In the midst of its recital of these reforms, the narrative features a brief assessment that identifies them as sin on the part of the king (12:30a). This note anticipates the fuller condemnation of Jeroboam's activity in 13:33–34. In this latter context, the text repeats the assessment of 12:30a and concludes that the sin will affect the dynasty (בַּיִת) of Jeroboam and result in its destruction from the face of the earth.

However, between the two recitations and narrative evaluations of Jeroboam's reform, the text preserves an intervening, two-scene prophetic story (13:1–32). In the first scene, an anonymous prophet interrupts Jeroboam's observance of his new festival at Bethel and delivers an oracle against the shrine and its altar in which he predicts their eventual defilement (13:1–10). In the second scene, the same prophet, having been deceived by another unnamed prophet from Bethel, violates Yahweh's instructions not to eat or drink during his mission and is subsequently killed by a lion (13:11–32). Interrupting the narrative condemnation of Jeroboam's cultic reforms (cf. 12:28–33; 13:33–34),[18] the shift in focus from the king to a pair of anonymous prophets is somewhat surprising. However, the episode, in its current place, serves an intriguing function at the center of the biblical account of Jeroboam's reign. As argued by Robert Cohn, the "Man of God interlude" is bracketed by scenes involving prophetic oracles from Ahijah (11:29–40; 14:1–16), their subsequent fulfillment (11:41—12:24; 14:17–18), and depictions of Jeroboam's cultic sins (12:25–33; 13:33–34).[19] The interlude thus stands at the climax of the account and separates the divinely sanctioned ascent of the king from his demise. In this central location it anticipates the king's eventual condemnation and serves as an illustration of the reversal of his dynastic status in the subsequent chapter. Just as the anonymous prophet suffers his grisly fate due to his disobedience of divine instructions, even under the influence of deception, Jeroboam will also be severely punished for his flagrant cultic violations.[20]

The final scene in Jeroboam's regnal account features a second prophetic interaction with Ahijah that confirms the narrator's negative evaluation of the king and develops more fully the nature of the demise of his dynasty. Given as a response to a request on the part of Jeroboam's wife regarding her sick son, Ahijah's oracle specifies the charges against the king and proclaims the end of his regime (14:7–16). For

---

intent to replace the celebration of Sukkoth (observed on the fifteenth day of the seventh month; 1 Kgs 8:2) in Jerusalem (Cogan, *1 Kings*, 360).

18. The repetition of key aspects of the reform (e.g. the installation of non-Levitical priests) on either side of the narrative (12:31; 13:33) and the repetitive nature of 13:33, which restates elements of 12:32, as a conclusion to the anonymous man of God scene has led some scholars to conclude that the frame is a *Wiederaufnahme* meant to facilitate the insertion of the episode into its present context. Given the association of the episode with the later centralization reforms of Josiah (cf. 2 Kgs 23), the interlude is frequently identified as a Deuteronomistic insertion into the Jeroboam account (cf. Campbell, *Of Prophets and Kings*, 90 n. 57–58; Cohn, "Literary Technique," 31 n. 15; Cogan, *1 Kings*, 367).

19. Cohn, "Literary Technique," 24.

20. Cohn, "Literary Technique," 33–34.

the present study, Ahijah's second oracle is significant in several ways. First, it again establishes the link between Jeroboam and David. In a historical review (14:7–8a), the prophet reminds the king of Yahweh's previous act of tearing the kingdom away from the house of David and giving it to Jeroboam. In this context, the appearance of the lexeme קרע ("tear") recalls the prophetic sign act of the torn garment from the designation scene and its connections to the Saul narrative. Further, the review introduces a significant political title (נָגִיד) to describe the status to which Yahweh had elevated Jeroboam. This title refers to an individual designated for kingship and appears elsewhere in Samuel-Kings in the depictions of the rises of Saul (1 Sam 9:16; 10:1), David (1 Sam 13:14; 25:30; 5:2; 6:21; 7:8), and Baasha (1 Kgs 16:2) to the throne.[21]

However, this comparison with David is immediately reversed in the oracle's summary of the charges levied against the king (1 Kgs 14:8b–9). Among the various transgressions, which include the worship of other deities, the veneration of molten images, and the direct rejection of Yahweh himself,[22] is the accusation that Jeroboam had not acted like David (וְלֹא־הָיִיתָ כְּעַבְדִּי דָוִד). Whereas David obeyed the divine commands, followed Yahweh wholeheartedly, and did only what was right in the eyes of God, Jeroboam is charged with apostasy. Given the characterization of Jeroboam in light of David, this specific charge is damning. Originally portrayed as a "*David redivivus*" and given the opportunity to receive a divinely supported dynasty like his predecessor (11:38), Jeroboam now stands as an anti-Davidic figure on the verge of receiving a proclamation of doom against his royal house.[23]

This proclamation of doom comes at the end of Ahijah's oracle in the form of a catalogue of curses that have far-reaching implications for Jeroboam's dynasty and the kingdom he created. First, according to the prophet, Jeroboam's descendants will be violently exterminated and their remains desecrated (14:10–11). The presentation of this ignoble demise features several phrases found in similar prophetic predictions of dynastic collapse (1 Kgs 16:3–4; 21:21–24; 2 Kgs 9:8–10): the bringing of evil against the royal house, the cutting off of every male associated with the dynasty,[24] the

---

21. The lexeme itself is a "passive actant noun" derived from the root נגד with the semantic meaning of one "placed in front" (Fox, *Semitic Noun Patterns*, 192–93; Huehnergard, "Qātîl and Qətîl Nouns," *8–11, *17). It most often describes an individual designated for kingship, though it can refer in late biblical texts to priestly officials (Jer 20:1; Dan 11:22; Neh 11:11; 1 Chron 9:11, 20; 2 Chron 31:13; 35:8) or other tribal military leaders (1 Chron 12:28; 13:1; 27:4, 16; 32:21; 2 Chron 11:11; 19:11; 26:24; 28:7). For discussions of the lexeme's significance in royal designation contexts as well as hypotheses regarding its historical development, see Campbell, *Of Prophets and Kings*, 47–61; Halpern, *Constitution of the Israelite Monarchy*, 1–11; and Mettinger, *King and Messiah*, 151–84.

22. The last charge is expressed through the idiom of placing the deity behind his back (וְאֹתִי הִשְׁלַכְתָּ אַחֲרֵי גַוֶּךָ).

23. Ash, "Ideology of the Founder," 16–24.

24. This element of the dynastic curse features the appearance of two unique constructions to express its masculine object and the totality of its scope. The first construction is a vulgar circumlocution that uses the image of "mural micturition" (מַשְׁתִּין בְּקִיר) to designate the male population (Campbell, *Of Prophets and Kings*, 62). Outside of its occurrences in the prophetic rejection speeches, the phrase appears elsewhere only in David's pledge to exterminate every male member of Nabal's household in

complete extermination of the dynasty itself, and the desecration of the corpses of those who perish either in the city or in the field. Next, Ahijah proclaims that Yahweh will also select and elevate a challenger to Jeroboam's throne who will complete the eradication of his dynasty (14:14). This elevation represents a dramatic reversal in which the one-time usurper now has his kingdom stripped from him and his descendants. Finally, the prophet concludes with an ominous anticipation of the ultimate downfall of the Northern Kingdom at the hands of Assyria centuries later (14:15–16). Notably, this conclusion introduces a formulaic reference to "the sins of Jeroboam that he committed and caused Israel to commit" (חַטֹּאות יָרָבְעָם אֲשֶׁר חָטָא וַאֲשֶׁר הֶחֱטִיא אֶת־יִשְׂרָאֵל) that will dominate the narrative evaluations of the rest of Israel's kings.[25] Through the extension of the curse beyond his dynasty and the ubiquitous prevalence of this formula in the Hebrew Bible, Jeroboam becomes the paradigm of covenant infidelity in the Deuteronomistic History and the architect of the ultimate doom of the Northern Kingdom.[26]

Following Jeroboam's death, Ahijah's oracle is fulfilled within one generation. Two years into the reign of Jeroboam's son Nadab, a usurper assassinates the king, ascends to the Israelite throne, and completely exterminates the house of Jeroboam (15:25–32). This final comprehensive downfall completes the reversal of the king's dynastic fortunes. What began with divine election and the promise of an enduring dynasty concludes with the dramatic upheaval of Jeroboam's royal house only two generations into its existence. Additionally, the implications of Jeroboam's covenant failings do not just end with the loss of his dynasty. Instead, these events also establish a pattern of political instability that will characterize the rest of the history of the Northern Kingdom.

(1 Sam 25:22, 34).

The second construction features a combination of two *Qal* passive participles (עָצוּר וְעָזוּב). The pair has been variously interpreted as a merism for two opposing groups of people, thus indicating all classes (*BDB*, 737; *HALOT*, 871), or as a hendiadys that depicts the lowest levels of society, thus indicating that the extermination will be total (Cogan and Tadmor, *2 Kings*, 107; DeVries, *2 Kings*, 179; Hobbs, *2 Kings*, 115). In either interpretation, the construction reflects the totality and finality of the predicted extirpation.

25. References to Jeroboam occur in negative evaluations for fifteen of Israel's eighteen kings: Nadab (1 Kgs 15:26, 30), Baasha (15:34; 16:2, 7), Zimri (16:19), Omri (16:26), Ahab (16:31), Ahaziah (22:53), Joram (2 Kgs 3:3), Jehu (10:29, 31), Jehoahaz (13:2, 6), Jehoash (13:11), Jeroboam II (14:24), Zechariah (15:9), Menahem (15:18), Pekahiah (15:24), and Pekah (15:28). The condemnation of Elah, the final member of Baasha's dynasty, does not feature an explicit mention of Jeroboam but does use a similar formula of sin done by the king and forced upon Israel by the king to describe his and his father's actions that result in the failure of their dynasty (16:13). The only other exceptions are Shallum, who receives no negative evaluation (perhaps due to the brevity of his reign), and Hoshea, who receives a limited negative evaluation. For a study of these negative evaluations, see Lamb, *Righteous Jehu*, 17–27.

26. Ash, "Ideology of the Founder," 16–24. Ash argues that Jeroboam's role as the *Unheilsherrscher* of the Northern Kingdom directly contrasts with David's role as the *Heilsherrscher* of Judah. This contributes to his overall scheme of the ideology of the founder, in which the fidelity of a dynasty's founder determines its success or failure.

Part 2: Covenant

Jehu: A Limited Extension

The second instance of an attempted royal covenant with a Northern king occurs in the context of Jehu's bloody ascension to the Israelite throne (2 Kgs 9–10). As with the account of Jeroboam's rise, the Jehu narrative features several parallels between the usurper and David, including the phenomenon of prophetic designation and the extension of a divinely sanctioned, dynastic promise. However, unlike Jeroboam's regime, Jehu's dynasty experiences a degree of stability due to his qualified fidelity to Yahweh.

Election: A Prophetic Anointing and a Bloody *Coup*

Like the rise of Jeroboam, Jehu's unusual ascent to the throne begins with an encounter with a prophetic figure. In Jehu's case, his encounter involves a young member of the northern prophetic guild who has been sent by the prophet Elisha to find Jehu at Ramoth-Gilead, where he and the Israelite army are currently fighting Aram, and to anoint him as king. In their encounter, the anonymous young man isolates Jehu from his fellow officers under the premise of a message for the commander and secretly carries out the anointing while the two are alone in a separate room (9:4–6). As part of the anointing ritual, the young prophet also delivers a set of instructions to the newly designated king in which he is tasked, under the authority of divine judgement, with the total eradication of the current ruling dynasty of Ahab (9:7–10).[27]

The presence of anointing in the context of Jehu's *coup* establishes the divine sanction at the foundation of his rule. As argued by Tryggve Mettinger, the ritual serves as a confirmation of the divine election of the king and his descendants to the throne. Based on ancient Near Eastern evidence, the anointing ceremony establishes a contractual agreement between Yahweh and his royal vassal in which the deity as performer pledges himself to his chosen representative.[28] This level of divine sanction serves ultimately to legitimize Jehu's irregular ascent to the throne. It also further distinguishes him from all other Northern kings since he is the only ruler among this group who is explicitly designated by means of this rite.[29]

---

27. Notably, much like Ahijah's oracle against Jeroboam discussed above, the young prophet's instructions feature elements found in other prophetic predictions of dynastic collapse (cf. 1 Kgs 14:10–11; 16:3–4; 21:21–24): the complete removal of the previous dynasty and the cutting off of every male member of Ahab's household (using the same constructions as the oracle against Jeroboam, see n. 24). The connection between these various oracles is made further explicit through the prophet's additional statement that Yahweh will make the house of Ahab like the previously eradicated dynasties of both Jeroboam and Baasha (2 Kgs 9:9).

28. For this argument, see Mettinger, *King and Messiah*, 185–232.

29. Given the importance of the ritual, some scholars conclude that anointing was a typical feature of the Israelite coronation ritual and is only explicitly mentioned in the text in cases of dynastic foundation or contested succession (Cogan and Tadmor, *2 Kings*, 106). However, the fact that the narratives of several kings who fit these categories (e.g. Jeroboam, Baasha, Omri, and Menahem) lack any mention of anointing severely challenges this hypothesis (Lamb, *Righteous Jehu*, 51–52).

The nature of Jehu's prophetic anointing is significant in the present study due to its establishment of a link between the future king and the figure of David. In Samuel–Kings, Jehu and David are two of only seven individuals who are anointed for monarchic rule: Saul (1 Sam 10:1), David (1 Sam 16:12–13; 2 Sam 2:4; 5:3), Absalom (19:11), Solomon (1 Kgs 1:39), Jehu (2 Kgs 9:6), Jehoash (11:12); and Jehoahaz (23:30).[30] However, among these seven figures, only Saul, David, and Jehu receive distinctly prophetic anointings.[31] In each case, all three individuals are anointed with oil in relative privacy by prophetic figures who are under explicit instructions from Yahweh to designate the ritual participant as king over Israel.[32] With this connection, Jehu is thus linked with two of Israel's most significant kings. Additionally, only David and Jehu are anointed while another king is in power, further establishing the parallel between the two figures.

Following the completion of the ritual, Jehu returns to his men and initiates his bloody *coup* against the house of Ahab and his crusade against their Baal cult, which dominate the rest of the biblical account of Jehu's reign (9:11—10:28). As with the anointing scene, aspects of these events are significant for their implications regarding the parallels between the Northern king and David. Much like David (cf. 1 Sam 18:7), Jehu is a military leader who receives widespread support throughout his ascent to the throne. His initial designation is marked by prophetic approval and the immediate acclamation of his military compatriots (2 Kgs 9:13). Further, nearly every stage of the *coup* is characterized by the defection of various individuals from the cause of Jehu's opponents resulting in a relative lack of resistance to his revolt. These include two of the current king's messengers (9:17–20), a group of eunuchs associated with Jezebel (9:32–33), and the rulers of Samaria entrusted with the care of Ahab's seventy sons (10:6–7). While some of these defections can be partially attributed to the fear of Jehu, especially those of the rulers of Samaria (10:4), it does not entirely explain the widespread support Jehu enjoys and the absence of resistance to his *coup* in the narrative.[33]

---

30. Additionally, Elijah is also instructed to anoint Hazael as king over Aram (1 Kgs 19:15). However, a later encounter between Elisha and Hazael, in which the prophet informs the Aramean official of his future kingship, lacks any mention of anointing (2 Kgs 8:7–15).

31. Nathan is present at Solomon's anointing, but the primary officiant is the priest Zadok (1 Kgs 1:39). In this regard, Solomon's priestly anointing parallels more closely the anointing of Jehoash (2 Kgs 11:12).

32. For these comparisons, see Campbell, *Of Prophets and King*, 17–23.

33. For this argument, see Lamb, *Righteous Jehu*, 88–91, 136–37. Lamb also argues that both David and Jehu share manifestations of the divine spirit shortly after their anointing. In Jehu's case, Lamb concludes that his manic chariot driving (9:20) serves as the confirmation of such a manifestation since the lexeme used to describe its manic quality (שׁגע) is also used to describe the nature of the anonymous prophet who anoints him (9:8). Further, he notes that wild or extraordinary behavior is often associated with spiritual manifestations in the Deuteronomistic History (Lamb, *Righteous Jehu*, 135–36). Likewise, Campbell also argues that, though not explicit, Jehu's commission requires the empowerment of Yahweh's spirit (Campbell, *Of Prophets and Kings*, 22). However, given the explicit references to spiritual empowerment in the anointing accounts of both Saul (1 Sam 10:6, 10) and David (1 Sam 16:13), a feature notably absent in the Jehu narrative, this potential parallel between

However, the violent nature of Jehu's revolt also raises a significant distinction between the king and David. Whereas David is depicted as innocent of the deaths of his rivals and their associates,[34] Jehu appears as an active and brutal participant in the various executions related to his gruesome rise. Nevertheless, certain features mitigate against the severity of this distinction. First, Jehu appears as initially reluctant to instigate his revolt and only begins to move forward following the initiative of other characters (cf. 9:13).[35] This places him initially within the same category as both David and Jeroboam who are largely passive in their respective ascents to the throne. Additionally, his active role in the *coup* is presented as having divine support. On three occasions Jehu appeals to prophetic oracles from Elijah as a defense for the brutality of his acts against the house of Ahab. After the assassination of Joram,[36] Ahab's son and the incumbent king of Israel, Jehu instructs his aide Bidkar to throw the king's corpse onto a field that had once belonged to Naboth. He then interprets the act as the fulfillment of a curse that he and Bidkar had once heard from the mouth of Elijah against their former master Ahab for his role in the death of the field's former owner (9:25–26).[37] Second, following Jehu's discovery of the disappearance of Jezebel's remains—save for her skull, hands, and feet—he again quotes the oracle against Ahab and claims that Jezebel's post-mortem desecration fulfills a scatological curse against the queen for her role in the murder of Naboth (9:36–37, cf. 1 Kgs 21:23). Finally, Jehu justifies the mass execution of Ahab's descendants at Samaria as a fulfillment of Elijah's general condemnation of Ahab's dynasty (2 Kgs 10:10). This prophetic defense is also echoed by the narrator in the final summary of Jehu's eradication of the house of Ahab (10:17). The plethora of prophetic citations, along with the violent nature of the instructions contained in Jehu's original commission (9:7–9), thus portrays the king as the executor of divine justice against Ahab's house.[38] This presentation likely

---

Jehu and David remains somewhat suspect.

34. To the point that he even twice refuses to take advantage of opportunities to kill Saul (1 Sam 24:3–7; 26:8–11) and either executes or condemns individuals who do kill his opponents (2 Sam 1:14–16; 3:28–29; 4:9–12).

35. Lamb, *Righteous Jehu*, 89–90. This is most evident in Jehu's first statement to his associates after their acclamation of his kingship in which he qualifies his subsequent activity as a response to the initiative of his officers (אִם־יֵשׁ נַפְשְׁכֶם, "if this is your wish"; 9:15).

36. The Hebrew text preserves two spellings of this king's name (יְהוֹרָם; יוֹרָם) reflecting the contrasting onomastic conventions of Judahite and Israelian Hebrew regarding Yahwistic theophorics. The different spellings occur in free variation throughout the text, even at times in the same narrative. For simplicity, this study uses the shorter form of the name since the abbreviated theophoric is more characteristic of Northern Hebrew (see Ahituv, *Echoes of the Past*, 264) and to prevent confusion with a Judahite king of the same name.

37. Jehu's quotation of Elijah's oracle is anticipated by the narrator's note that Joram's and Ahaziah's chariots met the chariot of Jehu in the vicinity of Naboth's plot (9:21).

38. Noting the totality of Jehu's violence, Stuart Irvine suggests that Jehu's *coup* reflects the ideology of the "holy war" contained in the biblical חרם traditions. Though the root חרם does not appear in 2 Kgs 9–10, an implicit appeal to this tradition, combined with the prophetic characterization of Jehu, would serve as a significant defense for his violent activities. It would also emphasize a contrast

explains Jehu's divergence from the pattern of passive ascent to kingship found within the David and Jeroboam narratives.

Promise and Failure: A Limited but Successful Dynasty

Unlike in the Jeroboam narrative, the dynastic promise to Jehu appears at the end of his account, after the completion of both his *coup* and his religious reform. In this context, it appears in the middle of a divine message, in which Yahweh commends Jehu for his obedience to his prophetic commission. According to the deity, Jehu has done "what is right in my [Yahweh's] eye" (הַיָּשָׁר בְּעֵינַי) and acted against the house of Ahab "according to all that is in my [Yahweh's] heart" (כְּכֹל אֲשֶׁר בִּלְבָבִי). As a result of this fidelity, Yahweh extends a limited dynastic promise to the king and his descendants (10:30). According to this promise, four generations of Jehu's sons will sit on the throne of Israel. This promise of dynastic stability further establishes the Davidic characterization of Jehu. Much like David, Jehu receives a promise of dynastic succession at the high point of his rule that is based on his prior fidelity to Yahweh.

However, the narrative qualifies the dynastic promise in two significant ways. First, the promise is framed by a larger negative evaluation that charges Jehu with following the sinful example of Jeroboam by continuing to participate in the golden calf cult at Bethel and Dan (10:29, 31). As stated above, the reference to the cultic sins of Jeroboam reflects a stereotypical formula used in the condemnation of nearly every Northern king. Given the positive nature of Jehu's commendation, this negative framing is surprising. Nevertheless, Jehu is distinguished among the rulers of Israel since, despite the negative framing, he remains the only Northern king to receive a positive evaluation. This feature instead places him in the rarified company of several of Judah's righteous kings. Outside of its appearance in Jehu's evaluation, references to "doing what is right in the eyes of Yahweh" characterize only the reigns of Judahite kings: David (1 Kgs 15:5), Asa (15:11), Jehoshaphat (22:43), Jehoash (2 Kgs 12:3), Amaziah (14:3), Azariah (15:3), Jotham (15:34), Hezekiah (18:3), and Josiah (22:2).[39] Further, the use of רַק followed by a reference to the continuation of improper cultic practices similarly qualifies the evaluations of Jehoash (12:4), Amaziah (14:3–4), Azariah (15:4), and Jotham (15:35)—the righteous, Judahite contemporaries to Jehu and his dynasty.[40] Finally, while Jehu is depicted as following in the sinful example of Jeroboam, his positive evaluation presents a stark contrast between the two kings. Whereas Jeroboam was instructed to "do what is right in the eyes of Yahweh" (1 Kgs

---

between Jehu and his dynastic predecessor whose treaty with Ben-Hadad at the battle of Aphek is condemned as a direct violation of a divine חרם command (1 Kgs 20). For this argument, see Irvine, "Rise of the House of Jehu," 106–12, 117–18.

39. Mullen, "Royal Dynastic Grant," 198.

40. Lamb, *Righteous Jehu*, 26.

11:33, 38) but ultimately failed (14:8), Jehu succeeded in maintaining a degree of fidelity to the will of the deity.

With its negative frame, the second qualification of the promise is the limitation of the scope of Jehu's dynasty. Whereas David is promised an indefinite dynasty, Jehu's is limited to only four generations.[41] While this does establish an unfavorable contrast to David, the length of Jehu's regime is nevertheless unique among the various monarchies of the Northern Kingdom. At five successive rulers, his dynasty outpaces the Omride dynasty, the next longest of Israel's various regimes, and its three generations of monarchic rule.[42] Further, Jehu's family rules Israel for over a century (102.5 years), more than double the duration of the Omride dynasty (48 years), and includes the Northern Kingdom's longest reigning monarch, Jeroboam II (41 years).[43]

The longevity and stability of Jehu's dynasty is even more astonishing given the narrative depiction of his descendants. In every case, the subsequent rulers of Jehu's family each receive an unqualified negative evaluation: Jehoahaz (13:2, 6), Jehoash (13:11), Jeroboam II (14:24), and Zechariah (15:9). However, three of these kings nevertheless experience great military successes often accompanied by positive interactions with the deity. During the reign of Jehoahaz, Yahweh delivers Israel from Aramean oppression after the king had entreated him for rescue (13:4–5). Although he remains weak from a military standpoint (13:7), this instance of divine intervention establishes a pattern of success against Aram that extends throughout the rule of Jehu's dynasty. Next, Jehoash defeats Aram three times and is able to restore territory taken from the Northern Kingdom during the reigns of his predecessors (13:25). Additionally, he even wins a significant victory against Amaziah, one of Judah's righteous kings (14:8–15). Finally, Jeroboam II further extends the borders of the Northern Kingdom by recovering additional territory from Aram. Notably, this victory is depicted as the fulfillment of an oracle given by a prophet named Jonah (14:25–27). This reference to an oracle indicates that, like his great-grandfather, Jeroboam II enjoyed a degree of prophetic support for his rule. Although the dynasty comes to a sudden end during the reign of Zechariah (15:8–12), the success of Jehu's descendants is striking alongside their continuation of the sins of Israel's previous kings.[44] Further, the stability of Jehu's dynasty also contrasts directly with the concomitant instability of the Judahite

---

41. The contrast between the promises has led to suggestions that the current form of Jehu's grant reflects a later limitation of an originally indefinite guarantee (Levenson, *Sinai & Zion*, 203–6) or an instance of *vaticinium ex eventu* (Bruegggemann, "Stereotype and Nuance, 20–21; Levenson, *Sinai & Zion*, 203; Mullen, "Royal Dynastic Grant," 197). However, noting similar non-eternal limitations in dynastic promises to Esarhaddon, Lamb argues for the originality of the limitation in Jehu's case and suggests that it could have served a crucial role in establishing the usurper's legitimacy in a context of political instability (Lamb, "Non-Eternal Dynastic Promise," 337–44).

42. The Omride dynasty consists of four kings but only three generations since Ahaziah and Joram are brothers (2 Kgs 1:17; 3:1).

43. For these calculations, see Lamb, *Righteous Jehu*, 174–76.

44. For a more extensive study of this combination of military success alongside negative evaluation, see Brueggemann, "Stereotype and Nuance," 16–28.

monarchy, which, despite the positive evaluation of several of its contemporary kings, experiences a gap in Davidic rule and the near extinction of the dynasty during the reign of Athaliah (11:1–20) as well as two royal assassinations (Joash [12:21–22] and Amaziah [14:19–21]) and a leprous king (Azariah [15:5]). The combination of success alongside cultic infidelity leads to the conclusion that "the dynasty of Jehu had endured solely by virtue of the royal grant that was given by Yahweh."[45] Indeed, this conclusion is shared by the biblical narrator in a postscript at the end of Zechariah's account, which quotes the original promise to Jehu followed by a reference to its fulfillment (וַיְהִי־כֵן; "and it was so"; 15:12).

Conclusion

Both Jeroboam and Jehu stand as significant figures in the history of ancient Israel due to their respective roles in establishing the Northern Kingdom and inaugurating its longest and most successful dynasty. This importance is reflected in the biblical depiction of both monarchs. In their respective narratives, both kings are explicitly designated for kingship by Yahweh through encounters with his prophets and both receive significant dynastic promises at key points in their reigns. This presentation notably establishes significant parallels between the two monarchs and the figure of David. These parallels create the possibility that one or both of these Northern kings could successfully participate in the role and benefits of divinely sanctioned kingship like David. However, neither ruler is fully able to accomplish this feat. Instead, both figures transgress cultic obligations and, as a result, experience limitations to the continuity of their respective dynasties.

The examples of Jeroboam and Jehu have several implications for an understanding of the biblical notion of covenant. First, they illustrate further the mechanics of the covenant in its royal form. As in Walton's characterization of the Davidic covenant, the two attempted Northern extensions demonstrate the central role of the king as the divinely selected representative of Yahweh's kingship over Israel and as the "covenant administrator" of its people. In this covenant economy, national success or failure is intimately tied to the behavior of the king. Second, they highlight the necessity of obedience for the full enjoyment of covenant benefits. In both cases, although the hope of dynastic stability is present, the Northern Kingdom is unable to experience the benefits of an enduring dynasty like its southern counterpart due to the failings of its rulers. Third, they reveal the importance of cultic fidelity as the defining characteristic for the role of the ruler in Israel's divinely sanctioned monarchy. Both kings are ultimately judged not by their diplomatic or military activities but rather by their ability or inability to maintain proper Yahwistic worship under their respective regimes. Jeroboam is negatively assessed by the writer for his role in establishing the calf image

---

45. Mullen, "Royal Dynastic Grant," 205.

cult, which subsequently serves as a stumbling block for his kingdom throughout the biblical narrative. Jehu, on the other hand, is commended for his eradication of the Baal cult established by his predecessors. Nevertheless, though obedient to his specific prophetic commission regarding Ahab and his dynasty, he too fails with respect to cultic fidelity and enjoys only a limited share of the covenant benefits granted to David. Finally, the example of Jehu also demonstrates aspects of divine faithfulness in the royal covenant economy. Although Jehu receives only a qualified positive evaluation and his sons are altogether portrayed as unrighteous kings, the dynasty nevertheless enjoys a period of stability and significant military success due to divine intervention. As concluded above, this success is entirely dependent on Yahweh's royal promise to Jehu. In this regard, such grace parallels Yahweh's faithfulness to the Davidic dynasty despite the rampant infidelity of several of its kings.

Bibliography

Ahituv, Shmuel. *Echoes from the Past: Hebrew and Cognate Inscriptions from the Biblical Period*. Jerusalem: Carta, 2008.

Ash, Paul S. "Jeroboam I and the Deuteronomistic Historian's Ideology of the Founder." *CBQ* 60 (1998) 16–24.

Brown, Francis, S. R. Driver, and Charles A. Briggs. *Hebrew and English Lexicon of the Old Testament*. Oxford: Clarendon, 1907.

Brueggemann, Walter. "Stereotype and Nuance: The Dynasty of Jehu." *CBQ* 70 (2008) 16–28.

Campbell, Antony F. *Of Prophets and Kings: A Late Ninth-Century Document (1 Samuel 1–2 Kings 10)*. Catholic Biblical Quarterly Monograph Series 17. Washington, DC: Catholic Bible Association, 1986.

Cogan, Mordecai. *I Kings*. AB 10. New York: Doubleday, 2001.

Cogan, Mordecai and Hayim Tadmor. *II Kings*. AB 11. New York: Doubleday, 1988.

Cohn, Robert L. "Literary Technique in the Jeroboam Narrative." *ZAW* 97 (1985) 23–35.

DeVries, Simon J. *1 Kings*. WBC 12. Waco, TX: Word, 1985.

Finkelstein, Israel. "A Corpus of North Israelite Texts in the Days of Jeroboam II?" *HeBAI* 6 (2017) 262–89.

Frisch, Amos. "Comparison with David as a Means of Evaluating Characters in the Book of Kings." *JHS* 11 (2011): 2–20.

García-Treto, Francisco O. "The Fall of the House: A Carnivalesque Reading of 2 Kings 9 and 10." *JSOT* 46 (1990) 47–65.

Halpern, Baruch. *The Constitution of the Monarchy in Israel*. HSM 25. Chico, CA: Scholars, 1981.

Hobbs, T. R. *2 Kings*. WBC 13. Waco, TX: Word, 1985.

Huehnergard, John. "Qātîl and Qǝtîl Nouns in Biblical Hebrew." In *Sha'arei Lashon: Studies in Hebrew, Aramaic, and Jewish Languages Presented to Moshe Bar-Asher*, edited by A. Maman, S. E. Fassberg, and Y. Breuer, 1:*1–*45. Jerusalem: Bialik Institute, 2007.

Hutton, Jeremy M. *The Transjordanian Palimpsest: The Overwritten Texts of Personal Exile and Transformation in the Deuteronomistic History*. BZAW 396. Berlin: Walter de Gruyter, 2009.

Irvine, Stuart A. "The Rise of the House of Jehu." In *The Land That I Will Show You: Essays on the History and Archaeology of the Ancient Near East in Honour of J. Maxwell Miller*, edited by J. Andrew Dearman and M. Patrick Graham, 104–18. JSOTSup 343. Sheffield: Sheffield Academic, 2001.

Kasari, Petri. *Nathan's Promise in 2 Samuel 7 and Related Texts*. Publications of the Finnish Exegetical Society 97. Helsinki: Finish Exegetical Society, 2009.

Knauf, Ernst Axel. "Jeroboam ben Nimshi: The Biblical Evidence." *HeBAI* 6 (2017) 290–307.

Knoppers, Gary N. *Two Nations Under God: The Deuteronomistic History of Solomon and the Dual Monarchies*. Vol. 1, *The Reign of Solomon and the Rise of Jeroboam*. Harvard Semitic Museum Monographs 52. Atlanta: Scholars, 1993.

Koehler, Ludwig, Walter Baumgartner, and Johann J. Stamm. *The Hebrew and Aramaic Lexicon of the Old Testament*. Translated and edited by Mervyn E. J. Richardson. 5 vols. Leiden: Brill, 2001.

Lamb, David T. "The Non-Eternal Dynastic Promises of Jehu of Israel and Esarhaddon of Assyria." *VT* 60 (2010) 337–44.

———. *Righteous Jehu and His Evil Heirs: The Deuteronomist's Negative Perspective on Dynastic Succession*. Oxford Theological Monographs. Oxford: Oxford University Press, 2007.

Leuchter, Mark. "Jeroboam the Ephratite." *JBL* 125 (2006) 51–72.

Levenson, Jon D. *Sinai & Zion: An Entry into the Jewish Bible*. New Voices in Biblical Studies. San Francisco: Harper & Row, 1985.

McKenzie, Steven L. *The Trouble with Kings: The Composition of the Book of Kings in the Deuteronomistic History*. VTSup 42. Leiden: Brill, 1991.

Mettinger, Tryggve N. D. *King and Messiah: The Civil and Sacral Legitimation of the Israelite Kings*. Coniectanea Biblica: Old Testament Series 8. Lund, Sweden: Gleerup, 1976.

Mullen, E. Theodore, Jr. "The Royal Dynastic Grant to Jehu and the Structure of the Book of Kings." *JBL* 107 (1988) 193–206.

Nelson, Richard D. *The Double Redaction of the Deuteronomistic History*. JSOTSup 18. Sheffield: Sheffield Academic, 1981.

Robker, Jonathan Miles. *The Jehu Revolution: A Royal Tradition of the Northern Kingdom and Its Ramifications*. BZAW 435. Berlin: De Gruyter, 2012.

Römer, Thomas. "How Jeroboam II Became Jeroboam I." *HeBAI* 6 (2017) 372–82.

Rückl, Jan. *A Sure House: Studies on the Dynastic Promise to David in the Books of Samuel and Kings*. Orbis Biblicus et Orientalis 281. Göttingen: Vandenhoeck & Ruprecht, 2016.

Schniedewind, William M. *Society and the Promise to David: A Reception History of 2 Samuel 7:1–17*. New York: Oxford University Press, 1999.

Sweeney, Marvin A. *I & II Kings: A Commentary*. OTL. Louisville: Westminster John Knox, 2007.

Waltke, Bruce K., and M. O'Connor. *An Introduction to Biblical Hebrew Syntax*. Winona Lake, IN: Eisenbrauns, 1990.

Walton, John H. *Covenant: God's Purpose, God's Plan*. Grand Rapids: Zondervan, 1994.

Wray Beal, Lissa M. *The Deuteronomist's Prophet: Narrative Control of Approval and Disapproval in the Story of Jehu (2 Kings 9 and 10)*. LHBOTS 478. New York: T. & T. Clark, 2007.

11

Israel's Relationship with Nature and with YHWH in the Book of Hosea[1]

Eric J. Tully

Throughout the Old Testament, YHWH's identity as creator ties the status of nature itself to the relationship between YHWH and his people. Genesis 1 and 2 declare that YHWH created the world to be "good." Nature is well-ordered and productive, sprouting vegetation, yielding fruit, and teeming with living creatures in the sea, on land, and in the sky (Gen 1:11, 20). God blessed his created world, and ordered it to produce food for humanity (Gen 1:22; 2:9; Ps 147:8–9). However, the inverse of this connection means that when the relationship between YHWH and his people is disrupted, then the created order is disrupted as well. Because of human rebellion against YHWH, the ground is cursed and does not easily produce food (Gen 3:17–18). Because of human sin, "the earth mourns and withers; the world languishes and withers . . . the wine mourns, the vine languishes" (Isa 24:4, 7). And all this is because "they have transgressed the laws, violated the statutes, broken the everlasting covenant" (Isa 24:5).[2] There is a connection between humanity's relationship to YHWH and humanity's relationship to nature and the created order.[3] This theme plays a

---

1. I learned the Hebrew alphabet from John Walton in Elementary Hebrew I at Moody Bible Institute. I'll never forget sitting next to Ken Way and singing John's alphabet song on those first days of class. I immediately knew that I wanted to be a teacher like John: creative, open to discussion and even disagreements in class, with high expectations and a love for the material. John has found a way to be an incredibly productive scholar *and* to invest significant time and energy in his students. I am grateful for the opportunity to contribute this essay in his honor.

2. Translations from *The Holy Bible: English Standard Version* (Wheaton, IL: Crossway, 2016). Other translations are mine, unless otherwise noted.

3. See Malchow, "Contrasting Views of Nature in the Hebrew Bible," 40–43, and Dell, "Covenant

significant role in the structure and message of the book of Hosea. One might say that it is the theological "backbone" of the entire book. In this essay, we will see that Israel's relationship with nature is closely linked to its covenant relationship with YHWH, a link that is highlighted by Hosea in a three-phase progression. First, Israel's distorted desire for a good relationship with nature motivates it to break its covenant relationship with YHWH. Then, YHWH responds to the broken covenant by breaking Israel's relationship with nature. Finally, when YHWH restores his covenant relationship with Israel, he also restores Israel's relationship with nature.

Chapters 1–3 serve as the introduction and interpretive grid for the book in three important ways. First, they establish the concept of marriage as a metaphor for covenant, which influences our reading of the oracles in chapters 4–14. Second, these introductory chapters focus on the concern over fertility and agricultural productivity as a temptation to pursue fertility religion, as a locus of YHWH's judgment, and as a sign of YHWH's blessing. Harmony with nature is foundational to Hosea's argument. Third, chapters 1–3 introduce the three-phase pattern which structures the oracles in chapters 4–14: accusation, temporal judgment, and eschatological restoration.[4] In the accusation phase, the prophet examines Israel's failures in the past. In the temporal judgment phase, he announces historical consequences in the near future. And in the eschatological restoration phase, he looks forward to YHWH's ultimate renewal of all things. These three phases structure the first set of oracles (4:1—11:11), the climactic section of the book (11:1–11), and the second set of oracles (11:12—14:8; see Table 1).[5] In the discussion which follows, we will look at the connection between Israel's (and by extension, humanity's) relationship with nature and the covenant relationship with YHWH according to each of these three phases, with a particular focus on the introductory oracles in Hosea 2:2–23 [4–25] since these are paradigmatic for the book.

---

and Creation in Relationship," 111–33.

4. Tully, "Hosea 1–3 as the Key to the Literary Structure and Message of the Book." See also Tully, *Hosea: A Handbook on the Hebrew Text*, 2–4.

5. Tully, "Hosea 1–3," 371. As with any structural analysis, these are general units. There are judgment oracles in Accusation sections, previews of restoration in Temporal Judgment sections, and so forth.

Part 2: Covenant

	Accusation	Temporal Judgment	Eschatological Reconciliation
Sign-Act 1:2—2:1 [1:2—2:3]	1:2–3	1:4–9	1:10—2:1 [2:1–3]
Application of Sign-Act 2:2–23 [2:4–25]	2:2–8 [2:4–10]	2:9–13 [2:11–15]	2:14–23 [2:16–25]
Sign–Act (3:1–5)	3:1 (Gomer and Israel)	3:2–4 (Gomer and Israel)	3:5 (Israel)
First Set of Oracles	4:1—8:14	9:1—10:15	11:1–11
Climax of the Book	11:1–4	11:5–7	11:8–11
Second Set of Oracles	11:12—12:14 [12:1–15]	13:1–16 [13:1—14:1]	14:1–8 [14:2–9]

Table 11.1: The Three-Phase Structure in Hosea

Accusation

In Deuteronomy 8, Moses gives the people of Israel a preview of the plentiful water, abundant crops, and natural resources that they can expect in the promised land (8:7–9). The intention is that when they eat and are satisfied, they will bless YHWH for the good land (8:10). However, Moses recognizes the temptation: when they have eaten and are full and have built good houses and become wealthy, they may forget YHWH and become proud (8:11–14). There will be a temptation to assume that they have procured the wealth for themselves (8:17). This self-dependence is precisely the opposite of the trusting devotion to which the Lord calls his people, and it leads them into all kinds of covenant violations.

The accusation found in Hosea 2:2–8 makes a point similar to Deuteronomy 8, but in retrospect—it has come to pass. The prophet examines Israel's history and finds that an inappropriate and incorrect perspective on YHWH's covenant gifts has led to apostasy. Israel has become proud in her wealth and has misattributed the gifts to competing deities. The connection between Israel's relationship to nature and the broken covenant with YHWH is highlighted by an alternating pattern (see Table 2):

v(v).	Relationship with YHWH	Relationship with Nature
2	Broken relationship YHWH calls Israel to end adultery	
3		YHWH threatens to make the land a wilderness
4–5a	Children of "whoredom" Mother has "played the whore"	
5b		Agricultural goods are Israel's motivation for infidelity
6–7a	YHWH will prevent Israel from finding her "lovers"	
7b–8		Israel is motivated to return to YHWH by agricultural goods and wealth; she has not known that he is the source

Table 11.2: Hosea's Accusation against Israel in 2:2–8 [4–10]

After explicitly accusing Israel, personified as mother and wife, of adultery and breaking the covenant, YHWH warns that he will strip her naked like the day she was born (2:2–3). The stripping (פשט) refers to an adulterous woman being divested of her possessions that had been granted by her husband.[6] Israel was "born" in the wilderness after coming out of slavery in Egypt and had nothing to her name; now YHWH will take her back to the time of her birth.[7] He will make the land like a wilderness when he removes its fertility and fruitfulness so that she has nothing. In 2:5, YHWH conveys Israel's attitude and motivations with representative speech—putting words in Israel's mouth that perfectly summarize her unfaithfulness. She says, "I will go after my lovers who give my bread, my water, my wool and my flax, my oil and my drink." She believes that her resources, agricultural produce, and resultant wealth come from her "lovers" rather than from YHWH.[8] When YHWH frustrates her pursuit of her lovers (2:7a), her mercenary perspective is confirmed when she decides to return to YHWH (2:7b), deciding that her situation was better when she was with him. She chooses her object of worship based on a simple calculus: who will be more successful at providing what she wants from nature? Her judgment that her current lovers have been less successful than YHWH is based on a skewed assessment of reality—YHWH is not just better at

---

6. See also Ezek 16:39 and 23:26.
7. Calvin, *Commentaries on the Twelve Minor Prophets*, 81.
8. Andersen and Freedman write that these items are not connected with sexuality (as in other passages in the prophets) but are items of payment—she is driven by greed, not lasciviousness; see Andersen and Freedman, *Hosea*, 232.

controlling nature, he is the *only* one who can bestow nature's gifts upon her. The tragic irony is that when she offered *YHWH's* gifts to other lovers she did not know that *he* had given her the grain, wine, oil, and precious metals (2:8).[9]

The mentions of "lovers" and "Baal" are references to Canaanite fertility deities competing with YHWH for Israel's loyalty. There is a direct link between Israel's theological and cultic commitments and her desire for nature to work on her behalf. Whereas Egypt and Mesopotamia are irrigated by rivers, the land of Palestine was completely dependent upon consistent rainfall—at the right time—for crops to survive and flourish. Although the lowlands of Israel were better for crops than the more challenging environment of the central hill country, it was still a challenge for ancient Israelite farmers to produce enough to survive.[10] This situation may explain Israel's propensity to slide into apostasy. There was enormous pressure to secure favor from gods who could ensure the fertility of the land and therefore the well-being of its people.[11] Baal was the most significant fertility deity in Canaan and the one mentioned most often in the Old Testament (including seven times in Hosea),[12] worshipped throughout Canaanite lands as well as in Egypt and in Mesopotamia.[13] Most of our knowledge of Baal comes from Ugaritic mythological texts found at Ras Shamra (ancient Ugarit) near the Mediterranean coast of Syria.[14] Baal was thought to have power over clouds, lightning, and storms and was therefore the god of precipitation, which ensured abundant crops. In the so-called "Baal Cycle" of the Ugaritic mythological texts, Baal is taken to the underworld, causing rain and fertility to cease. When he rises again, vegetation returns to life and fertility is restored.[15] Part of the attraction of fertility deities was the conviction that they could be manipulated by cultic activities into commanding nature for the worshipper's benefit.[16] The earliest mention of Baal in the Old Testament is the story of Israel's idolatry and immorality in the encounter with the Moabites at Baal-Peor (Num 25:1–9). Hosea mentions this episode in 9:10 and possibly alludes to it in 11:2.[17] Baal worship challenged orthodox faith from the beginnings of Israel's life as a nation (Judg 2:11, 13; 3:7) to the end of the pre-exilic period, climaxing with Elijah's contest with the prophets of Baal on Mt. Carmel (1 Kgs 17–18).

The presence of fertility religion in the northern kingdom is likely the background of Hosea's focus on nature and fertility in his condemnation of their broken

---

9. The irony is thick: "deluded into thinking that Baal is generous, his worshippers have to supply the metals to make him;" see Andersen and Freedman, *Hosea*, 243.

10. Ackerman, "Fertility Cult," 450.

11. Beitzel, *The New Moody Atlas of the Bible*, 58–64.

12. Hosea 2:10, 15, 18; 9:10; 11:2; and 13:1.

13. Herrmann, "Baal," 133.

14. See Gibson and Driver, *Canaanite Myths and Legends*.

15. Day, "Hosea and the Baal Cult," 205.

16. Dyrness, "Environmental Ethics and the Covenant of Hosea 2," 268.

17. Tully, *Hosea: A Handbook on the Hebrew Text*, 270.

covenant with YHWH. Israel has "prostituted" herself to these deities for a price, expecting to gain some control over nature so that it will produce abundantly for her, with the byproducts of security and wealth.

YHWH's gifts in nature were supposed to lead to faith and loyalty to himself, but they instead led to infidelity. The more Israel flourished, the more she built altars for rival deities (10:1), taking YHWH's gifts in nature and using them to fund the idolatrous cult. YHWH laments that his good gifts were abused by unfaithful people: "when they had grazed, they became full ... therefore they forgot me" (13:6).[18] This is likely an allusion to Deuteronomy 8:14. Using the same words (רום, לבב, and שכח) in the same order, Hosea suggests that YHWH had *already* provided the abundance of nature that they were seeking, but when he gave it to them, they turned away from him.

Hosea 13:6

שָׂבְעוּ וַיָּרָם לִבָּם עַל־כֵּן שְׁכֵחוּנִי

They were satisfied and their heart became proud. Therefore they forgot me.

Deuteronomy 8:14

וְרָם לְבָבֶךָ וְשָׁכַחְתָּ אֶת־יְהוָה אֱלֹהֶיךָ

Your heart will become proud and you will forget YHWH your God.

YHWH's covenant with Israel included material gifts of natural resources, productive crops, abundant food, fertility and offspring, and security (cf. Deut 28:1–14). These gifts were concrete expressions of YHWH's favor, intended to support and provide for his people in the land as well as to bolster their loyalty to him. If the people were in harmony with their creator, then they would be in harmony with nature. The created order would work *for* them rather than against them. But the prophet Hosea observes that this abundance led to pride on Israel's part. Even worse, they credited fertility deities for the abundance and then used YHWH's gifts to support their adulterous, misdirected worship. Their desire for harmony with nature, combined with a stunning lack of recognition of the true provider, motivated them to break harmony with YHWH.

Temporal Judgment

Not only is the natural world the catalyst for Israel's covenant breaking, it is also the locus of YHWH's discipline of Israel. Disruption of the natural world as a means of punishment is YHWH's typical pattern from the very beginning of the Old Testament canon. In Genesis 3, after the humans' disobedience against YHWH, their relationship with nature is damaged, resulting in animosity between serpent and human (3:15), difficulty with childbirth (3:16), and soil that frustrates human attempts at cultivation (3:18–19). The hostility between humans and animals is further increased in the

---

18. Translation from the ESV.

postdiluvian world, when YHWH states that the fear and dread of humanity will be upon every beast, bird, creeping animal, and fish (9:2).

The same pattern appears in YHWH's particular covenant with Israel. In Deuteronomy 28 (cf. also Lev 26), Moses announces that if Israel is loyal to YHWH's covenant, YHWH will bless their childbearing, agriculture, and livestock (4–6, 11). However, if they disobey and break the covenant, YHWH will ensure that nature works against them rather than in their favor. Their food will be cursed (17), along with their childbearing, agriculture, and livestock (18). There will be pestilence, disease, heat, drought, blight, and mildew (22). YHWH will prevent the rains and give them dust instead (24). Because of a lack of security, their enemies will take their animals and vineyards (30–31). They will weary themselves with extensive planting, but it will come to nothing because locusts will consume it (38). Grapes and olives will fail (39–40). An enemy nation will consume their grain, wine, and oil (51). Even worse, they will be so hungry and desperate that they eat their own offspring; a man will keep food from his own children and a woman will be so starving that she will eat the afterbirth of childbearing in secret rather than share it with her family (28:54–57). To summarize, YHWH will cause all the aspects of nature that should provide for Israel to work against it instead. A kind of enmity will exist between people and the created order, and the presumed abundance of creation will come to an end.

As a "covenant prosecutor," the prophet Hosea stands in the eighth century BC after the covenant disloyalty anticipated in Deuteronomy 28 comes to pass.[19] But he makes his case against Israel *before* the onset of the covenant curses threatened in Deuteronomy 28. Hosea's message is that in the imminent future, YHWH will punish Israel for her worship of the fertility deities by disrupting the mechanism of the created order so that it will no longer produce for Israel. In addition, he will destroy the gifts they have received previously. Thus, he announces the fulfillment of the Deuteronomic curses, focusing particularly on those that connect to Israel's relationship with nature.

The prophet begins his announcement of temporal judgment in Hosea 2:9–13.[20] Because Israel did not know that it was YHWH who gave her the grain, wine, and oil,[21]

---

19. Many critical biblical scholars date Deuteronomy to the seventh century BC or later, which would mean that Deuteronomy 28 does not anticipate covenant disloyalty but rather reflects it, see Weinfeld, *Deuteronomy 1–11: A New Translation and Commentary*, 77, and Nelson, *Deuteronomy*, 8. However, Deuteronomy itself claims authorship (substantially) by Moses (Deut 1:1). This is supported by later testimony in the Old Testament (1 Kgs 2:3; 2 Kgs 14:6; Ezra 3:2) and New Testament (Matt 19:7; Acts 3:22; Rom 10:19; 1 Cor 9:9). See Merrill, *Deuteronomy*, 22, Harrison, *Introduction to the Old Testament*, 646–48, and Wenham, "The Date of Deuteronomy: Linch-Pin of Old Testament Criticism," 15–18.

20. While the Accusation of the introduction (Hos 2:2–8) contains predominantly *qatal* verbs referring to the past, Hosea 2:9–13 looks to the imminent future with predominantly *yiqtol* and *weqatal* verbs. The *weqatal* (or irreal perfect) is commonly used to express predictive prophecy.

21. These three terms, in this order, make a possible allusion to Deuteronomy 28:51.

he will "snatch away" these blessings (2:8–9 [10–11]).[22] Calvin writes, "it was therefore necessary to reduce [Israel] to extreme want, that they might no longer pollute God's gifts, which ought to be held sacred."[23] The mentions of removing grain "in its time" and wine "in its season" may refer to the regularity of the growing season. Perhaps there has been great fruitfulness and the crops have come in when expected, but YHWH will demonstrate his supreme control over nature by devastating them. In this way, he will uncover Israel's nakedness and lewdness in the sight of her lovers (2:9–10 [11–12]) because she will be left without the covering of wealth and provision. He will ruin her vines and fig trees that she had credited to her lovers—the fertility deities—and turn them into a wild area where animals will devour them (2:12 [14]). The unit concludes with YHWH's explicit announcement in 2:13 [15] that this destruction of nature is punishment of Israel (see Table 3), leaving no doubt that Israel's infidelity to YHWH will cause the environmental upheaval.

	Relationship with Nature
v. 9	YHWH will take back the agricultural goods
v. 10	YHWH will "uncover" Israel
v. 11	YHWH will end her festival days
v. 12	YHWH will destroy her vines and fig trees; the animals will devour them
	Relationship with YHWH
v. 13	These actions are punishment for "lovers" and forgetting YHWH

Table 11.3: Two Connected Relationships

While the introduction to temporal judgment in Hosea 2:9–13 [11–15] sets expectations, the prophet goes into further detail in chapters 4–14. We can group these references in three categories. First, YHWH will cause the land to revert to a wild and disordered state. In Hosea 9:6, the prophet predicts that the people will go into exile, which will lead to wild prickly plants repossessing their precious things and thorns coming up in their tents. Similarly, 10:8 describes thorns and thistles overtaking their idolatrous altars. Ironically, Israel's false religion represents an attempt to take control of nature and subdue it, but when their religion leads to their defeat and destruction, nature subdues them instead.

A second judgment is the blocking of agricultural fertility. Hosea 4:1–2 says that there is no knowledge of God in the land, but rather swearing, lying, murder, stealing,

---

22. The verb נצל refers to taking something without the permission of the one possessing it.
23. Calvin, *Commentaries on the Twelve Minor Prophets*, 92.

and adultery. "Therefore, the land dries up and everything that lives in it languishes." The animals, birds, and fish all perish (4:3).[24] The word "therefore" in 4:3 is significant: it means that Israel's covenant failures have consequences for the natural world.[25] In Hosea 8:7, the prophet says that they sow wind, but "as for the standing grain—it does not have heads; it will not make flour; even if it does, strangers would devour it." This pseudosorites intensifies the hopelessness of the situation.[26] If they sow and harvest, they will not produce a crop ("heads"). Even if they produce a crop, they will not have grain. Even if they have grain, it will not make flour. But even if it *were* to produce flour, strangers will take it and eat it. Even should the people of Israel be able to circumvent YHWH's judgment and produce crops when he has set creation against them, they will still have nothing in the end. Likewise, in Hosea 9:2, "threshing floor and wine vat will not feed them, and new wine shall fail her." Finally, the prophet is clear that this devastation of agricultural fertility is not a coincidence: it comes from YHWH. Hosea 13:15 says, "an east wind will come, a wind from YHWH . . . and his spring will be dry, and his fountain will be parched." Throughout the Old Testament, an "east wind" (קָדִים) is a destructive gale which is always brought by YHWH.

Third, and finally, YHWH's temporal judgment of the natural realm involves obstruction of human fertility. It is not clear whether Canaanite fertility religion and the worship of Baal were thought to boost procreation.[27] However, Hosea makes this connection, emphasizing the loss of actual or potential children as a consequence of Israel's infidelity. In 4:10, the prophet speaks against the priesthood in the Northern Kingdom and claims that "they shall play the whore, but not multiply, because they have forsaken YHWH." They will fornicate, but it will not lead to offspring,[28] and their wombs will be as barren as their land. In 9:11, the prophet refers to childbirth in an unusual order: "no birth, no pregnancy, no conception!" The reversal creates a sense of intensity: not only will there be no birth, they will not even carry children in the womb. Not only will they not carry children in the womb, they will not even conceive!

---

24. The order of these three categories of animals may be significant. In Genesis 1 YHWH creates the fish (Gen 1:20a), the birds (1:20b), and the animals (1:24). He also gives humanity dominion over the fish, birds, and animals in Genesis 1:28. These three categories are reversed here in Hosea 4:3. Perhaps, like Zeph 1:2–3, this suggests the reversal, and undoing, of creation; see DeRoche, "The Reversal of Creation in Hosea," 403–4.

25. Hoffmeyer, "Covenant and Creation: Hosea 4:1–3," 144.

26. On the pseudosorites in Hebrew poetry see O'Connor, "The Pseudosorites: A Type of Paradox in Biblical Hebrew Poetry," 161–72; Patterson, "An Overlooked Scriptural Paradox: The Pseudosorites," 19–36.

27. Herrmann, "Baal," 135.

28. The verb פרץ refers to breaking out of confines, either in terms of possessions (Gen 30:30, 43) or in terms of population (e.g. Gen 28:14; Exod 1:12). Garrett suggests that perhaps the former is in view and that the priests are hoping that sacred prostitution will increase their wealth (Garrett, *Hosea, Joel*, 120). However, this may be over reading. The question of whether there *was* sacred prostitution in Israel is debated by scholars. For a view against see Ackerman, "Fertility Cult." For an argument for, see Day, "Hosea and the Baal Cult," 215.

The prophet then uses another pseudosorites: "even if they bring up children, I will bereave them until none is left" (9:12).[29] Even if they were somehow able to produce a child, YHWH will kill the child and bereave them. After praying that YHWH would "give them a miscarrying womb and dried up breasts" (9:14), the prophet uses another pseudosorites in 9:16. He says, "Their root is dried up; they will not bear fruit. Even though they give birth, I will kill the cherished of their womb." Finally, the killing of offspring is graphically described in 13:16, "they will fall by the sword, their infants will be smashed, and their pregnant women will be ripped open."

Thus, YHWH's coming judgment will systematically ruin and remove all the fertility, resources, food, and even children that Israel so desperately wanted from fertility deities. The people thought that these gods could secure greater flourishing and protect what they had already gained. By stripping these things away, YHWH shows the impotence of these imposter deities, while revealing himself to be the supreme creator who both gives and takes away the gifts that creation offers. When Israel breaks covenant relationship with YHWH, YHWH responds by breaking Israel's relationship with nature.

Eschatological Restoration

Thus far, we have seen that Israel's relationship to the natural world has been both a stumbling block to her covenant relationship with YHWH and the realm which YHWH targets in punishment. The reader of Hosea might be excused for thinking that this triangular relationship between YHWH, Israel, and the created order is just not working out. Remarkably, however, the prophet announces that YHWH is undeterred. He is not only determined to restore his relationship with his people, he is determined to restore their harmony with the created order completely and permanently.

In the final section of the book's introduction (Hosea 2:14–23 [16–25]), the prophet locates this dual restoration to YHWH and to nature in the eschatological future. The phrase "in that day" (בַּיּוֹם הַהוּא), found in Hosea 2:16, 18, and 21, is a common prophetic expression for speaking beyond the scope of history to the indeterminate time to come when YHWH will set all things right. There is a sense of finality to the situation: Israel will remember the Baals "no more" (2:17) and YHWH will betroth her to himself "in perpetuity" (לְעוֹלָם).

Much like the pattern in the accusation section of the introduction (2:2–8 [4–10]), here the prophet structures his prediction in an alternating pattern which links Israel's reconciliation to YHWH and to nature (see Table 4):

---

29. Translation from the ESV.

Part 2: Covenant

v(v).	Relationship with YHWH	Relationship with Nature
14	YHWH will coax his people back to him	
15		YHWH will return their vineyards
16–17	YHWH will remove the Baals from them	
18		YHWH will end their conflicts with animals and other humans
19–20	YHWH will establish a permanent relationship with them	
21–22a		YHWH will end their conflict with nature
23	Result: They will be YHWH's people; he will be their God	

Table 11.4: Eschatological Restoration in Hosea 2:14–23 [16–25]

In these verses, Hosea describes six actions that YHWH will take to restore his people. First, YHWH will coax Israel back to himself as in the early days of his relationship with her, symbolized by the wilderness (2:14). He uses the idiom "speak tenderly to her" (דִּבַּרְתִּי עַל לִבָּהּ), which is used elsewhere in circumstances in which there is a power differential between two parties and the party with lower status has faced some trauma. The party with higher status seeks to overcome the trauma and establish relationship.[30] Here, YHWH speaks rhetorically as though the discipline has already taken place, and now he woos and coaxes his people back again.

YHWH's second act of restoration is to return her vineyards (2:15a). This is a reversal of the judgment in 2:12, in which YHWH says he will desolate her vines and fig trees. In the eschatological future, she will once again have the vineyards that are not necessary for sustenance, but represent luxury. When he returns her vineyards, she will "answer" (ענה) as in the days of her youth (2:15b).[31] That is, she will respond to YHWH's coaxing (cf. 2:14) and turn back toward him in relationship.

Third, YHWH will remove the Baals from his people, and they will be remembered no more (2:16–17). YHWH's people will forsake competing deities and commit themselves to YHWH as their one true "husband" with allegiance and fidelity.

---

30. See Gen 34:3; 50:21; Judg 19:3; 1 Sam 1:31; 2 Sam 19:8; Isa 40:1; and Ruth 2:13; Tully, *Hosea: A Handbook on the Hebrew Text*, 57.

31. For a discussion of options on how to translate ענה, see Macintosh, *A Critical and Exegetical Commentary on Hosea*, 73. Analysis is somewhat difficult because ענה occurs in four different roots. The best option is to understand the verb as denoting responsiveness. See Delekat, "Zum Hebräischen Wörterbuch," 41, who argues that here it refers to a woman responding to her husband's desires.

Fourth, turning attention back to the natural realm, YHWH promises that he will end his people's conflicts with both animals and other humans. He states first in Hos 2:18a that he will "make for them a covenant" (וְכָרַתִּי לָהֶם בְּרִית) with the animals. Although the idiom בְּרִית + כרת is the standard formula for describing the creation of a covenant,[32] this covenant is unusual because there are three parties. YHWH is the initiator of the covenant. The second party is the people, indicated by "for them" (לָהֶם).[33] The third party is three groups of animals: wild animals of the field (חַיָּה), birds of the sky (עוֹף), and creeping creatures on the ground (רֶמֶשׂ). These designations, in this order, are important because they trigger an allusion to Gen 9:2.[34] Although in YHWH's original creation there was harmony between humans and animals, Gen 9:2 describes a postdiluvian world in which the "fear" (מוֹרָא) and "dread" (חַת) of humanity would now be on the animals and there would be discord between the two. Later, YHWH makes a covenant, spoken to Noah, that is actually between YHWH, Noah and his offspring, and "every living creature" (כָּל נֶפֶשׁ הַחַיָּה). The repetition of "every living creature" in the text does not allow us to miss the point that the animal kingdom is a participant in the covenant (Gen 9:9–10, 12, 15, 16). By alluding to Gen 9:2, Hos 2:18 announces another "covenant" or agreement that YHWH will make between humans and animals, ending their conflict and returning nature to its originally created state. Whitekettle writes, "Thus [Hos 2:18 (20)] is describing a lasting, constitutional change to the human/animal relationship. This would explain why the resolution involves all animals and why it uses something as formal and significant as a covenant as the mechanism."[35]

In the ancient world, wild animals evoked a sense of fear because they were a significant threat to life and civilization. We see references to this throughout the Old Testament. Wild animals were a direct danger to people (Judg 14:5; 1 Kgs 13:24; 2 Kgs 2:24; Jer 5:6) and to livestock (1 Sam 17:36; Jer 2:15). The fear of wild animals is also represented in metaphors representing dangerous enemies as animals (Prov 28:15; Isa 38:13; Lam 3:10; Amos 5:19), including in the book of Hosea (5:4, 10, 12; 13:7, 8).

However, the Latter Prophets teach that in the eschatological future, the created order will be transformed so that wild animals are no longer a danger to other animals or to people. Isaiah 11:6–9 promises a future under a Davidic ruler in which "they

---

32. The idiom is used in all three basic types of covenants in the OT: human with human, God with human, and human with God; see Robertson, *The Christ of the Covenants*, 8.

33. The nearest plural antecedent of the masculine plural pronoun is the "Baals" in 2:17 above, but this would be nonsensical. The pronoun must refer to the people in the wider context. The most common prepositions used to connect two parties in a covenant are עִם or אֵת ("with"), used a total of 33 times. The preposition לְ, used here, designates the party of covenant which is either future or potential, or when the party has lower status and no real agency or say in the matter.

34. For a detailed analysis of the allusion, see Whitekettle, "Freedom from Fear and Bloodshed: Hosea 2.20 (Eng. 18) and the End of Human/Animal Conflict," 219–36. Genesis 8:19 lists the same three groups of animals, but in a different order: חַיָּה < רֶמֶשׂ < עוֹף. Genesis 1:30 in the creation narrative also has similar language: וּלְכָל־חַיַּת הָאָרֶץ וּלְכָל־עוֹף הַשָּׁמַיִם וּלְכֹל | רוֹמֵשׂ עַל־הָאָרֶץ.

35. Whitekettle, "Freedom from Fear and Bloodshed," 232.

will not hurt or destroy in all my holy mountain."[36] Isaiah 35:9 states that no lion or ravenous beast will be found in the eschatological land of YHWH's people. In Ezekiel 34:28, YHWH's people will no longer be "prey" for the nations, "nor shall the beasts of the land devour them." Hosea 2:18 [20] joins these passages in anticipating an eschatological future in which YHWH makes an agreement between humanity and the animals so that their fundamental relationship is changed to one of harmony.

Not only will YHWH end his people's conflict with animals, he will also end their conflict with other humans. He will "abolish the bow, the sword, and war from the land" and give them safety (2:18b). In Hos 1:7, YHWH had said that he would *not* save them by bow, sword, war, or horses because of their unfaithfulness. But in the eschatological future, he will not need to save them because there will be peace.

A fifth restorative action of YHWH, found in Hos 2:19–20 [21–22], involves the establishment of a permanent relationship with his people. They will reflect his character (righteousness, justice, covenant love, mercy) and will "know" him. This will be a reversal of Hos 2:8, in which Israel did not "know" that YHWH was the creator and the source of all they had.

YHWH's sixth action will be to end his people's conflict with nature. YHWH stated in Hos 2:9 that he would obstruct the natural agricultural cycle and processes so that the land would no longer produce. However, now YHWH says that "on that day" (בַּיּוֹם הַהוּא), in his eschatological restoration, he "will answer the heavens, and they will answer the earth, and the earth will answer the grain, the wine, and the oil, and they will answer Jezreel" (2:21–22 [23–24]). The repeated verb "answer" (ענה) in these verses links back to 2:17, in which YHWH's people will "respond" (ענה) to him in relationship when he appeals to them and returns their vineyards. Now, he says in 2:21–22 that when his relationship with them is restored, he will "respond" to the heavens, reactivating them so that they produce rain once more. This will start a chain reaction: when the heavens "respond" to the earth with rain, it will respond by producing grain, wine and oil, which in turn will respond to the people on the land. Dyrness writes that the earth's fertility "is quite literally an 'answer' to God's promise. But so far from their religious practices being necessary to maintain this fertility—as the rituals of Canaanite religion were meant to 'maintain' the cycles of nature—this answer itself must be made and guaranteed by God."[37]

In the conclusion of this unit (2:23), we come full circle back to the sign-act in chapter 1 as the names of the prophet's children are reversed. YHWH's people will be reestablished in the land, shown mercy, and back in covenant relationship with him.

---

36. Tucker argues that neither Isa 11:6–9 nor Hos 2:18 [20] are eschatological or describe a transformation of nature. If they were, they would represent a rejection of the present world, which God created as good; Tucker, "The Peaceable Kingdom and a Covenant with the Wild Animals," 225. However, this view does not account for lived reality of animal threats nor the biblical-theological claim throughout the OT that though God created the world to be good, it has been damaged by human rebellion.

37. Dyrness, "Environmental Ethics and the Covenant of Hosea 2," 271.

Whereas the accusation (2:2–8 [4–10]) and temporal judgment (2:9–13 [11–15]) are focused on the nation of Israel *in history*, concretely relating to covenant obligations and covenant curses, this passage on eschatological restoration (2:14–23 [16–25]) is sweeping, permanent, and beyond the historical horizon. There is a transformation of humanity's fundamental relationship with animals, war is abolished, and harmony is realized in YHWH's relationship with his people.

The connection between reconciliation with YHWH and a life of fertility and flourishing is revisited in Hos 14:5–8 [6–9]. YHWH describes the results of reconciliation with rich metaphors drawn from nature and agriculture. He says in 14:5 [6], "I will be like the dew to Israel; he will blossom like the flower, and strike his roots like the tree of Lebanon." Just as dew allows for the growth of plants, relationship with YHWH creates conditions for life: "his shoots will go out; his splendor will be like the olive tree" (14:6 [7]). He continues in 14:7 [8], "they will produce grain, they will blossom like the vine."

Finally, the last verse in the book (prior to the postscript) represents an intimate conversation between YHWH and his people, fully reconciled (14:8 [9]). The verse is presented in alternating lines of dialogue.[38] First, Ephraim says, "What are idols to me?" In this rhetorical question with its obvious negative answer, YHWH's people (symbolized by Ephraim) express loyalty and trust in YHWH for security and fertility. YHWH speaks the next line, "I have answered (ענה) and I will watch over him." The verb "answer" recalls 2:21–22 [23–24], in which YHWH promised to restore humanity's productive relationship with nature. This prompts the people to respond, "I am like a luxuriant cypress"—a strong, healthy plant. YHWH poignantly answers, "Your fruit is found from me." This metaphor illustrates the restoration of YHWH's people to nature by stating explicitly that harmony and abundance come from *YHWH*. He is the creator of nature and has total control over it. He can disrupt it and he can restore it. If nature will once again produce for his people and benefit them, it will do so because he has caused it.

Conclusion

Hosea 2 functions as an interpretive lens for the entire book of Hosea, casting the prophet's accusation against Israel, announcement of judgment, and promise of future restoration in terms of her relationship to the natural world. These themes are continued to varying degrees in chapters 4–13 and then reemerge as the essential issue in chapter 14, the book's conclusion. By highlighting this nexus between YHWH and nature, the book of Hosea makes several theological contributions.

First, the focus on Israel's desire for harmony with nature, loss of that harmony, and eventual success serves as a polemic against Baal and the Canaanite fertility

---

38. See Tully, *Hosea: A Handbook on the Hebrew Text*, 350, and Macintosh, *A Critical and Exegetical Commentary on Hosea*, 576–77.

religion that continually tempted Israel. The competition between the worship of YHWH and the worship of Baal in particular is resolved without question in the course of the book: the fertility and resources of the land are YHWH's domain and all other deities are imposters, likened to adulterous lovers who "break up the home." Some contemporary scholars posit that Baal was the original fertility deity, and that YHWH eventually took on his characteristics in ancient religious thought.[39] Yet the book contends that it is the other way around: Baal is the pretender; this is YHWH's realm because he is the creator of the world.

Second, Hosea's focus on nature clarifies the way to a successful life. From the outset in 2:7 [9], fertility religion is presented as a gambit in which the people would worship certain deities because they were thought to have a better chance at providing the good life. It is significant that Hosea does not reject the connection between worship and concrete, physical flourishing in the natural world. Rather, he simply argues that it is only when one is faithful to YHWH—the creator—that one finds the good life. YHWH is not opposed to his people enjoying the gifts of creation. He has created the world to be good and has placed his people in it for their enjoyment. But they must be loyal to him. If they become proud, or give credit for those gifts to someone else, then their jealous God will see to it that they fail rather than flourish. For this reason, the postscript of the book (Hos 14:9 [10]), filled with words commonly associated with wisdom, is an effective summary of the book's entire argument. The wise person who seeks a successful life will only find it if they follow the ways of YHWH.

Finally, Hosea's focus on the connection between Israel, YHWH, and the world effectively ties YHWH's covenant with Israel into his great plan of redemption for the world. The grand narrative of creation, fall, judgment, and re-creation is seen in this book in microcosm. Israel functions as a representative for all of humanity at a particular point in history. That nation's relationship to the land—first as blessing, then as temptation, then as a locus of judgment, and finally as place of final restoration—embodies YHWH's sweeping plan on a global scale. Though Hosea speaks from the eighth century BC, he looks forward to a time when YHWH overcomes the determined rebellion of his people, reconciles all things to himself, and offers his people the permanent security and flourishing he had always intended for them.

Bibliography

Ackerman, Susan. "Fertility Cult." In *The New Interpreter's Dictionary of the Bible*, edited by Katharine D. Sakenfeld, 2:450–51. Nashville: Abingdon, 2006.
Andersen, Francis I., and David Noel Freedman. *Hosea*. AB 24. New York: Doubleday, 1980.
Beitzel, Barry J. *The New Moody Atlas of the Bible*. Chicago: Moody, 2009.
Calvin, John. *Commentaries on the Twelve Minor Prophets*. Translated by John Owen. Grand Rapids: Baker, 2003.

---

39. See for example, Dempsey, "Hosea's Use of Nature," 347.

Day, John. "Hosea and the Baal Cult." In *Prophets and Prophecy in the Ancient Near East: Proceedings of the Oxford Old Testament Seminar*, edited by John Day, 202–24. New York: T. & T. Clark, 2010.

Delekat, L. "Zum Hebräischen Wörterbuch." *VT* 14 (1964) 7–66.

Dell, Katherine. "Covenant and Creation in Relationship." In *Covenant as Context: Essays in Honour of E. W. Nicholson*, edited by A. D. H. Mayes and R. B. Salters, 111–33. Oxford: Oxford University Press, 2003.

Dempsey, Carol J. "Hosea's Use of Nature." *The Bible Today* 39 (2001) 347–53.

DeRoche, Michael. "The Reversal of Creation in Hosea." *VT* 31 (1981) 400–409.

Dyrness, William A. "Environmental Ethics and the Covenant of Hosea 2." In *Studies in Old Testament Theology*, edited by Robert L. Hubbard, Robert K. Johnston, and Robert P. Meye, 263–78. Dallas: Word, 1992.

Garrett, Duane A. *Hosea, Joel*. NAC 19A. Nashville: Broadman & Holman, 1997.

Gibson, John C. L., and G. R. Driver, eds. *Canaanite Myths and Legends*. Edinburgh: T. & T. Clark, 1978.

Harrison, R. K. *Introduction to the Old Testament*. Peabody, MA: Prince, 1969.

Herrmann, W. "Baal." In *DDD*, 132–39.

Hoffmeyer, Jeffrey H. "Covenant and Creation: Hosea 4:1–3." *Review & Expositor* 102 (2005) 143–51.

The Holy Bible: English Standard Version. Wheaton, IL: Crossway, 2016.

Macintosh, A. A. *Hosea*. ICC. Edinburgh: T&T Clark, 2014.

Malchow, Bruce V. "Contrasting Views of Nature in the Hebrew Bible." *Dialog* 26 (1987) 40–43.

Merrill, Eugene. *Deuteronomy*. NAC 5. Nashville: Broadman & Holman, 1994.

Nelson, Richard D. *Deuteronomy*. OTL. Louisville: Westminster John Knox, 2002.

O'Connor, Michael Patrick. "The Pseudosorites: A Type of Paradox in Biblical Hebrew Poetry." In *Directions in Biblical Hebrew Poetry*, edited by Elaine R. Follis, 161–72. JSOTSup 40. Sheffield: JSOT Press, 1987.

Patterson, Richard D. "An Overlooked Scriptural Paradox: The Pseudosorites." *JETS* 53 (2010) 19–36.

Robertson, O. Palmer. *The Christ of the Covenants*. Phillipsburg, NJ: Presbyterian & Reformed, 1980.

Tucker, Gene M. "The Peaceable Kingdom and a Covenant with the Wild Animals," in *God Who Creates: Essays in Honor of W. Sibley Towner*, eds. William P. Brown and S. Dean McBride Jr., 215–28. Grand Rapids: Eerdmans, 2000.

Tully, Eric J. "Hosea 1–3 as the Key to the Literary Structure and Message of the Book." In *An Excellent Fortress for His Armies*, edited by Richard E. Averbeck and K. Lawson Younger, 369–83. University Park: Pennsylvania State University Press, 2020.

———. *Hosea: A Handbook on the Hebrew Text*. Waco, TX: Baylor University Press, 2018.

Weinfeld, Moshe. *Deuteronomy 1–11*. AB 5. New York: Doubleday, 1991.

Wenham, Gordon J. "The Date of Deuteronomy: Linch-Pin of Old Testament Criticism." *Themelios* 11.1 (1985) 15–18.

Whitekettle, Richard. "Freedom from Fear and Bloodshed: Hosea 2.20 (Eng. 18) and the End of Human/Animal Conflict." *JSOT* 37 (2012) 219–36.

12

The Theological Implications of Covenant as Vassal Treaty in Israel

J. Harvey Walton

THE PURPOSE OF THIS study is to examine the language and imagery used in the Hebrew Bible to describe Israel's relationship with and cultic service to their God, especially that contained in Deuteronomy, the Deuteronomistic History, Ezekiel, and Malachi. The argument proposes that the rhetoric is intended to either reflect or establish a conception of Yahweh as a suzerain or emperor whom Israel serves as a vassal, and that Israel's cultic service—specifically, the various offerings—are depicted as tribute offered as tokens of fidelity and submission. This conception in turn may explain some of the Hebrew Bible's deviations from conventional ancient Near Eastern theological trends—specifically, the persistent emphasis on monolatry and the dubious status of the monarchy—which defy consensus among scholars.[1]

This study is not intended to suggest that the imagery of Yahweh as emperor and sacrifice as tribute is monolithic and systematic throughout the Hebrew Bible. Neither does it suggest or require that such conceptions were unique to Israel or that they even represented the common beliefs of historical Israelites. The point is rather to examine how the imagery contained in the various documents contributes to the argument presented by those documents (regardless of how unique, novel, or otherwise that argument may turn out to be).[2] This examination in turn requires properly appreci-

---

1. For presentation of this same idea and application to other aspects of Israelite theology, see Walton and Walton, *Lost World of the Israelite Conquest*, 220–29; Walton and Walton, *Demons and Spirits in Biblical Theology*, 89–91; Walton and Walton, *Lost World of the Torah*, 46–53; 72–74; 112–17.

2. "Ultimately [the biblical authors] were part of an ancient world culture, and we must assume some intellectual interplay and cross-fertilization of ideas. But when a biblical author expresses himself or herself in a text, the ideas really belong to that individual no matter how they might have been

ating what that imagery is and what significance it would have had in the ancient Near Eastern context in which it was composed.

Israelite theology and its relationship to Israelite political theory is a very complex topic, complicated further by the necessary distinction between the presentation of the ideas found in the texts and the historical realities as they would have been understood by the people involved. This study is interested only in analyzing the world-picture presented in the final redacted form[3] of the biblical documents; it is not interested in reconstructing the beliefs of historical people[4] and is not interested in the content and literary purpose of any of the (hypothetical) sources of those documents. Nonetheless, we still must establish some basic assumptions that underly this study and clarify the language and imagery that we will be examining.

Cultic Service and Divine-Human Relations

One of the most basic underlying assumptions of this study is that the cultic service to Yahweh advocated by the Hebrew Bible differs from the cultic service offered to gods in most other ancient Near Eastern literature. This implies that the "Israelites"—by which I mean the hypothetical people who espouse the beliefs of the implied authors of the biblical documents, who I will hereafter refer to as "Israelites" or "Israel" for brevity—have a different conception of divine-human relationships than their counterparts in the ancient Near East; that is, the hypothetical people who espouse the beliefs reflected in that literature, who I will hereafter refer to as "the ancient Near East (ANE)" for brevity. But in order to present that case, we need to briefly examine what the ANE conception of divine-human relations consisted of, and how Israel's conception differed.

Ancient Near Eastern religion centered around the idea that the gods had various needs and desires and that people had been created to provide for those needs. Civilization had been established by the gods and given to humanity for that purpose.[5] The role of the king, and of the various priests and officials who oversaw the institutions of the civilized world, was to ensure order and stability so that the needs of the gods could be met effectively and efficiently, thus guaranteeing the continued favor of the gods and the accompanying blessings of prosperity. If the humans failed to please the gods, the gods would become angry and either abandon the people to the

---

taken or cannibalized from other sources." Gnuse, *No Other Gods*, 130–31.

3. In most cases, for our purposes, this is also the Masoretic form that is the basis of English Old Testament translations, though text variants will be addressed if relevant. Translated biblical quotations throughout this work are from the NIV unless otherwise specified.

4. Presumably whoever was responsible for the form of the documents would have beliefs that concurred with their contents, but this study is concerned with the implied authors of the texts, not the historical authors/redactors.

5. So, for example: "Enlil, dwelling in his central shrine at Nippur, is taken care of by humanity, which has received civilization for that purpose." Wiggermann, "Agriculture as Civilization," 673.

predations of enemies or demons, or would take direct action and inflict curses and calamities on the people themselves. However, if the humans and the human world were compromised too extensively, the needs of the gods would not be met and the gods would suffer and starve. Thus there was a practical limit to the duress that the gods could inflict on the humans before the gods began to work against their own interests. This system produced a codependence between humans and gods, which Walton refers to as the "Great Symbiosis."[6] The driving engine of the Great Symbiosis was the sacrificial system, which was the means by which the humans fed and cared for the gods. In the ancient Near East, sacrifices were food offered to satisfy the gods so that the gods would not withdraw the blessings of order and prosperity that in turn allowed the humans to continue to meet the needs of the gods effectively.

The most important aspect of the symbiotic religious system for our purposes is the understanding that sacrifice provides something for the gods that will cause the gods to *suffer* if they have to go without it.[7] This is illustrated clearly in *Atrahasis*, where the gods have to go without sustenance for a week while the flood ravages the earth: "Their lips were feverishly athirst, they were suffering cramp from hunger."[8] When the gods retaliate for neglected offerings, then, they are effectively punishing the humans for causing them pain. The (potential) ability of the humans to inflict suffering on the gods allows the humans a degree of leverage to negotiate with the gods and compel the gods to do what the humans want. For example, elsewhere in *Atrahasis* the humans thwart the gods' plans to cull the numbers of humanity by neglecting the entire pantheon except for the one god who has the ability to end the various calamities; the offerings subsequently motivate the god to reverse the condition.[9] Some inscriptions also report kings reminding the gods of past service in exchange for favors, so for example: "Because I [. . .] quickly completed the pure temple, the exalted shrine, for the abode of the gods Anu and Adad, the great gods, my lords, and [thereby] pleased their great divinity [. . .] may they subdue under me all enemy lands, rebellious mountain regions, and rulers hostile to me."[10] Another inscription depicts the deity begging for food after having completed service to the king: "did I not vanquish your enemy? [. . .] what have you given me? There is no food for my banquet [. . .]. I am waiting for [it]."[11] An ancient Near Eastern proverb summarizes the implications of this leverage: "the man who does not sacrifice to his god can make the god run after him like a dog."[12] Of

---

6. Walton, *Ancient Near Eastern Thought*, 98–99.

7. "Every sacrifice was [. . .] presented to a divinity for its benefit or pleasure, something that was *necessary*, useful, or agreeable to that divinity." Bottéro, *Religion in Ancient Mesopotamia*, 125. Emphasis mine.

8. Lambert and Millard, *Atra-ḫasīs*, 97.

9. "He will be put to shame by the gift and will lift his hand." Lambert and Millard, *Atra-ḫasīs*, 69. (Line 1.398; see also lines 1.410; 2.ii.14; 2.ii.28).

10. Tiglath-Pileser 1 A.0.87.1; Grayson, *Assyrian Rulers of the Third and Second Millennium*, 29.

11. Excerpted from "3.5, The Word of Ishtar of Arbela"; Parpola, *Assyrian Prophecies*, 25–27.

12. Foster, *From Distant Days*, 387.

course, the gods are still powerful, so neglecting them is not necessarily a good idea—in *Erra and Ishum*, the god Erra plots to destroy humanity as retribution for contempt of himself and lack of care for the image of Marduk, for example—and many other texts make a point of demonstrating appropriately deferential piety. But the possibility of divine manipulation, while non-systematic and often understated, still remains a reality within the ancient Near Eastern religious system.

Israelite religion also has sacrifices offered to Yahweh, but in Israelite thinking Yahweh has no needs. This is stated most explicitly in Ps 50:9–13: "I have no need of [Heb. lit. "I will not take"] a bull from your stall or of goats from your pens [...] If I were hungry I would not tell you, for the world is mine, and all that is in it. Do I eat the flesh of bulls or drink the blood of goats?"[13] A similar expression of Yahweh's lack of needs is found in 2 Sam 7:6–7: "I have not dwelt in a house from the day I brought the Israelites up out of Egypt to this day [...] did I ever say to any of their rulers [...] 'Why have you not built me a house of cedar?'"[14] While biblical texts are neither systematic nor homogenous, nowhere in the Hebrew Bible does Yahweh say that he *does* need food or that he *does* need a house. If ancient Near Eastern cultic service provides for the needs of the gods—food and housing, through sacrifices and temples—and Yahweh does not need food or housing, then it would seem that Israel's cultic service to Yahweh serves a different purpose than cultic service offered to other ancient Near Eastern gods.

Many theologians do indeed recognize the difference, but propose that service to Yahweh meets a different *kind* of need than offerings to other gods. Various passages throughout (especially) the prophets are invoked to confirm that Yahweh is not really interested in food or housing. Some of the most notable examples are Hos 6:6 ("For I desire [*ḥāpēṣ*] mercy, not sacrifice, and acknowledgment of God rather than burnt offerings"); Ps 40:6 ("Sacrifice and offering you did not desire [*ḥāpēṣ*] [...] burnt offerings and sin offerings you did not require [*šā'al*]"); Isa 1:11 ("I have more than enough of burnt offerings [...] I have no pleasure [*ḥāpēṣ*] in the blood of bulls and lambs and goats"); and Ps 51:16 ("You do not delight [*ḥāpēṣ*] in sacrifice, or I would bring it; you do not take pleasure in [*rāṣâ*] burnt offerings"). Most of these passages

---

13. "Unlike other gods in the ancient Near East, the God of Israel does not accept sacrifice to appease an incessant appetite." DeClaissé-Walford et al., *The Book of Psalms*, 451. Likewise: "the language is comical, for it presupposes a rather weak and hungry God, waiting desperately for the next sacrifice to fill his belly [...] a superficial and formal offering of sacrifices, based on obedience to stipulations and nothing else, was tantamount to such a view of God." Craige, *Psalms 1–50*, 366. Psalm 50 is a liturgy that may have accompanied a covenant renewal ceremony: see ibid., 363–65; Goldingay, *Psalms 42–89*, 110. As such, it represents the essential expression of [Deuteronomistic] Israelite religion: "Just as the covenant was the very heart of the religion of Israel, so too Psalm 50 lies at the heart of the meaning of the Covenant" (Craige, *Psalms 1–50*, 367. See also Goldingay, Pss 42–89, 113: "the very definition of the covenant people as a whole lies here."). The sentiments of the Psalm are not peripheral or outlying ideas.

14. "A temple turns out to be unnecessary and unwanted. That David should propose such a grandiose gesture of patronage towards Yahweh [...] is taken as an affront." McCarter, *2 Samuel*, 197.

also eventually specify something that Yahweh wants instead (e.g., Mic 6:8: "what does the Lord require [*dāraš*] of you? To act justly and to love mercy and to walk humbly with your God"); or, alternatively, include a demand for Israel to stop doing something. Consequently, some interpreters approach these passages as implying, not that Yahweh has no needs, but that Israel has failed to identify Yahweh's needs properly—that is, Yahweh still requires the humans to supply something that Yahweh will suffer without, but the humans (Israel) do not understand what that something actually is. In this conception, Yahweh does not need food or housing, but he does need such things as worship, moral punctiliousness, or social justice, which Israel is supposed to provide. Yahweh will suffer (i.e., experience pain, lack, or loss; in context, this is usually asserted to consist of personal or vicarious psychological distress) if Israel does not provide these things, and so failure will be punished with abandonment and exile.

As popular as this conception is, there are several points at which it does not accord with the internal logic of the Hebrew Bible. First, and most importantly, this conception simply serves to psychologize the Great Symbiosis; it preserves the essential codependence of divine-human relationships and thereby ignores one of the most significant features of Israelite theology.[15] The rejection of offerings in fact reminds Israel that offerings *serve a purpose other than* meeting Yahweh's needs; it does not inform them that Yahweh has needs that offerings alone will not meet. Secondly, the language used in these passages is not indicative of neediness. The Hebrew word for "need" in terms of deprivation is *ḥāsēr* (see especially Deut 2:7, 15:8; Neh 9:21; Ps 23:1), but Yahweh is never the subject of this verb.[16] The verbs that define Yahweh's sentiments regarding offerings (negatively) or socio-ethical imperatives (positively) all fall within the semantic field of "ask," "want," or "enjoy,"[17] not "need" or "lack." Finally, all of the verbs that these passages apply negatively to offerings are also applied positively to offerings elsewhere. So, Yahweh does desire (*ḥāpēṣ*) sacrifices in Psalm 51:19; does demand (*dāraš*) sacrifices in Ezekiel 20:40; does ask for (*šā' al*) sacrifices in Deuteronomy 10:12–13 (implicit: "observe the Lord's commands and decrees");

---

15. Psalm 50, for example, does not condemn offerings unilaterally, but instead addresses a misconception about why they were necessary: "it would be odd for the psalm to abandon the idea of concrete offerings, because both the offerers and Yhwh would surely be glad to have such concrete expressions of gratitude [. . .] a material offering is apposite for them and therefore welcome to Yhwh, for what it says about their gratefulness, not because it will satisfy Yhwh's appetite." Goldingay, *Psalms 42–89*, 116.

16. Other Hebrew words indicating deprivation are *ṣōrek* (2 Chr 2:16) and *'ādar* (e.g. 1 Sam 30:19; 2 Sam 17:22; 1 Kgs 4:27). Neither of these take Yahweh as the subject, though Yahweh himself is *not* lacking [*'ādar*, implicitly lacking *for others*, as opposed to for himself] in Zeph 3:5.

17. See Talley, "חָפֵץ," 232 ("the word coveys a passionate emotion for an object"); *drš* with Yahweh as a subject usually occurs in a legal sense (i.e., "demand" rather than "need"; Denninger, "דָּרַשׁ," 995; *š' l* likewise refers to "ask" rather than "need" ("When God is the subject of *š' l*, the request often strengthens to a level of demand"; Beck, "אָלֹשׁ," 9); *rāṣâ* indicates what is or is not pleasing to God and what will produce divine acceptance and favor (or not); see Fretheim, "רָצָה," 1186.

and is pleased by (*rāṣâ*) sacrifices in e.g. Leviticus 1:4.[18] Further, when the Assyrian settlers in Samaria anger Yahweh in 2 Kgs 17:26–28, Israelite priests are employed to teach them "the rituals of the god of the land" (*mišpaṭ' ᵉlōhê hā' āreṣ*). However, the *mišpaṭ* in 2 Kgs 17 (NIV: "What [Yahweh] requires") does not consist of moral or social imperatives. The remainder of the passage specifies that the offense of the settlers refers to setting up shrines to other gods:[19] "But the Lord, who brought you up out of Egypt [. . .] is the one you must worship. To him you shall bow down and to him offer sacrifices [. . .] Do not worship other gods. Do not forget the covenant I have made with you, and do not worship other gods" (2 Kgs 17:36–38). The solution here that will stop Yahweh from killing the settlers is not social justice and no offerings are required;[20] instead it is both offerings and monolatry with no reference to moral performance or social justice.[21]

Statements that Yahweh does not want offerings, therefore, should not be read to mean that Israelite theology dismisses offerings as superfluous and unimportant.[22] Instead it means that Yahweh is not interested in offerings *as an end in themselves*. Passages such as Ps 50:8[23] and 1 Sam 15:13[24] indicate that the people and kings of Israel were diligent in performing offerings (though the returning generation was not, see Mal 1 and discussion below); the context of the complaints in both passages indicates that the problem was that the Israelites were less diligent in other things. According to ancient Near Eastern symbiotic thinking, offerings (food) and shrines (houses) *in and of themselves* are what the gods require because these serve to meet their needs, and the gods care very little about anything else as long as their needs continue to be met. For Yahweh, in contrast, offerings are a means to an end.

Sometimes the end that Yahweh desires can even be achieved through *not* providing sacrifices, as we see in the case of a lauded Israelite king who is *not* pious and diligent according to ancient Near Eastern categories: Hezekiah. He smashes all of the

18. *Niphal* stem throughout Leviticus does not change the essential meaning; for the sense of "accept [as an offering]" expressed in the *qal*, see Mal 1:10, 13.

19. See Cogan and Tadmor, *II Kings*, 210–11.

20. "The prophets indeed attacked the abuses of the sacrificial system (see Isa 1:11–15; 66:3; Jer 7:21–22; Hos 6:6; Amos 5:21–22; Mic 6:68), but as 1 Sam 2:29 says, "sacrifice and offering" are commanded by the Lord." Tsumura, *The First Book of Samuel*, 401.

21. Some interpreters, attempting to systematize these two ideas, suggest that immorality and social impropriety are inherent in idolatry and therefore a condemnation of idolatry should really be read as a call to socio-ethical reform. See for example Wright, *Old Testament Ethics for the People of God*, 25. This reading is often justified by a [very popular] misinterpretation of Ps 82, which is read as a statement that the gods were/should be killed for encouraging social injustice in their worshippers. For an alternative reading of Ps 82, see Walton and Walton, *Demons and Spirits in Biblical Theology*, 197–208.

22. Or as a purely human invention, which is a popular belief among modern interpreters who do not wish to believe that God could ever condone or require animal death.

23. Goldingay, *Psalms 42–89*, 114.

24. "*Though Saul acted religiously*, he actually did not listen to the voice of the Lord." Tsumura, *The First Book of Samuel*, 398 (emphasis mine).

shrines (2 Kgs 18:4; specified in 18:22 as shrines to Yahweh), after which he is promptly invaded by Assyria (2 Kgs 18:13). If Yahweh was a typical ancient Near Eastern god, this calamity would be interpreted as retribution for denying prerogatives to the gods. Foreign invasion is a clear sign of divine displeasure in the ancient Near East, which the commander of Sennacherib's army makes a point to note: "have I come to attack and destroy this place without word from the Lord? The Lord himself told me to march against this country and destroy it" (2 Kgs 18:25).[25] Hezekiah is also stricken with illness, another sign of divine disfavor (2 Kgs 20:1). However, despite destroying Yahweh's shrines and cutting off his sacrifices, Hezekiah is commended: "He held fast to the Lord and did not stop following him; he kept the commands the Lord had given Moses" (2 Kgs 18:5). Yahweh responds accordingly by delivering him from Sennacherib and by reversing his decree and healing Hezekiah's illness because Hezekiah "walked before [Yahweh] faithfully and with wholehearted devotion" (2 Kgs 20:3). By examining Ps 50 and 2 Kgs 18–20 we can see that, in Israelite theology, providing Yahweh with food and housing (offerings and shrines) does not by itself produce favor; conversely, denying Yahweh food and housing (by cutting off the offerings and destroying the shrines) does not by itself produce disfavor. Thus we see that the ancient Near Eastern symbiotic conception of divine-human relations is rejected in Israel.

At the same time, however, the sacrifices clearly serve some purpose, even though that purpose does not entail provision for Yahweh's needs in a codependent relationship. When Jer 7:22 says "I did not speak to your fathers or command them concerning burnt offerings and sacrifices" (ESV), it is not contradicting the content of Exodus and Deuteronomy, which in fact have quite a bit to say concerning burnt offerings and sacrifices. Instead, it goes on to say "But this command I gave them: 'Obey my voice, and I will be your God, and you shall be my people. And walk in all the way that I command you, that it may be well with you'" (ESV). As in the other passages discussed above, "obey my voice" and 'walk in the way I command" are not alternatives to sacrifices;[26] rather, they are the ends to which sacrifices—and by extension, the other stipulations of the Torah—are the means. That end cannot be reduced to the sacrifices themselves, as is the case in symbiotic religion, which is the point

---

25. Cogan and Tadmor point out that this is common Assyrian political rhetoric, not a reference to Isaiah 10:5–6 or an indication that Yahweh is enforcing a (hypothetical) loyalty oath by Hezekiah sworn in his name. Cogan and Tadmor, *II Kings*, 232. The destruction of shrines as the source of Yahweh's choice to join the Assyrian side is implied in 2 Kgs 18:22 (2 *Kings*, 231: "it may even be supposed that the reform was introduced in Judah without much popular support and so could have served the polemical purposes of the Assyrian speaker"). For Assyrians invoking sponsorship of enemy gods for political purposes in other campaigns, see Gnuse, *No Other Gods*, 159.

26. "Some of the polemic against sacrifice in the prophets can be explained as a way of saying 'I would rather have righteousness than sacrifice' [...] but the present verse [Jer 7:22], and the analogous texts in [Amos 5:21–24 and Hos 6:6; 8:13] do not lend themselves to this interpretation without violence." Holladay, *Jeremiah 1*, 261. Likewise, "it is unlikely that [Hos 6:6] represents God as rejecting the efficacy assigned to sacrificial practice elsewhere in the OT." Dearman, *Hosea*, 197.

of Jer 7:22–23.[27] However, the ends *also* cannot be reduced to moral or social engineering because, as seen above, the means to achieve the end explicitly also includes both sacrifices and monolatry, which have little to do with socio-ethical formation (and indeed contradict it, if modern humanistic concerns for animal rights and religious pluralism are also in view, as many theologians would prefer to be the case). The sacrifices are important; they serve a purpose; and that purpose is *not* symbiosis. Therefore we have to examine the internal logic of the Hebrew Bible itself to see what the sacrifices were supposed to do.

Sacrifice and Covenant

Israel's relationship with Yahweh is persistently described in terms of a *covenant* (Heb. *bᵉrît*). The term commonly refers to various kinds of social agreements (e.g., Gen 21:27; 2 Kgs 11:4) or political treaties (e.g., 1 Kgs 5:12; 15:19; 20:34); importantly for our purposes, it can refer specifically to a treaty between a suzerain and a vassal (e.g. Jos 9:11; 1 Sam 11:1; Ezek 17:13; Hos 12:1). Because of the language of "rebellion" occasionally employed in the context of this covenant and because of the imperial title assigned to Yahweh in Mal 1:14 (both discussed further below), the last of these is probably the most applicable. If this reading is correct, by this metaphor, Israel is described as a vassal to Yahweh.[28] References to various "commands," "decrees," and "statutes," as well as more nebulous injunctions to "obey [Yahweh's] voice" and "walk in [Yahweh's] ways" all refer to the stipulations of this treaty. The treaty itself is transcribed in Deuteronomy,[29] and referred to in Isa 1:2–3.[30] It is this metaphor, and not the paradigm of codependent symbiosis, that defines divine-human relations in Israel. Thus, whatever the Israelite sacrifices are intended to accomplish should conceptually parallel something that an ancient Near Eastern vassal would be expected to provide to their suzerain.

Sacrifices are explicitly described in the context of a political metaphor in Mal 1:8–14, which gives us insight into how they would have been understood. "'When you offer blind animals for sacrifice, is that not wrong? When you sacrifice lame or diseased animals, is that not wrong? Try offering them to your governor! Would he be pleased with you? Would he accept you? [. . .] For I am a great king,' says the Lord

---

27. "Obviously it is not [Yahweh's] will to offer burnt offering and sacrifice, not when those who offer it are so deaf to him." Holladay, *Jeremiah 1*, 262.

28. Or, at the very least, as subjects with a political duty to their ruler. The specific ideologies of empire vary throughout the ancient Near East, and the appropriation of the concept in Israelite theology is generic. In many cases "tribute" can substitute conceptually for "taxes," though the concept of rebellion (*mārad*) most commonly appears in imperial contexts.

29. See Kitchen and Lawrence, *Treaty, Law, and Covenant in the Ancient Near East*.

30. "Heaven and earth were invoked as witnesses when God made his covenant with Israel (Deut 4:26; 30:19; 31:28; 32:1; Ps 50:4; cf. Mic 6:1–2). Now they are invoked as witnesses to Israel's breach of that same covenant." Roberts, *First Isaiah*, 19.

Almighty, 'and my name is to be feared among the nations.'" This passage very clearly establishes a parallel conception between sacrifices offered to Yahweh and the tribute extracted by the regional governor (compare Neh 5:15). Tribute in the ancient Near East served a number of functions, but for our purposes, paying tribute demonstrated a posture of loyalty and submission towards the suzerain. Refusing to pay tribute is an act of rebellion (2 Kgs 17:4). Importantly, however, the suzerain does not "need" the tribute, in the sense that they will suffer privation if it is withheld; note that Nehemiah does not suffer lack or loss for refusing to "[demand] the food offered to the governor." The amount and quality of tribute that a ruler can extract is representative of their power and is boasted of in their inscriptions; the tribute reflects the ruler's authority and status. When Yahweh is complaining about the offerings he is receiving in Mal 1, he is accusing them of disregarding his status—the blind and defiled animals would not be suitable for even the governor (a relatively minor official), but Yahweh is the Great King, which is the preferred title of the Emperor (see further below).[31] The point is that the Israelites would not dare to present these animals to even someone of the rank of Nehemiah, let alone to someone of the rank of Cyrus.[32] It demonstrates a level of contempt that is almost worse than not offering any tribute at all (see Mal 1:10).[33]

Sacrifices in Israel, then, are conceived of as paying tribute to a suzerain as a gesture of loyalty, respect, and submission. This is reflected in some of the terms used for offerings. The word for the "tribute" that Hezekiah withholds from Assyria in 2 Kgs 17:4, also seen in several other political contexts (Judg 3:15–18; 2 Sam 8:2, 6; 1 Kgs 4:21; 2 Chr 28:6) is *minḥâ*. However, by far the most common usage for this term in the Hebrew Bible is for ritual offerings to Yahweh. The *minḥâ* is one of the prescribed sacrifices and is described in Lev 2 (NIV "grain offering"), but it can also refer to offerings more generically, i.e. those of Cain and Abel in Gen 4:3–5.[34] What is interesting for our purposes is that, in the rest of the ancient Near East, the typical words for political tribute have no currency in ritual contexts.[35] Further, it is not likely that the

31. See for example Hill, *Malachi*, 195.
32. See Verhoef, *Haggai and Malachi*, 218; Jacobs, *Haggai and Malachi*, 207–8.
33. Verhoef, *Haggai and Malachi*, 220.

34. We should clarify that this is not the same word for the "thank offering" (*tôdâ*) that Yahweh requests in Ps 50:14, 23. Psalm 50 juxtaposes offerings that satisfy hunger with offerings that reflect a relationship; it does not juxtapose offerings that reflect different kinds of relationships (i.e., loyal vassals versus rebellious vassals).

35. The primary Akkadian words for "tribute" are *biltu* (lit. "burden"; compare Heb. *mas*, Est 10:1; *maśśā*, 2 Chr 17:11), *maddattu*, and *tāmartu*; see CAD 2.234b–236a; 10.13a–14b; 18.113a–114b. A related term, *igisû*, refers to "gifts" that can be given to either kings or gods (CAD 7.42b–43b) and appears paired with "tribute" (CAD 2.36a; 7.43b). *Igisû* can also refer to taxes; this might be the meaning of *minḥâ* in 2 Chr 17:5 (where all Judah brings *minḥâ* to Jehoshaphat), and perhaps also in 2 Chr 17:11 where *minḥâ* is paired with *maśśā* (NIV: "gifts . . . as tribute"), just as *biltu* and *igisû* are paired in Akkadian texts. However, *minḥâ* often appears by itself to refer to tribute, but *igisû* does not. Compare *igisû* instead to Heb. *terûmâ*, which usually refers to cultic offerings or taxes paid to priests, but in Prov 29:4 refers to taxes levied by the king (see Wächter and Seidl, "תְּרוּמָה," 772–73).

Hebrew is adding political currency to a fundamentally religious term, because the Ugaritic cognate *mnh(t)* "lacks overt ritual associations."[36] Instead, taking a term with a technical political significance and applying it to a ritual context might be intended to add a political dimension to the religious actions.[37]

The concept of sacrifice as tribute fits well with the broader idea of Yahweh having no needs. Kings did demand tribute, but not because they would suffer privation if they had to go without it. The economy of the imperial state did not depend on an influx of resources from its territories, as was the case for example in European colonies; the collected tribute often wound up locked away in vaults or put on display as a demonstration of imperial might. The tribute existed so that the ruler could claim that it had been paid, and in doing so could demonstrate that he was worthy enough for his subjects to pay it. Tribute, then, serves to glorify the emperor and enhance his reputation, not to meet his personal needs.[38]

This *reputation* is what Yahweh is talking about in Mal 1:14 when he says "my name is to be feared among the nations." By disrespecting the sacrifices, the Israelites are effectively withholding tribute, which as seen above is construed as an act of rebellion. Rebellion in turn reflects poorly on the suzerain, who is seen as unable to assert control over his domains. Consequently, throughout the ancient Near East rebellion has a predictable response; the maligned emperor re-asserts his power and restores his sullied reputation by assembling an army and smashing the rebels into dust. Yahweh's response to rebellious Israel is the same, as described explicitly in Ezek 17:11–20:

> Say to this rebellious people [. . .] 'The king of Babylon [. . .] took a member of the royal family and made a treaty [*bᵉrît*] with him, putting him under oath [. . .] But the king rebelled [*mārad*] against him [. . .] Will he break [*pārar*] the treaty [*bᵉrît*] and yet escape? [. . .] Therefore this is what the Sovereign Lord says: As surely as I live, I will repay him for despising my oath and breaking [*pārar*] my covenant [*bᵉrît*] [. . .] I will bring him to Babylon and execute judgment on him there because he was unfaithful to me.'

---

36. Clemens, *Sources for Ugaritic Ritual and Sacrifice*, 68.

37. The word for "offering" [to the governor] in Mal 1:8 is *qārab* (hiphil); the same word is used for paying tribute in Judges 3:17–18 but is most commonly used for cultic offerings to Yahweh. Both the Hebrew *qrb* and its cognates, Akkadian *qerēbu* and Ugaritic *qrb*, are generic and can apply to both cultic and secular/legal contexts. See Gane and Milgrom, "קרב," 13.136.

38. While the success of empire did depend on the ruler's reputation, and the ruler's personal wellbeing was somewhat contingent on the success of empire, tribute was not akin to, say, a personal wage, wherein the ruler does not eat if it is not paid. The loss of the emperor's reputation will lead to a failure of the result he is attempting to achieve (empire), but it will not lead to personal privation in the same way that loss of food leads to personal privation of the gods. The emperor has a vested interest in the success of empire, as Yahweh also has a vested interest in Israel, but this interest should be conceptually distinguished from a dependence for basic necessities, which is represented by symbiotic religion.

Here the appointment of Zedekiah by Nebuchadnezzar and his subsequent rebellion (described in 2 Kgs 24:17–20) is compared with Israel's covenant infidelity,[39] with the consequences stressed as being identical; the rebels will be carried off to die in Babylon. The word for [political] rebellion here in Ezek 17:3 is *mārad* (see also e.g. Gen 14:4; 2 Kgs 18:7; 24:20), which is also used in Ezek 2:3 to describe Israel's relationship to Yahweh:[40] "Son of man, I am sending you to the Israelites, to a rebellious [*mārad*] nation that has rebelled [*mārad*] against me; they and their ancestors have been in revolt [*pāšaʿ*] against me to this very day." *Pāšaʿ* refers to political rebellion in e.g. 1 Kgs 12:19; 2 Kgs 3:5, 7; 2 Chr 21:8, 10. However, Israel's offenses are not usually withholding tribute, as in Mal 1; the more common offense for which Israel is accused of violating the covenant is idolatry. This is worth further examination.

Idolatry and Rebellion

Israelite theology conceives of its relationship to Yahweh as following the paradigm of a vassal's relationship to a suzerain, defined by their treaty, which is the covenant at Sinai. However, ancient Near Eastern vassal treaties do not commonly dictate which gods the vassals are allowed to serve. Assmann even suggests that the universality of polytheistic pantheons, albeit known by different names, is an underlying premise for the possibility of international treaties.[41] Yahweh, on the other hand, cares very much about who his vassals are making offerings to. Idolatry is the most common accusation against Israel, as seen for example in Ezek 20:32–38:

> You say, 'We want to be like the nations, like the peoples of the world, who serve wood and stone.' But what you have in mind will never happen. As surely as I live, declares the Sovereign Lord, I will reign [*mālak*] over you [. . .] I will bring you into the wilderness of the nations and there, face to face, I will execute judgment upon you. I will take note of you as you pass under my rod, and I will bring you into the bond of the covenant [*bᵉrît*]. I will purge you of those who revolt [*mārad*] and rebel [*pāšaʿ* ע] against me.

---

39. "Both fable and its earthly interpretation are suddenly transposed into an allegory of the relation between God and (the king of) Judah. The earthly suzerain, Nebuchadnezzar, will not let rebellious Zedekiah get away with treachery, how much less will the divine sovereign countenance the Judahite's breach of faith with *him*." Greenberg, *Ezekiel 1–20*, 322. This is in contrast to a more common interpretation that sees Yahweh condemning a breach of a treaty that Zedekiah has sworn in his name (*Ezekiel 1–20*, 320–22); "The natural—indeed obvious—construction of vs. 19 is to make 'my curse-oath . . . and my covenant' in YHWH's speech refer to his own covenant with Israel (as in 16:59), which the king was held responsible to maintain" (p. 322).

40. "Whether political or religious rebellion, *mrd* most frequently functions against the backdrop of covenantal relationships." Carpenter and Grisanti, "מָרַד", 1098.

41. "The conviction that these foreign peoples worshipped the same gods [. . .] must be reckoned among the major cultural achievements of the ancient world. The powerful influence of this insight can be seen in the field of international law and in the practice of forming treaties with other states and peoples." Assmann, *Moses the Egyptian*, 46.

A similar sentiment is expressed in Jer 22:8–9: "People from many nations will pass by this city and will ask one another, 'Why has the Lord done such a thing to this great city?' And the answer will be: 'Because they have forsaken [*'ʸāzab*] the covenant [*bᵉrît*] of the Lord their God and have worshiped and served other gods.'" The word for "breaking" the treaty that is used to describe Zedekiah's actions in Ezek 17:15–16 (and again in a political context in 1 Kgs 15:19; 2 Chr 16:3) is *pārar*, which is also used in collocation with *bᵉrît* to describe the actions of Israel in Deut 31:16, 20 and Jer 11:10, with the offense specified as idolatry: "these people will soon prostitute themselves to the foreign gods of the land they are entering. They will forsake [*'ʸāzab*] me and break [*pārar*] the covenant [*bᵉrît*] I made with them"; "when they eat their fill and thrive, they will turn to other gods and worship them, rejecting me and breaking [*pārar*] my covenant [*bᵉrît*]"; "They have followed other gods to serve them. Both Israel and Judah have broken [*pārar*] the covenant [*bᵉrît*] I made with their ancestors."[42] However, if Yahweh is seen as an emperor, and emperors do not care who their vassals worship, why does Yahweh care?

Many interpreters see the condemnation of idolatry as arising from ideological iconoclasm, which in turn is thought to be the foundational basis of monotheism in general: "[the] defining quality [of monotheism] lies not in the belief in one god as opposed to the belief in many gods, but in its radical and complete break from traditional religion [. . .] The decisive feature of monotheistic movements is their revolutionary, 'idolophobic,' or iconoclastic character."[43] Monolatry or monotheism, so the theory goes, arises as a radical counter-religion whose fundamental objective is an ideological purging of the mainstream tradition: "Monotheistic religions structure the relationship between the old and the new in terms not of evolution but of revolution, and reject all older and other religions as 'paganism' or 'idolatry.' Monotheism always appears as a counter-religion. There is no natural or evolutionary way leading from the error of idolatry to the truth of monotheism. This truth can only come from outside, by way of revelation."[44] Likewise, "monotheism is a kind of inner community discourse establishing distance from outsiders."[45] However, in the case of the Hebrew Bible at least, this does not appear to be the case; Israel's theological stance indeed developed through evolution,[46] arising naturally and necessarily from the innovative

---

42. Offenses other than idolatry on the part of Israel classified by use of the collocation *pārar* + *bᵉrît* are failure to be circumcised (Gen 17:14) or bringing the uncircumcised into the temple (Ezek 44:7), or generic violation of decrees (including implicitly those not to worship idols; Lev 26:15; Isa 24:5; Jer 31:32; Ezek 16:59). References to Yahweh "breaking the covenant" are found in Lev 26:44; Judg 2:1; Jer 14:21; and Zech 11:10. A generic reference to a "broken covenant" as a condition of distress is found in Isa 33:8.

43. Assmann, *Moses the Egyptian*, 39.

44. Assmann, *Moses the Egyptian*, 7.

45. Smith, *The Origins of Biblical Monotheism*, 154.

46. "The later dominant paradigm of a single national god with divine workers was only one version of devotion available in Iron Age Israel. Only later was the process of telescoping divinity into a single divine king with his servants completed." Smith, *The Origins of Biblical Monotheism*, 155.

use of a suzerain-vassal relationship to define divine-human relations. Most importantly for our purposes, the suzerain-vassal paradigm does not simply define Israel's relationship with Yahweh; it replaces the paradigm of symbiosis as a conceptualization of *divine-human relationships in general*. Serving gods other than Yahweh, then, is tantamount to swearing allegiance and paying tribute to *a different suzerain*. This in turn is something that ancient Near Eastern emperors care very much about. The succession treaty of Esarhaddon, for example, contains the explicit stipulation "[do not] set any other king or any other lord over yourselves, nor swear an oath to any other king or any other lord."[47] The difference between the paradigms has to do with the nature of the relationship between the parties. In divine-human symbiosis, any given deity wants its needs attended to, and as long as those prerogatives are supplied, he or she does not much care whether the humans are seeing to the needs of others as well. Feeding one god is not mutually exclusive with feeding another god.[48] Kings and emperors, on the other hand, desire loyalty, not food. Loyalty by nature is somewhat exclusive; see for example the argument of Matt 6:24. Further, at least in theory, part of the king's reputation hinged on his ability to provide for the security and stability of his (loyal) vassals. If a vassal feels like they need to seek support elsewhere, it does not speak highly of the competence of the emperor. This sentiment is expressed in 2 Kgs 1:3, 6, 16: "Is it because there is no God in Israel that you are going off to consult Baal-Zebub, the god of Ekron?" Israel, as a (theoretically loyal) vassal, is expected to rely on the emperor (Yahweh) for all of the services that his office is expected to supply; seeking those services elsewhere is an expression of disloyalty and therefore of rebellion.[49] Rebellious vassals, of course, would seek aid in the hopes of gaining independence, as Zedekiah petitions Egypt for in Ezek 17.

Normally a vassal acquires that status by virtue of having been conquered, or as an alternative to being conquered. Sometimes, however, vassals will patriate themselves voluntarily in order to gain benefits. The treaty between the Hittite emperor Mursili and his vassal Kupanta-Kurunta, for example, describes a king, Mashuiluwa, who swears allegiance to Hatti in order to secure military aid against rebels in his homeland, but subsequently rebels and is deposed. The treaty describes the emperor's successor, Mursili, instating the son of the deposed ruler, Kupanta-Kurunta, in his father's place.[50] The parallels to Israel's own situation are enlightening. Israel likewise does not picture itself as having been conquered or subjugated by Yahweh; rather, like Mashuiluwa, they accept the covenant voluntarily (Exod 24:7–8) with the expectation

---

47. Parpola and Watanabe, *Neo-Assyrian Treaties and Loyalty Oaths*, 71–72.

48. "The gods would not be jealous of attention paid to other gods as long as their own needs were being met and their position was not in jeopardy." Walton, *Ancient Near Eastern Thought*, 72.

49. "The answer to the king's question [. . .] predicts death for Ahaziah as a punishment for his offense, the disrespect shown to Yahweh by sending a mission to the god of Ekron." Fritz, *1 & 2 Kings*, 230.

50. Beckman, *Hittite Diplomatic Texts*, 69–71.

of benefits from the alliance; specifically, gifts of land and subsequent prosperity. Also like Mashuiluwa, they subsequently rebel and are summarily destroyed (Num 14:21–45). In the Hittite treaty, the emperor emphasizes that allowing the son of the rebellious Mashuiluwa to claim his father's throne is an unwarranted act of generosity:

> Now I, My Majesty, have not mistreated you, Kupanta-Kurunta, in any way. I have not turned you out. I have not taken the house of your father or the land away from you. I have given the house of your father and your land back to *you*, and I have installed *you* in lordship for the land [. . .] because your father Mashuiluwa offended against My Majesty, and you, Kupanta-Kurunta, were Mashuiluwa's son, even if you were in no way an offender—could not I, My Majesty, have deposed you right then, if My Majesty had been disposed to disfavor? I could even now have taken the house of your father away from you and have given [it] to someone else. I could have made someone else lord in the land.[51]

The next generation of Israelites is similarly reminded of the misdeeds of their parents (Deut 1:24–45) and is likewise offered the opportunity to accept the [same] covenant of their own volition (Josh 24:1–27). Specifically, they are reminded of what Yahweh has done for them[52] and invited to decide whether they would rather serve Yahweh or someone else: "Throw away the gods your ancestors worshiped beyond the Euphrates River and in Egypt, and serve the Lord. But if serving the Lord seems undesirable to you, then choose for yourselves this day whom you will serve, whether the gods your ancestors served beyond the Euphrates, or the gods of the Amorites, in whose land you are living" (Josh 24:14–15). Joshua continues to emphasize that idolatry will be a problem: "[Yahweh] will not forgive your rebellion (*peša'*) and your sins. If you forsake the Lord and serve foreign gods, he will turn and bring disaster on you and make an end of you, after he has been good to you [. . .] [Now] throw away the foreign gods that are among you and yield your hearts to the Lord, the God of Israel" (Josh 24:19–23). *Peša'* is the nominal form of *pāša'*, and refers to political rebellion in 1 Sam 24:11 and Prov 28:2. This passage indicates that a choice to serve the overlords—that is, the gods—of other nations will constitute political rebellion against their chosen overlord, Yahweh, who has been gracious and provided for them. Kupanta-Kurunta is similarly warned against disloyalty: "You shall not desire any other power over you. [In the future] protect My Majesty as overlord."[53] A different Hittite treaty explicitly commands the vassal not to pay tribute to another power: "The tribute that was imposed upon your grandfather and upon your father shall be imposed upon

---

51. Beckman, *Hittite Diplomatic Texts*, 71–74

52. Compare to the similar content of Hittite treaties: "Here it is demonstrated just why the [vassal] should be loyal to Hatti—either because he had been favored by the Great King, having received, say, basic sustenance or military assistance [. . .] or because he had been spared the severe punishment he deserved." Beckman, *Hittite Diplomatic Texts*, 3.

53. Beckman, *Hittite Diplomatic Texts*, 72.

you: They paid 300 shekels of refined gold [. . .] you shall pay it likewise. You shall not turn your eyes to another. Your ancestors paid tribute to Egypt, [but] you [shall not pay it]."[54] Paying tribute to powers other than the emperor constitutes rebellion. If offerings are tribute in Israel, then giving offerings to gods other than Yahweh likewise constitutes rebellion, for the same reasons, and is punished accordingly.

This comparison illustrates the extent to which service and gifts from Israel to gods other than Yahweh has been conceptually compared to service and gifts from a vassal to a ruler other than their suzerain in Israelite rhetoric, and thus illustrates the extent to which cultic service has been redefined in political terms. Divine-human relationships in Israel have not been psychologized or spiritualized relative to their ancient Near Eastern counterparts; rather, they have been *politicized*.[55] The political relationship of Israel to Yahweh is defined by the covenant. Tribute is demanded in the form of sacrifices and offerings, and sacrifices and offerings to other gods constitute rebellion, just as sending tribute and gifts to another king would do.

Monolatry in Israel, therefore, does not arise from a socially-fueled "counter-religion" whose objective is to purge itself from the cultural and theological trappings of outsiders in fire and blood.[56] Neither does it represent an enlightened progressive development from the more primitive religions of Israel's neighbors.[57] Polytheism is a sophisticated theological system with its own intricate internal logic,[58] as monotheism (or monolatry) also is.[59] The difference between them is substantive, not qualitative. At its most basic level, polytheism represents the pantheon as a divine bureaucracy, each member delegated to oversee a particular aspect of the world order.[60] The patron of any given component is easily identifiable and easily accessible, even across cultural boundaries where the deity remains the same despite being known by different names.[61] On the other hand, however, *human* government throughout the ancient world did not follow a similar model. Power in the human world is centralized in the king, not distributed more or less evenly throughout a bureaucracy. Conciliar government is fractious, anarchic, and inefficient, as opposed to the stability and consistency offered by centralization; Israel—according to the Deuteronomist, at least—recognized this political reality in the chaos of the judges period and demanded to rectify it with a

---

54. Beckman, *Hittite Diplomatic Texts*, 56.

55. "The God of the Exodus is [. . .] much closer to Pharaoh than to Aton or Amun, let alone Aristotle's unmoved mover, in being a primarily political figure [. . .] His 'wrath' and 'jealousy' are political affects, befitting a king who has entered into a treaty with a vassal." Assmann, *Moses the Egyptian*, 211.

56. For a summary of arguments to this effect, see Gnuse, *No Other Gods*, 138–41.

57. For summary of arguments to this effect, see Gnuse, *No Other Gods*, 136–38.

58. "The polytheistic religions of the ancient Near East and Ancient Egypt represent highly developed cultural achievements." Assmann, *Moses the Egyptian*, 45.

59. "Monotheism emerges and develops most fully in the context of serious intellectual struggles." Gnuse, *No Other Gods*, 131.

60. Walton, *Ancient near Eastern Thought*, 54–55.

61. Assmann, *Moses the Egyptian*, 47.

centralized government. According to the de facto practice of the ancient world, order in the human world is best sustained by a single king who delegates tasks through a subordinated hierarchy of bureaucrats; why should order in the divine world not be sustained in the same way? The theology of the Hebrew Bible represents a centralization of divine power, where the divine bureaucracy (designated by the terms *bĕnê ĕlôhîm* or *bĕnê ĕlîm*) are stripped of significance and reduced to extensions of the agency of the divine king, Yahweh,[62] just as bureaucrats and officials are reduced to extensions of the king in a human monarchy. There is level of irony that Israel's desire for autocracy in the human realm cannot be matched by a recognition of the same autocracy in the divine realm.[63]

Yahweh as King

The politicization of divine-human relations does not only necessitate demoting the pantheon to the status of bureaucratic officials of the single divine emperor; it also requires reexamining the status of Israel's human king. If Yahweh is the king, the human monarch cannot *also* be the king. Instead, if Yahweh is the emperor and Israel is his vassal, the human king (*melek*) should be given the status of the regent over the vassal state (Hebrew *melek* can also refer to a regent, e.g., 2 Kgs 3:4). This is indeed what we see when examine the conceptual status assigned by the Hebrew Bible to the Israelite monarchy.

Referring to deities as "king" is not uncommon in the ancient Near East, especially in hymnic literature. The title could either refer to the power and authority of the deity relative the humans—gods stood over the kings much like the kings and officials stood over the people—or it could indicate that the deity in question was the leader of the pantheon; that is, king of the gods.[64] Yahweh is no exception, and is referred

---

62. Stated explicitly in 1 Kgs 22:23; Job 1:20; 2:3 where Yahweh is given credit for his agent's actions.

63. Smith argues that Ugaritic—and by extension early Israelite—polytheism conceived of the pantheon as a reflection of the family as the dominant social unit. According to his theory, monotheism in Israel arose in response to the diminishing significance of family/clan/tribal units in the face of the monarchy. See Smith, *The Origins of Biblical Monotheism*, 164. If this theory is correct, the resistance of the [historical] Israelite people to the monotheistic religion—which the Deuteronomistic History itself acknowledges—might be explained by the similar resistance towards kings and emperors (demonstrated by frequent rebellions) described in the same documents.

64. Greenwood suggests that in early Assyrian thought the deity was conceived as a political emperor, as we also see in Israel; which he claims on the basis of the title *iššakku* ("regent") for the Assyrian monarch. According to his theory, as Assyria grew in power and prominence, the title of the monarch changed from *iššakku* ("regent") to *šarru* ("king"), thus indicating that the human ruler had assumed a role previously allotted to the deity, while the deity was redefined more abstractly and symbolically. He goes on to compare this development with Israel's request for a king (*melek*) in 1 Sam 8. Greenwood, *Then Aššur Will Hear His Prayers*, 32–34, 107. However, even the Assyrian "regents" offered sacrifices as food to their gods in a symbiotic relationship, rather than offering political service to a deity who required nothing of them but demanded loyalty and obedience for the sake of the deity's reputation, which indicates that Israel's political theology is still more or less unique even if this

to frequently as "king" (*melek*, or as the subject of the verbs *mālak* or *māšal*, "rule/reign [as king]"), especially in the psalms and prophetic literature. Superficially, this title supports the idea that Yahweh's status has been conceptually politicized and the human king reclassified accordingly. However, we should not necessarily place much technical significance on the various attributions of the title "king" to Yahweh, especially not in hymns, where the same designation could be applied to any deity by any ancient Near Eastern society regardless of the broader framework of divine-human relations or the relative status of the human ruler.[65] Nonetheless, a few occurrences of the title are worth brief examination.

Perhaps the most notable are the three passages where Yahweh's rule over Israel is juxtaposed with that of a human ruler. In Judg 8:23 Gideon claims that "I will not rule over (*māšal*) you . . . [but] the Lord will rule over you"; in 1 Sam 8:7 Yahweh complains that "[the Israelites] have rejected me as their king (*mālak*)"; in 1 Sam 12:12 Samuel announces that "you said to me, 'No, we want a king (*melek*) to rule over (*mālak*) us'—even though the Lord your God was your king (*melek*)." All of these are normally interpreted to indicate that the human king is usurping a function that Yahweh was supposed to perform. This in turn supports the idea that Yahweh's "rule" over Israel in these passages is being portrayed as conceptually similar to something a human *could* perform, and indeed normally *would* perform, since the request in 1 Sam 8:5 is for a king "such as all the other nations have." However, the problem with the request in 1 Samuel—which the Deuteronomist portrays negatively—is not usurpation per se; the elders are not specifically asking for Yahweh to step aside and allow a human to take over some or all of his functions.[66] The elders of 1 Sam 8 in fact want to do away with Israel's political conception of deity in exchange for the symbiotic conception held by their neighbors, thereby gaining the leverage over the deity that symbiotic sacrifice provides.[67] The problem is not that the Israelites want a *melek*, as opposed to some other kind of ruler;[68] the problem is that they want a *kind* of king ("such as all the other nations have") who is able to manipulate their God, specifically in terms of being able to call him out to battle. In Judges the condition of having "no king (*melek*) in Israel" is assessed negatively (Judg 17:6; 18:1; 19:1; 21:25).[69] A *melek* can be a faithful regent to Yahweh, as Samuel admonishes in 1 Sam 12:14-15: "If you fear the Lord and serve and obey him and do not rebel (*mārâ*) against his commands, and if both

---

theory is correct.

65. See Walton, *Ancient Near Eastern Thought*, 60–61.

66. For a discussion of various interpretations of what the request for a king entails, see Walton, "A King Like the Nations," 181–91.

67. Prior to the request for the king, leverage had been thought to be provided by the ark; after the loss of the ark in 1 Sam 4 this leverage was thought to be provided by Samuel, but the elders believe that his success will not be sustained by his sons. See Walton, "King Like the Nations," 195–99.

68. See discussion in Walton, "King like the Nations," 181–84.

69. In 1 Kgs 22:47, Edom is ruled by a ranking official (*nāṣab*; NIV "provincial governor") specifically in place of a king; however, this condition is never prescribed or recommended for Israel.

you and the king (*melek*) who reigns over you follow the Lord your God—good! But if you do not obey the Lord, and if you rebel (*mārâ*) against his commands, his hand will be against you, as it was against your ancestors." *Mārâ* usually refers to "rebellion" against Yahweh, though it also appears in social contexts (Deut 21:18, 20; Josh 1:18; Job 17:2); the term refers to disobedience or defiance of an authority figure.[70] Samuel's statement indicates that "not rebelling" is something the *melek* can theoretically do, which in turn means that simply *being* a *melek* does not in itself constitute *mārâ*. The title reserved for the emperor is *melek gādôl*, which is used for Sennacherib (2 Kgs 18:19, 28; Isa 36:4, 13) and also for Yahweh (Pss 47:2; 95:3; Mal 1:14) but never for Israelite kings.[71] There is nothing wrong with Israel having a human king, as long as that king is faithful to the stipulations of the covenant and thereby serves as a loyal vassal to the divine emperor (see especially Deut 17:14–20). The king is a regent of a divine suzerain, not an overlord in his own right with a divine sponsor, as was the case elsewhere in the ancient Near East.

Kings in Assyria and elsewhere in the ancient Near East served as viceroys of the gods on earth,[72] but even as they did so they held an elevated status that enfolded them into the divine sphere, even if they did not attain a full membership of the pantheon:

> The Neo-Assyrian royal titularies, narrative inscriptions, astrological prognostications and unctuously flattering correspondence hammer away at the theme of the unique proximity of the king to the divine realm and extol his god-like powers. The kings were summoned prenatally to kingship, suckled by goddesses, warned by eclipses and other portents of imminent personal hazards, and succored by upbeat, motherly prophecies uttered by goddesses. Kings like the gods strode into battle surrounded by the melammu, a radiant, terrifying nimbus devastating to foes [...] kings embodied godlike wisdom

---

70. See Carpenter and Grisanti, "מָרָה," 1100; "the subjects rebelling are always in some kind of subordinate position before another to whom they owe obedience." The noun form, *mᵉrî*, appears with an unspecified referent in Prov 17:11 (Heb. lit. "an evil [man] seeks only rebellion"; NIV has added "against God"), and in Job 23:2 *mᵉrî* describes Job's complaint concerning God's treatment of him.

71. "The Assyrian king [in 2 Kgs 18] is always designated as the *Great King*, a translation of the Akk. *šarru rabû*, the foremost title of every Assyrian king from the days of Shamshi-Adad I on [...] it originated in a north-Syrian title and was typical of the Hittite kings." Cogan and Tadmor, *II Kings*, 231. The Aramaic title for emperors in the Bible is "king of kings," used for Nebuchadnezzar in Dan 2:37 and Artaxerxes in Ezra 7:12. Hebrew "king of kings" is used for Nebuchadnezzar in Ezek 26:7; compare similar *melek śarim* (NIV "mighty king," lit. "king of princes") in Hos 8:10; for both titles comparable to *šarru rabû* see Wolff, *Hosea*, 144. Neither of these titles is used for either Yahweh or the Israelite king. NIV "Great King" in Hos 5:13 and 10:6 refers to Tiglath-Pileser III (see Wolff, *Hosea*, 115) and translates the Hebrew hapax *melek yārēb*, which is read as a scribal corruption of the [presumed] original Hebrew *melek rab* (יָרֵב מלב from רַב מַלְכִּי; see ibid., 104). Hebrew *melek rab* is also used of Yahweh in Ps 48:2, but never for the Israelite king. A nontechnical use of Hebrew *melek gādôl* (referring to a ruler of superlative power, though also not the Israelite king) appears in Jer 25:14; 27:7; Ps 136:17; and Eccl 9:14. Aramaic *melek rab* is used in the same nontechnical sense as a reference to Solomon in Ezra 5:11.

72. "In Assyria the main god is truly at the top of the hierarchy and the ruler is only his viceroy on earth." Holloway, *Aššur is King*, 65.

and could be characterized as the very image of the gods. The kings were not members of the state pantheon, but they dwelt in closer physical and ontological proximity to the gods than any other mortals.[73]

In a similar vein, "one could argue that the 'political dimension' of the sun-god was represented not only by images (ṣalmu) of Šamaš worshipped in temples, but also by the very person of the king, who functioned as a kind of "living image" of the sun-god (and perhaps a few other important deities as well)."[74] In this conception, the human king functions as the extension of the god itself into the political realm. In Israel, however, the "political dimension" of Yahweh remained invested in Yahweh himself; the human king is a deputy, but receives no unique semi-divine ontological status. The role of the ancient Near Eastern divine national patron and the [semi-]divine emperor are merged in Israel into the person of Yahweh, while the human king is reduced to a purely mortal regent of a vassal state. Kingship in Israel is not an office lowered from heaven to earth to enable the humans to better care for the gods, as in Mesopotamia; kingship in Israel is never lowered from heaven at all.[75] Yahweh remains the emperor over Israel; his human representative is chosen at a request from the people, not a cosmic decree of the gods. As such he serves essentially as a steward, his station granted somewhat arbitrarily and sustained conditional on continued fidelity, as we also saw in the case of the Hittite vassal.

Yahweh demands loyalty from his vassals and their regent, but we should not imagine that "loyalty" is something that will cause Yahweh to suffer if he has to go without it. The loyalty of the vassal serves to enhance the emperor's reputation, but we should not think that "reputation" is something that Yahweh will suffer without, either. Reputation is inherently tied to *revelation*, which is the motive behind all of Yahweh's actions towards Israel, including making a treaty with them (and, for some Christian and Jewish theologians, causing the record of those actions to be preserved as Scripture). Yahweh did not deliver Israel from Egypt and establish them as a nation because he wanted to receive anything from them in return. Likewise the reason was not to give anything *to* Israel: "Just as it pleased the Lord to make you prosper and increase in number, so it will please him to ruin and destroy you" (Deut 28:63). The same applies to the eventual restoration of Israel, stated explicitly in Ezek 36:22–23: "It is not for your sake, people of Israel, that I am going to do these things, but for the sake of my holy name [. . .] Then the nations will know that I am the Lord, declares the Sovereign Lord, when I am proved holy through you before their eyes." Yahweh's actions were not performed in order to motivate people to do [more or less specific] things; they were performed in order to communicate to the observers of those actions—or, more importantly for our purposes, to the readers of the documents that present and

---

73. Holloway, *Aššur is King*, 181–82.
74. Frahm, "Rising Suns and Falling Stars: Assyrian Kings and the Cosmos," 105.
75. Walton, *Ancient Near Eastern Thought*, 258–59.

interpret those actions—something about Yahweh, just as ancient Near Eastern emperors performed the actions of levying tribute or punishing rebels, and recorded those actions in inscriptions, in order to communicate something about themselves.

Conclusion

From this very brief overview, we can see that two of the most notable theological innovations of the Hebrew Bible—monolatry and the denigration of the office of kingship—are not arbitrary and are not each motivated by an independent or reactionary ideology. Instead the two ideas are related to each other, and both derive fundamentally from the idea that Yahweh has no needs. If Yahweh has no needs, the religious paradigm of the rest of the ancient Near East collapses. How are the people supposed to relate to such a god? The answer is that they relate to him in the same way they relate to their human emperor, presenting cultic service as tokens of loyalty and submission in gratitude for acts of past generosity and favor—in Israel's case specifically, the deliverance of the their ancestors from Egypt and the gift of the promised land. But if Yahweh is the king, the king does not share power, and these acts of deliverance—and the treaty that commemorates them—were brought about by Yahweh alone, and so it is Yahweh alone to whom Israel owes fidelity and service. Other gods are not to be worshipped for the same reasons that rulers other than the king are not to be acknowledged.

The idea that allows these two innovations to operate is the metaphor of divine-human relations expressed as a covenant. Through the covenant, Israel becomes a vassal to their divine emperor, Yahweh. Suzerains are not codependent on their vassals and the vassals do not serve to meet the suzerain's needs. Through the covenant, sacrifices are reclassified as gestures of fidelity and service, not as food. The refusal to offer similar service to other gods and the relatively low status of the Israelite king are both natural and necessary extensions of the covenant metaphor. It is the covenant, and not a disdain for other religions or dislike of monarchy as an institution, that shapes Israel's unique theology and stands at the heart of Israel's conception of deity. But the covenant metaphor itself is necessary because of the understanding that Yahweh has no needs. The covenant did not tell Israel that Yahweh had different kinds of needs than other gods, for things like universal worship, moral observance, or social justice; instead the covenant allowed Israel to serve a God who had no need for them at all yet nonetheless wished to make use of them to demonstrate a particular reputation to the nations. Understanding the covenant metaphor and its implications is necessary for the modern interpreter to understand and apply the nuances of the theology expressed in the Hebrew Bible.

Part 2: Covenant

Bibliography

Assmann, Jan. *Moses the Egyptian: The Memory of Egypt in Western Monotheism.* Cambridge: Harvard University Press, 1997.

Beck, John A. "שָׁאַל." In *NIDOTTE*, 4:7–10.

Beckman, Gary. *Hittite Diplomatic Texts.* SBLWAW 7. Atlanta: SBL, 1996.

Bottéro, Jean. *Religion in Ancient Mesopotamia.* Translated by Teresa Lavender Fagan. Chicago: University of Chicago, 2004.

Carpenter, Eugene E., and Michael A. Grisanti. "מָרַד." In *NIDOTTE*, 2:1098–99.

———. "מָרָה." In *NIDOTTE*, 2:1100–102.

Clemens, David M. *Sources for Ugaritic Ritual and Sacrifice.* Vol. 1, *Ugaritic and Ugarit Akkadian Texts.* AOAT 284/1. Münster: Ugarit-Verlag, 2001.

Cogan, Mordechai, and Hayim Tadmor. *II Kings.* AB 11. Garden City, NY: Doubleday, 1988.

Craige, Peter C. *Psalms 1–50.* WBC 19. Waco, TX: Word, 1983.

Dearman, J. Andrew. *Hosea.* NICOT. Grand Rapids: Eerdmans, 2010.

DeClaissé-Walford, Nancy, Rolf A. Jacobson, and Beth LaNeel Tanner. *The Book of Psalms.* NICOT. Grand Rapids: Eerdmans, 2014.

Denninger, David. "דָּרַשׁ." In *NIDOTTE*, 1:993–99.

Foster, Benjamin. *From Distant Days: Myths, Tales, and Poetry of Ancient Mesopotamia.* Bethesda, MD: CDL, 1995.

Frahm, Ekhart. "Rising Suns and Falling Stars: Assyrian Kings and the Cosmos." In *Experiencing Power, Generating Authority: Cosmos, Politics, and the Ideology of Kingship in Ancient Egypt and Mesopotamia*, edited by J. A. Hill et al., 97–120. Philadelphia: University of Pennsylvania Museum of Archeology and Anthropology, 2013.

Fretheim, Terence E. "רָצָה." In *NIDOTTE*, 3:1185–86.

Fritz, Volkmar. *1 & 2 Kings.* Translated by Anselm Hagedorn. Continental Commentaries. Minneapolis: Fortress, 2003.

Gane, R. E. and J. Milgrom. "קָרַב." In *TDOT* 13:135–48.

Goldingay, John. *Psalms.* Vol. 2, 42–89. Baker Commentary on the Old Testament Wisdom and Psalms. Grand Rapids: Baker Academic, 2007.

Gnuse, Robert Karl. *No Other Gods: Emergent Monotheism in Israel.* JSOTSup 241. Sheffield; Sheffield, 1997.

Grayson, A. Kirk. *Assyrian Rulers of the Third and Second Millennium.* RIMA 2. Toronto: University of Toronto, 1991.

Greenberg, Moshe. *Ezekiel 1–20.* AB 22. Doubleday: New York, 1983.

Greenwood, Kyle R. "Then Aššur Will Hear His Prayers: A Study of Middle Assyrian Royal Theology." PhD diss., Hebrew Union College-Jewish Institute of Religion, 2008.

Hill, Andrew E. *Malachi.* AB 25D. Doubleday: New York, 1998.

Holladay, William L. *Jeremiah 1.* Hermeneia. Philadelphia: Fortress, 1986.

Holloway, Steven W. *Aššur is King! Aššur is King! Religion in the Excercise of Power in the Neo-Assyrian Empire.* CHANE 10. Leiden: Brill, 2002.

Jacobs, Mignon R. *The Books of Haggai and Malachi.* NICOT. Grand Rapids: Eerdmans, 2017.

Kitchen, K. A., and Paul J. N. Lawrence. *Treaty, Law, and Covenant in the Ancient Near East.* 3 vols. Wiesbaden: Harrassowitz, 2012.

Lambert, W. G. and A. R. Millard. *Atra-ḫasīs.* Winona Lake, IN: Eisenbrauns, 1999.

McCarter, P. Kyle, Jr. *2 Samuel.* AB 9. Garden City, NY: Doubleday, 1984.

Parpola, Simo. *Assyrian Prophecies.* SAA 9. Helsinki: Helsinki University Press, 1997.

Parpola, Simo, and Kazuko Watanabe. *Neo-Assyrian Treaties and Loyalty Oaths*. SAA 2. Helsinki: Helsinki University Press, 2014.
Roberts, J. J. M. *First Isaiah*. Hermeneia. Minneapolis: Fortress, 2015.
Smith, Mark S. *The Origins of Biblical Monotheism*. Oxford: Oxford University Press, 2001.
Talley, David. "חָפֵץ." In *NIDOTTE*, 2.231–34.
Tsumura, David Toshio. *The First Book of Samuel*. NICOT. Grand Rapids: Eerdmans, 2007.
Verhoef, Pieter A. *The Books of Haggai and Malachi*. NICOT. Grand Rapids: Eerdmans, 1987.
Wächter, L., and T. Seidl. "תְּרוּמָה." In *TDOT* 15:770–77.
Walton, Jonathan H. "A King Like the Nations." *Bib* 96 (2015) 179–200.
Walton, John H. *Ancient Near Eastern Thought and the Old Testament: Introducing the Conceptual World of the Hebrew Bible*. 2nd ed. Grand Rapids: Baker Academic, 2018.
Walton, John H., and J. Harvey Walton. *Demons and Spirits in Biblical Theology*. Eugene, OR: Cascade Books, 2019.
———. *The Lost World of the Israelite Conquest*. Downers Grove, IL: InterVarsity, 2017.
———. *The Lost World of the Torah*. Downers Grove, IL: InterVarsity, 2019.
Wiggermann, F. A. M. "Agriculture as Civilization: Sages, Farmers, and Barbarians." In *The Oxford Handbook of Cuneiform Culture*, edited by Karen Radner and Eleanor Robson. Oxford: Oxford University Press, 2011.
Wolff, Hans Walter. *Hosea*. Translated by Gary Stansell. Hermeneia. Philadelphia: Fortress, 1974.
Wright, Christopher J. H. *Old Testament Ethics for the People of God*. Downers Grove, IL: InterVarsity, 2004.

Part 3

Context

13

Taking Care of Dead Kings
Isaiah 26 and the King of Life

Hannah Clardy

Introduction

ISAIAH 26:19, THE "RESURRECTION verse" of Isaiah, is a remarkable statement. It expresses in striking terms a vision of dead bodies rising out of the dust to new life, shouting for joy at the revivifying power of God. As the conclusion to a prayer of lament (Isa 26:7–19), its surprisingly corporeal picture of resurrection has long inspired hope among God's people and debate among scholars. This essay problematizes the popular "literal versus metaphorical" interpretive framework for the verse and proposes that the language and imagery of Isa 26:7–19 uses the categories of royal ancestor veneration to support its wider theme of the sovereignty of YHWH. It is offered with much gratitude to John Walton for his role in my life as a teacher, mentor, and friend. Among the many things that I have learned from him, perhaps the most lasting for me is the value of curiosity in reading Scripture and the joy of letting it surprise us.

An Interpretive Dichotomy

In the late nineteenth century, Bernhard Duhm popularized the apocalyptic label for Isaiah 24–27. For him, these dramatic chapters are best understood, not in the context of the classical prophets, but of the *Sibylline Oracles*, Daniel, and the Enochic literature.[1] This generic identification was strongly tied to authorship and date, and

---

1. Duhm, *Das Buch Jesaia,* 172. To be precise, Duhm was speaking here of the "apocalyptic"

Duhm considered it just as likely that Isaiah of Jerusalem wrote the book of Daniel as this "little book."[2] Indeed, with its depictions of cosmic judgment (e.g., 24:1–3) and vanquished beasts (27:1), it is not difficult to understand Duhm's approach to these distinctive chapters, and similar "apocalyptic" readings continue today.[3] Besides its apocalyptic literary style, the text contains several terms in the "associative field" of the resurrection of the dead, a central element in the eschatological developments of apocalyptic literature.[4] In Isa 26:19 alone, these terms include the verbs חיה (to live), קום (to rise), הקיץ (to wake up), the nouns מתים (dead ones), נבלה (corpse), טל (dew), אורת (lights), and the phrase עפר שכני (those who sleep in the dust). And modern interpreters are not alone in understanding Isa 26:19 as a reference to eschatological resurrection of the dead. Daniel 12:2 likely alludes to Isa 26:19, and other early "receptions" of Isa 26:19 also reuse it within the context of eschatological resurrection.[5]

However, a different interpretive tradition argues that Isa 26:19 does not refer to physical, embodied resurrection, but to national restoration. The representative "intertext" for this view is not Dan 12:2, but Ezek 37:1–14 (Valley of Dry Bones vision). Many who hold this view observe the *communal* context of Isaiah 26, which speaks of the whole nation rather than a faithful remnant only (cf. also Hos 6:1–3; Isa 52:1–2). Christopher Hays has recently identified a variety of texts from across the ancient Near East that use the language of "resurrection" or revivification to describe national restoration.[6] Despite these observations, it is difficult in this view to account for the reanimated corpses, which according to Sawyer, "no-one but a Sadducee, ancient or modern, could possibly misconstrue."[7] This sense grows when one considers supporting verses in the near context, e.g., YHWH's devouring of death forever (25:6) and the earth giving up its slain (26:21).[8]

---

sections of the text, as distinct from its "lyrical" sections, which he believed to be later additions.

2. Duhm, *Das Buch Jesaia*, 172.

3. In recent years, several studies have argued for a pre-exilic date for Isa 24–27, but the post-exilic, even post-Persian period still has adherents (e.g., Schmid, *The Old Testament*, 92, 202). The consensus regarding literary genre is that Isa 24–27 is "proto-" or early apocalyptic, though this is often vaguely defined.

4. Sawyer, "Hebrew Words for Resurrection," 218–34, esp. 234. Sawyer does not speculate about the date of Isa 26:19, but argues that, within the universe of discourse of its final form, resurrection was an issue of particular import.

5. The periphrastic rendering of the OG reflects this interpretation: "those who are in their graves will be raised" (ἐγερθήσονται οἱ ἐν τοῖς μνημείοις). Two Qumran texts, the "Messianic Apocalypse" (4Q521) and *Pseudo-Ezekiel* (see esp. 4Q385 frag. 2–3), reuse Isa 26:19 within a clearly eschatological framework. Cf. also Isa 25:8 // Rev 7:17; 21:4.

6. Hays, *Origins of Isaiah 24–27*, see esp. ch. 3. While some associate Isa 26:19 with the return from exile (e.g., Johnson, *From Chaos to Restoration*, 80–81), Hays argues that it is a reference to the end of Neo-Assyrian hegemony (*Origins*, 89–94).

7. Sawyer, "Hebrew Words for Resurrection," 234.

8. Hasel observes that the further mention of "bloodshed" and "the slain" of the earth in the immediately following context (vv. 20–21) is difficult to square with a merely political reading ("Resurrection," 274).

Both of the interpretive approaches to Isa 26:19 sketched above have reasonable support. And, although differing in their conclusions, both approaches ask the same question and present the same *either/or* choice. In both, the interpretation of Isa 26:19 is framed as *either* physical embodied resurrection, to be compared with Dan 12:2, *or* metaphorical national restoration, to be compared with Ezek 37:1–14. One of the pivotal factors in this discussion is the question of the date of composition, which follows similar lines: either the text is "late," and therefore a reference to the resurrection of the dead, or it is not "late," and therefore a metaphor for the restoration of the nation. In this case, this factor seems to be a particularly tenuous foundation since the brief verse, and indeed the whole of Isa 24–27, contains few historical clues. Moreover, in my view, claims about the early development of the belief in resurrection have often gone beyond the evidence and involve anachronistic imposition of Jewish and Christian beliefs onto this text. This characterization admittedly simplifies the situation, but nonetheless, this dichotomous interpretive framework for Isaiah 26 risks stifling other ways of approaching this passage.

This essay offers a number of related "intertexts" for Isaiah 26 that represent particular instances of the widespread practice of royal ancestor veneration. It will argue that the language of Isa 26:7–19 interacts with this ideology and celebrates the rule of a king quite unlike the ones represented by the dynastic lineages. By highlighting these texts, my aim is not to reject Daniel or Ezekiel as helpful intertexts for Isaiah 26, but to offer another conceptual frame that allows different questions and may help us move past the "physical versus metaphorical" approach to v. 19.[9] The first part surveys the *rpum* and their role as the royal dead as described in Ugaritic texts. In dialogue with evidence from Phoenicia and from the Mesopotamian practice of *kispum*, it asks how these texts portray the *rpum*'s effect on the world of the living and their role in maintaining societal stability. The second part considers the prayer of Isaiah 26 in light of this cultural context of royal ancestor veneration and argues that the prayer exploits these well-known categories in its celebration of YHWH as Israel's king, who will do far greater things for his people than even the most magnificent royal dynasty can offer.

Two notes are necessary on comparative method. First, I have chosen the term רפאים and its West Semitic cognates as an entry into the topic. Most known occurrences of the term outside the Old Testament are in Ugaritic texts, so the Ugaritic corpus constitutes the primary material for this study. It is important to acknowledge that the gaps in evidence are significant, and that if archaeologists were to discover, for example, ritual funerary texts from Moab, this could significantly change how we understand the *rephaim* or the "cult of the dead" in the Levant. Second, much of the

---

9. A comparatively small number of studies interact extensively with the ancient Near Eastern context of Isaiah 24–27, including Millar, *Isaiah 24–27 and the Origin of Apocalyptic*; Barker, *Isaiah's Kingship Polemic: An Exegetical Study in Isaiah 24–27*; McAffee, "Rephaim, Whisperers, and the Dead in Isaiah 26:13–19: A Ugaritic Parallel"; and Hays, *Origins*.

evidence considered, Ugaritic and Mesopotamian, significantly predates the book of Isaiah, on any reckoning. Because it would be hasty to assume direct borrowing, this essay neither presupposes this nor argues for a dependence relationship between the Ugaritic and biblical texts.[10] Sometimes the channels of cultural and religious influence are identifiable, but more often, we simply cannot know with certainty the processes through which this happened. Moreover, for practices as chronologically and geographically diffuse as ancestor veneration, it may be more helpful to conceptualize the comparative relationships in terms of a *network* or *environment* rather than a *process*.[11] Because the veneration of deceased royalty appears in various iterations, it is difficult to justify a single corpus as *the* relevant background of a biblical passage, and in the case of Ugarit, one that is never mentioned in the Old Testament itself.

Rephaim and Royal Ancestor Veneration

Evidence for funerary and mortuary rites in the ancient Near East spans millennia, taking different forms, from the elaborate descriptions of the Egyptian afterlife and its deities to the Mesopotamian apotropaic spells, and includes royal and popular expressions. It is not always clear if the dead were considered (semi-)divine, or if the practices directed toward them should be considered worship or commemoration, ritual or cult, funerary or mortuary.[12] These issues cannot be addressed here, and the term "veneration" is used for the sake of consistency but without the assumption of the kind of worship given to deities of the pantheon. Given the focal place of the *rephaim* in Isaiah 26, the discussion below will focus on the Ugaritic texts in which the *rpum* figure prominently, especially in their relationship to the living. It will also briefly discuss the similarities between the Ugaritic evidence and the *kispum* rite of Mesopotamia.

Rpum at Ugarit

The Hebrew term *rephaim* [pl.] and its Northwest Semitic cognates refers to a group of beings often associated with the dead. Although it has relatively few occurrences, the term is found in the Old Testament and in non-biblical texts dating from the late Bronze Age at Ugarit to the Persian period at Sidon (with one late Neo-Punic occurrence in the first century CE). In the Ugaritic corpus, the term *rpu[m]* appears in both mythological and cultic texts, some fifty times, although much of the evidence

---

10. It should be noted, however, that some argue for a particularly close literary relationship between Isa 24–27 and the Ugaritic Baal Cycle. For example, the only lexical parallel with Heb. *leviathan* in the ancient Near East is *litan* of Ugarit, and the creature's appearance in Isa 27:1 is strikingly similar to a passage in the Baal Cycle (*KTU* 1.5 i 1–3) (Barker, *Kingship Polemic*, 151, 152–70; cf. also Day, "God and Leviathan," 435).

11. Cf. "cognitive environment criticism" (Walton, *Ancient Near Eastern Thought*, 11).

12. Johnston points out the frequent imprecision in scholarly terminology related to cults of the dead, in particular in the somewhat arbitrary inclusion of necromancy (*Shades of Sheol*, 167–68).

is fragmentary.[13] The figures are associated with the underworld, and although their precise identity and function is debated, most scholars agree that the term designates a royal, (semi-)divine group inhabiting the underworld.[14] The chthonic figures sometimes appear with the sun goddess Šapšu, who is similarly associated with the underworld.[15] The Ugaritic King List (*KTU* 1.113, verso) contains a list of about fifteen royal names, each with the *'il*-prefix, suggesting divine status for the royal ancestors.[16] Regardless of their precise ontological status, what is important to evaluate here is the connection between the Ugaritic *rpum* and royalty, particularly as expressed in the Funerary Text (*KTU* 1.161) and the so-called "RPUM Texts" (*KTU* 1.20–21.22).

Ugaritic Funerary Text (*KTU* 1.161): This ritual text calls for mourning the death of an Ugaritic king and commemorates the inauguration of his successor, usually understood to be King Ammurapi III (ca. 1200 BCE).[17] The text opens by invoking the "*rpum* of the underworld" along with two recently deceased kings of Ugarit:

> The liturgy (book) of the nocturnal sacrifices:
> You are summoned, O "heroes" [*rpi*] of the underworld,
> You are invoked, O "gathered ones" of Didanu.
> Ulkn, the "hero" [*rp(u)*], is summoned,
> Trmn, the "hero" [*rp(u)*], is summoned,
> Sidanu-wa-Radanu is summoned,
> Toru 'Ilmn is summoned,
> The "heroes" [*rpim*] of old are summoned.
> You are summoned, O "heroes" [*rpi*] of the underworld,
> You are invoked, O "gathered ones" of Didanu.
> Ammittamru, the king [*m(l)k*], is summoned,
> Niqmaddu, the king [*(ml)k*], is summoned as well.
> (*KTU* 1.161, lines 1–12)[18]

The rhythmically repeated invocation is directed toward (or perhaps about) the *rpum*—first *en masse* as the *rpi arṣ* (*rpi* of the earth/underworld) (line 2) and the *qbitm qbṣ ddn* (gathered ones of Didanu) (3), then individually (*rpu*) as the proper

---

13. Whitaker, *Concordance*, 575. Almost half of these occurrences are from the title *dnil mt rpi*, which though likely related, constitutes a special case. The term has been vocalised in different ways and, like its Hebrew cognate, has a disputed etymology.

14. A notable exception is L'Heureux, who understands the Ugaritic *rpum* as living figures of an aristocratic or warrior class ("Ugaritic and Biblical Rephaim," 271–72).

15. E.g. the snake bite incantation (*KTU* 1.82, line 32). Compare the Ugaritic sun goddess Šapšu with the Mesopotamian sun deity Šamaš and their similar roles in association with the underworld (Healey, "The Sun Deity," 239–42).

16. A more recently published syllabic version of a corresponding king list (RS 94.2518) uses the dinger determinative, which supports this (semi-)divine status for the royal ancestors (Hays, *Death*, 108).

17. Its ritualistic repetition and parallelism has even been considered "quasi-poetic" (Pitard, "Ugaritic Funerary Text," 66).

18. All translations of the Funerary Text (*KTU* 1.161) are from Lewis, *Cults of the Dead*, 7–10.

names *ulkn* (4), *trmn* (5), *sdn w rdn* (6), *ṯr 'llmn* (7), and again *en masse*—the *rpim qdmym* (*rpim* of old) (8), *rpi arṣ* (9) and *qbitm qbṣ ddn* (10). Also invoked, using the same verb (*qra*),[19] are two kings of recent memory.[20] These kings, Ammittamru and Niqmaddu, are each designated as a "king" (*mlk*), and their names are known from elsewhere in the corpus.[21] The Ugaritic *rpum* appear to represent deceased royalty, "the mythic dead as opposed to the historical dead whose names were recorded in the king lists."[22]

After these invocations of the names of the *rpum* and the recent kings of Ugarit, the text calls for weeping (lines 13–17) and descent of Šapšu to the underworld (ארץ and עפר), the subterranean domain of the *rpum* and the dead kings (18–26):

> After your lord [(b)'lk], descend [rd] to the underworld [arṣ].
> Descend to the underworld [arṣ], down to the dust ['pr],
> Down [tḥt] to Sidanu-wa-Radanu,
> Down [tḥt] to Toru 'llmn,
> Down [tḥt] to the "heroes" (*rpim*) of old,
> Down [tḥt] to Ammittamru, the king,
> Down [tḥm][23] to Niqmaddu, the king, as well.
> (*KTU* 1.161, lines 21–26)

The names and titles from the opening invocations are largely repeated (except *ulkn* and *trmn*). Notice the two-part structure of the *rpum* sections, which enclose the call to mourn. Although the *rpum* and dead kings are invoked in the first section (lines 2–12), the second section (23–26) makes it clear that they remain denizens of the underworld. The Funerary Text concludes with a sevenfold offering (27–30) and sevenfold petition for peace (*šlm*) for the king and for the city of Ugarit (31–34).

One of the most obvious functions of the Funerary Text may be use in a funerary setting to mourn the death of a recently deceased king of Ugarit. The call to weep (lines 13–17) suggests that ritual mourning was involved. Some have suggested that it may also have served as a royal legitimation of the new king. If the *rpum* represent the royal dynasty of yore (*rpim qdmym*, lines 9, 24), the new king is presented as the manifestation of a long line of dynastic rulers, from the earliest *rpum* to his deceased father, a continuity which strengthens the claim to the throne. This legitimation

---

19. This use of the verb *qr'* is well represented (cf. *DUL*, 681, 770).

20. It is worth noting that in biblical Hebrew, the *hiphil* הזכיר "competes primarily with *qr'* 'to call'" (*TDOT* 1:384).

21. The ritual described by the text appears to mourn the death of Niqmaddu III and legitimate the reign of his successor, Ammurapi III, ironically the last known king of Ugarit (Lewis, *Cults of the Dead*, 32).

22. Suriano, *Politics*, 153–54; see also Levine and de Tarragon, "Dead Kings and Rephaim," 656.

23. This form appears to be a scribal mistake for *tḥt* (Lewis, *Cults of the Dead*, 26; Levine and de Tarragon, "Dead Kings and Rephaim," 653).

function is widely attested in the ancient world in different types of texts, including some royal genealogies.[24]

Most importantly for the present purposes, the Funerary Text likely functioned as a ritual petition for blessing upon the new king's rule. After the opening invocations and the call for mourning, the text concludes with a sevenfold offering and a sevenfold blessing upon King Ammurapi, the royal family, and the city of Ugarit. Whatever else may be said about the precise identity of the *rpum* in this text, it is clear that they are invoked along with two recently deceased rulers to bless and establish the peace of the city.

The "RPUM Texts" (*KTU* 1.20-21.22): This fragmentary collection appears to be three versions of a single text in which the *rpum* play a prominent role, though the place of these fragments within the larger literary tradition of Ugarit is uncertain.[25] In the first fragment (*KTU* 1.20), the *rpum* appear in parallel with the "gods" (*ilnym*) and the "dead" (*mtmtm*), which is consistent with their identity as "divinized" royal ancestors in the Funerary Text (*KTU* 1.161) and the King List (*KTU* 1.113). Wyatt interprets the *rpum* texts as descriptions of a communion ritual, which similar to the Funerary Text, is "probably the *kispum*," intended to solicit blessing for the living king.[26] Furthermore, the role of the *rpum*, insofar as it can be inferred from the damaged texts, involves what Wyatt calls a "soteriological function in maintaining society," which is also congruous with their role in the Funerary Text.[27] So while the *rpum* texts add little evidence with certainty, the identity and role of the *rpum* is at least consistent with the Funerary Text.

Appearances in Narrative Poetry/Epic: The *rpum* also appear in a few places in the poetic narrative literature. The epic of Keret includes a blessing formula for King Keret by the "*rpum* of the earth" and the "assembly of Dtn" (*KTU* I.15, III, 13-15), the same pair seen above in the Funerary Text. The narrative depicts Keret without an heir, so this blessing has been interpreted as a petition to the royal ancestors (*rpum*) for protection and perpetuation of the royal line.[28] Finally, the *rpum* appear at the end of the Baal Cycle, in a hymn to the sun goddess Šapšu (*KTU* 1.6 VI: 45-47). She is praised here as the ruler of the *rpum* (in parallel again with *'ilnym/'ilm/mtm*). Even though this text is damaged, Suriano observes that the sense relates somehow to the "wider theme of divine order that runs through the Ba'al Cycle," an order that extends even to, or indeed *from*, the dead ancestors.[29] Given the likely political function of the

---

24. Royal legitimation is also one of the many possible functions of the Ba'al Cycle. One version of this hypothesis infers that Ba'al's position *outside* the family of El may have bolstered the claims to sovereignty of a king without biological descent from the royal dynasty (cf. Barker, *Isaiah's Kingship Polemic*, 19-29).

25. Wyatt, *Religious Texts from Ugarit*, 314.

26. Wyatt, *Religious Texts from Ugarit*, 314.

27. Wyatt, *Religious Texts from Ugarit*, 315. Wyatt's gloss for *rpum*, "saviours," reflects this function.

28. Caquot and Sznycer, *Ugaritic Religion*, 20.

29. Suriano, *Politics*, 152.

Baal Cycle, the *rpum* are significant in their role of supporting the ruling dynasty and therefore in establish diving order.³⁰ These references to the *rpum* in Ugaritic texts are admittedly opaque, but together a picture emerges of a group of dynastic ancestors, whom the living invoke, provide offerings, and petition for stability and peace.

Rephaim at Sidon

Textual evidence for the *rephaim* outside the biblical and Ugaritic texts is scant. The only other known occurrences of the term are found on two Egyptian-styled sarcophagi of Sidonian kings from the Persian period. These inscriptions are different in some respects, but they include a similar curse on any would-be disturber of the royal burial place:

Tabnit, king of Sidon (KAI 13:6–8):

But if you in fact open up (what is) over me and in fact disturb [רגז תרגזן] me, may you have no seed among the living under the sun nor a resting-place with the shades [רפאם]!³¹

Eshmunazar, king of Sidon (KAI 14:6–8):

For should any ruler or any commoner open up (what is) over this resting-place, or lift up the box in which I lie or carry me away from this resting-place, may they have no resting-place with the shades [רפאם], and may they not be buried in a grave, and may they have no son or seed to succeed them.

One can reasonably infer from these curses that a desirable afterlife entailed leaving behind descendants, having a proper burial, and resting with the *rephaim*. The act of desecrating the burial place is described on Tabnit's inscription as "disturbing" (רגז) the deceased from their rest.³² This view of an honourable afterlife is resonant with descriptions from the Old Testament, especially the royal epilogues in the book of Kings.³³

Despite the location of these references to the *rephaim* on royal sarcophagi, it is not clear in this case that the reference is to deceased royalty alone. In fact, the inscriptions seem at pains to include *anyone* who might disturb their royal rest, both

---

30. Suriano, *Politics*, 152.

31. Both transliterations and translations are from Gibson, *Syrian Semitic Inscriptions*, 103, 106–7.

32. Greenfield, "Scripture and Inscription," 258.

33. Suriano observes that, while these inscriptions share key terminology with the biblical material, one significant difference is the use of *rephaim* (רפאם) in the former and the *fathers* (אבת) in the latter. And though these inscriptions are from fifth century Persian vassals, they reflect an older Levantine ideology of death-burial-inheritance and connection to the royal ancestors (*Politics*, 154–57, 158).

royal ("any ruler," כל ממלך) and non-royal ("or any person," וכל אדם) (*KAI* 14, line 4). It seems more likely that the term in this particular setting, in contrast to the *rpum* of Ugarit, refers to the dead more generally.

Ugarit and the Kispum

Not long after the Ugaritic texts began to be published, scholars noticed striking similarities between some of the Ugaritic texts and the widely-attested Mesopotamian *kispum* ritual, evidence for which has formed the basis of scholarly understanding of "cults of the dead." In its classic form, the *kispum* ritual included the presentation of food offerings and/or libations to the deceased and the invocation of the name of the deceased (*šuma zakārum*) by a relative, typically the eldest son (the *pāqidum*).[34] This patrilineal "care for the dead" honoured and perpetuated the memory of the deceased for the purpose of securing wellbeing for the living descendent(s), and sometimes pacifying the needy, aggrieved, or homeless dead who would otherwise cause harm to the living. This post-mortem care was constitutive of a blessed afterlife, without which the ghost is depicted as pitiful or angry.[35] Evidence exists for a popular *kispum* as well as *kispum* offerings for royalty.[36] There is less evidence for malevolent dead ancestors at Ugarit, and Mesopotamian *kispum* rites are directed toward attracting blessing and deterring evil.

The Genealogy of the Hammurapi Dynasty (GHD; BM 80328): This remarkable late Old Babylonian tablet appears to be a ritual text of a royal *kispum*, which names and invokes the royal ancestors for blessing. It lists the names of the long deceased, eponymous ancestors of tribal groups, one of which is *Di-ta-nu*, and the more recently deceased kings of the dynasty.[37] This genealogy also names those without "care-taker"

---

34. There is at least one clear instance of a father performing *kispum* rites for his son (Tsukimoto, "Peace for the Dead," 104).

35. The deprivation of proper post-mortem care forms the basis of curses like the one in Assurbanipal's account of the desecration of the tombs of Elamite kings: "I inflicted restlessness on their ghosts. I deprived them of funerary offerings and pourers of water." In incantations, the ghost (*eṭemmu*) of deceased kin is often malevolent, and in omens, is not a good sign (Bayliss, "Cult of Dead Kin," 117–18).

36. The *kispum* is attested from the Old Babylonian through the Late Babylonian periods, taking different forms, from the bi-monthly observation at Mari to a less regular practice in the Middle Babylonian period. The attitude toward the dead is not monolithic in the Mesopotamian sources, as the *kispum* can be directed toward appeasing the dead, honouring the dead, or both (see Hays, *Death*, 42; and Bayliss, "Cult of the Dead Kin," 123). Rituals for dead kings are also attested in Hatti and involved the invocation of the name and offerings for the dead king and his ancestors (Pitard, "Funerary Text," 67).

37. Scholars have long noted the correspondence between the names of the Genealogy of the Hammurapi Dynasty (BM 80328) and the Assyrian King List (AKL-A), particularly in the opening section with eponymous names of early tribes or topographies. These early names are thought to represent an old tribal tradition, to which a more "reliable record of the true dynastic pedigree" was joined (beginning with *Iptiyamūta* in line 11) (Finkelstein, "Hammurapi Dynasty," 112; 98–99;

or "rememberer" (*pāqidum* and *sāhirum*) to accept the food and drink offerings and bless the king of Babylon (*Ammiṣaduqa*).³⁸ As with the Ugaritic funerary text, this Babylonian genealogy may have had a royal legitimation function as well, but it is more focally directed toward the cultic function of the *kispum* or *kispum*-like ritual.³⁹

In the efforts to connect the evidence for an Ugaritic cult of the dead with the Mesopotamian *kispum* ritual, J. F. Healey compared the cultic function of the Genealogy of the Hammurapi Dynasty with that of the Ugaritic Funerary Text, arguing that they served a similar function, namely to invoke dead kings to bless the living.⁴⁰ In the Ugaritic Funerary Text, the *rpum* are closely associated with kings (*mlkm*), and both groups are invoked in the context of a ritual offering to bless the living king and his rule. Moreover, Healey suggested that Ugarit had a role similar to the Mesopotamian *pāqidum*, but there is less evidence for this.⁴¹ Similarly, Pitard found in the Funerary Text the three main elements of the *kispum*, namely the invocation of the names of ancestors (lines 2–12), food offerings (lines 13–17), and water libation (lines 20–26).⁴² Levine and de Tarragon also note that the Ugaritic funerary liturgy, though different in some respects, "shares common objectives with the *kispum*, or sacrifice of the dead."⁴³

It may be suggestive also that the kings associated with the two texts above, the Ugaritic Funerary Text and the Babylonian Genealogy, share a name. Hammurapi (and its various spellings) is a well-attested royal name, which many argue is, in this iteration, a patronymic ("my kin/uncle is a healer").⁴⁴ If it is the case that patronyms reflect the veneration and even deification of ancestors,⁴⁵ then the name of these kings encapsulates the very idea expressed in the ritual texts associated with them: the ancestors are "*rapi*," healers.

Wilson, *Genealogy and History*, 109). It may be significant that the Ugaritic *rpum* are also called "Didanites," a name similar to those found among the early "tribal" kings in these lists: *Di-ta-nu* (GHD), *Di-da-a-nu* (AKL-A), and *Didanu* (KAI 1.161).

38. The list seems at pains to include *every* possible menace to the living king, which along with dead kings, also includes the extended royal family and those who have died in service to the king (Lambert, "Hammurabi's Ancestors," 1).

39. Wilson, *Genealogy and History*, 114.

40. Healey, "MLKM/RP'UM and the KISPUM," 90.

41. Pope compares the Ugaritic "Duties of an Ideal Son" passage (*CTA* 17.1.26–34) with the Mesopotamian role of the *pāqidum* ("Cult of the Dead," 159–61). A wholly post-mortem interpretation probably overstates the responsibilities of the ideal son *after* the father's death. Although possibly incorporating funerary duties, this text is not itself a description of some Ugaritic equivalent of the *pāqidum* (Lewis, *Cults of the Dead*, 53–71).

42. Pitard, "Ugaritic Funerary," 67.

43. Levine and de Tarragon, "Dead Kings," 654.

44. The name also occurs as *Hammurabi* in its Mesopotamian logo-syllabic forms, particularly in texts from Alalakh, which sometimes use a sign (gal) that unambiguously represents this spelling (cf. Sasson, "King Hammurabi of Babylon," 902).

45. See van der Toorn, *Family Religion*, 226–31.

Summary

The texts discussed above represent different ancient societies, and the *kispum* texts in particular span millennia. Furthermore, the Ugaritic and Phoenician texts feature the cognate term *rp'm*, while the Mesopotamian texts use other terms for the dead. While allowing for genuine differences, there are nonetheless several summarizing points: 1) The West Semitic term *rephaim* and its cognates appear in different Levantine corpora (Ugarit, Israel, Sidon), often but not always associated with deceased royalty. 2) Ugaritic sources invoke these figures as part of the royal dynasty of yore and record food and drink offerings to them for blessing upon the living, particularly at the transition of royal power.[46] 3) There are significant parallels between the portrayal of deceased royalty in Ugaritic texts and the deceased of the Mesopotamian *kispum* ritual. Although the term *rephaim* and its cognates are attested only in the Levant, the appeal to ancestors for wellbeing was widespread throughout the ancient Near East, and the associated cultic practices share many of the basic components (invoking the name, providing offerings) and function (soliciting blessing or averting catastrophe).

Rephaim and Resurrection in Isaiah 26

Now we turn to Isa 26:7–19. This second part argues that this prayer uses and subverts the terminology of royal ancestor veneration in its celebration of YHWH's rule. In using these categories, the text is polemical, but it is more than merely a "polemic." The resurrection passage is less concerned with criticising the practice of ancestor veneration per se, and more concerned with conveying that YHWH's rule as living king is something altogether different and better. After briefly describing the theme of kingship in Isa 26:7–19, I will identify several elements that are part of the "semantic environment" of ancestor veneration. Finally, then, we will return to the resurrection statement and its message within this environment.

YHWH as Sovereign

Isaiah 26:7–19 is spoken in the voice of the community or a representative individual. Its genre is variously labelled as a communal complaint song,[47] communal prayer,[48] song of lament,[49] or often some mix of these. These labels reflect the eclectic quality of the text, which combines wisdom elements, "historical" recitation, and lament, all of which are expressed poignantly in first person address to YHWH.

---

46. This liminal and sometimes unstable period of the transition of power is particularly relevant if the Ugaritic texts are funerary rather than mortuary (see, e.g., Pitard, "Ugaritic Funerary Text," 66).

47. Sweeney, *Isaiah 1–39*, 341.

48. Hays and Irvine, *Isaiah the Eighth-Century Prophet*, 311.

49. Wildberger, *Isaiah 13–27*, 558.

Part 3: Context

The theme of divine kingship is focal throughout Isa 24–27, beginning especially with 24:21–23 ("YHWH of hosts reigns on Mount Zion in Jerusalem before his elders in glory"). The Zion scene continues in 25:6–12, in which YHWH serves as the royal host at a remarkable banquet. And, although the kingship theme is less appreciated in the communal prayer that follows, the prayer also develops this theme. The opening section (26:7–10) forms a meditation on the justice and righteousness of YHWH, whose rule brings wellbeing to the people of the world (cf. Isa 9:6[7]; Ps 72:1–4). These terms related to ideal kingship in Isa 26:7–10 are, therefore, not only part of a pious prayer, but a confession of allegiance to the rule of YHWH. It is into this context of YHWH's ideal and just rule that the pained lament (26:11–19) is spoken: "YHWH, other masters besides you have ruled over us."

"Invoking the Name" of YHWH

Besides the continued theme of kingship, the terminology of "name" and "memory" appears prominently in the prayer (vv. 8, 13, 14). The collocation of the noun שם ("name") and the verbal root זכר ("to remember, invoke") can indicate different actions, one of which is the invocation of the name of the dead. The collocation of "remembering/invoking (*hiphil*) the name" can be used in liturgical contexts in praise to God (Ps 20:8; cf. Isa 49:1), in cultic prohibitions against invoking the name of other gods (Exod 23:13; Josh 23:7), and in funerary or mortuary contexts, analogous to the *kispum* formulae.[50] This lexical cohesion is strengthened by the fact that the noun זֵכֶר ("memory") is found only here in the book of Isaiah (vv. 8, 14), which suggests its importance for the passage.

In Isaiah 26, the "invocation of the name" appears both positively, in reference to YHWH, and negatively, in reference to the "other masters." The prayer positively confesses the invocation of YHWH's name: "For your name [שמך] and your memory [זכרך] is the soul's desire" (v. 8). And "You alone, your name [שמך] do we invoke [נזכיר]" (v. 13), in contrast to invoking that of the "other masters [אדנים]." Instead of invoking the name of other masters, who fittingly remain anonymous, the community confesses allegiance to YHWH alone as king.

Negatively, the invocation of the name is denied to the "other masters" who are called "dead" and "*rephaim*" (v. 14). In this negative contrast, the prayer describes YHWH's act of erasing every memory (כל זכר) of them (v. 14b). Besides this repetition and pairing of "name" and "memory" terminology, v. 14 uses an additional term

---

50. Hebrew *hiphil* הזכיר is the "counterpart to Akk. *zakāru*" (*TDOT* 1:381). Cf. 2 Sam 18:18; Ps 45:17–18; Amos 6:10; and Ruth 4:10 (להקים שם המת). In 2 Sam 18:18, Absalom commissions his own stele since he is without "a son to invoke my name [הזכיר שמי]." Schmidt argues that Absalom's stele represents a *commemorative* act, not worship (*Israel's Beneficent Dead*, 127, 133; cf. Johnston, *Shades*, 191). Others see evidence here of something more than commemoration (Bloch-Smith, *Judahite Burial Practices*, 113). Another disputed case is 2 Kgs 9:34 and the treatment of Jezebel's remains. It seems that her royal status was the basis for "attending to" (פקד) her remains, or at least the attempt to do so.

connected with the care of the dead in God's act of "visiting with destruction" (פקדת ותשמידם). This root פקד is, of course, common in biblical Hebrew so on its own carries little weight. However, given the immediate context concerned with "invoking the name" and erasing the memory of contenders, it may in fact be a sort of "anti-*kispum*" statement that exploits the semantic range of the root—having the sense of its common Hebrew use of visiting for punishment *and* subverting the *pāqidum* role known from Mesopotamian sources. Given that the primary role of the *pāqidum* was to perpetuate the memory of the deceased, it seems unlikely to be coincidence here that YHWH plays the role of the *pāqidum* in reverse: instead of perpetuating the name of the deceased "other masters," he obliterates it. Without suggesting that YHWH is actually involved with a ritual for the dead, the language of the prayer calls to mind the practices associated with the care of the royal dead and univocally dismisses them in favour of invoking the name of the living king.

Resurrection in Isaiah 26:19

The resurrection statement of Isa 26:19 is actually the second of a pair of statements, so its meaning is constrained by its relationship to the other half.[51] More precisely, v. 19 is set in (mostly) positive opposition to its negative counterpart in v. 14. The negative counterpart, mentioned above in regards to the theme of kingship and the use of terminology related to care for the dead, is a statement against the "other lords":

Isaiah 26:14

מתים בל יחיו	They are dead; they will not live.
רפאים בל יקמו	They are *rephaim*; they will not rise.
לכן פקדת ותשמידם	To that end, you have visited them with destruction,
ותאבד כל זכר למו	and you have erased every memory of them.

From elsewhere in Old Testament poetry, it is clear that the *rephaim* refer to the dead, so the parallel terms here are not surprising.[52] The term sometimes refers simply to the dead *en masse*, with a negative association only in regards to the negativity of death itself (Ps 88:11; Job 26:5), but other times with a more negatively charged sense (e.g., the path of the adulteress and the fool: Prov 2:18; 9:18; 21:16).

---

51. This apparent contradiction between v. 14 and v. 19 is one reason that some take v. 19 to be a late addition with little meaningful connection to its literary context; e.g., Kaiser identifies the verse as a "contradiction to v. 14 and the tradition that lies behind it" (*Isaiah 13–39*, 217).

52. In Old Testament narrative, the term refers to the early inhabitants of Canaan and the Trans-Jordan (along with Anakim, Emim, Zamzummim, and Zuzim).

Part 3: Context

Within Isaiah, however, the *rephaim* occur in only one other text, namely the taunt song for the fall of the arrogant king of Babylon and his descent into Sheol (Isa 14:4–21). In this song, the *rephaim* appear as the dead kings of the nations, who are "stirred up" to receive the incoming king to the netherworld:

Isaiah 14:9

שאול מתחת רגזה	Sheol below is stirred up
לך לקראת בואך	to meet you when you enter.
עורר לך רפאים	It wakes up the *rephaim* for you,
כל עתודי ארץ	all the leaders of the earth.
הקים מכסאותם	It raises up [*hiphil*] from their thrones,
כל מלכי גוים	all the kings of the nations.

In apposition to *rephaim* are the "leaders of the earth" and "kings of the nations." The judgment includes slaughter for the royal descendants (14:21), to prevent them from having name or descendent. The *rephaim* are certainly not powerful here, but appear as weak deceased royalty ("weak, maggots, worms"). While we cannot assume that the *rephaim* in Isa 26:14 and 19 refer to the same figures as this taunt song, the theme of kingship, the use of *kispum*-like terminology, and the appearance of "other masters" in Isa 26 points toward a similar sense of deceased royalty.

If Isa 26:13–14, the first of the paired statements, constitutes a curse on other masters, its positive counterpart in v. 19 concludes the lament on a note of hope. Although it repeats much of v. 14 without the negative particle בל, it does not *merely* state its opposite. Note especially where the term *rephaim* occurs below:

Isaiah 26:19

יחיו מתיך	Your dead will live;
יחיו מתיך	as a corpse, they will rise!
הקיצו ורננו שכני עפר	Wake up and sing for joy, dust-dwellers,
כי טל אורת טלך	for your dew is the dew of light,
וארץ רפאים תפיל	but the land of the *rephaim* you will cast down.

The first clause of both verses uses the same verb (root חיה) and the same noun (מתים), and v. 19 simply omits the בל-negation and adds a second-person suffix ("your dead"). This creates a contrast between the dead of vv. 13–14 (the "other masters") and the dead of v. 19, who belong to YHWH.[53] The second clause of both verses also shares a verb (from קום), and follows the pattern of dropping the negation in v. 19.

However, unlike the first clause, the second clause of v. 19 does not repeat the noun (*rephaim*) of v. 14, but uses a different term—נבלה (corpse). This subtle difference is indicative of a more significant contrast between the dead masters and YHWH's people. The *rephaim* are thus not included in the positive counterpart to v. 14, but they do, in fact, appear later in v. 19, in the final three words of the prayer: וארץ רפאים תפיל. Due in large part to its connection with the immediately preceding positive statement, this final clause of the prayer is often read as a climactic statement of resurrection: *and the earth will give birth to the [dead] shades*. In this reading, not only do the dead corpses of God's people rise up to life, but the once dead *shades* (רפאים) are birthed to life again out of the earth. This is a powerful image, but it has difficulties—in regards to the semantic range of the verb נפל (*hiphil*),[54] the word order of the clause,[55] and the sense of the term *rephaim* from the immediate context. A preferable rendering is contrastive (see above), which has the support of the ancient versions.[56] When the cursed *rephaim* of vv. 13–14 are contrasted with YHWH's dead (v. 19), several striking differences emerge:

1) The first is that the rising of YHWH's dead is decidedly corporeal. In contrast to the *rephaim* or the ghosts, this vision is of a corpse coming to life, a fully embodied reanimation. In the Ugaritic and Mesopotamian sources discussed above, the deceased are honoured, invoked, appeased, petitioned, and feared. They are occasionally even said to come up (Samuel comes up [עלה] from the underworld, 1 Sam 28:14; Sheol raises [הקים] the *rephaim* from their thrones, Isa 14:9). However powerful, they are not described as regaining corporeality, and even the Ugaritic royalty are still located below; one must go down (ירד) to find them. They may be *rpum* or *ilm*, *elohim*, or

---

53. The syntax is open to interpretation here, and it is not impossible that the second person suffix is subjective and conveys the sense of "those whom you [YHWH] killed" (cf. Isa 5:25; Hos 5:13—6:3).

54. The verbal root נפל nowhere else has the sense of "giving birth" in *hiphil* or any other *binyan*. While allowing for the possibility of a rare or unique use, it is difficult to explain why the normal term ילד was not used (cf. Isa 26:17, 18), and ultimately does not seem likely that תפיל means "give birth" in Isa 26:19.

55. The word order of the clause (*waw* + noun phrase + verb) is more consistent with a disjunctive relationship ("*but* the land of the *Rephaim* you will cast down") than a conjunctive one ("*and* the earth will give birth to the shades"). See Beuken: "aber du hältst die Schatten zur Erde gefällt" (*Jesaja 13–27*, 362) and McAffee, "Whisperers," 93.

56. The ancient versions support this contrastive reading: OG: ἡ δὲ γῆ τῶν ἀσεβῶν πεσεῖται ("but the land of the ungodly will fall"); Tg. Jon.: וְרַשִׁיעַיָּא דִיהַבְתָּא לְהוֹן גְּבוּרָן וַאֲנוּן עֲבַרוּ עַל מֵימְרָךְ לְגֵיהִנָּם תִּמְסַר ("and the wicked to whom you have given might, and they transgressed against your Memra, you will hand over to Gehenna").

"ghosts" (*eṭemmu*). But the conclusion to this prayer expresses something qualitatively different from the royal ancestors, namely the re-embodied life of YHWH's dead.

2) The next clause of v. 19 strengthens this contrast, with its choice of the term קוץ (*to wake up*). The *rephaim* in the underworld may be disturbed from their post-mortem sleep, but often this is described as being "stirred" or "bothered" (רגז) (Samuel in 1 Sam 28:15 [*hiphil*]; the *rephaim* in Isa 14:9; the dead king of the Phoenician sarcophagus [*KAI* 13:6–8]). The contrast with the *rephaim* is that, while they are "stirred up" (or occasionally awakened עור), the dead here wake up to genuine life.

3) Lastly, the risen people of YHWH will sing for joy (רנן), which contrasts with the low whispers of the dead (Isa 29:4). The difficult line in the lament (26:16) seems to speak of "pouring out" an incantation or of speaking in hushed tones in despair.[57] But again, the contrast is stark: while the royal inhabitants of the underworld may manage a subterranean whisper, the risen people of God will shout for joy at their life above the dust.

Conclusion

If I am correct in seeing the categories of ancestor veneration used in Isa 26 as a negative foil for the life-giving power of Israel's God, it remains to be argued elsewhere for the date of the text. Mortuary practices are attested across the ancient Near East, from the third millennium stretching into the Hellenistic period and beyond.[58] It goes beyond the evidence of the text itself to claim that a full-fledged cult of the dead existed in ancient Israel or Judah, and the mention of such a cult in Isa 26 may function in more ways than simply censure or critique. I have argued that the evidence for royal ancestor veneration in both the Levant and Mesopotamia, especially the role of the *rpum* at Ugarit, provides relevant "intertexts" for understanding Isa 26 and the concerns of its praying community. The people of Ugarit invoked and sacrificed to the long dynastic line of dead kings for the peace (*šlm*) of their society, and before them, the Mesopotamians for the peace of theirs. One often overlooked line of Isaiah's prayer confesses, "YHWH, you will establish peace (שלום) for us" (26:12). This prayer, though spoken by a suffering people, gives voice to the hope that YHWH is the sole giver of life and peace. His people invoke the name of a living king, who in his "upside down" kingdom, lowers the lofty from their thrones and raises the needy from the dust.

---

57. McAffee argues cogently for an incantation background for the term לחש in 26:16 ("Whisperers," 87–91).

58. Oppenheim mentions a Seleucid text which speaks of "pronouncing the name [*za-kar šu-mu*]" of the dead ("Assyriological Gleanings," 38 n. 2).

Bibliography

Barker, William. *Isaiah's Kingship Polemic: An Exegetical Study in Isaiah 24–27*. FAT 2/70. Tübingen: Mohr/Siebeck, 2014.

Bayliss, Miranda. "The Cult of Dead Kin in Assyria and Babylonia." *Iraq* 35.2 (1973) 115–25.

Beuken, Willem. *Jesaja 13–27*. HThKAT. Freiburg: Herder, 2007.

Bloch-Smith, Elizabeth. *Judahite Burial Practices and Beliefs about the Dead*. JSOTSup 123. Sheffield: Sheffield Academic, 1992.

Caquot, André, and Maurice Sznycer. *Ugaritic Religion*. Iconography of Religions. Sec. XV, Mesopotamia and the Near East 8. Leiden: Brill, 1980.

Day, John. "God and Leviathan in Isaiah 27:1." *BSac* 155 (1998) 423–36.

Duhm, Bernhard. *Das Buch Jesaia*. 4th ed. Göttingen: Vandehoeck & Ruprecht, 1922.

Finkelstein, J. J. "The Genealogy of the Hammurapi Dynasty." *JCS* 20 (1966) 95–118.

Gibson, John C. L. *Phoenician Inscriptions*. Vol. 3 of *Textbook of Syrian Semitic Inscriptions*. Oxford: Clarendon, 1982.

Greenfield, Jonas C. "Scripture and Inscription: The Literary and Rhetorical Element in Some Early Phoenician Inscriptions." In *Near Eastern Studies in Honor of William Foxwell Albright*, edited by Hans Goedicke, 253–68. Baltimore: Johns Hopkins, 1971.

Hasel, Gerhard. "Resurrection in the Theology of Old Testament Apocalyptic." *ZAW* 92 (1980) 267–84.

Hays, Christopher B. *Death in the Iron Age II and in First Isaiah*. FAT 79. Tübingen: Mohr/Siebeck, 2011.

———. *The Origins of Isaiah 24–27: Josiah's Festival Scroll for the Fall of Assyria*. Cambridge: Cambridge University Press, 2019.

Hays, John and Stuart Irvine. *Isaiah the Eighth-Century Prophet: His Times and His Preaching*. Nashville: Parthenon, 1987.

Healey, J. F. "MLKM/RP'UM and the KISPUM." *UF* 10 (1978) 89–91.

———. "The Sun Deity and the Underworld: Mesopotamia and Ugarit." In *Death in Mesopotamia*, edited by B. Alster, 239–42. Copenhagen: Akademisk Forlag, 1980.

Johnson, Dan. *From Chaos to Restoration: An Integrative Reading of Isaiah 24–27*. JSOTSup 61. Sheffield: Sheffield Academic, 1988.

Johnston, Philip. *Shades of Sheol: Death and Afterlife in the Old Testament*. Downers Grove, IL: InterVarsity, 2002.

Kaiser, Otto. *Isaiah 13–39*. Translated by R. Wilson. OTL. Philadelphia: Westminster, 1974.

Lambert, W. G. "Another Look at Hammurabi's Ancestors." *JCS* 22.1 (1968) 1–2.

Levine, Baruch A. and Jean-Michel de Tarragon. "Dead Kings and Rephaim: The Patrons of the Ugaritic Dynasty." *JAOS* 104 (1984) 649–59.

Lewis, Theodore J. *Cults of the Dead in Ancient Israel and Ugarit*. HSM 39. Atlanta: Scholars, 1989.

L'Heureux, Conrad. "The Ugaritic and Biblical Rephaim." *HTR* 67 (1974) 265–74.

McAffee, Matthew. "Rephaim, Whisperers, and the Dead in Isaiah 26:13–19: A Ugaritic Parallel." *JBL* 135 (2016) 77–94.

Millar, William. *Isaiah 24–27 and the Origin of Apocalyptic*. HSM 11. Missoula, MT: Scholars, 1976.

Olmo Lete, Gregorio del, Joaquín Sanmartín, et al. *A Dictionary of the Ugaritic Language in the Alphabetic Tradition*. 3rd rev. ed. Translated by Wilfred G. E. Watson. Handbook of Oriental Studies. Sec. 1, The Near and Middle East 112. Leiden: Brill, 2015.

Oppenheim, A. Leo. "Assyriological Gleanings I." *BASOR* 91 (1943) 36–39.

Pitard, Wayne T. "The Ugaritic Funerary Text RS 34.126." *BASOR* 232 (1978) 65–75.

Pope, Marvin. "The Cult of the Dead at Ugarit." In *Ugarit in Retrospect: Fifty Years of Ugarit and Ugaritic*, edited by Gordon Douglas Young, 159–79. Winona Lake, IN: Eisenbrauns, 1981.

Sasson, Jack M. "King Hammurabi of Babylon." In *Civilizations of the Ancient Near East*, edited by Jack M. Sasson, 2:901–15. 1995. Reprint, Peabody, MA: Hendrickson, 2001.

Sawyer, John. "Hebrew Words for the Resurrection of the Dead." *VT* 23.2 (1973) 218–34.

Schmid, Konrad. *The Old Testament: A Literary History*. Translated by Linda Maloney. Minneapolis: Fortress, 2012.

Schmidt, Brian. *Israel's Beneficent Dead: Ancestor Cult and Necromancy in Ancient Israelite Religion and Tradition*. FAT 11. Tübingen: Mohr/Siebeck, 1994.

Suriano, Matthew. *The Politics of Dead Kings*. FAT 2/48. Tübingen: Mohr/Siebeck, 2010.

Sweeney, Marvin A. *Isaiah 1–39 with an Introduction to Prophetic Literature*. Forms of the Old Testament Literature 16. Grand Rapids: Eerdmans, 1996.

Toorn, Karel van der. *Family Religion in Babylonia, Syria and Israel: Continuity and Change in the Forms of Religious Life*. Studies in the History and Culture of the Ancient Near East 7. Leiden: Brill, 1996.

Tsukimoto, Akio. "Peace for the Dead, or *kispu(m)* Again." *Orient* 45 (2010) 101–9.

Walton, John H. *Ancient Near Eastern Thought and the Old Testament*. 2nd ed. Grand Rapids: Baker Academic, 2018.

Whitaker, Richard E. *A Concordance of the Ugaritic Literature*. Cambridge: Harvard University Press, 1972.

Wildberger, Hans. *Isaiah 13–27*. Translated by Thomas H. Trapp. Continental Commentaries. Minneapolis: Fortress, 1997.

Wilson, Robert R. *Genealogy and History in the Biblical World*. Yale Near Eastern Researches 7. New Haven: Yale University Press, 1977.

Wyatt, N. *Religious Texts from Ugarit: The Words of Ilimilku and His Colleagues*. 2nd ed. Biblical Seminar 53. Sheffield: Sheffield Academic, 2002.

14

Jesus and Ritual Impurity in Mark's Gospel

Seth M. Ehorn

In his essay on "Purification" in the *Oxford Handbook of Early Christian Ritual*, Thomas Kazen notes that: "[B]oth archaeology and textual evidence suggest extensive observance of purity rules and purification rituals [by Jews], including frequent, perhaps daily, immersions in stepped pools (*miqwa'ot*) far from the temple as part of 'household religion.' No decrease in these practices can be shown until after the Bar Kochba revolt."[1]

Therefore, it is not surprising that many scholars question Jesus's observance of purity rules and purification rituals. In the earliest gospel, Mark, Jesus never visits a *miqwa*. Moreover, he engages in a heated debate with scribes and Pharisees over issues of purification and Torah observance and he disagrees with them (Mark 7:1–15; cf. *m. Yoma*).[2]

On the basis of material such as this, scholars disconnect Jesus from issues and concerns of ritual impurity. For example, John Meier claims that "apparently, for Jesus ritual impurity . . . is not an issue at all."[3] Brigitte Kahl also claims that Jesus does not intend to address issues of ritual impurity.[4] James Dunn draws a similar conclusion with regard to Mark's gospel:

---

1. Kazen, "Purification," 225.

2. I note, however, that in an apocryphal gospel (P.Oxy 840), Jesus claims, "I am clean; for I washed in the pool of David, and having descended by one staircase I ascended by another, and I put on white and clean garments, and then I came and looked upon these holy vessels." Cited from the *editio princeps*: Grenfell and Hunt, *The Oxyrhnchus Papyri*, 7.

3. Meier, *Law and Love*, 414–15.

4. Kahl, "Jairus," 61–78.

> Over against such concerns [for purity in Second Temple Judaism] we have the striking sequence of episodes set out by Mark. Jesus touches a man with skin disease (leprosy—Mark 1.40–45), in evident disregard for the seriousness of the man's impure condition, and declares him clean prior to any examination by a priest or offering of sacrifice (Lev. 13–14) . . . He is touched by and heals a women with a haemorrhage (5.24–34), and thus in a state of perpetual impurity (Lev. 15.25–27), and grasps by the hand the little girl already pronounced dead (Mark 5.41) . . . In short, even if Mark has highlighted the theme by his structuring of the narrative and sharpening of the issue, the theme itself is clearly and firmly rooted in the tradition. It is not a matter of much doubt that Jesus was remembered as casual in regard to purity ritual.[5]

My aim in this essay is to revisit the following question: was Mark's Jesus concerned with issues of ritual impurity? Much of the discussion of this question gravitates toward the handwashing incident in Mark 7:1–23. However, as Dunn observes, the careful reader of Mark's gospel will have already noted that Jesus has several interactions with ritually impure individuals in Mark 1–6. These interactions clearly have a bearing on Jesus's relationship to purity laws. After briefly considering three kinds of ritual impurity in Jewish Scripture and their development and application in the Second Temple Period, I examine three stories in Mark 1–6 where Jesus comes into contact with people who are ritually impure. These interactions, although often taken as evidence that Jesus was less than strict on issues of ritual impurity, demonstrate that a key part of his mission included directly addressing issues of ritual impurity.[6]

It is a pleasure to contribute this chapter to a volume honoring John Walton's long, fruitful career as an Old Testament scholar and teacher. John was my teacher (Wheaton College Graduate School, 2008–2010) and then my colleague (Wheaton College, 2015–2019) and his work continues to stimulate my thinking. As a New Testament scholar, I have selected a topic that bridges Old Testament purity issues with New Testament texts. Although I focus more on the New Testament in its Second Temple Jewish context, I hope that the honoree will find something of interest in this essay.

Ritual Impurity in Jewish Scripture and Second Temple Judaism

Because I am concerned with ritual impurity as it was understood and practiced in the Second Temple period, it is important to survey (very briefly) not only what Jewish Scripture teaches on the subject but also how Jews living in the Second Temple period interpreted and lived out these legal traditions. The latter, especially, will help to situate Jesus within his social context and assess the question of his interest in or indifference to issues of ritual purity. I begin with a brief analysis of Num 5:2, which mentions three kinds of impurities:

5. Dunn, *Jesus Remembered*, 789.
6. See esp. Kazen, *Purity Halakhah*, 197–98.

צַו אֶת בְּנֵי יִשְׂרָאֵל וִישַׁלְּחוּ מִן הַמַּחֲנֶה כָּל צָרוּעַ וְכָל זָב וְכֹל טָמֵא לָנָפֶשׁ:
Command the Israelites to put out of the camp everyone who has skin diseases, or has a discharge, and everyone who is unclean by contact with a corpse.
(Num 5:2, NRSV with modifications)

Ritual Impurity through Skin Disease

The first issue of ritual impurity mentioned in Num 5:2 refers to someone with a skin disease. The issue is identified as "leprosy" in many English translations (NRSV, NET, NKJV, ESV). However, the Hebrew צרע and the LXX's λέπρα refer to the full range of skin disorders that render someone ritually impure.

These skin diseases also receive significant attention in Leviticus 13–14. The discussion of skin diseases in Leviticus includes information on identifying and resolving skin diseases (13:1–44); guidance for how the afflicted should live (13:45–46);[7] a ritual for cleansing the afflicted (14:1–21); and additional legislation about clothing and buildings touched by the afflicted (13:47–59; 15:22–54). Amid these details, Leviticus is surprisingly silent on the questions of the transmission of skin diseases, or purification after contact with someone with צרע or λέπρα. As Myrick Shinall notes, "[i]f Jews dreaded the touch of lepers as much as New Testament exegetes often claim, Leviticus's lack of instructions for managing this impurity is surprising."[8]

Given this silence, it is important to note that Leviticus presupposes a setting in the wilderness, in the Israelite encampment surrounding the tabernacle (i.e., holy space). By extension, later readers might reasonably apply the legislation to Jerusalem and the temple, but it its applicability outside Jerusalem is uncertain.[9] In light of the connection of the legislation with holy space, Jacob Milgrom's systematization of purification rituals is useful. Because the purification rituals associated with צרע or λέπρα are extensively discussed in Leviticus, Milgrom assigns it atop a hierarchy of impurities communicated to others.[10] But, as Milgrom notes, it is not contact with the impurity itself that presents a problem, as purification rituals can be performed. Only contact with holy objects (e.g., holy vessels, priests, the sanctuary) is problematic.

---

7. What is clear from the text, especially 13:45–46, is that one afflicted with צרע or λέπρα adopts a behavior similar to someone in mourning: they wear torn clothing (Gen 37:29; Josh 7:6; Judg 11:35; etc.), they have unkempt hair (Lev 10:6; 21:10; Job 1:20; etc.), they cover their upper lip (Ezek 24:17; 24:22), and they cry out "Unclean! Unclean!" as a form of lament. Noted by Shinall, "Social Condition," 919, but see also Milgrom, *Leviticus*, 803–4 and Maccoby, *Ritual and Morality*, 125.

8. Shinall, "Social Condition," 919.

9. Shinall, "Social Condition," 918.

10. Milgrom, *Leviticus*, 1000–4.

Part 3: Context

Ritual Impurity through Bodily Discharges

The second issue of ritual impurity addressed in Num 5:2 relates to bodily discharges (זוב), primarily genital discharges, especially semen and vaginal blood.[11] For present purposes, the regulations about women are most relevant—particularly the purity laws regulating the *zabah*, which refers to a woman with an irregular genital discharge. The purification process following an irregular genital discharge is described more fully in Lev 15:25–30. Since the text explicitly stipulates that objects on which the *zabah* lies and sits become unclean (15:26), it is a matter of dispute whether the *zabah* transmits impurity directly. However, on analogy with the male transmitting impurity through touch (15:11), it is very likely that the *zabah* was thought to transmit impurity through touch as well.[12]

In the Second Temple period and beyond, the question of the transmission of impurity by touch appears to have developed or, at least, become a matter of legal dispute. For example, it is noteworthy that the Septuagint tradition of Leviticus departs from the Hebrew text on the issue of touch in Lev 15:27:

πᾶς ὁ ἁπτόμενος αὐτῆς ἀκάθαρτος ἔσται, "the one who touches *her* will be unclean"

וכל הנוגע בם יטמא, "whoever touches *these things* shall be unclean"

Whereas the Hebrew text refers to objects that the *zabah* touches, the Greek tradition refers explicitly to touching the woman with an impurity. The Mishnah also stipulates that a *zab* (and, by extension, a *zabah*) cannot touch or be touched without communicating impurity (*m. Zabim* 5:1). By contrast, the Dead Sea Scrolls provide evidence of both a utopian and an actual/realistic approach to ritual impurity. As Cecilia Wassen demonstrates, the Temple Scroll stipulates that "those afflicted with a discharge" shall have a separate place outside the city (11Q19 46.16–18; cf. 45.7–17; 48.14–17).[13] The rationale for the isolation appears to be that the *zab* or *zabah* is impure and, therefore, precautions must be taken to prevent touching and transmission of impurity. Conversely, 4QTohorot describes ritually impure individuals who come into contact with others and describes circumstances wherein they *touch* others without spreading impurity (4Q274 1.10–12). Although fragmentary, the larger context of 4Q274 has led some scholars to believe that the *zab* (and by extension, the *zabah*) "does not transmit impurity through touch of his hand when he has washed them."[14] If Milgrom is correct in his analysis of Leviticus, this understanding at Qumran seems to mirror the Hebrew text of Lev 15:11.[15] In summary, Jews did not have a monolithic

---

11. Kazen, "Purification," 226.

12. See discussion of this issue in Milgrom, *Leviticus*, 936.

13. I note that Josephus (*Ant.* 3:261) could also be used to support this quarantine perspective, but given that Josephus seems to be repeating Mosaic law and not describing actual practice, this evidence must be used with caution. See Wassen, "Hemorrhaging Woman," 650–51.

14. Wassen, "Hemorrhaging Woman," 654.

15. Note also Milgrom's (*Leviticus*, 936) conclusion cited earlier.

view on whether a *zabah*'s touch spread impurity. Certainly, some Jews maintained that it did. It may be wise, following the Septuagint tradition, to think that early readers of Mark shared this view.

Ritual Impurity through Contact with a Corpse

The third issue of ritual impurity addressed in Num 5:2 concerns contact with a corpse. Like other forms of ritual impurity, contact with a corpse was inevitable for most ancient Israelites. Corpse impurity is presented as the most serious type of impurity even though, like the other impurities already discussed, it only brought about a temporary state of impurity to the one affected. Unlike the previous impurities, the majority of biblical discussion of corpse impurity is found in Numbers (5:1–4; 19:11–22; 31:19–24) rather than Leviticus. As Thomas Kazen notes, the regulations appear to be straightforward: contact with a corpse (i.e., touching), including a bone or a grave, renders a person impure for seven days (19:11, 16; cf. 31:19). Moreover, entering the same enclosed space as a corpse renders one impure (19:14–15). The logic of this principle is that whatever overshadows the corpse (e.g., a tent or building) can also overshadow a person and cause them to become impure (cf. *m. 'Ohal.* 15:10; 11Q19 49:5–21).

The solution to this impurity is given in Num 19:12: the affected person should wash with water on the third and seventh day. Moreover, the water used for washing was to be mixed with the ashes of a heifer as well as cedar wood, hyssop and scarlet wool (19:6, 17)—elements associated with purification rituals elsewhere in Jewish Scripture (cf. Lev 14:4–7; Ps 51:7). Thus, this impurity can be remedied by ablutions and time, but failure to do so was severe, including the grave consequence of being cut off from Israel (Num 19:13). Like the previous discussions, the legislation presupposes the wilderness setting. However, it is clear that the "tent" (אהל) of Num 19:14 was later interpreted as "house" (בית or οἰκία; e.g., 11Q19 49:5–19; LXX Num 19:18). This natural development of thought, even to this minor extent, shows that corpse impurity was still considered a significant issue in the Second Temple period.

Finally, one major misconception that must be addressed before turning to Mark's gospel is the idea that contracting or coming into contact with ritual impurity somehow demonstrates a lack of concern for issues of ritual impurity. This is simply false. As Paula Fredricksen helpfully notes,

> most people were in a state of impurity most of the time. Menses, semen, childbirth, burial of the dead: all of these (more-or-less inevitable) occurrences rendered a person 'impure.' Impurity, in other words, was a (natural) state that a person moved into and out of. It implied no 'sinful' condition or permanent status; rather, it simply limited a person's access to the temple. The remedy for impurity was purification—usually some combination of washing and waiting.[16]

---

16. Fredricksen, *When Christians Were Jews*, 38.

Part 3: Context

Jonathan Klawans agrees, noting that "there are three distinct characteristics of ritual impurity. (1) The sources of ritual impurity are generally natural and more or less unavoidable. (2) It is not sinful to contract these impurities. And (3) these impurities convey an impermanent contagion."[17] Accordingly, for someone—e.g., Jesus—to come into contact with a ritually impure individual is completely normal and does not, by itself, tell us much about that person's perspective on ritual purity.

Jesus and Ritual Impurity in the Gospel of Mark

In the early chapters of Mark's gospel, we see Jesus encounter the three different kinds of impurity discussed above and we see his reactions. After looking at the examples from Mark 1–6, I briefly discuss the hand-washing incident of Mark 7 because it provides an overt authorial perspective on Jesus's relationship to Torah. I conclude that Jesus is not indifferent to ritual impurity but rather he engages directly with issues of ritual impurity in his ministry, helping ritually impure individuals overcome and, indeed, remove their impurity because of his own holy status.

Ritual Impurity through Skin Disease (Mark 1:40–45)

The story of the man who approaches Jesus in Mark 1:40, asking if Jesus is willing to cleanse him (θέλης δύνασαί με καθαρίσαι), is the first significant encounter involving touch which Jesus has with a ritually impure person in the Gospel (cf. Matt 8:1–4; Luke 5:12–16).[18]

> *A leper* [λεπρός] came to him begging him, and kneeling he said to him, "If you are willing, you are able *to cleanse* [καθαρίσαι] me." **41**Becoming angry [reading ὀργισθείς rather than σπλαγχνισθείς], Jesus stretched out his hand and touched him, and said to him, "I am willing, *be cleansed* [καθαρίσθητι]!" **42**Immediately *the leprosy* [ἡ λέπρα] left him, and *he was made clean* [ἐκαθαρίσθη]. **43**And he sent him away immediately after speaking harshly to him, **44**saying to him, "See that you say nothing to anyone; but go, show yourself to the priest, and offer for *your cleansing* [τοῦ καθαρισμοῦ σου] what Moses commanded, as a testimony to them." **45**But he went out and began to proclaim it freely, and to spread the word, so that Jesus could no longer go into a town openly, but stayed out in the country; and people came to him from every quarter. (Mark 1:40–45, NRSV with modifications)

It is noteworthy that in the immediately preceding context, Mark claims that Jesus "*cured* [ἐθεράπευσεν] many who were sick with various diseases" (1:34). But in this

---

17. Klawans, *Impurity and Sin*, 23.
18. Note the "man with an *unclean* spirit" (ἄνθρωπος ἐν πνεύματι ἀκαθάρτῳ) of 1:23–25 speaks to, but does not touch, Jesus.

story, he switches to the verb καθαρίζω and cognate terms (four times in the story!), never using θεραπεύω to describe the miracle or healing. That is, Mark is telling a story about a man with a ritual impurity issue (λέπρα), and not just a story about one of Jesus's healings.

The text has a notorious text-critical issue that affects the meaning of the passage. In Codex Bezae, ὀργισθείς ("becoming angry") appears in the place of the participle σπλαγχνισθείς ("being moved with pity") (cf. also the Latin witnesses and the Diatessaron, cited as positive evidence in NA28). Despite the weak external attestation, the parallel passages in Matt 8:3 and Luke 5:13, which both omit any reference to Jesus's emotion (either compassion or anger), should also count as early evidence in support of ὀργισθείς.[19] That is, it is easier to imagine that Matthew and Luke omitted a reference to "anger" rather than "compassion" in their version(s) of Mark.[20] Adding to the evidence, other passages from Mark have been treated similarly by his co-evangelists. For example, in Mark 3:5 Jesus looks around "with anger" (μετ' ὀργῆς), a description missing from the Synoptic parallels (Matt 12:12; Luke 6:9).[21] This line of reasoning has convinced several modern translation committees (not to mention many commentators) to translate Mark 1:41 as something like "Jesus was indignant" (e.g., NIV 2011).

On the assumption that ὀργισθείς is the earliest recoverable text, what was Jesus angry about?[22] Many options have been offered, but few are convincing. For example, Robert Guelich concludes that:

> [i]f the anger was not directed at the man or his actions and if it does not play a formal role in the narrative, it must stem from the setting of the illness and what it represented as a distortion of God's creature by the forces of evil.[23]

Explanations such as this one search beyond the text itself for an explanation that absolves Jesus of his angry disposition—a form of exegetical anger management. Similarly, France concludes that "the anger was not directed against the man himself [which] is implied by [Jesus's] immediate compassionate response."[24] But this hardly seems a fair characterization of the Markan context where Jesus subsequently "sends him away immediately after speaking harshly to him" (ἐμβριμησάμενος αὐτῷ

---

19. Cranfield, *Mark*, 92. See also P.Egerton 2:15–16v, where the same story is retold without "anger."

20. See Ehrman, "Angry Jesus," 77–98. For a strong, but ultimately less convincing treatment of σπλαγχνισθείς as the earliest recoverable text, see Williams, "Case for ὀργισθείς," 1–12. Williams argues that the orthographic similarity between the majuscule script of ΧΠΛΑΓΧΝΙΘΕΙΣ and ΣΠΛΑΓΧΝΙΣΘΕΙΣ suggest that ὀργισθείς may have been a one-off copyist mistake in MS D (although Williams also notes that "both accidental and deliberate elements" must explain the alteration) (6).

21. See also Mark 10:14, where Jesus is "indignant" (ἠγανάκτησεν) and Matthew and Luke omit the emotion (Aland §253).

22. I note that Lake, "ΕΜΡΙΜΗΣΑΜΕΝΟΣ and ΟΡΓΙΣΘΕΙΣ," 197–98, argues that the participle refers to the man with λεπρός and not Jesus. But this ignores the clear flow the passage where there is no indication of a change of grammatical subject between ἥψατο and λέγει.

23. Guelich, *Mark*, 74.

24. France, *Mark*, 118.

εὐθὺς ἐξέβαλεν αὐτόν, 1:43).²⁵ Whatever ἐμβριμησάμενος means, and it is debated, interpreters generally agree that it is a harsh word. Attempts to disassociate Jesus's anger with the man appear futile. But the issue of ritual purity provides another interpretive possibility. It is noteworthy that when this man interacts with Jesus, he says, "if you are willing, you are able to cleanse me" (ἐὰν θέλῃς δύνασαί με καθαρίσαι). Jesus's response mirrors the request: "I am willing, be cleansed" (θέλω, καθαρίσθητι). The concern with "willingness" is a significant and somewhat neglected aspect of the exchange.

In his response, as noted already, Jesus is presented as willing to engage with a ritually impure man. This contrasts with Bart Ehrman's preferred explanation of the text, which helpfully compares Jesus in other "angry" contexts but imprecisely parallels Mark 1:41 with Mark 9:23.²⁶ In the latter text, Jesus has just descended from the Mount of Transfiguration when he has an encounter with a desperate man who asks him, "if you *are able* to do anything, have pity on us" (εἴ τι δύνῃ, βοήθησον ἡμῖν σπλαγχνισθεὶς ἐφ᾽ ἡμᾶς). Despite similarities with Mark 1:41, in 9:23 the man questions Jesus's *ability* to heal and Jesus responds sharply, "if you are able?" (τὸ εἰ δύνῃ). It is not Jesus's ability, but his willingness that is questioned in 1:41: is Jesus willing to solve problems concerning issues of ritual purity? Following the man's question, Jesus becomes angry but, nevertheless, touches him and speaks to him, "I am willing, be cleansed."

How can we be certain that Jesus is concerned about ritual purity? Mark tells us that Jesus told the man to go and present himself to the priests for inspection (Mark 1:44; cf. Matt 8:4; Luke 5:14), thus following the purity stipulations of Lev 14:2–7 (cf. *m. Neg.* 14). Jesus's statement that the purpose of the priestly inspection was to be "for a witness to them" (εἰς μαρτύριον αὐτοῖς) makes sense precisely in this context. Mark's use of the expression εἰς μαρτύριον αὐτοῖς with a (possible) sense of hostility in 6:11 and 13:9 has led many interpreters to infer a similar hostile sense in 1:44.²⁷ But this is an unlikely reading. Luke's adoption of Mark 6:11 reflects a negative interpretation of "against them" (ἐπ αὐτούς, Luke 9:5), but the preposition ἐπί never follows μαρτύριον in Mark's gospel. Similarly, Mark 13:9 is not as clearly negative/hostile as some interpreters assert. Both Matthew and Luke read εἰς μαρτύριον αὐτοῖς positively, meaning that "the witness is an opportunity for the disciples to preach the gospel to the rulers (cf. Matt 10:18–20; Luke 21:12–15)."²⁸ Thus, it is best to take εἰς μαρτύριον αὐτοῖς in Mark 1:44 with σεαυτὸν δεῖξον τῷ ἱερεῖ καὶ προσένεγκε, providing evidence that Jesus was a law observant Jew who was concerned with ritual purity in his ministry.

From this first encounter with a ritually impure man, already we can begin to draw some important conclusions. First, it is clear that the story presents Jesus as

---

25. The verb ἐκβάλλω can have either a positive (Mark 1:12) or negative sense (1:34, 39). Given the context of Mark 1:40–45, the more negative sense is probably correct here.

26. Ehrman, "Angry Jesus," 94, is aware that the parallel is imprecise: "Jesus is angered when anyone questions his authority or ability to heal—or his desire to heal."

27. E.g., Broadhead, "Mark 1,44," 260–65.

28. Cho, *Royal Messianism*, 124; Gundry, *Mark*, 104, also reads αὐτοῖς in a neutral sense.

respecting the Jewish purification laws, including seeking an examination from a priest and offering a sacrifice (cf. Lev 13–14). Second, although Jesus "touches" (ἅπτω) the man with λέπρα, this does not necessarily prove that "Jesus was remembered as casual in regard to purity ritual."[29] The fact that Jesus, as a healer, touches his patient is a normal aspect of healing stories in Mark. Moreover, as noted earlier, the commonality of coming into contact with ritual impurities was neither problematic nor abnormal. Rather, his response to the man and his healing of the man tell us much more. When the man questions Jesus's willingness to cleanse him (which would imply touch), Jesus affirms that he is willing. Here, Jesus does not react indifferently or negatively to ritual impurity, but agrees to remove impurity.

Ritual Impurity through Bodily Discharge (Mark 5:24b–34)

The story of a ritually impure woman with a bodily discharge and the death of a young girl in Mark 5:21–43 are connected literarily and topically. First, Mark's story about the ritually impure woman with a bodily discharge is sandwiched between the story of the death of Jairus's daughter (Mark 5:21–24a, 35–43). As is generally acknowledged, Markan "sandwiches" or intercalations—the literary phenomenon that Mark begins one story, introduces a second story, and then returns to the first story—often present characters and themes together for consideration.[30] Second, and more important for present purposes, the stories are connected because they each center on someone who is ritually impure. The first story is found in Mark 5:24b–34 (cf. Matt 9:20–22; Luke 8:42b–48).

> 24b And a large crowd followed him and pressed in on him. 25 Now there was a woman having a flow of blood for twelve years. 26 She had endured much under many physicians, and had spent all that she had; and she was no better, but rather grew worse. 27 She had heard about Jesus, and came up behind him in the crowd and touched his cloak, 28 for she said, "If I but touch his clothes, I will be made well." 29 Immediately her spring of blood stopped; and she felt in her body that she was healed of her disease. 30 Immediately aware that power had gone forth from him, Jesus turned about in the crowd and said, "Who touched my clothes?" 31 And his disciples said to him, "You see the crowd pressing in on you; how can you say, 'Who touched me?'" 32 He looked all around to see who had done it. 33 But the woman, knowing what had happened to her, came in fear and trembling, fell down before him, and told him the whole truth. 34 He said to her, "Daughter, your faith has made you well; go in peace, and be healed of your disease." (Mark 5:24b–34, NRSV with modifications)

---

29. Pace Dunn, *Jesus Remembered*, 789.

30. Among the vast literature on Markan intercalations, see Edwards, "Markan Sandwiches," 193–216.

Here Mark introduces another ritually impure person into the narrative: a woman "having a flow of blood for twelve years" (γυνὴ οὖσα ἐν ῥύσει αἵματος δώδεκα ἔτη, 5:25) or a "spring a blood" (ἡ πηγὴ τοῦ αἵματος, 5:29). Although Mark does not specify the location of the flow of blood, the fact that these descriptions mirror LXX Lev 15:25 and 12:7, both of which describe women with genital discharges, suggests this is an irregular genital discharge.[31] There are obvious editorial features of the story that relate to Mark's intercalation of this story with the story about Jairus's daughter (5:21–24a, 35–43, to be discussed below), but the key datum for present purposes is that the woman is presented as ritually impure, with an ongoing bodily discharge.[32]

There is some disagreement in the ancient sources about the need for quarantine and/or about the problem of a *zabah* touching someone else.[33] Even if her touch was thought to impart impurity to others, typically this problem could still be resolved for the one affected by washing and waiting. However, as Mark's narrative indicates, the woman's condition spanned twelve years (5:25), which would create a problem for her following the rules for purification. In any event, we still have an interaction between the woman and Jesus that provides some data for assessing the question of Jesus's perspective toward ritual impurity.

Mark's story sets up the encounter by having the woman approach Jesus from behind and touch his clothes, which was apparently a common practice during his ministry (cf. Mark 3:10; 6:56). But why does the woman approach Jesus in this way? Adela Yarbro Collins suggests several possibilities:[34]

- The woman was ashamed to reveal her ailment in public;
- The woman was afraid of Jesus because she stole power without his consent;
- The woman was knowledgeable of different interpretations of purity *halakhah*;
- The woman was afraid that Jesus would be upset and reverse the healing;
- The woman was awed by Jesus's power.

It is very likely that this story illustrates the woman's reluctance to approach Jesus directly with a problem of ritual impurity. Just like in the story of the man with λέπρα, it is not Jesus's ability to heal the woman that is in question. Rather, it is Jesus's desire to heal this woman that is unknown or in question. Thus, the woman's approach to Jesus may reflect her uncertainty about whether Jesus would be interested in helping her.

Support for this interpretation comes from the intercalation of this story with the death of Jairus's daughter (Mark 5:21–43). In the story of the raising of Jairus's daughter, after a report comes that the girl is dead, some unnamed men ask, "why

---

31. Haber, *Purify Themselves*, 132–33.

32. *Pace* Fonrobert, *Menstrual Purity*, 191–95, who argues that a healing story has been transformed into a story about Jewish ritual impurity in its reception.

33. See Wassen, "Ritual Purity," for the evidence and full discussion.

34. Collins, *Mark*, 283–84.

bother the teacher anymore?" (5:35). This clearly demonstrates their lack of faith in contrast with the woman with the genital discharge (5:34), but it also introduces the question of Jesus's concern for the girl who died: is Jesus *willing* and/or *able* to help in this situation? The men in the story presume the answer is "no." Given the parallels elsewhere in this intercalation, it seems reasonable to conclude that Jesus's willingness or ability to heal the woman with the genital discharge is also a key factor in the way she approaches Jesus. Because the story explicitly states that she possessed "faith" that Jesus could heal her (5:34), we are left with the option that she may have doubted Jesus's willingness to engage with her due to her impurity.

Much scholarly commentary has focused on the fascinating inverse flow of power out of Jesus. In Tom Holmén's words, "[Jesus's] purity has become contagious."[35] Or, as Candida Moss has shown through comparison with Greco-Roman healing traditions, Jesus's "porosity" serves the twin functions of facilitating the woman's cure and standing "as a marker of a hidden, divine identity."[36] Moss further notes, "[p]orosity was viewed positively in the context of ideas about divine beings concealing themselves in human form."[37] In the larger context of Mark's gospel this is an especially intriguing observation because Mark is simultaneously concealing and revealing the identity of Jesus throughout his narrative. I will return to this observation in the conclusion, but here it is important to note that Jesus's status as God's Son or "the holy one of God" (Mark 1:24) may play an important role in these interactions.

After Jesus seeks out the woman who touched him, the woman responds with "fearing and trembling" (φοβηθεῖσα καὶ τρέμουσα) and "falls before him" (προσέπεσεν αὐτῷ, 5:33). Then, after she "told him the whole truth" (5:33–34), Jesus commends the woman, telling her that "your faith has made you well; go in peace, and be healed of your affliction" (ἡ πίστις σου σέσωκέν σε· ὕπαγε εἰς εἰρήνην καὶ ἴσθι ὑγιὴς ἀπὸ τῆς μάστιγός σου).

The text of Mark is silent on whether Jesus instructed the woman to perform the prescribed rituals of sacrifice following her healing/cleansing. However, as with the previous story, the woman's ritual impurity and its source are resolved through her physical contact with Jesus. As noted above, it is debated by scholars whether her contact with Jesus would have spread impurity to him.[38] But, in any case, the story is clear that "power had gone forth from him" (5:30) and removed her impurity.

---

35. Holmén, "Purity Paradigm," 2723; see also Blomberg, *Contagious Holiness*.

36. Moss, "Flow of Power," 519.

37. Moss, "Flow of Power," 518. In addition to Greco-Roman texts, Moss also cites the Transfiguration as an example where divine glory cannot be contained within the human body and, therefore, leaks out.

38. See, esp. Wassen, "Hemorrhaging Woman," 641–60.

Part 3: Context

Ritual Impurity through Contact with a Corpse (5:21–24a, 35–43)

The third important story for assessing Jesus's attitude to ritual impurity is woven together with the story of the women with the genital discharge. In Mark 5:21–24a, 35–43 (cf. Matt 9:18–19, 23–26; Luke 8:40–42a, 49–56) Jesus comes into contact with a corpse.[39]

> ²¹When Jesus had crossed again in the boat to the other side, a great crowd gathered around him; and he was by the sea. ²²Then one of the leaders of the synagogue named Jairus came and, when he saw him, fell at his feet ²³and begged him repeatedly, "My little daughter is at the point of death. Come and lay your hands on her, so that she may be made well, and live." ²⁴So he went with him. And a large crowd followed him and pressed in on him.
>
> ³⁵While he was still speaking, some people came from the leader's house to say, "Your daughter has died. Why trouble the teacher any further?" ³⁶But Jesus, ignoring the message, said to the leader of the synagogue, "Do not fear, only believe." ³⁷He allowed no one to follow him except Peter, James, and John, the brother of James. ³⁸When they came to the house of the leader of the synagogue, he saw a commotion, people weeping and wailing loudly. ³⁹When he had entered, he said to them, "Why do you make a commotion and weep? The child is not dead but sleeping." ⁴⁰And they laughed at him. Then he put them all outside, and took the child's father and mother and those who were with him, and went in where the child was. ⁴¹He took her by the hand and said to her, "Talitha cum," which means, "Little girl, get up!" ⁴²And immediately the girl got up and began to walk about (she was twelve years of age). At this they were overcome with amazement. ⁴³He strictly ordered them that no one should know this, and told them to give her something to eat. (Mark 5:21–24, 35–43, NRSV with modifications)

In Mark's story of Jairus's (unnamed) daughter, a report comes that "your daughter has died" (ἡ θυγάτηρ σου ἀπέθανεν, 5:35). Jesus "ignores the message" (παρακούσας τὸν λόγον, 5:36) and enters the house of the dead girl, which would render him ritually impure.[40] Although the text does not draw attention to the ritual impurity issue, it would be a mistake to ignore it. Based on the survey of corpse impurity issues above, it would have been obvious to most (and perhaps all) early readers of Mark's gospel that Jesus's close proximity with the girl involved ritual impurity.

There is some question about the status of the girl, because Jesus says that "the child is not dead, but asleep" (5:39). However, the mention of "a commotion and those who were weeping and loudly wailing" (θόρυβον καὶ κλαίοντας καὶ ἀλαλάζοντας πολλά, 5:38) suggests she really was dead. Why, then, does Jesus say that the little girl is "not

---

39. Due to the intercalation of this story, noted above, the corpse contact story is treated as a single unit here.

40. There is debate about the meaning of παρακούω, but the clear meaning of the word in all its LXX (1 Esd 4:11; Esth 3:3, 8; 4:14; 7:4; Tob 3:4; Isa 65:12) and NT (Matt 18:7) instances is "to ignore."

dead but asleep" (5:39)? Although "sleep" was a common metaphor for death, Mark's syntax (i.e., "not . . . but") requires a more careful explanation than simply claiming that sleep equals death. Many scholars accept Robert Guelich's explanation that Jesus's words must be interpreted "in light of the approaching miracle."[41] However, it is also possible that Jesus's declaration cushions a marriage-aged girl against societal ostracism, particularly that caused by corpse impurity, by publicly saying that she "is not dead but asleep" (5:39), by removing everyone from the healing context (except for her parents and a few of his own disciples) (5:40), and then performing the healing/resurrection more privately. In light of the theme of reintegrating social outcasts into society elsewhere in context (e.g., 5:34), it is possible and, perhaps, even likely that Jesus's comment that she is "sleeping" should be understood as an effort to protect her public status.[42]

As with Jesus's other interactions discussed here, this encounter involves *touch*. Jesus speaks to her "while grasping the hand of the child" (κρατήσας τῆς χειρὸς τοῦ παιδίου, 5:41) and he says "Little girl, get up!" (τὸ κοράσιον . . . ἔγειρε, 5:41). By resurrecting the young girl, Jesus demonstrates his healing power over the most severe form of ritual impurity. Additionally, the text describes him as willing to engage with the girl even when the characters of the story doubt his willingness or ability (cf. 5:35).

The Hand-Washing Incident (Mark 7:1–23)

Beyond these three healing narratives in Mark 1–6, the hand-washing incident in Mark 7 is important for the topic of Jesus and impurity because it presents a potential threat to the interpretation offered thus far. First, the language of cleanness (καθαρίζω) in 7:19 must be distinguished from the types of impurities discussed already. Daniel Boyarin helpfully notes that Mark's authorial comment that Jesus declared that "all foods are clean" (καθαρίζων πάντα τὰ βρώματα, 7:19) has been widely misunderstood. In Jewish law, there is a clear distinction between what is "clean" and what is "kosher," although the two could overlap. Specifically, Boyarin notes that "the system of purity and impurity laws and the system of dietary laws are two different systems within Torah's rules for eating, and Mark and Jesus knew the difference."[43] The language of "clean" in this passage should not be confused with the purity language and discussion elsewhere in Mark.

Second, the passage also raises the question of Jesus's relationship to Torah. Whereas many interpreters understand Mark 7:1–23 as a clear example of Jesus

---

41. Guelich, *Mark*, 302. This perspective is preferable to Pesch, *Das Markusevangelium*, 296, who argues that an original healing story developed into a resurrection story in the tradition.

42. This interpretation was suggested to me in a personal conversation with Andrew Kelley. At the time of our conversation, he could not recall if this was an original insight or if it was something he read elsewhere.

43. Boyarin, *The Jewish Gospels*, 113.

abrogating the law, the passage should be understood in a different way.[44] Three times in the text Jesus excoriates his opponents for prioritizing human traditions rather than God's commandments (7:8, 9, 13) and he goes on to prove his claim with an illustration using the example of a financial "gift" (κορβᾶν) one makes to God in order to get out of the obligation to care for one's parents (Mark 7:10–13; cf. Exod 20:12). Here Jesus draws attention to a tradition that allows his contemporaries to side-step the law of Moses. These Pharisees practiced Torah as well as an additional set of stipulations to help them practice it—something Mark refers to as "the traditions of the elders" (τὴν παράδοσιν τῶν πρεσβυτέρων, 7:3). Jesus, on the other hand, practices Torah alone. This is not a debate about *whether* to keep Torah, but about *how* to keep it. Thus, the hand-washing incident poses no real threat to the earlier discussion and, in fact, it strengthens it.

Conclusion

It is difficult to speak for other people, let alone purport to know their thoughts or intentions. But, one of John Walton's favorite maxims—"the Bible is *for us*, but *not to us*"—may help explain some of scholarly views I have discussed (and, at times, disagreed with) in this chapter. Issues of ritual purity and impurity do not register high on matters of relevance to many contemporary readers of the Bible, including some scholars. Indeed, for some Christian readers the notion that Jesus did not participate in the Jewish systems of ritual purity is welcome (or assumed). Nevertheless, we must let the text be the text. What are some implications of Walton's maxim with regard to Jesus and ritual impurity in Mark's gospel?

First, Mark's gospel presents Jesus as engaged with three of the most significant kinds of ritual impurity: skin diseases (Mark 1:40–45), bodily discharges (Mark 5:25–34), and contact with a corpse (Mark 5:21–24, 35–43). As noted above by Fredricksen, Klawans, and others, coming into contact with impurity was common and often unavoidable for most people in antiquity. Because of this reality, it would be wrong to assume that Jesus's contact with ritual impurities means that he was lax or indifferent on ritual impurity generally.[45] On the contrary, Jesus directly engages people with issues of impurity even when they question his willingness to do so.

Second, as Joel Marcus has noted, "[i]n the course of Mark's Gospel, Jesus treats nearly the same three categories of sufferers [as Num 5:2] in exactly the same order: a man with scale-disease (1:40–45), a *zaba* (5:25–34), and a corpse (5:35–43)."[46] While this may be a mere coincidence, Mark's larger engagement with exodus and new exodus themes (which would include the book of Numbers) certainly bolsters the claim that Mark has intentionally structured the early part of his narrative to include Jesus's

---

44. Boyarin, *The Jewish Gospels*, 107.
45. *Pace* Kazen, *Purity Halakhah*, 197–98.
46. Marcus, *Mark*, 367–68.

interactions with three ritually impure individuals. One possible implication of this framing of the narrative is that Mark intends readers to conclude that engaging directly with ritual impurity was a core part of Jesus's ministry. This suggestion may be further supported by the observation that both Matthew and Luke have followed Mark in their presentation of Jesus in this way. In addition to adopting Mark's stories discussed above, Matthew includes a unique expansion in the story of the commissioning of the Twelve disciples: "And preach as you go, saying, 'The kingdom of heaven is at hand.' Heal the sick, raise the dead, cleanse the lepers, cast out demons" (Matt 10:7–8). Here two of Jesus's actions connected to ritual impurity are passed on to his followers.

Third and finally, the fact that Jesus comes into contact with ritually impure persons and removes their impurities has a narrative explanation within the gospel of Mark. Following his baptism and identification as "the Son of God" (Mark 1:11), one of Mark's characters addresses Jesus as "the holy one of God" (ὁ ἅγιος τοῦ θεοῦ) in 1:24. It is significant that this description comes from "a man with an unclean spirit" (ἄνθρωπος ἐν πνεύματι ἀκαθάρτῳ, 1:23) who seems to have an understanding of Jesus's identity beyond that of other human characters in the story. As Hodges and Poirier conclude, "Jesus's identity as the holy one pits him against the debilitating power of disease, for impurity cannot withstand the presence of the holiness itself."[47] As God's holy one, Jesus encounters and removes ritual impurity throughout these early chapters of the gospel of Mark. Thus, I think it is fair to conclude that Mark's Jesus is not indifferent or casual with regard to ritual impurity, but rather is consistently opposed to it.

Bibliography

Blomberg, Craig L. *Contagious Holiness: Jesus' Meals with Sinners*. New Studies in Biblical Theology. Downers Grove, IL: InterVarsity, 2005.

Boyarin, Daniel. *The Jewish Gospels: The Story of the Jewish Christ*. New York: New Press, 2012.

Broadhead, E. K. "Mark 1,44: The Witness of the Leper." *Zeitschrift für die neutestamentliche Wissenschaft und die Kunde der älteren Kirche* 83 (1992) 260–65.

Cho, Bernardo K. *Royal Messianism and the Jerusalem Priesthood in the Gospel of Mark*. Library of New Testament Studies 607. London: T&T Clark, 2019.

Collins, Adela Yarbro. *Mark: A Commentary*. Hermeneia. Minneapolis: Fortress, 2007.

Cranfield, C. E. B. *The Gospel according to Mark: An Introduction and Commentary*. Cambridge Greek Testament Commentary. Cambridge: Cambridge University Press, 1959.

Dunn, James D. G. *Christianity in the Making*. Vol. 1, *Jesus Remembered*. Grand Rapids: Eerdmans, 2003.

Edwards, James R. "Markan Sandwiches: The Significance of Interpolations in Markan Narratives." *NovT* 31 (1989) 193–216.

---

47. Hodges and Poirier, "Jesus as the Holy One of God," 184.

Part 3: Context

Ehrman, Bart. "A Sinner in the Hands of an Angry Jesus." In *New Testament Greek and Exegesis: Essays in Honor of Gerald F. Hawthorne*, edited by Amy M. Donaldson and Timothy B. Sailors, 77–98. Grand Rapids: Eerdmans, 2003.

Fonrobert, Charlotte Elisheva. *Menstrual Purity: Rabbinic and Christian Reconstructions of Biblical Gender*. Stanford: Stanford University Press, 2000.

France, R. T. *The Gospel of Mark*. New International Greek Testament Commentary. Grand Rapids: Eerdmans, 2002.

Fredricksen, Paula. *When Christians Were Jews: The First Generation*. New Haven: Yale University Press, 2018.

Grenfell, Bernard P., and Arthur S. Hunt. *The Oxyrhnchus Papyri*, Part. 5: *Edited with Translations and Notes*. London: Oxford University Press, 1908.

Guelich, Robert A. *Mark 1–8:26*. WBC 34a. Dallas: Word, 1989.

Haber, Susan. *They Shall Purity Themselves: Essays on Purity in Early Judaism*, edited by Adele Reinhartz. Early Judaism and its Literature 24. Atlanta: Society of Biblical Literature, 2008.

Hodges, Horace Jeffrey, and John C. Poirier. "Jesus as the Holy One of God: The Healing of the *Zavah* in Mark 5.24b–34." *Journal of Greco-Roman Christianity and Judaism* 8 (2011–12) 151–84.

Holmén, Tom. "Jesus and the Purity Paradigm." In *Handbook for the Study of the Historical Jesus*, edited by Tom Holmén and Stanley E. Porter, 3:2709–44. Leiden: Brill, 2011.

Kahl, Brigitte. "Jairus und die verlorenen Töchter Israels: Sozioliterarische Überlegungen zum Problem der Grenzüberschreitung in Mk 5,21–43." In *Von der Wurzel getragen: Christlich-feministische Exegese in Auseinandersetzung mit Antijudaismus*, edited by Luise Schottroff and Marie-Theres Wacker, 61–78. Biblical Interpretation Series 17. Leiden: Brill, 1996.

Kazen, Thomas. *Jesus and the Purity Halakhah: Was Jesus Indifferent to Impurity*. Coniectanea Biblica 38. Stockholm: Almqvist, 2002.

Kazen, Thomas. "Purification." In *The Oxford Handbook of Early Christian Ritual*, edited by Risto Uro, Juliette J. Day, Rikard Roitto, and Richard E. DeMaris, 220–44. Oxford: Oxford University Press, 2018.

Lake, Kirsopp. "ΕΜΡΙΜΗΣΑΜΕΝΟΣ and ΟΡΓΙΣΘΕΙΣ, Mark 1,40–43." *HTR* 16 (1923) 197–98.

Klawans, Jonathan. *Impurity and Sin in Ancient Judaism*. Oxford: Oxford University Press, 2000.

Maccoby, Hyman. *Ritual and Morality: The Ritual Purity System and its Place in Judaism*. Cambridge: Cambridge University Press, 1999.

Marcus, Joel. *Mark 1–8*. AB 27. New Haven: Yale University Press, 2002.

Meier, John P. *A Marginal Jew: Rethinking the Historical Jesus*. Vol. 4, *Law and Love*. Anchor Bible Reference Library 4. New Haven: Yale University Press, 2009.

Milgrom, Jacob. *Leviticus 1–16*. AB 3. New York: Doubleday, 1998.

Moss, Candida R. "The Man with the Flow of Power: Porous Bodies in Mark 5:25–34." *JBL* 129 (2010) 507–19.

Pesch, Rudolf. *Das Markusevangelium*, Vol 1. Handkommentar zum Neuen Testament 2. Freiburg: Herder, 1976.

Shinall, Jr., Myrick C. "The Social Condition of Lepers in the Gospels." *JBL* 137 (2018) 915–34.

Wassen, Cecilia. "Jesus and Hemorrhaging Woman in Mark 5:24–34: Insights from Purity Laws from the Dead Sea Scrolls." In *Scripture in Transition: Essays on Septuagint, Hebrew Bible, and the Dead Sea Scrolls in Honor of Raija Sollamo*, edited by Raija Sollamo, Anssi Voitila, and Jutta Jokiranta, 641–60. Supplements to the Journal for the Study of Judaism 126. Leiden: Brill, 2008.

Wassen, Cecilia. "The Jewishness of Jesus and Ritual Purity." *Jewish Studies in the Nordic Countries Today* 27 (2016) 11–36.

Williams, Peter J. "An Examination of Ehrman's Case for ὀργισθείς in Mark 1:41." *NovT* 54 (2012) 1–12.

15

On Identifying the "Dragon's Spring" in Jerusalem (Neh 2:13)

Kyle H. Keimer

Introduction

It is with great pleasure that I offer this article to my former teacher. John's teaching and research have been a source of great interest and cause for reflection over the years, and I can think of no better honor than to dedicate an article about context to him. In Neh 2:13, during his night journey, Nehemiah passes by עֵין הַתַּנִּין "the dragon's spring," a location mentioned only here in the Bible. In this paper, I will discuss various views on the identification of this spring and offer an explanation for the name's origin, a point that has not generally received attention.

The Text of Nehemiah 2:13

Nehemiah 2:13–15 relates the night journey taken by Nehemiah to inspect the city walls of Jerusalem:

וָאֵצְאָה בְשַׁעַר־הַגַּיְא לַיְלָה וְאֶל־פְּנֵי עֵין הַתַּנִּין וְאֶל־שַׁעַר הָאַשְׁפֹּת וָאֱהִי שֹׂבֵר בְּחוֹמֹת יְרוּשָׁלַם־הַמְפֹרוּצִים וּשְׁעָרֶיהָ אֻכְּלוּ בָאֵשׁ: וָאֶעֱבֹר אֶל־שַׁעַר הָעַיִן וְאֶל־בְּרֵכַת הַמֶּלֶךְ וְאֵין־מָקוֹם אֲשֶׁר לַבְּהֵמָה לַעֲבֹר תַּחְתָּי:
וָאֱהִי עֹלֶה בַנַּחַל לַיְלָה וָאֱהִי שֹׂבֵר בַּחוֹמָה וָאָשׁוּב וָאָבוֹא בְּשַׁעַר הַגַּיְא וָאָשׁוּב:

¹³I went out by the Valley Gate at night, past the Dragon's Spring, and to the Dung Gate, and I inspected the walls of Jerusalem that were broken through and its gates which were burned with fire. ¹⁴Then I passed to the Spring Gate

and to the King's Pool, but there was no place for the beast under me to pass. ¹⁵So I went up by the valley at night and I inspected the wall. Then I turned back and I entered by the Valley Gate, and so returned.

The six places mentioned in the text have largely eluded unanimous identification. A number of the locations appear elsewhere in the Hebrew Bible (Dung Gate: Neh 3:13–14; 12:31; Valley Gate: Neh 2:15; 3:13; 2 Chr 26:9; Spring Gate: Neh 2:14; 3:15; 12:37), but the "king's pool" and "dragon's spring" appear only here. The "valley" (*naḥal*) is generally identified as the Kidron Valley, but this is not definite. As such, debate has raged on the specific route and direction taken by Nehemiah as well as the extent of Jerusalem in the fifth century BC. While I will turn to these matters below, it is necessary to first evaluate the transmission of the word *tannîn*, "dragon, serpent," as the LXX appears to translate *tĕēnîm* "figs" instead when it says πηγῆς τῶν συκῶν. Moreover, some English translations add to the confusion by emending *tannîn* to *tannîm* to provide a reading of "jackal('s) well" (ASV, NIV, RSV), though this emendation is without textual support.¹ Josephus (*Ant.* 11.168–71) omits the night journey so there is no additional reference by which to clarify the matter.

So which reading is to be preferred: *tnyn* or *t'nym*? If the issue is morphological in nature, the switch requires not only the elision of the *'aleph*, but also the transition of *nun* to *mem*. The likelihood that such changes resulted from scribal error or that there are variant textual traditions for this name are not compelling. More intriguing is the possibility that what we are actually seeing is a case of homophony in Hebrew in which there was a presumed similarity in sound between Hebrew *hattannîn* and *hattĕēnîm*. The Septuagintal translator heard the latter, resulting in a "fig spring" instead of a "dragon's spring." Without access to the ancient spoken language, however, this can be merely conjecture. Nevertheless, the LXX translates *tannîn* as δράκων in 14 of 16 instances;² this word was apparently understood, lending support to the idea that the homophony was between Hebrew words, not between Hebrew and Greek. Similarly, in the two instances in which Hebrew *tĕēnîm* is used—Amos 4:9 and Jer 5:17—the LXX renders συκῶν, so neither is there any confusion between these words.

Linguistically, there is no good reason to favour the LXX's apparent Vorlag over the MT. In fact, I will argue that conceptually, the MT's *tnyn* is the original and fits with expectations and failed expectations ascribed to Jerusalem in the exilic and postexilic periods.

---

1. Such English translations may have in mind Ezek 29:3; 32:2 and/or Lam 4:3 where m/n emendations due to conflation have stronger textual support.

2. Gen 1:21 (has κήτη—"sea monster"); Exod 7:9, 10, 12; Deut 32:33; Isa 27:1; 51:9 (the end of the verse is missing); Jer 51:34 (LXX 28:34); Ezek 29:3; 32:2; Ps 74:13 (LXX 73:13); 91:13 (LXX 90:13); 148:7; Job 7:12; Neh 2:13; Lam 4:3.

Part 3: Context

Locating the Dragon's Spring

Late Medieval sources were divided over where to locate the Dragon's Spring as summarized in Quaresmius's AD 1639 *Terrae Sanctae Elucidatio*.³ He cites Boniface (AD 1573) and Adrichomius (AD 1590) both of whom place it on the eastern side of the southeastern ridge known as the City of David. Boniface specifically identifies the Dragon's Spring with the Virgin's Well, what is today known as the Gihon Spring. Villalpandus (AD 1604) believed the Dragon's Spring was northwest of the Western Hill near "Mt. Calvary" (or the Church of the Holy Sepulchre). All of these individuals were influenced by the line of the Ottoman city walls finished in AD 1541 that included the Western Hill but excluded the City of David; this line was erroneously presumed to follow the line from the time of Nehemiah. Slightly earlier Father Anselm Minorita (1514), with whom Quaresmius agrees, identified the Dragon's Spring with En Rogel, a second spring located about 400 m south of the southern extent of the City of David ridge.

In the nineteenth century, Robinson believed that the Dragon's Spring was another name for the Gihon "fountain," a dried-up water source in the upper stretches of the Hinnom Valley.⁴ In the early twentieth century, Dalman returned to Father Minorita's identification and believed the Dragon's Spring was to be equated with En Rogel.⁵ This identification was particularly attractive because it made a connection between the "serpent's stone" (אֶבֶן הַזֹּחֶלֶת) in 1 Kgs 1:9 and Neh 2:13.⁶ But, since Braslavi's 1971 article which argues against this identification, it has been widely recognized that En Rogel is, in fact, too far south to fit the context of Nehemiah's night ride around Jerusalem.⁷ Less widely discussed, however, is his claim that עֵין הַתַּנִּין should be equated with what he calls the "Shiloah Spring," which is the pool located at the outpouring of what today is known as Hezekiah's Tunnel (or, the Siloam Tunnel) at the southwestern side of the City of David ridge.⁸ The source of the water flowing through Hezekiah's Tunnel is the Gihon Spring, located to the north and on the eastern side of the City of David ridge.

---

3. Quaresmius, *Terrae Sancta*, 291. I thank my colleague Prof. Alanna Nobbs for her help translating the Latin of Quaresmius.

4. Robinson, *Biblical Researches*, 513–14. Robinson differentiated between what he called a "spring," which was the location from which water emanated, and a "fountain," which was a location from which water issued, but may not be the source of that water.

5. Dalman, *Jerusalem*, 166.

6. Niehr, "Tannin," 731, posits a potential relationship between the "serpent's stone" of 1 Kgs 1:9 and Josephus' "serpent's pool" (*BJ* 5.108), even though, according to him, neither this association nor any possible confusion between *tannîn* "dragon" and *tannîm* "jackals" can be determined.

7. See Fensham, *Ezra and Nehemiah*, 166.

8. Braslavi, "En Tannin," 93. Compare the unfounded and unexplained suggestion of Blenkinsopp (*Ezra-Nehemiah*, 222) that while Braslavi's "identification with the Pool of Siloam ... is topographically more feasible ... it is safer to assume an allusion to a source of water in the Tyropeon now dried up."

On Identifying the "Dragon's Spring" in Jerusalem (Neh 2:13) —Kyle H. Keimer

Braslavi's use of the term "Shiloah Spring" follows from Josephus (*BJ* 5.140), who refers to the Shiloah/Siloam spring as between the Western Hill and the City of David.[9] Braslavi equates the Dragon's Spring with Josephus's Shiloah Spring, then he suggests that the Shiloah Spring was another name for the Gihon Spring before Hezekiah's Tunnel was cut.[10] Over the course of the First Temple period, says Braslavi, the name "Shiloah" disappeared. And after the cutting of Hezekiah's Tunnel, the name "Dragon Spring" was equated with Shiloah because the tunnel was winding like a snake.[11]

I agree with Braslavi's identification of the Dragon's Spring in Neh 2:13 as the location where Hezekiah's Tunnel issues forth from under the City of David today; there can be no other possibility when the topography, archaeology, and textual sources are considered. Nehemiah 2:13–15; 3:1–31; and 12:31–39 all list a number of specific locations in Jerusalem of the fifth century BC, and although none are unambiguously identified archaeologically, a clear identification of the Dragon's Spring on the southwestern side of Jerusalem could provide a starting point by which additional locations mentioned in the text could be identified. Additionally, what is clear archaeologically is that the Western Hill of Jerusalem (the so-called Mishneh) was not occupied in the Persian period.[12] Any possibility that there was a Dragon's Spring located on the southwestern side of the Western Hill, in the Valley of Hinnom, must be rejected. This leaves only the outlet of Hezekiah's Tunnel as a viable candidate for the Dragon's Spring.

That the Dragon's Spring of Neh 2:13 cannot be equated with the modern Gihon Spring on the eastern side of the City of David ridge is also clear from the archaeology. Reich and Shukron's excavations around the Gihon Spring did not turn up any Persian period pottery. They posit that in the days of Hezekiah the inner cell of the Spring

---

9. For a recent discussion of the name Siloam along with matters of identification and interpretation see Phillips, "The Pools of Siloam."

10. Braslavi, "En Tannin," 93. The moniker "Hezekiah's Tunnel" derives from a traditional interpretation that connects the underground tunnel with a reference to Hezekiah directing the waters of the Gihon to the west side of the City of David (2 Chr 32:30). Modern archaeological investigation has not reached a consensus on the dating of "Hezekiah's Tunnel" and whether or not it is actually the feature being referred to in the biblical text, or whether some other component of Jerusalem's water system, e.g., Channel II, is the referent (See Hom, "Where Art Thou" for a recent summary).

11. Braslavi, "En Tannin," 93.

12. See Ristau *Reconstructing Jerusalem*, 13–88 for the most recent and comprehensive summary of the archaeology of Persian period Jerusalem. In his synthesis of the various excavations in Jerusalem Ristau notes that there is good evidence for the construction of fortifications already in the fifth century BC, as the book of Nehemiah maintains (*Reconstructing Jerusalem*, 40). After this time, the sparse evidence of occupation from the early Persian period (i.e., sixth- to early fifth-centuries BC) outside of the line of apparent fortifications ceases; no doubt because people moved inside the city at that point. Additionally, Ristau cites Macalister and Duncan and Shiloh as positing postern gates in the eastern fortification line, in Areas G and D1 according to Shiloh's nomenclature which could potentially be identified with some of Jerusalem's gates mentioned in Neh 3 and 12.

Additional analysis of both old and recent excavations in Jerusalem have also shown that in a number of locations the ruined buildings from the Babylonian destruction were partially cleared, resulting in squatters' houses (Shalev and Gadot, *Looking for the Missing Link*).

Tower which surrounded the Gihon Spring was filled in, only to be uncovered again in the Hasmonean period.[13] The Gihon Spring—the source of the water—was inaccessible in the Persian period. The only place inhabitants of Jerusalem could apparently access water was at the outlet of Hezekiah's Tunnel.[14]

Tannîn in the Hebrew Bible and ANE

The origin of the name "Dragon's Spring" has not been satisfactorily determined.[15] Ugaritic texts from the Late Bronze Age mention a *tunnānu*, which can be translated as "dragon" or "snake" that is apparently multi-headed. There is also a Tunnan, who appears to be an antagonist to an unclear protagonist in KTU 1.83, a text which recounts the binding of Yamm.[16] Elsewhere, in the Baal Epic *tnn* is paralleled with Lītānu (biblical Leviathan) and referred to as a "fleeing serpent" and a "twisting serpent" (KTU 1.5 1:1–2; 1.3.III.37–42). These parallel statements are mirrored in Isa 27:1 which refers to Leviathan as a *tannîn*.

Millar notes that Isa 27:1 "is almost a direct quote from Ugaritic text 5.1.1–5,"[17] though as Anderson adds, "it seems . . . that the Ugaritic myth influenced the Israelite poetic tradition from early times, perhaps as early as the Song of the Sea (Exod 15:1–18), and in all likelihood by the time of the cultic recitations connected with the acclamation of Yahweh as king in Zion (e.g., Ps 93)."[18]

Tannînîm in the Hebrew Bible are generally understood to be "(sea) monsters," or, when singular, a specific reference to Leviathan (Gen 1:21; Isa 27:1; 51:9; Pss 74:13–14; 148:7; Job 7:12; Jer 51:34). The term, however, may also refer more generally to "serpents" (Exod 7:9–10, 12; Ps 91:13) and even potentially "crocodiles" (Ezek 29:3; 32:2), though a direct identification as a real animal may extend beyond what ancient authors were communicating. A *tannîn* was a creature that was entirely under the authority of YHWH, but which represented chaos in the ancient world. Dekker notes that "the representation of *tunnānu* in Ugaritic incantation texts presupposes a representation of the creature as a demonic power that is still present and against which people have to protect themselves."[19]

---

13. Reich and Shukron, *History of the Gihon Spring*, 217.

14. There is no archaeological evidence to suggest one way or the other that the underground tunnel leading down to Warren's Shaft and the Stone Cut Pool was still accessible in the Persian period. If it were still functioning people could potentially have reached the waters of Gihon.

15. The English "dragon" comes from the Greek *drakōn,* which is the word generally used in the LXX to translate *tannîn*.

16. Smith and Pitard, *Baal Cycle*, 248–60 for the connection between *tnn* and Yamm.

17. Millar, *Isaiah 24–27*, 55.

18. Anderson, *From Creation*, 197.

19. Dekker, *God and the Dragons*, 23.

Heider says that the use of *tannîn* in Neh 2:13 "is difficult to place" among the other references to *tannînîm* in the Hebrew Bible and Near Eastern literature.[20] But it is the appearance of the *tannîn* in "cosmic" contexts about creation or re-creation that is of importance for understanding why this term was applied to the outlet of Hezekiah's Tunnel in Persian period Jerusalem.

A Dragon and a Cosmic Mountain

Already in the Monarchic/Pre-Exilic period, Jerusalem was clearly conceptualized as a cosmic mountain. That is, a mountain "involved in the government and stability of the cosmos."[21] Such mountains often can be: 1) the meeting place of the gods; 2) the source of water and fertility; 3) the battleground of conflicting natural forces; 4) the meeting place of heaven and earth; and 5) the place where effective decrees are issued.[22]

It is precisely this belief, as viewed through the lens of the Babylonian destruction of Jerusalem and YHWH's Temple, along with the unfulfilled expectations of renewal/redemption into the days of Nehemiah that leads to the juxtaposition of the ideas of Jerusalem as holy, ordered place, and Jerusalem as chaotic place. A "dragon" spring, or conceptually speaking, a "chaos" spring, finds its best home in the early Post-Exilic Period. Such a name forms a nice bridge not only between a Zion Tradition that saw Jerusalem as inviolable and the home of YHWH forever and the heart-wrenching cries of Lamentations,[23] but also between a sense of judgment and hope embodied in much of the prophetic warnings from the monarchic and exilic periods and the unfulfilled reality of a prominent Persian-period Jerusalem.

This is the time—the mid- to late-sixth-century BC—when many passages in the book of Isaiah—particularly in chapters 40–55—remind Israel/Judah that YHWH is in control and is the God of creation (Isa 40:21–22, 26; 42:5; 44:24; 45:7, 12, 18; 48:13). As He brought order to chaos originally, so will he bring order to chaotic Israel in the form of redemption from the Exile.[24] Chaos reigns, but not forever. Isaiah 45:14–25 "glorifies Jerusalem's restoration and the reconstruction of the temple as a temporal victory but, more than this, as a cosmic victory and act of re-creation."[25]

The rebuilding of the temple in the late-sixth-century BC brings to a completion the unending, or unresolved state of mourning as expressed throughout the book of Lamentations. Judah had been "cut off from access to God's presence"; the Babylonian

---

20. Heider, *Tannin*, 836.
21. Clifford, *The Cosmic Mountain*, 3.
22. Clifford, *The Cosmic Mountain*, 3. Levenson (*Sinai and Zion*, 111–37) expands upon these ideas showing how pervasive was the idea of Jerusalem/Zion as a holy and cosmic mountain.
23. Roberts, *Solomon's Jerusalem*.
24. Stuhlmueller 1970: 193–208.
25. Ristau, *Reconstructing Jerusalem*, 96.

destruction of Jerusalem marked a national, political, and religious death for Judah.[26] All that had been ordered had been brought to chaos. Even though specific cosmic language is lacking in Lamentations, the tenor of the poems that comprise the book illustrate the mindset of those attempting to make sense of their circumstances. Jerusalem, in particular—God's chosen town—was decimated; the Temple wherein YHWH rested was destroyed. Chaos marked a city that was once the pinnacle of order.

Where Lamentations lacks explicit creation language, Ps 74 makes the connection between the destruction of Jerusalem and cosmogonic language explicit, albeit in a recollection of YHWH's power to bring order from chaos, even as this order is not fully experienced for the psalmist either.[27]

> [2c]Remember Mount Zion, where you have dwelt. [3]Raise up your steps to the perpetual ruins; the enemy has destroyed everything in the sanctuary! ... [12]Yet God my king is from of old, working salvation in the midst of the earth. [13]You divided the sea by your might; you shattered the heads of the dragons (*tannînîm*) on the waters. [14]You crushed the heads of Leviathan; you gave him as food to the creatures of the wilderness. [15]You split open springs and streams; you dried up strong rivers. [16]Yours is the day, yours also the night; you have established the heavenly lights and the sun. [17]You have set up all the boundaries of the earth; you have made summer and winter ... [22]Arise, O God! Defend your cause. Remember how the foolish scoff at you all day! [23]Do not forget the clamour of your enemies, the uproar of those rising up against you, which goes up continually! (Ps 74:2c–23)

In the book of Isaiah, God is king of the universe, and his domain is the entire universe (Isa 37:16; 44:24; 42:5; 45:12, 18; 51:12, 13; 54:5; 66:1). Isaiah 65:17a says, "For behold, I create new heavens and a new earth ..." But he also reigns specifically from Jerusalem (Isa 24:23b). In detailing the theme of God's/YHWH's kingdom in the book of Isaiah, Abernethy notes that "on the one hand, God's kingdom is universal—all of heaven and earth is the realm of God's kingdom. On the other hand, there is a particularized view of God's kingdom—Zion is its centre point."[28] Regardless of when one wishes to date the composition of Isa 40–66, the cosmic language, aspiration for order, and promise of God's control would have spoken to Judahites in the Exilic and Post-Exilic periods.[29]

---

26. Berlin, *Lamentations*, 16.

27. We may also consider Ps 44:20 if *tannim* is to be read as *tannîn* as some MSS indicate.

28. Abernethy, *The Book of Isaiah*, 172.

29. The matter of the compositional and/or redactional history of the book of Isaiah is outside the scope of this paper. Regardless of how one understands these matters, most scholars would agree that any so-called Deutero-Isaiah (or Deutero-Isaianic school) would have an original context no later than the Babylonian period.

Abernethy,[30] citing Stromberg,[31] notes that Isa 65:18-25 details that God will bring about the "restoration of Jerusalem and its people, extremely long life, ownership and use of the land, productive labour, success in birth, attentiveness from the Lord, and safety from threatening animals." Abernethy adds, "God will be creating a reality where all is as it should be; distress and turmoil will be no more."[32] Moreover, as Berges notes, in Isa 40–55 "the waters of chaos and destruction are converted in her to the four life giving rivers which assure fertility and prosperity."[33] Jersualem's spring, the Gihon, is one of the four rivers that emanates from the Garden of Eden (Gen 2:13). The idea of Jerusalem as the center of the world is often latent in the Hebrew Bible, and at times very explicit (e.g., Isa 2).[34] The Temple's construction mirrors Gen 1;[35] Jerusalem was and is the dwelling place of YHWH, who is reigning from Mt. Zion (Isa 24:23).

Such hope is visible elsewhere in Isa 52:7-12, which has God returning to reign from Jerusalem, where his house is (52:11-12). Isaiah 66:19-24 sees all nations coming to God's holy mountain to worship him. The ideas of a new Exodus and a flourishing Jerusalem because of God's re-established kingship centered at Jerusalem offer an (ideal) call to return to Jerusalem, but it is an incomplete stitching of reality and expectation as is clear from Neh 2:13.[36]

In fact, by the fifth century BC Haggai's vision of a renewed Davidic line through Zerubbabel (Hag 2:20-23) had not been fulfilled, nor had the material wealth mentioned in Hag 2:6-9 been forthcoming. The land was not bearing abundant produce as promised (Neh 5:1-9; Mal 3:10; Zech 8:12). Life in Jerusalem in the Persian period was not ideal or easy. The idea of a *tannîn*, "dragon" spring would be entirely at home for the jaded inhabitants of Jerusalem in the late sixth to mid-fifth centuries. No doubt this name is a conscious and ironic moniker bestowed to the outlet of Hezekiah's Tunnel in light of Isa 33:20-22, Ezek 47:1-12, Zech 14:8, and Joel 4:18.[37] The idea in these passages of a river of life-giving water flowing from Jerusalem is even connected to the primordial paradise of Eden by Ezekiel (Ezek 28; Gen 2:6, 10-14). But into the days of Nehemiah, no such life was yet flowing from Jerusalem. The hoped-for river of life

---

30. Abernethy, *The Book of Isaiah*, 174.

31. Stromberg, *Isaiah after Exile*, 91-95, esp. 94.

32. Abernethy, *The Book of Isaiah*, 174.

33. Berges, *Zion and the Kingship*, 104. Cf. Ego, *Die Wasser der Gottesstadt*.

34. See Levenson, *Sinai and Zion*, 130-31, who alludes to the fact that the sacrality of the Gihon and a connection between Eden and Jerusalem were already established in the days of David in the tenth century BC. He also cites Ps 36:8-10, which connects Eden and Gihon and Jerusalem (p. 132).

35. Walton, *Genesis 1*, 100-110; "The Temple in Context;" *The Lost World*, 78-86; Levenson, *Sinai and Zion*, 141-45.

36. See Berges *Zion and the Kingship*, who focuses on the ideal expressed in Isa 40-55.

37. These, and in particular Isa 33, may hearken back to an original Canaanite motif in which waters flow from the tent of El, the unstormable compound as Clifford suggests (*The Cosmic Mountain*, 158). See Day, *God's Conflict with the Sea*.

flowing from the cosmic Jerusalem wherein YHWH dwelt was still viewed as a chaotic trickle of what was likely a fading hoped-for reality.

Conceptually, there is good reason to understand how/why a name such as the "Dragon's Spring" arose. But there are also specific physical and topographic features that likely combined with the conceptual to cement the name for at least a few generations until Nehemiah arrived.[38] First, Hezekiah's Tunnel is winding, which could draw from allusions to the winding serpent Leviathan in the Baal Myth and in Isa 26:20—27:1. Second, the water carried by Hezekiah's Tunnel just issued forth from a large fissure in the bedrock. Since the Gihon Spring itself was covered over in the Persian period, there would have appeared to be an unknown water source emanating from underground, which is where *tannînîm* lived. Third, and without overstating my case, there may also be an aspect of physical geography being drawn upon for theological statement, and that is that the output of Hezekiah's Tunnel is over 100 m lower in elevation than the top of Mt. Moriah / the Temple Mt. It is nearly at the bottom of the Tyropoen Valley, and thus closer to the underworld, where Chaos monsters live. Fourth, Jerome notes that there was on occasion a loud sound emanating from Hezekiah's Tunnel. Perhaps such sound was associated with a dragon, something which we can only conjecture because we have no idea what sound(s) ancient people ascribed to dragons.

With the reordering of Jerusalem/the cosmos through the actions of Nehemiah, the classical concept of Jerusalem as a cosmic mountain appears to shift. At least by the second century BC, the idea that life giving water flowed from directly beneath the deity's temple (Ezek 47:1–12; Joel 3:18) gave way to the idea that at least in one instance that water flowed from underneath the cosmic mountain (1 En. 26:2). As Clifford notes, 1 En. 26:1–5, which follows God's mountain-garden throne in chapters 24–25, attests to a different concept of the cosmic mountain.[39] No doubt this passage is drawing directly from the physical geography of Jerusalem and working to remove any negative connotation associated with the former days of chaos.

Conclusions

Jerusalem was a sparsely inhabited squatter town in the sixth- to mid-fifth centuries BC. It was only in the days of Nehemiah and after that any stability emerged along with administrative consolidation.[40] The conceptual progression we can trace moves from: 1) Jerusalem as a cosmic mountain with YHWH's Temple, from which order flows; 2) Babylonian destruction of Jerusalem—de-creation to a state of chaos; 3)

---

38. There are interesting passing remarks in late antique sources about a Dragon Spring in Jerusalem (see Phillips, "The Pools of Siloam"). It may be that this name continued for a very long time in the local imagination.

39. Clifford, *The Cosmic Mountain*, 182–89.

40. Ristau, *Reconstructing Jerusalem*, 89.

Expressions of lament and separation from YHWH are related to Jerusalem; 4) hope for restoration and order is expressed and/or re-expressed by a number of prophets; 5) the Temple is rebuilt but the hoped for complete restoration of Israel and David's line is not achieved—full order is not restored and the hope of (4) is tempered with continuing expectation, frustration, and (economic, political, and religious) failure, ultimately giving way to the idea that Jerusalem is still in a state of chaos. The name "Dragon's Spring" most likely appears at this time; 6) Nehemiah arrives and finds a chaotic Jerusalem, albeit with a functioning Temple and starts to restore order through the construction of fortifications and favourable religious and political moves (along with Ezra); and, 7) eventually, Israel regains autonomy under Hasmonean rule and the last element of chaos, the Dragon Spring, which issues from the bottom of YHWH's mountain, is reconceptualized in 1 Enoch as an element of order/paradise signalling that order has been fully re-established.

The "Dragon's Spring" highlights the penchant that people have had throughout history to lose hope in the face of waiting and in the face of (seemingly) bad circumstances. People forgot that YHWH's pace is not their pace. The hoped for fulfillment of visions and oracles spoken by Israel's prophets were ultimately considered fulfilled, and when this happened, the dragon and all that it represented was reconceptualized and replaced.

Bibliography

Abernethy, Andrew T. *The Book of Isaiah and God's Kingdom: A Thematic-Theological Approach.* New Studies in Biblical Theology 40. Downers Grove, IL: InterVarsity, 2016.

Anderson, Bernhard W. *From Creation to New Creation: Old Testament Perspectives.* Minneapolis: Fortress, 1994.

Berges, Ulrich. "Zion and the Kingship of YHWH in Isaiah 40–55." In *'Enlarge the Site of Your Tent': The City as Unifying Themes in Isaiah: the Isaiah Workshop*, edited by Archibald L. H. M. Van Wieringen and Annemarieke van der Woude, 95–119. Oudtestamentische Studiën 58. Leiden: Brill, 2011.

Berlin, Adele. *Lamentations: A Commentary.* OTL. Philadelphia: Westminster, 2002.

Blenkinsopp, Joseph. *Ezra-Nehemiah: A Commentary.* OTL. Philadelphia: Westminster, 1988.

Braslavi, Joseph. "En-Tannin (Neh 2:13)." *EI* 10 (1971) 90–93 (Hebrew).

Clifford, Richard J. *The Cosmic Mountain in Canaan and the Old Testament.* HSM 4. Cambridge: Harvard University Press, 1972.

Dalman, Gustaf. *Jerusalem un sein Gelände.* Gütersloh: Bertelsmann, 1930.

Day, John. *God's Conflict with the Dragon and the Sea: Echoes of a Canaanite Myth in the Old Testament.* University of Cambridge Oriental Publications 35. Cambridge: Cambridge University Press, 1985.

Dekker, Jaap. "God and the Dragons in the Book of Isaiah." In *Playing with Leviathan: Interpretation and Reception of Monsters from the Biblical World*, edited by Koert van Bekkum, et al., 21–39. Themes in Biblical Narrative 21. Leiden: Brill, 2017.

———. *Zion's Rock-Solid Foundations: An Exegetical Study of the Zion Text in Isaiah 28:16*. Oudtestamentische Studiën 54. Leiden: Brill, 2007.

Ego, Beate. "Die Wasser der Gottesstadt: Zu einem Motiv der Zionstradition und seinen kosmologischen Implikationen." In *Das biblische Weltbild und Seine altorientalische Kontexte*, edited by Bernd Janowski and Beata Ego, 361–89. FAT 32. Tübingen: Mohr/Siebeck, 2001.

Fensham, F. Charles. *The Books of Ezra and Nehemiah*. NICOT. Grand Rapids: Eerdmans, 1982.

Heider, G. C. "Tannin תנין." In *DDD*, edited by Karel van der Toorn, et al., 834–36. 2nd ed. Grand Rapids: Eerdmans, 1999.

Hom, Mary Katherine Yem Hing. "Where Art Thou, O Hezekiah's Tunnel? A Biblical Scholar Considers the Archaeological and Biblical Evidence Concerning the Waterworks in 2 Chronicles 32:3–4, 30 and 2 Kings 20:20." *JBL* 135 (2016) 493–503.

Levenson, Jon D. *Sinai and Zion: An Entry in the Jewish Bible*. Minneapolis: Winston Press, 1985.

Millar, William R. *Isaiah 24–27 and the Origins of Apocalyptic*. HSM 11. Missoula, MT: Scholars, 1976.

Niehr, H. "תַּנִּין tannin." In *TDOT* 15:726–31.

Phillips, Elaine A. "The Pools of Siloam: Biblical and Post-Biblical Traces." *TynBul* 70 (2019) 41–54.

Quaresmio (Quaresmius), Francisco. *Historica Theologica et Moralis Terrae Sanctae Elucidatio*. Antwerp: Moreti, 1639.

Reich, Ronny and Shukron, Eli. "The History of the Giḥon Spring in Jerusalem." *Levant* 36 (2004) 211–23.

Ristau, Kenneth A. *Reconstructing Jerusalem: Persian-Period Prophetic Perspectives*. Winona Lake, IN: Eisenbrauns, 2016.

Roberts, J. J. M. "Solomon's Jerusalem and the Zion Tradition." In *Jerusalem in Bible and Archaeology: The First Temple Period*, edited by Andrew G. Vaughan and Ann E. Killebrew, 163–70. SBL Symposium Series 18. Atlanta: SBL, 2003.

Robinson, Edward, *Biblical Researches in Palestine, Mount Sinai and Arabia Petræa: A Journal of Travels in the Year 1838*. London: Murray, 1841.

Shalev, Yiftah, and Yuval Gadot. "Looking for the Missing Link—New Evidence for Persian and Hellenistic Jerusalem and Its Implications." Paper presented at the Annual Meeting for the American Schools of Oriental Research, San Diego, Nov. 21, 2019.

Smith, Mark S., and Wayne T. Pitard. *The Ugaritic Baal Cycle*. Vol. 2, *Introduction with Text, Translation and Commentary of KTU/CAT 1.3–1.4*. VTSup 114. Leiden: Brill, 2009.

Steinmann, Andrew E. *Ezra and Nehemiah*. Concordia Commentary. Saint Louis: Concordia Publishing House, 2010.

Stromberg, Jacob. *Isaiah after Exile: The Author of Third Isaiah as Reader and Redactor of the Book*. Oxford: Oxford University Press, 2011.

Stuhlmueller, Carroll. *Creative Redemption in Deutero-Isaiah*. Analecta Biblica 43. Rome: Biblical Institute, 1970.

Walton, John H. *Genesis 1 as Ancient Cosmology*. Winona Lake, IN: Eisenbrauns, 2011.

———. *The Lost World of Genesis 1*. Downers Grove, IL: InterVarsity, 2009.

———. "The Temple in Context." In *Behind the Scenes of the Old Testament: Cultural, Social, and Historical Contexts*, edited by Jonathan S. Greer, John W. Hilber, and John H. Walton, 349–54. Grand Rapids: Baker Academic, 2018.

16

Metaphor and Meaning in Psalm 23
Provisions for "a Table in the Presence of My Enemies"[1]

ADAM E. MIGLIO

"One of the qualities essential to being good at reading poetry is ...
a capacity for surprise. It's easy to become so mired in our likes or dislikes that
we can no longer recall ... that person inside of us who once responded to poems ...
without any preconceived notions of what we wanted them to be."
—CHRISTIAN WIMAN

"Where there is an overlapping of purposes, there is an overlapping
of metaphors and hence a coherence between them."
—LAKOFF AND JOHNSON[2]

PSALM 23 IS A short, if much-discussed poem that is as vivid as it is well-known. It is packed with complex figurative language, yet the poem's familiarity can make it difficult to read without predetermination regarding its meaning. One effective way for readers to encounter the poetry of the Hebrew Bible afresh is through exposure to the ancient world in which this literature was composed. Hundreds of thousands of cuneiform sources help to provide a window into this "lost world."

---

1. The abbreviations for primary Near Eastern sources follow the system in the *Assyrian Dictionary of the Oriental Institute of the University of Chicago* (CAD).

2. Share and Wiman, *The Open Door*, 8. Lakoff and Johnson, *Metaphors We Live By*, 96.

These sources allow readers of the Hebrew Bible to get "behind" the text and, in turn, offer the potential to generate innovative readings "in front" of the text. The stimulating interpretive possibilities catalyzed by Near Eastern sources are, at least in part, what has inspired John H. Walton's insistence that even if the Old Testament was written *for* 21st-century readers, it was not written not *to* them. By comparing the Old Testament with ancient Near Eastern sources he has repeatedly sought to defamiliarize the familiar in order to help contemporary readers approach the Old Testament from new perspectives; this brief foray into Ps 23:5a is offered as a tribute to him with the utmost respect and in friendship.

YHWH as Host of a Festal Meal

The opening four verses of Psalm 23 explore the well-known metaphor of YHWH as a shepherd. They survey the landscape and experiences of life on the go through the steppe. The fifth verse, however, marks a transition. It introduces the imagery of YHWH arranging a meal for the psalmist amidst enemies. This figural language in verse five, in which YHWH is the host of a meal amidst enemies, has proved challenged interpreters. The wide array of explanations for this metaphor, which is tersely described as transpiring "before my enemies," attests to its difficultly for commentators.[3] Interpreters have compared the festal imagery in Ps 23:5[4] with various ancient Near Eastern ritualized meals–whether victory banquets at palaces, eating at the king's table, or even ceremonial supping with the dead;[5] yet, these comparisons fail to convincingly explain why the meal is described as "before my enemies." In the present essay, therefore, I will propose a new explanation for Ps 23:5a, namely that it employs imagery taken from the Near Eastern practice in which kings furnished foodstuffs to their dependents "on the road." I will consider how such royal provisions were meals of symbolic significance that not only served to sponsor palace dependents but also to broadcast royal largess. Thereafter, by way of conclusion, I will briefly reflect on how the metaphors of YHWH as *host* and the metaphor of YHWH as *shepherd* have a shared entailment in this poem—kingship.

---

3. The shift between the two dominant metaphors in the poem is further encoded by the formal structure, which changes from tri-cola in verses 1–4 to quadra-cola in verse 5-6 (see below). Commentators have explained this (seeming) transition to imagery of a host in numerous ways. For example, suggestions range from redactional histories that reconstruct the addition of verses 5–6 (Klaus-Peter), to arguments that shepherding imagery is the only image that suffuses the poem (Mittmann), to attempts to locate altogether different literary themes as central to the poem such as "new exodus" (Freedman and Barré and Kselman), to emendations (Dahood).

4. By the use of the word festal, feast or feasting I simply intend a "... social event oriented toward abundant display and communal consumption with ritualizing tendencies" (Fu and Altmann, "Feasting," 15). For a more thorough discussion of literature pertaining to feasting, see further Fu and Altmann, "Feasting," 1–32.

5. E.g. Barré and Kselman, "New Exodus," 104–15; Loretz, "Nekromantie," 97–123; Klaus-Peter, "Feasting and Foodways," 241–48.

Royal Provisions "for the Road" in the Ancient Near East: Practice and Ideology

The well-documented royal practice (and associated ideology) of making provisions for dependents "on the road" in Mesopotamian sources provides an instructive point of comparison for the image of YHWH preparing food and drink amidst enemies in Ps 23:5a. As a matter of practicality, Mesopotamian monarchs provided their dependents with provisions "for the road." That provisioning troops met practical needs does not require extensive demonstration. Kings frequently mobilized food and drink for troops (and at times their pack-animals)[6] as travel provisions (Akkadian *ṣidītum*).[7] Countless archival sources reveal troops' expectations for royal provisions as well as their discontent when such provisions were (perceived to be) insufficient or simply not supplied. For example, in one instance from the Old Babylonian period, two separate representatives from Mari who oversaw the same cadre of troops wrote to the king recounting the troops' frustrations with their provisions. The crux of the complaint was practical: the troops had not been provisioned with flour by a local king who was responsible for their rations and, as a result, the troops were intent on leaving their post if they went without their rations.[8]

At the same time, the necessary logistics of provisioning troops became a vehicle for political ideology. Kings self-reflectively fashioned their royal responsibility into a literary *topos* in palace propaganda. The act of provisioning troops came to be a means to signal royal largess and patronage. The symbolic importance of the king's provisions may be observed, in part, through the ideological narratives of royal compositions. Royal inscriptions, especially those of the Neo-Assyrian monarchs, boasted of the abundant provisions that the king made for his troops and, in turn, how the troops responded with loyal service to their sovereign. For example, the Neo-Assyrian monarch Sargon II (722–25 BC) bragged that he supplied his "men with rich and ample food, and they joyfully prepared sufficient travel provisions (*ṣudû*)." Likewise, his son and successor, Sennacherib (705–681 BC), propagandized about the ample preparations he made for his troops and their animals for a military campaign: "I made the warriors embark on boats and I issued travel provisions (*ṣidītu*) to them. I (also) loaded grain and straw for the thoroughbreds with them." And the literary motif of the king's generous benefaction toward the troops was also reinforced in

---

6. For example, a Neo-Assyrian letter (SAA 5.250) mentions a significant amount of grain that had been inventoried for pack-animals, soldiers, and several high-level functionaries (*turtānu* and *rab šaqê*), who were hole up at an Assyrian stronghold near a battlefront in eastern Mesopotamia (see the discussion of this letter by Fales, "Grain Reserves," 25), though what is not clear from the letter is if the rations were to be a minimal hoard for the battle or if they represented a plentiful supply for the offensive.

7. *Ṣidītum* (typically comestibles), but also at times other provisions (tools, clothing, sandals); *CAD Ṣ ṣidītu*, pp. 172–74.

8. ARM 26.313, 314, 356.

detailed artistic depictions that adorned Neo-Assyrian palaces. Food preparations for the troops in the camp was a muse for the king's craftsmen, who illustrated the bravado of the royal inscriptions on palatial reliefs.[9] And that the royal duty of provisioning troops played an important part in the Neo-Assyrian ideology of kingship is further demonstrated by the way in which the palace chancelleries innovated this literary motif. For example, by the reign of Esarhaddon (681–69 BC), Sennacherib's son, the motif had creatively evolved such that he baldly insisted that amidst the fierce warfare, "I did not (even) store up travel provisions for my campaign."[10] Esarhaddon's scribes inverted his father's and grandfather's boasts about furnishing substantial provisions for the Assyrian military into a "humblebrag." Esarhaddon underscored his natural abilities (and divine favor) as the only explicable reasons for his military successes.

That provisioning troops was understood as a symbol of royal largess, at least by troops for whom it was furnished, can be observed by returning to the aforementioned Old Babylonian dossier concerning flour rations. What is interesting about this dossier is the fact that royal provisions are inextricably connected with feasting at the king's table. In this dossier, the overseer of the troops was frustrated by the lack of rations provided by the king, and he perceived this lack as a failure of the king to perform his royal duty. As a result, this overseer made his frustrations known by absenting himself from the king's festal meals (*naptanū*): "I am speaking with him (i.e. the king) about furnishing the troops with flour, but he is not respo[nding]. So I have not gone to his

---

9. Fales and Rigo, "Everyday Life." There are no Neo-Assyrian depictions of the king feasting at a common table within the camp (Fales and Rigo, "Everyday Life," 425) yet a few reliefs are connected with ritualized behaviors (see Reade 2005). Also, it is certainly clear from the Old Babylonian sources that royal feasting was hardly confined to the palace; there were "moveable feasts," and as such this practice could transpire in foreign contexts. One curious, often overlooked, instance of portable feasting is documented by archival sources from the ancient city of Mari. According to these sources, the palace would furnish a feast "on the road" for the sovereign and his entourage (e.g. ARM 11.24, 74, 215 and 250). The distributions for the *magarrû šarrim* were not dramatically different from the provisions made for the more typical meal of the king (*naptan šarrim*), though Burke notes that the amounts of foodstuffs are fewer than the *naptan šarrim* and less diverse (ARM 11, p. 139)—the primary difference between the *naptan šarrim* and *magarrû šarrim* being the absence of certain less-portable and more-perishable foodstuffs in the latter. It is difficult to infer from the extant administrative sources what specific rituals accompanied the practice of feasting "on the way" or what formalized customs these meals may have involved beyond the consumption of the foodstuff by the king and his entourage. Yet it seems noteworthy that administrative entries pertaining to the *magarrû šarrim* are occasionally included on the same tablets that record the more luxurious feast of the *naptan šarrim*, or "meal of the king" (e.g. ARM 9.71, 121, and 216).

10. RIMA 1, lines 63ff. Similarly, if in poetic form, the *Zimri-Lim Epic* accentuates the austerity of the conditions on campaign, both for the king and his troops, in order to call attention to the sovereign's character and skills on the battlefield. "Until the king accomplished his objective, And he trampled Ida-Maras under his feet, He only drank from the water skin, Allotted among the soldiers, he (too) is distressed by everything. Great are the soldiers, who went out with him: Like the wild ass (eating) the straw in the steppe, His men devour flesh, They take heart (and) gain strength." This portion of *The Zimri-Lim Epic* foregrounds how the king inspired his troops as he fearlessly participated alongside them despite the adverse conditions, such as a lack of choice provisions, on the battlefield.

festal meal (*naptanum*) for eight days because he is not providing flour for me."¹¹ The overseer's demonstration against the king's festal meals was a fitting form of protest, since communal feasting at the king's table was more than a coincidental aspect of subsistence; rather, this custom was enmeshed with fundamental cultural, social, and political realities. Festal meals with the king helped to (re)construct or maintain social and political roles.¹² To be invited to eat at the king's table (Akkadian *paššur šarrim* or Hebrew *šulḥan hammélek*)¹³ marked the honored status of the guest(s), while at the same time the abundance of foodstuffs conveyed the largess of the king.¹⁴ Thus the overseer's absence from the festal meals was a logical indication of his disapproval of the king's unwillingness/inability to provision the troops with their flour rations; the overseer simply could not affirm the potentate's wealth, strength, and benevolence by feasting with him since the king had failed to furnish the troops with their rations.¹⁵

YHWH and Metaphorical Entailment of Kingship in Psalm 23

The practice and ideology of royal provisions for dependents on campaign may provide a helpful point of comparison for the figural language of YHWH preparing food amidst enemies in Ps 23:5a. When read against the backdrop of the Mesopotamian customs discussed above, YHWH appears in Ps 23:5a as the one who plentifully

---

11. *ARM* 26.313.

12. An individual's social rank readily affected how he feasted and, at the same time, feasting could be a part of an ongoing negotiation of social or political positions. As Fu and Altmann, succinctly state, "the feast and foodways [were] constitutive elements in the construction of community, in the production of social roles, and in the development and maintenance of the state" ("Feasting," 9–10). See also Wiessner and Schiefenhövel, *Food and the Status Quest*.

13. For helpful treatments, see Sasson, "The King's Table"; Charpin, "Les usages politiques"; MacDonald, "Not Bread Alone."

14. The logistics required to disburse provisions for sovereigns and their servants of all types (e.g. messengers, troops, caravans, etc.) helped to contribute to the production of thousands of cuneiform administrative tablets known from Syro-Mesopotamia. And from the advent of writing in Syro-Mesopotamia, at least, it is clear that those who controlled surplus distributed it to the personnel in their employ as an expression of social differentiation. As Peter Damerow comments, already at the turn of the third millennium the re-provisioning of surplus and socio-political status went hand-in-hand: "[At this time,] food production and distribution were no longer primarily matters of individual effort ... [A] person's status could not be significantly altered by his own initiative. For a considerable part of the population the status quest was, by definition of social role, in vain" (Damerow, "Food Production," 167).

15. Similar customs may have been paralleled in the world of ancient Israel, as best can be discerned, from a few characteristically terse Hebrew narratives. For example, a royal meal "on the road" may be alluded to in 1 Kgs 20:12, where the Aramean king may be described feasting "on the road" while besieging Samaria (although, the phase בסכות is equivocal, referring either to a geographical locale in Trans-Jordan or a sprung structure, like a tent). 2 Sam 13:23–28 may also envision a royal meal "on the road," when Absalom invited his brother, the prince, to feast as a part of his nefarious plot to attack and kill him amidst the revelries. It is tempting, too, to see in the narrative of David bringing his brothers food on the battlefront a critique of Saul's failure as a king as well as a foreshadowing of David's ascent (1 Sam 17).

provides for his dependents "on the road." The image of YHWH as host evokes his largess as well as the care his dependents receive while abroad.[16] The metaphor draws on the source-domain of royal patronage or provisioning to conceptualize YHWH. In this way, the metaphor in Ps 23:5a is congruent with the image of YHWH as shepherd found in the preceding verses. That is, the theme of kingship is also suggested by the metaphor of YHWH as a shepherd.[17] Royal associations with shepherding are ubiquitous in the ancient Near East; to be a king was to be like a shepherd. In Ps 23, shepherding and kingship most overtly converge in the reference to the "rod/scepter" (שבט), which designates both a herding implement and a royal accoutrement.[18] If the understanding of Ps 23:5a proposed herein is correct, then, the shepherd and host metaphors in this poem overlap and, hence, focus attention on a central theme—kingship. The first four verses of the poem may pivot away from the figurative language of shepherding to that of hosting a meal, but both the metaphor of YHWH as shepherd and the metaphor of YHWH as host entail the notion of YHWH's kingship and therein the poem finds a coherence.

Appendix: A Translation of Psalm 23

[1] A Psalm of David:

YHWH is my shepherd (so) I lack nothing,
[2] He provides me rest in verdant[19] pasture,
He directs me to waters of tranquility.[20]

---

16. Freedman ("Twenty-Third Psalm") long ago noted that Ps 23:5a is literally connected with Ps 78:19. Ps 78:19 uses imagery of God arranging a table in the steppe (אל לערך שלחן במדבר) to allude to the exodus. That such a memory would be recalled in this Psalm seems fitting, even if the passing allusion is coincidental to the poem's primary interest in the theme of kingship. That the exodus is the *central* concern in the poem seems tendentious (cf. Barré and Kselman, "New Exodus," 98, who have tried to make this case by finding mention of new covenant in Ps 23:6).

17. Pardee, in my estimation, is correct to identify royal concerns as central to this poem; see also Tanner, "King Yahweh."

18. Power, "The Shepherd's Two Rods," 434–42; see further Tanner "King Yahweh." Cf. the iconography of Assurnasirpal's 'Banquet' Stele, which combines shepherd imagery with warrior imagery with a text focused on feasting (the king holds a crook-like scepter in one hand and a mace in the other).

19. The use of the lemmata דשא (verdant, vs. 2) and רויה (abundant, vs. 5), which have complimentary semantics, help to provide a coherent focus on YHWH's provisions "for the road" across the two dominant metaphors in the poem.

20. The phrases מי מנחות and מעגלי־צדק are construct chains that produce equivocal meanings. For example, מי מנחות may designates waters characterized by their tranquil flow or that produce tranquility for those who encounter them. Likewise, מעגלי־צדק may indicate the "right paths" or "paths of righteousness" (for the latter, see Abernathy). No doubt they are intended to invite reflection on the possibilities of more than one meaning; I have tried to retain the ambiguity in the English translation above.

³He restores me to life,
He guides me in (the) right paths,
(He does this) for it is his way.²¹

⁴For while I go along,
(Even) in a valley as dark as death,²²
I will not fear disaster.

For you are with me,
(So are) your rod and your staff;
They comfort me.

⁵You spread out before me a table,
In the presence of my enemies,
You anoint my head with oil,²³
(And) my drink is abundant.

⁶Ah, goodness and kindness will follow me,
All of my life;²⁴

---

21. The "name-theology" of the Hebrew Bible is intimately connected with YHWH's character and deeds.

22. I prefer to take the form צלמות from a root צלם, as a feminine, plural segholate noun meaning "darkness" (cf. Akkadian ṣalmum I "dark" [AHw 1078]; see also Van Acker). Alternately, an initial element in this form could be taken as from the Hebrew root צלל ("shadow") followed by a form of the root מות ("death") (e.g. Freedman, "Psalm" n 13). Regardless of the etymology, the evocation of death may be in view by wordplay as indicated by my translation if not by actual reference (Pardee, 275).

23. Anointing with oil was practiced in numerous ritualized situations, some of which included feasting. For example, such situations included arrangements for marriage (e.g. El Amarna 11, 31), feasting at economic transactions (e.g. ARM 8.13), religious rituals, military campaigns (e.g. KUB 30.42 i 8–14; Laroche 1971:162), and royal coronations (e.g. 1 Sam 10; 2 Kgs 9). An interesting example comes from a recently published letter from Mari, ARM 33.117 (= M.8242+ M.14182). In this missive an official recounted meeting up with tribal guests, perhaps for a syssitia-like feast: "I had them [the Yamina tribes] eat a meal; I anointed their heads with oil." (8) níg-gub [naptanam] ú-ša-ap-ti-šu-nu-ti 9) qa-qa-da-ti-šu-nu ì-giš ap-⌈šu⌉-úš!; cf. ARM 33.118–19). Aside from the variety of contexts for such practices, it is sufficient to note that there were generalized rituals of anointing amidst feasting in the ancient Near East akin to that hinted at in Psalm 23.

24. The precise significance of the image in which טוב וחסד are the agents in pursuit of the psalmist is difficult. One option is to emphasize the depiction of "goodness and kindness" (טוב וחסד) in pursuit (רדף) as compared with the alternative, and more readily intelligible image of enemies bearing down (e.g. Ps 7:6; 31:16). In this case, it would seem that "goodness and kindness" were being personified (cf. Ps 89:14b; for additional reference, see Barré and Kselman, "New Exodus," 102–4; Freedman has even suggested that the poem envisions these qualities as lesser supernatural beings, such as angels ["Twenty-Third Psalm," 298–99]). Whether טוב וחסד are literarily personified (i.e. as a figure of speech) or were conceptualized as a metaphysical reality is not resolvable. At the same time, this personification could be patterned after the imagery used to describe kings on military campaigns, making verse 6a a continuation of the imagery in the preceding verse. In verse 6, however, the image would be a

> I will return[25] to YHWH's house,
> For the extent of (my) days.

Bibliography

Adam, Klaus-Peter. "Feasting and Foodways in Psalm 23 and the Contribution of Redaction Criticism to the Interpretation of Meals." In *Feasting in the Archaeology and Texts of the Bible and the Ancient Near East*, edited by Peter Altmann and Janling Fu, 223–55. Winona Lake, IN: Eisenbrauns, 2014.

Abernathy, Andrew T. "'Right Paths' and/or 'Paths of Righteousness'? Examining Psalm 23.3b within the Psalter." *JSOT* 39 (2015) 299–318.

Barré, Michael L, and John S Kselman, SS. "New Exodus, Covenant, and Restoration in Psalm 23." In *The Word of the Lord Shall Go Forth: Essays in Honor of David Noel Freedman in Celebration of His Sixtieth Birthday*, edited by Carol L Meyers and Michael Patrick O'Connor, 97–127. American Schools of Oriental Research Special Volume Series 1. Winona Lake, IN: Eisenbrauns, 1983.

Beaulieu, Paul-Alain. *The Reign of Nabonidus, King of Babylon, 556–539 B.C.* Yale Near Eastern Researches 10. New Haven: Yale University Press, 1989.

Charpin, Dominique. "Les usages politiques des banquets d'après les archives mésopotamiennes du début du deuxième millénaire av. J.-C." In *Le banquet du monarque dans le monde antique*, edited by Catherine. Grandjean, Christophe. Hugoniot, and Brigitte Lion, 31–52. Tables des hommes. Rennes: Universitaires de Rennes, 2013.

---

variation on the trope in royal compositions wherein the king's military exploits were accompanied by divine support. For example, in the Old Babylonian *Epic of Zimri-Lim*, Addu and Erra go on either side of the king (cf. *ARM* 26.199 and the prophetic imagery which may personify the battering ram and siege engine going alongside the king as symbols of divine support). In the first millennium, one might compare, among others, the Sippar Cylinder of Nabonidus, in which hepatoscopic texts pronounce the favorable outcome of Sin and Shamash going at the king's side into battle (Beaulieu, *Reign*, 19–22, 64; see also, the inscription of Adad Guppi, which invokes the great gods to go at Nabonidus's side). Alternately, Michaël Guichard has considered the role of deities and supernatural beings at royal feasts as witnessed by their depiction on luxury vessels attested in the palace inventory. As he summarizes, "Un des grands intérêts des textes de Mari est de montrer que les génies Lahmum, Lamassatum, Uridum et les animaux sauvages étaient pour ainsi dire associés d'une manière en partie volontaire, en partie aléatoire par la réunion des pièces d'un service de vaisselle stocké dans un même coffre portatif. Même si les thèmes traités étaient au fond assez banals, quand les pièces étaient disposées dans la scène du banquet, ils produisaient peut-être un certain effet . . . [C]es images réunies convoient un message à ceux qui assistaient aux banquets et peut-être surtout confortait le roi dans son rôle de roi : en effet au centre de la scène était le roi. Les Lamassatum témoignaient qu'il jouissait de la protection divine et connaissait la bonne fortune ; les Lahmum étaient les gardiens et les garants de l'abondance procurait par son règne ; par leur silhouette athlétique ils évoquaient l'éternelle force et jeunesse du pouvoir" ("Génies protecteurs," 13–14). It is too tempting not to speculate that this aspect of Near Eastern festal traditions might be behind the imagery in Ps 23:6.

25. Given the imagery of verses 5–6 as "on the road," I tentatively prefer the interpretation by the MT of ושבתי as from the root שוב, rather than that of the LXX (καὶ τὸ κατοικεῖν με, which represents a form of ישב). The use of ב + שוב in this poem is unusual, but not unintelligible. Moreover, it would seem that the image is that of a devotée returning to the temple (with gifts?) in response to the divine favor demonstrated while "on the road." Additionally, the use of this root in verse 6 would repeat it from verse 3, where last YHWH was addressed in the 3rd person: YHWH restores (שוב) the psalmist's life and the psalmist returns (שוב) to YHWH's house.

Dahood, Mitchell J. *Psalms 1–50*. AB 16. Garden City, NY: Doubleday, 1965.
Damerow, Peter. "Food Production and Social Status as Documented in Proto-Cuneiform Texts." In *Food and the Status Quest: An Interdisciplinary Perspective*, edited by Polly Wiessner and Wulf Schiefenhövel. Providence, RI: Berghahn, 1996.
Fales, Frederick Mario. "Grain Reserves, Daily Rations, and the Size of the Assyrian Army: A Quantitative Study." *SAAB* 4.1 (1990) 23–34.
Fales, Frederick Mario, and Monica Rigo. "Everyday Life and Food Practices in Assyrian Military Encampments." In *Paleonutrition and Food Practices in the Ancient Near East: Towards a Multidisciplinary Approach*, edited by Lucio Milano, 413–37. HANE/M 24. Padova: S.A.R.G.O.N., 2014.
Freedman, David Noel. "The Twenty-Third Psalm." In *Pottery, Poetry, and Prophecy: Studies in Early Hebrew Poetry*, 275–302. Winona Lake, IN: Eisenbrauns, 1980.
Fu, Janling, and Peter Altmann. "Feasting: Backgrounds, Theoretical Perspectives, and Introductions." In *Feasting in the Archaeology and Texts of the Bible and the Ancient Near East*, edited by Janling Fu and Peter Altmann, 1–31. Winona Lake, IN: Eisenbrauns, 2014.
Guichard, Michaël. "Génies protecteurs dans l'art et les textes: l'imginaire à la table du roi de Mari." In *Entre dieux et hommes: anges, démons et autres figures intermédiaires*, edited by Thomas Römer, Bertrand Dufour, Fabian Pfitzmann, and Christoph Uehlinger, 1–14. OBO 286. Göttingen: Vandenhoeck & Ruprecht, 2017.
Lakoff, George and Mark Johnson, *Metaphors We Live By: With a New Afterword*. Chicago, IL: University of Chicago Press, 2003.
Loretz, Oswald. "Nekromantie und Totenevokation in Mesopotamien, Ugarit und Israel." In *Religionsgeschichtliche Beziehungen zwischen Kleinasien, Nordsyrien, und dem Alten Testament*, edited by Bernd Janowski, Klaus Koch, and Gernot Wilhelm, 285–318. OBO 129. Göttingen: Vandenhoeck & Ruprecht, 1993.
MacDonald, Nathan. *Not Bread Alone: The Uses of Food in the Old Testament*. Oxford: Oxford University Press, 2008.
Mittmann, Siegfried. "Aufbau und Einheit des Danklieds Psalm 23." *ZTK* 77 (1980) 1–23.
Pardee, Dennis. "Structure and Meaning in Hebrew Poetry: The Example of Psalm 23." *Maarav* 5–6 (1990) 239–80.
Power, Edmond. "The Shepherd's Two Rods in Modern Palestine and in Some Passages of the Old Testament." *Bib* 9 (1928) 434–42.
Sasson, Jack M. "The King's Table: Food and Fealty in Old Babylonian Mari." In *Food and Identity in the Ancient World*, edited by Cristiano Grottanelli and Lucio Milano, 179–215. SHANE 9. Padova: S.A.R.G.O.N., 2004.
Share, Don and Christian Wiman, eds. *The Open Door: One Hundred Poems, One Hundred Years of "Poetry" Magazine*. Chicago: University of Chicago Press, 2012.
Tanner, Beth. "King Yahweh as the Good Shepherd: Taking Another Look at the Image of God in Psalm 23." In *David and Zion: Biblical Studies in Honor of J. J. M. Roberts*, edited by Bernard Frank. Batto and Kathryn L. Roberts, 267–84. Winona Lake, IN: Eisenbrauns, 2004.
Van Acker, David. "צלמות An Etymological and Semantic Reconsideration." *JNSL* 43/2 (2017) 97–123.
Wiessner, Polly, and Wulf Schiefenhövel, eds. *Food and the Status Quest: An Interdisciplinary Perspective*. Providence, RI: Berghahn, 1996.

17

The Patriarchs' Altar-Building as Anticipation of the Israelite Conquest

Benjamin J. Noonan

Introduction

IT IS WELL-KNOWN THAT patriarchal religion differs from Israelite religion as expressed in the Sinaitic Covenant.[1] God specifically tells Moses that he did not fully reveal himself to the patriarchs as Yhwh, but as El Shaddai (Exod 6:23), a statement that well suits the patriarchs' frequent usage of names other than Yhwh with reference to God. Without an established priestly system and central divine sanctuary, the patriarchs practiced worship relatively freely, and some of their practices would even be banned later in the Mosaic law.[2]

One interesting practice of patriarchal religion is altar-building. Abraham (Gen 12:6–9; 13:14–18; 22:1–19),[3] Isaac (Gen 26:23–25), and Jacob (Gen 33:18–20; 35:1–7) each constructed open-air altars throughout the land of Canaan. In most instances there is no explicit mention of sacrifice, which has prompted a variety of explanations for these altars. Some see them as expressions of worship and piety,[4] and oth-

---

1. It is with great thanks that I offer this article as a tribute to John. I am indebted to him for all he has taught me about the Hebrew Bible, especially how to interpret it within its cognitive environment. Furthermore, I would not be the teacher, scholar, and person I am today without his investment in me over the years, first as a student at Wheaton College and now as a colleague. My hope is that this article reflects the same careful attention to the biblical text, thorough research, and consideration of the Hebrew Bible's original context that John masterfully exemplifies in his own scholarship.

2. Fleming, "Religion," 680–82; cf. Moberly, *Old Testament of the Old Testament*, 91–96.

3. For convenience's sake, I use the name "Abraham" for both "Abram" and "Abraham" throughout this article.

4. E.g., Wenham, *Genesis 1–15*, 280; Sarna, *Genesis*, 92; Zwickel, "Altarbaunotizen," 533–46; Leder,

ers consider them memorials of God's faithfulness.[5] The most intriguing suggestion, however, is that the patriarchs' altars represent territorial claims to the land. Augustine Pagolu puts forth this possibility in his *The Religion of the Patriarchs*: "Building altars may have established a claim to the land promised, since there is no evidence of the patriarchs building altars outside Canaan."[6]

Yet, as plausible as this hypothesis is, it remains largely undeveloped in the scholarly literature and uninformed by the ancient Near Eastern and canonical contexts of the altar-building accounts (*Altarbaunotizen*). So, in this article I reexamine the rationale behind the patriarchs' altar-building, arguing that comparative study and the book of Genesis itself support the hypothesis that the patriarchs' altars mark both sacred space and geographical territory. By building altars throughout Canaan, the patriarchs set portions of the land apart for God's purposes in anticipation of the Israelites' conquest of the land.

The Content of the Patriarchal Altar-Building Accounts

As a backdrop to the rest of my analysis, I begin by summarizing the content of each of the patriarchal altar-building accounts. The book of Genesis contains seven narratives in which the patriarchs build altars: four accounts regarding Abraham (Gen 12:6–7, 8–9; 13:14–18; 22:1–19), one regarding Isaac (Gen 26:23–25), and two regarding Jacob (Gen 35:1–7).

The first account of the patriarchs' altar-building appears in Gen 12:6–7, immediately after Abraham's arrival in the land of Canaan. Abraham travels to Shechem, where the tree of Moreh was located (Gen 12:6). At Shechem God appears to Abraham and promises to give the land to his descendants (Gen 12:7). This promise occurs just after the explicit reminder that the Canaanites lived in the region at that time (Gen 12:6; cf. Deut 11:30), emphasizing that the fulfillment of the divine land promise would come at a later time.

Genesis 12:8–9 reports the next altar-building account. Abraham continues on from Shechem until he arrives in the hill country between Bethel (on the west) and Ai (on the east) (Gen 12:8). There he pitches his tent and builds an altar (Gen 12:8). He also calls upon the name of Yhwh, a detail not mentioned previously in the account of Abraham's altar-building at Shechem (Gen 12:8). After remaining for some time between Bethel and Ai, Abraham eventually departs for the Negev, where no mention is made of any altar-building (Gen 12:9).

"'There He Built an Altar,'" 58–83.

5. E.g., Jacob, *Genesis*, 345; Aalders, *Genesis*, 1:271–72; Procksch, *Genesis*, 98.

6. Pagolu, *Religion of the Patriarchs*, 54; cf. Westermann, *Genesis 12–36*, 155; Cassuto, *From Noah to Abraham*, 328–29; Deurloo, "Way of Abraham," 98–99.

Abraham builds his next altar after a brief sojourn in Egypt (Gen 12:10–20) and after he and Lot have separated (Gen 13:7–12).[7] God again appears to Abraham and promises him the land of Canaan (Gen 13:14–17), but the promise is more detailed than earlier in that God also promises to make Abraham's offspring as numerous as the dust of the earth (Gen 13:16). Furthermore, God specifically says he will give the land to both Abraham and his descendants (לְךָ אֶתְּנֶנָּה וּלְזַרְעֲךָ; Gen 13:15) rather than simply Abraham's descendants as earlier (לְזַרְעֲךָ אֶתֵּן אֶת־הָאָרֶץ הַזֹּאת; Gen 12:7). Abraham then settles at Hebron (Gen 13:17–18). There he builds an altar but is not explicitly said to call upon the name of Yhwh as he did previously (Gen 13:18; cf. Gen 12:8).

Abraham constructs his final altar at Moriah, later identified as the site of the Jerusalem temple (2 Chr 3:1),[8] in response to God's command to sacrifice his son Isaac there (Gen 22:1–19). Unlike all the other altar-building accounts in the Ancestral Narratives, Abraham builds the altar at Moriah explicitly for sacrifice.[9] Yet, the text recounts Abraham's construction of the altar very similarly to the other altar-building accounts (וַיִּבֶן שָׁם אַבְרָהָם אֶת־הַמִּזְבֵּחַ; Gen 22:9). Furthermore, like some of the other altar-building accounts, it includes a theophany (Gen 22:1–2; cf. Gen 22:11–12, 15–18), and Abraham names the place יְהוָה יִרְאֶה 'Yhwh will provide' (Gen 22:14). No explicit promise of the land is given, although God does say Abraham's descendants will possess the gate of their enemies (Gen 22:17).

Years later, Isaac builds his sole altar at Beersheba and calls upon the name of Yhwh (Gen 26:25). He does so in response to a theophany, in which God promises to bless Isaac and multiply his descendants but makes no explicit promise of land (Gen 26:24). The references to Isaac's pitching a tent and his servants' digging a well (Gen 26:25) together reflect the patriarch's intent to settle in Beersheba, and indeed he stayed there for quite some time (cf. Gen 28:10). Although presumably in the same general region, there is no evidence that Isaac built the altar at the exact same location where his father had settled and earlier planted a tamarisk tree (cf. Gen 21:32–34).

Jacob builds both of his altars after returning to Canaan from his sojourn in Paddan-Aram. He encamps near the city of Shechem and purchases a plot of land, where he pitches his tent to settle for a while (Gen 33:18–19). Here, without any prompting from a theophany or the like, he sets up an altar.[10] Then, rather than calling upon the

---

7. Although Abraham does not build his next altar until after he and Lot separate, on his way back from Egypt he does return to the altar that he built between Bethel and Ai. There he calls upon the name of Yhwh as he had done previously (Gen 13:3–4).

8. On the issues surrounding the connection between Moriah and the Temple Mount at Jerusalem, see Kalimi, "Land of Moriah," 345–62; Mathews, *Genesis 11:27—50:26*, 290–91.

9. There are several other notable differences between this altar-building account and the others. It differs in that it entails more participants (Gen 22:3), includes dialogue (Gen 22:5, 7–8), and mentions many specific details surrounding the altar's construction, including a time reference (Gen 22:4), the materials used for the altar-building and sacrifice (Gen 22:3, 6), and the details of the altar's construction and arrangement of the sacrifice (Gen 22:9–10). Cf. Klingbeil, "Altars, Ritual, and Theology," 507–13.

10. Given the use of the verb נצב rather than בנה, some argue that the text should read וַיַּצֶּב־שָׁם

name of Yhwh, he names the altar אֵל אֱלֹהֵי יִשְׂרָאֵל 'God, the God of Israel' (Gen 33:20). There is no evidence that Jacob settled at the exact same location in Shechem as his grandfather Abraham did (cf. Gen 12:6–7), especially because Jacob purchases the plot of land from the native inhabitants in order to settle there (Gen 33:19).[11]

Genesis 35:1–7 represents the very last altar-building account in the book of Genesis. God commands Jacob to build an altar at Bethel so that he may fulfill his earlier vow, now that he has returned from Paddan-Aram (Gen 35:1; cf. Gen 28:20–22; 35:3). After building the altar as commanded, Jacob names the location of the altar—rather than the altar itself—אֵל בֵּית־אֵל 'God, the House of God' (Gen 35:7). Jacob's altar-building echoes his earlier setting up of a standing stone at Luz, when he had similarly named the place בֵּית־אֵל 'Bethel' on his way to Paddan-Aram (Gen 28:18–19).

The Context of the Patriarchal Altar-Building Accounts

Having summarized the content of the patriarchal altar-building accounts, I now situate them within their ancient Near Eastern and canonical contexts. I begin with the ancient Near Eastern context, in which altars marked sacred space and geographical territory. Then I explore the different canonical contexts of the patriarchs' altar-building: humanity's priestly commission, the territorial claims of the Primeval History's city-building, and the patriarchs' land acquisition.

Altar-Building in the Ancient Near East

The first context that must be understood to make sense of the patriarchs' altar-building is the ancient Near Eastern cognitive environment of altars. Altars in the ancient Near East provided a place for the worshipper to make offerings to the deity and thereby experience the deity's presence. Offerings could take a number of forms, including animal sacrifice, incense, foodstuffs, and libations. The form of the altar depended on the type of offering for which the altar was built.[12] Regardless of the type, however, altars functioned as a place to make offerings to the gods and served as a focal point of communication between the human and divine realms.[13]

מַצֵּבָה instead of וַיַּצֶּב־שָׁם מִזְבֵּחַ (e.g., *BHS*; Westermann, *Genesis 12–36*, 529; Dillmann, *Genesis*, 371; Skinner, *Genesis*, 416). However, such an emendation is not supported by any of the ancient versions, which all read מִזְבֵּחַ 'altar' rather than מַצֵּבָה 'standing stone': θυσιαστήριον (Septuagint), *ara* (Old Latin), *altari* (Vulgate), מדבח (Targums Onqelos and Pseudo-Jonathan), and ܡܕܒܚܐ (Peshitta). Furthermore, the verb נצב is used elsewhere for setting up stones (2 Sam 18:17), and the contextual mention of Jacob's pitching his tent (Gen 33:19) matches the circumstances of the patriarchs' other acts of altar-building (cf. Gen 12:8; 13:4, 18; 26:25). See Pagolu, *Religion of the Patriarchs*, 71.

11. Pagolu, *Religion of the Patriarchs*, 71.

12. Forms include rock altars, open-air altars, enclosed altars, incense altars, presentation altars, and libation altars. See Haak, "Altars," 1:80–81; Galling and Lohmann, *Altar*.

13. Haak, "Altars," 1:80–81. This function of altars may even be evident in their shape, which could

Similarly, the Hebrew Bible depicts an altar as a place where the worshipper can make an offering to God and experience his presence. Whether making an offering to gain God's favor or to be restored to him, the purpose of the offering was communion with God.[14] The earthen-altar law demonstrates the close connection between altars and God's presence in that God says he will come to those who make offerings on an earthen altar (Exod 20:24–26);[15] the placement of altars in the tabernacle (Exod 27:1–8; 30:1–21) and temple (1 Kgs 6:22; 7:48) likewise demonstrates that altars enabled the Israelites to experience God's presence. Thus, just as in the rest of the ancient Near East, ancient Israelite altars served as a point of communication between the human and divine realms and provided a connection between deity and the worshipper—in short, they established sacred space.[16]

At the same time, because sacred space occupies physical terrain and creates divisions of geographic space,[17] ancient Near Eastern altars could also mark territory. The establishment of an altar at a particular location set that location apart and demarcated territory. Thus, the inhabitants of the ancient Near East—including the Israelites—tended to build altars at the borders of geopolitical territories. Jeroboam, for example, set up cult sites with altars at Dan and Bethel, marking the northernmost and southernmost boundaries of his kingdom (1 Kgs 12:26–33).[18] As another example, the eastern tribes' so-called "altar of witness" arguably also marked territorial boundaries (Josh 22:9–34).[19]

The use of altars to mark territory belongs to the broader ancient Near Eastern usage of monuments to claim land, including kings' construction of victory stelae at the limits of their dominion (cf. 1 Sam 15:12; 2 Sam 8:3) and the use of standing stones to mark geographical boundaries (cf. Gen 31:45–53; Isa 19:19).[20] These monuments could have ritual functions in addition to claiming territory: victory stelae were often the recipients of ritual activity, including sacrifice, and as places of worship standing stones frequently marked the immanence of deity.[21] Thus, the ancient Near East at-

---

be understood as resembling a ziggurat or the cosmic mountain (Albright, "Babylonian Temple-Tower," 139; Morales, *Tabernacle Pre-Figured*, 232–33).

14. These two aspects of offering represent the "gift theory" and "communion theory" of sacrifice. Another aspect of sacrifice is consecration of one's self or some object to God, but it is not as common in the Hebrew Bible and does not apply to the Ancestral Narratives. Cf. Averbeck, "Sacrifices and Offerings," 708–9.

15. Tigay, "Presence of God," 205–9; Pitkänen, "From Tent of Meeting," 28.

16. Dohmen, "מִזְבֵּחַ *mizbēaḥ*," 8:211–12; Levine, "*lpny YHWH*," 199.

17. Brereton, "Sacred Space," 12:7982.

18. Rainey and Notley, *Sacred Bridge*, 169.

19. Noort, "Streit um den Altar," 156–61.

20. Cf. Durand, *Culte des pierres et les monuments commémoratifs*, 93–141, 155–71; Kupper, "Inscriptions triomphales akkadiennes," 92–106; Graesser, "Standing Stones," 37–39.

21. Shafer, "Assyrian Royal Monuments," 133–59; Graesser, "Standing Stones," 44–48.

tests to a strong tradition of constructing monuments that fused sacred space and geopolitical territory.

To summarize, the peoples of the ancient Near East built altars to establish sacred space. Wherever they built an altar, they could commune with the deity and experience the divine presence. But, by virtue of the inherent intersection between sacred space and geographical territory, altars could frequently mark geographical boundaries and lay claims to land. In light of their ancient Near Eastern context, then, the patriarchs' altars most probably mark sacred space and lay claim to the land.

Humanity's Priestly Commission

The second context to consider is humanity's priestly commission. The first two chapters of the book of Genesis describe God's establishment of creation as a temple, in keeping with the ancient Near East's conception of the cosmos as a divine sanctuary.[22] The Garden of Eden, furthermore, serves as the locus of God's presence in the world, as indicated by the use of divine sanctuary imagery and terminology associated with Israel's later sanctuaries.[23] There, God creates humanity as his priests tasked with expanding the sacred space of the garden. Humanity's priestly role is reflected in God's command to tend the garden using the verbs עבד and שמר (Gen 2:15), two terms used together elsewhere only with reference to priestly duties (Num 3:7–8; 8:25–26; 18:5–6; Ezek 44:14; 1 Chr 23:32).[24]

Notably, God's call of Abraham in Gen 12:1–3 closely mirrors humanity's commission in Gen 1:28 in that both entail God's blessing, descendants, and the provision of geographical territory for carrying out God's purposes. The various reiterations of God's promise to Abraham throughout the Ancestral Narratives also contain these same elements of humanity's commission (Gen 17:2, 6, 8; 22:17–18; 26:3–4, 24; 28:3–4; 35:11–12).[25] This indicates that the patriarchs are depicted as new "Adams" who are given the same task that Adam was: to establish sacred space as God's priests.

---

22. Walton, *Genesis 1 as Ancient Cosmology*, 101–19, 178–92; Beale, *Temple and the Church's Mission*, 29–66.

23. Walton, *Genesis*, 180–83; Wenham, "Sanctuary Symbolism," 19–25; Beale, *Temple and the Church's Mission*, 66, 70–80; contra Block, "Eden: A Temple?," 3–29. Connections include the rivers that flow from Eden (Gen 2:10–14; cf. Ezek 47:1–12; Rev 21:1–2), the tree of life (Gen 2:9; 3:22; cf. Exod 25:31–40; 1 Kgs 6:18, 29, 32; 7:20–22), the cherubim (Gen 3:24; cf. Exod 25:18–22; 26:31; 1 Kgs 6:29, 32–35; 8:6–7; Ezek 41:18), the precious materials found near Eden (Gen 2:11–12; cf. Exod 25:7, 11–39; 28:9–12, 20; 1 Kgs 6:20–22; 1 Chr 29:2), the orientation of Eden toward the east (Gen 3:24; cf. Ezek 40:6), and the usage of the Hitpael of הלך with reference to God "walking" (Gen 3:8; cf. Lev 26:12; Deut 23:15 [23:14]; 2 Sam 7:6–7).

24. Walton, *Genesis*, 172–74; Malone, *God's Mediators*, 52–53; Beale, *Temple and the Church's Mission*, 66–70.

25. Beale, *Temple and the Church's Mission*, 94–96; Wright, *Climax of the Covenant*, 21–26.

Indeed, the patriarchs' actions—not the least of which is their construction of altars—frequently resemble those of priests.[26]

If the patriarchs serve as priests who carry out God's original commission for humanity, the land of Canaan can be seen as a new "Garden of Eden" granted by God to aid the patriarchs in their establishment of sacred space. Just as the Garden of Eden was a starting point from which Adam and Eve were to extend its sacred space,[27] so is Canaan a starting point for Abraham's call to be a blessing to the nations (cf. Gen 12:3).[28] Within this framework, the patriarchs build altars to establish centers of sacred space, not merely as a pious response to God's activity on their behalf.[29] That the patriarchs' altars serve as loci of sacred space is evident from their association with trees as well as the altar-building accounts' use of the term מָקוֹם 'place' and terminology connected with the later tabernacle and temple.

First, several of the locations where the patriarchs build altars are said to contain trees or be located near trees, including the אֵלוֹן מוֹרֶה 'oak of Moreh' at Shechem (Gen 12:6), the אֵלֹנֵי מַמְרֵא 'oaks of Mamre' near Hebron (Gen 13:18), and הָאַלּוֹן 'the oak' near Bethel (Gen 35:8).[30] These trees probably look back to the "Tree of Life" found in Eden (Gen 2:9; 3:22) and reflect the arboreal imagery common to ancient Near Eastern temples, including Israel's later sanctuaries.[31] These trees' sacred quality is further demonstrated by paralleling the altar-building accounts with the similar narrative of Abraham's planting of a tamarisk tree at Beersheba (Gen 21:32–34).[32] Given the tamarisk tree's usage in the ancient Near East to cleanse people, objects, and space

---

26. Malone, *God's Mediators*, 58–60. In addition to building altars, the patriarchs experience theophanies and receive divine instruction (Gen 12:1–3; 13:14–17; 15:1, 4–5, 7, 9, 13–16, 18–21; 17:1–16, 18–21; 18:10, 13–14; 21:12–13; 22:1, 12, 15–18; 26:2–5, 24; 28:13–15; 31:3; 32:29 [32:28]; 35:1, 9–12; 46:2–4), make sacrifices (Gen 15:10; 22:13; 31:54; 46:1), set up cult objects in the form of standing stones (Gen 28:18; 31:45; 35:14), intercede on behalf of others (Gen 18:22–33; 20:7, 17), and purify themselves as expressed by the cultic term טהר (Gen 35:1).

27. Walton, *Genesis*, 186.

28. Beale, *Temple and the Church's Mission*, 96; Williamson, "Promise and Fulfillment," 17–18. Notably, the Hebrew Bible elsewhere compares the land of Canaan with the Garden of Eden (Gen 13:10; Isa 51:3; Ezek 36:35; Joel 2:3) (Alexander, "Beyond Borders," 39–41).

29. Riecker, "Theologischer Ansatz," 526–30; contra Zwickel, "Altarbaunotizen," 533–46.

30. On the usage of אֵלוֹן with reference to sacred space, cf. Judg 9:6, 37; 1 Sam 10:3. Possibly also to be included here is the סְבַךְ 'thicket' at Moriah (Gen 22:13) since this rare term is elsewhere associated with forests (Isa 9:17 [9:18]; 10:34; cf. the use of the related term סְבָךְ in Ps 74:5) (Beale, *Temple and the Church's Mission*, 102).

31. Beale, *Temple and the Church's Mission*, 102–3; Longman, *Immanuel in Our Place*, 20–21.

32. The parallel nature of this narrative to the altar-building accounts is evident in the short nature of the account, usage of the term שָׁם 'there' also found in each of the altar-building accounts (Gen 21:33; cf. Gen 12:7–8; 13:18; 22:9; 26:5; 33:20; 35:1, 3, 7), the mention of calling upon the name of Yhwh (Gen 21:33; cf. Gen 12:8; 13:4; 26:25; 33:20; 35:7), and the reference to Abraham's sojourn among the native inhabitants of the land (Gen 21:34).

from evil and to reestablish equilibrium with deity, Abraham probably plants this tree to establish sacred space.³³

Second, the book of Genesis frequently associates the patriarchs' altar-building with the word מָקוֹם 'place'. This term often appears with reference to sacred sites, especially the temple where God chooses to place his name (e.g., Gen 28:11, 16–17, 19; Exod 20:24; Deut 12:5; 15:20; 16:15–16; 17:10; 31:11).³⁴ It is significant, then, that the text uses מָקוֹם with reference to the patriarchs' altar-related activity at Shechem (Gen 12:6), the hill country between Bethel and Ai (Gen 13:3–4), Hebron (Gen 13:14), Moriah (Gen 22:3–4, 9, 14), and Bethel (Gen 35:7). Regardless of whether this term demonstrates that the patriarchs constructed altars in places already considered sacred,³⁵ מָקוֹם's cultic connotations link the patriarchs' altars with sacred space.

Third, the altar-building accounts use terminology associated with both the tabernacle and temple. The patriarchs pitch their tents (אֹהֶל) as they journey throughout Canaan (Gen 12:8; 13:3; 26:25; 33:19; 35:21) and build their altars. Notably, the only other places in the Hebrew Bible where the terms אֹהֶל 'tent' and מִזְבֵּחַ 'altar' occur together are the descriptions of the tabernacle (Exod 28:43; 29:44; 30:18; 38:30; 40:7, 30, 32; Lev 3:8, 13; 4:7, 18; 16:20, 33; Num 18:3; 1 Kgs 2:28–29).³⁶ Similarly, the terms בַּיִת 'temple' and מִזְבֵּחַ 'altar' frequently occur together within descriptions of the temple (1 Kgs 6:22; 7:48; 8:31; 2 Kgs 11:11, 18; 16:14; Isa 56:7; 60:7; Ezek 40:47; 45:19; 47:1; Zech 14:20; 1 Chr 22:1; 2 Chr 4:19; 6:22; 23:10; 26:19; 28:24; 29:18; 33:4, 15). Thus, the association of the terms אֹהֶל and מִזְבֵּחַ with sacred space outside the book of Genesis links the patriarchs' altars with sacred space.³⁷

Given the many connections between the patriarchal altars and sacred space, the patriarchs' construction of altars is best viewed within the context of humanity's priestly commission. The patriarchs build altars in accordance with God's intent for people to serve as his priests and establish sacred space in the world. In this way, the patriarchs' altar-building aligns with God's original purposes for humanity and serves to establish centers of sacred space throughout the land of Canaan.

The Territorial Claims of the Primeval History's City-Building

The third context to explore is the contrast between the patriarchs' altar-building and the city-building recounted in the Primeval History. David J. A. Clines rightly observes

---

33. Umbarger, "Abraham's Tamarisk," 189–200; cf. *CAD* B 239–42; *AHw* 127. In the Akkadian fable *The Tamarisk and the Palm*, the tamarisk claims that he is the chief exorcist (*rab-maš-maš-a-ku-ma*) and thereby renews the house of the god (*bīt ili ú-da-aš*) (VAT 10102:26), demonstrating that the tamarisk was used to purify a place so that it could be used as sacred space for the deity.

34. Gamberoni and Ringgren, "מָקוֹם *māqôm*," 8:537–43.

35. Such a notion is far from proven; see Pagolu, *Religion of the Patriarchs*, 55–56.

36. The Septuagint translates the Hebrew term אֹהֶל as σκηνή, elsewhere used of the tabernacle (e.g., Exod 27:21; 29:4; Lev 1:1; Num 1:1).

37. Beale, *Temple and the Church's Mission*, 96–97.

that the Ancestral Narratives function as the mitigation element of the Tower of Babel narrative.[38] The account of the Tower of Babel, in turn, represents the culmination of the various building projects recounted in the Primeval History.[39] Because in Genesis the term בנה 'to build' is largely limited to city-building accounts and altar-building accounts,[40] the canonical shape of the book of Genesis juxtaposes the primeval city-builders' activity with the patriarchs' altar-building and requires that the latter be read against the backdrop of the former.[41]

There are three city-building accounts in the Primeval History. Cain builds a city and names it after his son Enoch (Gen 4:17); Nimrod establishes his kingdom of Babel, Uruk, Akkad, and Kalneh and also builds Nineveh, Rehoboth-Ir, Calah, and Resen (Gen 10:10–11); the post-deluge population constructs a city with a ziggurat at Babel (Gen 11:1–9). Each of these building projects is geopolitical in nature in that the cities constructed encompass geographical territory and represent the urbanization of civilization. At the same time, the Primeval History never divorces these cities' geographical territory from sacred space, especially because the ziggurat constructed at Babel—the culmination of the Primeval History's city-building—bridges the human and divine realms.[42]

Furthermore, the Primeval History depicts all three of these city-building accounts negatively despite their positive contribution to civilization.[43] Cain's defiant building of a city despite God's pronouncement that he would be a wanderer (cf. Gen 4:12, 15) casts Cain's city-building in a negative light.[44] Similarly, the second city-building account portrays the construction of Nineveh, Rehoboth-Ir, Calah, and Resen negatively in light of Nimrod's characterization and connection with Babel and Shinar (Gen 10:8–12).[45] Finally, God's response at the Tower of Babel is best under-

---

38. Clines, *Theme of the Pentateuch*, 85.

39. Leder, "'There He Built an Altar,'" 67; O'Connor, "Biblical Notion of the City," 19.

40. Noah's altar-building is included here (Gen 8:20). The only exception to this pattern is the threefold metaphorical use of בנה with reference to "building" families (Gen 2:22; 16:2; 30:3).

41. Leder, "'There He Built an Altar,'" 59–60; Klingbeil, "Altars, Ritual, and Theology," 508; Dillmann, *Genesis*, 222. Several elements contribute to the contrast between the Primeval History's city-building accounts and the patriarchs' altar-building accounts. For example, both accounts use the verb קרא 'to call' in conjunction with שֵׁם 'name', but in very different ways: in the Primeval History humans name the cities (Gen 4:17; 11:9) whereas in the Ancestral Narratives the patriarchs call upon the name of Yhwh (Gen 12:8; 13:4; 21:33; 26:25). As another example, the builders construct the city and ziggurat for themselves (לָנוּ) (Gen 11:4), but the patriarchs build their altars for Yhwh (לַיהוָה) (Gen 12:7–8; 13:18).

42. Cf. Walton, "Mesopotamian Background," 155–75.

43. Leder, "'There He Built an Altar,'" 68.

44. Mathews, *Genesis 1—11:26*, 284–85; Hamilton, *Chapters 1–17*, 238. This interpretation is supported by the text's emphasis on Cain's pride and murder (cf. Gen 4:5–9), traits amplified in his descendant Lamech (Gen 4:19, 23–24) and therefore characteristic of his line despite the positive advances in civilization it brings.

45. Hom, "'. . . A Mighty Hunter before YHWH,'" 63–68.

stood as an act of divine judgment, which requires that the builders' actions be seen negatively as well.[46]

If the Primeval History's city-building accounts integrate geopolitical territory with sacred space, and if the patriarchs' altar-building counters the negative building activity of the Primeval History, then the patriarchal altars should also mark both sacred space and geopolitical territory. Such a function is in accordance with the typical functions of ancient Near Eastern altars and demonstrates that in carrying out humanity's priestly commission the patriarchs claim geographical territory.

The Patriarchs' Acquisition of Land

The final context to examine is the patriarchs' acquisition of the land. As the patriarchs sojourn, they not only build altars but also claim plots of land for themselves. In doing so they assume their descendants' permanent settlement in the land and anticipate the later conquest of Canaan, in accordance with God's promise of land (cf. Gen 15:13–16). Furthermore, because they trust in God's promises the patriarchs acquire land legally and in cooperation with the native inhabitants, rather than forcibly.[47] The patriarchs claim the land legally in two main ways: by purchasing it and by appropriating it for use.

First, the patriarchs acquire territory by purchasing it for a price. Abraham comes to own a field in Machpelah, located to the east of Mamre, after a series of negotiations with the local Hethites.[48] The Hethites initially try to simply give him the land, but Abraham insists on paying 400 shekels for it to ensure that he genuinely owns it (Gen 23:3–16). The narrative concludes with a clear statement of Abraham's ownership of the field (Gen 23:17–20), emphasizing the scope of Abraham's ownership (the

---

46. Cf. Strong, "Shattering the Image of God," 625–34; Lacocque, "Whatever Happened in the Valley of Shinar?," 29–41.

47. Cf. Habel, *Land Is Mine*, 125–30. The clearest example of this is Abraham's defeat of the alliance of kings in Gen 14. Abraham attacks the four rulers (Amraphel of Shinar, Arioch of Ellasar, Kedorlaomer of Elam, and Tidal of Goyim) who have made war against the Transjordan and Canaan. Then, he pursues his enemies from Hebron, which is just 23 miles northeast of Beersheba, all the way to Dan and beyond (Gen 14:13–15). Given the Hebrew Bible's use of the expression "from Dan to Beersheba" with reference to the entire land of Canaan (Judg 20:1; 1 Sam 3:20; 2 Sam 3:10; 17:11; 24:15; 1 Kgs 5:5 [4:25]; 2 Chr 30:5), Gen 14 portrays Abraham as Canaan's conqueror and legitimate possessor (cf. Gen 14:21). Yet, Abraham explicitly refuses to take anything but his allies' share of provisions and wages (Gen 14:24). Instead, he aligns himself with the king of Salem, Melchizedek, who recognizes that God alone is the source of Abraham's strength and all that he has (Gen 14:19–20). Abraham thereby rejects any opportunity he has to claim the entire land, instead trusting that God will give it at the right time. See Walton, *Genesis*, 425–26; Kuruvilla, *Genesis*, 179–82.

48. Here I distinguish the בְּנֵי־חֵת (Gen 23:3, 5, 7, 16), descended from Heth the son of Canaan (Gen 10:15; 1 Chr 1:13), from the Anatolian Hittites (Josh 1:4; 1 Kgs 10:29; 2 Kgs 7:6; 2 Chr 1:17). The similarity of the name of these indigenous inhabitants of Canaan with the name of the Anatolian Hittites is coincidental (Hoffner, "Contributions of Hittitology," 28–37; Singer, "Hittites and the Bible Revisted," 725–26).

field, the cave in the field, and the trees in the field) and describing the field as a אֲחֻזָּה 'landed property', a term often used for the land that God promises to give the patriarchs and Israelites (e.g., Gen 17:8; Lev 25:24; Josh 22:4, 9, 19).[49] The use of the field as a family burial plot (Gen 23:19; 25:9; 49:29–32) confirms the territorial nature of this purchase in that burial places cross-culturally mark claims to land.[50]

Jacob also acquires land near Shechem by purchasing it.[51] After leaving Paddan-Aram, he comes to Shechem and encamps within sight of the city. Then he purchases הַשָּׂדֶה 'the open field' where he has pitched his tent from the sons of Hamor for a hundred qesitahs (Gen 33:18–19). He presumably buys this land because he wants to settle there for some time but, given the field's location in the vicinity of Shechem, has no legal right to settle there unless he purchases it from the native inhabitants. Use of the verb קנה 'to buy' (Gen 33:19) emphasizes Jacob's legal acquisition of the field by purchasing it, making that land a permanent possession to be passed on to his descendants.[52]

Second, the patriarchs obtain territory by inhabiting and appropriating the land. Both Abraham and Isaac come to acquire wells—a form of landed property—in Canaan. Abraham claims a well in the vicinity of Beersheba by virtue of digging the well and using it, as Abimelek acknowledges (Gen 21:25–32).[53] Isaac reclaims some of these same wells years later, after the Philistines had stopped and filled them with earth, by redigging them and giving them the names his father had given them; the latter act asserts the right of the original owner and therefore Isaac's right to the wells as Abraham's heir.[54] In addition, Isaac claims new territory for himself. He procures new wells at both Rehoboth and Beersheba by digging them, an act that gives him the ownership right to the wells (Gen 21:22, 25, 32–33).[55]

Jacob acquires burial plots near Bethel and Bethlehem. Unlike his grandfather Abraham, who purchased his burial plot from the local inhabitants, Jacob simply claims his burial plots by burying Rebekah's nurse Deborah (Gen 35:8) and his wife Rachel (Gen 35:20) at these locations. Both sites are apparently far enough away from

---

49. Jeyaraj, "Land Ownership in the Pentateuch," 43–44; Habel, *Land Is Mine*, 123.

50. Cf. Stavrakopoulou, *Land of Our Fathers*, 29–53. On the connection between burial places and geographical territory, see Pearson, *Archaeology of Death and Burial*, 124–41.

51. Jacob may allude to his acquisition of the field in Gen 48:22, where he states that he gives Joseph שְׁכֶם אַחַד עַל־אַחֶיךָ. However, it is not entirely clear that שְׁכֶם here should be translated as 'Shechem', especially because Jacob's claim that he took it from the Amorites with his sword and bow does not match the account earlier in Genesis or later in Joshua (Gen 33:19; Josh 24:32).

52. Jeyaraj, "Land Ownership in the Pentateuch," 66–67.

53. Genesis 21:30 states that Abraham gives the seven ewe lambs to Abimelek not as payment, but to testify that Abraham is the rightful owner of the land because he found the spot for the well and dug it himself (Jeyaraj, "Land Ownership in the Pentateuch," 41–42).

54. Jeyaraj, "Land Ownership in the Pentateuch," 56.

55. Isaac tries unsuccessfully to claim several wells in the valley of Gerar (Gen 26:19–21). Perhaps this is because the wells are close enough to the Philistines' settlement that the native inhabitants could assert their rights to it (Jeyaraj, "Land Ownership in the Pentateuch," 56–57).

any local settlements for Jacob to have to legally purchase them, so he is able to appropriate the land for himself simply through use. Jacob's ownership of these burial plots is reflected in his naming of Deborah's burial site, which asserts his rights and authority over that portion of the land, and his setting up of a standing stone over Rachel's tomb. Furthermore, as was the case with Abraham's acquisition of the field at Machpelah, the funerary nature of the sites demonstrates his ownership because burial places frequently mark claims to land.[56]

The patriarchs' acquisition of land by both purchase and use anticipates the future fulfillment of God's promise to give their descendants the land.[57] Acquiring land is not their primary goal, but it is something that they do amidst their other activities, and they do so in recognition that God remains the ultimate owner of the land. This territorial dimension again demonstrates that the patriarchal priestly commission entails claiming geographical territory and thereby provides a framework for viewing the patriarchs' altar-building.

Exposition of the Patriarchal Altar-Building Accounts

Thus, ancient Near Eastern altars were used to mark sacred space and, by virtue of this role, claims to land. The canonical context of the patriarchs' altar-building—specifically humanity's priestly commission, the territorial claims of the Primeval History's city-building, and the patriarchs' acquisition of land—likewise demonstrate that the patriarchs concern themselves with both establishing sacred space and claiming geographical territory. The task remains to see whether the patriarchal altar-building accounts support the notion that the altars mark land claims in addition to sacred space. So, I turn now to an exposition of the patriarchal altar-building accounts.

The difficulty in determining the function of the patriarchs' altar-building stems in part from the abbreviated nature of ritual texts.[58] Yet, the patriarchal altar-building accounts can be described in terms of their various elements: the location where the patriarch builds the altar, the newness of that location vis-à-vis the patriarch's itinerary, the patriarch's settlement at that location, a theophany, the giving of the land promise, and an invocation. The following table summarizes these elements:

---

56. Cf. Stavrakopoulou, *Land of Our Fathers*, 81–102.

57. Williamson, "Promise and Fulfillment," 29–30.

58. Klingbeil, "Altars, Ritual, and Theology," 507–8. Most of the patriarchal altar-building accounts do not provide information such as how the altars were built, what kind of altars were built, how the altars were utilized, or the like. As I noted earlier, the exception is Gen 22:1–19.

Passage	Patriarch	Location	Movement to a New Place?	Settlement?	Theophany?	Land Promise?	Invocation?
12:6–7	Abraham	Shechem	Yes	No	Yes	Yes	No
12:8–9	Abraham	Bethel/Ai	Yes	Yes	No	No	Yes
13:14–18	Abraham	Hebron	Yes	Yes	Yes	Yes	No
22:1–19	Abraham	Moriah	Yes	No	Yes	No	Yes
26:23–25	Isaac	Beersheba	Yes	Yes	Yes	No	Yes
33:18–20	Jacob	Shechem	Yes	Yes	No	No	Yes
35:1–7	Jacob	Bethel	No	Yes	Yes	No	Yes

Table 17.1: Synopsis of the Patriarchal Altar-Building Accounts

Examining the patriarchal altar-building accounts in terms of these elements makes it much easier to discover what patterns are present—and are not present—across all the accounts. So, I now present what the patriarchal altar-building accounts do not have in common and explore what, in light of the above elements, they all do have in common. Doing so will shed significant light on the probable function of the patriarchs' altars.

What the Patriarchal Altar-Building Accounts Do Not Have in Common

Interpreters have offered a variety of explanations for the patriarchs' altar-building, such as that it suits their wandering lifestyle[59] or serves as a response to a theophany.[60] However, these kinds of explanations do not work because the Ancestral Narratives do not consistently associate the patriarchs' altars with their wandering lifestyle or theophanies.

First, the patriarchs do not build an altar in every location where they sojourn.[61] Abraham sojourns in several different locations throughout his lifetime: near the tree of Moreh in the vicinity of Shechem (Gen 12:6), in the hill country between Bethel and Ai (Gen 12:8; 13:3–4), in the Negev (Gen 12:9), in Egypt (Gen 12:10), near the trees of Mamre in the vicinity of Hebron (Gen 13:18), Gerar (Gen 20:1), and Beersheba (Gen 21:31). Yet, he does not build any altars while sojourning in the Negev, Egypt, Gerar, or Beersheba. Isaac sojourns in Gerar (Gen 26:1, 6, 17) and Beersheba

---

59. E.g., Pagolu, *Religion of the Patriarchs*, 54–55; Albertz, *History of Israelite Religion*, 1:36–37.
60. E.g., Zwickel, "Altarbaunotizen," 533–46.
61. Cf. Pagolu, *Religion of the Patriarchs*, 54.

(26:23) but only builds an altar at the latter. Finally, Jacob sojourns in Beersheba (Gen 28:10), Paddan-Aram (Gen 28:5), Shechem (Gen 33:18), Bethel (Gen 35:1), Migdal-Eder (Gen 35:21), and Hebron (Gen 35:27; 37:14). Of these, he only builds altars at Shechem and Bethel.

Second, the patriarchs' construction of altars is not always connected with moving to a new place.[62] Jacob builds an altar at Bethel only when he returns there, in fulfillment of his vow (Gen 35:7); the first time he arrives in Bethel he does not settle there permanently and sets up a standing stone rather than an altar (Gen 28:18). After leaving Egypt Abraham returns to the very same altar he had previously constructed in the hill country between Bethel and Ai (Gen 13:3–4). Although the text does not explicitly say so, presumably he uses it for worship as he did the first time he was there in light of the mention of Abraham's calling upon the name of Yhwh (Gen 13:4).[63]

Third, there is no clear link between the patriarchs' altar-building and an intention to settle for a long time. The text explicitly mentions the patriarchs' settling down in most, but not all, of the altar-building accounts. Abraham pitches his tent (וַיֵּט אָהֳלֹה) between Bethel and Ai (Gen 12:8) and also pitches his tent (וַיֶּאֱהַל) and settles (וַיֵּשֶׁב) near Mamre (Gen 13:18); Isaac pitches his tent (וַיֵּט־שָׁם אָהֳלוֹ) at Beersheba (Gen 26:25); Jacob encamps before the city (וַיִּחַן אֶת־פְּנֵי הָעִיר) and settles in the field where he pitches his tent (נָטָה־שָׁם אָהֳלוֹ) at Shechem (Gen 33:18–19). However, Abraham is never said to settle at Shechem, in the hill country between Bethel and Ai the second time he sojourns there, or at Moriah; rather, the subsequent narratives highlight Abraham's movement to other locations (Gen 12:9; 13:5–7; 22:19). Similarly, Jacob moves on from Bethel after building an altar there (Gen 35:16). Thus, it cannot be said that the patriarchs build altars where they settle down for a longer period.[64]

Fourth, the patriarchs do not always build altars in response to a theophany or the land promise.[65] Abraham builds an altar in conjunction with both a theophany and promise of land only at Shechem (Gen 12:6–7) and Mamre (Gen 13:14–18), and God appears to him in conjunction with his altar-building at Moriah (Gen 22:1–19). But, Abraham builds an altar in the hill country between Bethel and Ai without any theophany or promise of the land (Gen 12:8). Furthermore, both Isaac and Jacob build altars in response to a theophany but without any promise of land: God appears to Isaac at Beersheba and promises to multiply his descendants but says nothing about land (Gen 26:23–25), and God reveals himself to Jacob and commands him to go to Bethel but likewise does not mention land (Gen 35:1–7).

---

62. Cf. Pagolu, *Religion of the Patriarchs*, 54.

63. Cf. Pagolu, *Religion of the Patriarchs*, 57.

64. Contra Pagolu, *Religion of the Patriarchs*, 54–55, 70–71; Albertz, *History of Israelite Religion*, 1:36–37.

65. Cf. Pagolu, *Religion of the Patriarchs*, 54.

Part 3: Context

What the Patriarchal Altar-Building Accounts Do Have in Common

Although the patriarchal altar-building accounts cannot be explained in terms of the patriarchs' wandering lifestyle or responses to theophanies, the accounts do share several common threads. By observing what the accounts have in common, it becomes evident that the patriarchs always build altars in connection with God's purposes for the land of Canaan.

First, the patriarchs build altars within Canaan, and never outside the land.[66] No mention is made of building altars when the patriarchs are in Egypt (Gen 12:10), Philistia (Gen 20:1; 26:1, 6, 17), or Paddan-Aram (Gen 28:5), all regions outside the promised land of Canaan. In this regard, it is significant that the patriarchs' altar-building takes place at key junctures in their sojournings. Abraham builds altars at Shechem and Moriah (Gen 12:7; 22:9), which mark the beginning and end of his sojournings.[67] Similarly, whenever they leave and then return to the land, the first thing the patriarchs do upon returning to Canaan involves an altar: after leaving Egypt Abraham returns to the altar he built between Bethel and Ai (Gen 13:3–4), Isaac builds an altar at Beersheba after sojourning in Gerar (Gen 26:25), and Jacob builds an altar at Shechem after returning from Paddan-Aram (Gen 33:20).

Second, the places where the patriarchs build altars are arguably strategic locations in the land of Canaan. Shechem, Bethel, Hebron, Jerusalem, and Beersheba were all located along the National Highway (i.e., the Central Ridge Road), the only major thoroughfare in ancient Canaan to fall entirely within the boundaries of the land and the main highway through the central hill country.[68] These locations represent the most important sites in the heartland of Canaan, with Shechem and Beersheba marking the northern and southern boundaries of that territory.[69] Furthermore, all these sites are locations of great historical significance, as is evident from their importance for both biblical and extra-biblical history, as well as religious significance, as is evident from the existence of prominent sanctuaries at each site.[70]

Third, the altar-building accounts contain or occur alongside references to the land's inhabitants who serve as obstacles to the land promise's fulfillment. The very first altar-building account notes that the Canaanites were in the land during Abraham's sojournings at Shechem (Gen 12:7). Similarly, Abraham's construction of an altar at Hebron comes immediately after the statement that the Canaanites and Perizzites were in the land (Gen 13:7) and after Lot's self-removal from the land of Canaan, an event

---

66. Pagolu, *Religion of the Patriarchs*, 54.
67. Cf. Kuruvilla, *Genesis*, 255.
68. Dorsey, *Roads and Highways*, 117–19; Aharoni, *Land of the Bible*, 57–58.
69. Cf. Deurloo, "Way of Abraham," 98–99, 106.
70. For summaries of the historical and religious significance of these sites, see Toombs, "Shechem," 5:1174–86; Campbell, "Shechem," 4:1345–54; Brodsky, "Bethel," 1:710–12; Kelso, "Bethel," 1:192–94; Ferris, "Hebron," 3:107–8; Ofer, "Hebron," 2:606–9; King, "Jerusalem," 3:747–66; Shiloh et al., "Jerusalem," 2:698–716; Manor, "Beer-Sheba," 1:641–45; Herzog, "Beersheba," 1:167–73.

that made it possible for Abraham to receive the land (Gen 13:7–12).[71] Isaac builds an altar at Beersheba in the aftermath of his conflict over wells with the Philistines, a conflict that entailed rights to the land (Gen 26:12–22).[72] Jacob constructs an altar near Shechem within sight of the Canaanite city (Gen 33:18), the same place where he later comes into conflict with the native inhabitants after Dinah is raped (Gen 34:30). Lastly, when Jacob builds the altar at Bethel the text distinguishes between Jacob and the native inhabitants in that God sends a terror upon the surrounding towns so that they pose no threat to Jacob (Gen 35:5).

Fourth, each altar-building account contains either the land promise or an invocation, but not both. This suggests that the land promise and invocation have similar roles in the patriarchal altar-building accounts; if so, the invocation must designate the land as set apart for God's purposes just as the land promise does. Indeed, both the act of calling upon the name of Yhwh and the naming of the altar or altar-site—the two forms of invocation found in the patriarchal altar-building accounts—have such a purpose. To call upon the name of Yhwh is to invoke God to act in accordance with his promises as well as to proclaim who he is and what belongs to him.[73] Thus, when Abraham calls on the name of Yhwh between Bethel and Ai (Gen 12:8) and Isaac calls upon the name of Yhwh at Beersheba (Gen 26:25), they proclaim God's ownership of the area set apart by the altar.[74] Similarly, because a name represents the essence of the thing it designates, to name something is to assign it a particular purpose.[75] So, when Jacob calls the altar he builds at Shechem "God, the God of Israel" (Gen 33:20) and the place where he sets up the altar at Bethel "God, the House of God" (Gen 35:7), he proclaims that these locations belong to God and are to be used for God's purposes.

Synthesis

Thus, the patriarchs do not build altars simply because it suits their worship habits, nor do they exclusively build altars in response to a theophany or the land promise.

---

71. On Lot's self-removal from the land of Canaan, see Helyer, "Separation of Abram and Lot," 77–88.

72. That the conflict over the wells relates to habitation of the land is indicated by Isaac's closing remark, made after resolution of the conflict, that God had given him room so that he might flourish in the land (Gen 26:22).

73. Brongers, "Wendung $b^e\check{s}\bar{e}m$ jhwh," 12–14; Millar, *Calling on the Name of the Lord*, 19–26; cf. Walton, *Genesis*, 278–79. Outside the book of Genesis, קרא בְּשֵׁם can mean 'to invoke' (1 Kgs 18:24 [2×], 25–26; 2 Kgs 5:11; Joel 3:5 [2:32]; Zech 13:9; Ps 116:4) or 'to seek after' (Isa 41:25; 44:5; 64:6 [64:7]; 65:1; Jer 10:25; Zeph 3:9; Ps 79:6; 80:19 [80:18]) when people are the subject; however, it also means 'to proclaim' (Exod 33:19; 34:5; Isa 12:4; Ps 105:1; 116:13, 17; 1 Chr 16:8) or 'to designate' (Isa 43:7; 45:3–4; 48:1) in a number of instances, especially when God is the subject. Thus, calling upon the name of Yhwh represents more than a technical term for prayer or worship, as is sometimes argued (contra Pagolu, *Religion of the Patriarchs*, 107–9).

74. Brongers, "Wendung $b^e\check{s}\bar{e}m$ jhwh," 12–13.

75. Seymour, "Personal Names and Name Giving," 108–20.

Instead, they build altars at strategic sites in the land of Canaan amidst reference to the land's inhabitants who serve as obstacles to the land promise. Furthermore, each act of altar-building is accompanied by a designation that the accompanying location is set apart for God's purposes, either in the form of an explicit land promise or an invocation. These patterns confirm that the patriarchs build altars not merely to worship but also to lay claim to portions of the land. Such a conclusion sits well with both the ancient Near Eastern and canonical contexts of the patriarchs' altar-building. Comparatively, ancient Near Eastern altars marked sacred space and laid claim to geographical territory; canonically, the book of Genesis situates the patriarchs' altar-building within the framework of their establishment of sacred space and acquisition of portions of Canaan.

The patriarchs' altar-building also sits well with both ancient Near Eastern and modern mobile pastoralists' means of claiming land: traversing between strategic locations that they mark and use as their own. By frequenting key sites—especially sites that serve as centers of religious ritual—mobile pastoralists establish a network of territorial nodes that bring together the non-contiguous expansive stretches of land in between.[76] Such a practice is demonstrated by textual and archaeological evidence from ancient Near Eastern locales like Mari and the Cis-Jordan;[77] the charting of modern Bedouin populations likewise shows that mobile pastoralists hold together their stretched territory by frequenting key sites.[78]

The result of the patriarchs' altar-building, then, is the dotting of the land of Canaan with altars, analogous to staking territory by placing flags in the ground.[79] By building these altars the patriarchs declare God's sovereignty and ownership of the land and anticipate their descendants' possession of Canaan on behalf of their divine suzerain.[80] Such anticipation is no less contrary to the land promise than is Jeremiah's purchase of his uncle's field just prior to the exile (Jer 32:1–15). Just as Jeremiah could be confident that one day the land would once again be inhabited by his people and therefore could purchase the field in anticipation of the fulfillment of God's promise, so could the patriarchs be confident that one day the land would be their ancestors' and therefore could

---

76. In contrast with modern conceptions of territory as discretely bounded, ancient Near Eastern territory was conceived of as non-contiguous (Smith, "Networks, Territories, and the Cartography," 832–49).

77. Miglio, *Tribe and State*, 76–81; van der Steen, *Tribes and Territories in Transition*, 295–305.

78. van der Steen, *Tribes and Territories in Transition*, 102–31.

79. Beale, *Temple and the Church's Mission*, 99; Longman, *Immanuel in Our Place*, 20.

80. Leder, "'There He Built an Altar,'" 78–79; cf. Kennedy, *Seeking a Homeland*, 52–53. It is important to distinguish this anticipation from the fulfillment of the land promise. The different iterations of the land promise consistently emphasize its future fulfillment by mentioning the patriarchs' descendants (Gen 12:7; 13:14–17; 15:7, 17–21; 17:4–8; 26:2–5; 28:13–15; 35:11–12) and by noting that the patriarchs see themselves as sojourners (Gen 23:4; 28:4; 47:9; cf. Gen 17:8; 35:27; 37:1; Exod 6:4; Acts 7:5; Heb 11:9). Thus, the patriarchs' acquisition of territory—whether by building altars or other means—symbolically anticipates the land promise's fulfillment rather than actually fulfilling it in some way (cf. Williamson, "Promise and Fulfillment," 28–30; Turner, *Plot in Genesis*, 95–104).

claim portions of the land in anticipation of the fulfillment of the land promise. Both the patriarchs and Jeremiah acknowledge that the land was ultimately not theirs and that they are vassals helping God to accomplish his purposes through the land.

Association of altars and territory appears elsewhere in the Hebrew Bible with reference to the conquest, confirming that the patriarchs' altar-building anticipates the Israelites' possession of the land. God commands the Israelites to destroy the Canaanites' altars, pillars, and cult objects when they enter the land. Then they are to worship at the place he chooses לָשׂוּם אֶת־שְׁמוֹ שָׁם 'to place his name there' (Deut 12:2–7), a phrase belonging to the ancient Near Eastern tradition of using monuments to claim land.[81] Thus, the Israelites must remove all pagan items of worship not only because those items could entice them to worship other gods, but more importantly because the Canaanite altars represent the claims of those pagan gods to the land. The message here is that God is claiming the territory he has won by conquest and expunging all previous claims upon that territory. The Israelites are to worship at the place God chooses so that they do not forget that their continued occupancy of the land is dependent on the recognition that it belongs to God their suzerain.[82]

Conclusion

Throughout the years interpreters have suggested many different reasons for the patriarchs' altar-building: to facilitate worship, to serve as memorials, and to claim geographical territory. However, to date their proposals have been rather cursory, without much consideration of the ancient Near Eastern context of altar-building or the canonical context in which the altar-building accounts occur. Thus, the rationale behind the patriarchs' altar-building remains disputed and underexplored, up until now.

In this article I have demonstrated that the patriarchs' altars both establish sacred space and lay claim to the land of Canaan. The ancient Near Eastern and canonical contexts of the altar-building accounts support such a notion: in the ancient Near East altars marked sacred space and laid claim to territory, and the book of Genesis presents its altar-building accounts within the framework of humanity's priestly commission and the patriarchs' acquisition of land in Canaan. The altar-building accounts themselves confirm this purpose in that the patriarchs always build altars in the land of Canaan and designate the sites where they build altars as set apart for God's purposes. By building altars, therefore, the patriarchs declare God's ownership of the land and anticipate the Israelites' conquest of Canaan.

---

81. "Placing the name" reflects the ancient Near Eastern tradition of writing one's name on votive stelae, victory stelae, building inscriptions, and foundation deposits in order to lay claim to a particular territory. The Hebrew phrase שׂוּם שְׁמוֹ שָׁם לְשַׁכֵּן שְׁמוֹ שָׁם and its synonymous reflexes לָשׂוּם שְׁמוֹ שָׁם (cf. Deut 12:5) and לִהְיוֹת שְׁמִי שָׁם are a calque of the Akkadian phrase *šuma šakānu* used in such monuments (Richter, *Deuteronomistic History and the Name Theology*, 96–126). This further establishes a connection between the patriarchs' altar-building and Deut 12:2–7.

82. Richter, *Deuteronomistic History and the Name Theology*, 210–11.

Bibliography

Aalders, G. Charles. *The Book of Genesis*. 2 vols. Translated by William Heynen. Grand Rapids: Zondervan, 1981.

Aharoni, Yohanan. *The Land of the Bible: A Historical Geography*. 2nd ed. Translated by Anson F. Rainey. Philadelphia: Westminster, 1979.

Albertz, Rainer. *A History of Israelite Religion in the Old Testament Period*. 2 vols. Translated by John Bowden. OTL. Louisville: Westminster John Knox, 1994.

Albright, William F. "The Babylonian Temple-Tower and the Altar of Burnt-Offering." *JBL* 39 (1920) 137–42.

Alexander, T. Desmond. "Beyond Borders: The Wider Dimensions of the Land." In *The Land of Promise: Biblical, Theological, and Contemporary Perspectives*, edited by Philip S. Johnston and Peter Walker, 35–50. Downers Grove, IL: InterVarsity, 2001.

Averbeck, Richard E. "Sacrifices and Offerings." In *Dictionary of the Old Testament: Pentateuch*, edited by T. Desmond Alexander and David W. Baker, 706–33. Downers Grove, IL: InterVarsity, 2003.

Beale, G. K. *The Temple and the Church's Mission: A Biblical Theology of the Dwelling Place of God*. New Studies in Biblical Theology 17. Downers Grove, IL: InterVarsity, 2004.

Block, Daniel I. "Eden: A Temple? A Reassessment of the Biblical Evidence." In *From Creation to New Creation: Biblical Theology and Exegesis*, edited by Daniel M. Gurtner and Benjamin L. Gladd, 3–29. Peabody, MA: Hendrickson, 2013.

Brereton, Joel P. "Sacred Space." In *The Encyclopedia of Religion*, edited by Lindsay Jones, 12:7978–86. 15 vols. 2nd ed. Detroit: Macmillan Reference, 2005.

Brodsky, Harold. "Bethel (Place)." In *ABD* 1:710–12.

Brongers, H. A. "Die Wendung $b^e\check{s}\bar{e}m$ jhwh im Alten Testament." *ZAW* 77 (1965) 1–20.

Campbell, Edward F., Jr. "Shechem." In *NEAEHL* 4:1345–54.

Cassuto, Umberto. *From Noah to Abraham: Genesis VI 9—XI 32*. Vol. 2 of *A Commentary on the Book of Genesis*. 2 vols. Translated by Israel Abrahams. Jerusalem: Magnes, 1964.

Clines, David J. A. *The Theme of the Pentateuch*. 2nd ed. JSOTSup 10. Sheffield: Sheffield Academic, 1997.

Deurloo, Karel Adriaan. "The Way of Abraham: Routes and Localities as Narrative Data in Gen. 11:27—25:11." In *Voices from Amsterdam: A Modern Tradition of Reading Biblical Narrative*, edited by Martin Kessler, 95–112. SemeiaSt. Atlanta: Scholars, 1994.

Dillmann, August. *Die Genesis*. 6th ed. Kurzgefasstes exegetisches Handbuch zum Alten Testament 11. Leipzig: Hirzel, 1892.

Dohmen, Christoph. "מִזְבֵּחַ *mizbēaḥ*." In *TDOT* 8:209–25.

Dorsey, David A. *The Roads and Highways of Ancient Israel*. ASOR Library of Biblical and Near Eastern Archaeology. Baltimore: Johns Hopkins University Press, 1991.

Durand, Jean-Marie. *Le culte des pierres et les monuments commémoratifs en Syrie amorrite*. Florilegium marianum 8. Paris: Société pour l'étude due Proche-Orient ancien, 2005.

Ferris, Paul Wayne, Jr. "Hebron (Place)." In *ABD* 3:107–8.

Fleming, Daniel E. "Religion." In *Dictionary of the Old Testament: Pentateuch*, edited by T. Desmond Alexander and David W. Baker, 670–84. Downers Grove, IL: InterVarsity, 2003.

Galling, Kurt, and Paul Lohmann. *Der Altar in den Kulturen des alten Orients: Eine archäologische Studie*. Berlin: Curtius, 1925.

Gamberoni, Johann, and Helmer Ringgren. "מָקוֹם *māqôm*." In *TDOT* 8:532–44.

Graesser, Carl F. "Standing Stones in Ancient Palestine." *BA* 35 (1972) 33–63.

Haak, Robert D. "Altars." In *OEANE* 1:80–81.

Habel, Norman C. *The Land Is Mine: Six Biblical Land Ideologies.* Overtures to Biblical Theology. Minneapolis: Fortress, 1995.

Hamilton, Victor P. *Chapters 1–17.* Vol. 1 of *The Book of Genesis.* 2 vols. NICOT. Grand Rapids: Eerdmans, 1990.

Helyer, Larry R. "The Separation of Abram and Lot: Its Significance in the Patriarchal Narratives." *JSOT* 26 (1983) 77–88.

Herzog, Ze'ev. "Beersheba: Tel Beersheba." In *NEAEHL* 1:167–73.

Hoffner, Harry A., Jr. "Some Contributions of Hittitology to Old Testament Study." *TynBul* 20 (1969) 27–55.

Hom, Mary Katherine Y. H. "'. . . A Mighty Hunter before YHWH': Genesis 10:9 and the Moral-Theological Evaluation of Nimrod." *VT* 60 (2010) 63–68.

Jacob, Benno. *Das erste Buch der Tora: Genesis.* Berlin: Schocken, 1934.

Jeyaraj, Baskaran. "Land Ownership in the Pentateuch: A Thematic Study of Genesis 12–Deuteronomy 34." PhD diss., University of Sheffield, 1989.

Kalimi, Isaac. "The Land of Moriah, Mount Moriah, and the Site of Solomon's Temple in Biblical Historiography." *HTR* 83 (1990) 345–62.

Kelso, James L. "Bethel." In *NEAEHL* 1:192–94.

Kennedy, Elisabeth Robertson. *Seeking a Homeland: Sojourn and Ethnic Identity in the Ancestral Narratives of Genesis.* Biblical Interpretation Series 106. Leiden: Brill, 2011.

King, Philip J. "Jerusalem." In *ABD* 3:747–66.

Klingbeil, Gerald A. "Altars, Ritual, and Theology—Preliminary Thoughts on the Importance of Cult and Ritual for a Theology of the Hebrew Scriptures." *VT* 54 (2004) 495–515.

Kupper, Jean-Robert. "Les inscriptions triomphales akkadiennes." *OrAnt* 10 (1971) 92–106.

Kuruvilla, Abraham. *Genesis: A Theological Commentary for Preachers.* Eugene, OR: Resource Publications, 2014.

Lacocque, André. "Whatever Happened in the Valley of Shinar? A Response to Theodore Hiebert." *JBL* 128 (2009) 29–41.

Leder, Arie C. "'There He Built an Altar to the Lord' (Gen 12:8): City and Altar Building in Genesis." *OTE* 32 (2019) 58–83.

Levine, Baruch A. "*lpny YHWH*—Phenomenonlogy of the Open-Air Altar in Biblical Israel." In *Biblical Archaeology Today, 1990: Proceedings of the Second International Congress on Biblical Archaeology,* edited by Avraham Biran and Joseph Aviram, 196–205. Jerusalem: Israel Exploration Society, 1993.

Longman, Tremper, III. *Immanuel in Our Place: Seeing Christ in Israel's Worship.* The Gospel according to the Old Testament. Phillipsburg, NJ: P&R, 2001.

Malone, Andrew S. *God's Mediators: A Biblical Theology of Priesthood.* New Studies in Biblical Theology 43. Downers Grove, IL: InterVarsity, 2017.

Manor, Dale W. "Beer-Sheba (Place)." In *ABD* 1:641–45.

Mathews, Kenneth A. *Genesis 1—11:26.* NAC 1A. Nashville: Broadman & Holman, 1996.

———. *Genesis 11:27—50:26.* NAC 1B. Nashville: Broadman & Holman, 2005.

Miglio, Adam E. *Tribe and State: The Dynamics of International Politics and the Reign of Zimri-Lim.* Gorgias Studies in the Ancient Near East 8. Piscataway, NJ: Gorgias, 2014.

Millar, J. Gary. *Calling on the Name of the Lord: A Biblical Theology of Prayer.* New Studies in Biblical Theology 38. Downers Grove, IL: InterVarsity, 2016.

Moberly, R. W. L. *The Old Testament of the Old Testament: Patriarchal Narratives and Mosaic Yahwism.* Overtures to Biblical Theology. Minneapolis: Fortress, 1992.

Morales, L. Michael. *The Tabernacle Pre-Figured: Cosmic Mountain Ideology in Genesis and Exodus*. BTS 15. Leuven: Peeters, 2012.

Noort, Ed. "Der Streit um den Altar: Josua 22 und seine Rezeptionsgeschichte." In *Kult, Konflikt und Versöhnung: Beiträge zur kultischen Sühne in religiösen, sozialen und politischen Auseinandersetzungen des antiken Mittelmeerraumes*, edited by Rainer Albertz, 151–74. AOAT 285. Münster: Ugarit-Verlag, 2001.

O'Connor, Michael. "The Biblical Notion of the City." In *Constructions of Space II: The Biblical City and Other Imagined Spaces*, edited by Jon L. Berquist and Claudia V. Camp, 18–39. LHBOTS 490. London: T&T Clark, 2008.

Ofer, Avi. "Hebron." In *NEAEHL* 2:606–9.

Pagolu, Augustine. *The Religion of the Patriarchs*. JSOTSup 277. Sheffield: Sheffield Academic, 1998.

Pearson, Michael Parker. *The Archaeology of Death and Burial*. Texas A&M University Anthropology Series 3. College Station: Texas A&M University Press, 1999.

Pitkänen, Pekka. "From Tent of Meeting to Temple: Presence, Rejection and Renewal of Divine Favour." In *Heaven on Earth: The Temple in Biblical Theology*, edited by T. Desmond Alexander and Simon Gathercole, 23–34. Carlisle, UK: Paternoster, 2004.

Procksch, Otto. *Die Genesis*. 2nd ed. Leipzig: Deichertische, 1924.

Rainey, Anson F., and R. Steven Notley. *The Sacred Bridge: Carta's Atlas of the Biblical World*. 2nd ed. Jerusalem: Carta, 2014.

Richter, Sandra L. *The Deuteronomistic History and the Name Theology: l^e šakkēn š^{e}mô šām in the Bible and the Ancient Near East*. BZAW 318. Berlin: de Gruyter, 2002.

Riecker, Siegbert. "Ein theologischer Ansatz zum Verständnis der Altarbaunotizen der Genesis." *Bib* 87 (2006) 526–30.

Sarna, Nahum M. *Genesis*. JPS Torah Commentary. Philadelphia: Jewish Publication Society, 1989.

Seymour, Timothy P. "Personal Names and Name Giving in the Ancient Near East." *UCLA Historical Journal* 4 (1983) 108–20.

Shafer, Ann. "Assyrian Royal Monuments on the Periphery: Ritual and the Making of Imperial Space." In *Ancient Near Eastern Art in Context: Studies in Honor of Irene J. Winter by Her Students*, edited by Jack Cheng and Marian H. Feldman, 133–59. CHANE 26. Leiden: Brill, 2007.

Shiloh, Yigal, et al. "Jerusalem: The Early Periods and the First Temple Period." In *NEAEHL* 2:698–716.

Singer, Itamar. "The Hittites and the Bible Revisted." In *"I Will Speak the Riddles of Ancient Times": Archaeological and Historical Studies in Honor of Amihai Mazar on the Occasion of His Sixtieth Birthday*, 2 vols., edited by Aren M. Maeir and Pierre de Miroschedji, 2:723–56. Winona Lake, IN: Eisenbrauns, 2006.

Skinner, John. *A Critical and Exegetical Commentary on Genesis*. 2nd ed. ICC. Edinburgh: T&T Clark, 1930.

Smith, Monica L. "Networks, Territories, and the Cartography of Ancient States." *Annals of the Association of American Geographers* 95 (2005) 832–49.

Stavrakopoulou, Francesca. *Land of Our Fathers: The Roles of Ancestor Veneration in Biblical Land Claims*. LHBOTS 473. London: T&T Clark, 2010.

Steen, Eveline J. van der. *Tribes and Territories in Transition: The Central East Jordan Valley in the Late Bronze Age and Early Iron Ages: A Study of the Sources*. OLA 130. Leuven: Peeters, 2004.

Strong, John T. "Shattering the Image of God: A Response to Theodore Hiebert's Interpretation of the Story of the Tower of Babel." *JBL* 127 (2008) 625–34.
Tigay, Jeffrey H. "The Presence of God and the Coherence of Exodus 20:22–26." In *Sefer Moshe: The Moshe Weinfeld Jubilee Volume*, edited by Chaim Cohen et al., 195–211. Winona Lake, IN: Eisenbrauns, 2004.
Toombs, Lawrence E. "Shechem (Place)." In *ABD* 5:1174–86.
Turner, Laurence A. *Announcements of Plot in Genesis*. JSOTSup 96. Sheffield: Sheffield Academic, 1990.
Umbarger, Matthew. "Abraham's Tamarisk." *JESOT* 1 (2012) 189–200.
Walton, John H. *Genesis*. NIV Application Commentary. Grand Rapids: Zondervan, 2001.
———. *Genesis 1 as Ancient Cosmology*. Winona Lake, IN: Eisenbrauns, 2011.
———. "The Mesopotamian Background of the Tower of Babel Account and Its Implications." *BBR* 5 (1995) 155–75.
Wenham, Gordon J. *Genesis 1–15*. WBC 1. Waco, TX: Word, 1987.
———. "Sanctuary Symbolism in the Garden of Eden Story." In *Proceedings of the Ninth World Congress of Jewish Studies, Jerusalem, 4–12 August, 1985: Division A: The Period of the Bible*, 19–25. Jerusalem: World Union of Jewish Studies, 1986.
Westermann, Claus. *Genesis 12–36: A Commentary*. Translated by John J. Scullion. Continental Commentaries. Minneapolis: Augsburg, 1985.
Williamson, Paul R. "Promise and Fulfilment: The Territorial Inheritance." In *The Land of Promise: Biblical, Theological, and Contemporary Perspectives*, edited by Philip S. Johnston and Peter Walker, 15–34. Downers Grove, IL: InterVarsity, 2001.
Wright, N. T. *The Climax of the Covenant: Christ and the Law in Pauline Theology*. Edinburgh: T&T Clark, 1991.
Zwickel, Wolfgang. "Die Altarbaunotizen im Alten Testament." *Bib* 73 (1992) 533–46.

18

Jesus the Slave
The Gender of a Christological Metaphor in Luke and Paul

Caryn A. Reeder

> It is better to die than to be degraded as a slave.
> —Publilius Syrus, *Sententiae* 489[1]

Publilius of Syria was enslaved in Rome in the first century BCE. He was well educated and clever, and as a result he was lucky enough to be manumitted by his owner. After receiving his freedom, Publilius Syrus gained recognition as a dramatist and moralist. By Roman standards, he lived a slave success story. And yet, despite his visible success, Publilius Syrus would have preferred death to the dishonor of slavery.

In the Roman Empire's slave society, status as slave, freed slave, or freeborn was fundamental to social identity (Gaius, *Inst.* 1.9).[2] The particular system of slavery practiced in Rome was chattel slavery. Slaves were legally defined as property. Therefore, slaves did not possess their own legal rights (for instance, marriage; making a will; or protecting their own bodies from assault). Slaves' external powerlessness correlated with a perceived inability to exercise reason or self-control. From an elite Roman perspective, slaves were more animal-like than human (cf. Plutarch, *Cat. Maj.* 21.1). Enslavement represented a living death.[3]

---

1. Translation from Wiedemann, *Slavery*, 71.

2. On identification of the Roman Empire as a slave society, see Bradley, *Slavery*, 12–16; and Morley, "Slavery," 284.

3. Diodorus Siculus 13.58.2; Seneca, *Ep.* 77.18; Ulpian, *Digest* 35.1.59.2, 50.17.209; Bradley, *Slavery*, 25–27; Glancy, *Slavery*, 77–78.

The realities and representations of slavery in the Roman Empire provide an essential context for interpreting the metaphor of enslavement in New Testament Christology. The metaphor appears in several traditions. In Mark 10:41–45, Jesus exhorts his disciples to become servants and slaves of all because he himself came to serve and give his life as a ransom for many. Jesus does the work of slaves by washing the disciples' feet in John 13:3–17. In 1 Pet 2:18–24, Jesus's death is compared with the violence regularly experienced by household slaves. In the texts that are the focus of this study, Jesus identifies himself with slaves who serve at the owner's table in Luke 22:27, and Paul presents Jesus's life and death as dishonorable enslavement in Phil 2:5–8.

Within Roman constructions of enslavement, the representation of Jesus as slave suggests he has no power, status, freedom, or legal rights. He is less than human. For the earliest audiences of these texts, the identification of Jesus as slave would have been quite shocking.[4] The dissonance only increases with the considerations of gender. The recognition of the intersection of masculinity with slavery in Roman understanding is relatively recent in classical scholarship, and its implications for interpreting the metaphor of Jesus as slave in the New Testament remain largely unexplored. In this essay, I develop the correlation of slavery with gender in Roman thought to analyze the representation of Jesus as slave in Luke 22:24–27 and, more briefly, Phil 2:5–11.

I offer this paper in humble appreciation of John Walton, who has taught generations of students the importance of cultural, literary, social, and historical contexts for interpreting the biblical text. Walton encourages us to consider, question, and celebrate the "high-context communication" reflected in the Bible—to boldly explore the shared histories, cultures, languages, and experiences of a text's author(s) and earliest audiences as a framework for our interpretation of the text.[5] Walton's approach to the Old Testament is no less important for New Testament research, and I am ever grateful for his influence over my own formation as a biblical scholar.

Gender, Slavery, and the Roman Empire

According to the constructions of gender among the Roman elite, an enslaved person embodied the precise opposite of ideal masculinity.[6] Roman constructions of slavery and gender intersect, therefore, in significant ways. Arguably, as central systems of social organization within the Roman Empire, gender and slavery fundamentally depend upon and define each other.

---

4. So Combes, *Metaphor of Slavery*, 46–47, 68–69; Hellerman, *Reconstructing Honor*, 136–42. Despite attempts to argue the opposite (see Martin, *Slavery*, 2–32, 50–55; Conway, *Behold the Man*, 99–100), in the Roman world slavery was not desirable, and comparisons of freeborn elites with slaves were neither normative nor acceptable.

5. Walton, *Lost World*, 15–17.

6. See Cohen, "High Cost," 145–49; McDonnell, *Roman Manliness*, 159; Reeder, *War and Peace*, 28.

Roman definitions of gender reflect a single-sex system in which masculinity provided the measure of humanity.[7] The ideal human was the wealthy, politically active, freeborn Roman man.[8] He had no living father or legal guardian to oversee his life. Rather, he exercised authority over others as *paterfamilias* and patron, and he was a public benefactor.[9] These economic and political expectations prevented the majority of the population from attaining the ideal, making "ideal masculinity" better understood as "elite masculinity."

Masculinity was essentially a public performance which had to be learned, practiced, and constantly, consistently maintained. The elite man avoided unmanly traits like slouching, sneezing, or short, mincing steps; he walked and talked like a man.[10] He displayed masculine discipline in his austere dress, diet, and behavior.[11] He exhibited courage in the face of danger.[12] He acted as the penetrator rather than the penetrated in sexual encounters, and he proved his virility by begetting children.[13] Finally, the ideal man modeled moral behavior.[14]

> On entering the senate house Prusias stood in the doorway facing the members, and putting both his hands on the ground he bowed his head to the ground in adoration of the threshold and the seated senators, with the words, "Hail, you savior gods," making it impossible for anyone after him to surpass him in unmanliness (ἀνανδρία), womanishness (γυναικισμός), and slavishness (κολακεία). (Polybius, *Histories* 30.18.5 [Paton and Olson, LCL, modified])

The contrast of masculinity with femininity in Polybius's story of Prusias is a common element in Roman texts. However, in Rome's single sex system of gender, freeborn women were more-or-less masculine, as evidenced by their exercise of self-control, power over others, public benefaction, reason, and courage.[15] By contrast, even adult male slaves lacked the basic attributes of masculinity. Within the Roman single-sex system of gender, the inverse of an honorable, powerful, disciplined, freeborn, elite male was a slave.

---

7. McDonnell, *Roman Manliness*, 2; Boatwright, "Women and Gender," 108–10.

8. On the construction of ideal masculinity in the Roman world, see Gleason, *Making Men*, 58–71; McDonnell, *Roman Manliness*, 167–72; Foxhall, *Studying Gender*, 68–70, 91–94, 108–9; Wilson, *Unmanly Men*, 21–28.

9. Valerius Maximus 8.13.5; Tacitus, *Ann.* 2.72–73; Plutarch, *Aem.* 39.6–9.

10. Cicero, *Off.* 1.128–29; Valerius Maximus 8.13, ext. 1; Quintilian, *Inst.* 11.3.19, 32, 63, 72, 80–81, etc.; Polemon, *Physiognomy* 2.1.192–94, 50.1.260.

11. Dionysius of Halicarnassus, *Ant. rom.* 14.9.8; Livy 5.6.4–5; Tacitus, *Agr.* 29, *Ann.* 15.48; Suetonius, *Aug.* 24.1.

12. Polybius 10.3.5–7; Sallust, *Bell. Cat.* 6.5; Valerius Maximus 3.2.24; Livy 7.17.3–5.

13. Polybius 6.37.9; Valerius Maximus 6.1.10; Tacitus, *Ann.* 2.41; Plutarch, *Pyrrh.* 28.3.

14. Polybius 35.4.8–9; Sallust, *Bell. Cat.* 3.3, 9.1–2; Tacitus, *Agr.* 9.5.

15. Valerius Maximus 3.2.2, 8.3.1; Tacitus, *Ann.* 1.57, 1.69, *His.* 1.3; Appian, *Hist. rom.* 7.5.29.

As in Polybius's analysis of Prusias, the unmanliness of slavery is consistent and pervasive in Roman sources. For Valerius Maximus, manliness (*virtus*) is fundamentally opposed to captivity, submissiveness, and enslavement (3.2.7, 3.2.12).[16] To be conquered by Rome was consistently represented as a loss of manliness to enslavement.[17] Tacitus claims that Vitellius lost the honorable *virtus* he displayed during his military postings upon his return to Rome, becoming instead shamefully slavish (*Ann.* 6.32). Cassius Dio's Boudica reverses the standard Roman rhetoric, claiming the Britons, whether man, woman, or child, are honorably manly, but the Romans, enslaved as they are to the womanish Nero, have emasculated themselves with luxury (62.6).

The figurative (and, sometimes, literal) emasculation of slaves reflects the brutality of enslavement across the Empire.[18] The system of slavery in the Roman Empire benefited slave owners. Slaves were bodies for the owners' use and pleasure—the independent personhood of slaves was only rarely recognized.[19] Slaves had no capacity for personal honor.[20] They carried out work that would be demeaning for the freeborn. They were treated in dishonorable ways, with casual violence, intentional floggings and brandings, and sexual abuse.[21] They were not granted the privileges of freedom: legitimate marriage; rights over their own children; sexual chastity; owning property independently of their owners' authority; or making wills.[22] The power dynamics, legal status, and rhetoric of slavery combined resulted in dehumanization.[23] Because of the correlation of humanity with masculinity, slaves were un-gendered.[24]

Jesus the Slave

Various New Testament texts recognize the harsh realities of enslavement in the Roman Empire. Slaves in Jesus's parables in the Gospels are beaten and abused (Matt 18:23–24; Mark 12:2–5; Luke 12:45–48, 17:7–10). The household codes in Eph 6:9

16. See also Valerius Maximus 2.7.9; Livy 26.2.10–11; Quintilian, *Inst.* 11.3.83; Pliny, *Ep.* 1.8.8–9.

17. Diodorus Siculus 11.1.3–4; Tacitus, *Agr.* 21.3–4, *Hist.* 2.17–18; Appian, *Hist. rom.* 12.1.2.

18. See Bradley, *Slavery*, 176–81; Hezser, *Jewish Slavery*, 180–83; Glancy, *Slavery*, 10–29; Reeder, *Slavery*, 5–12.

19. Glancy, *Slavery*, 9–16, particularly addresses the identification of slaves as "bodies"; see also Rev 18:13; Cicero, *Ep.* 16.16; Pliny the Younger, *Ep.* 3.19.3; P. Oxy. 3.494; Bradley, *Slavery*, 7–8. Admissions of slaves' humanity come in Seneca, *Ep.* 47; Plutarch, *Cat. Maj.* 5.2; Pliny the Younger, *Ep.* 8.16.

20. See esp. Bradley, *Slavery*, 24, 27; Morley, "Slavery," 280–83; Combes, *Metaphor of Slavery*, 27n16; Reeder, *War and Peace*, 28.

21. For instance, Diodorus Siculus 5.38; Varro, *Rust.* 1.17.4–7; Seneca, *Ira* 3.32.1; Pliny, *Nat.* 18.4.21; Plutarch, *Cat. Maj.* 4.4, *Conjugalia Praecepta* 16; P. Oxy. 42.3070; *Digest* 48.19.10.

22. These legal restrictions, often simply assumed in the sources, are explicitly addressed in, e.g., Seneca the Elder, *Controversiae* 4, pref. 10; Pliny the Younger, *Ep.* 8.16; Gaius, *Institutes* 2.86–88; and note the cooption of the privileges of the freeborn by slaves in funerary inscriptions (ILS 1583, 8438). See further Bradley, *Slavery*, 4–6, 27.

23. Note Seneca, *Dial.* 9.8.7–8, and *Ep.* 12.3; ILS 9455; *Digest* 11.4.1.

24. So also Hezser, *Jewish Slavery*, 84; Glancy, *Slavery*, 24–26.

and 1 Pet 2:18–20 associate the experience of slavery with injustice and suffering. Jesus's instructions to the disciples in Mark 10:41–45 identify slavery as the opposite of (human perceptions of) greatness, and Paul suggests that his own self-identification as a slave made his message unacceptable to general audiences (2 Cor 4:3–5).

While masculinity is not explicitly referenced in these texts, the concerns of masculinity—self-control, power, and social honor—are present, and would have been easily recognizable for a first century audience in the Roman Empire. The ungendering of enslavement in Roman thought offers a particularly fruitful context for examining the metaphor of Jesus as slave in the Gospel of Luke and Paul's letter to the Philippians. The Gospel of Luke and Paul's letters have attracted significant attention for their portrayals of gender in general.[25] The connection of masculinity with slavery, however, has not been explored. The inclusion of Luke 22:24–27 and Phil 2:5–11 in an analysis of gender in the Gospel and Paul's letters adds an important element to the discussion.

Luke 22:24–27

In the Gospel of Luke, the story of Jesus is firmly contextualized in the Roman Empire, from simple references to Roman-style roof tiles in 5:19 and the representation of Anna as a *univira* in 2:36–37, to more complicated integrations of (and challenges to) imperial ideology (as in 2:1–14).[26] Gender is one aspect of this contextualization. Some portrayals of masculinity in Luke seem to reflect imperial norms. The characterization of Jesus as a wise twelve-year-old, a man of authority, and a prophet-man who is powerful in speech and action, identifies him with aspects of Roman manhood (2:46–47, 7:6–8, 24:19). Examples of elite masculinity can be found in Jesus's parables and in certain stories in the Gospel (e.g., 7:1–10, 12:39–40, 19:12–14). For a number of scholars, then, the Gospel of Luke upholds hegemonic masculinity, narrating the story of Jesus to fit the Roman ideal.[27]

However, what is perhaps the most obvious representation of Jesus in the guise of an ideal Roman man in Luke 24:19–21 actually disrupts the ideal, arising ironically as it does through the disciples' doubt concerning Jesus's identity following his crucifixion. There are significant challenges to elite masculinity in the Gospel.[28] The active role taken by women in the narrative inversely reflects on the masculinity of

---

25. For instance, Conway, *Behold the Man*, 67–88, 128–42; Wilson, *Unmanly Men*; Westfall, *Paul and Gender*.

26. See further Danker, *New Age*, 3–9; Wilson, *Unmanly Men*, 21–28; Reeder, *War and Peace*, 12–14.

27. D'Angelo, "ANHP Question," 58–62; Scaer, *Lukan Passion*, 45–53, 90–106; Conway, *Behold the Man*, 127–32.

28. Wilson, *Unmanly Men*, 193–94; Reeder, *War and Peace*, 70–71.

Zechariah and the male disciples (1:26–55, 10:38–42, 24:8–11).[29] Alongside the reflections of ideal masculinity in the parables are disruptions of the central concerns of (male) violence and status (11:21–22, 14:7–14, 14:31–33). Moreover, Jesus explicitly limits his adult, male disciples from the traditional masculine role of the *paterfamilias* (9:57–62, 14:26). He tells them to become like little children (18:17), and in various parables the disciples are represented by slaves (12:35–38, 12:41–48, 17:7–10).

> There was an argument among them about which one of them seemed to be the greatest. Jesus said to them, "The kings of the nations rule over them, and the people who have authority over them are called benefactors. But you are not to be like this. Rather, the greatest among you must be like the youngest, and the ruler must be like the servant. For who is greater, the one who reclines at table or the one who serves? It's the one who reclines, right? But I am among you as one who serves." (Luke 22:24–27, author's translation)

This story, set during Jesus's last meal with his disciples before his arrest, uses a dinner scene as a teaching tool. Meals form a significant narrative setting and vehicle for Jesus's teachings in Luke.[30] These texts often explicitly address the expectations and practices of dining in Roman society, particularly with respect to honor and status.[31] The positions of guests in the dining room, the services provided to individual guests, and the quality of food and drink given to different guests depended upon and determined a person's status. A guest's status held practical consequences for that person's life in terms of access to the host's resources, the ability to make relationships with important people, and the social honor or dishonor that came with a guest's position in the room.[32]

The surprise of the Pharisees (and others) at Jesus's habit of eating with tax collectors and sinners in Luke expresses the more common expectation that diners would be of a similar status (5:30, 7:39, 15:2, 19:7).[33] Likewise, in contrast to the use of meals to raise social status, Jesus instructs guests to seek out the lowest position in the room, and hosts to invite those who cannot repay their investment (14:7–14).[34] The subver-

29. See Carroll, "Gospel of Luke," 372.

30. E.g., Luke 5:29–31, 7:36–50, 11:37–52, 16:19–31, 24:28–43. On meals in Luke's Gospel, see esp. Smith, "Table Fellowship," 613–38; Barreto, "Gospel on the Move," 177–86.

31. See Smith, "Table Fellowship," 619–20; Green, *Luke*, 547–63.

32. Cicero, *Att.* 353.2, 407A.4; *Fam.* 13.3; Valerius Maximus 2.1.9; Juvenal, *Sat.* 3.82–85, 5.24–173; Pliny, *Ep.* 2.6.1–5; Suetonius, *Calig.* 39.2; Plutarch, *Mor.* 679B; Dunbabin, *Roman Banquet*, 13, 39–43; Hellerman, *Reconstructing Honor*, 25–28.

33. See further Smith, "Table Fellowship," 635–37; Barreto, "Gospel on the Move," 180.

34. Smith, "Table Fellowship," 617–20, 635–38, points out parallels with Plutarch, *Quaest. conv.* 1.2, 1.3, 616c–f, and *Sept. sap. conv.* 148f–149f. However, as Smith notes, Luke's message is distinctive in the inclusion of the poor, disabled, and sick—social outsiders who would not be welcomed to Plutarch's dinners. The only people of significantly unequal status at a Roman banquet would be the slaves who serve and entertain the diners, and the hosts' clients who, despite their need for economic and social assistance, are participants in the system of status and reciprocity (and who also offer the

sion of social status is reinforced by the parable of the great dinner and in the general promise of feasting for the poor and Gentiles (1:53, 6:20–21, 13:28–29, 14:15–24). Jesus's message to his disciples during his last meal with them in chapter 22 reflects this "great reversal."[35] The importance of displays of social status, wealth, and power in Roman constructions of masculinity adds the (unrecognized) issue of gender to the great reversal. Jesus's dining habits and teachings during and about meals in Luke offer a challenge to gender norms.

In Luke 22:24–27, the concerns of gender are highlighted by the disciples' argument and Jesus's recognition of normative constructions of power and status, only to be overturned: The great should become like the youngest, and the leader as the one who serves (as Jesus himself models). The challenge to elite masculinity here is reinforced by the implications of enslavement. The vocabulary of Luke 22:24–27 reflects servanthood (διακονέω), a term used throughout the Gospel for preparing and serving food, rather than slavery (δοῦλος, δουλεύω).[36] Nonetheless, the contrast of reclining to eat with serving a meal evokes the concerns of slavery and freedom in the Roman world (as the connection of serving a meal, διακονέω, with slaves, δοῦλος, in Luke 17:7–10 indicates). In frescoes and mosaics, plays, poems, and letters, slaves wash diners' hands and feet, prepare the meal and the tableware, serve the food, and care for the diners' needs. Slaves entertain the guests and clean up after them.[37] The guests, meanwhile, recline, relax, and receive the benefit of the slaves' work. Reclining to dine was the privilege of the elite, and symbolic of elite masculinity.[38]

Visual representations of meals separate slaves from the diners physically. The portrayals minimize the slaves' status through relative sizing, posture, and position.[39] Verbal descriptions of dinner parties clarify the gendered implications of such images. In Seneca, *Ep.* 47, a dinner offers a means to critique the excesses of Roman society, including the dehumanization of slaves. According to Seneca's exaggerated story, a

---

host the opportunity to display his wealth and power).

35. So González, *The Story*, chapters 3 and 6; see also Smith, "Table Fellowship," 628–29.

36. διακονέω occurs clearly in this sense in Luke 4:39, 10:40, 12:37, and 17:8 (and therefore this meaning is also likely for the remaining occurrence in 8:3). See further Via, "Women," 37–44; Gooder, "*Diakonia*," 40 (analyzing the lexical work of John N. Collins); Hentschel, *Diakonia*, 286–88.

37. See Aristophanes, *Vesp.* 1208–1210; Plautus, *Most.* 308–9, and *Pers.* 791–93; Horace, *Ep.* 1.5, and *Sat.* 2.8.10–13; Plutarch, *Mor.* 201c.

38. There is some uncertainty over women's presence during Roman meals (see Dunbabin, *Roman Banquet*, 23, 67–68), but Roller, *Dining Posture*, 105–22, argues persuasively that wives, concubines, prostitutes, and female slaves did normally recline with the men to whom they were (legitimately) sexually available. In any case, reclining is clearly presented as an elite masculine prerogative in, e.g., Diodorus Siculus 19.22.2; Cicero, *Fam.* 362.2–3; Valerius Maximus 2.1.2; Columella, *Rust.* 11.1.19; Apuleius, *Metam.* 1.22; Aulus Gellius, *Noct. att.* 2.2.9–10; and through the disruption of social norms in Seneca, *Ep.* 47.15–16; Petronius, *Satyricon* 70. See further Dunbabin, *Roman Banquet*, 11–13; Roller, *Dining Posture*, 16. There is a certain tension between the masculine privilege of reclining to dine and austerity in diet as an expression of masculine discipline (e.g., Caesar, *Bell. gall.* 2.15, 4.2; Livy 23.18.11–12; Plutarch, *Mor.* 201C).

39. See Dunbabin, *Roman Banquet*, 151; Roller, *Dining Posture*, 19–22, 29–30, 85.

diner overeats to the point that he vomits it all back up, all while silent, hungry slaves stand around the dining room. The slaves each have a specific job: carving the meat, serving the wine, cleaning up diners' vomit, picking up scraps from the floor, and spying on the guests. In *Constant.* 2.15, Seneca emphasizes the shame of such tasks—they offend the honor due a freeborn man (*pudor ingenuo*). Slaves who sit on the floor beneath the guests, eating the scraps dropped by the diners, are utterly debased by Roman standards (a judgment reflected in the depiction of the poor man, Lazarus, in Luke 16:20–21).

These two passages in Seneca contrast the dishonor of serving at a dinner with masculine honor. In *Constant.* 2.15.1, the work of the slaves is compared with a freeborn man being lashed, having an eye gouged out, or being mocked in the forum. Seneca's overall argument associates true manliness with enduring such indignities, but this context only reinforces the fundamental dishonor of enslavement. Even for Seneca, slaves, particularly slaves who serve at meals, represent the opposite of honorable masculinity.[40] The un-gendering of the slaves is explicit in *Ep.* 47 in the emasculation of adult male slaves, "boys" (*puer*) forced to shave their beards and wear women's dress, with the implication of postprandial sex with the owner.[41] For the slaves in Seneca's stories, a dining room is a space of humiliation and dehumanization.

The un-gendering of slaves in the service of (elite male) diners is not unique to Seneca. Other writers also identified the tasks of preparing, managing, serving, and entertaining at a dinner as unworthy of an honorable man (Polybius 30.26.4–9; Diodorus Siculus 21.16.2–3).[42] The work of slaves at a dinner was unpleasant and dishonorable on its own (Petronius, *Satyricon* 31–36; Martial, *Epigrams* 3.82.8–17); the representation of slaves as dirty thieves further marks their dishonor (Horace, *Sat.* 2.4.78–80, who judges such a slave to be nauseating to a freeborn man; Pliny, *Nat.* 33.6). In addition, the slaves might be beaten for simple mistakes, a physical reminder of their unmasculine inability to protect from or retaliate against abuse.[43] The simple act of standing at a dinner (rather than reclining) underscores the distinction between enslavement and freedom (Livy 24.16.11–13; Seneca, *Ben.* 3.27.1).[44] Explicitly in the feminization of slave bodies and implicitly in the menial, dishonorable tasks the slaves performed, Greek and Roman authors use dinner service to contrast freeborn honor with the debasement of slavery.

---

40. Notably, Seneca does not tell Roman men to be like slaves. Rather, they should endure shameful treatment (like that experienced regularly by slaves) with the fortitude of a freeborn, elite man.

41. Compare also Plautus, *Pseud.* 1271–1273; Cicero, *Cat.* 2.10; Juvenal, *Sat.* 5.56–61; Dunbabin, *Roman Banquet*, 154–55; Roller, *Dining Posture*, 22, 30.

42. By contrast, hosting a dinner was an honorable demonstration of a man's status (e.g., Sallust, *Bell. Jug.* 85.38–40; Pliny the Younger, *Ep.* 1.15; Plutarch, *Aem.* 28.7–9); cf. Hentschel, *Diakonia*, 289.

43. Martial, *Epigrams* 3.94; Petronius, *Satyricon* 34; Seneca, *Ira* 40.2; Plutarch, *Mor.* 461B, *Cat. Maj.* 21.3.

44. See Dunbabin, *Roman Banquet*, 11; Roller, *Dining Posture*, 85–87.

This context sharpens the message of Luke 22:24–27. Those who serve at a dinner are abased, emasculated, and abused. Those who recline, as the οὐχί in verse 27 anticipates, are clearly greater than those who serve—a recognition of normative masculinity that draws attention back to the disciples' disagreement over their relative greatness in verse 24. The reference to the exercise of power over others in verse 25 further reinforces the overtones of gender. Some interpretations suggest that Jesus's words in Luke 22:25 critique unjust rule (kings who "lord it over" subjects, and the implication that "benefactor" is an undeserved title).[45] However, κυριεύω more likely refer to the normal exercise of ruling power, whether it is just or oppressive, and εὐεργέτης to the standard benefaction of the elite in Roman society, practiced as a demonstration of status (a display, therefore, of manliness, as the middle or passive of καλέω implies).[46] The critique, then, is not concerned with unjust practices, but with the values of honor, status, and authority. The disciples should not engage with such performances of normative masculinity. Instead, they must become like the one who serves at a dinner—that is, they must identify with the slaves who carry out dishonorable tasks, experience abusive treatment, and care for the needs of others, for the benefit of others and not themselves.[47]

This interpretation is supported by the accompanying claim that the greatest among the disciples should become like the youngest (cf. Luke 9:46–48). Children, even freeborn children, held low status in Roman constructions of maturity and masculinity. They were small, incomplete adults, constrained by physical and rational weakness, fear, and a lack of self-control.[48] For the greatest among the adult male disciples to become like the youngest children would mean giving up their own positions of authority and self-governance to assume a low status of dependency on and subordination to others.

"I am among you as one who serves" (Luke 22:27): Luke's Jesus does not ask the disciples to do more (or less) than he himself does (as he has, in fact, just done in offering the disciples bread and wine in vv. 17–20).[49] He claims the position of a debased, emasculated, abused slave for himself. In Roman context, Jesus is unmanly (as the crucifixion

---

45. Compare the NRSV and NIV translations, and see Conway, *Behold the Man*, 142.

46. On κυριεύω (and the parallel term καταχυριεύω in Mark 10:42) as a basic representation of the legitimate rule of a king or other authority, see Clark, "Meaning," 100–104. Green, *Gospel of Luke*, 767; Bovon, *Luke*, 173–74; and Carroll, *Luke*, 438–39, adopt the interpretation suggested here (though with slightly different emphases); as Bovon concludes, Jesus is "subverting the human system of authority and the exercise of power" (p. 174). Unfortunately, none of these commentators explore the image of the one who serves as a slave at a meal. Note that Lull, "Servant-Benefactor," interprets the text as a call for the disciples to become benefactors, defined by Jesus's example as those who serve the community.

47. Cf. Gooder, "*Diakonia*," 40 (drawing on the work of John J. Collins).

48. Seneca, *Clem.* 14, *Const.* 12.2, *Ira* 2.21; Green, *Gospel of Luke*, 391–92, 769; Reeder, *War and Peace*, 28–29, 44–48.

49. Compare Luke 12:35–38, and see further Hentschel, *Diakonia*, 288. Nelson, "Flow of Thought," 117–18, argues that since Jesus also hosts the dinner, his identification with the slave who serves is complicated. But this complication also makes visible the message of the parable in Luke 12.

is about to prove).⁵⁰ In serving meals and becoming like the youngest, the leadership of Jesus and his adult male disciples is, as Joel Green says, "wholly unconventional."⁵¹ It is a redefinition of leadership (one which is rewarded in vv. 28–30).⁵²

The unconventionality extends to gender. Notably, in Luke's Gospel a number of people actively serve Jesus and the disciples: Peter's mother-in-law (4:39); Mary Magdalene, Joanna, Susanna, and many other women (8:1–3); Martha (10:38–42). The instruction to the disciples to serve in the same way identifies these women as models for the men to follow.⁵³ In Luke 22:24–27 (as throughout the Gospel), Jesus subverts the expectations of honorable masculinity for himself and his followers. They adopt an unexpected, dishonorable persona, setting aside the concerns of status, power, and honor that were central to masculinity in favor of serving like the women, and like slaves.⁵⁴

Philippians 2:5–11

The interpretation of Luke 22:24–27 as a subversion of normative masculinity develops from a broader understanding of slavery and dinners in the Roman world. What is, I have argued, implicit in Luke's representation of Jesus and the disciples is explicit in the Christological hymn in Phil 2:5–11. This text has been analyzed with respect to its possible pre-Pauline origins and Paul's potential edits, its purpose in Philippians, its significance for early Christology, and more. Amid these concerns, attention to the gendered implications of Phil 2:5–11 has been lacking.⁵⁵ However, in Roman context, the identification of Jesus as a crucified slave raises serious questions concerning his masculinity. My analysis here accordingly focuses on this concern in verses 5 through 8.⁵⁶

> Have this attitude among yourselves which was also in Christ Jesus, who, though he was in the form of God, did not consider equality with God something to exploit, but emptied himself by taking the form of a slave, becoming

---

50. On the unmasculinity of Jesus in the Gospel of Luke, see especially Wilson, *Unmanly Men*, 194–95, 241.

51. Green, *Gospel of Luke*, 767–68 (see also Nelson, "Flow of Thought," 118).

52. Nelson, "Unitary Character," 615–17.

53. See Via, "Women," 45, 57 (and also Smith, "Table Fellowship," 631, though he does not comment on the question of gender).

54. Cf. Carroll, "Gospel of Luke," 372; Wilson, *Unmanly Men*, 21.

55. Conway, *Behold the Man*, 80, identifies Phil 2:9–11 as a portrayal of Jesus's (imperial) apotheosis and ruling power; she does not address vv. 5–8. Hellerman, *Reconstructing Honor*, insightfully analyzes Phil 2:5–11 in terms of Roman honor. While he notes that honor was the privilege of freeborn Roman men (e.g., 11, 34), however, he does not address the implications of Phil 2:5–11 for gender. Shaner, "Rape and Robbery," 362, does explicitly comment on questions of gender in Phil 2:5–8, comparing this depiction of Jesus with the "subjugated, degraded, female body" representing conquered peoples in imperial reliefs.

56. My discussion is, therefore, limited. For more complete analyses of the text and its various issues of interpretation, see Martin, *Carmen Christi*; Fee, *Philippians*, 191–229; Keown, *Philippians*, 351–448.

in human likeness. And being found in appearance as a human, he humiliated himself, becoming obedient to the extent of death—the death of the cross. (Philippians 2:5–8, author's translation)

Though Jesus Christ was in the "form of God" (μορφὴ θεοῦ), he takes the form of a slave (μορφὴ δούλου; Phil 2:6–7).[57] For an audience in Roman Philippi, this imagery would be unsettling (to say the least).[58] Becoming a slave was feared across the Roman Empire. While many slaves were born into slavery, freeborn people faced the dangers of kidnapping and capture in war. Stories of freeborn people who were enslaved by one means or another emphasize the emasculating shame of the loss of power, the privilege of chastity, and the ability to protect one's own body against physical abuse.[59]

In some of these stories, the new slaves attempt suicide to save themselves from the shame of slavery (especially rape).[60] In the popular story of a Spartan boy captured in war, however, suicide is the response to the general work of slaves. According to Plutarch's version, so long as the boy was given jobs that could be done honorably by a freeborn man, he obeyed. But when tasked with a shameful job, work that would dishonor a freeborn man, the boy killed himself (*Apoph.* 69.38).[61] Plutarch's story recalls the manly reputation of the Spartans (a significant concern throughout *Apoph.* 69). In the context of the Roman Empire, the story reinforces masculine honor, and the inability of slaves to attain (or maintain) masculinity.

Unlike the Spartan boy, Jesus is not enslaved through capture in war—he chooses this identity, as is apparent in his refusal to use his equality with God to his own advantage (ἁρπαγμός), his self-referential emptying (ἑαυτὸν ἐκένωσεν), and his "taking" the form of a slave.[62] The voluntary nature of Jesus's actions mark them as distinctly different from the normal experiences of enslavement. Nonetheless, for an audience in Roman Philippi, Jesus's rapid descent from the form of God to the form of a slave would be perceived as humiliating and degrading.[63] The realities and representations of enslavement also provide a particular meaning to the idea of emptying in verse 7.

---

57. This imagery may be influenced by Isaiah's servant songs (see Keown, *Philippians*, 355–56).

58. See O'Brien, *Philippians*, 222–23; Fee, *Philippians*, 213; and Hellerman, *Reconstructing Honor*, 136–40.

59. E.g., Diodorus Siculus 1.48.2, 13.58.1–2, 17.35.3–17; Chariton, *Callirhoe* 2.9.6–7; Seneca, *Ira* 3.29.1, *Phoen.* 571–76; Bradley, *Slavery*, 32–39; Glancy, *Slavery*, 73–80. Consequently, status anxiety was expressed in various ways across the Empire (see Briggs, "Bondage and Freedom," 121; Glancy, *Slavery*, 71–72).

60. Diodorus Siculus 13.90.2; Valerius Maximus 3.2.12, 6.1, ext. 1, 3; Philo, *Prob.* 114–19; Josephus, *J.W.* 7.380–387; Reeder, *War and Peace*, 116–17.

61. See also Philo, *Prob.* 114; Seneca, *Ep.* 77.14–15. Plutarch also relates a version in which the enslaved Spartan is a woman (*Mor.* 242D [30]).

62. See further O'Brien, *Philippians*, 216; Keown, *Philippians*, 399–400, 416.

63. So Combes, *Metaphor of Slavery*, 69; Briggs, "Bondage and Freedom," 118; Hellerman, *Reconstructing Honor*, 136–42.

The contrast between the position of God and the position of a slave surely incorporates power, authority, self-control, honor (and the ability to live honorably), and even a fundamental sense of personhood into Jesus's kenosis.[64]

The description of Jesus's enslavement continues in verse 8 with the claim that Jesus humbled himself, ἐταπείνωσεν ἑαυτόν. ταπεινόω has a broad range of meaning. It is a positive virtue in the Bible.[65] This usage is comparatively rare, however; ταπεινόω more often carries the sense of humiliation. It represents abuse, including rape, and the oppressive treatment of slaves in the Septuagint.[66] In the Septuagint and Greek literature, a person of superior status or ability might forcibly humble or humiliate someone socially or politically.[67] For Plutarch, a person could be humiliated by working at dishonorable tasks or presenting themselves as cowardly, poor, and powerless (*Ant.* 83.1; *Cat. Min.* 21.4; *Per.* 2.1; [*Lib. ed.*] 2). More generally, ταπεινόω refers to an undesirably low social status (Aristotle, *Nic. Eth.* 1124b.26; Plutarch, *Per.* 24.4, *Sull.* 3.4), as suggested by Paul's representation of his own humiliation in 2 Cor 11:7.

Outside the New Testament (and Prov 13:7), ταπεινόω is not used with a reflexive pronoun. However, in the Gospels Jesus instructs his disciples to humble themselves (ταπεινόω ἑαυτόν; Matt 18:4, 23:12; Luke 14:11, 18:14). The act of humbling oneself contrasts with the standards of honor in Roman society.[68] In light of the range of meaning of ταπεινόω and its specific context alongside self-emptying and enslavement in Phil 2:6–8, ταπεινόω in verse 7 may be best translated as humiliation.[69] That is, the reference is not to an attitude of humility, but the social humiliation of enslavement. This includes a loss of masculinity. Manliness inflicts humiliation on others by its superior show of strength and power; manliness is lost in humiliation (cf. Diodorus Siculus 12.2.1; Plutarch, *Alex.* 71.1–3).

The sense of abasement in Jesus's slavery and self-humiliation is supported by the reference to obedience, ὑπήκοος. This particular term generally indicates the obedience of a social inferior to a superior (as in Prov 4:3; Acts 7:39; 2 Cor 2:9).[70] More specifically, it describes the enslavement of defeated enemies (Deut 20:11; Josh 17:13).[71]

---

64. Cf. Martin, *Carmen Christi*, 194–95; O'Brien, *Philippians*, 216–17; Hellerman, *Reconstructing Honor*, 135–36; Keown, *Philippians*, 406–8. On the long history of interpretation of kenosis, see Martin, *Carmen Christi*, 165–94.

65. Ps 18:27; Sir 3:18; Pr Azar 16; Jas 4:10; 1 Pet 5:6; Keown, *Philippians*, 344–45, 415.

66. For instance, Gen 15:13, 16:9, 31:50, 34:2; Exod 1:12; Deut 21:14, 22:24, 26:6; Judg 19:24; 1 Sam 12:8; 2 Sam 13:12. ταπεινόω also represents self-abasement and punishment for sin (e.g., Lev 16:29; 1 Kgs 8:35; Isa 2:9, 3:17; Lam 1:8; Hos 5:5).

67. Similarly, defeat in war is described as humiliation. See Judg 4:22; 1 Sam 7:10–13; Est 6:13; 2 Macc 8:35; Aristotle, *Pol.* 3.1284a.40; Polybius 3.85.7, 9.37.10; Plutarch, *Alcib.* 13.1, *Cim.* 12.1, *Them.* 22.3.

68. See also Hellerman, *Reconstructing Honor*, 143.

69. See Martin, *Carmen Christi*, 199, 217; Combes, *Metaphor of Slavery*, 92.

70. See also ὑπακοή in 2 Cor 10:5–6; Philem 21; 1 Pet 1:2; and ὑπακούω in Gen 16:2, 27:13; Lev 26:14; Deut 17:12; 1 Pet 3:6.

71. Cf. Aeschylus, *Pers.* 234; Diodorus Siculus 12.26.2; Pausanias 3.2.3.

The household codes in Eph 6:1, 5 and Col 3:20, 22 connect the cognate verb ὑπακούω with childhood and enslavement. Likewise, the obedience required of slaves gives significance to the metaphorical enslavement to sin and righteousness in Rom 6:12, 16–17. Across these references, obedience is not a term of equality, but subordination. The inclusion of obedience with its echoes of enslavement disrupts the representation of Jesus's volition in Phil 2:5–8. Once Jesus was "found" as a human/slave, he had no choice but obedience; his obedience confirms his enslavement.[72]

Cicero opposes honorable (Roman) freedom with obedient enslavement (*pareo* and *servio*) in Rab. Post. 22. Slavery is more generally connected with obedience throughout Greco-Roman sources.[73] While obedience in itself does not necessarily have gendered implications, when it is tied to slavery it affirms the oppression of the social system. The Spartan captive in Plutarch, *Apoph.* 69.38, was obedient (ὑπήκοος) only so long as his work was honorable. Once he was charged with a dishonorable task—that is, with the normal work of a slave—he killed himself rather than obey. In Phil 2:8, however, Jesus the slave is obedient to the point that he dies the most shameful death possible, crucifixion.

In Seneca's version of the story of the Spartan captive, the boy proves his essential masculine honor by suicide. For Seneca, even slaves and animals have life; manliness lies in the choice and manner of death (*Ep.* 77.6, 14–15). Jesus's death in Phil 2:8 is fundamentally opposed to such manly honor.[74] Crucifixion publicly, visibly demonstrated Rome's power over the bodies of slaves and conquered peoples. This method of execution was dishonorable and disgraceful (cf. Valerius Maximus 1.7.4, 2.7.12).[75] Crucifixion unmanned its victims, in Brittany Wilson's analysis.[76] Paul identifies the crucifixion of Jesus as a foolish message in 1 Cor 1:18–31, and a scandal (or stumbling stone) in Gal 5:11. In Phil 2:8, crucifixion marks the apex of Jesus's humiliation.[77] By the standards of the Roman Empire, Jesus is abased, humiliated, and unmanned in his obedient enslavement to the point of death.

Of course, in the message of the gospel it is precisely in the apparent conquest of Jesus on the cross that Jesus conquers. In Phil 2:9–11, because of his obedience Jesus is exalted to the highest status, and receives the name above all names—Yahweh's

---

72. Cf. Hellerman, *Reconstructing Honor*, 143.

73. See, e.g., Xenophon, *Oec.* 13; Plautus, *Capt.* 345–50, 402–17; Livy 30.16.7.

74. Contra Keown, *Philippians*, 417.

75. See also O'Brien, *Philippians*, 229–30; Hellerman, *Reconstructing Honor*, 144–47; Keown, *Philippians*, 419–20.

76. Wilson, *Unmanly Men*, 21, 190–91. See also Conway, *Behold the Man*, 67.

77. Martin, *Carmen Christi*, 221–22; Combes, *Metaphor of Slavery*, 92. Conway, *Behold the Man*, 70–73, argues that noble martyr traditions give New Testament authors a way to interpret Jesus's death as manly. But crucifixion is not a means of death in noble martyr traditions; rather, crucifixion represents an unmanly, weak, and shameful death. Jesus's death may sometimes be presented as a manly noble death (though see Wilson, *Unmanly Men*, 190–91, 206–7, on this point), but this is not the case in Phil 2:8.

name (Isa 45:23).[78] Colleen Conway argues on the basis of verses 9 through 11 that Paul represents Jesus according to ideal, hegemonic Roman masculinity.[79] However, the vocabulary of enslavement, humiliation, obedience, and crucifixion in the first half of the text raises serious questions concerning this conclusion. The exaltation of Jesus certainly restores his original status, but the complete Christology of Phil 2:5–11 holds humiliation and exaltation in tension.

In Phil 2:5–11, Paul undermines Jesus's masculinity by depicting him in the acts of self-emptying, willing enslavement, self-humiliation, and obedience even to the point of crucifixion. Notably, in the greeting of this letter Paul presents himself and Timothy as slaves (1:1). He calls the Christians of Philippi to be like Jesus by being unified with each other; doing nothing out of selfish ambition or "empty-glory" (κενοδοξία); in humility (ταπεινοφροσύνη) regarding others as better than themselves; putting the needs of others above their own; and always obeying (ὑπακούω; 2:2–4, 12). In other words, in their imitation of Jesus, the Philippians should reject Roman ideal masculinity.[80] Their self-emasculation will, like Jesus's, be honored by God (cf. 3:20–21).[81]

Christology, Gender, and Slavery

Even accounting for local variance across the Roman Empire, the fundamental commonality of constructions of elite masculinity around the values of power, discipline, and honor emasculates and, consequently, dehumanizes slaves. The New Testament Christology of Jesus as slave therefore disrupts the expectations of honorable masculinity in the Roman world. The intersection of gender and slavery in Roman understanding marks the representations of Jesus in Luke 22:24–27 and Phil 2:5–11 as deeply, thoroughly unmasculine.

Moreover, Jesus's essential unmanliness provides a model for the disciples in Luke and for the Philippian Christians. Those who are "in Christ" should not pursue the values and expectations of normative masculinity, but instead take on the identity of slaves who work for the benefit of others. The challenge of this message is marked in a first century context. It is no less challenging or important today. What might Jesus's disruption of the privileging of power and status mean for us? In a society in which public presentation matters just as much as in the Roman world, how might we give up selfish ambition and self-glorification to glorify and support others? Who are the

---

78. Hellerman, *Reconstructing Honor*, 151–52, also sees a reference to the emperor and imperial cult in κύριος.

79. Conway, *Behold the Man*, 80. Conway does not address verses 5 through 8. Shaner, "Rape and Robbery," 362–63, presents a more nuanced argument on this point.

80. Cf. Hellerman, *Reconstructing Honor*, 148–54.

81. The reversal from humiliation to exaltation is a common theme in the New Testament (e.g., Matt 18:4, 23:12; Luke 1:52; Jas 4:10; 1 Pet 5:6). See further O'Brien, *Philippians*, 252–53.

equivalents of the youngest and those who serve in menial, dishonorable tasks in our society, with whom Christian leaders today should identify?

With respect to this final question, I return to the example of John Walton. John models the *imitatio Christi* that Paul proclaims in Phil 2:1–5 through his support for current and former students in general, and more specifically for women (who remain underrepresented in biblical studies). The number of women at John's annual breakfast for current and former students is truly remarkable—visible proof of John's willingness to set aside personal glory to serve others, including those who haven't always had advocates (notable here as well is the list of student researchers John acknowledges in *The Lost World of Adam and Eve* as influences on his writing, nearly all of whom are women). I am deeply grateful for his influence in my life as teacher, mentor, and friend.

Bibliography

Barreto, Eric D. "A Gospel on the Move: Practice, Proclamation, and Place in Luke-Acts." *Int* 72 (2018) 175–87.

Boatwright, Mary T. "Women and Gender in the Forum Romanum." *Transactions of the American Philological Association* 141 (2011) 105–41.

Bovon, François. *Luke 3: Commentary on 19:28—24:53*. Translated by James Crouch. Hermeneia. Minneapolis: Fortress, 2012.

Bradley, Keith. *Slavery and Society at Rome*. Cambridge: Cambridge University Press, 1994.

Briggs, Sheila. "Paul on Bondage and Freedom in Imperial Roman Society." In *Paul and Politics: Ekklesia, Israel, Imperium, Interpretation*, edited by Richard A. Horsley, 110–23. Harrisburg, PA: Trinity, 2000.

Carroll, John T. "The Gospel of Luke: A Contemporary Cartography." *Int* 68 (2014) 366–75.

Carroll, John T. *Luke: A Commentary*. NTL. Louisville: Westminster John Knox, 2012.

Clark, Kenneth Willis. "The Meaning of [Kata]Kyrieyein." In *Studies in New Testament Language and Text*, edited by George Dunbar Kilpatrick and J. K. Elliott, 100–105. NovT Supplement 44. Leiden: Brill, 1976.

Cohen, Edward E. "The High Cost of Andreia at Athens." In *Andreia: Studies in Manliness and Courage in Classical Antiquity*, edited by Ralph M. Rosen and Ineke Sluiter, 145–65. Mnemosyne Supplement 238. Leiden: Brill, 2003.

Combes, I. A. H. *The Metaphor of Slavery in the Writings of the Early Church: From the New Testament to the Beginning of the Fifth Century*. JSNTSup 156. Sheffield: Sheffield Academic, 1998.

Conway, Colleen M. *Behold the Man: Jesus and Greco-Roman Masculinity*. Oxford: Oxford University Press, 2008.

D'Angelo, Mary Rose. "The ANHP Question in Luke-Acts: Imperial Masculinity and the Deployment of Women in the Early Second Century." In *A Feminist Companion to Luke*, edited by Amy-Jill Levine, 44–69. London: Sheffield Academic, 2002.

Dunbabin, Katherine M. D. *The Roman Banquet: Images of Conviviality*. Cambridge: Cambridge University Press, 2003.

Fee, Gordon D. *Paul's Letter to the Philippians*. NICNT. Grand Rapids: Eerdmans, 1995.

Foxhall, Lin. *Studying Gender in Classical Antiquity*. Key Themes in Ancient History. Cambridge: Cambridge University Press, 2013.

Glancy, Jennifer. *Slavery in Early Christianity*. Minneapolis: Fortress, 2006.

Gleason, Maud W. *Making Men: Sophists and Self-Presentation in Ancient Rome*. Princeton: Princeton University Press, 1995.

González, Justo L. *The Story Luke Tells: Luke's Unique Witness to the Gospel*. Grand Rapids: Eerdmans, 2015.

Gooder, Paula. "*Diakonia* in the New Testament: A Dialogue with John N. Collins." *Ecclesiology* 3 (2006) 33–56.

Green, Joel B. *The Gospel of Luke*. NICNT. Grand Rapids: Eerdmans, 1997.

Hellerman, Joseph H. *Reconstructing Honor in Roman Philippi:* Carmen Christi *as* Cursus Pudorum. SNTSMS 132. Cambridge: Cambridge University Press, 2005.

Hentschel, Anni. *Diakonia im Neuen Testament*. WUNT 226. Tübingen: Mohr/Siebeck.

Hezser, Catherine. *Jewish Slavery in Antiquity*. Oxford: Oxford University Press, 2005.

Keown, Mark J. *Philippians 1:1—2:18*. Evangelical Exegetical Commentary. Bellingham, Wash.: Lexham, 2017.

Lull, David John. "The Servant-Benefactor as a Model of Greatness (Luke 22:24-30)." *NovT* 28 (1984) 289–305.

Martin, Dale B. *Slavery as Salvation: The Metaphor of Slavery in Pauline Christianity*. New Haven: Yale University Press, 1990.

Martin, R. P. *Carmen Christi: Philippians ii.5-11 in Recent Interpretation and in the Setting of Early Christian Worship*. Cambridge: Cambridge University Press, 1967.

McDonnell, Myles. *Roman Manliness: Virtus and the Roman Republic*. Cambridge: Cambridge University Press, 2006.

Morley, Neville. "Slavery Under the Principate." In *The Cambridge World History of Slavery, Volume 1: The Ancient Mediterranean World*, edited by Keith Bradley and Paul Cartledge, 265–86. Cambridge: Cambridge University Press, 2011.

Nelson, Peter K. "The Flow of Thought in Luke 22.24-27." *JSNT* 43 (1991) 113–23.

Nelson, Peter K. "The Unitary Character of Luke 22.24-30." *NTS* 40 (1994) 609–19.

Polybius. Translated by W. R. Paton and S. Douglas Olson. 6 vols. Loeb Classical Library. Cambridge: Harvard University Press, 2010–2012.

Reeder, Caryn A. *Gendering War and Peace in the Gospel of Luke*. Cambridge: Cambridge University Press, 2018.

Reeder, Caryn A. *Slavery in the New Testament*. Grove Biblical 93. Cambridge: Grove, 2019.

Roller, Matthew B. *Dining Posture in Ancient Rome: Bodies, Values, and Status*. Princeton: Princeton University Press, 2006.

Scaer, Peter J. *The Lukan Passion and the Praiseworthy Death*. New Testament Monographs 10. Sheffield: Sheffield Phoenix, 2005.

Shaner, Katherine A. "Seeing Rape and Robbery: ἁρπαγμός and the Philippians Christ Hymn (Phil. 2:5-11)." *BibInt* 25 (2017) 342–63.

Smith, Dennis E. "Table Fellowship as a Literary Motif in the Gospel of Luke." *JBL* 106 (1987) 613–38.

Via, E. Jane. "Women, the Discipleship of Service, and the Early Christian Ritual Meal in the Gospel of Luke." *Saint Luke's Journal of Theology* 29 (1985) 37–60.

Walton, John H. *The Lost World of Adam and Eve: Genesis 2–3 and the Human Origins Debate*. Downers Grove, IL: IVP Academic, 2015.

Part 3: Context

Westfall, Cynthia Long. *Paul and Gender: Reclaiming the Apostle's Vision for Men and Women in Christ*. Grand Rapids: Baker Academic, 2016.
Wiedemann, Thomas. *Greek and Roman Slavery*. London: Routledge, 2005 (1981).
Wilson, Brittany E. *Unmanly Men: Refigurations of Masculinity in Luke-Acts*. Oxford: Oxford University Press, 2015.

19

The Sword of YHWH

*The Human Use of Divine Weapons
in the Ancient Near East and the Hebrew Bible*

Charlie Trimm

Introduction

JOHN WALTON HAS BEEN a pioneer in helping evangelicals understand the importance of the ancient Near Eastern context for Old Testament studies. Even though I never had the opportunity to take a class from him during my doctoral program at Wheaton College, his influence on me at that time was immense, both through his publications and through my work as his teacher's assistant. I am personally grateful to him for the introduction to the world of ancient Near Eastern iconography I acquired when he assigned me to compile a picture index for the massive five volume *Zondervan Illustrated Bible Backgrounds Commentary*. As I have remained in touch with him over the years I have benefited first-hand from his strong desire to help younger scholars flourish.

In light of his interest in the ancient Near East and its role in helping us understand the Old Testament, I am honored to contribute this study of a common phenomenon in both the ancient Near East and the Old Testament: divine weapons. These weapons range from human weapons to weapons appropriate only for gods, such as lightning. However, their divine status did not mean that they had no impact on human life; as John Walton says, "Life was religion and religion could not be compartmentalized within life."[1] Since the king was appointed by the warrior god to lead the nation, a common symbol of kingship throughout the ancient Near East was the

---

1. Walton, *Ancient Near Eastern Thought*, 47.

transfer of the divine weapon to the king for his use in battle. After briefly surveying this ancient Near Eastern evidence for the human use of divine weapons in battle, the paper will look at the Hebrew Bible's depiction of YHWH's divine weapons.

ANE Divine Weapons

Before examining the Old Testament, we will begin by looking at the passing of divine weapons to kings in several ancient Near Eastern cultures.[2] References to divine weapons are sparse in Hittite and West Semitic literature. In a prayer to the Sun-goddess of Arinna, Hattusili referred briefly to previous kings "to whom the Storm-god had given the weapon."[3] Weapons found in sanctuaries in Ugarit might have been viewed as divine weapons.[4] A king of Alalakh employed a divine weapon against his enemies.[5]

However, divine weapons are abundant in Egypt and Mesopotamia, especially in Egyptian reliefs (Figure 1 and Figure 2).[6] A relief of Seti I records Amun's words to Pharaoh while the god holds out a sword to the king: "Receive unto yourself the scimitar, (O) mighty king, as your mace has smitten the Nine Bows!"[7] Ramses III wrote that Amun promised to give him his sword. "I give to you my Sword as a shield for your breast, while I remain as the magical protection of your body in every battle."[8] Later in Egyptian history, Sheshonq I chronicled that Amun told him "With my mighty sword, you have struck every land in a feat of victory."[9]

In early Mesopotamia, Sargon the Great boasted that he "conquered fifty governors with the mace of the god Ilaba."[10] Naram-Sin employed several divine weapons in his attacks against his enemies: "by means of the weapons of the god Dagān, who magnifies his kingship, Narām-Sîn, the mighty, conquered Armānum and Ebla."[11] The Babylonian king Samsu-iluna claimed he received a weapon from the gods: "on account of this the gods An, Enlil, Marduk, Enki, and goddess Inanna determined as his destiny (and) gave to him a mighty weapon that has no rival (and) a life that like

---

2. For more on divine weapons and other connections king made with mythic material, see Trimm, *Fighting for the King and the Gods*, 606–17.

3. SBLWAW 11.21 (CTH 383) in Singer, *Hittite Prayers*, 100.

4. Vidal, "Ugarit at War (4)."

5. #1 in Wiseman, *The Alalakh Tablets*, 25.

6. Masetti-Rouault, "Armes et armées des dieux," 219–29; Töyräänvuori, "Weapons of the Storm God," 147–80.

7. Epigraphic Survey, *Reliefs and Inscriptions at Karnak 4*, 51, plate 15.

8. "Medinet Habu Pylon, Southern Triumphal-Scene and Topographical List" in Kitchen, *Ramesside Inscriptions: Translated & Annotated: Setnakht, Ramesses III, and Contemporaries*, 72.

9. SBLWAW 21.48 in Ritner, *The Libyan Anarchy*, 204.

10. Lines 15–18 of E2.1.1.2 in Frayne, *Sargonic and Gutian Periods*, 13.

11. Lines i.30—ii.7 of 2.1.4.26 in Frayne, *Sargonic and Gutian Periods*, 133.

(that of) the gods Nannu and Utu is eternal."[12] The divine weapon also played a role in legal proceedings as a place to swear oaths: if the oath-taker broke the oath, then the divine weapon would assault them.[13]

Figure 19.1: Amun Holding Divine Weapon before Ramses III
Medinet Habu, Egypt; Photo courtesy of author

Figure 19.2: Horus Holding Divine Weapon before Ramses II
*Beirut National Museum; Photo courtesy of Roman Deckert/Wikimedia Commons
(https://commons.wikimedia.org/wiki/File:NationalMuseumBeirut_RamsesII-BasaltStele-Tyre-13cBC_RomanDeckert31102019.jpg)*

The clearest connection between the use of the divine weapon to defeat divine enemies and its deposition with a king is found in a Mari prophecy by Adad to

---

12. Lines 77–89 of 4.3.7.8 in Frayne, *Old Babylonian Period*, 391.

13. On the use of divine weapons in legal contexts, see Harris, "The Journey of the Divine Weapon," 217–24; Stol, "Renting the Divine Weapon as a Prebend," 561–83; Kitz, *Cursed Are You!*, 56–61.

Zimri-Lim. After disclosing how he had taken away land from the king, Adad declared that he had given his weapons to the king. "I restored you to the th[rone of your father's house], and the weapon[s] with which I fought with Sea I handed you. I anointed you with the oil of my luminosity, nobody will offer resistance to you."[14] A pair of reliefs found in a temple at Aleppo might also refer to the handing over of the divine weapon to the king.[15] In one relief the storm god is portrayed as an armed divine warrior by himself, while in the other relief the storm god and the king both appear unarmed but in martial poses. Most likely, the missing weapon would have been physically present in the temple itself. A parallel to support this is the Mari letter that reports that the weapons of Addu had arrived in Terqa in the temple of Dagan.[16]

Neo-Assyrian texts also refer frequently to divine weapons being granted to the kings and used in battle. Shalmaneser III boasted that "With the exalted might of the divine standard which goes before me (and) with the fierce weapons which Aššur my lord gave to me, I fought (and) defeated them."[17] Ishtar gave Esarhaddon "a strong bow (and) a mighty arrow", while Ashur provided him with "a terrible staff to strike the enemy."[18] Another important aspect of the divine weapon was the placement of the divine weapon in a conquered location as a reminder of the power of Ashur.[19] For example, after conquering Illubru, Sennacherib settled foreigners in the city and said that "I installed the weapon of the god Aššur, my lord, inside."[20]

Finally, even the neo-Babylonian texts, which refer to warfare far less than the Assyrian texts, frequently refer to divine weapons. Nabopolassar recorded that Marduk "made (me) hold a mighty staff to subdue the unsubmissive."[21] In another inscription he stated that he killed Assyrians "with the mighty weapon of the awe-inspiring Erra, who strikes my enemies with lightning."[22] Likewise, Neriglissar said that Marduk "let my hands hold an *ušparu*-staff, who subdues the enemy."[23] Vari-

---

14. SBLWAW 12.2/A.1968/FM 7.38; translation from Nissinen, *Prophets and Prophecy in the Ancient Near East*, 22. However, the historical context of this scenario is complicated; for a discussion see Ballentine, *The Conflict Myth and the Biblical Tradition*, 115–16; Tugendhaft, *Baal and the Politics of Poetry*, 47–61.

15. For a summary of the reliefs, see Töyräänvuori, "Weapons of the Storm God," 161–62.

16. A.1858/LAPO 18 982; translation in Sasson, *From the Mari Archives*, 257.

17. Lines i.44–45 of A.0.102.2 in Grayson, *Assyrian Rulers of the Early First Millennium BC II*, 16.

18. Lines Rev. 28, 33–35 of Esarhaddon 98 in Leichty, *The Royal Inscriptions of Esarhaddon*, 184–85.

19. For more on this, see Holloway, *Aššur Is King! Aššur Is King!*, 160–77.

20. Line iv.89 of Sennacherib 17 in Grayson and Novotny, *The Royal Inscriptions of Sennacherib, Part 1*, 136.

21. Riva, *The Inscriptions of Nabopolassar, Amel-Marduk, and Neriglissar*, 75.

22. Riva, *The Inscriptions of Nabopolassar, Amel-Marduk, and Neriglissar*, 88.

23. Riva, *The Inscriptions of Nabopolassar, Amel-Marduk, and Neriglissar*, 119.

ous temple records even refer to deified weapons, such as a divine staff and divine quiver, in ritual and legal contexts.[24]

In sum, throughout the ancient Near East not only is the idea of a divine weapon common, but the motif of a god giving a divine weapon to a human (always a king) is also widespread. This provides us with a solid foundation to now turn to the Old Testament and compare and contrast the evidence found there.

Divine Weapons in the OT

We will begin our study of the Old Testament by examining the divine weapons ascribed to YHWH.[25] The most common human weapon associated with YHWH is the sword. The Israelites were concerned about YHWH attacking them with a sword (Exod 5:3). In the covenant curses YHWH threatens Israel that he will destroy them with the sword if they mistreat the poor (Exod 22:24 [Heb 22:23]) or break the covenant (Lev 26:25; cf. v. 33). One of the more extended descriptions of this judgment is found in Deuteronomy.

> "If I sharpen my flashing sword and my hand takes hold on judgment, I will take vengeance on my adversaries and will repay those who hate me. I will make my arrows drunk with blood, and my sword shall devour flesh—with the blood of the slain and the captives, from the long-haired heads of the enemy." (Deut 32:41–42)[26]

The poetic texts frequently also ascribe a sword to YHWH. Psalms frequently refers to YHWH using (or threatening to use) a sword or bow against an enemy (Ps 7:12–13 [Heb 13–14]; 17:13). Likewise, prophetic texts frequently refer to YHWH's sword that he uses in judgment (Isa 66:16; Jer 12:12). The target of YHWH's sword varies in the prophetic texts. Sometimes YHWH's sword comes against Israel (Jer 29:17; Ezek 12:14). Frequently foreign nations are the target.

> "And the Assyrian shall fall by a sword, not of man; and a sword, not of man, shall devour him; and he shall flee from the sword, and his young men shall be put to forced labor." (Isa 31:8)

> "For my sword has drunk its fill in the heavens; behold, it descends for judgment upon Edom, upon the people I have devoted to destruction. The LORD has a sword; it is sated with blood; it is gorged with fat, with the blood of lambs

---

24. Beaulieu, *The Pantheon of Uruk During the Neo-Babylonian Period*, 351–53.

25. A variety of other references close to the topic of divine weapons will be set aside for the purposes of this study. For example, Gideon's men called out "a sword for YHWH and for Gideon" (Judg 7:20), but this is an ironic reference since the men are not carrying swords. In addition, this refers to human weapons being used on behalf of God, not a divine weapon used by God.

26. All Bible translations are from the ESV.

and goats, with the fat of the kidneys of rams. For the LORD has a sacrifice in Bozrah, a great slaughter in the land of Edom." (Isa 34:5–6)

"Who stirred up one from the east whom victory meets at every step? He gives up nations before him, so that he tramples kings underfoot; he makes them like dust with his sword, like driven stubble with his bow." (Isa 41:2)

One remarkable text refers to Israel as the sword and bow of YHWH against a foreign nation (Zech 9:13). An unusual example involves defeating Leviathan: "In that day the LORD with his hard and great and strong sword will punish Leviathan the fleeing serpent, Leviathan the twisting serpent, and he will slay the dragon that is in the sea" (Isa 27:1)

YHWH is only rarely connected with other hand to hand weapons. Isaiah refers to Assyria as "the rod of my anger" (Isa 10:5).[27] One of the more extended texts describing his weaponry is missing a sword but includes a spear.

"You stripped the sheath from your bow, calling for many arrows. Selah. You split the earth with rivers. The mountains saw you and writhed; the raging waters swept on; the deep gave forth its voice; it lifted its hands on high. The sun and moon stood still in their place at the light of your arrows as they sped, at the flash of your glittering spear." (Hab 3:9–11)

YHWH also attacks his enemies with distance weapons, primarily the bow. Ironically, the first story of a divine weapon involves YHWH putting down his bow after the flood (Gen 9:13). However, he still used a bow on other occasions (Deut 32:23). YHWH's arrows are compared to thunder (2 Sam 22:15//Ps 18;14[Heb 15]; Ps 77:17[Heb 18]; 144:6; Zech 9:14) and famine (Ezek 5:16). Suffering caused by YHWH is sometimes described as the arrows of YHWH striking someone (Job 6:4; Ps 38:2[Heb 3]; Lam 3:12). The author of Lamentations describes YHWH killing his people with his bow (Lam 2:4; 3:12). However, his distance weapons also target the enemy (Ps 64:7). Finally, Jeremiah attributed the role of a slinger to YHWH: "For thus says the LORD: 'Behold, I am slinging out the inhabitants of the land at this time, and I will bring distress on them, that they may feel it'" (Jer 10:18).

YHWH Giving a Weapon to a Human

The Old Testament clearly refers to divine weapons belonging to YHWH. However, the main research question for this paper is whether YHWH ever gave these weapons to Israelites in the same way that the other ancient Near Eastern deities did. We will begin with some texts that approach this idea, but are fundamentally different. David talks about YHWH teaching him to fight (2 Sam 22:35//Ps 18:34[Heb 35]). The

---

27. For a study of how this reverses the motif in Assyrian royal annals of the Assyrian kings being weapons of their gods, see Salo, "Assur als Werkzeug Gottes im Alten Testament," 61–84.

servant in Isaiah speaks of God preparing him in martial terms. "He made my mouth like a sharp sword; in the shadow of his hand he hid me; he made me a polished arrow; in his quiver he hid me away." (Isa 49:2). However, neither of these examples include giving a divine weapon to a human.

The Old Testament contains several clearer cases of YHWH giving a weapon to a human. In the first, a sword is prepared and then given to the one killing, but it is not said specifically to be YHWH's sword (Ezek 21:9–11 [Heb 14–16]). In another case, the anointed one is appointed by YHWH to be king, who will defeats his enemies with a rod of iron. While the text does not record that YHWH gave the anointed one this weapon, one could logically deduce that this is the case (Psalm 2).

It is also possible that the "commander of YHWH's army" in Joshua 5:13–15 gave his sword to Joshua as part of a royal ritual.[28] Thomas Römer argues that the general gave Joshua this weapon because it would explain the origin of the weapon that Joshua held up in a later battle (Josh 8:18, 26).[29] However, the text provides no indication that the general handed Joshua a weapon and the words of the general focus attention on the need for Joshua to submit to YHWH's instructions, not on giving Joshua greater ability to fight. The word describing the weapon differs between the two texts well: the general has a sword (חרב), but Joshua later holds up a javelin (כידון).[30] While it is possible that the two words are synonyms,[31] the traditional understanding of the כידון as a javelin is most likely correct.[32] Therefore, it is unlikely that this text should be read as a divine weapon ritual text.

The clearest case of YHWH giving a weapon to a king is found in Ezekiel. However, instead of an Israelite king, it is a Babylonian king who receives YHWH's weapon!

> "And I will strengthen the arms of the king of Babylon and put my sword in his hand, but I will break the arms of Pharaoh, and he will groan before him like a man mortally wounded. I will strengthen the arms of the king of Babylon, but the arms of Pharaoh shall fall. Then they shall know that I am the LORD, when I put my sword into the hand of the king of Babylon and he stretches it out against the land of Egypt." (Ezek 30:24–25)

As part of his judgment against Israel, YHWH frequently employs the foreign nations as his weapon. As noted above, Isaiah refers to Assyria as the rod of YHWH's anger. However, this text goes one step further by not only describing the enemy nations

---

28. Other spirit beings who have swords include the cherubim at the garden of Eden (Gen 3:21) and the angel of YHWH that met Balaam (Num 22:23) and David (1 Chr 21:16).

29. Römer, "Joshua's Encounter with the Commander of Yhwh's Army," 49–64.

30. Römer explains the discrepancy by supposing that the two texts were written independently, but this would seem to destroy the main support for his position.

31. Calabro, "'He Teaches My Hands to War,'" 58.

32. The word appears elsewhere as a weapon of Goliath (1 Sam 17:6, 45) and in several generic lists of weapons (Job 39:23; 41:29[Heb 21]; Jer 6:23; 50:42). The LXX is inconsistent in translating the word, but uses γαίσῳ in Josh 8:18, which means javelin.

as weapons, but as giving his sword to the enemy king. A verse earlier in the chapter might also have a further reference to divine weapons: "I am against Pharaoh king of Egypt and will break his arms, both the strong arm and the one that was broken, and I will make the sword fall from his hand" (Ezek 30:22). Since Egyptian mythology refers to Pharaoh using a divine weapon (see references above), then perhaps this sword that Pharaoh can no longer use is a divine weapon.

The clearest case of YHWH giving an Israelite human leader a divine weapon occurs in the exodus narrative. When YHWH addressed Moses at the burning bush, he commanded Moses to perform a series of signs with his shepherd staff (Exod 4:2–4). A little later, he ordered Moses to take "this staff" with him when he went to Egypt (Exod 4:17), and the narrator records that he left with "the staff of God" (Exod 4:20). It appears that YHWH consecrated Moses' staff to become the staff of God, which Moses then employed before several of the plagues.[33]

However, even this case is not the same as a divine weapon in other ancient Near Eastern cultures. First, Moses only used the staff after YHWH instructed him how to use it each time. In the exodus narrative Moses does not have independent use of the staff to use it as he wills: each time he uses it, he uses it following the instructions of YHWH. This continues with the first episode of water from the rock, in which Moses used the staff only after God told him to use it (Exod 17:1–7). After the exodus narrative, Moses gains some measure of independent use of the staff. The battle against the Amalekites functions as a transition point in the narrative (Exod 17:8–16). While Joshua leads the troops in the valley, Moses was on the mountaintop supporting them. However, the text is somewhat ambiguous concerning the details: does he raise his two hands (symbolizing prayer) or the staff of God? I argue elsewhere that the narrative intentionally creates this ambiguity (what I call a macro-level Janus parallelism) as a way to show this transition. The staff of God motif recalls the exodus narrative, where the focus is on the power and initiative of God. The raising of Moses' hands looks forward to the time when God's people employ more initiative and trust in YHWH. The miracles of the exodus are not a promise that God will continue to do these miracles for Israel in the future. The connection of the staff of God with these non-repeating miracles implies that God giving a divine weapon to a human leader would not be a normal pattern.[34]

Second, he was eventually censured by YHWH when he used the staff incorrectly (Num 20:1–13). As previously, YHWH instructed Moses concerning the staff of God. In this case, he was to take the staff of God and speak to the rock. However, Moses hit the rock twice instead. While YHWH still provided water for the people, he condemned Moses and Aaron for not treating him as holy. This rather obscure statement has led to a variety of interpretations. One of the more common is that the problem

---

33. For more on this, see Trimm, *"YHWH Fights for Them!,"* 101–6.
34. See Trimm, "God's Staff and Moses' Hand(s)," 198–214.

lies in Moses hitting the rock with his staff rather than talking to it.[35] However, in at least half of the previous cases Moses also did not follow the instructions YHWH provided and he was not condemned. It is more likely that the problem lies in Moses' words: he claimed the miracle for himself by saying "shall we bring water out of this rock?" (Num 20:10).[36] This story illustrates that YHWH's divine weapon has strong limits: it cannot be used autonomously but only in the way that YHWH directs and for his glory.[37] This is parallel to the teaching about the Ark of the Covenant: its mere presence will not guarantee victory (1 Sam 4–6).

The Old Testament does not inform us why YHWH does not usually give his divine weapons to his human rulers. As seen above, it is not because he does not have divine weapons: the Old Testament contains abundant evidence that YHWH possesses a variety of such weapons. The theory I would propose is that this is part of an Old Testament theme of YHWH desiring his people to be weak according to standard measures of strength so that they trust him. In this case, the Israelite king could not place his trust in an object that would guarantee victory through the presence of the deity.[38] This theme appears in a variety of places in the Old Testament.

1. Unlike the other nations whose gods commanded their kings to conquer the world, YHWH gave land to other nations and prohibited Israel from taking that land (Deut 2:8–15).

2. YHWH promised to save the non-Israelite nations, like Assyria and Egypt, and not make them Israel (Isa 19). Nations could follow YHWH without being a part of Israel.

3. YHWH would attack Israel directly when they sin (Deut 2:8–15). The divine warrior would not automatically be on their side in battles.

---

35. For one interpretation that focuses on this aspect of the story, see Kok, *The Sin of Moses and the Staff of God*.

36. Olson, *Numbers*, 126–27; Cole, *Numbers*, 327–28. For the argument that Moses was condemned for both his actions and his words, see Burnside, "Why Was Moses Banned from the Promised Land?," 111–59. Jacob Milgrom argues that Moses speaking at all was the cause of the punishment in Milgrom, "Magic, Monotheism, and the Errors of Moses," 251–65; Milgrom, *Numbers*, 448–56. For an interesting narrative geographical argument that Moses was not allowed to use the staff in this account while he was in Exodus 17:1–6 because of geological differences (striking a rock in the location of the Exodus account would never bring water, while it possibly might cause water to flow from hidden pockets in the area of the Numbers account), see Beck, "Why Did Moses Strike Out?," 135–41.

37. Moses raising his hand with the staff before hitting the rock might refer to Moses' defiant attitude; see Wong, "'And Moses Raised His Hand' in Numbers 20,11," 397–400; Sonnet, "Nb 20,11: Moïse en flagrant délit de 'main levée'?," 535–43.

38. For other ways that Israelite kings were different from other ancient Near Eastern kings, see Walton, *Ancient Near Eastern Thought and the Old Testament*, 267–68; Hallo, "The Bible and the Monuments," xxi–xxvi.

4. Israel was to trust YHWH for their military power, not to become a military powerhouse. The law of the king prohibited the king from accumulating many horses and chariots (Deut 17:16). In that same line of reasoning, YHWH commanded Joshua to hamstring the captured horses and burn captured chariots (Josh 11:6).

5. Unlike other kings who wrote their own law, the king was commanded to copy for himself a copy of YHWH's law, not to make his own law (Deut 17:18–20).

6. The image of God has been democratized in Israel (Genesis 1). Rather than only the king being in the image of God, all humans (including all non-Israelites) are in the image of God.

7. Finally, the location of the land YHWH gave to Israel indicated weakness. If YHWH was sovereign over all the world, he could have given any land to his people. If he wanted Israel to become a powerful empire, he could have given Israel the area around the Nile or in Mesopotamia, where the rivers and the flat land were conducive for an empire. Instead, he gave Israel the land of Canaan with its many mountains and the relatively worthless Jordan River. Most problematically, Canaan occupied the heavily contested land bridge between Egypt and the Levant, leaving Israel frequently under attack from marauding imperial armies.

Conclusion

In sum, the ancient Near East frequently refers to the motif of divine warriors giving their weapons to kings to enable them to defeat their enemies. The Old Testament clearly portrays YHWH as a divine warrior who fights his enemies with divine weapons. However, the motif of handing his divine weapons over to humans is largely missing from the Old Testament. Besides a few questionable cases that might refer to the practice, two texts clearly refer to the practice. However, in both cases the normal practice seen elsewhere in the ancient Near East is not followed. In one case, YHWH gives his sword to Israel's enemy Babylon to empower them to fight against Israel. In the other case, YHWH gave his weapon to Moses, but only in carefully scripted ways. Further, Moses was rebuked for using the staff illegitimately. Moses' use of a divine weapon was not a paradigm for future rulers, but part of the foundational history of Israel. The reason for this avoidance of providing human rulers with divine weapons most likely is based on the common Old Testament theme of YHWH desiring his people to be weak according to common standards of strength so that they would trust him more.

Bibliography

Ballentine, Debra Scoggins. *The Conflict Myth and the Biblical Tradition*. Oxford: Oxford University Press, 2015.

Beck, John A. "Why Did Moses Strike Out? The Narrative-Geographical Shaping of Moses' Disqualification in Numbers 20:1–13." *WTJ* 65 (2003) 135–41.

Burnside, Jonathan P. "Why Was Moses Banned from the Promised Land? A Radical Retelling of the Rebellions of Moses (Num 20:2–13 and Exod 2:11–15)." *ZABR* 22 (2016) 111–59.

Calabro, David. "'He Teaches My Hands to War': The Semiotics of Ritual Hand Gestures in Ancient Israelite Warfare." In *War and Peace in the Jewish Tradition*, edited by Yigal Levin and Amnon Shapira, 51–61. Routledge Jewish Studies Series. London: Routledge, 2012.

Cole, R. Dennis. *Numbers*. NAC 4. Nashville: Broadman & Holman, 2000.

Epigraphic Survey. *Reliefs and Inscriptions at Karnak 4: The Battle Reliefs of King Sety I*. Oriental Institute Publications 107. Chicago: Oriental Institute, 1986.

Frayne, Douglas. *Old Babylonian Period (2003–1595 BC)*. RIME 4. Toronto: University of Toronto Press, 1990.

———. *Sargonic and Gutian Periods (2334–2113 BC)*. RIME 2. Toronto: University of Toronto Press, 1993.

Grayson, A. Kirk. *Assyrian Rulers of the Early First Millennium BC II (858–745 BC)*. RIMA 3. Toronto: University of Toronto Press, 1996.

Grayson, A. Kirk, and Jamie Novotny. *The Royal Inscriptions of Sennacherib, King of Assyria (704–681 BC), Part 1*. RINAP 3/1. Winona Lake, IN: Eisenbrauns, 2012.

Hallo, William H. "The Bible and the Monuments." In *The Context of Scripture: Monumental Inscriptions from the Biblical World*, edited by William W. Hallo, xxi–xxvi. Leiden: Brill, 2003.

Harris, Rivkah. "The Journey of the Divine Weapon." In *Studies in Honor of Benno Landsberger on His Seventy-Fifth Birthday*, edited by Hans G. Güterbock and Thorkild Jacobsen, 217–24. Assyriological Studies 16. Chicago: University of Chicago Press, 1965.

Holloway, Steven W. *Aššur Is King! Aššur Is King!: Religion in the Exercise of Power in the Neo-Assyrian Empire*. CHANE 10. Leiden: Brill, 2002.

Kitchen, K. A. *Ramesside Inscriptions: Translated & Annotated: Setnakht, Ramesses III, and Contemporaries*. Ramesside Inscriptions 5. Malden, MA: Blackwell, 2008.

Kitz, Anne Marie. *Cursed Are You! The Phenomenology of Cursing in Cuneiform and Hebrew Texts*. Winona Lake, IN: Eisenbrauns, 2014.

Kok, Johnson Lim Teng. *The Sin of Moses and the Staff of God: A Narrative Approach*. Studia Semitica Neerlandica 35. Assen: Van Gorcum, 1997.

Leichty, Erle. *The Royal Inscriptions of Esarhaddon, King of Assyria (680–669 BC)*. RINAP 4. Winona Lake, IN: Eisenbrauns, 2011.

Masetti-Rouault, Maria Grazia. "Armes et armées des dieux dans les traditions mésopotamiennes." In *Les armées du Proche-Orient ancien (IIIe–Ier mill. av. J.-C.): Actes du colloque international organisé à Lyon les 1er et 22 décembre 2006, Maison de l'Orient et de la Méditerranée*, edited by Philippe Abrahami and Laura Battini, 219–29. British Archaeological Reports Series 1855. Oxford: John and Erica Hedges, 2008.

Milgrom, Jacob. "Magic, Monotheism, and the Errors of Moses." In *The Quest for the Kingdom of God: Studies in Honor of George E. Mendenhall*, edited by Herbert B. Huffmon, Frank A. Spina, and A. R. W. Green, 251–65. Winona Lake, IN: Eisenbrauns, 1983.

———. *Numbers*. The JPS Torah Commentary. Philadelphia: Jewish Publication Society, 1990.
Nissinen, Martti. *Prophets and Prophecy in the Ancient Near East*. SBLWAW 12. Atlanta: Society of Biblical Literature, 2003.
Olson, Dennis T. *Numbers*. Interpretation. Louisville: John Knox, 1996.
Ritner, Robert K. *The Libyan Anarchy: Inscriptions from Egypt's Third Intermediate Period*. SBLWAW 21. Atlanta: Society of Biblical Literature, 2009.
Riva, Rocío Da. *The Inscriptions of Nabopolassar, Amel-Marduk, and Neriglissar*. Studies in Ancient Near Eastern Records 3. Berlin: De Gruyter, 2013.
Römer, Thomas. "Joshua's Encounter with the Commander of Yhwh's Army (Josh 5:13–15): Literary Construction or Reflection of a Royal Ritual?" In *Warfare, Ritual, and Symbol in Biblical and Modern Contexts*, edited by Brad E. Kelle, Frank Ritchel Ames, and Jacob L. Wright, 49–64. SBL Ancient Israel and Its Literature 18. Atlanta: Society of Biblical Literature, 2014.
Salo, Reettakaisa Sofia. "Assur als Werkzeug Gottes im Alten Testament." In *Religion und Krieg*, edited by Rüdiger Schmitt, 61–84. MARG 22. Münster: Ugarit-Verlag, 2015.
Sasson, Jack M. *From the Mari Archives: An Anthology of Old Babylonian Letters*. Winona Lake, IN: Eisenbrauns, 2015.
Singer, Itamar. *Hittite Prayers*. SBLWAW 11. Atlanta: Society of Biblical Literature, 2002.
Sonnet, Jean-Pierre. "Nb 20,11: Moïse en flagrant délit de 'main levée'?" In *The Books of Leviticus and Numbers*, edited by Thomas Römer, 535–43. Leuven: Peeters, 2008.
Stol, Martin. "Renting the Divine Weapon as a Prebend." In *The Ancient Near East, A Life! Festschrift Karel Van Lerberghe*, edited by Tom Boiy, Joachim Bretschneider, Anne Goddeeris, Hendrik Hameeuw, Greta Jans, and Jan Tavernier, 561–83. Leuven: Peeters, 2012.
Töyräänvuori, Joanna. "Weapons of the Storm God in Ancient Near Eastern and Biblical Traditions." *Studia Orientalia* 112 (2012) 147–80.
Trimm, Charlie. *Fighting for the King and the Gods: A Survey of Warfare in the Ancient Near East*. Resources for Biblical Literature 88. Atlanta: Society of Biblical Literature, 2017.
———. "God's Staff and Moses' Hand(s): The Battle against the Amalekites as a Turning Point in the Role of the Divine Warrior." *JSOT* 44 (2019) 198–214.
———. *"YHWH Fights for Them!": The Divine Warrior in the Exodus Narrative*. Piscataway, NJ: Gorgias, 2014.
Tugendhaft, Aaron. *Baal and the Politics of Poetry*. Ancient Word. London: Routledge, 2018.
Vidal, Jordi. "Ugarit at War (4): Weapons in Sanctuaries." *UF* 43 (2013) 449–57.
Walton, John H. *Ancient Near Eastern Thought and the Old Testament: Introducing the Conceptual World of the Hebrew Bible*. 2nd ed. Grand Rapids: Baker, 2018.
Wiseman, D. J. *The Alalakh Tablets*. Occasional Publications of the British Institute of Archaeology at Ankara 2. London: British Institute of Archaeology at Ankara, 1953.
Wong, K. L. "'And Moses Raised His Hand' in Numbers 20,11." *Bib* 89 (2008) 397–400.

20

David's Census and the Fate of the Canaanites

Joshua T. Walton

Introduction

KING DAVID IS ONE of the most positively portrayed figures in the Hebrew Bible. As many scholars have pointed out, the literary traditions of David shaped by the biblical authors go to great lengths to idealize his reign and to glorify the Davidic dynasty.[1] Yet despite this process of idealization, there are two clear instances in which David's actions were deemed explicitly sinful.[2] The first is the Bathsheba incident (2 Sam 11–12), the sin of which appears clear and inexcusable (and conveniently omitted by the Chronicler). The second instance, recorded in 2 Sam 24 (see also 1 Chr 21),[3] is David's census of Israel. This second episode is surprising. At face value, there appears to be nothing inherently wrong with taking a census of the people; and yet, every character in the story, including David himself, acknowledges his transgression (2 Sam 24:11). Even Joab, not remembered as the most godly of individuals by the biblical authors, immediately recognizes the sinfulness of the action. That the pro-David biblical authors included this account attests to their recognition of the sinfulness of David's action, and their need to describe the divinely invoked consequences. Despite this, David's exact sin in counting the men of Israel and Judah has eluded scholarly

---

1. See Knapp, *Royal Apologetic*, 161–248; Bar-Efrat, "From History to Story," 45; Halpern, *David's Secret Demons*; Baden, *The Historical David*; McCarter, "The Apology of David." Although some scholars (e.g. Campbell, "2 Sam 21–24") have suggested that certain waves of tradition preserved in the biblical text have a less idealistic view of King David.

2. Although one could convincingly argue for many more implicit critiques of David's actions.

3. The main focus of this essay will be on the narrative as presented in 2 Sam 24. There are some important differences between the texts (see, e.g., Auld, "David's Census"), but these textual variations are less significant for the broader argument of the present study.

consensus, which collectively concedes that David's offense in census-taking is neither explicitly mentioned nor immediately apparent. John Walton has been a long-time champion for the usefulness of comparative ancient Near Eastern literature for helping the reader to make sense of seemingly difficult passages, such as David's census. In particular, Walton has argued that the Bible and other ancient Near Eastern literature share a common cultural environment that should be investigated using "cognitive environment criticism," to combine background, cultural, and comparative studies.[4] In the following, I apply Walton's methodological principles to better understand the concept of "census" in the ancient Near East and I argue that David's sin was the violation of the divine command to drive out the Canaanites from the land, and instead enacting the formal incorporation of these Canaanite populations into his newly formed state.

Previous Interpretations

There are three main ways that scholars have tried to deal with the situation. The first suggests that the sin derived from some ancient taboo against counting or a general conception that counting was an activity reserved for the deity.[5] By counting the people David was infringing upon God's sovereignty.[6] This response is not satisfying, as many commentators have noted, because there are many example of counting and census taking in the Bible (e.g., Exod 30; 2 Chr 2; Ezra 2; Num 1; Num 31), none of which receive divine rebuke.[7]

A second suggestion is that the sin is procedural, that is, in how David conducted the census. This explanation hypothesizes that David failed to levy an appropriate ransom payment (*kōper*) as mandated by Exod 30:12.[8] According to this interpretation, purity requirements were necessary as part of census-taking, based in part on parallels from Mari, where the verb to take a census is derived from the Akkadian root *ebēbum*–meaning to be clean or pure.[9] Because registering the population in a census was for the conscription of soldiers as a prelude to war, in which purity violations were inevitable, a ransom to absolve those future violations was necessary. David's sin was an inevitable purity violation, which he failed to protect against by collecting the precautionary *kōper*.[10]

---

4. Walton, *Ancient Near Eastern Thought*, 11.

5. See Speiser, "Census and Ritual Expiation"; Frazer *Folk-Lore in the Old Testament*.

6. Park, "Census and Censure," 36.

7. See Neufeld, "Sins of the Census," 198; Firth *1 & 2 Samuel*, 540; Evans, *1 and 2 Samuel*, 247. It is also possible that the authors of these passages, which are not part of the Deuteronomistic history/tradition, may have other goals and agendas.

8. Tsumura, *The Second Book of Samuel*, 341; Weinfeld, "The Census in Mari," 297; Klement, *2 Samuel 21–24*, 178; Schenker, *Der Mächtige im Schmelzofen*, 18; Bergen, *1,2 Samuel*, 475. This is also the explanation settled upon by early rabbinic commentators and Josephus.

9. Speiser, "Census and Ritual Expiation."

10. McCarter, *II Samuel*, 513–14.

However, such a payment is not explicitly mentioned in the case of other censuses, none of which end in a disastrous plague, and the punishment would seem extreme as a response to a procedural faux pas.[11] Greenwood further argues that the collection of the *kōper* in Exod 30 had a particular function (for the construction of the tabernacle) and was not intended as a lasting ordinance or binding institution.[12]

Most commentators focus on a third explanation, and find fault with why David decided to undertake a census. According to this line of thought, David did not trust in God by evaluating the military might of Israel on his own. The sin here was pride or hubris, perhaps with David trying to usurp Yahweh's authority in matters of state.[13] A derivation of this idea considers David as trusting in numbers and his own talent for military organization instead of putting his faith in Yahweh.[14] However, if the offense was David's pride or hubris, then it is unclear why the entire community was punished. In this case, Greenwood rightfully questions "why this particular occurrence would have resulted in consequences more harsh than other examples of hubris."[15] In a variation, Greenwood points to David's motivations and posits that by commanding a census David made plans to organize corvée labor for construction of the temple—an unauthorized project that he had been forbidden from completing.[16] None of these solutions is particularly satisfying, and none of them adequately explains Joab's opposition.[17]

There is another possibility for identifying David's sin that to my knowledge has not yet been proposed. Rather than David's sin residing in what, how, or why he conducted the census, the sin lies in who David was counting and the implicit connotation that counting a population represented a means of incorporating new groups into an expanding state or empire. If we understand David's census as including an accounting of foreigners living within the borders of Israel, then the violation was incorporating the local Canaanite populations into the broader Israelite socio-political community. Mettinger already linked David's census with the incorporation of Canaanite territories, with the suggestion that "This census was evidently a step taken in order to confirm the Israelite supremacy over these new dominions."[18] Similarly, Adler had considered the sin "for failing to carry out God's injunction concerning the conquest of the seven nations who inhabited Canaan (Deut 20:17)," and specifically

11. Adler, "David's Last Sin," 93.

12. Greenwood, "Labor Pains," 469.

13. Firth, *1 & 2 Samuel*, 541; Tsumura, *Second Book of Samuel*, 341; Adler, *David's Last Sin*, 91; Brueggemann, "2 Samuel 21–24," 393; Evans, *1 and 2 Samuel*, 247; Omanson and Ellington, *Handbook on First and Second Samuel*, 1179–80; Klement, *II Samuel 21–24*, 178.

14. Klement, *II Samuel 21–24*, 179; Stolz, *Das erste und zweite Buch Samuel*, 301; Auld, *I & II Samuel*, 609; Cartledge, *1 & 2 Samuel*, 700.

15. Greenwood, "Labor Pains," 468.

16. Greenwood, "Labor Pains."

17. See discussion of this in Adler, "David's Last Sin," 91–92.

18. Mettinger, *Solomonic State Officials*, 131.

noted the Jebusites as still occupying Mt. Moriah, from one of whom, Araunah, the plot for the temple must be purchased to halt the divine plague.[19] Whereas Adler suggests that the failure of Israel to drive out the Jebusites from Mt. Moriah was the broad transgression inciting the plague, he does not link the census to the deliberate incorporation of these people into the Israelite community. To provide further support that David's sin was the official incorporation of the Canaanites into the kingdom of Israel, it is important first to examine the various purposes and functions of the census in the ancient Near East.

Purpose and Function of Census Taking in the Ancient Near East

There are many accounts of census taking in the ancient Near East. Broadly, census records from the ancient Near East relate to taxation, military conscription, corvée labor, and land apportionment.[20] In many cases, the entirety of the evidence comes in the form of lists of names, with little insight into the broader ideology or functions behind the processes. There are two instances, however, where ancient texts provide a window into the broader political functions of censuses within society. These functions move beyond the practical elements of ascertaining and mobilizing manpower, into the realm of national identity and political and administrative incorporation. The two examples, the *tēbibtum* in Mari, which originated in the early second millennium BCE, and census-taking by Neo-Assyrian kings of the early first millennium BCE, bookend the historical setting of the Davidic narrative and suggest a broader ancient Near Eastern conceptualization of census-taking that transcended a particular time period or culture. It would be anachronistic to speak of citizenship in the ancient Near East, especially with the modern baggage accompanying that term, but ancient censuses certainly seem to have functioned as a form of official incorporation of a conquered or foreign people into the administrative and bureaucratic structures of a state/empire.[21]

Mari Evidence

The first example comes from the much-discussed Mari census documents, the bulk of which date to the reign of Zimri-Lim in the eighteenth century BCE. The Mari census has been of particular interest to biblical scholars because one of the terms, *tēbibtum*, derives from the Akkadian *ebēbum*, broadly meaning 'to be clean,' or, in the causative,

---

19. Adler, "David's Last Sin," 94. Evans likewise notes that "Araunah was a Jebusite, one of the original inhabitants of Jerusalem. That his land was purchased and not requisitioned shows the way in which these inhabitants appear to have been absorbed into, rather than enslaved by, the conquering Israelite community," but she doesn't link this incorporation to David's sin (Evans, *1 and 2 Samuel*, 249).

20. Hurowitz, "Census."

21. Liverani, *Assyria*, 203.

'to purify.' As such, it has commonly been seen as an example of the cultic nature of counting, and an analog for the commandment in Exod 30 that any census required a ransom of a half-shekel per individual,[22] although no cleansing ritual has been found in association with the *tēbibtum*.[23] Durand has also noted that nouns derived from the verb *ebēbum* cannot simply be equated with notions of purity.[24] In the context of Mari, the *Chicago Assyrian Dictionary* suggests that the verb should be translated "to clear a person or property of legal or financial claims."[25]

More reasonably, broad functional links for the purpose of military conscription and land allocation exist between the *tēbibtum* and biblical census.[26] Rather than focusing exclusively on some of the nuances of the *tēbibtum*, it is instructive to look at the broader way censuses were used across the diverse populations governed by the kings of Mari. Functionally, the *tēbibtum* served as a clear indicator that those undergoing the count entered into a new political structure or order. To the population being registered, their conscription was a sign of allegiance to a higher political power.[27] As such, an important element of the census ceremony involved the swearing of a loyalty oath to the king.[28] Luke further notes that such incorporation was not always voluntary, and that failure to assemble for conscription could have dire consequences.[29]

One of the interesting features of the Mari documents is that they also provide a window into who was not counted or included in a census, as well as local pushback against census operations, a number of which have been collated by Diego Fracaroli. *ARM* I:6 makes it clear that it was possible to achieve the goals of military conscription without conducting a formal census. In this letter, Samsi-Addu wrote to his son Yasmah-Addu:

> Concerning the census of the Yaminites you wrote to me: It is not convenient to take a census of the Yaminites. If you take a census of them, their Rabbean brothers who dwell on the other bank, in the Land of Yamhad, will hear and become concerned about them. To their land they will not come back. So do

---

22. Kupper, *Les Nomades*.
23. Sasson, *From the Mari Archives*, 125 n.14.
24. Durand, *Les documents épistolaires*, 333.
25. *CAD* E, 6. Certainly one could suggest that incorporating new members into a political entity via census could involve the dissolution of any legal or financial claims held through previous alliances or relationships.
26. Speiser, "Census and Ritual Expiation," 20; Weinfeld, "The Census in Mari," 293.
27. Durand, *Les documents épistolaires*, 334.
28. Luke, "Light from Mari," 79–80; Fleming, *Democracy's Ancient Ancestors*, 73–74. Similar oaths (*adê*) were required of foreign kings by the Assyrians, and should be expected if part of the role of the census was to incorporate foreign elements into the state or empire. Although the *adê* is unique to the Neo-Assyrian Empire, functionally similar oath protocols (under the designations *riksu/rikiltu* or *isiktum*) are attested in the Middle Assyrian and Old Babylonian periods respectively. Lauinger "The Neo-Assyrian *Adê*," 100.
29. Luke, "Light from Mari," 82.

not take census of them. Issue a strict order to them: Give them a strict order in this manner: Give them a strict order in this manner: 'The king will undertake a military campaign and everybody, including youngsters, should be assembled. The local chief who does not assemble his troops, the one who leaves a man has violated the king's oath.'[30] Give them a strict judgement in this manner, but do not take census of them.[31]

Thus there was a clear difference in the mind of the king between counting the people in the form of a census (*ubbubim*), and conscripting them for military aid (here represented by the phrase "issue them strict orders (*šipṭum*),"[32] just as later Assyrian kings could demand support from vassals without incorporating them into the empire. That a census was used for conscription but was not the only means to obtain manpower suggests that the census carried with it other connotations—connotations that Samsi-Addu wished to avoid to preclude trouble. In another example, *ARM* I:87, Samsi-Addu noted that registering certain groups of people (specifically nomads) was demanding and troublesome.[33] It makes sense that a nomadic group would be challenging to incorporate into the kingdom, and that their mobility would make the imposition of duties such as taxation, corvée, and military service arduous to enforce.[34]

The kings of Mari seem to have been particularly sensitive to incorporating various nomadic or semi-nomadic tribal populations. Fleming suggests that different tribal groups were exempt from the census (but still responsible for providing soldiers) depending on which king and which tribe were in power.[35] However, by avoiding the census these groups also lacked the benefits accompanying formal acceptance into the kingdom. To return to the anachronistic language of citizenship, a census was a count that a polity takes of its citizens. Thus including people in a census (and likely imposing on them the associated loyalty oath) was akin to granting them "citizenship," understood as a form of official administrative and bureaucratic incorporation with its associated benefits and obligations. As indicated, there were certain instances evidenced in the Mari letters, where such an incorporation might be counterproductive or undesirable. Indeed, Joab certainly seems to take this perspective in the biblical account of David's census.

---

30. *Asak šarrim īkul*. Lit. to eat the *asakkum* of the king. See Charpin, "Manger un serment" in support of the given translation.

31. For editions of this letter see Fracaroli, "Fear of Census," 16–17; Fleming, *Democracy's Ancient Ancestors*, 95; Durand, *Les documents épistolaires*, 342–44.

32. See *CAD* Š3, 92–93.

33. Fracaroli, "Fear of Census," 19.

34. See Durand, *Les documents épistolaires*, 338.

35 Fleming, *Democracy's Ancient Ancestors*, 88ff; see also Durand, *Les documents épistolaires*, 335.

Neo-Assyrian Evidence

A similar argument can be constructed from the Neo-Assyrian royal inscriptions. Although some of the language and traditions discussed below can be attested as early as the Middle Assyrian Empire (ca. twelfth to eleventh century BCE), a majority of the evidence dates to the eighth century BCE. In his seminal 1993 article, "Assyrians on Assyria in the First Millennium BCE," Peter Machinist asked the fundamental question of "What for the Neo-Assyrians constituted 'Assyrians?' What groups were seen as included in this term and on what basis? Was there, in other words, a way of defining membership in the Assyrian state?"[36] Machinist broadly framed Assyrians, at least from the perspective of the royal inscriptions, as individuals who accepted the order imposed by the Assyrian king as the representative of the Assyrian god, and who obeyed his dictates. From a practical point of view, Machinist noted that this obedience took specific forms, for instance in the provision of taxes, tribute, and service.[37] Similarly, Fales has argued for three separate uses of the term "Assyrian" in Neo-Assyrian literature: 1) As an institutional-hierarchical marker used to identify members of the Neo-Assyrian state; 2) As a generic positional-institutional marker used to describe the condition of belonging to, or being forcibly included within the complex of the Assyrian population; 3) As a typological/qualitative value in opposition to other identity markers.[38] Fales's suggested second use, as a positional-institutional marker, is most relevant for examining the mechanisms for incorporating new populations into the larger imperial complex. The mechanism for this incorporation was counting (*manû*).[39]

The Assyrian royal inscriptions deal with the issue of Assyrian-ness through a number of sovereignty idioms, by which the king expresses his dominance over his opponents. One such phrase is of particular significance, in which a conquered people are accounted (*manû*) to/with (*ana/itti*) the people of Assyria. (Note that the cognate Hebrew root [*mnh*] is used 2 Sam 24:1). In this usage, the *Chicago Assyrian Dictionary* defines *manû* as "to consider a person, region, an object as belonging to a specific class, region, or destination."[40] This definition explicitly encompasses the incorporation and categorization of persons, places, and things—one apparent function of "counting" in the form of census-taking. In a variant idiom, various duties (taxes, the Assyrian yoke, corvée labor) are imposed on a conquered people "like the Assyrians" (*kî ša assurî*). These particular idioms associate Assyrian political identity

---

36. Machinist, "Assyrians on Assyria," 79; more recently see Fales, "Composition and Structure of the Neo-Assyrian Empire."
37. Machinist, "Assyrians on Assyria," 102.
38. Fales, "Composition and Structure of the Neo-Assyrian Empire," 70–71.
39. Fales, "Composition and Structure of the Neo-Assyrian Empire."
40. *CAD M1*, 224–26.

with the performance of certain duties assessed on a population through the process of counting, that is, a census.

As one would expect with a census, once an Assyrian king "counted" a conquered population as "people of my land," he would then "impose upon them the yoke of my lordship" (*nīr bēlūtīya ēmissunūti*). Liverani makes the terms of this incorporation more explicit by naming the newly conquered people "Assyrians," but seeks to distinguish between "Old Assyrians" and "New Assyrians." Still, both categories of Assyrian were subject to the same authority (God and king) and obligations (labor, soldiers, taxes).[41] This act of incorporation became more common in the Neo-Assyrian period in the context of territorial expansion, but was also attested earlier in the Middle Assyrian period, particularly for foreign soldiers incorporated into the Assyrian military.[42] One earlier example comes from the royal inscriptions of Adad-Nirari III (late ninth/early eighth century BCE), who brought a captured king and his troops back from campaign, and "granted them Assyrian cities and counted their number (*minussu amnu*)."[43] Liverani cites many additional examples of the theme of incorporation, in all of which the verb *manû* plays a central role.[44] Thus, in the case of Assyria, counting a population in the form of a census and imposing on them accompanying duties, served as a mechanism for officially incorporating that group into the state or empire, at least from an administrative and bureaucratic perspective.

Fate of the Canaanites

Understanding David's census as a mechanism of annexing the Canaanites not only fits with general cultural and historical parallels from the ancient Near East, but also works on a literary level, meshing well with intertextual themes and evidence within the biblical narrative trajectory.[45] If we understand census-taking as a mechanism for incorporating outsiders into a multi-ethnic kingdom, it is possible to read 2 Sam 24 as the conclusion to a broader motif of Israel vs. the local population of Canaan. The proposed interpretation also solves a problem introduced in 2 Sam 24:1. Commentators have wondered why it is that Yahweh[46] would incite David to sin only to pun-

41. Liverani, *Assyria*, 203–4.
42. Liverani, *Assyria*, 204.
43. Grayson, *Assyrian Rulers*.
44. Liverani, *Assyria*, 204–6.

45. Note that for this study we are particularly interested in the D narrative regarding the fate of the Canaanites, and its ensuing incorporation into the narrative of DtrH. Schwartz has convincingly argued for competing narratives across the sources regarding the literary question of the fate of the Canaanites. See Schwartz, "Reexamining the Fate of the 'Canaanites.'" However, the fate of the Canaanites presents both a literary and an historical problem.

46. Emended to Satan by the Chronicler in an interesting and oft-discussed variation that is beyond the scope of this essay. See Walton and Walton, *Demons and Spirits*, 212–14; and a brief review of previous literature in Stokes "The Devil Made David Do it."

ish him and the community for that offense. A common solution lies in the opening phrase: "And again the anger of Yahweh burned against Israel,"[47] suggesting, as many commentators have noted, that Yahweh used David's census as an occasion to punish Israel for their sin.[48] Bergen specifically suggests that the reason must have "stemmed from a violation of some aspect of the Torah."[49] In fact, both Israel and David have sinned. Israel's failure to drive out the Canaanites and other local inhabitants of the land is a clear violation of the commandments of Deut 7:1 and 17:20.[50] This failure necessitated David's sin of finding another means of dealing with them—annexation.

Reading David's census as an attempt to incorporate the local Canaanite populations into the broader socio-political entity of early Israel brings to a conclusion a literary arc that deals with ancient Israel's "Canaanite Problem." This narrative arc answers with the essential question: "What was the ultimate fate of the Canaanites?" In Exod 3 the biblical text introduces the reader to the "seven nations of Canaan."[51] As Yahweh spoke to Moses from the burning bush he promised to deliver the Israelites from the hands of the Egyptians and to bring them to "the land flowing with milk and honey—the place of the Canaanites, and the Hittites, and the Amorites, and the Perizzites, and the Hivites and the Jebusites."[52] This list of nations, the local populations of Canaan, is mentioned again later in Exod 3:17, as well as in Exod 13:5 when the Israelites prepare to leave Egypt, as part of the fulfillment of Yahweh's promises to Israel's ancestors (13:11). Exodus 23:23–28 provides divine promises that Yahweh will send his angel ahead of Israel to drive out these inhabitants, a promise reiterated in Exod 33:2 and 34:11, the latter attached to the preconditions of Israel obeying Yahweh's commandments.[53]

More importantly for the Deuteronomistic history is the continuation of this theme in the book of Deuteronomy. The narrative of Deuteronomy begins with the Israelites breaking camp to enter and possess "the hill country of the Amorites and all its neighboring towns, in the Arabah, in the mountains, in the Shephelah, in the Negev and along the coast—the land of the Canaanites and Lebanon, as far as the great river, the Euphrates" (Deut 1:7). A recurring theme in Deuteronomy is that Yahweh will go with Israel and drive out the nations that inhabit the land (4:38). The best summary of the divine command to drive out these seven nations comes in Deut 7:1–2:

47. Unless otherwise noted all translations are my own.

48. Douglas, "Numbers after Samuel," 146; Evans, *1 and 2 Samuel*, 247; Auld, *I & II Samuel*, 604.

49. Bergen, *1, 2 Samuel*, 474. More specifically than a violation of Torah, a violation of D (although it must be noted that not every violation of D in the DtrH is necessarily punished.

50. See Frankel, *The Land of Canaan*, 268–77 for a more detailed discussion of conquest law.

51. Depending on the passage all seven, or the same nations, will not always be listed. Exodus frequently cites the six listed here or fewer, with the Girgashites added in Deuteronomy.

52. Exodus 3:8. Note that the Girgashites are absent from this verse, but are included elsewhere.

53. Note again, that these early mentions of the seven nations originate outside of D, but certain themes from these earlier references are reinterpreted by D. See Schwartz, "Reexamining the Fate of the 'Canaanites,'" 153–57.

"When Yahweh your God brings you into the land you are entering therein to possess, and drives out before you many nations—the Hittites, and the Girgashites, and the Amorites, and the Canaanites, and the Perizzites, and the Hivites, and the Jebusites, seven nations larger and mightier than you—and when Yahweh your God has delivered them to you and you have defeated them, then you must devote them to ḥērem.[54] Make no treaty with them, and show them no mercy." Deuteronomy 20:17 reiterates that these nations were to be devoted to ḥērem so that they might not lead Israel into sin and idolatry. The next mention of these nations comes in Josh 3:10, when the command to drive out the local populations is reiterated. These nations were listed as opponents of the Israelites throughout Joshua (9:1; 11:3; 12:8). Contrary to the claims of Josh 24:11, this group of local inhabitants was not fully eradicated by the Israelite conquest, as is made clear by Josh 13 and Judg 1. By Judg 4 there was a Canaanite king oppressing Israel from Hazor, attesting to the persistence of local populations and political structures.

By the ninth century BCE these Canaanite populations no longer existed as a recognizable political entity. At the time of their conquest of the southern Levant, the Assyrians recognize the Philistine city-states on the coast, the Transjordanian kingdoms of Ammon, Moab, and Edom, a kingdom of Israel (*Bit-Humri*), and a kingdom of Judah. As a political entity, the Canaanite city-states have ceased to exist. From an archaeological perspective, however, Canaan persisted well into the Iron Age, especially in urban northern sites in the valleys around Megiddo and in rural environs.[55] This "New Canaan" was the dominant material-cultural entity in the northern lowlands well into the period of the Israelite monarchy, and reinforces ideas of a failed conquest.[56] But what happened to these Canaanites who occupied much of the northern valleys? Clearly at some point they were politically incorporated into the Northern Kingdom of Israel, while still maintaining some of the identity markers

---

54. The Hebrew term ḥērem, frequently used with its verbal form ḥrm and translated as "destroy completely" or "devote to destruction" refers to something that is forbidden or set apart and dedicated to the deity. The practice of ḥērem is generally understood as a form of prohibition or ban used to set aside a target as an offering to the deity or temple, which implies either their destruction or dedication to temple service (see Giesen, "ḥrm," 180–89). Walton and Walton (*Lost World of the Israelite Conquest*, 170) have argued against translations of destruction, preferring "removal from human use," since not everything committed to ḥērem is necessarily destroyed. Giesen ("ḥrm," 195) similarly argues that "where the balance of power permitted, the result was not necessarily the extermination of the Canaanites, but at least their dispossession and expulsion"; however, even with this understanding I believe it is apparent that the underlying tone of the term is best linked to concepts of sacrifice that imply destruction. Note that the dedication of Gibeonites as wood cutters and water carriers for the house of Yahweh, and later Solomon's enlistment of the Canaanite populations for temple construction, could both be seen as a dedication of those populations to God, which would fulfill the sacrificial nature of ḥērem. This dedication of service matches, for instance, the dedication of Samuel to service in fulfillment of Hannah's vow in 1 Sam 1. No matter which translation of the term is applied, the Israelites at the time of David's census have still clearly failed in their duties to enact ḥērem.

55. Finkelstein, "City-States to States," 77; Finkelstein, "New Canaan"; Na'aman, "Memories of Canaan," 135–36.

56. Or, as some critical scholars prefer, no conquest or a literary conquest created by later authors.

of their Canaanite origins. How then, did these independent local entities become a part of Israel?

Annexation of Canaanite Populations

Based on these parallels, it is possible to reconstruct a situation whereby, from the perspective of the biblical text, David tried to consolidate his empire in the last years of his life, part of which involved the official incorporation of local Canaanite populations into Israel, a process achieved by means of a census.[57] Support is lent to this conclusion by an examination of Joab's itinerary. In 2 Sam 2:2, David commanded Joab to register (*pqd*) "all the tribes[58] of Israel from Dan to Beer Sheva." The itinerary he followed, as described in 2 Sam 24:5–7, suggests the incorporation of non-Israelite populations living within its borders. The route described encompassed what is assumed by the authors to comprise the boundaries of the Davidic Kingdom: from Aroer in the south, through Gilead to Dan in the North,[59] skirting the Phoenician coastal holdings of Sidon and Tyre, through the Canaanite and Hivite cities of the northern valleys and returning to Beer Sheva.[60] The inclusion of the Hivite and Canaanite city states already led Alt to conclude that "the towns of the western plains which, although neither Israelite nor Judean, were nevertheless obliged to provide troops and thus must have been allied to the kingdoms and possessed the same rights."[61] Certainly, the distinct mention of the "Hivites and Canaanites" seems to directly support the incorporation of a socially and perhaps politically distinct pre-Israelite population.[62] Firth further suggests that "the journey from Gilead took Joab's group outside Israelite territory as they would have gone through Geshur and Maacah into southern Lebanon, though David had subjugated these regions."[63] The itinerary itself then is evidence that the extent of this registration went beyond what had previously been considered "Israel."

Further textual support for this interpretation appears in 2 Chr 2. Here Solomon "counted (*spr*) all the foreigners who were in the land of Israel, *after the census (spr) that David his father had counted (spr)*, and there were found 153,600" (2 Chr 2:16).

57. Note that David is not just counting foreigners, he is counting "all of Israel" with the explicit connotation that Israel now includes local populations that would previously not have been identified as such.

58. Note following McCarter that some manuscript traditions have "Israel and Judah" and others omit the "of all the tribes of" (McCarter, *II Samuel*, 504).

59. The text here is unclear. McCarter (*II Samuel*, 504), following Skehan ("Joab's Census," 44), reconstructs "below Hermon." Firth reconstructs the Hebrew as an unknown place name "Tahtim-Hodsi" (Firth, *1 & 2 Samuel*, 540. See also Bergen, *1,2 Samuel*, 476). Others have reconstructed "Kadesh in the land of the Hittites," but this seems improbable from both an historical and literary perspective. McCarter's interpretation fits well with the geographical location of the Hivites in Joshua 11:3.

60. McCarter, *II Samuel*, 509–10.

61. Alt, *Essays on Old Testament History*, 289; see also Klement, *II Samuel 21–24*, 174.

62. Tsumura, *The Second Book of Samuel*, 342.

63. Firth, *1 & 2 Samuel*, 544.

Second Chronicles specifically notes David as having numbered the foreign men (*hāʾănāšim hagêrim*) in his previous census. If the incorporation of the Canaanites into Israel's political administrative system was the purpose of the census, this could also explain Joab's initial opposition to the plan. As the general of David's army, Joab might rightfully have been hesitant to incorporate formerly hostile local elements into the military, or he might worry about the way in which other Israelite tribes might react to this maneuver.

If David's sin was one of incorporation, granting Canaanites legitimacy and membership in the broader political community of ancient Israel, then it is also clear why this was such an egregious transgression in the eyes of the Deuteronomist. The Israelites were clearly commanded to drive out and annihilate the local populations, not incorporate and assimilate them. From the literary perspective of the Deuteronomist, such behavior was a clear violation of divine commands, commands that David should have been aware of (and in fact was, as portrayed by his own admission of guilt), and thus worthy of divine retribution. The fact that these populations remained was not just a sin of David's, but of the entire nation. The plague that struck the land recalls the plague that ran through Israel's encampment in Num 25, which Yahweh similarly sent as a response to the incorporation of foreigners in the community.

From a literary perspective, this story also marks the end of the narrative arc of the Canaanites. Second Samuel 24 is one of the last references to the local populations of Canaan in the Hebrew Bible with the last occurring in the reign of Solomon in 1 Kgs 9:20.[64] This final reference is set up as Solomon's rectification of David's folly. Following David's death, Solomon assumed the throne and conducted a census of his own (2 Chr 2), although without the same penalties and negative reactions attributed to his father's attempt. The lack of divine censure would make sense if the foreign elements had already been officially incorporated. Solomon's census also followed existing precedent for how to incorporate local populations. The Bible provides a model for the appropriate incorporation of foreigners into the community in the event that the Israelites were unable to drive them out. This model was established with the Israelite treaty with the Gibeonites in Josh 9. According to this passage, having been tricked into making a covenant with the Gibeonites, the Israelites solved the problem by appointing them servants designated as "cutters of wood and drawers of water" in service to Yahweh. Deuteronomy 20:11 also suggests that in warfare, when the Israelites attacked a city, they should make the inhabitants an offer of peace. If accepted, these subjugated populations should be subjected to forced labor. The final mention of the Canaanites in the land mentioned in 1 Kgs 9:20–21 appears to present a similar solution to the problem posed by David's incorporation of the Canaanites: "All the people who were left from the Amorites, the Hittites, the Perizzites, the Hivites, and the Jebusites, who were not of the people of Israel—their descendants who were left after them in the land, whom the people of Israel were unable to devote to

---

64. With the parallel passage of 2 Chr 8:7.

the ḥērem—these Solomon drafted for compulsory heavy labor, until today."[65] Second Chronicles 2 similarly links Solomon's census of the foreign men with their assignment as carriers and quarriers. Enslavement of the local population for heavy labor (which is likely a hyperbolic description of the drafting of corvée labor) was seen as an acceptable alternative to the ḥērem.

Conclusions

Thus, the Deuteronomistic historian's account of David's census was able to deal with multiple problems: 1) The Canaanites were in fact never driven from the land, as recorded in Josh 13, Judg 1, Judg 4, 2 Kgs 9 and corroborated by the archaeological record. This was a failing of the Israelite community as a whole, and caused Yahweh's wrath to burn against Israel. 2) David solved this problem politically by officially incorporating the Canaanites into the administrative structure of an emerging Israelite polity. As he neared the end of his reign this was a logical and necessary step to stabilize the kingdom in preparation for his successor. David accomplished this incorporation by means of an official census of the foreign population in direct violation of the order to drive out these people, and elicited harsh rebuke from Yahweh in the form of a plague. 3) Solomon provided the theologically appropriate conclusion to this problem by assigning the incorporated populations to forced labor, in accordance with a previously established mechanism for incorporating inhabitants of the land who were not driven out or annihilated. After this, Canaan and the local populations continued to exist ethnically, but ceased to exist as a meaningful socio-political entity and thus functionally disappear from the biblical text.

In conclusion, David's sin in conducting the census was not a question of how or why he conducted it, but rather whom he decided to count, and what counting a population meant politically in ancient kingdoms. His incorporation of foreign elements into the administrative system of Israel violated the commands to drive out these people. This sin was immediately apparent to the Deuteronomistic authors, and therefore in need of a divine rebuke. It was these very same foreign elements that led the people to worship other gods and to turn from Yahweh throughout the ensuing accounts of the Israelite monarchy.

---

65. See again 2 Chr 8:7 for the parallel passage.

Part 3: Context

Bibliography

Adler, J. "David's Last Sin: Was It the Census?" *JBQ* 23 (1995) 91–95.

Alt, Albrecht. *Essays on Old Testament History and Religion*. Garden City, NY: Doubleday, 1968.

Auld, A. Graeme. *I & II Samuel: A Commentary*. OTL. Louisville: Westminster John Knox, 2011.

———. "David's Census: Some Textual and Literary Links." In *Textual Criticism and Dead Sea Scrolls Studies in Honour of Julio Trebolle Barrera*, edited by Andrés Piquer Otero and Pablo A. Torijano Morales, 19–34. Journal for the Study of Judaism Supplements 157. Leiden: Brill, 2012.

Baden, Joel. *The Historical David: The Real Life of an Invented Hero*. New York: Harper Collins, 2013.

Bar-Efrat, S. "From History to Story: The Development of the Figure of David in Biblical and Post-Biblical Literature." In *For and Against David: Story and History in the Books of Samuel*, edited by A. Graeme Auld and Erik Eynikel, 45–56. Bibliotheca Ephemeridum theologicarum Lovaniensium 232. Leuven: Peeters, 2010.

Bergen, Robert. *1, 2 Samuel*. NAC 7. Nashville: Broadman & Holman, 1996.

Brueggemann, Walter. "2 Samuel 21–24: An Appendix of Deconstruction." *CBQ* 50 (1988) 383–97.

Campbell, Antony F. "2 Samuel 21–24: The Enigma Factor." In *For and Against David: Story and History in the Books of Samuel*, edited by A. Graeme Auld and Erik Eynikel, 347–60. Bibliotheca Ephemeridum theologicarum Lovaniensium 232. Leuven: Peeters, 2010.

Cartledge, Tony W. *1 & 2 Samuel*. SHBC. Macon, GA: Smith & Helwys, 2001.

Charpin, D. "Manger un Serment." In *Jurer et Maudire: Pratiques Politiques et Usages Juridiques du Serment dans Le Proche-Orient Ancien*, edited by S. Lafont, 85–96. Paris: L'Harmattan, 1997.

Douglas, Mary. "Reading Numbers after Samuel." In *Reflection and Refraction: Studies in Biblical Historiography in Honour of A. Graeme Auld*, edited by Robert Rezetko et al., 139–54. VTSup 113. Leiden: Brill, 2007.

Durand, Jean-Marie. *Les documents épistolaires du palais de Mari*. Vol. 2. Paris: Cerf, 1998.

Evans, Mary J. *1 and 2 Samuel*. New International Bible Commentary; Old Testament Series 6. Peabody, MA: Hendrickson, 2000.

Fales, Frederick M. "The Composition and Structure of the Neo-Assyrian Empire: Ethnicity, Language, and Identities." In *Writing Neo-Assyrian History: Sources, Problems, and Approaches*, edited by G. B. Lanfranchi et al., 45–90. State Archives of Assyria Studies 29. Helsinki: Neo-Assyrian Text Corpus Project, 2019.

Finkelstein, Israel. "City-States to States: Polity Dynamics in the 10th–9th Centuries B.C.E." In *Symbiosis, Symbolism, and the Power of the Past: Canaan, Ancient Israel, and Their Neighbors from the Late Bronze Age through Roman Palaestina*, edited by William G. Dever and Seymour Gitin, 75–83. Winona Lake, IN: Eisenbrauns, 2003.

———. "New Canaan." *EI* 27 (2003) 189–95.

Firth, David G. *1 & 2 Samuel*. Apollos Old Testament Commentary 8. Nottingham, UK: Apollos, 2009.

Fleming, Daniel E. *Democracy's Ancient Ancestors: Mari and Early Collective Governance*. Cambridge: Cambridge University Press, 2004.

Fracaroli, Diego. "Fear of Census: State Policies and Tribal Ideology in the Mari Kingdom during the Period of Samsi-Addu." In *Reconstruyendo el Pasado Remoto: Estudios Sobre el Proximo Oriente Antiguo en Homenaje a Jorge R. Silva Castillo*, edited by Diego A. Barreyra and Gregorio del Olmo Lete, 13–21. Barcelona: Editorial AUSA, 2009.

Frankel, David. *The Land of Canaan and the Destiny of Israel: Theologies of Territory in the Hebrew Bible*. Winona Lake, IN: Eisenbrauns, 2011.

Frazer, James. *Folk-Lore in the Old Testament*. London: Macmillan, 1918.

Giesen, G. "ḥrm." In *TDOT* 5:180–203.

Grayson, A. Kirk. *Assyrian Rulers of the Early First Millennium BC I (1114-859 BC)*. RIMA 2. Toronto: University of Toronto Press, 1991.

Greenwood, Kyle. "Labor Pains: The Relationship between David's Census and Corvee Labor." *BBR* 20 (2010) 467–77.

Halpern, Baruch. *David's Secret Demons: Messiah, Murderer, Traitor, King*. Grand Rapids: Eerdmans, 2001.

Klement, Herbert H. *II Samuel 21–24: Context, Structure, and Meaning in the Samuel Conclusion*. Europäische Hochschulschriften. Reihe XXIII, Theologie 682. Frankfurt: Lang, 2000.

Knapp, Andrew. *Royal Apologetic in the Ancient Near East*. Writings from the Ancient World Supplement Series 4. Atlanta: SBL Press, 2015.

Kupper, J.R. *Les nomades en mesopotamie au temps des rois de Mari*. Bibliothèque de la Faculté de philosophie et lettres de l'Université de Liège 142.). Paris: Les Belles Lettres, 1957.

Lauinger, Jacob. "The Neo-Assyrian *Adê*: Treaty, Oath, or Something Else?" *JANEBL* 19 (2013) 99–116.

Liverani, Mario. *Assyria: The Imperial Mission*. Winona Lake, IN: Eisenbrauns, 2017.

Luke, K. "Light from Mari on David's Census." *IJT* 32 (1983) 70–89.

Machinist, Peter. "Assyrians on Assyria in the First Millennium." In *Anfänge Politischen Denkens in der Antike: Die Nahöstlichen Kulturen und die Griechen*, edited by Kurt A. Raaflaub. Schriften des Historischen Kollegs. Kolloquien 24. Munich: Oldenbourg, 1993.

McCarter, P. Kyle, Jr. "The Apology of David." *JBL* 99 (1980) 489–504.

———. *II Samuel*. AB 9. Garden City, NY: Doubleday, 1984.

Mettinger, Tryggve. *Solomonic State Officials: A Study of the Civil Government Officials of the Israelite Monarchy*. Coniectanea biblica: Old Testament Series 5. Lund: Gleerup, 1971.

Na'aman, Nadav. "Memories of Canaan in the Old Testament." *UF* 47 (2016) 129–46.

Neufeld, Ernest. "The Sins of the Census." *Judaism* 43 (1994) 196–203.

Omanson, Roger, and John Ellington. *A Handbook on the First and Second Books of Samuel*. New York: United Bible Society, 2001.

Park, Song-Mi. "Census and Censure: Sacred Threshing Floors and Counting Taboos in 2 Samuel 24." *HBT* 35 (2013) 21–41.

Sasson, Jack. *From the Mari Archives: An Anthology of Old Babylonian Letters*. Winona Lake, IN: Eisenbrauns, 2015.

Schenker, Adrian. *Der Mächtige im Schmelzofen des Mitleids: Eine Interpretation von 2 Sam 24*. OBO 42. Göttingen: Vandenhoeck & Ruprecht, 1982.

Schwartz, Baruch. "Reexamining the Fate of the "Canaanites" in the Torah Traditions." In *Sefer Moshe: The Moshe Weinfeld Jubilee Volume*, edited by Chaim Cohen et al., 151–70. Winona Lake, IN: Eisenbrauns, 2004.

Skehan, Patrick W. "Joab's Census: How Far North (2 Sm 24,6)?" *CBQ* 31 (1969) 42–49.

Speiser, E. A. "Census and Ritual Expiation in Mari and Israel." *BASOR* 149 (1958) 17–25.

Stokes, R. E. "The Devil Made David Do It . . . Or *Did* He? The Nature, Identity, and Literary Origins of the *Satan* in 1 Chronicles 21:1." *JBL* 128 (2009) 91–106.

Part 3: Context

Stolz, Fritz. *Das Erste und Zweite Buch Samuel*. Zürcher Bibelkommentare: AT 9. Zurich: TVZ, 1981.

Tsumura, David. *The Second Book of Samuel*. NICOT. Grand Rapids: Eerdmans, 2019.

Walton, John H. *Ancient Near Eastern Thought and the Old Testament*. Grand Rapids: Baker Academic, 2018.

Walton, John H., and J. Harvey Walton. *The Lost World of the Israelite Conquest*. Downers Grove, IL: InterVarsity, 2017.

———. *Demons and Spirits in Biblical Theology: Reading the Biblical Text in Its Cultural and Literary Context*. Eugene, OR: Cascade, 2019.

Weinfeld, Moshe. "The Census in Mari, Ancient Israel and in Rome." In *Storia e Tradizioni di Israele: Scritti in Onore di J. Alberto Soggin*, edited by Daniele Garrone and Felice Israel, 293–98. Brescia: Paideia, 1991.

21
―――

The Lost World of Lexical Semantics
Samson's Spectacle in Judges 16:25

Kenneth C. Way

Historical Backgrounds

John H. Walton is the consummate mentor, investing valuable time and creative ideas in his students to inspire them and to form them into independent Christian scholars. The following study serves as an example of how he mentored me as an undergraduate Bible/Theology student at Moody Bible Institute in Chicago, Illinois. After writing some word studies for his Hebrew Exegesis class in fall 1996, Walton encouraged me to adapt a paper for presentation at the Midwest Regional ETS meeting, conveniently hosted by Moody Bible Institute on March 14–15, 1997. The title of the paper was "The Semantic Range of צ/שׂחק and Its Implications for Judges 16:25."[1] To my surprise, it merited the "Student Paper Award" that year—a distinction made possible only because of Walton's generous guidance.

Around that same time, Walton was writing his concise and accessible essay on "Principles for Productive Word Study" for *NIDOTTE* in which he draws many examples from Hebrew lexemes, including צחק, and he carefully leverages common uses of the English language to illustrate and clarify complex linguistic phenomena by analogy.[2] I attempt to model the same approach in the essay below, which essen-

---

1. See Theological Research Exchange Network no. ETS-0248.
2. See Walton, "Principles for Productive Word Study" in *NIDOTTE* 1:161–71. Walton eloquently defines the task of lexical analysis: "Word study is a step in the process of exegesis; it does not comprise the whole of the process. The authority of the Scripture is not found in the words, though each word has an important role to play; rather, the authority is embodied in the message—that tapestry for which words serve but as threads that derive their significance from being viewed within the tapestry rather than being explored on the skein" (*NIDOTTE* 1:171).

tially retains its original form, save the bibliographic updates in the footnotes. Because popular word studies often lack methodological sophistication (betraying ignorance of contributions by James Barr and others),[3] the discipline of lexical semantics can be considered a "Lost World." By applying Walton's principles, I attempt to reclaim that world and to model his productive approach.

Lexical Problem

Judges 16 recounts the story in which the Philistines gather to offer praise and sacrifices to their god Dagon in celebration of the captivity of their enemy, Samson. When the attendants are in high spirits, they shout, "'Call Samson so that he may entertain us [וישחק־לנו].' So they called Samson out of the prison, and he acted obscenely before them [ויצחק לפניהם]" (Judg 16:25).[4] The composer uses two different verbs to describe the activities taking place in this verse, though they are often considered simply variant spellings of the same verb.[5] But is his choice of spelling arbitrary, or are there reasons motivating his distinction? These two verbs are related by a sibilant phoneme variation (ש/צ), but their meanings are rarely, if ever, distinguished. In fact, most contemporary English translations assign the same (or similar) meaning to both verbs.[6] But is the difference between them merely orthographic, or is it also semantic? Careful discussion on this question is scant in the literature.[7] For this reason, it is incumbent on interpreters to engage in careful word study. I will demonstrate through synchronic analysis that there is semantic differentiation between these two related roots. I will then explore how a phoneme shift took place (from צ to ש), and how certain archaic usages are preserved in the צ-form. Such analysis requires cataloguing all occurrences of שחק/צ and identifying their nuances. Once these nuances are synchronically established, one is better prepared to explain and translate Judges 16:25.

---

3. See Noonan, *Advances*, 66–87.

4. This is my suggested translation from the MT. For evaluation of the variants and additions of the Greek Versions, see Marcos, *Judges*, 48, 98*.

5. E.g., Bartelmus claims that "the alternation . . . in Jgs. 16:25ff. demonstrates the synchronic exchangeability of the two variants" (*TDOT* 60). Brenner comments that שחק in Judg 16:25 is "a true synchronic variant of ṣḥq in the same verse" ("On the Semantic Field of Humor, Laughter, and the Comic in the Old Testament" in Radday and Brenner, *On Humor and the Comic*, 47). Block similarly notes that the verse employs "two variations of the same verb . . . both of which mean 'to laugh'" (Block, *Judges, Ruth*, 466).

6. E.g., see CSB, ESV, NASB, NET, NIV, NJPS, NKJV, NLT, NRSV, etc.

7. In 1997, when I presented this study, there was a lack of critical discussion on Judges, and lexical reference works on שחק/צ were few or forthcoming—situations that have changed dramatically since that time. In addition to *NIDOTTE* (1:165; 3:796–97 [#7464], 1228–30 [#8471]), the available lexical resources now include the completed *DCH* (7:112; 8:120–21) and *TDOT* (14:58–72); *TLOT* does not include these roots. Commentaries have also proliferated on Judges 16:25 in the years following; e.g., see Block, *Judges, Ruth*, 466; Butler, *Judges*, 310, 318, 353; Chisholm, *Commentary on Judges and Ruth*, 385, 429–30; Niditch, *Judges*, 167, 171; Way, *Judges and Ruth*, 139; Webb, *The Book of Judges*, 408, 411; etc.

Lexical Base

The lexical base consists of sixty-eight occurrences. The שׂ-form occurs fifty-three times: as a verb, it appears thirty-six times in the *qal*, *hiphil*, and *piel* stems, and as a substantive (שׂחוק) it appears seventeen times.[8] The צ-form occurs only fifteen times: as a verb, it appears thirteen times in the *qal* and *piel* stems, and as a substantive (צחוק) it appears twice.[9] In Table 1, the two roots are arranged in columns so that nuances can be distinguished by stems and collocations.

	שׂחק	צחק
qal	+ אל: Job 29:24	
	+ ב: Prov 1:26	+ ב: Gen 18:12
	+ ל: Job 5:22; 39:7, 18, 22; 41:21[29]; Pss 2:4; 37:13; 59:9[8]; Prov 31:25; Hab 1:10	+ ל: Gen 21:6
	+ על: Job 30:1; Ps 52:8[6]; Lam 1:7	
	Uncollocated: Prov 29:9	Uncollocated: Gen 17:17; 18:13, 15(2x)
	Infinitive construct forms: Judg 16:27; Job 8:21; 12:4[2x]; Ps 126:2; Prov 10:23; 14:13; Eccl 2:2; 3:4; 7:3, 6; 10:19; Jer 20:7; 48:26, 27, 39; Lam 3:14	Infinitive construct forms: Gen 21:6; Ezek 23:32
hiphil	+ על: 2 Chr 30:10	
piel		+ את: Gen 26:8
	+ ב: 2 Sam 6:5; Job 40:29[41:5]; Ps 104:26; Prov 8:30, 31; Zech 8:5	+ ב: Gen 39:14, 17
	+ ל: Judg 16:25a	
	+ לפני: 2 Sam 2:14; 6:5, 21; 1 Chr 13:8; Prov 8:30	+ לפני: Judg 16:25b
	Uncollocated: 1 Sam 18:7; 1 Chr 15:29; Job 40:20; Prov 26:19; Jer 15:17; 30:19; 31:3[4]	Uncollocated: Gen 19:14; 21:9; Exod 32:6

Table 21.1: Lexical Base

---

8. For the infinitive construct forms as substantives, see Even-Shoshan, *New Concordance*, 1130. In addition, a variant spelling of Isaac's name (ישׂחק) occurs four times (Ps 105:9; Jer 33:26; Amos 7:9, 16).

9. For the infinitive construct forms as substantives, see Even-Shoshan, *New Concordance*, 983. Another nominal derivative is the name Isaac (יצחק) occurring 108 times with wide distribution.

Part 3: Context

Synchronic Analysis

This table may now provide an outline for sense differentiation by starting with the category at the top left and working towards the bottom right. That final category (צחק in *piel*), however, requires closer analysis than the other categories in order to appreciate the composer's intentional word choices in Judges 16:25.

First, the *qal* stem: the root שׂחק occurs in the *qal* stem thirty-three times. This form of the verb שׂחק carries a negative nuance and means "to deride/ridicule." This applies both to the occurrences with prepositions and to the one without. The negative denotation is confirmed by its parallel use with the verb לעג, "to mock" (5x).[10] As a substantive (infinitive construct), however, שׂחק can be used either positively or negatively. That is, it denotes "pleasure/laughter" (9x),[11] as well as "laughingstock, object of ridicule" (8x).[12]

The root צחק occurs in the *qal* stem eight times. The verbal forms carry the positive/neutral sense "to laugh"; whereas, the substantives are, once again, either positive (Gen 21:6, "laughter")[13] or negative (Ezek 23:32, "ridicule"). It is also noteworthy that the (six) positive/neutral occurrences are all used in wordplays pertaining to the name Isaac (יצחק, "he laughs").[14]

The sole attestation of the *hiphil* stem is in 2 Chronicles 30:10. In this context, שׂחק is paralleled with לעג, "to mock"[15] so that a negative sense is required. This nuance relates to the use in *qal*, and it makes sense causally (thus, "to cause ridicule"). It is therefore rendered, "they made a mockery of them," or as NRSV, "they laughed them to scorn." That the chronicler uniquely uses the *hiphil* in this verse instead of the *qal*-form may be a characteristic of LBH,[16] but it is difficult to explain without any other *hiphil*-occurrences in the Hebrew Bible.

Unlike in the *qal* and *hiphil*, the occurrences in the *piel* stem (the function of which is debated)[17] cannot be divided according to positive/negative criteria. שׂחק occurs nineteen times in the *piel* stem and basically means "to play." The contextual nuances that "play" may take include celebration (2 Sam 6:5, 21; 18:7; 1 Chr 13:8;

---

10. Pss 2:4; 59:8[9]; Prov 1:26; Jer 20:7; and 2 Chr 30:10 (*hiphil* stem).

11. See Job 8:21; Ps 126:2; Prov 10:23; 14:13; Eccl 2:2; 3:4; 7:3, 6; 10:19.

12. See Judg 16:27; Job 12:4(2x); Jer 20:17; 48:26, 27, 29; Lam 3:4. See also *DCH* 8:120, 121; Way, *Judges and Ruth*, 139 ("looking at the spectacle of Samson" [הראים בשׂחוק שמשון]; Judg 16:27).

13. Brenner translates this verse negatively ("On the Semantic Field of Humor, Laughter, and the Comic in the Old Testament," in Radday and Brenner, *On Humor and the Comic*, 50), but the context favors a positive nuance (cf. *DCH* 7:112).

14. See Whedbee, *The Bible and the Comic Vision*, 76–77, 80–81, 88, 91–93. Additionally, Bartelmus observes that the root may onomatopoeically express the sound of laughter (*TDOT* 59–60).

15. Both of these verbs are *hiphil* masculine plural active participles with prepositions.

16. See Brenner, "On the Semantic Field of Humor, Laughter, and the Comic in the Old Testament" in Radday and Brenner, *On Humor and the Comic*, 47, 48; Walton, "Principles for Productive Word Study" in *NIDOTTE* 1:165.

17. See discussion in Noonan, *Advances*, 97–104.

15:29), rejoicing (Prov 8:30–31),[18] entertainment (Judg 16:25a),[19] dueling (2 Sam 2:14),[20] joking (Prov 26:19), and merrymaking (Jer 15:17; 30:19; 31:3[4]).

Finally, the use of צחק in the *piel* stem: the seven occurrences in this category are most provocative for the lexicographer because they each occur in contexts that are notoriously ambiguous. I would suggest that the reason for this is that צחק in the *piel* stem has a euphemistic function. Simply stated, "Euphemism is the substitution of a less charged word for one that may be taboo, offensive or disagreeable."[21] The following discussion explains and defends the euphemistic use of צחק in five discrete passages.

Genesis 26:8 provides what is, perhaps, the clearest instance of euphemism in this category. The verse recounts how king Abimelech looked down from a window and saw Isaac "fondling"[22] his wife Rebekah (יצחק מצחק את רבקה אשתו). The response in the following verses indicates that the activity (מצחק) between Isaac and Rebekah was of such a nature that it convinced Abimelech of their married status. It is implicitly evident that צחק is used as a reference to some sort of physical intimacy in this verse.[23] It is unclear whether את is functioning as a preposition ("with") or as a particle marking the definite direct object.[24] In either case, מצחק could function euphemistically for sexual activity. An English example that may serve to illustrate the euphemism here is the term "petting."

Another example of this use of צחק occurs in the story related by Potiphar's wife in Genesis 39. She calls her household servants and says, "See, he has brought to us a Hebrew man to screw with us [לצחק בנו]! He came in to me to lie with me, and I cried out with a loud voice" (Gen 39:14). Later on, when Potiphar arrives, she also tells him, "The Hebrew servant, whom you have brought to us, came in to me to screw with me [לצחק בי]" (Gen 39:17). Her twisted story utilizes לצחק ב two times along with other choice expressions. Both of her expressions "he came in to me"

---

18. See von Rad, *Wisdom in Israel*, 50, 170, 316.

19. In his discussion about the occupations of slaves, Hoffner suggests: "Since such temple 'entertainment' often involved acrobatics and feats of strength Samson was able to grasp the pillars that supported the temple roof without arousing suspicion" ("Slavery and Slave Laws in Ancient Hatti and Israel" in Block, *Israel: Ancient Kingdom or Late Invention?*, 143).

20. See *DCH* 8:121 ("have a contest, make gladiatorial play, sport"); Sukenik, "Let the Young Men," 110–16; Trimm, *Fighting for the King and the Gods*, 277–79; de Vaux, "Single Combat in the Old Testament" in de Vaux, *The Bible and the Ancient Near East*, 129–31; Yadin, *The Art of Warfare*, 266–67, 362. Hoffner suggests that Abner's word choice was a "euphemistic *terminus technicus*" for the combat of (teams of) champions (Hoffner, "Hittite Analogue," 221).

21. Minkoff, "Coarse Language in the Bible?" 24–25.

22. NJPS; NRSV; Hamilton, *Genesis: Chapters 18–50*, 189; and cf. "caressing" in CSB, NASB; NET, NIV; NLT; Westermann, *Genesis 12–36*, 421; "have sexual pleasure" (*DCH* 7:112); "playing around" (Whedbee, *The Bible and the Comic Vision*, 90). Walsh suggests that Isaac was "tickling" Rebekah in a manner that suggested their married status (Walsh, *Fruit of the Vine*, 235).

23. Cf. Wenham, *Genesis 16–50*, 190.

24. Waltke and O'Connor discuss the ambiguity of את in *IBHS* §10.3.

(בא אלי; vv. 14, 17)[25] and "to lie with me" (לשכב עמי; v. 14)[26] are well-established idioms that can refer to sexual intercourse. It would be difficult to misunderstand what Potiphar's wife means by using this string of euphemisms; and again, she uses צחק in this sexually charged context.

In Genesis 19:14, Lot says to his sons-in-law, "'Get up! Get out of this place, because YHWH is about to destroy the city!' But he was like a jester [כמצחק] in the eyes of his sons-in-law." The meaning of צחק here is ambiguous, but such is the nature of euphemism. Of course, it has not gone without suggestion that the sons-in-law perceived Lot as making a pass at them,[27] but צחק need not be understood only as a sexual euphemism. Some euphemisms originate with sexual connotations, but then shift to broader meanings (e.g., the English expression, "screwing around"). In this verse, the sons-in-law most likely consider Lot's claim to be "in bad taste"—the worst sort of coarse jesting.[28]

The same form occurs in Genesis 21:9–10, where "Sarah saw the son of Hagar the Egyptian, whom she had born to Abraham, messing around [מצחק]. So she said to Abraham, 'Drive out this maid and her son, for the son of this maid shall not inherit with my son Isaac.'" Some of the Versions add the clarifying phrase "with Isaac her son" after מצחק.[29] Even if this addition is not preferred on text-critical grounds,[30] the context still indicates that Ishmael's action was in some way related to Isaac. The question at hand, however, concerns the nature of Ishmael's activity. What is the meaning of מצחק? Was Ishmael merely playing with Isaac or was he "playing Isaac—that is, pretending to be Isaac"[31]? Or was he dancing on the occasion of a feast for Isaac's weaning?[32] Or was he "performing athletic feats," as some have suggested?[33] None of these options can really account for Sarah's reaction in verse 10. It is clear that מצחק

---

25. Cf. Gen 16:2, 4; 29:21; 30:3, 16; 38:9; Deut 21:13; 22:13; 2 Sam 3:7; Ezek 23:44.

26. Cf. Gen 19:32, 34, 35; 30:15, 16; 39:7–12; Exod 22:15[16]; Deut 22:22–30; 2 Sam 11:1.

27. See Coote and Ord, *The Bible's First History*, 131.

28. See *DCH* 7:112 ("one who jests"); cf. CSB, ESV, NIV, NJPS, NKJV, NLT, NRSV. For the phrase "in bad taste," see Walton, *Genesis*, 478.

29. See LXX and Vulgate.

30. The addition (which is longer than and disambiguates the MT) is favored by NLT; NRSV; Gal 4:29; Speiser, *Genesis*, 153, 155; Westermann, *Genesis 12–36*, 336–37, 339. However, the addition is not preferred by ESV; NASB; NET; NIV; NJPS; NKJV; Hamilton, *Genesis: Chapters 18–50*, 75; Sarna, *Genesis*, 146; Wenham, *Genesis 16–50*, 77, 82.

31. Exum and Whedbee, "Isaac, Samson, and Saul: Reflections on the Comic and Tragic Visions," in Radday and Brenner, *On Humor and the Comic*, 127; Whedbee, *The Bible and the Comic Vision*, 81. See also Hackett, "Rehabilitating Hagar" in Day, *Gender and Difference*, 20–21 ("Isaac-ing"); Walsh, *Fruit of the Vine*, 235.

32. See Jubilees 17:4, "Sarah saw Ishmael playing and dancing, and Abraham rejoicing with great joy, and she became jealous of Ishmael" (Charles, *The Apocrypha and Pseudepigrapha*). For the banquet setting of Isaac's weaning (and for the scenes in Exod 32:6 and Judg 16:25), see Walsh, *Fruit of the Vine*, 232–37.

33. Sasson makes this argument from Genesis 16:12; 21:20 in "Worship of the Golden Calf" in Hoffner, *Orient and Occident*, 154; cf. Hamilton, *Genesis: Chapters 18–50*, 79.

was behavior that was offensive to Sarah.[34] Instead of an explicit statement describing Ishmael's behavior, the text uses a *piel* participle of צחק to say implicitly that what he did was unacceptable and met with disgust on Sarah's part. To use an English euphemism again, one could say that Ishmael did something "in bad taste;" that is, he acted inappropriately.[35] This may have been something with sexual overtones or even a reference to physical abuse (note that Paul interprets מצחק with διώκω, "to persecute," in Gal 4:29).

Finally, Exodus 32 recounts the story of the golden calf where Aaron declared a festival at which the Israelites "sat down to eat and drink; then they rose up to party [לְצַחֵק]" (Exod 32:6).[36] Some traditional interpreters suggest that the festivities in this chapter are characteristic of the Canaanite fertility cult,[37] and many other interpreters believe that צחק in this verse refers to unrestrained sexual activity.[38] Current scholarship recognizes that the demonstration of such ideas may include some presuppositions that reevaluation could prove to be unfounded.[39] Alternatively, another scholar suggests, "Rather than wild abandoned acts, the scene that unfolds before the calf was probably an *orderly* ritual . . . that consisted of a (ritual) banquet followed by sports, miming, and antiphonal singing to honor the gods."[40] This latter interpretation is problematic because it fails to account for the narrator's comment in verse 25: "Moses saw that the people were running wild because Aaron had let them get out of control."[41] The context does not favor לְצַחֵק of verse 6 to refer to "orderly" festivities. One needs further information to clarify whether this euphemism with צחק is veiling sexually explicit behavior or some cultic behavior that was unacceptable or even syncretistic.

---

34. That is, it was "insulting behavior" (Wenham, *Genesis 16–50*, 376) or "making fun" (NLT).

35. Again, see Walton, *Genesis*, 496.

36. Or "to revel" (*DCH* 7:112; NRSV).

37. E.g. Hvidberg, *Weeping and Laughter*, 146–48; Moberly, *At the Mountain of God*, 46, 196 n. 7; Noth, *Exodus*, 248; Pedersen, *Israel: Its Life and Culture*, 4:468–69; cf. NLT ("indulged in pagan revelry").

38. E.g., Brenner, "On the Semantic Field of Humor, Laughter, and the Comic in the Old Testament" in Radday and Brenner, *On Humor and the Comic*, 47 n. 6 ("a euphemism for lewd activity"); Cassuto, *A Commentary on the Book of Exodus*, 414 ("fertility and the inchastity connected therewith"); Childs, *The Book of Exodus*, 566 ("religious orgy"); Clements, *Exodus*, 207 ("an orgy which included sexual immorality"); Durham, *Exodus*, 422 ("sexual play"); Hyatt, *Exodus*, 305 ("a fertility ceremony, probably with obscene rights"); Paul, "The Shared Legacy" in Paul, *Divrei Shalom*, 313 ("the religious orgy . . . which has decidedly sexual connotations"); van der Toorn, "Female Prostitution," 202 ("unmistakable euphemism for sexual activities").

39. See Albertz, *A History of Israelite Religion*, 1:331–32 n. 109; Janzen, "The Character of the Calf and its Cult," 597–607.

40. Sasson, "Worship of the Golden Calf" in Hoffner, *Orient and Occident*, 152 (italics added).

41. For the term פרע see 2 Chr 28:19 and Prov 29:18 (cf. Prov 1:25; 4:15; 8:33; 13:18; 15:32). Moberly argues that verse 25 indicates the writer's disapproval of their worship and that "If the people cast off restraint in the presence of an image which was the symbol of fertility, the implications are obvious" (*At the Mountain of God*, 196 n.7); cf. 1 Cor 10:7.

The uses of צחק in these five passages acquires cohesion if one accepts the euphemistic function in the *piel* stem. Each one of the examples is deliberately vague in meaning. Indeed, linguists rightly explain that euphemism is "close to the border between speaking and being silent."[42] The remaining occurrence of צחק in the *piel* stem is, of course, in Judges 16:25b, and it is treated separately at the conclusion of this study.

Thus, five categories of meaning are established for the sixty-eight occurrences of שׂחק/צ. The resulting nuances, based on synchronic analysis, are now summarized in Table 2.

	שׂחק	צחק
qal	to ridicule	to laugh
hiphil	to cause ridicule	
piel	to play	euphemistic function

Table 21.2: Synchronic Nuances

Potential Solutions

Now that these two lexemes are compared and contrasted synchronically, a question remains concerning their diachronic (etymological) relationship.[43] I indicate above that a phoneme shift takes place in which the fricative sibilant (שׂ) replaces the affricate (צ).[44] This evolutionary shift in spelling/pronunciation is an intra-Hebrew phenomenon that relegates צחק to the status of an archaism.

A foray into comparative Semitics demonstrates that the צ-form is etymologically primary, rather than the שׂ-form.[45] That is, צחק has cognates in Ugaritic, Aramaic, Amorite, and Arabic,[46] all with the basic sense, "to laugh;"[47] whereas, שׂחק

---

42. Ellingworth and Mojola, "Translating Euphemisms in the Bible," 143.

43. For definitions of the terms "synchronic" and "diachronic," see Noonan, *Advances*, 39–40; Walton, "Principles for Productive Word Study" in *NIDOTTE* 1:163–64.

44. Whereas GKC explains this as "commutation" (§19a), Waltke and O'Connor simply term it "interchange of consonants" (*IBHS* §5.8).

45. See Brenner, "On the Semantic Field of Humor, Laughter, and the Comic in the Old Testament" in Radday and Brenner, *On Humor and the Comic*, 46–48.

46. Other cognates include Syriac, Mehri, Soqotri, and Harari; see Murtonen, *Hebrew in its West Semitic Setting*, 2:358. For the Ugaritic cognate see also *DUL* 771; *UT* 429, 473 in the glossary.

47. Murtonen, *Hebrew in its West Semitic Setting*, 2:358.

does not occur in the near cognates at all.⁴⁸ This suggests that biblical Hebrew צחק is the archaic representative preserving the Proto-Semitic root.

But why would this archaic form be preserved in certain biblical contexts? It is a well-recognized linguistic phenomenon that figures of speech can preserve archaic forms. I would suggest that all the occurrences of צחק (in both *qal* and *piel*) can be explained as archaisms which are preserved by three figures of speech—namely, paronomasia, hendiadys, and euphemism.

Paronomasia. צחק is used in a wordplay on the personal name "Isaac" (יצחק, "he laughs"). This wordplay occurs seven times in the *qal* stem, and is used exclusively in Genesis.⁴⁹ The spelling of the name Isaac becomes the basis for this wordplay because it preserves the archaic צ-form. The preservation of an archaism in a personal name is also observed in English surnames such as "Wainwright," freezing the archaic occupation of "wagon-worker."⁵⁰ In a similar way, the name Isaac preserves a word that is no longer in common usage. Therefore, the name Isaac becomes the occasion for wordplays with the archaic root צחק.

Hendiadys. Another occurrence of צחק is in Ezekiel 23:32. It is essential to note that "scorn and derision" (לצחק וללעג; omitted by LXX) in this verse is a hendiadys,⁵¹ because hendiadys has a linguistic capacity to freeze archaic terminology. Take, for example, the English hendiadys "beck and call." The combination "beck and call" occurs frequently, even though "beck" (an English archaism) no longer occurs by itself. Of course, this example does not prove that the hendiadys in this passage freezes an archaic form, but it simply demonstrates the possibility of this phenomenon occurring in language generally.⁵²

Euphemism. The euphemistic use of צחק is demonstrated above for the occurrences in the *piel* stem only. Euphemisms are not only expressed by means of foreign, high level, and technical language, but they are also expressed by means of archaic terminology.⁵³ Thus, it is linguistically conceivable that archaic צחק is preserved

---

48. Murtonen, *Hebrew in its West Semitic Setting*, 2:418.

49. Gen 17:17; 18:12, 13, 15(2x); 21:6(2x).

50. One can observe this phenomenon in many English surnames (e.g., Cooper, Smith, Sheppard, Glover, Weaver, Potter, etc.). Not only do names have the capacity of preserving archaisms, but names can also acquire euphemistic nuances (cf. "Fanny").

51. See Cook, "Structure and Significance of Hendiadys." He does not include Ezekiel 23:32 in his list (pp. 100–107), but it could still qualify. Through personal correspondence in 1997, Cook notes that this phrase could be persuasively argued as a hendiadys ("mocking laughter"), though it may be better classified as syntheton. Either classification could freeze archaic terminology.

52. For other English examples, note how "wax and wane," "to and fro," and "fire and brimstone" are expressions that preserve or freeze archaisms. In Mishnaic Hebrew לשׂאת ולתת ("to negotiate;" literally, "to take and to give") is a hendiadys that freezes the archaic vocalization (i.e. the standard biblical Hebrew spelling) of the *qal* infinitive construct forms; however, the same forms are vocalized independently as לישׂא ("to marry") and ליתן ("to give") in Mishnaic Hebrew (see Jerusalmi, *Basic Pirqé Avoth*, 29).

53. See Ellingworth and Mojola, "Translating Euphemisms in the Bible," 142.

through the means of euphemism. For example, one may refer to a toilet as the "john." This designation may originate in the life of Sir John Harrington, who developed Britain's first flushing toilet in the late sixteenth century CE.[54] This use of the word "john" is a euphemism that has a semantic connection to an archaic context. This example demonstrates how euphemisms have the capacity to preserve archaisms.

Furthermore, צחק is not the only Semitic lexeme that carries the nuance "to laugh" in addition to a euphemistic usage. For example, the Akkadian ṣâḫu (ṣiāḫu), although not an obvious cognate (lacking the third radical), provides an example of another term that can mean both "to laugh, to smile" and "to be alluring, to act coquettishly."[55]

Therefore, צחק is always used in a figure of speech—either wordplay, hendiadys, or euphemism. This is an important observation because each of these figures of speech has the capacity to freeze archaic forms. That is why archaic צחק is preserved in biblical Hebrew.

Now if this analysis of צחק is correct, then one can infer that the normal range of meaning for this lexeme was transferred to שחק. One could even speculate that this shift took place because of the distasteful nuances that became attached to צחק (in the *piel* stem).

There are numerous examples of words that cease to be used in their original sense when they acquire euphemistic meanings. Take, for instance, the English word "gay." When it acquired a euphemistic meaning (as "homosexual"), it ceased to be used in its original sense (as "happy"). Of course, "gay" does not provide a perfect analogy to שׂ/צחק; it only demonstrates how an acquired euphemism can be the occasion for a change in usage.[56]

When a word acquires a euphemistic meaning, the common response is to attach the non-euphemistic part of the semantic range to a close synonym. For example, the word "donkey" (rather than "ass") is generally the preferred designation because of the pejorative sense that "ass" acquired in American English.[57] But concerning שׂ/צחק, I suggest that rather than shifting to a different lexeme that was semantically related, the normal meaning of צחק shifted to a lexeme that was phonetically related (thus, the sibilant shift from צ to שׂ).

---

54. See https://en.wikipedia.org/wiki/John_Harington_(writer) and http://www.todayifoundout.com/index.php/2010/08/why-the-toilet-is-sometimes-called-a-john/ (accessed on March 25, 2020).

55 *CAD* vol. 16 (Ṣ), 64–65; cf. *HALOT* 3:1019; Paul, "The Shared Legacy," in Paul, *Divrei Shalom*, 313; van der Toorn, "Female Prostitution," 202.

56. For other English examples, cf. "faggot" (pejorative) and "intercourse." In Modern Hebrew, חשפנות was originally coined for "archaeology," from חשׂף, "to uncover" (Ben-Yehuda, *Dictionary*, 17, 111), but the word quickly came to mean "strip tease" (Alcalay, *Dictionary*, 3627) and apparently did not enter Modern Hebrew usage; thus the preferred term for "archaeology" is now the borrowed lexeme ארכאולוגיה (Alcalay, *Dictionary*, 188). I must thank Ayelet and Noam Hendren for their assistance with the Modern and Mishnaic Hebrew examples (both here and above).

57. Cf. "bitch" for another example.

English speakers are also accustomed to using phoneme shifts as a reaction to semantic change. The word "damn" used to be a perfectly acceptable word that referred to God's eternal judgment. But when it began to be used as profanity, "damn" became unacceptable for use in polite company. The English phoneme shift to "darn" or to "dang" is not a reassignment of the original semantic range of "damn," but it comprises a more polite form of the expletive. This example and many others[58] may demonstrate how a semantic change can effect a phoneme shift.

The English examples that I offer throughout this study are only illustrations. They do not prove my proposals; they merely clarify general linguistic phenomena. I have not been able to identify other instances in either Hebrew or cognate languages where a distasteful nuance becomes the occasion for a phoneme shift. Perhaps this can be a subject for future research.

Reading Judges 16:25

So what aspects of "Samson's spectacle" (שחוק שמשון; v. 27) are specified in Judges 16:25? When the Philistines shouted, "Call Samson so that he may entertain us [וישחק־לנו; v. 25a]," the word used was שחק in the *piel* stem: this is normal Hebrew usage. Then the text says that "they called Samson out of the prison, and he acted obscenely before them [ויצחק לפניהם; v. 25b],"[59] in which צחק is used in the *piel* stem. I am suggesting that the only reason archaic צחק would be chosen is for euphemistic purposes. Therefore, the composer intends these two verbs to convey different meanings. שחק refers to the Philistines's cruel intentions (literally, "that he may play for us"),[60] whereas, צחק represents Samson's unexpected actions.

If צחק indeed preserves a euphemistic usage in the *piel* stem, then Samson does not offer the entertainment that the Philistines are expecting.[61] When the Philistines bring him out for their amusement, Samson perhaps responds with obscene gestures or behavior considered to be in bad taste. Since a euphemism intends to conceal, it is difficult to pinpoint a specific gesture or behavior in the cultural *milieu* of ancient

---

58. Cf. the phoneme shifts "hell/heck," "God/gosh," etc.

59. Each of the collocations in this verse is unique, occurring nowhere else.

60. Walton et al. speculate about the Philistines's intentions: "The 'entertainment' provided by Samson was probably not connected to his wit or his strength, but to his blindness. Putting obstacles in the way and striking or tripping him would be only a few of the cruel possibilities for tormenting a blind person in an unfamiliar place" (*IVPBBCOT*, 270).

61. Many scholars have observed that the immediate context is saturated with literary reversals and paronomasia. See Exum and Whedbee, "Isaac, Samson, and Saul: Reflections on the Comic and Tragic Visions," in Radday and Brenner, *On Humor and the Comic*, 136, 148–50, 156; Halton, "Samson's Last Laugh," 61–64 (but note the critiques in Chisholm, *Commentary on Judges and Ruth*, 429–30 n. 158); Kim, *Samson Cycle*, 362–63, 375–77; Segert, "Paronomasia in the Samson Narrative," 455, 460. Baker points out a number of word plays in Judges, especially those featuring sibilants (see Baker, "Double Trouble," 32–33, 36, 45–50).

Philistia/Israel.[62] However, that the nature of Samson's response is insulting, offensive, or obscene would be the implication of the term צחק.

Bibliography

Albertz, Rainer. *A History of Israelite Religion in the Old Testament Period*, vol. 1: *From the Beginnings to the End of the Monarchy*. Translated by John Bowden. OTL. Louisville: Westminster John Knox, 1992.

Alcalay, R. *The Complete English-Hebrew Dictionary*. New enlarged ed. Jerusalem: Massada, 1990.

Baker, Robin. "Double Trouble: Counting the Cost of Jephthah." *JBL* 137 (2018) 29–50.

Ben-Yehuda, Ehud, ed. *Ben-Yehuda's Pocket English-Hebrew Hebrew-English Dictionary*. New York: Pocket, 1964.

Block, Daniel I., ed. *Israel: Ancient Kingdom or Late Invention?* Nashville: Broadman & Holman, 2008.

Block, Daniel I. *Judges, Ruth*. NAC 6. Nashville: Broadman & Holman, 1999.

Botterweck, G. Johannes, Helmer Ringgren, and Heinz-Josef Fabry, eds. *Theological Dictionary of the Old Testament*. Vol. 14. Grand Rapids: Eerdmans, 2004.

Butler, Trent. *Judges*. WBC 8. Nashville: Nelson, 2009.

Cassuto, U. *A Commentary on the Book of Exodus*. Jerusalem: Magnes, 1967.

Charles, R. H. *The Apocrypha and Pseudepigrapha of the Old Testament*. Oxford: Clarendon Press, 1913.

Childs, Brevard S. *The Book of Exodus: A Critical, Theological Commentary*. OTL. Philadelphia: Westminster, 1974.

Chisholm, Robert B., Jr. *A Commentary on Judges and Ruth*. Grand Rapids: Kregel, 2013.

Clements, Ronald E. *Exodus*. Cambridge Bible Commentary. Cambridge: Cambridge University Press, 1972.

Clines, David J. A., ed. *The Dictionary of Classical Hebrew*. 9 vols. Sheffield: Sheffield Phoenix, 1993–2016.

Cook, J. A. "The Structure and Significance of Hendiadys in the Old Testament." Deerfield, IL: Trinity Evangelical Divinity School, M.A. Thesis, 1992.

Coote, Robert B., and David Robert Ord. *The Bible's First History: From Eden to the Court of David with the Yahwist*. 1989. Reprint, Eugene, OR: Wipf & Stock, 2017.

Day, Peggy L., ed. *Gender and Difference in Ancient Israel*. Minneapolis: Fortress, 1989.

Durham, John I. *Exodus*. WBC 3. Waco, TX: Word, 1987.

Ellingworth, Paul, and Aloo Mojola. "Translating Euphemisms in the Bible." *BT* 37.1 (1986) 139–43.

Even-Shoshan, Abraham, ed. *A New Concordance of the Old Testament Using the Hebrew and Aramaic Text*. Jerusalem: Kiryat-Sefer, 1993.

Gesenius, W., E. Kautzsch, and A. E. Cowley. *Gesenius' Hebrew Grammar*. Oxford: Clarendon, 1910.

Gordon, Cyrus H. *Ugaritic Textbook*. Analecta Orientalia 38. Rome: Pontifical Biblical Institute, 1965.

Halton, Charles. "Samson's Last Laugh: The Ś/ŠḤQ Pun in Judges 16:25–27." *JBL* 128 (2009) 61–64.

---

62. Cf. hand gestures for communicating the F-word in the modern cultural *milieu*.

Hamilton, Victor P. *The Book of Genesis: Chapters 18–50*. NICOT. Grand Rapids: Eerdmans, 1995.

Hoffner, Harry A., ed., *Orient and Occident: Essays Presented to C. H. Gordon on the Occasion of his Sixty-fifth Birthday*. AOAT 22. Kevelaer: Butzon und Bercker; Neukirchen-Vluyn: Neukirchener, 1973.

Hoffner, Harry A. "A Hittite Analogue to the David and Goliath Contest of Champions?" *CBQ* 30 (1968) 220–25.

Hvidberg, Flemming Friis. *Weeping and Laughter in the Old Testament: A Study of Canaanite-Israelite Religion*. Leiden: Brill, 1962.

Hyatt, J. P. *Exodus*. New Century Bible. Grand Rapids: Eerdmans, 1971.

Janzen, J. "The Character of the Calf and its Cult in Exodus 32" *CBQ* 52 (1990) 597–607.

Jerusalmi, Isaac. *Basic Pirqé Avoth: A Philological Commentary*. Cincinnati: Hebrew Union College-Jewish Institute of Religion, 1968.

Kim, Jichan. *The Structure of the Samson Cycle*. Kampen: Kok Pharos, 1993.

Koehler, Ludwig, and Walter Baumgartner. *The Hebrew and Aramaic Lexicon of the Old Testament*. Vol. 3. Leiden: Brill, 1996.

Marcos, Natalio Fernandez. *Judges*. BHQ 7. Stuttgart: Deutsche Bibelgesellschaft, 2011.

Minkoff, Harvey. "Coarse Language in the Bible? It's Culture Shocking!" *BRev* 5.2 (1989) 22–27, 44.

Moberly, R. W. L. *At the Mountain of God: Story and Theology in Exodus 32–34*. JSOTSup 22. Sheffield: Sheffield, 1983.

Murtonen, A. *Hebrew in Its West Semitic Setting: A Comparative Survey of Non-Masoretic Hebrew Dialects and Traditions*. Vol. 2. Studies in Semitic Languages and Linguistics 16. Leiden: Brill, 1989.

Niditch, Susan. *Judges: A Commentary*. OTL. Louisville: Westminster John Knox, 2008.

Noonan, Benjamin J. *Advances in the Study of Biblical Hebrew and Aramaic: New Insights for Reading the Old Testament*. Grand Rapids: Zondervan, 2020.

Noth, Martin. *Exodus: A Commentary*. Translated by J. S. Bowden. OTL. Philadelphia: Westminster, 1962.

Olmo Lete, Gregorio del, Joaquín Sanmartín, et al. *A Dictionary of the Ugaritic Language in the Alphabetic Tradition*. 3rd ed. Leiden: Brill, 2015.

Oppenheim, A. Leo, and Erica Reiner, eds. *The Assyrian Dictionary of the Oriental Institute of the University of Chicago*, Vol. 16/Ṣ. Chicago: Oriental Institute, 1962.

Paul, Shalom M. *Divrei Shalom: Collected Studies of Shalom M. Paul on the Bible and the Ancient Near East, 1967–2005*. CHANE 23. Leiden: Brill, 2005.

Pedersen, Johannes. *Israel: Its Life and Culture*. 4 vols. in 2. Translated by A. Møller and A. I. Fausbøll. London: Oxford University Press, 1953.

Radday, Yehuda T., and Athalya Brenner, eds. *On Humor and the Comic in the Hebrew Bible*. JSOTSup 92. Sheffield: Almond, 1990.

Rad, Gerhard von. *Wisdom in Israel*. Translated by James D. Martin. Nashville: Abingdon, 1972.

Sarna, Nahum M. *Genesis*. JPS Torah Commentary. Philadelphia: Jewish Publication Society, 1989.

Segert, Stanislav. "Paronomasia in the Samson Narrative in Judges XVII–XVI." *VT* 34 (1984) 454–61.

Speiser, E. A. *Genesis*. AB 1. Garden City: Doubleday, 1964.

Sukenik (=Yadin), Yigael. "Let the Young Men, I Pray Thee, Arise and Play Before Us." *JPOS* 21 (1948) 110–16.

Toorn, Karel van der, "Female Prostitution in Payment of Vows in Ancient Israel." *JBL* 108 (1989) 193–205.

Trimm, Charlie. *Fighting for the King and the Gods: A Survey of Warfare in the Ancient Near East*. Resources for Biblical Study 88. Atlanta: Society of Biblical Literature, 2017.

VanGemeren, Willem A., ed. *New International Dictionary of Old Testament Theology and Exegesis*. 5 vols. Grand Rapids: Zondervan, 1997.

Vaux, Roland de. *The Bible and the Ancient Near East*. Translated by Damian McHugh. Garden City: Doubleday, 1971.

Walsh, Carey Ellen. *The Fruit of the Vine: Viticulture in Ancient Israel*. HSM 60. Winona Lake, IN: Eisenbrauns, 2000.

Waltke, Bruce K., and M. O'Connor. *Introduction to Biblical Hebrew Syntax*. Winona Lake, IN: Eisenbrauns, 1990.

Walton, John H. *The NIV Application Commentary: Genesis*. Grand Rapids: Zondervan, 2001.

Walton, John H., Victor H. Matthews, and Mark W. Chavalas. *The IVP Bible Background Commentary: Old Testament*. Downers Grove, IL: InterVarsity, 2000.

Way, Kenneth C. *Judges and Ruth: Teach the Text Commentary Series*. Grand Rapids: Baker, 2016.

Webb, Barry G. *The Book of Judges*. NICOT. Grand Rapids: Eerdmans, 2012.

Wenham, Gordon J. *Genesis 16–50*. WBC 2. Dallas: Word, 1994.

Westermann, Claus. *Genesis 12–36*. Translated by John J. Scullion. Continental Commentaries. Minneapolis: Fortress, 1985.

Whedbee, J. William. *The Bible and the Comic Vision*. 1998. Reprinted, Minneapolis: Fortress, 2002.

Yadin, Yigael. *The Art of Warfare in Biblical Lands in the Light of Archaeological Study*. Two volumes. New York: McGraw-Hill, 1963.

22

The Victory of YHWH in the Temple of Dagon (1 Samuel 5:1–5)

JONATHON WYLIE

FIRST SAMUEL 5:1–5 NARRATES YHWH's victory over Dagon inside Dagon's own temple (בית). This scene is at the center of the so-called Ark Narrative (henceforth, AN) of 1 Sam 4:1b–7:1, which recounts the capture of the ark by the Philistines, its deadly sojourn in Philistia, and its eventual return to Israel.[1] My contention in this essay is that there is symbolic significance in the fact that YHWH defeats Dagon *in Dagon's temple.* In view of the fact that ancient temples were not only a place of worship but also representative and constitutive of a people's cosmology, YHWH's victory in Dagon's temple proclaims his dominion not only over Dagon himself but over the entire Philistine cosmos.

The genesis of this article came a few years ago as I was writing my doctoral dissertation, in which I made a brief comment about the cosmic reaches of YHWH's victory in Dagon's temple.[2] When I was invited to contribute to this volume in honor of Prof. Walton, it seemed fitting to develop the idea for this occasion. As readers will see, this essay is heavily influenced by Prof. Walton's illuminating work on ancient

---

1. Since the publication of Leonhard Rost's seminal 1926 monograph *Überlieferung von Thronnachfolge Davids*, there has been widespread (though not universal) agreement that the AN originated as an independent text. In Rost's formulation, the original narrative included most of what is now 1 Sam 4:1—7:1 and 2 Sam 6, and served as a *hieros logos* explaining how the ark came to Jerusalem. I find Rost's hypothesis that the AN was formerly independent compelling, but I am ambivalent about whether the independent text included anything that is now in 2 Sam 6 (see Wylie, "He Shall Deliver," 31–63). For summaries of the issues pertaining to the AN's composition- and redaction-history, see Miller and Roberts, *Hand of the Lord*, 18–26; Campbell, "Yahweh and the Ark;" and Eynikel, "Relation."

2. Wylie, "He Shall Deliver," 84–85.

temples, and this study may be seen as an application of his ideas to a text that, to my knowledge, has not previously been considered through this lens.[3] I never had the pleasure of studying with Prof. Walton in a formal setting, but I have learned much from his writings, lectures, and our occasional conversations. He has been a blessing and an example to me in several ways, and I am honored to dedicate this essay to him.

The Role of the Ark in the AN

The AN begins with a pair of battles between the Israelites and Philistines near Aphek and Ebenezer in the Sharon plain. After losing the first battle, the Israelite elders ask, "Why has YHWH defeated us today before the Philistines?" They instantly propose that the ark of YHWH be retrieved from Shiloh "so that he [or it] may enter into our midst and save us from the hand of our enemies" (1 Sam 4:3). Despite the expectations of Israelites and Philistines alike (1 Sam 4:5–9), the ark does not improve Israel's fortunes in the second battle. In fact, the results are worse than before. This time, some 30,000 troops are slain, the Elide priestly family is killed, and, worst of all, the ark is captured by the Philistines (1 Sam 4:10–11, 12–22).

It is well known that, in the cognitive environment of the ancient Near East, warfare was a contest of human armies and a contest between the gods of the warring parties.[4] This is why the Israelites bring the ark from Shiloh. In the AN, the ark is virtually inseparable from YHWH, and the elders assume that its proximity will make YHWH more present and therefore more potent.[5] More specifically, the Israelites view the ark as a war palladium, representing and ensuring the presence of YHWH.[6] The expectation shared by Israelites and Philistines alike (1 Sam 4:5–9) is that the presence of the ark in the Israelite camp all but guarantees a victory for Israel.[7]

When these expectations are thwarted by Israel's loss in the second battle, the death of the priestly clan, and especially the capture of the ark by the Philistines,

---

3. See especially Walton, "Creation in Genesis 1:1—2:3;" *Genesis 1*, 100–121; *Ancient Near Eastern Thought*, 73–96.

4. Campbell, *1 Samuel*, 75. Prof. Walton has written extensively on the concept of cognitive environment; see Walton, *Genesis 1*, 1–16; "Interactions," 333–39.

5. Importantly, the elders' question—"Why has YHWH defeated us today before the Philistines?" (1 Sam 4:3)—reveals that they believe that YHWH was already active on the battlefield even while the ark remained in Shiloh. The ark does not make YHWH *become* present but it does make him *more* present, and perhaps (Israel hopes) more favorable. The ark symbolizes YHWH but it does not contain him.

6. The ark has a similar military function in Num 10:35–36; 14:44; and 2 Sam 11:11.

7. One is left to wonder why Israel did not bring the ark to the first battle. The best answer, in my view, is more narratival/theological than historical: the narrator wants to raise questions about the ark's (and YHWH's) power, first by presenting defeat in the ark's absence and then by presenting defeat in its presence. The ark's presence at the second battle heightens the anticipation that Israel will be victorious. This expectation, in turn, enhances the sense of devastation when it is unmet. See further discussion at McCarter, *I Samuel*, 109; Campbell, *1 Samuel*, 67; Brueggemann, *First and Second Samuel*, 30.

urgent theological questions arise. If the ark is representative of YHWH and his might, its capture and Israel's defeat inevitably evoke reflection: Has YHWH succumbed to the Philistines and their god? Is he still sovereign? If he is, why has he not given Israel the victory?

Sacred objects and images were frequently captured by victorious armies in the ancient Near East. In the following pages, I present a brief survey of ancient texts produced by victorious and vanquished parties. This survey will shed light on the theological implications of the capture or loss of sacred objects. The insight we glean from this survey, in turn, will illuminate the theological aims of the AN in general and of YHWH's victory in Dagon's temple in particular.

Theological Implications of the Capture and Loss of Sacred Objects

As was just noted, capturing the statue of a vanquished enemy's god was a common element of ancient Near Eastern warfare. The practice is abundantly attested, both in biblical and non-biblical texts. In the aftermath of his defeat of Ursa the Urartian, for instance, Sargon II boasts of plundering Ursa's gods and goddesses:

> I totally conquered, and devastated his land. Of Urzana, of Musasir,—Haldia, his god, Bagbartu, his goddess, together with the great wealth of his temple, and 6,110 people, 12 mules, 380 asses, 525 cattle, 1,285 sheep, his wife, his sons, his daughters, I carried off.[8]

In a biblical example, David is said to have taken the idols of the Philistines following one of his battles with them (2 Sam 5:21).

Ancient texts indicate that victorious parties comprehended the significance of taking an enemy's god in various ways, and the differing perspectives could lead to different treatments of the images. One view was that the capture of an enemy's statue was a clear indication that the victorious god had vanquished the enemy's deity. This view often resulted in victorious kings offering captured images to their own deities as booty. Tiglath-Pilesar I's treatment of the images he captured from the land of Sugi illustrates this practice:

> At that time I presented the twenty-five gods of those lands, which I had captured with my hand and had taken away, as gifts to the temple of Belit (Ninlil), the mighty consort, the beloved of Assur, my lord, and (to the temples) of Anu and Adad, and the Assyrian Ishtar,—the sanctuaries of my city Assur and of the goddesses of my land.[9]

---

8. Luckenbill, *ARAB II*, §176.

9. Luckenbill, *ARAB I*, §234. For additional examples of kings presenting plundered statues to their own god as booty, see Miller and Roberts (*Hand of the Lord*, 10 and 91 n. 75), who also cite the passage above.

Taken to the extreme, the view that one deity had conquered another could result in the destruction or disposal of captured statues by those who plundered them. This was the course that Assurbanipal took when he sacked Elam. He claimed,

> The sanctuary of Elam I destroyed totally (lit., to non-existence) . . . Its gods (and) goddesses I scattered (*lit.* counted) to the wind(s). Their secret groves, which no stranger (ever) penetrates, whose borders he never (over)steps,— into these my soldiers entered, saw their mysteries, and set them on fire.[10]

Deuteronomy's insistence that Israel burn the statues of foreign nations is another attestation of the practice of destroying enemies' sacred objects (Deut 7:5, 25). Given the close relationship between a god and its statue,[11] the act of destroying an image was tantamount to denying that god's existence.

An alternative perspective that victorious parties frequently maintained was that their enemy's god had forsaken his/her people in order to ally him-/herself with them (that is, with the victors). The most common explanation for the god's defection is that the god had become angry with his/her people. Hence, Assurbanipal justifies his war against Shamash-shum-ukîn by saying: "Because of the evil deeds which he did to my house, his gods have been angry with him, they have left him, they have sought other (lands)."[12] Here, the god is not so much captured as welcomed. A biblical example of this reasoning appears in 2 Kgs 18:21–25, where the Rabshakeh claims that YHWH is displeased with Hezekiah and Judah and is therefore now on Assyria's side.

However a victorious party treated the sacred objects they plundered, the very act of taking those objects was, to their minds, a symbolic expression of a new sociopolitical and theological reality. Taking the image of an enemy's god was a sign of the subjugation of that god's land and people. In some cases, it was an indication that the god has forsaken his/her native people and sided with the enemy. In others it was a testament to the superiority of the victorious people and god.

Turning to the responses of vanquished peoples, the fact that the ancients understood warfare to involve both humans and their gods inevitably led to theological questions in the wake of a god's capture. Unwilling to concede that their god had been overwhelmed by enemies, defeated parties typically attributed their defeat and their god's "departure" to the displeasure of the god, usually because of sin. The following texts of Esarhaddon and Assurbanipal, respectively, are good examples:

> Before my time the great lord Marduk became angry. He went in (to his temple), and his heart was enraged against Esagila and Babylon, he was furious. Through the anger of his heart and the fury of his soul, Esagila and Babylon

---

10. Luckenbill, *ARAB II*, §810.
11. Walton, *Ancient Near Eastern Thought*, 74–77.
12. Luckenbill, *ARAB II*, §1104.

became wasteland and were like the open country. Its gods and goddesses departed, leaving their shrines and going up to heaven.[13]

The goddess Nanâ, who had been angry for 1,635 years, and who had gone and dwelt in Elam, a place not suitable for her, now, in these days, when she and the gods, her fathers, had named me for the rulership of the lands, she intrusted [sic] to me the return of her divinity, with the words: "Assurbanipal shall bring me out of wicked Elam, shall bring me into Eanna."[14]

In other cases, peoples who lost their gods determined that the god had simply gone on a trip. The best illustration of the latter strategy is in the *Prophecy of Marduk*, which narrates and explains a series of (ostensibly) intentional departures that Marduk made from Babylon.[15] According to the text, when Mursilis I of Hatti captured the image of Marduk (1595 BC), Marduk himself orchestrated the whole event: "I [Marduk] gave the command. I went to the land of Hatti. I questioned Hatti. The throne of my Anu-ship I set up within it. I dwelt within it for 24 years, and I established within it the caravan of trade of the Babylonians."[16] In this case, what was seen by Marduk's Babylonian devotees as a catastrophe is reframed as a trip to strengthen international trade networks. The text proceeds to explain the time when Marduk's image was carted off to Assyria by Tukulti-Ninurta I (1225 BC). Again, the text insists that it was Marduk's will to be in Assyria and that he always returns home to Babylon: "I am Marduk the great lord. I alone am lord of destinies and decisions. Who has taken this road? Wherever I went, from there I returned."[17] The text makes these historical points in order to address the recent defeat of Babylon by the Elamites and the capture (once again) of the image of Marduk (1150 BC). In keeping with the text's strategy, it asserts Marduk's sovereignty in this new situation: "I myself gave the command. I went to the land of Elam, and all the gods went with me—I alone gave the command."[18] However much the *Prophecy of Marduk* may spin historical events, the fact that the text relentlessly asserts Marduk's sovereignty in the face of events that called it into question shows the theological dilemma that the loss of a sacred object presented to ancient communities. The god's capture brought forth concerns about the strength of the god and his intentions. It fell to ancient theologians to provide consolation by reaffirming the god's sovereignty.

---

13. Luckenbill, *ARAB II*, §662.
14. Luckenbill, *ARAB II*, §812.
15. All surviving tablets date to the seventh century BC, but the text likely originated in the reign of Nebuchadnezzar I (1125–1104 BC). For additional discussion of this text, see Borger, *Gott Marduk*; Miller and Roberts, *Hand of the Lord*, 11–14; Longman, *Fictional Akkadian Autobiography*, 132–42; Roberts, "Nebuchadnezzar I's Elamite Crisis;" and Sugie, "Reception."
16. Miller and Roberts, *Hand of the Lord*, 12.
17. Miller and Roberts, *Hand of the Lord*, 12.
18. Miller and Roberts, *Hand of the Lord*, 13.

Part 3: Context

Returning to 1 Sam 5:1–5, the foregoing survey sheds light on why the Philistines capture the ark and set it up in Dagon's temple. If the Philistines view the ark as representative of a deity whom Dagon has defeated, then they place the ark in Dagon's temple as a trophy of Dagon's strength and success, perhaps with the expectation that YHWH will venerate Dagon.[19] Alternatively, and in my view more likely, the Philistines deposit the ark in Dagon's temple because they intend to revere the God of Israel alongside Dagon—not necessarily as an equal to Dagon but as a deity who has partnered with Dagon and promoted his cause. This would be consistent with the Philistines' respectful attitude toward the ark in 1 Sam 4:6–8, where they realize that the ark has arrived at the battlefield and fear that YHWH will do to them what he did to the Egyptians earlier in Israel's history. The possibility that the Philistines intend to honor the ark finds lexical support in the fact that they set it up *beside* the statue of Dagon (ויציגו אתו אצל דגן), not in front of or opposite it (e.g., לפני or מול). The arrangement seems to be one of co-regency, or at least of regent and vice regent.

As for how the Israelites may have interpreted the catastrophes of the battle of Ebenezer, it is apparent both from the AN and from the comparative texts surveyed above that the loss of a sacred image evoked pressing theological questions: Is our god still sovereign, or is he defeated? If he is in control, why has this misfortune happened to us? The AN explicitly raises the question of "why?" in 1 Sam 4:3, immediately following Israel's loss in the first battle. Curiously, the narrative never gives an explicit answer to that question.[20] On the other hand, the text raises the question of YHWH's sovereignty only implicitly through calamitous events, but it answers this question forcefully in 1 Sam 5–6. After the first battle, the elders' question is "Why has YHWH defeated us today before the Philistines?" (1 Sam 4:3). They are not yet questioning YHWH's dominion. Given the length to which the remainder of the AN goes to vindicate YHWH's might, however, it seems that Israel's question becomes starker after the outcome of the second battle. The question after the second battle is no longer *why* but *whether*—whether YHWH is himself defeated.

---

19. So McCarter, *I Samuel*, 125.

20. The question of why YHWH abandoned Israel in 1 Sam 4 is especially pressing in a hypothetically independent text commencing at 1 Sam 4:1 (see above, n. 1). In the current arrangement of texts, the sin of the Elides and the prophecy against them (1 Sam 2:12–17, 22–25, 27–36) seems to provide the reason for the catastrophes in 1 Sam 4 (see Willis, "Anti-Elide Narrative;" Miller and Roberts, *Hand of the Lord*, 18–22; McCarter, *I Samuel*, 25–26). However, it should be noted that the devastations of 1 Sam 4 are far more extensive than what is anticipated by 1 Sam 2:27–36. The latter passage envisions the demise of the Elides alone; it does not seem to expect widespread destruction for Israel. In fact, the oracle expects the Elides to be in distress while YHWH bestows prosperity upon Israel. This raises the question of whether 1 Sam 2:27–36 (and the sin of the Elides more generally) should be identified as the reason for the catastrophes in 1 Sam 4. It is more likely, in my view, that the prophecy against the Elides in 1 Sam 2:27–36 finds its fulfillment in Saul's slaughter of the priests of Nob (1 Sam 22) and the eventual election of Zadok over Abiathar, a descendant of Eli (1 Kings 2:26–27). For further discussion, see Campbell, "Yahweh and the Ark," 35; Eynikel, "Relation;" Leuchter, "Something Old, Something Older;" McCarter, *I Samuel*, 91–93; and Wylie, "He Shall Deliver," 46–50.

The Victory of YHWH in the Temple of Dagon (1 Samuel 5:1–5) —Jonathon Wylie

As the scene shifts to Philistia, the AN turns to responding to this question, emphatically vindicating YHWH's sovereignty. The Philistines take the ark to Ashdod and set it up in Dagon's temple (1 Sam 5:1-5). On the following two mornings, the Ashdodites enter the temple and find their god prostrate before the ark. On the second morning, they find him face down before the ark with his hands and head cut off, lying on the threshold of the sanctuary (1 Sam 5:3-4). The AN continues to demonstrate YHWH's dominion in the following scenes as the "hand of YHWH" executes a deadly plague upon the Philistines and their land (1 Sam 5:6-12). The Philistines pass the ark from Ashdod to Gath to Ekron, but wherever it goes it brings death and pandemonium. The plague finally compels the Philistines to return the ark to Israel (1 Sam 6:1-14), where it continues to evince its power and holiness (1 Sam 6:15—7:1).

YHWH's victory over Dagon in the latter's temple is the turning point of the narrative. Whatever the reason for the catastrophes of 1 Sam 4, 1 Sam 5:3-4 shows that they were not the result of any weakness in YHWH nor of any strength in the god of the Philistines. Yet, if the sole purpose of 1 Sam 5:2-5 is to show that YHWH is not powerless against the Philistines and their god, then, strictly speaking, this scene is not essential to the story. For an AN lacking this passage would still prove YHWH's dominion—first, over the Philistines (and thus, over Dagon; 1 Sam 5:6-12; 6:1-14), and then over the Israelites (1 Sam 6:19-20)—even if somewhat less dramatically.[21] Of course, we cannot assume that every element of a text must make a unique contribution. Even so, the observation that a text devoid of 1 Sam 5:2-5 would still vindicate YHWH's sovereignty does compel me to consider whether the scene in Dagon's temple may communicate more than initially meets the (modern Western) eye. Indeed, when we consider this scene in the light of ancient conceptions of temples, we see that the location of YHWH's victory is an important element of this pericope's meaning.

Theomachy, Temple, Cosmos

The AN presents the scene in Dagon's temple laconically and with mysterious undertones. The narration is terse, and the events unfold at night without any witnesses. There is no explicit account of the engagement between YHWH and Dagon. These factors make the contest in 1 Sam 5:3-4 distinctive in comparison with other divine battles in ancient literature, which dwell at length on the taunts the gods exchange, their weaponry, the contests themselves, and the outcomes.[22] Nevertheless, it is quite clear that the scene in Dagon's temple is a theomachy—a conflict between the gods.

---

21. Citing the redundancy between 1 Sam 5:1 and 2, and the etiology in 1 Sam 5:5, some scholars have proposed that 1 Sam 5:2-5 may be interpolated (e.g., Campbell, *Ark Narrative*, 83-85; Zwickel, "Dagons abgeschlagener Kopf"). It is likely that the etiology in verse 5 is secondary (Geoghegan, *Time, Place, and Purpose*, 88-89, 120-24), but I am unconvinced that the rest of the pericope is. As I hope to show below, 1 Sam 5:2-4 is quite integral to the AN.

22. Compare, for instance, the showdown between Baal and Yamm (*KTU* 1.2 i–iv; 1.3 i), in which these elements are developed.

The fact that, on the second morning, the Ashdodites find their deity's dismembered head and hands on the threshold of the temple is proof of a violent confrontation.

In a survey of ancient texts, Prof. Walton has shown that "In the cognitive environment of the Ancient Near East, the gods become involved in conflict under a variety of circumstances and at various levels: among themselves on an individual or corporate level, with entities or nonentities representing threat, or with humans."[23] Accordingly, what is at issue in one theomachy is not necessarily at issue in another. This raises the question of what, precisely, the theomachy in 1 Sam 5:3–4 is about.

Walton categorizes ancient Near Eastern theomachies according to the following typology:

1. Dissatisfied class revolt among the divine proletariat concerning roles
2. Order vs. Disorder in the macrocosmos (*Chaoskampf*)
    a. Initial establishment of order (cosmogony)
    b. One-time threat from chaos monster
    c. Renewal on a seasonal or daily basis
3. Struggle for rule among the gods between individual competing claimants
4. Generational coup seizing rule among the gods[24]

The conflict between YHWH and Dagon falls into the third category, in which "what is at stake is control of the divine realm."[25] Dagon's posture following the conflicts supports this conclusion. On both mornings, the priests of Dagon find him "fallen face to the earth before the ark of YHWH" (והנה דגון נפל לפניו ארצה לפני ארון יהוה). There are two possible interpretations of this phrase. One interpretation is that Dagon bows in submission to YHWH. The phrase נפל לפני ("fall before") commonly has this meaning.[26] Alternatively, and in my view more likely, the phrase indicates that Dagon is dead, even when this phrase describes Dagon's posture after the first night's confrontation. All occurrences of נפל ארצה in which נפל is a participle, as in 1 Sam 5:3–4, refer to individuals who have "fallen slain."[27] Moreover, such a meaning is consistent

---

23. Walton, "Creation in Genesis 1:1—2:3," 49.

24. Walton, "Creation in Genesis 1:1—2:3," 49.

25. Walton, "Creation in Genesis 1:1—2:3," 51. The contests between Baal and Yamm (*KTU* 1.2 iv) and Seth and Horus (*AEL II*, 214-23) are among the most well-known exemplars of this type of theomachy, but attestations are extant from across the ancient Near East. Walton adds that theomachies in this category "do not represent cosmic conflict but political conflict" ("Creation in Genesis 1:1—2:3," 51; see also Smith, "Interpreting the Baal Cycle;" Wyatt, *Myths of Power*). That is, these texts serve to legitimate royal claims to power. There can be no doubt that the AN does speak to political issues, but, unlike the theomachies involving Baal and Yamm or Seth and Horus, I do not see 1 Sam 5:1–5 promoting royal ideology, at least not directly. See below (conclusion) on the AN's function within 1–2 Samuel's dialogue on Israel's human leadership.

26. E.g., Gen 44:14; 50:18; Josh 5:14; 2 Sam 14:4, 22; 19:18; etc. For another text that speaks of YHWH subduing other gods and the resulting submission of those gods and their nations to YHWH's rule, though with very different language, see Zeph 2:11.

27. See Judg 3:25; 2 Chron 20:24. Even when נפל is not a participle, the phrase נפל ארץ/ארצה

The Victory of YHWH in the Temple of Dagon (1 Samuel 5:1–5) —Jonathon Wylie

with the AN's emphasis on YHWH's utter sovereignty; there is no theological space in this text for a rival god, even a subordinate one. If the latter interpretation is correct, then Dagon is slain during the ark's first night in his temple (1 Sam 5:3). YHWH's victory on the second night is a *fait accompli*; his dismemberment of Dagon's statue underscores and proves what has already been achieved (1 Sam 5:4).[28] However we understand the phrase דגון נפל לפניו ארצה לפני ארון יהוה, there can be no doubt that, by the second morning, headless Dagon is dead.

If the catastrophes of 1 Sam 4 called YHWH's sovereignty into question, then 1 Sam 5:3–4 insists that those catastrophes were *not* outside YHWH's control. This response does not explain why YHWH allowed the devastation, but it does extinguish any doubt about YHWH's own power. To be sure, this is a meaningful point in its own right. Yet, my contention is that, to an ancient audience, our passage meant still more. Specifically, I propose that there is significance in the fact that the theomachy takes place not in some nondescript place in the world but in a sacred space—in Dagon's own temple.

Ancient peoples from Egypt to Mesopotamia, from the third millennium BC until the Byzantine period, understood temples to be much more than brick-and-mortar buildings.[29] The temple stood at the center of the cosmos, holding heaven and earth together. It had metaphysical reaches and cosmological functions because, in a sense, the temple *was* the cosmos, or at any rate, an icon of it. To the ancient mind, a temple was an *imago mundi* and a microcosm of the created universe.[30] What Levenson says of the Jerusalem temple applies to ancient conceptions of temples across the ancient Near East: the temple "is the world *in nuce*, and the world is the Temple *in extenso*."[31]

Writing of the way in which temples dominated the landscape of ancient Egypt, Assmann notes that "it was possible to conceive of Egypt as a single huge temple, the 'temple of the entire world.'"[32] He proceeds to comment on the way in which the architecture and iconography of Egyptian temples replicated the cosmos:

> Essentially, the floor of these later temples represented the earth, and the ceiling the sky. Columns took the form of plants rising from the earth, and the dados of the walls were decorated with marsh plants or with processions

---

frequently (but not always) refers to falling slain, e.g., Lev 26:7–8; 1 Sam 14:13; 17:49; 2 Sam 3:34; etc.

28. On YHWH's dismemberment of Dagon, see Delcor, "Jahweh et Dagon." 1 Sam 5:4b presents notorious text critical difficulties. MT reads: וראש דגון ושתי כפות ידיו כרתות אל המפתן רק דגון נשאר עליו, "And the head of Dagon and his two hands were cut off upon the threshold; only Dagon was left to him." For the last clause, LXX reads πλὴν ἡ ῥάχις Δαγων ὑπελείφθη, "only the spine of Dagon was left." Most likely, we should read רק גוו דגון נשאר עליו, "only the trunk of Dagon was left to him," with גוו having been omitted from MT by haplography with דגון (McCarter, *I Samuel*, 119).

29. See the collection of essays in Boda and Novotny, *From the Foundations to the Crenellations*, which explores temples and temple texts from across the ancient world.

30. Meyers, *Tabernacle*, 171.

31. Levenson, "Temple and World," 285.

32. Assmann, *Search for God*, 27.

of 'fecundity figures,' personifications of telluric fruitfulness that always face the inner part of the temple, bearing offerings. As the sky, the ceilings were decorated with stars or with astronomical representations. Between the floor and the ceiling, between earth and sky, stretched the decorations on the walls with their endless cult scenes filling this stony cosmos *in effigie* with action and life.[33]

The remains of the temple to Horus in Edfu illustrate Assmann's comment. The top of the inner shrine is pyramidal in shape, symbolizing the primordial hill, the first dry land to emerge from the primeval waters at the dawn of creation. Supporting the massive temple are columns depicting plants growing out of the waters of creation, and reeds and papyri are carved in relief within the shrine.[34] In a comprehensive monograph on the symbolism of the Edfu temple, Finnestad notes that "The parallelism demonstrated between the cosmos and the temple shows that the Egyptians developed the cosmological aspect of the temple intentionally and coherently . . . This monumental edifice is the Egyptian exposition of the sacred nature of the cosmos."[35]

The relationship between temple and cosmos is manifest in Mesopotamian texts and architecture as well. In Assyria and Babylonia, the cosmic function of temples is proclaimed in their very names: É.ab.ša.ga.la, "House which stretches over the midst of the sea;" É.an.ki, "House of heaven and the underworld;" E.dur.an.ki, "House, bond of heaven and the underworld."[36] It is apparent from these names, and many others like them, that the temple sits at the hub of the cosmos, functioning as the meeting place of the heavens above and the netherworld or fertile primordial waters below.[37]

The link between temple (or tabernacle) and cosmos appears in biblical literature as well, though the link is often subtle. Pentateuchal scholars have long noted a typological relationship between Genesis 1 and the tabernacle.[38] Wenham, similarly, has argued that "The garden of Eden is not viewed by the author of Genesis simply as a piece of Mesopotamian farmland, but as an archetypal sanctuary, that is a place where God dwells and where man should worship him. Many of the features of the garden may also be found in later sanctuaries particularly the tabernacle or Jerusalem temple."[39] In his seminal essay on Israel's temple theology, Levenson observes that

---

33. Assmann, *Search for God*, 35; cited by Walton, *Genesis 1*, 106.

34. Lundquist, "What is a Temple?" 87.

35. Finnestad, *Image of the World*, 78. The Edfu temple was a relatively late construction (Ptolemaic period), but precisely by this fact we can see the way in which this temple demonstrates the enduring commitment to architectural traditions with more ancient roots. For the Edfu temple, despite its relative youth, incorporates architectural and iconographic grammar of more remote times (Kemp, *Ancient Egypt*, 152).

36. For additional examples, see Walton, *Genesis 1*, 103.

37. See further discussion in Hurowitz, *I Have Built*, 335–37.

38. Blenkinsopp, *Prophecy and Canon*, 61–62; Weinfeld, "Sabbath, Temple, and the Enthronement of the Lord," 502–3.

39. Wenham, "Sanctuary Symbolism," 19.

the number seven dominates the narrative of the construction and dedication of the temple in 1 Kgs 6–8, and argues that the completion of the temple recalls and even completes the creation of the world.[40]

Given the cosmic importance of the ancient temple, it is no surprise that texts routinely depict the temple as a sort of cosmic control room, the place from which the heavenly king orchestrates justice, peace, and fecundity.[41] Hence, as Gudea prepares to build a temple for Ningirsu, the latter exclaims:

> When you bring your hand to bear for me I will cry out to heaven for rain.
> From heaven let abundance come to you,
> Let the people receive abundance with you.
> With the founding of my temple
> Let abundance come!
> The great fields will lift up their hands to you,
> The canal will stretch out its neck to you.[42]

In like fashion, upon the completion of his rebuilding of the temple of Anu and Adad, Tiglath-Pileser I prays:

> [M]ay Anu and Adad graciously turn unto me, may they take pleasure in the lifting up of my hand, may they give ear unto my fervent supplication. Copious rains, and years of abundance and plenty during my reign, may they grant. May they bring me back in safety from battle and combat. May they bring into submission under my feet all the lands of my enemies, haughty lands and princes who hate me. And may they shower kindly blessings upon me and upon my priestly seed.[43]

The dedicatory inscription from Ekron indicates that seventh century BC Philistines also linked temples with blessing: "The temple (בת) which *'kyš* son of Padi, son of *Ysd*, son of Ada, son of Ya'ir, ruler of Ekron built for *PTGYH* his lady. May she bless him, and keep him, and prolong his days, and bless his land."[44] Finally, Solomon's prayer of dedication over the temple in Jerusalem reveals similar convictions about the function of that temple (1 Kgs 8:31–53). The king names several key ways in which YHWH will maintain order and justice by means of the temple: judging the guilty and vindicating the righteous (vv. 31–32); granting forgiveness of sin and restoring the land after it is lost (vv. 33–34); causing rain to fall after a period of drought brought on by sin (vv. 35–36); healing diseases and expunging pestilences caused by sin (vv. 37–40); acting

---

40. Levenson, "Temple and World," 289. If Levenson is correct in hearing an echo of Gen 1 in 1 Kgs 6–8, then this relationship recalls *Enuma Elish*, in which *Esagila* is constructed after the creation of the world and as the pinnacle of it.
41. Lundquist, "What is a Temple?" 97; Walton, *Ancient Near Eastern Thought*, 88–90.
42. Gudea Cylinder A: xi.5–13; cited by Walton, *Ancient Near Eastern Thought*, 88.
43. Luckenbill, *ARAB I*, §263.
44. See Gitin, Dothan, and Naveh, "Royal Dedicatory Inscription," 9; my translation (J.W.).

on behalf of the YHWH-fearing foreigner (vv. 41–43); giving Israel victory in battle (vv. 44–45); and restoring from exile (vv. 46–53).

If the temple is the locus of order and prosperity, then, naturally, the destruction, violation, or neglect of a temple is disastrous.[45] The book of Lamentations is illustrative. Here, the destruction of Jerusalem and the temple is cataclysmic; devastation is associated with the return to chaos: gardens are laid waste (Lam 2:6), mothers eat their children (Lam 4:10), those who formerly enjoyed luxury sit in heaps of ash (Lam 4:5). Similarly, the prophet Haggai declares that the struggles of the post-exilic community in Yehud are the consequence of neglecting to rebuild the temple (Hag 1:4–11). Once the temple is rebuilt, YHWH vows to bless his people (Hag 2:19).

What the foregoing discussion points toward is a "homology," an intimate connection and fundamental sameness between shrine and cosmos.[46] The temple is an icon, a type, a mimesis of the "true(r)" cosmic temple.[47] Because the temple is a microcosm of the world, we may conclude that whatever happens within the temple has implications in the cosmos. In the AN, then, Dagon's temple becomes YHWH's temple, which means that Dagon's world becomes YHWH's world.

The Victory of YHWH in the Temple of Dagon

One may question the extent to which the foregoing conceptions were operative for the temple of Dagon. We admittedly have no certain indication that the Philistines thought of Dagon's temple along these lines.[48] But as the diverse provenance of the primary texts cited above suggests, the idea that the temple is a cosmic symbol is not an idiosyncrasy of one particular community. These ideas were held across the

45. Lundquist, "What is a Temple?" 97.

46. Eliade, *Sacred and Profane*, 57, 165; Levenson, "Temple and World," 296; Walton, *Ancient Near Eastern Thought*, 83.

47. Hence, in Wis 9:8, Solomon acknowledges to God that "You have given command to build a temple on your holy mountain, and an altar in the city of your habitation, a copy ($\mu\acute{\iota}\mu\eta\mu\alpha$) of the holy tent that you prepared from the beginning" (NRSV). And the author of Hebrews, a bit later, says "Christ did not enter a sanctuary made with human hands, a mere copy ($\dot{\alpha}\nu\tau\acute{\iota}\tau\upsilon\pi\alpha$) of the true one, but he entered into heaven itself, now to appear in the presence of God on our behalf" (Heb 9:24 NRSV). As late as the fourth century AD, Gregory of Nyssa wrote that the tabernacle was "a sanctuary with beauty of indescribable variety," adding that God counseled Moses not to represent the tabernacle's beauty "in mere writing but to imitate in material construction that immaterial creation, employing the most splendid and radiant materials found on earth" (*Life of Moses* 1.49).

48. In truth, we know very little about this particular temple or its services. Apart from this passage, it is referenced elsewhere only in 1 Chron 10:10 and 1 Macc 10:84; 11:4. The passage in 1 Macc narrates Jonathan Maccabee's destruction of a temple of Dagon in Azotus (Hellenistic Ashdod). The reference in 1 Chron is almost certainly influenced by Judg 16:23 and (especially) 1 Sam 5:1–5, and therefore does not provide independent evidence of a historical cult of Dagon among Iron I Philistines (see Machinist, "Biblical Traditions," 72–73 n. 42). No buildings were uncovered in the excavations at Ashdod that can be confidently identified as the remains of this temple. In fact, if it were not for a handful of biblical texts, we would not even know the Philistines worshiped Dagon. For a recent discussion of 1 Sam 5:1–5 from a historical and archaeological perspective, see Emanuel, "Dagon Our God."

The Victory of YHWH in the Temple of Dagon (1 Samuel 5:1–5) —Jonathon Wylie

ancient Near Eastern world (though, no doubt, with nuances from one time and place to another). In any case, the AN was not intended for Philistines but for Israelites, and Israel certainly viewed its sacred spaces in the ways presented above. It is reasonable to suppose, therefore, that YHWH's victory in the house of Dagon would have been understood to have ramifications not only within the confines of that particular building but also on a much larger, cosmic scale. This insight, I suggest, has implications both for the AN itself and for the larger book of Samuel.

Commentators have tended to see YHWH's vindication in 1 Sam 5 unfolding in two distinct scenes: first, he displays his might in the divine realm (1 Sam 5:1–5), and then in the earthly one (5:6–12). For instance, in their very enlightening volume on the AN, Miller and Roberts draw the following conclusions about 1 Sam 5:1–5:

> The superiority of Yahweh in the divine realm has been established first. The Philistine victory did not mean as one might have supposed (Israelite or Philistine), that Dagon was mightier than Yahweh or Yahweh subject to Dagon. On the contrary, Yahweh rules in the divine world. And, as the next section will manifest, that rule extends to and has implications for the human sphere also.[49]

The point is correct as far as it goes, but it requires nuance following the discussion above. Given the homology between temple and cosmos, and in view of the unity that a temple maintains between heaven and earth, YHWH's rule in the "divine realm" cannot be separated from his rule in the terrestrial one. The rigid separation of heaven and earth—"divine world" and "human sphere"—is a modern distinction, not an ancient one. To our story's ancient audience, YHWH's ascendancy in Dagon's temple was simultaneously his ascendancy in all Philistia.

In 1 Sam 5, then, we cannot draw too sharp a line between the two scenes that comprise the chapter (1 Sam 5:1–5, 6–12). YHWH's enthronement in the temple of Dagon proclaims and portends his domination of all Philistia. Dagon now is dead, even non-existent. As Klein put it, he is "without a head for thinking or hands for acting."[50] Critically, it is YHWH who has rendered him that way. And while Dagon's hands are cut off, the hand of YHWH is heavy against the Philistines, doling out plague, death, and fear (1 Sam 5:6–12).[51] YHWH's domination of Philistia is not something distinct from his victory in Dagon's temple but rather part and parcel of it. If, as we have seen, the temple was the control center for the cosmos, then YHWH's victory over Dagon in Dagon's temple puts him at the Philistine helm. What the Philistines experience as pandemonium is, in fact, perfectly orchestrated by the one who rules their temple and world.

---

49. Miller and Roberts, *Hand of the Lord*, 46

50. Klein, *1 Samuel*, 50.

51. "The (heavy) hand of YHWH" is a major motif in 1 Sam 5–6 (5:6, 7, 9, 11; 6:3, 5, 9). The contrast with Dagon's severed hands cannot be missed.

Part 3: Context

The foregoing elucidation of the significance of YHWH's victory in Dagon's temple also sheds light on the theological and political function of the Ark Narrative in its canonical location. The book of Samuel is deeply interested in governance and leadership. That is to say, 1–2 Samuel is concerned with the question of what form of governance, and which particular leader, is best for Israel. To a large extent, the answer is determined by another question: Who can most adequately protect Israel from Philistine incursions? Thus, as 1–2 Samuel proceeds to narrate Israel's transition from a theocracy under Samuel's intercession, to kingship under Saul, and finally to kingship under David, the traditions within the book legitimize (and/or delegitimize) each leader on the basis of how capably he subdues the Philistine threat to Israel.[52] YHWH's victory in the house of Dagon, with its symbolic assertion of YHWH's sovereignty over the Philistines, serves as a prolegomenon to this political narrative. It implies that any individual who seeks to establish his government in Israel by successfully fighting the Philistines must do so as an agent of YHWH, who rules the Philistine world.

Bibliography

Assmann, Jan. *The Search for God in Ancient Egypt.* Translated by David Lorton. Ithaca, NY: Cornell University Press, 2001.

Blenkinsopp, Joseph. *Prophecy and Canon: A Contribution to the Study of Jewish Origins.* University of Notre Dame Center for the Study of Judaism and Christianity in Antiquity Studies 3. Notre Dame: University of Notre Dame Press, 1977.

Boda, Mark J., and Jamie Novotny, eds. *From the Foundations to the Crenellations: Essays on Temple Building in the Ancient Near East and Hebrew Bible.* AOAT 366. Münster: Ugarit-Verlag, 2010.

Borger, Rykle. "Gott Marduk und Gott-König Šulgi als Propheten: Zwei prophetische Texte." *Bibliotheca Orientalis* 28 (1971) 3–24.

Brueggemann, Walter. *First and Second Samuel.* Interpretation. Louisville: Westminster John Knox, 1990.

Campbell, Antony F. *The Ark Narrative (1 Sam 4–6, 2 Sam 6): A Form-Critical and Traditio-Historical Study.* SBLDS 16. Missoula, MT: Scholars', 1975.

———. *1 Samuel.* FOTL 7. Grand Rapids: Eerdmans, 2003.

———. "Yahweh and the Ark: A Case Study in Narrative." *JBL* 98 (1979) 31–43.

Delcor, M. "Jahweh et Dagon (ou le Jahwisme face à la religion des Philistins, d'après 1 Sam. V)." *VT* 14 (1964) 136–54.

Eliade, Mircea. *The Sacred and the Profane: The Nature of Religion.* Translated by Willard R. Trask. New York: Harcourt, 1959.

Emanuel, Jeffrey P. "'Dagon Our God': Iron I Philistine Cult in Text and Archaeology." *JANER* 16 (2016) 22–66.

Eynikel, Erik. "The Relation between the Eli Narratives (1 Sam. 1–4) and the Ark Narrative (1 Sam. 1–6; 2 Sam. 6:1–19)." In *Past, Present, Future: The Deuteronomistic History and the Prophets,* edited by Johannes C. de Moor and Harry F. van Rooy, 88–106. Oudtestamentische Studiën 44. Leiden: Brill, 2000.

---

52. For further discussion, see Wylie, "He Shall Deliver."

Finnestad, Ragnhild Bjerre. *Image of the World and Symbol of the Creator: On the Cosmological and Iconological Values of the Temple of Edfu*. Studies in Oriental Religions 10. Wiesbaden: Harrassowitz, 1985.

Geoghegan, Jeffrey C. *The Time, Place, and Purpose of the Deuteronomistic History: The Evidence of "Until this Day"*. Brown Judaic Studies 347. Providence: Brown University Press, 2006.

Gitin, Seymour, Trude Dothan, and Joseph Naveh. "A Royal Dedicatory Inscription from Ekron." *IEJ* 47 (1997) 1–16.

Gregory of Nyssa. *The Life of Moses*. Translated by Abraham Malherbe and Everett Ferguson. Classics of Western Spirituality Series. New York: Paulist, 1978.

Hurowitz, Victor. *I Have Built You an Exalted House: Temple Building in the Bible in the Light of Mesopotamian and Northwest Semitic Writings*. JSOTSup 115. JSOT/ASOR Monograph Series 5. Sheffield: JSOT, 1992.

Kemp, Barry J. *Ancient Egypt: Anatomy of a Civilization*. New York: Routledge, 2006.

Klein, Ralph. *1 Samuel*. WBC 10. Grand Rapids: Zondervan, 2000.

Leuchter, Mark. "Something Old, Something Older: Reconsidering 1 Sam. 2:27–36." *JHS* 4 (2003) Article 6. http://www.jhsonline.org/Articles/article_28.pdf.

Levenson, Jon D. "The Temple and the World." *Journal of Religion* 64 (1984) 275–98.

Longman, Tremper, III. *Fictional Akkadian Autobiography: A Generic and Comparative Study*. Winona Lake, IN: Eisenbrauns, 1991.

Luckenbill, Daniel David. *Ancient Records of Assyria and Babylonia*. 2 vols. Chicago: University of Chicago Press, 1926–27.

Lundquist, John M. "What Is a Temple? A Preliminary Typology." In *The Quest for the Kingdom of God: Studies in Honor of George E. Mendenhall*, edited by Herbert B. Huffmon et al., 205–20. Winona Lake, IN: Eisenbrauns, 1983.

Machinist, Peter. 2000. "Biblical Traditions: The Philistines and Israelite History." In *The Sea Peoples and Their World: A Reassessment*, edited by Eliezer D. Oren, 53–83. University Museum Monograph 108. University Museum Symposium Series 11. Philadelphia: University Museum, University of Pennsylvania, 2000.

McCarter, P. Kyle, Jr. *I Samuel*. AB 8. Garden City, NY: Doubleday, 1980.

Meyers, Carol L. *The Tabernacle Menorah: A Synthetic Study of a Symbol from the Biblical Cult*. Piscataway, NJ: Gorgias, 2003.

Miller, Patrick D., and J. J. M. Roberts. *The Hand of the Lord: A Reassessment of the "Ark Narrative" of 1 Samuel*. Baltimore: Johns Hopkins University Press, 1977.

Roberts, J. J. M. "Nebuchadnezzar I's Elamite Crisis in Theological Perspective." In *The Bible and the Ancient Near East: Collected Essays*, 83–92. Winona Lake, IN: Eisenbrauns, 2002.

Rost, Leonhard. *Überlieferung von Thronnachfolge Davids*. BWANT 42. Stuttgart: Kohlhammer, 1926.

Smith, Mark S. "Interpreting the Baal Cycle." *UF* 18 (1986) 313–39.

Sugie, Takuma. "Reception of the 'Marduk Prophecy' in Seventh-Century B.C Nineveh." *Orient* 49 (2014) 107–13.

Walton, John H. *Ancient Near Eastern Thought and the Old Testament: Introducing the Conceptual World of the Hebrew Bible*. Grand Rapids: Baker Academic, 2006.

———. "Creation in Genesis 1:1—2:3 and the Ancient Near East: Order out of Disorder after *Chaoskampf*." *CTJ* 43 (2003) 48–63.

———. *Genesis 1 as Ancient Cosmology*. Winona Lake, IN: Eisenbrauns, 2016.

———. "Interactions in the Ancient Cognitive Environment." In *Behind the Scenes of the Old Testament: Cultural, Social, and Historical Contexts*, edited by Jonathan S. Greer, John W. Hilber, and John H. Walton, 333–39. Grand Rapids: Baker, 2018.

Weinfeld, Moshe. "Sabbath, Temple, and the Enthronement of the Lord: The Problem of the Sitz im Leben of Genesis 1:1—2:3." In *Mélanges bibliques et orientaux en l'honneur de M. Henri Cazelles*, edited by André Caquot and M. Delcor, 501–12. AOAT 212. Kevelaer: Butzon & Bercker, 1981.

Wenham, Gordon J. "Sanctuary Symbolism in the Garden of Eden Story." In *Proceedings of the Ninth World Congress of Jewish Studies, Jerusalem, August 4–12, 1985, Division A: The Period of the Bible*, 19–25. Jerusalem: World Union of Jewish Studies, 1986.

Willis, John T. "An Anti-Elide Narrative Tradition from a Prophetic Circle at the Ramah Sanctuary." *JBL* 90 (1971) 288–308.

Wyatt, N. *Myths of Power: A Study of Royal Myth and Ideology in Ugaritic and Biblical Tradition*. Münster: Ugarit-Verlag, 1996.

Wylie, Jonathon E. "'He Shall Deliver My People from the Hands of the Philistines': The Theological and Political Uses of the Philistines in the Book of Samuel." Ph.D. diss., University of Wisconsin-Madison, 2018.

Zwickel, Wolfgang. "Dagons abgeschlagener Kopf (1 Samuel V 3–4)." *VT* 44 (1994) 239–49.

www.ingramcontent.com/pod-product-compliance
Lightning Source LLC
Chambersburg PA
CBHW080407300426
44113CB00015B/2422